Paddington Boy

DAVID FRITH

CricketMASH

PADDINGTON BOY

by David Frith

Published by

CricketMASH,

Amstelveen, Netherlands

www.cricmash.com

May 2021

Cover Design: Maha #smahaart

ISBN: 9 7894922030 5 2

To my daughter Julianne,
who has been my salvation through the darkest time

FOSTER & SONS

CHAPTER ONE

The indictment had never been clearly express
And it seemed that the Snark had begun,
And had spoken three hours before anyone guessed
What the pig was supposed to have done.

LEWIS CARROLL

MY usefulness was at an end, cut short as if by an assassin's shot. Then, from the comments that fortified me through the dark days and nights, came words from someone I had never met. In a wide-ranging letter, he wrote: 'I apologise on behalf of all cricketing people for the hurt caused to you and your family.'

From the steady deluge of correspondence over all the years, this extraordinary remark in early 1996 stands out as the one least expected. Why would a member of the cricket community be apologising to me?

The legions of cricket-followers include many earnest and generous people. With them in mind, in 1979 I had created *Wisden Cricket Monthly*, a magazine that would be entertaining and informative, meeting the needs of cricket-lovers and the players themselves, and just the sort of publication that I, as a so-called cricket fanatic, craved.

Now, a wearying 17 years and 202 editions later, it was all over, and I was stunned. Midst secrecy and intrigue, the new owners of John Wisden, J.Paul Getty jnr and his son Mark, had cut me adrift, six years short of normal retirement. While it meant relief from ceaseless concentration on every daily detail of what was happening in cricket, a punishing self-imposed discipline, my dismissal threatened the security I'd worked so hard to achieve. It snatched away privileges that go with the pursuit of full-time accredited cricket journalism and editorship, modest privileges which had been hard earned. With an immature pension fund, I was in no position to stop working.

The operation had been conducted with all the impersonal efficiency of a state execution. The world's longest-serving cricket magazine editor, I was also the senior editor among sports magazines in Britain. Who had been so keen on squeezing me out? And why? I'd been puzzled by the way I was being treated by the new management. I felt rising alarm during months of desperation. Then it dawned on me that this was probably exactly how it had been orchestrated since the Getty acquisition of John Wisden & Company early in 1993. There could be no other explanation.

There was something odd about the attitude of the American billionaire and his son. I had a staff of only three full-time employees, one of whom, taken on in 1988 as a sort of office manager, was now quietly meeting with the new owners. He was suddenly elevated to 'managing director', was given an 'enhancement' which embraced a shiny new car, while my deputy editor was appointed to my editorial board, all of this and a great deal more being rubber-stamped without the courtesy of any consultation with me. I was the founder of the magazine, a director since the start back in 1979, a shareholder too, and of course by far the longest-serving employee.

My deputy, Steven Lynch, was dismayed at his relative demotion in the pecking order and was considering leaving (he would have been difficult to replace adequately, and I was made to feel a nuisance for stressing this to the other board members). I was getting no response to my letters of concern. Beyond all this, I was granted no annual salary review – not even in line with inflation – in April 1995, and my query about an upgrade for my eight-year-old company car was flatly ignored. What was going on? I asked myself over and over as the months ground on. The insulting refusal to treat me as a colleague was threatening sanity. What price now the assurances from the outgoing owners of Wisden that all jobs were safe? We were a cottage industry, yet the new owners were imposing a dispassionate 'big business' overview that made little sense to three out of four of us.

The new management had set up the former (junior) office manager as their sole communicant in the Guildford office. I was not willing to stand by and watch morale crumble. This was the company I'd set up. After 14 years, *WCM* was more than a magazine. It had become a part of many people's lives. Family aside, it was practically my whole life. For thousands of readers it was a monthly creation that they seemed to want always to be there.

'*WCM* takes a worldly, open-minded and critical view of our sport, and it's fun to read,' wrote a reader from Pennsylvania after my departure was made public. Another, from Melbourne, wrote: 'You always spoke the truth and shamed the devil, especially on the subject of the West Indies born-again Bodyliners and electronic umpiring. If there was a fashionable view, it could be almost guaranteed you wouldn't hold it!' Another, from Kent: 'You have created a magazine which has genuinely changed the whole market for periodicals, while also jolting *The Cricketer* out of its cosy little corner.' Another, from India, after my successor as editor had produced three issues: 'Most of the writing is too cute by half and lacks authority. I also find the design horrible and wonder why new editors always feel they have to make sweeping changes, this after the magazine had undergone an excellent facelift just a few issues back. Maybe it is a sign of insecurity. But why must the reader suffer?'

These remarks were some comfort after the axe had fallen. The 17 chocolate-coloured binders on the shelf reflected the affection and dedication I felt towards a game that some identified as an obsession, others as an addiction (which sounds even worse). 'It wasn't just the cricket which I learnt to appreciate so richly,' wrote a Derbyshire reader, 'but the human insight and the historical perspective. I would be arrested by a piquancy of phrase or psychological insight.'

Two other 'obituaries' enabled me to come a little closer to terms with this trauma: 'The editorials remind me of the depth and sincerity of your commitment to the game, with a determination to hold to the values that mean something rather than seeking the easy and popular way forward – or out.'

Following this letter from London came one, to my astonishment, from Turkey (though not from a Turk): 'Our sincere thanks for your splendid magazine and for your courageous editing, which has been greatly valued in this present world of all journalism travelling on the same bus and no-one daring to take a different stand or to offer another view.'

I accept that I may have done myself a disfavour by quoting from these letters. My enemies in cricket – and there were a few – may suggest that they were solicited or invented, or that it was immodest of me to have referred to them. But they are part of my story, and would otherwise have turned to dust in a drawer.

As significant as any of the cascade of letters that came in following the euphemistic announcement by Wisden's eminence grise Matthew Engel of my 'early retirement' was one from Sir Derek Birley, eminent educationalist, Yorkshire-born, and author of the challenging cricket book *The Willow Wand* (published 1979, the year my *WCM* was born), a volume largely ignored by the timorous reactionary cricket Press. He wrote: 'Cricket, I fear, has lost none of its capacity for hypocrisy through becoming a branch of showbiz, merely acquired a different set of dubious values to be two-faced about. It is a great pity that one who so patently combines idealism with enthusiasm for the game should be caught up in this way.

'You are reported as feeling very tired,' he continued, 'this I can well believe, and I know also that you must feel very hurt. It is a sad irony that you have so long and so much come to personify the magazine and what it stands for that people should apparently confuse your giving an airing to Mr Henderson's views with approving them.'

Who is this Mr Henderson to whom Sir Derek refers? Was he a major figure in my ultimate 'severance' from *Wisden Cricket Monthly*? When the poor chap (Wisden's company secretary) who had been sent (alone, of course) to tell me that I was finished was asked to identify the reason, he muttered something about my not contributing to the last Wisden management committee meeting. (Just about all they ever talked about at that table was *Wisden Cricketers' Almanack*: the magazine, it seemed to me, was something of an irritant, and I was thinking about leaving the 'committee'.) When pressed, the messenger of doom said, 'And there was that business last year.'

'That business' has become known as the Henderson Affair. It was a 'media beat-up' at a slack time for news. It was a phenomenon that featured stomach-churning distortions, hypocrisy and duplicity, had some eminent people ducking for cover, and insignificant figures talking big, 'soapboxing', enhancing their own reputations, their eyeballs ablaze with insincerity. Target Frith became the order of the day. Hammer the arrogant colonial. Let's portray him as a racist, a Nazi, a Fascist, a bigot.

The thrust of Henderson's article had been national identity, a tiresome subject perhaps, but unquestionably one of considerable topical importance. I sensed its significance years previously because wherever I went, from the mid-1980s, be it a county match or Test or a club dinner or cricket society gathering, inevitably somebody would raise the question of the composition of the England team: 'Look at the number of foreign-born players!' And when England were going through a long losing patch, I was not the only cricket-writer to sense that the foreign-born were, in some quarters, taking the brunt of the blame. Clearly it was an area for study: a subject of major significance to anyone who had experienced life in two cultures, affiliation to two countries. Was the public's perception in this complex matter unrealistic? Was it unfair? It was a *compassionate* subject at base, and that is why I gave space to the Henderson article in the July 1995 edition of *WCM*.

I wish I hadn't bothered. His style was somewhat harsh, and it proved too sensitive a subject, even in an age of ever-increasing grossness. It would have taxed the writing skills and powers of human insight of John Arlott, my dear friend and mentor. But John was now dead. And with the dark events of 1995-96, whole areas of my feelings for cricket and respect for my fellow man died too.

CHAPTER TWO

London was like some huge prehistoric animal, capable of enduring terrible injuries, mangled and bleeding from many wounds, and yet preserving its life and movement.

WINSTON CHURCHILL

THE earliest memory: Derry, the Airedale, standing guard at the end of the frilly pram; or the view along the cream frontages of Westbourne Terrace, not far from Lord's, from a second-floor balcony, where my grandmother was in domestic service. The recently-delivered male child, born into an England drifting towards war, soon came to the startling realisation that he was exclusively him. No interchange. This was the body and this was the mind and soul that would be his for ever, or at least until a German high-explosive bomb ended it all. Nobody could appropriate this persona; nor could he swap places with anybody else. I am me! This was the emergence and recognition of the soul.

From perusal of a stack of expensive birth, marriage and death certificates acquired over the years, and ignoring the fact that several generations back there were, not all that unusually, a few crosses, or 'marks', instead of signatures, I ought to have inherited some manual dexterity, for the occupations listed on the certificates include scale-maker, engineer, master fishmonger, glassblower, leather-case-maker and meat-carver. There was a coachman, a groom, a horse-drawn cab-driver, motor-washer, packing-case-maker, porter, soldier, tramcar conductor. And there was more than one labourer and a milliner, a telegraph engineer, cabinetmaker, blacksmith, gardener, cutler and master bootmaker.

The meat-carver was my father, employed in London's West End at the time of my arrival. Ted Frith was born in 1909 in Bethnal Green, and had moved in the right direction, away from the dingy, gas-lit streets where the barrel-organs and the pub babble were the only manifestations of cheer. Bubble'n'squeak and cocoa and bread with beef dripping formed the staple diet. They were an 'underprivileged' family, three boys and four girls, two of whom died in infancy, while a third, Susannah, died at 17 in 1918, not a victim of the 'flu epidemic, as my father always seemed to believe, but of tuberculosis, known as the 'White Death'.

Susannah Frith, victim of the 'White Death'

Lung disease, furthered by poor diet and crowded living space, was the family curse. Poor Ted always believed that his mother was Irish, but she wasn't. She was London-born. Both his parents succumbed to TB, within five weeks of each other in 1921. Dad was certain his father had died of a broken heart after losing his wife, Susan, who was born in Bromley-by-Bow into the Gillbe family. Her facial image is preserved in one precious surviving photograph, probably the only one she had taken during her 41 years.

My father's mother Susan

George Ernest Frith, my grandfather, enlisted in the East Surrey Regiment in September 1914 and made it to lance-corporal before being discharged on health grounds three years later. He must have been quite ill, for Britain needed every fighting man it could muster at that critical stage of the Great War. The only surviving photo shows him in his 'Old Contemptibles' uniform, jug of ale in hand, cigarette dangling from his lips, laughing chirpily, probably at the bar of the *Nag's Head* (later *O'Neill's*) in Caledonian Road, a favourite pub. A cousin of his, Charlie Frith, was killed near Arras while serving in the Rifle Brigade. His body was never recovered. Before the war he had been the uniformed doorman at the Russell Hotel in London. He left a wife and two children.

Lance-Corporal George Frith

So, in 1921, when only 12, my future father, Ted, was whisked off to a Shaftesbury Home for orphans, set up by the great benefactor Lord Shaftesbury in Bisley, Surrey (Coldingley Prison now occupies the site), while his surviving sister, Nell, and two brothers, George and Alec, were taken elsewhere to other places of care and tuition.

Dad never quite cast off the anguish of those haunting losses and the rawness of new surroundings and the coarse voices, following the soul-crushing collapse of family life, deprived though it had been. As he wrote in his unpublished autobiography, he 'came from nothing, had nothing, and had nothing to look to for the future'. His hair crew-cut to banish the nits, he threw himself into woodwork lessons and made some robust forays into swimming and boxing, football and water polo under the kindly eye of a custodian. He learned bee-keeping, French-polishing, upholstery and gardening, endured the cane on his backside, benefited from some painful vaccinations and dental care, enjoyed the open spaces, returned some 'poor to average' academic results, and made illicit forays to the village pub, the Hen & Chickens.

In 1924, when 15, he left Bisley in just the clothes he stood in, with a toothbrush and £1.10.0 in his pocket. He found employment as a pageboy in a red pillbox hat at a London hotel. When he was ready to face the wider world, his first task was to trace Nell and George, Alec having turned up at Bisley just before he left.

He walked to Cornwall from London – fuelled by a small tin of sugar – seeking brother George down Bodmin way (the eldest brother had changed his name, and there were murmurs about how he may have killed a man and pushed the car over a cliff). Soon poor little Nell too was traced, and began to earn her living as a chambermaid. On the birthday which they shared, two years apart, my father gave his younger sister a tortoiseshell comb and she gave him a brass tie-pin.

Helped briefly by the Salvation Army, Ted Frith had become a fiercely independent young man, possessed of the vital combination of cunning, reverence and charm needed to persuade some caterers in London to employ him and train him. He then met my future mother, who felt rather sorry for him as well as being drawn by his ivory smile, shining cleanliness, sportsman's physique and improving speech. She bought him a monogrammed 18-carat signet ring for £5.15.0 at Brooks, in Wardour Street, and they were married in Paddington Parish Church, St James's, Sussex Gardens on September 1, 1934 (a miniature woman's shoe and two horseshoes made of ivory and a pink satin ribbon survive from the occasion). They honeymooned in Cliftonville, on the furthest tip of the Kent coast. I came along two years later, and the Second World War began two days after their fifth wedding anniversary.

Mum was born four months before my father, on March 17, 1909 – St Patrick's Day, hence 'Patricia'. Her full names were Lilian Patricia Ethel, but she soon abandoned the first name. She had one sister, Edie, two years older, who was to play a large role in our lives. The girls' parents were John Valentine Thomas, born in 1875, on St Valentine's Day, at High Wood, a property in Roehampton, demolished by developers late in the 20th Century. There is only one surviving picture of him: a dark- haired man clad in waistcoat, standing by a horse. J.V.Thomas died from rheumatic fever in March 1921, aged 46, when my mother was 12. It was revealed recently that his father came from Sennybridge, in Wales. At a cricket society gathering around 2010, I told the audience of my pleasure at having discovered this trace of Welsh blood, at which one of the guests removed his Wales Rugby Grand Slam tie and insisted that I should take it. I was only too proud to join a kind of brotherhood.

So, 16 years before I was born three of my four grandparents died within 38 days in 1921. (This was almost as grievous as Winston Churchill's losses that same year: his brother-in-law took his own life, his mother died, as did his manservant, and his little daughter Marigold.)

All the more reason for me to treasure the one grand-parent who remained: Rhoda Jane Thomas, who also had a traumatic youth. Her mother died at 34 from diphtheria when she, Rhoda, was only 17, and her father, John Wood, 36, finding it all too much, hanged himself in his fishmonger's shop in Fulham months later, in 1890. Young Rhoda found work as a domestic servant, while her six younger siblings went into the care of grandparents.

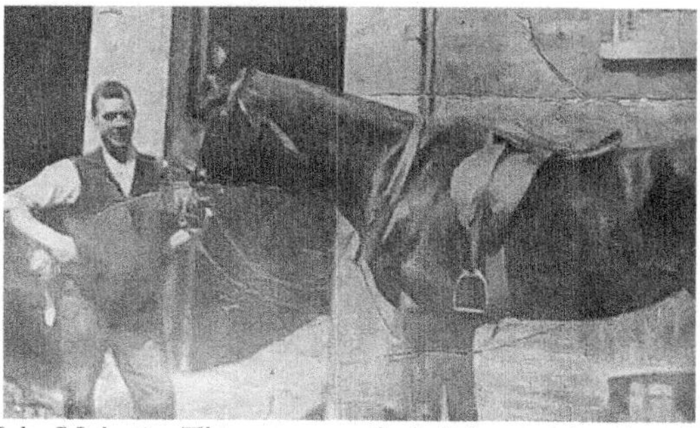

John Valentine Thomas, my mother's father: another short life

Rhoda was 'in service' around London and in Brasted, Kent and Bexhill-on-Sea, Sussex before marrying J.V.Thomas, that son of a Welshman, and a fellow High Wood employee, on August 27, 1904, at St Mary Magdalene Church, Southwark.

The Grandma Rhoda I knew, until she died suddenly in 1943, when I was six, was – from my infant's perspective – a rather large lady. Sad-faced and forever weary, she had her grey hair swept back into a bun, rarely combing it to its full length, and covering it with a black straw hat when she lumbered off to the shops.

Grandma had rheumatism, a legacy of scrubbing steps on cold, damp mornings, and she used an ointment with an overpowering aroma. Often she humoured her fair-haired grandson by sitting on the staircase and playing 'buses', and singing, in her rare lighthearted moods, songs from her late-Victorian and Edwardian heyday: *Two Little Girls in Blue, The Honeysuckle and the Bee, Goodbye Dolly Gray, Pack Up Your Troubles, The Old Bull and Bush, Hold Your Hand Out Naughty Boy*, honest, uncynical melodies. The tune that really stirred me was Soldiers of the King. I stamped up and down the hall, toy gun at the shoulder. It was a time of patriotism and military pride. Memories of the Boer War and the Great War were still there for older folk, and Hitler's war, now raging around us, was going to be won. Wasn't it?

The naval giants, Beatty, of the jauntily-angled cap-peak, and Jellicoe, were Grandma's heroes, along with Kitchener. Her voice trembled when she recalled the eerie, evil Zeppelin airships in London's night sky, and she still despised the old Kaiser. There was the occasional reference to Mafeking, and, with poignancy, Nurse Edith Cavell, murdered by the Germans. And she had spent plenty of evenings in music-halls, judging from the constant references to Little Tich and Marie Lloyd, Harry Champion and Gus (*'Alf a Pint of Ale*) Elan. But she never mentioned Jack the Ripper, who had prowled in the darkness not far from where she lived when she was in her teens. Nor did she speak of her father, the fishmonger who hanged himself after his wife died.

It is not just odd but creepy to 'hear' the voice of someone who was wafted away well over half-a-century ago, and even more so when only four words are all that remain. Grandma called me 'Davit', and was always urging me to drink my milk, which she pronounced 'melk'. 'Dreadful' was pronounced 'dretful', and she sometimes thought me 'mischeevus'.

I don't remember any hugs. The only hugger in the family was Auntie Edie. She squeezed me a lot. She never had any children of her own; and she hugged lots of people, it seems; probably too many for her own good.

With Grandma Rhoda, the only grandparent I knew

So there we were: Pat and Ted Frith, with their three-year-old son, and Mum's sister and their mother, soon to be joined by Uncle Fred (Grandma's brother), a sullen old man who resembled John Le Mesurier (Dad's Army) and had been at sea as a cook, proud to have served on Admiral Jellicoe's mighty flagship HMS Iron Duke in the First World War.

We were all squeezed into 80 Lynton Road, Rayners Lane, Harrow, a neat semi-detached on one of the faintly elegant housing developments that spread north-west out of London during the 1930s, later described by the whimsical John Betjeman as 'Metroland'. Bay windows at the front, pebbledash walls, handkerchief of a front garden, about a sixth of an acre at the back, a couple of young fruit-trees, with similar dwellings front, back and either side as far as the eye could see. The developers, T.F.Nash, had considerately dotted the new streets with copper beech saplings. From such family archives as there are, a Times Furnishing (High Holborn branch) invoice shows a houseful of furniture, plus lino, rugs and (for £1.7.6) a 4ft 6ins spiral spring mattress all purchased for £147.9.0. For under £600 for the house, with a big mortgage, Pat and Ted achieved happiness in their blue heaven. But not for long.

There were simply too many people in that little house, though I couldn't know it, for at my tender age what was there to compare it with? Grandma and Auntie Edie could presumably have stayed in London, in Conduit Mews. However, here they were, in Lynton Road with us, and it's now too late to find out why the new parents weren't allowed to be alone in suburbia with their bouncing baby boy.

I'd landed at Gloucester Terrace, Paddington, a noble stack of column-fronted four-storey terrace buildings, No. 268 then being a nursing-home. It was less than a mile from Lord's Cricket Ground, where the 150th anniversary of MCC was about to be celebrated. My birth took place around 2pm on Tuesday, March 16, 1937, and I was delivered by a Dr Golding, weighing in at 9lb 2oz and attracting the nickname 'Carnera' from the nursing staff after the 'Ambling Alp', the behemoth Italian heavyweight boxer then in the news. Cow & Gate figured prominently in my early diet, so the weight remained healthy. The top tune of the hour was *Pennies from Heaven*; Stanley Baldwin was Prime Minister; Australia had just stolen the Ashes from under England's nose by winning the last three Tests (skipper Bradman 270, 212 and 169) from a two-down position; and I had the rarity of an Edward VIII stamp on my birth certificate, though that irresponsible monarch had abandoned the throne four months previously.

A wartime boyhood has one advantage: it compels you to grow up fairly fast. The alternative was to withdraw in terror into a permanent state of immutable infancy. The German bombing raids, night after shocking night, tore at my mother's nerves. And even though Harrow took only a small fraction of the deadly bombardment that pulverised so much of London and surrounds, enough incendiaries and high-explosives whistled down and enough ear-splitting anti-aircraft gunfire went off from nearby ack-ack batteries to convince all but the most boozed-up optimist that there was no way we could reasonably expect to survive much longer.

My downstairs cot was placed in the inner corner of the dining-room at 80 Lynton Road, up against the dividing wall of the house, close to the chimney stack, the area most likely to withstand a house collapse if it took a bomb. Outside was the Anderson shelter, sunk in concrete a few feet into the ground, with curved corrugated-iron roof covered in earth. It was damp-smelling, and claustrophobic, by no means proof from a direct hit but a safer place to be if the house should come crashing down.

Grandma, in particular, didn't like it in the shelter, and was usually caught unprepared and in need of persuasion. One night, after a wailing siren alarm, she wouldn't retreat to the Anderson until she had located her false teeth (there was a popular contemporary giggle on this theme: 'Come on, Grandma. They're dropping bombs, not mince-pies!'); and one other night she had her head in the gas-oven, cleaning the burners. When she was finally made to hear the calls to evacuate the house, she banged her head and had to be helped, dazed and reeling, down the darkened path to the shelter.

My parents on honeymoon, 1934

Even a small boy couldn't fail to discern the agony behind his mother's sweet smile. She flinched and stifled squeals each time the scream of falling bombs gave way to an explosion which made the house and its occupants tremble. The four-year-old tried to help, but the best he could muster was: 'Don't worry, Mummy. They're only dropping bombs!' The sheer absurdity of it, coupled with the suggestion that at least the little chap was apparently not crippled by fear, probably helped in some small way.

I was certainly familiar with terror. That dining-room with its heavy blue-green drapes drawn across the French windows may have been gloomy, particularly bearing in mind what dreadful things always seemed to be going on out there in the apocalyptic night, but upstairs, when I was parked in my cot at the foot of my parents' bed in the front bedroom, when no air-raid was in progress, it was still tense for a child who knew well enough what might happen at any time. The babble one night was so great down below in the dining-room (the sitting-room at the front, with its rounded bay, immaculate carpet, green/silver lounge suite, and standard lamp, was scarcely ever used) that nobody – apart from me, alone upstairs – heard the air-raid siren. As it wailed, the laughter, the clinking of glasses and the schhhhh of the soda-siphon downstairs went on unabated. Mum, Dad, Auntie Edie and Grandma were oblivious to the flock of German bombers on their way to demolish No.80. I called out. I screamed out. I screamed more loudly. I was too petrified even to think of trying to break out of the cot. The din they were making downstairs, blending with whatever was on the wireless – probably *Bandwagon* or *Variety Bandbox*, or Tommy Handley, Colonel Chinstrap, Fumph the Spy, and Mrs Mopp sustaining the morale of the nation with the hilarious ITMA, or perhaps the sweet music on *Henry Hall's Guest Night* – all this put them out of range of my desperate shrieks. Something more penetrative was needed, and it came with the ominous drone of the bombers through the blackness overhead, and the first raucous rounds of flak.

The door was flung open. A burst of light beamed from the landing, and Dad was whisking me out of bed and into his strong, safe arms. Mum fretted and apologised and managed a chuckle, and soon we were all snugly back in the garden shelter, with its stale air and flickering candles.

It was even more frightening when Dad wasn't there, even with the female comfort and compassion of Mum, Grandma and Auntie Edie. Rejected by the Royal Air Force and the Army's officer recruitment because of his meagre education and his colour-blindness, Ted Frith was now a £3-a-week fireman, firstly with the AFB (Auxiliary Fire Brigade), then the LFB (London), which was eventually absorbed into the NFS (National Fire Service). Home on brief periods of leave, his eyes red-rimmed, his face and neck flecked with cinder burns, he smelt of oil and smoke. His waterproof uniform, black and heavy, was usually still damp. His private torment was changing him before our very eyes.

From the idylls of peacetime suburbia, untried young men from all over Britain and the Commonwealth had donned uniform and been hurled into conflict and turmoil that would scar their psyches for ever. Dad spared us most of the gory details, restricting his accounts of the nightly horror to the faintly humorous. There was the man who emerged from bomb wreckage in the City of London, grinning vacuously and holding his torn-off ear in his hand. There were tales of firemen hopelessly trapped by live cables as they fought to pull hoses across flaming landings, desperately axeing down doors to get to trapped civilians; and of others, Dad included, 100ft skywards on turntable ladders, training hoses with frail expectation onto buildings that were raging furnaces while bombs whistled down all around their heads, the firefighters roaring their curses up into the night sky. At least soldiers, sailors and airmen usually had the chance, sooner or later, to retaliate. Not so the battered, traumatised firemen on the home front.

One day Dad had his picture in the evening paper: a blurred figure sky-high up the ladder, directing hose-water down onto a burning building in the Strand. And at least we saw him every few days. Mr Farquhar from across the street was fighting with the Cameron Highlanders many miles away and didn't come home on leave for years.

Little DF holds the Luftwaffe at bay

The first major action had come when the London docks were raided, the firemen being summoned from the Palace Theatre halfway through Oscar Asche's *Chu Chin Chow*, a show for which they'd been given tickets.

During the great City Blitz, which started on December 29, 1940, Dad was given up as lost. East London was ablaze, countless souls trapped within a mammoth ring of flames. Thousands of the Luftwaffe's fire-bombs rained down after the bombardment of high-explosives. At ground level, water supplies were destroyed, and the Thames tide was too low to be of any use. It would have been total wipe-out had poor weather in Germany not forced a halt to further aircraft take-offs. Historic buildings and innocent men, women and children were obliterated, but by the grace of God my father was not among the 13,500 Londoners killed by German bombing by the end of 1940.

He told of the odd bit of pilferage that went on, and made us laugh by recalling one fireman's practice of timing a brick through a shop window – preferably a jeweller's – just as the whistling of a falling bomb gave way to the explosion. This time the bomb was a dud, and the isolated sound of a brick through a window soon brought a policeman running.

Less amusing was his description of being hurled across a room by a bomb blast. His torso was damaged quite badly. Later he suffered a broken foot, which was a long time in plaster.

Dad kept a diary in 1941. The entries were sporadic and brief, but they painted a picture:

March 15: Started week's annual. Went to Mrs Squires, 354 Cherryhinton Road, Cambridge.

March 16: My nerves seem shot to pieces lately.

April 2: Acted on guard of honour for Mr Menzies [Australian Prime Minister, who had come to meet Churchill, and said in a radio broadcast: 'I am here to tell you in your own lovely country that we are with you. You must never think yourselves alone.'] and Mr Morrison [Minister of Home Security].

April 16: Worst London raid. Numerous fires, minor and heavy HiEx [high explosives]. Newport Buildings, Maples, Waring & Gillows, Leicester Sq, etc, Selfridges, St Pauls.

April 17: Home on leave. Damn good sleep. Felt no good for gardening.

April 19: Bad London raid. East End worst. 12 midnight slackened off. Livened up 1am to 5am.

May 4: Still getting out bodies from Newport Buildings and Alfred Place from the raid on 16th April.

May 8: Still feel upset over Newport Buildings.

May 10: Worst blitz again. Big Ben, Houses Parliament, Westminster Abbey, Old Bailey, British Museum. 50,000 gallons oil. Got 33 bombers down. Home 1pm. Rudolf Hess landed in Scotland by parachute from Nazi plane with broken ankle. Hope more of 'em come.

May 11: Felt terrible with oil fumes in stomach, was sick with belching.

May 13: As I'm writing this, David comes up and sits on my lap, then starts sobbing. I ask him what is the matter. He says 'I feel sad when I think of you out in the air- raids.' The wireless is playing. I expect the sad music made him sad.

May 28: What a war. No sweets, choc, lemons, cheese, fruit and very short of fags, but yet we all take it in a fine spirit, the spirit that will win the war.

June 8: Phoned up station to report sick with traumatic arthritis of left hand.

June 10: Uncle Fred died at 9.5am. Pat, Mum and I were present. He died very peaceful.

June 13: Uncle Fred buried, Eastcote Lane. Mourners Pat, Mum, Lizzie [sister to Fred and Grandma] and me.

June 14: Shelter all finished now and cemented. Got medicine for my bad nerves which is getting worse. David lost his cold.

July 14: [his 32nd birthday] : Tommy our cat died with cat 'flu.

July 26: Started second week of annual. Painted up outside of house. Took another cat home, name 'Skipper'.

July 29: Went to Bodmin [Cornwall] with Pat and David.

August 6: 'Skipper' our other cat died with germ from 'Tommy'.

Sept 2: To attend court for rates summons.

Sept 10: Made David a board and easel.

Sept 11: Made David a scooter.

Sept 12: Made David 12 soldiers and 12 sentry boxes.

Sept 15: Went to Dr McKeown for more medicine to ease my bad nerves.

Oct 16: Saw Dr McKeown, told me he can't do anything about my nerves, only rest. What a hope.

Oct 17: Very cold and rain. I will try and dig the garden when I can. Can't do much at this stage. Still got pain in chest and my left ankle.

Dec 29: Anniversary of the big City 'Blitz' of 1940. I was riding the pump.

And so into 1942:

January cash account: Got none now to balance.

Jan 8: DP and pump now on the run from Shaftesbury Avenue so we now do 48 hours there.

Jan 14: Received back-pay as LFB. My pay is now £4.12.0, i.e. 62/ – pay, rent 10/-, extra hours 10/-, cost of living 10/-.

Jan 15: Woke up to see 1 inches snow on ground and after a short while was frozen over.

Jan 19: Bill [Edie's husband] came home with the sad news that he has 5 days embarkation leave. [Dad possibly felt sad because Uncle Bill's presence was to be so extended.]

Jan 27: Bill left Central Hotel Marylebone for ?Gibraltar.

Feb 5: We have had a terrific amount of snow up to now. We have had a severe winter.

April 7: Started on Pat's boat 'Santa Maria'. Hands not so steady now as they used to be in 1938 but I'll manage, blast the Luftwaffe. Much better with the extra hour of daylight now.

April 9: The Russians are still doing remarkable well thank God. They have deffinately saved us from something terrible because it all looked bad when I reflect my mind back to the time before Germany advanced on Russia. Japan, the yellow swine, seem to be getting it all their own way with us and America, but they'll slip up one day I hope. America seems very quiet. They don't seem to do much.

April 14: Fags are now 6d more. 'Players' will cost 2/ – for 20, 'Weights' etc will cost 1/6d for 20 now.

April 15: Had a letter from Clare Hall Hospital, South Mimms telling me Nellie [his sister] is on the danger list. I must see her tomorrow.

April 24: Went to visit Nellie again. She was much brighter. Doctor has drawn 32ozs fluid from her lung. The worst thing she said was, 'Your sister will never get better, unless a miricle is performed. She is eaten up with it.'

May 6: Went to visit Nellie again. She looks brighter, but she isn't really. She has lost 4lbs more, now she's 6 stone 4lbs.

May 31: Went to visit Nell. She looks ever so much better, but the sister said she isn't.

June 1: It was announced on the wireless today that we had sent over to Germany 1050 bombers, 1000 alone raided Cologne. We lost 49 all-in. My what a welcome bit of news. Now we can see something for the couple of years we've been waiting, and if we get it in the neck in return, well we've had it before and we can take it.

June 3: Over 1000 bombers were over Germany again last night, this time over Essen, that's where Krupps arms factories are. Took Pat and David to the Zoo [Regents Park].

June 4: It has been a sweltering hot week, I mean over 80° in shade.

June 22: Churchill is in America and I think something big is in the air. I took the slide I made to Bishop Creighton Home Settlement, 378 Lillie Road, Fulham SW6.

June 23: Pat and I sowed some seeds Jillronald [a peculiar coded message relating to the conception of my forthcoming baby brother]. Michael George William was born at 10.14pm weighing only 4¾ lbs, premature birth of 7 months and one day 25/1/43 [i.e. retrospective entry seven months later].

August 1: Bill Ryan's [Auntie Edie's husband] brother George came home for 21 days' leave from the Navy after being out to sea for 3 years. We all went out and had a few. Edie got in her usual mood; I rowed with her, she walked out, Pat got upset, Edie came back, we all went to bed at 03.00 hours.

August 15: Entered marrow and 6 tomatoes in flower & veg show. Won 1st marrow and 2nd tomatoes.

Sept 4: A terrible fight is going on in Russia, Jerry is using 1,000,000 men, 1000 planes and hundreds of tanks. Where will this bloody war all end and when will this 2nd Front start.

Sept 7: David started at school for the first time today and I'm dying to get home on Wed. to find out if he likes it.

Sept 11: Pat is feeling fine, showing a little. She has definately gone off smoking and all drinks except coffee, milk and water.

Oct 10: David had a nasty attack of tonsillitis, was sick, but he bears up fine.

Oct 15: Went on a commando exercise to Hadley Woods. Very hard going man-handling the pumps across the brook and through the forest.

Oct 26: I'm at North Ealing station and the air raid warning is just sounding, it's pouring of rain like Hell, and old Jerry likes to sneak in on the low cloud days, he's dead scared of the RAF. Heavy gun-fire locally.

Nov 9: Oh boy! I'll say there's something big in the air, listen, the 8th Army have pushed Rommel out of Egypt and have routed the Axis forces, we have captured thousands of prisoners and guns and hundreds of tanks, this is the end of Rommel in the Western desert.

Nov 11: Took David to London. Very, very foggy. Harrow buses stopped through it.

Nov 12: Pat is feeling fine. She sure is getting bigger, her varicose veins are causing a pain in her buttock and she now has to wear crepe bandages.

Nov 15: Civil Defence Day to remember our defeat of the Luftwaffe. The bells sound lovely. I went to St Pauls to see our parade and I went cold all over.

Nov 26: I went and took Nellie away from Dansbury Manor, Welwyn now she is fit to leave. She doesn't like her digs at 1 Oxford Road, Chiswick.

Dec 18: Riding the salvage van and had 3 shouts, the last one at 02.05 in Cork Street, and what a blaze, 2nd and 3rd floors gutted.

Dec 25: Had 4 shouts. DP smashed up in Northumberland Avenue, Leading Firemen Andrews and Turner taken to hospital with burns from Archer Street fire at 07.00 hours.

Dec 26: Off today, had a decent time. David did enjoy himself, bless him.

Dec 29: Pat got sciatica and a cold. Mum is not feeling too well, and I've got a cold and it seems like the 'flu. A small amount of snow, the first this winter.

Dad didn't keep a diary in 1943, but resumed writing in the eventful year of 1944. The preceding 1941-42 chronicles, meanwhile, have triggered some vivid boyhood recollections.

That first entry, for March 15, 1941, the day before my fourth birthday, tells of the brief holiday in Cambridge under a News Chronicle scheme to afford some respite to exhausted firefighters and their families. Any expectation that Cambridge would be a haven of peace was quickly quashed though: there was a bomb crater in Mrs Squires' garden. 'Pat upset' is the sobering entry.

My own trauma in Cherryhinton Road stemmed from having forgotten to bring my Teddy bear, an oversight which left me lonely and close to panic. I've no memory of what we did or where we went during the few days in Cambridge, but the panic, unrelieved by Mum's caring sympathy, of being without Teddy at bedtime is easily recalled all these years later. Poor timid little fellow.

Three months further, sombre Uncle Fred died, in the rear bedroom. Dad shaved him, and the funeral went ahead without me. Over half-a-century later I obtained Fred Wood's death certificate and was taken back at seeing the causes of death listed as heart and kidney ailments, cirrhosis of the liver, and *syphilis*. 'Well, he was a sailor,' I was told when the subject came up in later family discussion. (Oddly enough, Fred's estranged wife was named Phyllis).

A few weeks after that we went to Cornwall for a break, as recorded briefly in Dad's diary. His elder brother George, always a man of mystery, lived down there with his wife Harriet, a kindly, jovial lady, and their snowy-haired children Joey, Jimmy and Rosie. Uncle George (now calling himself Joe Watson) served in the Home Guard, while Dad's younger brother Alec saw Army postings all over England, and for a time was in the same Ox & Bucks unit in which Essex and England fast bowler H.D.'Hopper' Read was an officer.

It was the first great train journey of my life. We chugged through wide, summery fields and past gently-sculpted hills, through tunnels, in and out of strange railway stations, people getting into and out of the carriage, a pretty girl in light-blue Air Force uniform absorbing me for a time, people passing along platforms, one a stooped man in a cap and long coat who was ashen-faced and sad-looking and surely about to breathe his last. Perhaps, with Uncle Fred's recent passing still in mind, I studied this wretched old man and for the first time my thoughts on death intensified.

There were uplifting features to the epic journey. I had just stuck together a miniature, coloured, cut-out cardboard model of a Mosquito aircraft (like the one that Keith Miller was flying, as I discovered much later). My tiny aeroplane meant as much to me as that Teddy bear. Such are the playthings of a boy in wartime.

The exhilaration of sticking my head out of the train window and feeling the wind rush into my face, watching my Mosquito on the window ledge doing close to 100 mph, with stanchions whooshing past and the odd speck of hot coal grit getting into the eye: this was really nothing compared to sitting on Uncle George's lap and gripping the wooden steering-wheel as he drove us in his old automobile into Bodmin. And there, in a field by the caravan and lean-to tent where we all slept, I had to run as fast as my solid little legs would take me when a snorting bull headed my way. The notion of going to the lavatory out past the bushes was distasteful, but no more than my own remark to Mum that evening, when I queried with mild alarm and suspicion, and quite loudly, 'Mum, are these people gypsies?' The delightful Aunt Harriet certainly was: a 'queen' in reality, and a credit to the clan.

Shy I may have been, but there seems also to have been a developing pattern of unfettered utterance. In a doctor's waiting-room we sat opposite a woman with only one leg. 'Mum,' I chimed, loudly enough for the amputee to hear, 'look at that lady. She's got one leg and no leg!' If nothing else, the logic was faultless.

Then, on a London Underground station, I saw a huge Guinness poster curving up the far wall. Thrilled at the product-recognition, I yelled: 'Mum, look! There's Grandma's Guinness!' The old lady was with us at the time, and she frowned with embarrassment. I failed to see why I should be told to 'Shhhh!' I was merely stating the obvious. What was so wrong about Grandma drinking Guinness, especially as I was always allowed to deal with the quarter-inch left in the bottom of the bottle? The taste was wonderful. It was not as if I had designs on Auntie Edie's gin or her martinis, though the cherries on the sticks were fair game.

That winter, I was taken on a visit to Dad's fire station. I was already fairly steeped in the lore: the cry of 'Taut sheet!' when somebody was about to plunge from a high window-ledge in a blazing building down into a broad safety sheet held by rescuers; and the leg-over-shoulder 'fireman's lift'. Early in January 1942, when Dad was stationed in Shaftesbury Avenue (a station rebuilt after a 1940 raid and again in the 1970s) – a curious follow-up, nominally speaking, to his earlier orphan's shelter in the Shaftesbury home at Bisley – I spent time upstairs in the recreation room, watching the firemen play snooker and jabbing the table myself, and I looked through the window down at the derelict yard where they kept pigs. Dad's special mates Lionel Gray and Dick Milton were there that afternoon, and I was allowed to slide down the slippery brass 'fireman's pole', used by the firemen to hasten their journey down to the appliances on the ground floor when the alarm-bells rang. It seems unlikely that any other five-year-olds have had the exhilarating experience of sliding down the pole. None could have been prouder.

Dad transferred from station to station throughout the war (Charing Cross, Dollis Hill, Peter Street, Holland Park, Clipstone Street, Brewery Road, North Ealing, Long Acre, Kensington) and escaped death yet again when he switched leave with another fireman the night in October 1940 when 72 Station (Shaftesbury Avenue) was destroyed by bombs that also wrecked the Palace Theatre.

When Dad wrote, on January 19, 1942, that Uncle Bill had five days' embarkation leave, he didn't mean it was 'sad' news that he would be with us, of course. He meant that it was sad that he was about to embark: that's to say, return to the battle front. These two men were not always the dearest of friends. I was horrified to hear Dad say one night, as he switched his ring to his right hand, that he was going to sort Bill out when he got back from an outing with Edie, both predictably over the limit. From upstairs, in the middle of the night, I heard raised voices, then bumping and banging of furniture. The fist fight was brief, but it was a symptom of the tensions in this household when all the strains and duress of war erupted as people endeavoured to co-exist under one roof, many of them prone to jealousy and alcoholic oblivion.

Auntie Edie's wedding: Uncle Bill's parents, Charlie, Bill, Edie, Gradnma, Mum, Dad and the four-year-old mock naval officer

Auntie Edie had clearly been 'one for the boys'. Her pre-war Joan Crawford looks were still visible in a framed photo on the sideboard: slightly protuberant eyes, tight curls permed, perhaps more of a Bette Davis of a young woman. I often wondered what she saw in Bill Ryan, who was balding and squat, with no noticeable charm about him. They married at St Paul's, Eastcote Lane, in April 1941, Bill in his Army uniform, Edie in suit and hat, fox-fur at her shoulder, given away by Dad, in his smart fireman's uniform, in the absence of Edie's long-dead father. Bill's old cockney parents were there, as was his brother Charlie, also in Army uniform, home on leave. Mum looked stylish. And to complete the military picture, I wore my naval uniform, complete with officer's peaked cap, the same outfit I wore on a trip to London, when Dad walked me down Whitehall and I saluted the Cenotaph with due gravity. That same salute was directed at all the Servicemen I passed in street, bus or tube train, and each time that those heroes returned the salute, shivers ran down my short spine.

It was a great improvement on the earlier civilian status when, clad in overalls and a bus-driver's cap, I squeezed into my pedal-car and pointed a toy gun at the sky to impress my slightly blank-faced grandmother as she stood at the kitchen door in her white-spotted blue pinafore.

Before Uncle Bill went back to war, he took me out for a 'treat'. We were off to the pictures. Trouble was, nothing on show appealed to me. Even at four or five years of age you have a fairly precise idea of what you do and don't want. So as we took buses to Rayners Lane and South Harrow and Ruislip, I found one excuse after another to decline seats in these cinemas. The framed stills on display outside were all I had to go on, and the stills from *Blood and Sand* (Tyrone Power and Rita Hayworth) were definite turn-offs. Who wanted blood? And look at that snorting bull. (Sitting through that depressing film years later, I saw the point of that rejection of it as a child.) My tastes were all attached to Walt Disney. *Snow White* and *Pinocchio* remained for some years the most bewitching films I had seen. (Top film preferences now, all these years later, are *Treasure Island* and *The Titfield Thunderbolt*).

Understandably Uncle Bill's patience now snapped. He became quite brusque. And I don't think he ever wanted to see me again after it was discovered back home that the toy Churchill tank with rubber tracks that he'd bought me, and which I'd been pulling around everywhere on a string, had been left on the top deck of the bus.

Off he trudged, to rejoin the Somerset Light Infantry, to labour with the Eighth Army through North Africa and Egypt and Italy and Greece, taking his rifle with him, that weapon he stood in the corner of our hall and which I'd quietly caressed. Back to the hideous, screaming mortar attacks Private Bill Ryan went, the terror of which he had described to his small nephew: trapped in a trench, with only a helmet for protection as the German death packages whooshed and whined in his general direction; moans all through the night from wounded men – often an enemy trap – their torn bodies smothered with maggots.

He was under instructions to bring me back a German soldier's helmet – the small incendiary bombs and chunks of oil bomb Dad brought home were never sufficient – and that expectancy helped little David brave it through the ongoing months and years of this bewildering disruption known as the Second World War. What would I do when Uncle Bill brought that trophy home? Goosestep down Lynton Road, wearing this Jerry tin-hat? Or maybe better just to sit and gaze at it, shuddering, in the hallway? The choice was never fulfilled. Uncle Bill did return one day, but apart from his kitbag and that much-used gun and some souvenir shell fragments, he was empty-handed. He said he despised the cowardly Italians ('Eye-ties') and he said he'd killed plenty of Germans. But of a helmet there was no sign. There was no excuse and, to my shame, I never forgave him.

He did try one final peace offering. I was taken to see his old parents over in Merlins Avenue. His mother had a funny old hat on and swathes of clothing, her legs bandaged up like Grandma's, while Mr Ryan sat in the corner beneath a canary in a cage, a friendly old boy in waistcoat and spotted scarf, half-visible in a cloud of pipe-smoke. But even this excursion was ruined when Uncle Bill went into the backyard and showed me how to wring a goose's neck. He simply picked it up by the head, as if it were some undersized German soldier, and twirled it, snapping its vertebral column instantly. I came close to fainting.

Meanwhile, Auntie Edie was drinking steadily – cocktails, gin-and-Its, martinis and, when unavoidable, brown ale – and continued to spoil her nephew at every turn. Working in Chiltern delicatessen near Baker Street station, she served the rich and famous (Bud Flanaghan, Vic Oliver, Bebe Daniels, Sam Costa, Billy Cotton and Hermione Gingold were some of the names that recurred) and she served the Frith family too in that time of severe food rationing. Mum's surviving ration-book has spare coupons for Bacon & Ham and Cooking Fats including Lard & Dripping, unused at Miles the butchers and the Watford Co-op. Courtesy of Edie, meats, bacon and cheeses were unwrapped, drink galore, and bars of Cadbury's chocolate. Little chance that a boy might waste away with this and the Guinness dregs constantly available.

She brought more than exotic provisions home, too. One evening she turned up with a Dutch Serviceman, who not only failed to radiate charm but launched me upon a prejudice against the Dutch that prevailed for some years, for when I succeeded him in the lavatory on the landing I found that he had vomited and had not been very conscientious about clearing up.

Auntie Edie brought other things home that were more useful. There were American comics, in colour, featuring Popeye and the fascinating Katzenjammer Kids. There was a four-inch plaster figure of a German soldier (to throw pebbles at). And a magazine, perhaps the Saturday Evening Post, with a cover picture, Norman Rockwell-style, that haunted me. From the bleak mess that was our war-torn world, I was bewitched by a radiant picture of a white-uniformed milkman crossing a trim lawn past a white picket fence. He was placing some bottles of milk onto a sunlit patio, his smile as joyous as the flowering-cherry trees that skirted the street. It was a picture of peacetime, and I wondered what it would be like, and whether I'd ever experience such blissful serenity and innocence.

Auntie Edie kept everyone's spirits up by a variety of means. In my case, occasional brave sorties into London took in visits to Hamleys in Regent Street, a toyshop of awesome size, where she spent freely on me, sweet little Dinky toy vehicles primarily. A stately black Buick became a favourite, and almost needed tyre retreads after so much running and skidding in and out around the chair-legs and down by the bulbous supports of the sideboard and table.

I managed somehow to avoid any burdensome complexes, even though Mum often beamed embarrassingly that I had 'girl's skin', so smooth and blemish-free was it, while Auntie Edie used to claim that I had a 'titty nose'. She would perch me in her bed, sometimes being none too careful how she wore her satin top, and as I took in the dull dado that ran high around the dull wallpaper, she would chuckle, 'Well, me old lubbadicks, what you been doing?' To which there never seemed much to report. A variant on the quaint 'lubbadicks' was 'sconya'.

Evidence of a crude latent cunning emerged when Mum caught me in the larder with my fingers in the jar of mustard pickles. What was I doing? In a flash the answer came: 'God told me to do it!' I was pardoned, while the yellow substance trickled down my chin.

On quiet nights, when I was alone in the cot at the foot of my parents' bed, I could see the moonlit rooftops on the houses across the road, and when there was no blurred drone coming up from the wireless downstairs, I could hear the distant barking of a dog, unaccountably comforting. The pik-pik-pik-pik-t'pik of my father's approaching footsteps down Lynton Road was the most compelling sound in my world. Hardly a motor-car was seen or heard then, and not all that many footsteps. But I always recognised his. And the sound of the key in the lock of the front door made my heart beat faster.

After one heavy snowfall, I lay on the cold pathway at the side of the house and tried to cover myself with snow, planning to jump up when he was almost upon me. Dad simply said, as he saw my backside sticking up from the lumps of grey snow, 'What the deuce are you doing?'

Mum was always urging me to remember the Russians as I knelt to murmur my bedtime prayers. With a picture of Stalin's reassuring countenance strongly in mind (if only we'd known then of his murderous deeds) the script went: 'And please, God, thank the Russians for helping us' – a simple gesture from a junior citizen of a nation that stood alone through months of terrifying peril until it became clear that not only the Empire but the mighty Americans and Russians were coming in to make life difficult for those hateful enemies of ours, Hitler and Mussolini and Tojo. My new pyjamas, courtesy of Auntie Edie, had a Russian Cossack collar, warm in winter, when to leave the coal-fire in the dining-room was to run the gauntlet of a freezing kind of damnation in a house where a couple of wall-mounted electric fires, expensive to run, were the only other source of warmth, apart from the cosy hot-tank in the airing-cupboard in the poky black-and-white-tiled bathroom. Bath- time brought the toy submarine into play.

Dad's diary housed frequent references to his sister Nell, who took a long time to die from tuberculosis. Two years younger than Dad, but sharing his July 14 birthday, she was a sweet-natured girl, who had worked pre-war as a waitress at the ABC Cafe in Chiswick. She had forged a friendship with a married man, Jim, who used to visit her in hospital and at home with us during Aunt Nell's spell of remission.

Mum was terrified that her young son and his baby brother might catch TB from their infected aunt, and her war on germs intensified. Cups and knives and forks were scalded and rinsed in disinfectant, and the slightest cough had my poor mother rigid with fear. It was in many ways a precursor of the frightening Covid-19 scourge of recent times. Ever since those long-ago days of poor Aunt Nell I have drunk left-handed from cups and avoided cracked crockery.

Nell was laid up for much of her adult life, which led to her reading hundreds of books. A surviving diary from 1946 points to her tastes: J.B.Priestley, Arnold Bennett, Agatha Christie, Peter Cheyney, Daphne du Maurier, Thackeray, Galsworthy, Dickens, Dumas, Shaw. She also knitted a lot, sometimes 'all day'. Other times she 'could not stop crying all day'. Visits to her in hospital gladdened her dull, painful existence, and were noted: Pat (Mum), Ted (Dad), Edie and Bill (always bearing sherry or whisky), Aunts Flo and Lou (Mum's aunts), one or two friends, and 'my Jim', whose time with her was the most precious. Crosswords came in useful, and they played cards, Nell sometimes recording that she won threepence off Jim. Every few days her pencilled scrawl refers to palpitations, indigestion, haemorrhoids, troublesome coughing, headaches, depression. She recorded her temperature most days, and it was seldom below 100°. I thought of her nearly half-a-century later when writing the biography of Archie Jackson, Australia's promising colt alongside Don Bradman, who was a victim of TB.

When the weather relented Nell sat in the garden. She and my mother corresponded weekly. Suddenly, from the sad monotony of the diary entries, Nell writes, shakily, on April 27, 1946: 'Cup final. Listened in to match. Very good. Derby County 4-1 [against Charlton Athletic].' I'd listened as well, in our garden, the wireless commentary blaring out through the French doors.

The handwriting gets shakier. Once in a while she wrote to her other brothers, George and Alec, down in Cornwall. George, by now a scrap-metal dealer living near Bodmin, once sent her £10, a sizable sum. In the autumn of 1946, Nell received letters from nine-year-old me; their literary merit must have been slight, but the one she received on October 29 was described as 'nice'.

Towards the end of that year, her last full year on earth, one entry reads: 'Pat came. Let myself down by crying.' Soon it was Christmas ('We had a grand time – opened whisky'), and nine months later she was finally out of her cruel misery. Dad had tickets for the World Speedway Championship at Wembley Stadium that September evening, and I expected him to call it off. But we went. It helped take his mind off the loss of his kid sister, who had taken so long to die from the 'White Death'. Poor Nell.

My baby brother's arrival, foreshadowed so slickly in my father's retrospective entry in his diary on June 23, 1942, was dramatic for being two months premature. He barely troubled the scales at under 5lbs. It was something of a miracle that my mother, her nerves shattered by over two years of air-raids and anxiety for her husband, had been able to produce a baby at all. I pencilled a note of congratulations and handed it to her in the hospital: 'Dear Mummy, I hope you are feelling well. Thank you for getting my Michael for me and I hope he is well. Daddy says I have been a good boy and he has bought me a dartboard. I am exited and looking forward to you both coming home. Fondest love, David.'

Something there for a sub-editor to work on.

Michael George William, almost six years younger than I, was cute in his tininess, and upon his homecoming I was persuaded – I think by the irrepressible Auntie Edie – to plant a kiss on his bare bottom during a nappy-change (probably one of the superstitious practices that saturated our family culture). The baby reacted with an anal emission. I got away just in time, but it rendered me even more cautious, circumspect and shy. This incident was really a token of our future fraternal relationship: fractious.

This war was now truly global. Uncle Bill was soldiering either in North Africa, Italy or Greece, and the newspaper and crackling wireless bulletins brought us drama from all parts. When my parents went out, I was given the adult responsibility of memorising any fresh war news, as delivered by those toffish BBC newsreaders Stuart Hibberd, Bruce Belfrage, John Snagge and Alvar Lidell ('Al Varley Dell', I fondly believed, until I saw the name written years later). When Mum and Dad came home, I was able to announce with a sense of efficiency but unsteady voice that 'we bombed Berlin last night; no losses, but a lot of German planes were shot down'. In November 1941 I was the first member of the household to hear the ghastly news that HMS *Ark Royal* had been sunk. When the mighty German battleship *Bismarck* went down, I may have been as thrilled as any of the grown-ups, but now, six months on, with the loss of the British showpiece aircraft-carrier, I might have been tempted to think of the war as some kind of football match, where we score then they equalise. But I wasn't.

For amusement, I sometimes camped under the table, with the table-cloth well down, and made my own 'wireless broadcasts', the family beyond barely able to conceal their giggles, while I did so much want to be taken seriously.

Some of those early images of war had permanent, haunting impact: the newspaper photograph of German soldier corpses strewn across a frozen Russian road, and, later, the Australian airman, on his knees, blindfolded, with a Japanese soldier, sword raised, about to behead him. The cinema newsreels told their stories in moving monochrome: flashing artillery batteries at night in the desert, troops sprinting, crouched over, bayonets fixed. Where was Uncle Bill? And battleships tossed on seas so wild that it made cinema-goers queasy just to watch. There was Winston Churchill again, Homburg hat and cigar in place, stepping through the bomb wreckage, and our sacred, beloved King and Queen smiling upon their subjects, who cheered and waved in the completely acceptable deferential manner of the time. And the newsreel shots of the American landing-craft reaching the beaches of the Pacific, the doors crashing down to let the troops wade ashore, thrilled me deeply.

I had gazed in wonderment at the vapour-trails against the vivid blue sky during the dogfights of the Battle of Britain, and heard the clatter and screaming engines as the Spitfires and Hurricanes wheeled and dived, jousting with the Messerschmitts, the most tangible display of Good versus Evil to be seen over England in the entire duration. By 1944, any seven-year-old who couldn't tell a Messerschmitt from a Heinkel or a Junkers from a Dornier wasn't really worth knowing. And when Dad took me to see a shot-up, crash-landed Heinkel 111 in Hyde Park, that impotent, shattered grey monster, inert on the grass, German markings so alien in a London setting, was a sight that would remain forever beyond compare, beyond even the bulky barrage balloons, which looked like writhing, legless elephants when grounded.

Auntie Nell, another victim of the wretched scourge

Back home, the sounds emerging from the upright wireless-gramophone, with the morning sunlight catching the thinnest coating of overnight dust on the walnut top, could be very gripping. Middle Eastern music was exotic, but all kinds of vacillating war reports floated in, heavy with static, intense as any sporting broadcasts I would ever hear in the peacetime decades to come.

Auntie Edie saw to it that this serious stuff never hung in the air for long. She had all those pre-war dance-band records: Jack Payne, Ambrose, Roy Fox, Geraldo, *Amapola, Isle of Capri, It's a Sin to Tell a Lie, Smoke Gets in Your Eyes.* And she would do a little foxtrot in the small space between the dining table and the fireplace, either with the vision of her absent husband, or whoever was handy.

While it was always a great relief to wake in the morning and know that we had survived another night of bombing, I had trouble with my eyelids, which sometimes became sealed tight with 'sleep'. Those impatient, slightly panicky minutes while I waited for Mum to rescue me with cotton-wool and a boracic solution fleetingly gave me an understanding of the anguish suffered by those blind London kids in the Blitz, the youngsters for whom Dad and other firemen made wooden toys in their rare spare time.

Then there was the problem of Sundays. On Sundays the wireless became funereal. There seemed so little to do. The church music was depressing. And after Grandma died in June 1943 – suddenly she was gone; the Victorian link severed; I knew she was far from well; I was shielded from the final drama – Sundays meant visits to the cemetery in Eastcote Lane, where the rows of gravestones posed awkward thoughts for a six-year-old and the vases stuffed with mournful hydrangeas deflated the spirits.

Mondays were little better. We always had cold meat that day, clever utilisation of the leftovers of the premium meal of the week, the Sunday roast joint. Cold meat was OK, until that Monday when Mum cut her finger while carving it, and a droplet of blood fell on my allocation. I went off it completely and was too polite to explain why.

We continued to escape falling bombs, but there was catastrophic destruction a few streets away. A semi-detached in Capthorne Avenue was hit when a couple were at the Odeon cinema, and their two infants perished. It added to my anxiety whenever we ventured to the cinema, but the only incident occurred as we walked home after seeing *I'll Be Your Sweetheart* (which contained so many of Grandma's favourite melodies). Dad spotted a blazing chimney in a house in Kings Road. For a veteran of so many London infernos, extinguishing it was a simple job.

The fiercest action remained in and around the city, where searchlight beams sought frantically to embarrass the German bombers as they rumbled across the night sky. There is no stronger period memory than of being lifted up to see the angry red glow in the distance as London burned and suffered. 'Don't go back into that, Daddy. Don't go!' If I didn't actually say that to him, I thought it.

In time, daylight raids became rarities, but it was still a tense business going into London by day. Dad took me in again when Salutes to the Services were staged: Trafalgar Square almost festive in its celebratory fervour, Nelson still unscathed up there on his stratospheric column, and me proudly clutching my cheap, painted, cut-out tin aircraft all the way back to the suburbs, only seven stops on the Metropolitan Line from Baker Street to Rayners Lane, the train's windows blurred by the yellowing shatterproof latticework stuck all over them.

Dad's 1942 diary testifies that my schooling began on September 7, when I was five. Roxbourne School was not far away: right out of the house, along

Lynton Road, left at the brick public air-raid shelter, into Widdicombe Avenue, past Exeter Road, and right into Torbay Road. Little traffic to avoid, no muggers or child-molesters in the neighbourhood, the only dangers, as we were soon warned, being the 'butterfly' bombs the Luftwaffe sometimes dropped, with children particularly in mind. Pick one of these intriguing and peculiar objects up and you would lose a hand at the very least.

The alleyways backing the rows of houses were an alternative route, where we could linger, and flick cigarette-cards against the fence, the one closest taking the lot. That way I came near to collecting a full set of *Kings & Queens of England* (Richard the Lionheart, Henry V and Charles I were favourites) and *Film Stars* (Madeleine Carroll and Gary Cooper were the pick). I was also keen on *Aircraft of the Royal Air Force*, naturally enough, and even the tranquillising Wills's *Garden Flowers*. The bearded sailor on the Player's Navy Cut cigarette packet itself was yet another stirring symbol of British history, virtue and indomitability.

How those mothers must have worried. When the air-raid sirens wailed, you ran fast on to school or back home, whichever was nearer. In the school grounds there was a long tunnel of a shelter, narrow and gloomy and stuffy and almost certainly a home for rats. And to add to the inconvenience, we had to squeeze our faces into our smelly, rubbery 'Mickey Mouse' gas-masks.

The war would eventually draw to an end, or so everybody went on believing for sanity's sake. But something that was to touch me for life began in that school playground, for it was there that I first picked up a cricket bat. In the five years at Roxbourne that initial touch of a bat-handle and a tennis-ball flourished into a serious interest that grew in due course almost out of control. Still, it was preferable to picking up one of those evil butterfly bombs.

Miss Mead and Miss Rees (who taught us to sing *All Through the Night* in Welsh as well as English) were my main teachers, with Miss Ramsay a stern but sensitive headmistress. My artistic and literary pretensions were soon budding.

My first book materialised, a diminutive four-page work entitled *Scrubbing Brush Island*, something about an elephant and some buns. Miss Ramsay said she'd store it in the school's treasury of keepsakes, but when I went back over 40 years later to reclaim my literary masterpiece, there was no sign either of it or Miss Ramsay.

I graduated quickly from messy poster paints, and drew a soldier, almost as big as myself, with his rifle as authentic as could be, thanks to my familiarity with Uncle Bill's .303.

My special pals were Colin Glass, Richard Hewitt and George Cridlan, so in no fashion might I have been regarded as a loner . . . at that stage. Ralph Lidyard was the cricket know-all. He was ahead of me in strokeplay, in bowling the off-break, and in his knowledge of cricketers. I had vowed to overtake him within the year . . . and in due course, perhaps everybody else in the world, if I could only manage it.

Ralph was even ahead of me in cigarette-cards. And he teased. 'Betcha you don't know who this one is!' he said as he flashed a 1938 Player's card. I'd just caught a glimpse of the caption, 'C.Washbrook', before he slid his thumb across it. Thinking as fast as I could, I mumbled 'Colin Washbrook?' 'No!' he yelled triumphantly. 'Tis!' 'Tisn't!' 'Tis!' 'Tisn't!' 'Betchawotchalike! Let me see!'

He did, purring, 'It's *Cyril,* not Colin!'

What a long, long road lay ahead (though I have never been daunted by long roads) if everything that needed to be learnt was to be learnt.

Why, already I was stumbling over the English language. Uncle Bill, apart from teaching me how to tell the time (a boring necessity in the lifetime ahead), had perfected my ABC for me. But please, Miss Mead, how can b-u-s-y be the way to spell 'bizzy'? To complicate life further, I 'froze' during my maiden stage appearance, as a shepherd in the Nativity play. This shyness would have to be overcome somehow.

The perfectionist in me was emerging. I found it hard to hold hands with the other children in drill and playground games because one boy's hand, when touched, felt so dry and rough that the uneasiness ran right up my arm and made me catch my breath. And the first girl to take an interest in me – Beryl – was repulsed because I objected to the faint down on her arms and upper lip. When we were asked to choose a school outing, Beryl went for the Muir Mathieson concert (the composer/conductor, whose name appeared on so many film credits, gallantly performed with his broken arm in plaster), while I was carried off in another direction – the Tower of London or perhaps Windsor Castle. Cheaper, too.

At the age of nine or so I became infatuated with Anne, and in time this led to one chaste peck on the cheek. An anonymous Valentine's Day card came, covered in sweet little red hearts, and I wanted to believe it was from Anne, though I hadn't the nerve to find out; but it was probably from Beryl.

Mum, Dad and Auntie Edie had the *Tithe Farm* pub as their watering-hole, a walkable distance from home. I was usually parked outside, to stare at a mammoth stuffed pig in a glass display case, or to talk to other lads while their parents sipped their cares away inside. It was at the *Tithe Farm* that my parents got talking to a pilot from the nearby RAF base at Northolt, and he promised to buzz our house next time he went on a mission. He must have given an appointed time, for we were all ready in the garden that afternoon. The noise was intimidating, the split-second giant shadow heart-stopping, and the thrill massive. My young school-friends were clearly envious of the privilege I'd enjoyed.

The *Tithe Farm* was not always the site for incipient pleasure. Auntie Edie and Uncle Bill once left me outside, and the siren suddenly began wailing and screaming to warn of an impending air- raid. The shocking noise went through my head like a lance, and it took me a while to control my hysteria. The odd-smelling plaster miniature Lightning bomber (with camouflaged wings) which I was clutching, a present from Mum, was no comfort, and I wondered not so much if the truculent promises of ultimate Allied victory would ever come to pass but whether my nerves, like my poor mother's, would be frayed beyond repair before the end came.

The most grotesque nightmare of the war came with a bout of German measles that laid me up in delirium. For a time my tortured mind placed me inside a U-boat, of all places, the panic doubling the emission of perspiration from my germ-racked body. Mum, of course, was out of her mind at the sight of her prostrate son. But it was all soon over.

Dad was always in control. He towelled me down during this illness, and was swiftly in action another time when the pile of sand I was standing on collapsed and my back slid down the splintery fence, gathering a collection of dirty wooden 'needles' around the spinal flesh. It took him some time, with sterilised needle and tweezers, to remove the debris and bathe the small holes in the flesh. His sturdy fingers, anything but delicate, were as decisive of movement as when he yanked out my loose baby teeth (sixpence a time as my prizemoney). He should have been a doctor. He wanted me to be. His shortage of education debarred him. My education was to leave me with no excuse.

Midway through boyhood I started to wonder about God. Dear old Aunt Flo, Mum's maiden aunt, lived in Stockwell after the war years spent at Huntley & Palmers in Reading. She served the Salvation Army for decades, and bought me *The Story of Jesus* for my seventh birthday, a 'pop-up picture' book. While the pop-up full-colour tableau of the Sermon on the Mount was compelling, I found myself even more tightly mesmerised by the Feast of the Apostles, and in particular by the slinking figure of Judas in the background. How many Judases lurked waiting ahead of me?

More immediately, what did God look like? I could see the handsome, gentle, bearded Jesus, and was impressed – even to the point of attending Sunday School for a few dreary weeks – but God seemed by all accounts to be the One we should all be obedient to if we wanted a long and healthy life (even if many of the dead soldiers must have been believers). But where was He . . . or She? I decided that that was Him up there in that enormous, fleecy summer cloud formation. But no, I reasoned, that was only one of loads of clouds around the world. Logic triumphed. God was probably that exquisite crystal powder-pot on Mum's dressing-table. It was at that glass-topped dressing-table, with its two wing mirrors, that I had first seen what the back of my head looked like. Now I replicated the crystal powder-bowl by mirror reflection. But that couldn't be right. There is only one God, Aunt Flo said. Lifting the heavy crystal lid, I saw and smelt aromatic pink face-powder. The quest for a glimpse of the Almighty was to continue. I knew He was there somewhere, even if He permits some surprising behaviour by Nature and by humans.

On New Year's Day 1944 my father began a fresh diary, but only after some brief reflections on 1943: 'Last year was bad: – Michael was born premature, I broke my foot, I got an ulcer, Mum died, Michael & David had whooping cough, Michael bronchitis. I couldn't get a diary. We also have a lot of good news. Germany bombed to Hell, Italy out of the war, we take Sicily, Tunisia, North Africa, a load of islands, Scharnhorst sunk 26/12/42, Russia doing marvellous, 2000 tons of bombs on Berlin 29/12/43.'

In that 1943-44 winter Dad was laid up for weeks with the duodenal ulcer. He had to consume only milk, custard and eggs (which necessitated a 'priority' on his ration-book). Like his stricken sister Nell, he read a lot: novels with wartime-issue yellow dustjackets, and, memorably, Malory's *La Mort d'Arthur*, from which he would read heroic extracts in a halting voice: '"Gramercy," said King Arthur, "for this journey; and wit you well," said King Arthur, "I shall acquite you of your goodnesse." And ever the Queene beheld Sir Launcelot, and wept so tenderly that shee sanke almost downe upon the ground for sorrow . . .'

The spirit of those Knights of the Round Table lived on in many an English home and heart. The Germans simply could not be allowed to trample over all this.

Some 1944 extracts from Ted Frith's diary, which reads at times like a series of Air Ministry communiqués:

January 14: For the past hour and half our heavy bombers have been passing over to Germany, very frequent sound these days after black-out. Pulled my old shed down, I want the wood for new one.

Jan 15: It's 7.50pm, the alert has sounded, guns going like mad, Jerry is going over overhead, and the fog is as thick as can be. You can't see your hand in front of you. Last night Berlin was again bombed by light force. Sneak raider dropped a bomb on London cinema 7 killed NO ALERT.

Jan 19: Visited David's school & saw him at work & spoke to his teacher, she gave a very good report of him & said he was the best boy in the class. Churchill home after his illness in North Africa.

Jan 20: Ede, David and I went to Winter Garden Theatre [Drury Lane] & saw *Where the Rainbow Ends.*

Jan 21: 2300 tons dropped on Berlin on its 105th raid. London had its 712 alert, lasted 2 hours, very heavy gunfire & it appeared to be a minor blitz.

We'll see in the morning press, shrapnel dropped like rain.

Jan 29: 'The wireless has gone funny' the expression we use just before a raid warning – is in progress just now 8.15pm.

Feb 3: The alert has just sounded, it's a moonlight night, our fighters are just going over to intercept.

Feb 4: We had a further alert at 5am. Very heavy gunfire. Bombs were dropped on London. 70 Nazis came over, 8 down, 20 reached London. Yesterday USA sent out 1100 planes to Wilhelmshaven.

Feb 13: It's getting a habit with Jerry, we put up a hellaver barrage & when one dived we thought he was going to drop his lot but he dived to dodge guns.

Feb 14: We're out of coal & no delivery for a week, 4cwts per month we're allowed, we are making good use of electric fires.

Feb 16: Berlin very heavily raided, 2500 tons of bombs rained down in 30 mins, the heaviest raid in history of any war or any country. Good luck. Keep it up. Remember London, Coventry, etc.

Feb 19: It was mainly over this way, Ealing, Acton, Wembley, Alperton, Eastcote & Wealdstone, the latter very heavy, big fires were started. Flares lit the sky & all kinds of weapons were used, it was very noisy, like hell let loose & none brought down.

Feb 22: 12th week of sick leave. I was able to buy 1 lb (5) lemons today the first for years. Edie came home drunk again, that's Thurs, Fri, Sat, Mon & Tues she has come home late & drunk. God knows what has come over her, she looks terrible.

Feb 23: He dropped bombs on Harrow-on-the-Hill (West St), houses destroyed at Eastcote Lane (by Corbins Lane) very hot barrage. Edie drunk again. I shall code her in future as E.D.

Feb 26: Phew!! No alert last night, what a change. Edie didn't go to work but saw Dr McKeown, she is very repentant, promises again NO DRINKING OR NO SMOKING.

March 2: The war is now costing Britain £18,000,000 per day. Stuttgart raided by RAF last night, we sent 600 planes out & lost only 4. I queued up for 8 oranges and 7 lemons today 10/6.

March 8: USAAF made another very heavy raid on Berlin. Pat went to London to buy slippers & corsets, I made some cakes. E.D.

March 11: Lovely warm day with hot sun. Getting low on coal again. Edie came home at 11pm drunk as Hell, I gave her a good rousing & told her I give her two weeks to get out if she remains like this.

March 12: Edie still drunk & is drinking all day, she was in the dining room all night with the light on.

March 13: Very windy all day. Pat's washing was blown down 3 times. Made meat safe. [Refrigerators were still only for the wealthy.] Edie still blind drunk.

March 16: 6 days ago America said they will knock out the Luftwaffe within 30-60 days. Let's hope they are right.

March 17: Alert No.722 at 9pm. Clear starry night no moon, little gunfire, a few planes, lasted 35 mins, no incidents. David's party today [a day late, but it was Mum's birthday anyway].

March 24: Short alert at 12.15am this morning. Soon after 2 bombs were dropped somewhere rather near. Last night RAF sent 1000 bombers to Frankfort.

March 25: One bomb near to us. Took David to London to see 'Salute the Soldier' week.

March 26: I took David to Hyde Park to see the Tattoo, millions of people were there.

March 27: The pain in my right side has been very severe the last 3 days & if something is not done about it soon I'll go mad.

April 4: Saw doctor today & he said the X-ray seems satisfactory & gave me oil of belladonna to take before meals & at bedtime.

April 9: Bill sent Edie table cloth, planted out beans & tomato seeds.

April 12: Edie's at it again, stuck in the dining room all day blind drunk. We can't stand it much longer. I'll sling her out before long. Took David to see

Snow White & 7 Dwarfs at Ruislip.

April 14: Ede went to work today & came home asking for forgiveness. I had to give it to her, but how long for I don't know.

April 20: Pear and plum trees now in full bloom, apple trees have lots of buds. Busmen and Manchester gas works are out on strike now. It gets on one's nerves.

April 27: Reported back to duty, strange it was too. Seems a nice place & blokes seem OK so far.

May 8: When the heck is this 2nd Front going to start? We are all waiting.

May 13: 'Tiny' our rabbit died.

May 22: Phoned Dr Simpson to visit David, after examining him he thinks its German measles, thank God it's no worse than that.

May 23: Things in Italy going very good, Russia quiet, Far East also very good. David is much better, but no rash out yet. Planted out cabbage, spinach, caulis & sprouts.

May 24: David is much better now, still no spots yet, the doctor has given him a tonic. Michael now has 10 teeth & quite well.

May 26: I have planted out over 650 plants & that's about enough.

June 6: AT LAST THE 2nd FRONT HAS BEEN OPENED ON NORTHERN FRANCE, ALL SEEMS OK.

June 7: We have occupied Caen 10 miles inland using tanks there. Gen. Montgomery is leading them in, 11,000 planes, 4000 ships & thousands of small craft used for the landing, very little oppersition from Jerry, no activity over our coast: I guessed that something was in the wind.

June 14: Michael immunised today. David now fit to go back to school. I was taken very bad at 5.30pm & was sent home to bed. McKeown called & put me on 4ozs milk per hour for 3 days.

June 15: A plane seemed to skim our roof, misfiring all the time, it crashed in Hillingdon.

June 16: Now disclosed Jerry is using pilotless planes & he has let loose quite a lot & we have to expect a lot of sleepless nights now. I know now we had a narrow squeak.

June 18: Coming home from cemetery tonight Spitfire shot one down at Harrow? Several I heard explode.

June 20: We have started sleeping in the shelter again & we all had a lovely night.

June 21: One 'doodlebug' dropped on North Harrow yesterday & did we hear it. We have some nice comfortable nights in the shelter now.

June 23: We are still bombing Pas de Calais very heavy. Jap Fleet gets a beating from USA Fleet.

June 26: One dropped at West Harrow & the blast blew out some (4) windows in Rayners Lane.

June 28: One came right over the house this afternoon. I don't know where it landed. Rose, Maureen & Janice came to stop.

June 30: [Nine more alerts.] North Harrow caught a nasty blow last night, hitting British Restaurant & one hears of these 'buzz' bombs from people every day, very sad tales are told too.

July 2: Went to London today & saw some bomb damage, Tottenham Court Rd is terrible. Raining all day.

July 15: Jerry seems to be cutting his 'Buzz Bombs', we don't seem to get many alerts these days.

July 20: I saw one streak overhead at 10.30am, went to Acton Lane. Another at 11.45 red hot & low. Attempt on Hitler's life with dynamite, he was only slightly burnt, hard luck.

July 22: One past over Lynton Road tonight (I was on leave) when Jerry [a relative of Uncle Bill's] and I was coming back from pub.

July 23: I was on the 4pm job at Nevern Square & did more rescue work. I should say it's the worst damage I've seen with one bomb.

July 29: Just now I'm beginning to be a little scared of B.Bombs these days after seeing so much damage & casualties. High Street Kensington yesterday: – 35 killed 64 injured.

July 30: Pat phoned & said one had dropped at West Harrow.

August 1: This BB business is doing a helluver lot of damage, I'm afraid I'm getting a bit browned off, but I've got to stick it & put up with it, after all there is a war on & I'm a fireman.

August 2: One dropped in Philbeach Gdns on our ground, we got 7 out including 2 dead & now there are 10 still missing.

August 3: One dropped last night in South Harrow. More windows at Rayners Lane broken. I was on leave today & had a dam good sleep, my body aches.

August 6: Pat is now thinking of evacuating with kids to Derby.

August 20: Phew! he sent over a load today, owing to very low cloud, one dropped in the park only 50 yards from our observation post. Not one injured. I was on working party at Euston LMS to help evacuees.

August 21: Very windy & rain all day, one dropped in Holland Park breaking some of our station windows. E.D.

August 26: Things are much better to get except beer, there's a shortage of that everywhere.

Sept 8: Went away to Dartmouth today 5 hours on train, arrived very tired.

Sept 9: Michael is flabagasted at all the sights to greet his eyes, ships, trains, cows, etc.

Sept 11: David & I went out hazel-nutting collected about 3lb to take home with us, had a few long walks.

Sept 20: Jerry has started V2. He sends them over in day, no alert is sounded. Makes a huge crater.

Sept 27: Our air-troops have been withdrawn from Arnham, very heavy losses. It will go down in history as a great & glorious action.

Oct 7: I went to see Nell at hospital this evening, she is bringing up blood, she looks pretty bad to me.

Oct 11: Aachan refuses surrender terms, now we'll show 'em how to raze a town to the ground.

Oct 22: A terrific explosion woke us home at Harrow on Fri night, it was V2 rocket & it dropped behind *Adam & Eve* pub at Hayes, 18 injured no killed.

Nov 8: Heard from Bill, says most of his old company wiped out.

Nov 21: A V2 dropped in Battersea at 11.15pm & it simply rocked the station.

Nov 28: White paper out about UK war effort, 4,500,000 houses damaged (1 in 3 in the country) 60,000 civilians killed 80,000 injured 22,000,000 people mobilised. Cost of war up to now is [£]22,000 millions, all the world praises the U.Kingdom.

Nov 30: I win £1 if war isn't over today. Well Dickson has paid me his 10/ – Feinmessen is at Euston so I'm waiting to hear from him & give me his 10/–

Dec 18: Hoorah! Bill is home for 5 weeks.

Dec 22: Underground drivers threaten a strike over Xmas day if they're not given 2 days holiday, what a bloody lot we Englishmen are.

Dec 25: Freezing very hard, 1/4in of frost. Underground are on strike, I couldn't get to station so I'm off today as well. We've taken a little lost ground in Belgium & Germany.

So he won a few bob, with some regret, because the war had stretched beyond 1944, though the expectation of peace was still strong. Even a boy could feel it. But more death and devastation were to come before the ultimate jubilation of VE Day and VJ Day.

Reference to the new shed – my father was so very adept in carpentry, model galleons too – conjures up visions of the Great Mice Massacre. I was laid up with some ailment or other when some of my 60 tame mice (a tribe of white, brown and black darlings which I'd bred from little pink blobs from three original sixpenny purchases) gnawed through their wooden cage and scattered behind Dad's tool benches, and behind the coal bunkers. In spite of my quavering protest, my father argued that they must not be allowed to breed wild to infestation levels. So he set about picking them off – with a little too much relish for my liking – with his Webley air-pistol. As I lay in my sick-bed, a shudder shot through my body at every 'clack!' of the gun.

The theatre outing in January 1944 was evidently pleasant enough, which was more than could be said of the pantomime put on by the firemen a couple of years earlier. Dad had worn a false black beard, a weird hat, cape and green pantaloons, and terrified his son, who sat with his mother in the stalls. No amount of reassurance soothed, and I ended up under the seat, praying for this outrage to end.

Kids' birthdays were celebrated with gusto. My seventh was marked a day late with a party on March 17, Mum's 35th birthday. Colin, Richard and George were there, together with half the juvenile population of Lynton Road, most of the residents having moved in during the 1930s and quickly started families. The mixture of exhibitionism and shyness at these parties always made for alternating silence and uproar, and the juvenile jinks – pinning tails on donkeys, musical chairs, pass-the-parcel, scholarly but brief quizzes – usually ended when somebody was sick all over the carpet. I don't recall ever being sad when the parents arrived to collect their offspring.

These parties, home and away, became more serious after I got my two pairs of boxing-gloves one Christmas. Fighting was exciting, and fun, until the burlier Colin planted a few straight lefts on my nose. Boxing with Dad was no better. It was hard to get past his longer reach, even when he fought from the kneeling position. And when I did land one on him, I felt bad.

Small gifts went back and forth at the children's parties. Birthdays and Christmases in the Frith household were, war or no war, glamorous affairs. And I cannot pretend I didn't do well. Dad made so many toys himself, and the smell of fresh paint became evocative ever after. One year a slim edition of *Treasure Island* was backed up by a beautiful Dad-made wooden model of Captain Smollett's *Hispaniola*, which I stared at on the Christmas tree without quite being able to accept that it would soon be mine. (The book's illustrations of the ruthless pirates were to come in useful for scaring my annoying little brother.)

So eager was my father to give me the kind of jolly Dickensian Christmas that he had craved and missed in his deprived childhood that he left a note purportedly written by Father Christmas, complete with sooty smudge-marks, and a drained brandy-glass from which the thirsty old boy with the flowing white beard had allegedly drunk. I was happily fooled.

Sick with excitement, I would fumble and feel for the presents in the darkness of the early hours, having taken ages to get to sleep. The boxing-gloves were so irresistible that I slid them into my bed well before dawn came up. I'd guess at the titles of the books: Just William books, building into a long run in the late 1940s, and the *Empire Youth Annual,* full of inspirational patriotic stuff, and *Heroes of the Sea.*

A toy sweet-shop and post office amused me for a time: tiny jars of sugary delights, a counter window, miniature postage stamps, forms of all colours, an official-looking rubber stamp. But the thought of having most of the merchandise left still unsold at the end of a day's trading convinced me I lacked the temperament to be a shopkeeper.

Even better than any birthday or Christmas was D-Day: June 6, 1944, when the Allies launched their long-awaited, unimaginably gigantic and perilous attack on occupied France.

Dad was not the sole gardener. I was prodding the carrots section of my vegetable patch with a hoe when old Mrs England next door, who dressed even more mournfully than Grandma, poked her head over the fence by the sweet-peas and made herself heard above the roar of the aircraft overhead: 'David, go and tell Mummy to put the wireless on!'

As those great Dakotas droned southwards, some towing gliders, all with three distinctive white bars across their wings, the voices of Eisenhower, Montgomery and Churchill were intoning that this was it: the greatest counter-punch in history. Many hundreds of thousands – millions – of husbands, fathers and young shavers were charging at the hated enemy's fortifications. Soon the supremely thrilling sight of the landing-barges hitting the Normandy beaches was beaming from our cinema screen. Was the war about to end? Not quite. But that smiling milkman and sunlit peacetime lawn over in America might soon be replicated in battered, weary old England.

As Dad's diary records, the deadly flying-bombs – V1s – were the next threat. One jagged its raucous way across the sky one afternoon at the back of the house, seemingly uneven in flight-path (or perhaps I was swaying with apprehension), flame from the single jet barely perceptible. The engine cut-out, which everybody dreaded, occurred when it was almost out of sight. It then plunged to earth to the west of us with its deadly weight of explosive. Its successor, the V2 rocket, was thought to be faster than sound and was therefore blasting its random victims to kingdom come before anybody knew it was coming. What a merciful, lethal weapon. The war wasn't yet won.

The boys in the street and at school continued with their war games. The small hands held either an imaginary rifle or a wooden one, and the fabricated sound of automatic gunfire had to be mastered: 'Huh-uh-uh-uh-uh! You're dead!' If there was an art to being shot, it eluded our gang: melodramatic hugging of the chest with agonised gyrations before the final collapse (carefully) to the ground. One sunny afternoon, during an ambush on the little wooded traffic island where Newquay Crescent meets Kings Road, I almost trod on a small white rubber thing which a sophisticated boy named Davidson (whose unmarried sister had brought shame on the family by falling pregnant) identified as a condom – a 'frenchie'. Red double-decker buses passed right by that island, but under wartime regulations their headlights were restricted to mere slits. The 'lovers' would have been safe.

Happily ignorant of all things adult apart from their capacity to drink, smoke, swear and kill, I had engaged in an innocent experiment for a minute or two one evening in the air-raid shelter. Dad's diary happens to pinpoint it: June 28, 1944, when Rose, a sister or sister-in-law of Uncle Bill's, parked her two little girls with us. While the adults might have been at the pub, I placed my cigarette-cards on display by the entrance to the shelter, on the pathway by the cabbages that grew to enormous bulk and were smothered in creepy yellow caterpillars. It began to rain quite heavily. One of the little girls – who may have known more than I did about life – suggested we 'rub bellies'. It seemed a pointless exercise really. That was all there was to it. In the morning my cards were fatally soggy, and the caterpillars had multiplied.

The trip to Devon in September was a delight, from the intensity of the train journey to the beauty of Dartmouth and Dittisham. An old sea salt at Dartmouth told us, as we looked across the water, about the son he had just lost in the merchant navy, victim of a torpedo, like so many brave and defenceless merchantmen. Dittisham, the picturesque village, and the rose-fringed cottage where we stayed, must have conjured up idyllic visions for Mum of what a perfectly peaceful existence might have been, even if we were city/suburban folk by upbringing. During that fortnight of bliss we saw Paignton Zoo and Torquay and, much to my mother's despair, Plymouth, which, although Francis Drake's monument on the Hoe was unscathed, had suffered almost as grievously as London. (According to my notes in an exercise-book of the time, Drake used to play 'bowels'.) Mum was unprepared for the sight of the bomb carnage, and was badly shaken. There must have been deep depression at the awareness that all of England, not just London, was gradually being destroyed.

When the males went out on a rabbit shoot in the serene Devonshire wilderness, I spoiled it by hurling stones whenever I saw a bobtail, depriving the men of a level shot. I can't recall whether I was trying to claim a rabbit of my own with a pebble on the head or trying to scare them off before the shotguns killed them.

One noble theme touched me powerfully in Cornwall, and that was the legend of King Arthur and his Knights of the Round Table, first found during that convalescence of my father's. It touched me because it had clearly touched him, from the time as a teenager when he walked to Cornwall from London in search of his brother and found himself in Tintagel, with its rocky clifftops. Now, in 1944, when Good versus Evil was the concept that governed all deed and thought, Arthur was, like Elizabeth I, Drake, Nelson and Wellington, a perfect patriotic vision and symbol of Strength and Virtue. Men and boys then would never have given a moment's consideration to flawed heroes. In those dark times it was all square jaw, steady gaze, shining armour and the British flag. This code was to remain functional, with never more than a fleeting adjustment, for ever more. I see red when a cricketer or footballer of the 1990s weeps just because his team was defeated.

Cheeringly, on the train journey home, there was Rocky Marciano. At least, the American GI who called 'Here, buddy!' and gave me some chewing-gum as we stretched our legs on the platform at one of the stops looked every bit like the future world heavyweight champ. Or was it Lou Costello?

A school exercise-book from 1944 is gently revealing: 'I wear a blue lumber- jacket and grey trousers,' I pencilled. 'I see my Dad off after I have eaten my breakfast.' Later: 'I know a policeman who is very big. He wears a helmet and it is a bit to small for him.' The critical faculty emerging at seven? And: 'A postman comes to our house every morning and he is a nice man. He wears a navy blue cap with a red stripe round it. You would always find him with his buttons shineing.' Then a Pythonesque 'The boy who sits next to me is called Brian.' And an optimistic statement of intent: 'I am going to stick a tall flag in my garden when its peace.' And the less-than-honest child: 'I like my milk, I like brown bread, That is why my cheeks are red.' Probably symptoms of a loner show in: 'I like to go in buses on my own. Usually I go in the little box where the people keep their cases when all the seats are full.' This is followed by: 'The bus that serves this area is the 114. It goes from Rayners Lane to Edgware . . . If I could change the name of my road because I didn't like it I would call it Shortman Road.'

'Three little gentlemen in coats of red rode their horses up to bed' earned me a green (Husky house) star, a kind of first-up literary award. There can seldom have been a simpler view of a soldier than: 'A soldier wears a kaki uniform and on his back he has some package. He's also got a knife and on his belt he's got some little bags with bullets in. Sometimes when he's in battle he has a bottle of water. On the end of his rifle he's got a bannet. His rifle is very heavy.' (Personal experience.)

Christmas '45 was clearly documented (with a precocious semi-colon): 'On Christmas Eve I had a bath, that night I could not get to sleep. Anyway at last I did. It did not seem a minute I was asleep when I woke up. I had a very big surprise for I had Mickey Mouse Annual for the third time running; and Rupert for the second time. I also had a pair of cowboy's trousers with fur on the front. I had a Christmas pudding and a turkey for dinner. As it was Jesus's birthday, when it was bedtime I read a little bit of the bible.'

Then, on January 18, 1945, came another creed for life:

Good, better, best,
Never be at rest
'Til the good is better
And the better, best.

Now the autobiographical jottings continued in pen. There was A Dream: 'I dreamt I had to join the army. As soon as I got to the billets, the officer shouted "Who are you" I said "I have come to join the army" "Alright" he said "you will go to France." I saluted and went to a hut which was the billet. Next morning I went to France and when I came home I was tattered and torn. When I woke up, as it was Saturday I played soldiers.'

This masterpiece earned a 'Quite good'.

With the war grinding to its conclusion at long last, 1945 became the greatest year in many people's lives, including mine. Dad wrote another diary, but only up to late June, when life must have been blissful, drained at last of its long-term scary daily and nightly drama, though a new set of anxieties would present itself ere long.

Having sold six of his model galleons for £25, he went out and bought 'a load of decoration materials for the house'. It was still only January, but he was hoping for some good weather so he could start the painting during periods of leave. Just as the snow was beginning to thaw, another heavy lot fell: 'David and I have had a great deal of snowballing and he has had the time of his life.'

At this point he calculated that London had endured 1230 alerts, 487 of them from those deadly V1 flying-bombs.

And so to the run-in to victory:

January 13: I detest this new station (A.19), it's cold, very cold grub rotten. I'm trying to get out.

Jan 17: Warsaw captured by Russians, marvellous.

Jan 19: Rain, sleet, wind & snow, that's the weather we're having today.

Jan 25: A rocket exploded in the air over Dollis Hill this morning & blew me against door. Russians now only 150 miles from Berlin.

Feb 1: Blimey! A rocket burst in the air over Rayners Lane 4.30am this morning, what a bang, poor Mick screamed, I had him in my arms in about 2 or 3 seconds, Pat visited WC.

Feb 4: I've started painting out the hall & stairs now and I've got Column Officer [Percy] Thomas to help me.

Feb 15: We are giving Germany a really terrific bombing these days, Dresden had 650,000 incendiary bombs and thousands of tons of HEs.

Feb 17: Hoorah I get transferred to A.8 Kensington next Friday, Oh to get shot of A.19 Dollis Hill, The Mortuary.

Feb 18: Beautiful day today 65° in bedroom. Dave & I went to see Nell & she's very much better, it won't be long before she's out. Monty has advanced another 2 miles.

Feb 21: Started decorating up the dining room, Col/Off [Column Officer]

Thomas is now plain Mr [Percy] Thomas. He's out of the Service.

Feb 27: Very few rockets these days, bloody good job too.

March 1: Michael fell & cut his head yesterday & today David caught Mick's small finger (right hand) in kitchen door.

March 5: We now have on London piloted planes, rockets & fly-bombs, yet no one worries except Pat.

March 17: Pat's birthday (36). David had a lovely party today 18 kids, hard days work for me, we all enjoyed it.

March 21: Fetched Nell away from Staines. Berlin twice last night. Terrible damage and casualties at Packards by rocket bomb, another burst over Harrow, cracked kitchen window.

March 22: Still I haven't put my seeds in, I'm waiting for rain to break the soil up.

March 24: Monty has struck & very hard too, crossed the Rhine, biggest airbourne assult yet, bigger than Arnham or D-Day.

March 29: Blackout imposed on Monty's moves, Patton is sending mad tank columns spearheads in the thick of Germany.

April 2: My pear tree is now in full bloom the best yet, so is the plum, just planted seeds.

April 3. Monty is tearing into Germany, prisoners coming in at rate of 20,000 per day, town after town is falling to Allies.

April 4: Lionel Gray [fellow fireman] 3.15 Green Park Stn. Took David with me, Lionel wanted to see me with a view to opening up a shop with him, I haven't decided to yet. Maybe.

April 12: Weather still very lovely 82° in the shade, the fruit trees at home show promise of a good crop.

April 13: President Roosevelt died at 11.50pm last night what a terrible shock to the world.

April 19: NFS are now emptying & disconnecting dams, a good sign. Blackout done away with as from next Mon, very good.

April 20: Americans have captured the horrible prison torture camp at Belsen, the Press is full of terrible pictures of it specially Kramer the Hun.

April 29: Partisans have killed Mussolini & 18 others, Berlin nearly completely captured.

May 1: Hitler is dead, he 'died at his battle post in Berlin' Admiral Donetz is the new Feuhrer, he orders fight on. Ha Ha.

May 3: The sirens will not sound again, weve 'ad it, Germans surrendering all over the place, the crack has come at last.

May 4: Gone sick with fibrositis (stiff neck). Well it's all over bar the shouting, Pat said she would be drunk on VE night, just now she is as sick as a dog mostly excitement.

May 7: At 2.41 am this morning Germany signed unconditional surrender, to take effect from tommorrow midnight.

May 8: What a day, Churchill spoke on wireless 3pm, the King 9pm, the kids in Lynton Road had a party in road, I made bonfire & burnt Hitler.

May 9: Took David to London, saw King & Queen, London has gone mad, all jolly & merry, weather warm, we queued up to go into Westminster Abbey. Got my new civvy suit.

May 10: Sign of the times, I'm taking down our shelter, Pat is as pleased as Punch, Goering captured, Nazi fleet surrender.

May 11: I guess from now on there won't be a lot to put in this war diary now.

My father went back to his diary on June 28 to list the fates of members of the 'Nazi gang', complete with his own versions of spelling: Hitler dead? Goebels dead, Himmler dead, Goering, Rippontrop, Von Keitel, Kesselring, Rundstudt and 'Haw- Haw' all captured, Laval in Spain awaiting arrest, etc, etc.

'I left the NFS,' wrote this unsung hero, 'on June 17th & started as manager of John Lewis & Co snack-bar. General Election is in full swing, Conservative are sure to get in . . .' How wrong could one be? And he explains – on behalf of all of us – how hard it was to get used to the cessation of siren alerts and the sound of violence and murder as bombs fell. 'Never again,' he reflects, 'will we be annoyed with the sight of the Anderson shelter blocking the view of the garden . . . It's lovely rushing out of the house each morning at 7.15 to catch the workmans [train] to work & rushing home again, just like pre-war days.'

The concrete pit where the shelter stood was converted by Dad into a fish-pond, where two golden carp swam easily around, glorying in the honoured names of Monty and Winnie. In the hard winter of 1946-47 they survived for many days under an impenetrable two-inch crust of ice. The little colony of frogs was less hardy, less fortunate. When relief came they were stiff, long-legged corpses.

At the end of 1945, Dad planted his final entry into his diary on the war theme: further fates ('John Amery hanged, Gen.Patton killed in crash, Labour Government in, Atom bombs dropped, now at Taylors restaurant') and reflections on those final dramatic weeks: 'Hitler's body has not yet been found, maybe he has fled to Japan. The Japs are getting a big thrashing now, Okinawa has fallen . . . Emporer Hirorito [Hirohito] will take supreme command of all his forces, he will no doubt commit hari-kari rather than unconditional surrender.'

And there was a telling pointer to the Frith family's medium-term fate: 'The housing shortage is very bad & so is the food problem, we have had fats cut down & meat also, potatoes have been terrible scarce we've queued for 1 hour for only 3lb, it was bad.' Perhaps there was a faraway place where things weren't so bad?

Of all my father's 1945 diary entries (which, incidentally, he read again 38 years later, when he was 74, and inscribed on the front cover: 'What a true stark war diary') four entries trigger outstandingly vivid impressions.

I was sitting alongside him in bed, looking over his arm as he read his paper, the *Daily Mirror*, with the memorable *Jane* and *Garth* and *Ruggles* cartoon strips, when Mum came in with the stunning news that the American President had died. Franklin D. Roosevelt, strong, kindly, decent man, had long been sick and worn-out, but it was cruel that he was not spared to see the Allied victory.

Still, we had our Montgomery and Eisenhower, and all the other military, naval and air force chiefs, and supreme among all our heroes Winston Churchill, whose growling, rousing, defiant speeches boomed across the living-rooms of the land, seeing his people through when all seemed lost. That influence was to be lasting and maybe even a little character-forming for many – and bulldogs would for ever more be representative of the great struggle. A 'fight them on the beaches' and 'we shall never surrender' stance was going to be adopted towards all the cheats and adversaries one was inevitably going to encounter in the life ahead. The desecration of his Westminster statue 75 years later was a foul outrage.

In the early days of the war a boy could manage to smile (Grandma stands anxiously by the door) . . .

The newsreel footage of the strung-up corpses of Mussolini and his mistress sparked booing and vengeful hissing from the audience. Poor Uncle Bill, still on some far distant land, was being kept waiting for his demobilisation to England; otherwise he would have joined in with us.

As for the street party, we ate and drank well at the long trestle table, and the Hitler effigy Dad made was convincing. He threw one of his fireman's practice explosives onto the huge bonfire and proved to all the neighbours that a certain woman was not as deaf as she pretended. And we had races, though I just stood by the finishing-line, chewing my fingernails. Auntie Edie saw none of this. She was as drunk as she'd ever been, poor thing, and collapsed after throwing an empty gin bottle from an upstairs window.

. . . but by Victory Day 1945 he had developed a neurotic nail-biting (far left)

As for the VE Day celebrations in London, a boy sensed that these mental pictures would last him for life, barring acute senility. Grown-ups filled every square-foot of pavement and road, laughing, singing, making any silly, euphoric noise that their voice-boxes could devise. Every Allied uniform seemed visible, European and Commonwealth. There seemed no danger of violence or theft or discord. It was innocent joy, unfettered.

The grand parade was like a variety show: the King and Queen, Field Marshal Montgomery in his beret, Churchill taking the plaudits like some rotund batsman who had just scored 200 before lunch. And towards the rear was a jeep manned by laughing Yanks who had scrawled 'Nuts and Bolts' across the windscreen, just in case anybody had become too serious.

We'd been spared from the greatest human conflict yet known. We had prevailed. We had been blessed. I was proud to be the son and the nephew of heroes. What now?

CHAPTER THREE

I much prefer the past. It was much happier.

BRIAN WILSON

WHILE Dad, in his uniform, was the centre-stage hero, it was becoming clearer to me that the inner heart of the family was, and always had been, my mother. She endured the many stresses of her husband's hazardous five-year ordeal amidst the bombing carnage; she feared for the safety of her two little sons; she worried about her alcoholic sister and warrior brother-in-law; she mourned her mother and uncle; she dreaded TB contagion from her sister-in-law; she bore the sadness of a cousin's death from beriberi while a prisoner of the Japanese. The heroism on foreign fields from Mum's side of the family had come from cousin Tinky, who saved his soldier mates in the Dunkirk evacuation. It was not so much on foreign fields as waters, for their escaping motor-launch had broken down. They were sitting ducks for German dive-bombers, but Tinky, the only one with mechanical knowhow, eventually managed to get the engine to cough back to life, and back to the White Cliffs and comparative safety they putt-putted.

Mum was proud of what she considered to be a cockney background, though she was born in Aybrook Street, too far west of Bow Bells for that kind of pedigree.

She had inherited a set of expressions that probably died with her generation: 'Got the 'ump?' (Are you fed up?); 'cocky packet' (smartarse); 'soppy 'ay'p'th' (Silly you); and among a small selection of cockney back-slang terms 'Evach a kool' (Have a look), and rhyming slang: 'apple and pears' (stairs). I wish she had talked more about her childhood, but, perhaps because her mother 'worked her fingers to the bone' in service and she lost her father so young, she was disinclined to reminisce, apart from the odd story. One which she told often was about the monkey in London Zoo who was being teased by visitors. He turned his back, peed into a brown paper bag, and then tossed the 'bomb' through the bars, splashing his tormentors.

For years her mother had worked for the McClure family in Conduit Mews. Mum had no resentment about her as she referred to the supposed upper classes as 'knobs'. Her distinctive handwriting was surprisingly firm and stylish. And whenever I left the house, there was always a loving 'Mind 'ow you go, love!'

If there was a conflict in her make-up, it was that she sought respectability while exuding no trace of stuffiness or snobbery, no pretence. Like most young women in the 1930s, she idolised Ronald Colman, Lew Ayres and Leslie Howard, with a dash of Continental taste for Anton Walbrook and Maurice Chevalier, and could listen all evening to Rudy Vallee and the velvety Bing Crosby, and Al Bowlly, South African- born, who was killed in the Blitz, or, a bit later, to Donald Peers. And among the bevy of film stars whose hairstyles her generation adopted she liked Zasu Pitts and Tallulah Bankhead, probably because they never took themselves too seriously. At a party, Mum would be in the thick of *Roll Out the Barrel* – much to her son's embarrassment – and yet, to confound us all, no music moved her more (even though she would mimic hilariously the sopranos who trilled and warbled from the wireless) than the spine-tingling *Nuns' Chorus* from Johann Strauss's Casanova.

She was a suburban Madonna. Her smile was as sweet as the wartime Queen's; she resembled that lady. To look at, Dad was more Randolph Scott than the King. Together, in their pre-war nonchalance, my parents looked simply perfect in their stylish holiday outfits, stepping along the seaside promenade. Why should they have wanted to spoil their freedom by having kids?

When the house filled up during those wartime years, swear-words sometimes rent the air, though only 'bloody' and 'bugger', nothing foul. It was not contagious. My parents never heard their little angel utter one unacceptable word – except for the time when I found a hole in my sock as I left the house. I was for some reason already in a grim mood, and when I looked down and saw the flesh of my heel where wool should have been, I blurted out: 'And now I've got a bloody hole in my sock!' Mum burst out laughing, but I blushed all the way to the bend in the street.

Her outstanding attribute, aside from her perpetual and undemonstrative affection, was her jollity. And yet her cheerfulness was linked oddly to an Olympian capacity to worry. The frivolity in the carefree young pre-war wife was crushed by wartime terror. Thoughtlessly, I came home with sixpenn'orth of fish for the cat. It was the ugly head of a hake, and my love of wordplay led to my announcing that I'd got a 'head-hake'. Mum almost collapsed. Her boy had had whooping cough and German measles. What now? Was it TB? (Remember poor Aunt Nell.) 'No, Mum, the fish is a "hake"!'

Beyond infancy, we only ever once clung physically to each other, and that was when she was demonstrably and deeply upset about something. As she sat on the staircase and fought against her tears, I touched her arm, anguished at her distress, especially as I think I had been partly to blame. She embraced me, and soon I knew it was all right, and I pulled away.

As 1946 unfurled, a full life beckoned. There was endless joy emanating from the wireless. The vibrant voice of the Forces' Sweetheart, Vera Lynn, had carried us through the years of fear. *We'll Meet Again* was an anthem in itself, but *Yours* was the recording that would forever more scoop me up from wherever I was and place me back in the dining-room at 80 Lynton Road, with Auntie Edie singing with Vera to her Bill across the seas. *There'll Always Be An England* stirred the soul, and had us thinking for many years yet, though not necessarily forever, that the assurance in the song's title might be depended upon. Gracie Fields had touched us with her Lancashire bounce, and George Formby's hilarious accent as he plinked his ukulele made England seem such a harmless, gormless place. Tommy Trinder, a fireman in *The Bells Go Down*, had given us an inkling of the perils that had beset Dad night and day during the Blitz. The nonsense emitted by Enoch & Ramsbottom in *Happidrome* was a welcome contribution; same with Robb Wilton and Wee Georgie Wood. The Western Brothers were drawling away with their 'cads' duet; Cyril Fletcher performed his *Odd Odes*; Elsie and Doris Waters (Gert and Daisy) went on and on like the neighbours down the road; 'Two Ton' Tessie O'Shea bellowed away, slapping her banjo; the Andrews Sisters, and Bebe Daniels and Ben Lyon, brought gusts of fresh American exuberance, and Charlie Kunz played his piano with a knowing touch which my heavy-handed father envied. All this uplifting of spirits, with the lovable midget 'Big-Hearted' Arthur Askey always buzzing around, enabled people better to endure mournful-looking politicians like Stafford Cripps and Ernest Bevin as well as the ongoing frustration of food rationing in the Austerity years, with the Radio Doctor grinding on about cures for constipation, and while the 'spivs', the 'wide boys', the 'barrer boys' surreptitiously sold their nylon stockings and other knockdown wares, usually stolen.

A certain Captain X put a spring into my post-war step. When I tied that cape (dishcloth) round my shoulders, I could leap up three steps at a time. Captain X could even bound the length of the house down the narrow side-path in three seconds. And it didn't involve having to talk. Accused often of being too serious and too quiet, I'd explained that I didn't want to use up all my breath by speaking, believing implicitly that God had given each of us a lifetime ration of words, and they should therefore be used sparingly.

A more mature activity than Captain X was the Wolf Cubs. Once more into uniform, with braided cap, throat-scarf, woggle, and badges galore sewn on as knots and signalling and breeding silk-worms and other skills were mastered. There we crouched, on the floor of the little hut perched by the railway bridge at Rayners Lane, chanting our DYB DYB and DOB DOB in obedience to our Akela. She sometimes took us to larger accommodation, a chilly Nissen hut, where other cubs came, and we prepared acts. My sketch based on Just William would have enchanted the lot of them if only the four of us, sitting in an imaginary motor-car, had not completely forgotten our words.

A full life it was. Horse-chestnuts were gathered in the autumn for conker contests (today banned for being too dangerous). Last year's conkers, kept in the airing cupboard, were always tougher, and a soaking in vinegar helped too. Already the inventive needs for survival in this demanding, competitive world were being addressed.

Indoors, just because the war had ended it didn't mean we suspended our soldier games. Dozens of the leaden heroes bedecked the carpet; the toy Howitzer cannon fired its matchsticks until they were all mown down, flat, dead.

More constructively, there were jigsaws (Dad even made one of our own design with his fret-saw) – *The Three Caballeros*, Donald Duck, José Carioca, courtesy of Walt Disney (whom I ranked only behind Churchill, Montgomery and Dad among magnificent men). Then, on wintry evenings by the fireside, there were games of *Monopoly*, which Dad always won. And it hurt. Once, when he popped outside to refill the coal-scuttle, I took a furtive peep at the next Chance card in the pile. As I replaced it, I caught sight of Dad's face peering reprovingly from the darkness through the French windows. It scared the wits out of me, and I felt even worse when he came back into the room . . . and said nothing.

Peace in our suburban back garden, 1946. Mum can smile once more.
DF, in cub uniform, tries to be a good big brother

Solitary pursuits were safer. I spent hours at my Home Cricket board game, rolling the dice, shifting the counter, scoring another single, weathering another lbw appeal. There was also Bayko, a forerunner of Lego, and preferable to the metallic Meccano set, the plaything of Peter Oliver, who lived over at the back, and whose parents over-indulged him. He had a Hornby train set too.

Paradise was a thick slice of bread and jam, steaming cocoa, and a good book. The comics were utterly vital – *Beano, Radio Fun, Knockout, Film Fun*: Our Ernie, Desperate Dan, Korky the Cat, Billy Bunter, Laurel and Hardy, Lord Snooty, Stonehenge Kit, Tiger Tim. But the colourful, blissful charm of Alfred Bestall's *Rupert Bear* gradually gave way to Just William. Christmases and birthdays produced a flow that amounted finally to 25 titles from the Lancastrian spinster Richmal Crompton's pen, with graphic illustrations by Thomas Henry. I had no ambitions to emulate William Brown, the scruffy, rebellious 11-year-old, though I rather liked the cut of his smooth and handsome brother Robert, and was later fortified to learn that the stories had been written in the 1920s with an adult readership in mind. The 'Outlaws', Ginger, Douglas and Henry, became my friends, while Violet Elizabeth Bott said it all about prissy, bad-tempered girls. The inscriptions in my William books range from 'To David from Mum and Dad' through 'From Mum with best wishes' to a warmer 'With best love, Mum, March 16th, 1946'.

It was less easy combining the nibbling of bread-and-jam with puffing into a mouth-organ, but that's the way it was when Danny Kaye, the sensation from America, was tickling us via the radio airwaves and singing *Balling the Jack*. It was easier to follow on a mouth-organ than was *The Nuns' Chorus*.

Music is in the blood of most of us. Dad and brother George, when young, had had a black-up minstrel act, the Jolly Boys, which they unleashed in pubs and in the street, singing and tap-dancing. Aware that all kinds of music stirred me, I then took a step further by constructing a miniature stage, complete with drawing curtains and a battery-powered lighting system, scarcely dazzling. The actors – toy soldiers and what-have-you, even a few farm animals – stood fixedly, and the scripts were hardly Shakespearean, but the charge for entering beyond my blanket partition to see the show was a penny, and I must almost have recovered my expenditure from the local kids.

While *Children's Hour* with 'Uncle Mac' was outgrown, the wireless remained the key entertainment source: *Just William*, *In Town Tonight*, *Workers' Playtime*, *Ignorance is Bliss*, *Much Binding in the Marsh*, *Music While You Work*, Wilfred Pickles' *Have a Go*, Jewell & Warris, newcomer Bill Kerr's strange Australian drawl, ingenuous programmes all of them. Dad even got a request put out in my name on Sandy Macpherson's show.

But one programme was paramount: *Dick Barton, Special Agent.* Each evening at a quarter-to-seven, *The Devil's Gallop* pounded out of the BBC's Light Programme wavelength, and all red-blooded boys sat close with tense breath. Dick Barton and his trusty assistants Snowy and Jock evaded all kinds of threats from all manner of villains during that riveting quarter-hour – Good versus Evil yet again. The mental images bred from the dialogue and sound-effects were the ultimate test of a youngster's power of imagination. Half-a-century later I learned that the *Daily Worker* had branded Barton a 'crypto-Fascist', and it was all an anti-Marxist plot. If only the dozen Rules of Conduct drawn up for the serial by the BBC were applied to real life. Among other things, Dick Barton's 'violence is restricted to clean socks [punches] on the jaw'; 'in reasonable circumstances, he may deceive but he never lies'; 'sex, in the active sense, plays no part in the Barton adventures'; and 'swearing and bad language generally may not be used by any character. This ban ranges from "bloody" through "God", "damn" and "Hell" to ugly expressions currently heard in certain conversations but not considered admissible for child usage in middle-class homes'. Not in the Frith household, at any rate.

As for the cinema, there were the noisy Saturday morning 'flicks' for kids only, all cowboys and Indians, cartoons and heart-stopping serials, and there were evening outings with Mum and Dad in the one-and-ninepennies at the Odeon, Rayners Lane: Charlie Chaplin eating his boot in *The Gold-Rush*; Spencer Tracy groaning away with *Goodbye Leetle Feesh* before horrifyingly disappearing beneath the waves in *Captain Courageous*; Bambi and Dumbo drawing teardrops of a different kind; more beloved Disney in Song of the South, with dear old Uncle Remus singing *Zip-a-Dee-Doo-Dah*; then *Peter and the Wolf* (with a bit of culture in Prokofiev's captivating musical compositions) and Willie the Giant in *Fun and Fancy Free*, whose blundering stupidity made even a 10-year-old feel superior.

Sonje Henie, twirling on ice-skates, was boring; Carmen Miranda, with a pile of fruit-salad on her head, flapping her eyelashes as she gurgled 'Eye-eye-eye-eye-eye-eye like you vaireee much', was ridiculous; Humphrey Bogart and Edward G. Robinson and Sydney Greenstreet in gloomy movies like *Key Largo* and *The Maltese Falcon* were too slow-moving and left young legs jumpy; James Mason and Margaret Lockwood in *The Wicked Lady* were little better. But we all wanted to be out of the house whenever possible for the sheer joy of no longer having to cower in fear of high-explosive bombs.

This Happy Breed melted the heart; *The Last of the Mohicans* was captivating because Dad was in it (Randolph Scott really); *Tarzan* and *Zorro* and *Robin Hood* (Cornell Wilde) gave us plenty of material to act out in street games (or on that traffic island). Then there was Danny Kaye – persuasively described somewhere, everywhere, as a genius – in *Up in Arms*; and Irving Berlin's *This is the Army, Mr Jones* for the benefit of those of us whose souls would forever tingle at matters military. Most beneficial, though, were the rib-tickling doses of Abbott & Costello and Laurel & Hardy. Their knockabout routines were crudely re-enacted in the playground and on the roadside kerb for days afterwards.

That kerb in Lynton Road was kept warm through summer evenings by our young backsides as we talked, and played with the fivestones we'd moulded out of clay: Horses in the Stable (tossing one up and flicking the others between the fingers of the spread hand) and Nelson's Column (gathering four widely-spaced fivestones before the tossed stone came down and was caught). Pam, the nine-year-old icy blonde from three doors away, usually went off in a huff, and after his chemistry-set blew up in his face we never saw much of 'Junior', son of the Hayters, an American family. Colin Brunt used to take me upstairs to see his sister, who lay in a coma for months, just staring at the ceiling from her prone position on the bed. It was always a relief to return to the street.

There was just so much activity. Outgrowing hopscotch, we slammed a football around in winter snow and slush, annoying neighbours in the spring when the heavy ball bounced into their beds of daisies and marigolds. Billy-carts clack-clacked along the pavement in summer, and home-made sledges were tugged along in the snow, the youngest and the weakest doing the tugging. The roadway was ours, for cars were a rarity. Neighbours creaking off to their vegetable allotments on their bicycles didn't bother us. Battalions of kids on roller-skates screeched down the street, often brandishing sticks in the midst of a primitive hockey game. But best of all were the bicycles. On these, we were astride stallions. We had speed. We had power. We had collisions.

I used Dad's heavy bike until I scored a shiny new Raleigh of my own. He thought I was merely borrowing his for sedate rides to the shops. When one of his brown 'puncture-proof' tyres burst and he nearly broke his neck, he got really angry. He knew from examining the fierce wear on the tyre that I'd been mistreating his sole means of personal transport by skidding it round a thousand sharp bends in our 'speedway' tournaments.

Speedway was the first obsessive sporting passion. My parents had been pre-war Wembley patrons, with Mum keen on Lionel van Praag, an Australian dasher with Errol Flynn moustache and a flowing white scarf. Dad took me to Wembley Stadium every Thursday evening in summer when the Lions raced at home. There were 80,000 cheering fans there with us, filling the terraces, giving the tumultuous Lions' Roar and twirling their noisy wooden rattles.

Even the stewards, in their berets, looked glamorous as they filed into the arena to the military-brass strains of *The Entry of the Gladiators*. We always positioned ourselves near the starting/finishing tape, where we could see the faces beneath the coloured helmets and behind the goggles and scarves – or at least see the nose and eyes: of the likes of Tommy Price and George Wilks, and the comically- named Alf Bottoms, and chubby Roy Craighead, who became a hero one night when he puffed and pushed his clapped-out motor-bike halfway round the stadium to claim a vital point for finishing third. That was the spirit that won the war!

Most of all, though, our admiration was directed towards Bill Kitchen, the man in the red helmet, the calm and astute skipper, one of the many pre-war returnees, whose maturity showed as he either won his races or shepherded his blue- helmeted No.2 into a first-and-second maximum for five points.

A crumpled programme from that first meeting, July 11, 1946, shows that Bill won three of his five heats, came in behind team-mate Price in another, and gave best to West Ham's Malcolm Craven in the other: 13 points out of 15, which was his par. Wembley won 57-39, after the Dare-Devil Peggy Trio had entertained us during the interval with all kinds of stunts, climaxing with one-legged Peggy herself surviving the Death Dive from a 75ft tower while 'enveloped in flames'. Nobody at school would believe that.

A week later, Bill Kitchen crashed and was hurt. This made me more circumspect in our next street speedway bicycle meeting.

The Belle Vue match brought the classy Jack Parker to Wembley. Rumour had it that this pre-war England team-mate was an even better rider than Bill Kitchen. Well, Bill beat him over the four laps in Heat 11, but Parker did for him in Heat 13, sealing the match. I studied my Wembley Supporters' Club lapel badge questioningly, and the red-and-white scarf, but my loyalty never seriously wavered. So committed was I that I'd stood by the bend and collected handfuls of flying cinders, which I kept in a milk-bottle as a souvenir. Down by that wire fence, the smell of the high-octane fuel was intoxicating, in the best possible sense.

Thursday-night Mecca: Wembley Stadium speedway, late 1940s. Dad and I were nearly always down by the starting tape

During the next two summers Dad and I hardly missed a Wembley speedway meeting, even when Auntie Nell died, and even when matches were transferred to Harringay while Wembley Stadium was host to the 1948

Olympic Games. Dad even took me to the club members' outing at Rye House, where our famous speedway idols took part in an undignified donkey race.

Some of the riders featured on pre-war cigarette-cards were still in action – Colin Watson, king of the 'draggers' (left knee on ground around the bends), Eric Chitty the Canadian, Ron Johnson the Aussie, Bill Kitchen, Jack Parker, George Wilks, Malcolm Craven – but Mum and Dad spoke nostalgically about Tom Farndon, who was killed riding at New Cross, and Bluey Wilkinson, a ginger-haired Australian, who had died in a motor-bike crash on the road. Gus Kuhn now ran a motor-cycle shop in Clapham, having gained too much weight and too many years. Looking at the cigarette-cards, I wondered how a chap could end up with a name like Acorn Dobson. Then I started a scrapbook, planting in some of the captions with my John Bull printing set, and began to understand what it was that touched sport with so much glamour: its great array of personalities and archival potential.

Aussie Vic Duggan became the man to beat, and then Wembley found two exciting youngsters in Split Waterman and Freddie Williams. The World Championship final in September became the attraction of the year. None of the riders could have felt more nervous that I did on the tube train to Wembley Park that evening, and along Olympic Way to the inviting twin-turreted stadium. Vic Duggan won the 1948 Championship, roaring in for one second place and four firsts to take a *Sunday Dispatch* prize of £200 and the trophy. With Australia having bowled England out for 52 in the Oval Test match a month earlier, my admiration for the Bradmans, Lindwalls and Duggans was rising fast.

Another sport was looming large. Dad and a friend got tickets for some big boxing matches, and while I listened to commentary by Raymond Glendenning or Stewart MacPherson on the wireless, with W. Barrington-Dalby's apparently learned between-rounds summaries, my father was up in the bleachers, or sometimes (because he had a passing acquaintance with promoter Jack Solomons through the restaurant) nearer ringside as Gus Lesnevich thrashed Freddie Mills at Harringay in 1946, and Joe Baksi half-killed Bruce Woodcock in the same ring in 1947, and Britain at last got the better of America when Mills beat Lesnevich at White City in 1948 to take the world cruiserweight title. Dad got me signed photos of Mills and Baksi when they too went into the Rupert Street, Soho restaurant he was now managing. He demonstrated some of the manoeuvres he had seen, especially Freddie Mills's 'chopper' punch: 'Bosh!'

He probably deemed pro boxing rather too savage and bloody for his son's personal gaze, and took me instead to the England v Switzerland amateur programme at the Empire Pool, Wembley. They were tedious bouts, apart from the heavyweight, in which a slow-moving sack of an Englishman named Brian Harper stopped to push back his long hair, and while both gloves were by his forehead his Swiss opponent, a lanky, spindly specimen named Jost, threw a ramrod left that almost decapitated the squat Englishman. Harper was later to change his name to Brian London and joined the ranks of British heavyweights who earned fame with their glass jaws and horizontal posture.

Freddie Mills: 'Bosh!'

All this, of course, was aimed at turning a callow boy into a man who was fit to take on any physical threat that might come his way. When six or seven, I'd shed a tear after a playground bully landed one on me. Far from going down himself to sort the bully's father out, Dad urged me in very strong terms to go and hit the kid back, even though 24 hours would separate his punch and mine. I slept poorly that night, but carried out my orders next day, stepping up to my tormentor and flailing two or three punches at him before we both burst into tears. Though clearly satisfied that justice had been done, Dad was less impressed at my tearful reaction. I resolved never to disappoint him on that score ever again.

I disappointed him at times when, having waited at Rayners Lane station to meet him or Auntie Edie at the end of a day's work, I walked home with her if she arrived first. His feelings for his sister-in-law were ambivalent after the tension her wartime binges had inflicted on our household.

Upon reaching double figures in March 1947, I felt ready to embark on what I called 'adventures'. These were any journey, by bike or bus, which took me out of sight of the house.

West Harrow was a favourite place because of the spacious park and shallow pond where boys sailed little boats and where I could make the best of a penny bag of lemonade powder that shot frissons through the tastebuds.

Alexandra Park was another green haven, where we had speedway 'Tests' on our bikes and played cricket on grass (I slogged my first fifty there) or tried to fly our kites (mine came from an army disposal shop) or made do with a bit of French cricket. The air-raid siren at the *Tithe Farm* pub across the road was now silent. And further afield was Ruislip Lido, where I saw a poisonous yellow-and-black adder writhing through the reeds. My net scooped up orange-bellied newts and inch-long fish called sticklebacks, which were shaken stupid in a jam-jar swinging from the handlebars on the homeward journey.

It was on one such adventure that a couple of the gang began mocking a returned soldier who was obviously shellshocked – 'bomb happy' – to judge from his disoriented behaviour and the grotesque scar across the top of his head. He wore an army tunic and talked manically to himself, and I was branded a spoilsport for voicing disapproval at the taunting.

No outdoor 'adventure' quite compared with a private visit to the British Museum soon after the war ended. Next-door neighbour Mr Kane, an elderly Irishman with a tobacco-yellowed moustache, was an attendant at the Museum. He offered to show me around weeks before it was ready to be reopened to the public, and if the experience failed to enthuse me for the Egyptian studies that lay ahead at school, I was awestruck by the giant Greek columns at the entrance and by the great mummy cases and the painted images in the shadowy corridors, the dust and staleness overwhelming.

The 1946-47 winter was ghastly. In addition to the longish grey flannel shorts, knee-length socks, pullover and snake-clasp belt, we needed overcoats, and balaclavas over hair that was parted – in a pattern for a lifetime – on the left. Making slippery slides on the pavement by repeatedly skidding over a few feet of frozen ground began to lose its appeal: too many complaints from the adults anyway. The most important phenomenon in the street became the grimy coalman, with his horse-drawn cart heavy with black bags bulging with coke and anthracite. From late January, when the Arctic freeze set in for weeks on end, the prospect of dying from chilblains or hypothermia taxed all but the completely unimaginative. Fireside was the place to be, looking through the dining-room windows at the robins as they fought over their fried bread and bacon-rind.

Death almost came not from hypothermia but under the wheels of a towering double-decker bus when my bike slid over on the ice in Warden Avenue. Tangled up in seat and crossbar, I lay helpless as the bus bore down. One constructive thought swiftly hit me before the bus: I was lying on the icy road right outside Dr McKeown's surgery, so medical assistance – or the last rites – would surely be quickly to hand. However, the bus driver proved to be a man of unusual skill. He feathered the brakes perfectly and brought the red monster to a halt inches from my head. Life was to proceed. Perhaps God was guiding me from that crystal powder-bowl after all.

This escape and the recent nightly Luftwaffe threats were early links in a chain of brushes with death which were to include two near-drownings; two brake failures; a bolt of lightning; a head blow from a falling coconut; an over-dosed smallpox vaccination; a petrifying blind landing in the black of night during a tropical storm; hanging on to the neck of a stampeding horse during our honeymoon; a reprieve from decapitation by a heavy flying surfboard; coaxing a small car across a flooded creek with fast-moving water halfway up the doors; trapped in a 'frozen' hotel lift; a spinning car on a snow-covered dual carriageway; almost crushed by a falling beech tree during the hurricane; and a heart stoppage of over half a minute during a pacemaker operation.

The peaceful summer of 1947 was warm to hot, and the sticky flypapers filled up fast. I had picked up my first wireless broadcast of cricket during the winter, scattered, scratchy bits of commentary or summary from the Ashes Tests in Australia, where England were enduring their first post-war thrashings. In 1947 the South Africans came, and, abandoning my makeshift golf on the back lawn, which had entailed battering one of my baby brother's little wooden building-blocks with a stick (no golf ball being available), I moved on from being fascinated by the sound of one of the Springbok names, 'Nourse', to be touched by the descriptive powers of a 33-year-old commentator from Hampshire, John Arlott, whose voice was still rather too taut and urgent, but was not to be ignored. Had I but known it, this man was to have an enormous impact on my life in the years far ahead.

Meanwhile, the focus of attention, especially for a boy living north-west of London, was Denis Compton. He and his sidekick, Bill Edrich, tormented the South African bowlers, and all the others, all through that golden summer, chalking up over 7000 runs between them. Without having yet seen him most of us were transformed into Denis while batting in the roadway against the high-bouncing tennis-ball. We knew that when winter returned we could switch from being Compton the Middlesex batsman to Compton the Arsenal footballer. And at night, with head covered by the blanket to ensure complete detachment in my land of privacy and fantasy, I had sumptuous partnerships with him, matching him stroke for stroke as we took our stand into the hundreds, hair (both of us) smooth with Brylcreem. It made a change from the fantasies in which I was a knight in shiny armour, rescuing a sweet and helpless girl from danger while humming a bagpipe version of *Scotland the Brave*.

This cricket thing intensified when one of the teachers, the dreamy Mr Hawkins, broke away from the lesson, as was his habit, and told us the story of how Warwick Armstrong's seemingly unbeatable Australian team were overthrown by old Archie MacLaren and his handpicked assortment of veterans and youngsters at Eastbourne in 1921. Mr Hawkins, soft of voice, with a sad face made sadder by a drooping moustache, remembered that the summer of '21 brought such heat that the soles of his plimsoles stuck to the pavement. And when he'd finished recalling that famous cricket match, he dwelt on one of its heroes, Aubrey Faulkner. I leaned forward on my desk and lapped it up, and when, over 40 years later, I wrote *By His Own Hand*, a study of cricket's suicides, I could understand fully how my teacher had been so fascinated by Faulkner.

Further discovery of London followed, many an outing starting on a misty morning. On a school excursion I climbed up the steps to the top of the Monument and was stirred by the narrative of the Great Plague and the Great Fire of 1666. With Dad, I took in Cleopatra's Needle, ancient and imposing on the Thames embankment, and also the Serpentine in Hyde Park, and Westminster Abbey again, with its haunting tomb of the Unknown Warrior. Then came the bomb-scarred Houses of Parliament, with the statues of Oliver Cromwell and, astride a great horse, Richard the Lionheart. The king's sword had been buckled by shrapnel, which I solemnly refused to see as comical.

How St Paul's Cathedral came to be spared, apart from a peripheral hit, nobody could ever explain. We went inside, to be overwhelmed by the upward view of the dome, and down in the crypt the massive black carriage from the Duke of Wellington's funeral, made from melted gun-metal. The Iron Duke and Lord Nelson are buried there, and father and son were now duly and truly reverent.

Into Madame Tussaud's waxworks we stepped, just down from the Baker Street delicatessen where Auntie Edie worked (how her razor-sharp bacon-slicer made me shudder). Inside Tussaud's we were fooled by the attendant in the foyer who was really only a wax model, and by the 'model' that suddenly sprang to life and threatened to bite the pointed finger. The magical experience of 'meeting' the kings and queens, Dickens and Churchill, showbusiness figures and sportsmen, made such an impression that forever more I was urging people to make this their first sightseeing target when in London. The Chamber of Horrors – 'Children must be accompanied by an adult' – had the desired effect: the glassy eyes of murderers and of the beheaded followed the visitor down the dimly-lit aisles. The tableau *When Did You Last See Your Father?* (velvet-clad son of a Royalist being interrogated by stern Roundheads) caused a doting boy to linger and wrestle with his own emotions. Until recently he had many times wondered if he would ever see his own father again. As for *The Death of Nelson*, I remember turning my face away before Dad noticed my tearful eyes.

The principal novelty at Tussaud's was the model of Sleeping Beauty, which actually 'breathed', a bellows device causing her chest to heave up and down. No exhibit, though, had a more stiffening impact than the Nazi gang. There, life-size and in his rotten brown shirt and swastika armband, was – take a deep breath - Adolf Hitler, the most hated man not just in Lynton Road but in the entire world. Alongside him were the creepy runt Goebbels and the fat Reichsmarschall Hermann Goering, in Luftwaffe uniform. And, most fascinating because his hairy hands looked so real, Rudolf Hess. Someone had earned his fee planting all those black hairs into the wax.

If all the film and stage stars, sportsmen too, who went into the restaurant Dad ran in Soho had turned up at once, the place would almost have rivalled Tussaud's as an attraction. Googie Withers, Jack Warner, Hugh McDermott and Max Wall (who was then a heart-throb) were regulars. So were Muriel Pavlow, Bonar Colleano, Max Adrian, and Kathleen Harrison (who was to live beyond 100, and was so like Mum in spirit, speech and good humour). Terry-Thomas, the gap-toothed comedian whose career was about to escalate, once forgot his coat, and later left a signed photo to add to Dad's collection: 'Dear Ted, A million thanks for returning my jacket. How careless of me and how kind of you. Sincerely, Terry.'

'Dear Ted, A million thanks . . .'

One celebrity I did catch was 'Prince Monolulu', the outrageous pseudo-Abyssinian prince and racing tipster, bedecked in feathers and dazzling waistcoat, whose cry of 'I gotta horse!' had been familiar nationally since he allegedly won the unthinkable sum of £35,000 at the 1935 Derby and lost it all next day. He was the first black man I'd ever seen. Standing on the footpath after leaving the restaurant, he looked down at me, shook hands at Dad's behest, and uttered a few remarks that a 10-year-old failed to absorb for future recital. If only Denis Compton had been a diner at Dad's Rupert Street establishment. Colourful to the end, poor Monolulu choked to death in hospital in 1965, when he was 82, having failed to cope with a chocolate given him by Jeffrey Bernard.

August was holiday time. We set off in a coach to Cliftonville, Margate, where Mum and Dad had honeymooned in 1934, and rented a couple of rooms in a guesthouse. The charabanc ride was a joy (in 1948 we passed close to the St Lawrence ground, Canterbury, where the Australians were bowling Kent out for 51: why couldn't we have stopped for an hour or two?). And after adjusting to our new environment, we took our pleasures seriously: deckchairs on the sand, clothing anything but relaxed and informal; donkey rides for us kids; the Punch and Judy show; seductive sixpenny dishes of cockles, gritty, saturated in vinegar, coated in salt and pepper; Dreamland funfair in the evening; or a concert at The Oval, a bandstand surrounded by deckchairs: completely innocent entertainment.

With brother Michael (Mick, then Mike)

There was a large, bald chap at the guesthouse who gasped 'Corn in Egypt!' any time somebody said something the least bit remarkable. And after a week of cricket on the damp sand and enough sun on the bare torso to cause terrible discomfort (calamine lotion was the solution), my ardour for the sea-front diminished in an instant when a drowned youngster's limp, white- tinged-blue body was dragged from the water. Dad, of course, tried to help, but it was too late.

Back home, I dug up from the garden the small bottles of perfume I was attempting to manufacture, one full of crushed rose-petals, the other containing mashed banana. But after a fortnight underground, the one smelt of stale roses, the other of rotten banana, and the contents looked horrible.

My entrepreneurial ambition was dashed. Nothing for some time replaced it.

Learning to drive: Cliftonville Sands, 1947

Auntie Edie loved the West End shows. She and Bill went to see the Crazy Gang, and Noel Coward's *Blithe Spirit* (which brought guffaws from Dad, who thought it was all about boozing). They also saw the spectacular musicals *Annie Get Your Gun* and *Oklahoma!*, coming home bedazzled by the sight of the glamorous young Princess Margaret in the Royal box.

In November 1947 the elder princess, Elizabeth (future Queen), married her Philip, and I managed to view the wedding on a small television set in a Rayners Lane shop-window, near where Mum and I had run to shelter in a shop when an air-raid siren started to wail. This became an even more dramatic stretch of pavement when I took off down the hill, out of control, on roller-skates. I had no brakes and knew of no technique for arresting the wild acceleration towards Village Way . . . other than to swerve into the parade of shops.

I finished in a heap beneath the ironmonger's doorway display, brooms and buckets everywhere, mothballs bouncing down the hill. Life was safer on the bike.

I guess life was becoming altogether too perplexing around this time, for one evening I slipped into a kind of trance as a few of us lads stood around talking about this and that. Next thing I knew, one of them was jabbing my shoulder and saying: 'What's the matter with you?' I shook my head and asked him what he meant. 'You were just standing there,' he insisted, 'and you were saying "What are we made for? What are we made for?" Over and over.'

Is this how Denis Compton does it?

I covered my embarrassment and confusion by pretending I had merely been trying to tease them. We went on chatting about speedway or Denis Compton or Freddie Mills, but the experience left me wondering what it was that had got hold of me. Quite apart from that, what *were* we made for?

If 1947 was an engrossing year, 1948 was even better, especially on the sporting front. Dad's boss invited us up to his impressive home in Muswell Hill to watch the Cup final on his television set, an item which was still in only a small proportion of homes. In an immaculate sitting-room full of people, with the chintz curtains keeping out half the afternoon light, we saw Blackpool's hopes shattered by Manchester United, four goals to two, after I had murmured a preference for United unaware that there was a huge tide of sentiment, not only in that room but across the nation, in support of Stanley Matthews, the wizard Blackpool outside-right who had never won an FA Cup-winner's medal. Bad luck, Stan; but I glowed at the wisdom of my random forecast.

It became a matter of searching for people who had television. The next bit of TV-viewing was at Colin Glass's house. His parents occupied a rare plane not only for having the sole television set in the district, so far as I could tell, but they owned a car too, one of those slightly absurd, tall and narrow Ford Populars, all black duco and chrome. Firstly, there had been an incomprehensible drama called *Thark* – five minutes of that was more than enough – which might misleadingly have persuaded a boy that he would certainly not be wasting much time in future sitting in front of this grey, flickering picture. But it was much better when Colin promised that there would be some cricket on, and I hurried round to see Bradman's Australians maintain their summer-long grip over England. Hassett's dropped catch off a hook by Washbrook (Cyril, of course) had us giggling.

There was some casual cricket to be played around the fringe of Rayners Lane Sports Ground, elevated by the presence of an Australian boy whose name (Don) we found rather intimidating, even though his skill was nothing out of the ordinary. The real Don, Australia's immortal little skipper, was soon registering the most famous duck in cricket history, in what turned out to be his final Test innings, at The Oval, in the August of 1948. And it was not the only shock of the day, for England had already been bowled out for 52 (Lindwall 6 for 20), a sensation which diverted me from a reverie I was having on the Rayners Lane railway bridge, gazing towards the church spire over at Harrow- on-the-Hill. A man, in an evident state of shock, was reading the news of England's humiliation in his afternoon paper as he stood, half-paralysed, by the railway station exit. How ludicrously far-fetched it would have seemed had somebody told me that one day I would enjoy the friendship of both Don Bradman and Ray Lindwall, as well as replicating Ray's Oval bowling figures when I played for their club, St George (then 12,000 miles away and unknown to me).

Cricket had to share 1948 with the Olympic Games which were staged in war-battered London's austere environment. Fanny Blankers-Koen, the Dutch athlete, won undying fame. But, personal recollection always dominating, I remember this shoestring extravaganza for the particle of glamour gifted to our neighbourhood by the herculean Canadian weightlifter who was billeted over the back, in Lulworth Gardens, and by a visit to Lyons Sports Ground at Sudbury Hill to see some of the hockey. As Pakistan beat France 3-1 (why shouldn't they have made it look easy: they had no roller-skates strapped to their feet), we were suddenly inspired to get our own street Olympics going.

I made an Olympic torch from an empty cocoa tin with Mum's copper-stick rammed into the base, stuffed it with cotton-wool, soaked it with paraffin, and ran down Lynton Road, proclaiming our Games open. Recruiting little chaps from as far away as the next street, I got my select committee to draw up a programme of events: weightlifting, running, cycling, boxing, wrestling, hockey, football, hurdling, and the hazardous pursuit of fencing with our crude wooden Robin Hood swords. Plus, of course, cricket.

By the start, we had only five takers, one for each of the rings in the Olympic symbol, and the four-day programme was all over in one evening of curtailed activity. The cycling was messed up when John Lister fell off halfway round the block and demanded a rerun. Refused. And at the end of it all we couldn't get the foul-smelling torch to light again. Still, we sent little Geoffrey down the length of the street with it. He came from Wiltshire, and had a funny accent. Little remained of the much-vaunted Olympic spirit by the time we'd finished.

Things were warming up, however, as the days at junior school ran out, and interests continued to broaden. Dad got me a stamp album from a shop in Wembley; not an empty one but an album already stuffed with exotic examples, like the Falkland Islands faults, 1945 atomic-bomb commemoratives from China, the striking Danzig issues, young Farouk from Egypt, and the still-frightening image of Adolf Hitler. Abyssinia to Zululand, a geography and history lesson. Stamps were ordered on approval from a dealer, and sixpences and shillings from pocket-money were invested.

Dad took us on a secret trip one evening, and when we were level with a department store window he stopped dead and pointed. 'That's for you, David. It's being delivered tomorrow.' I followed his finger, and checked with him in high-pitched incredulity: 'That? A piano?' Yes, and I was soon to start lessons.

Well, I never did. No real interest. Instead, Dad, disappointed again, himself hammered the ivories at every opportunity, and I settled for a beautifully-crafted bow-and-arrows set for passing my exam. Later, when I became enraptured by some Freddie Gardner records, I yearned to play the saxophone, but never did anything about it.

There was a fearful shock in store when we returned from the annual Margate holiday. Jeff Boyd, one of our gang, had been killed when his bicycle careered down a hill, round a bend, and into a car. He was tossed through the windscreen. Fancy that, after surviving all those air-raids. Only a year earlier, Dad read from his newspaper at the guesthouse breakfast-table that Bronco Wilson, the cumbersome heavyweight Wembley speedway rider, had been killed. I was beginning to dread holiday time for the grief it seemed to bring.

Dad had some tension of his own to cope with around this time. A girl named Rita Green was murdered in Soho, close to his shop, and he'd seen a suspicious-looking man, carrying a Gladstone bag, hurrying away around the time of the killing. Dad told the police, but was understandably if illogically scared that his name might appear in the papers. It all gave me the creeps too, and Lord knows what effect it had on poor Mum, the world's Number 1 worrier.

The cricket and football were coming along nicely, but academic matters were what counted now: the 11-Plus exam that would determine whether I went to an 'ordinary' school like Eastcote Lane or to the heady wonders of a grammar school.

Since the day, six years earlier, when I had grasped the spelling of 'busy' and gone on to tell the teacher (no-one else knew) that the natives of Australia were 'abbora- guy-nees', I'd put all I had into my studies. Now fingers were crossed.

I won the scholarship, and, with Colin, was offered to Harrow County Grammar School, a bus-ride away. Ralph 'Know-all' Lidyard made it to

Merchant Taylors'. Mum and Dad took me to the school's open day, and it came as a surprise that there was not a straw boater in sight. The Harrow School, the one where F.S.Jackson and Archie MacLaren and Winston Churchill attended, up on the hill, was not far away, though a million miles in another sense. Ours was in Gayton Road, and in later years changed its name to Gayton, and produced Angus Fraser, Mark Ramprakash, Michael Portillo and Clive Anderson, having provided a pre-war education for the comical Cardew Robinson. The school's foundation stone had been laid by Britain's Fascist leader Oswald Mosley, as Harrow's MP (1918-22). The columned sandstone entrance, surmounted by a somehow formidable clock, together with the high ceilings rendered the place quite overwhelming.

It was time to decide once and for all which of the pronunciations I'd been hearing all these years was correct – 'Harrer' or 'Harrow'. It was time, too, to get measured for smart green cap and blazer, with school motto beneath the badge: *Virtus Non Stemma*, which appealed more as life went on: 'Tis Worth not Birth, in the words of the school song: 'Be this our battle-cry. Stand up for truth! Be honest! Spurn a lie!' That would do me.

Masters in flowing black gowns, imposing architecture (some of it), science laboratories with bunsen burners and test-tubes, rugby in the field down the road, with a bald-headed coach in long black shorts who had played for his county and maybe even England; then home on the bus, case heavy with books, when it was absolutely dark at 4pm: all this was the new order. And when I forgot to take a worm to biology lesson, I was made to write 100 times: 'An hermaphrodite is a creature with both sex organs.' Not the easiest thing to grasp.

The next step up in punishment was the cane, a thin birch rod which stung badly (so I heard) and which I planned to avoid best I could. To help alleviate the anxiety of this threat, I bought an orange ice-stick each day from the vendor by the school gates.

It was not until almost half-a-century had passed that I discovered that the headmaster, Dr Alex Simpson, had kept wicket for Scotland in the 1920s and 1930s. In fact he was in the line-up in 1930 to face the Australians in the very match (at the Grange Club, Edinburgh) which followed the Headingley Test in which young Don Bradman had scored his record 334. The Don took the field against Scotland, but the match was wrecked by rain, and my old headmaster did not even step onto the field of play.

He had played against the 1926 Australians, at the North Inch ground, Perth, where Arthur Mailey had him caught for 2 (Simpson was very much the tailender), and also against New Zealand, Indian and South African touring teams; he also played against the 1934 Australians (no Bradman this time), catching Ponsford and Chipperfield and being bowled for a duck by the tricky Fleetwood-Smith. How I wish I had known all this in 1948 and had had the nerve to 'interview' him.

Few sports were not tasted: putting at Margate

Music lessons were ruined when Mr Thorn began inserting two fingers into our mouths to show exactly how wide our jaws should open when singing. Just as intimidating was the sight of the senior boys under the showers after rugby. All that fur around their private parts: surely not!

As this new life began to change me without my fully realising it, to my astonishment I found my parents adopting an almost reverential attitude towards me. Proud they were, and conscious of their own shortage of formal education, but to begin regarding me as some sort of mastermind was a bit rich. Dad couldn't seem to make up his mind, as years passed, whether to feel unequivocally glad that I was getting the sort of education he'd missed or to vent his unease at the 'intellectual' gap opening up between us. As a seven- or eight-year-old, with the sweetest of intentions, I had picked him up over his quaint mis-spelling of certain words, such as 'deplict' and 'heighth', and he in turn said he'd clip me around the ear if he ever again heard me say 'Look at them birds.'

Anyway, there had been something much bigger on all our minds since Dad had come home one evening and posed this question to Mum, my brother and me: 'How would you like to live in Australia?' He might well have seemed to be seeking opinions, but his mind was already made up. He was fed-up with Edie and Bill still being with us, fed-up with the ongoing drabness and poverty of poor exhausted old England, fed-up with the continuation of food rationing, and fed-up with the evident lack of opportunity for his two boys and himself. An Australian acquaintance in London had fanned his enthusiasm and steered him through the Australia House brochures, and he was ready.

What did I feel? I had an open mind. I'd miss Auntie Edie, if not as much as Mum would. I'd probably miss Colin. I'd probably never see old

Aunt Flo again, or her sisters Louie (with her dyed ginger hair and her gentle husband Jim, whose tongue poked out most of the time and who wanted me to adopt his hobby of making alabaster models of parrots), and Lizzie, severest of the old sisters, her white hair combed back. She too had an interesting husband: Uncle Bert, all ears and tobacco-stained moustache, had given my mother away at her wedding, and was celebrated in family folklore for having narrowly escaped decapitation as he leaned well out of a train window, waving goodbye, huge gramophone trumpet under his arm, unaware that the train was about to enter a tunnel.

I supposed I'd miss the privet hedges touched by snow on moonlit nights. And never again would I gaze all a'wonder through the toilet window at next door's roof and the blue sky which extended to eternity. But it all sounded a bit exciting, and probably the sky was even bigger in Australia.

Before long we were selling the furniture – or much of it – with me manning the telephone and booking in the prospective buyers. Then we had to adjust the departure date when it was clear we wouldn't be ready to board Orontes early in January 1949. And just as well. She almost sank in a dreadful storm, and most of her crockery was smashed.

I was made to stand up in class by a teacher with unruly hair and a bow-tie who had struck me as slightly exhibitionist when he'd shown off his rowing eight to us down at Putney. 'Frith is leaving us, boys,' he intoned. 'He's running out on his country.' To their credit, the class did not raise a mass sneer, but Mr (I've understandably forgotten his name) pursued his point a little further, while I reddened and fought against rising panic and indignation.

At least Dr Simpson, stern but kindly Scot, gave me a good headmaster's reference, even though I'd been at the school for no more than four months, and with Dad's ears ringing with his restaurateur boss's challenging words ('You'll be back inside 18 months, Ted, you mark my words') we were, at last, ready to go.

The short span of life (Horace wrote) forbids us to take on far-reaching hopes. But then Quintus Horatius Flaccus, wise Roman muse that he was, had never known the thrill of sailing off to the land of Bradman.

CHAPTER FOUR

There is a time for departure even when there's no certain place to go.

TENNESSE WILLIAMS

TEN days out on the high seas, according to an entry in Dad's 1949 diary, 'We're all getting well and truly brown now and people on board are showing a new look of life, all very cheerful.'

Not before time. Leaving had been upsetting. Friends and neighbours had drifted in to say goodbye, and as we boarded the taxi, one of those cute black pre-war jobs with small nose, half-open cockpit, and roomy cabin, old Ma England came out to wave farewell, looking even sadder than usual.

We stayed overnight in the imposing Kings Cross hotel, and Auntie Edie and Aunt Flo came up for last-minute goodbyes. Emotions were highly charged. I went to my room early, but I know the tears flowed. Breakfast was all shiny cutlery and white tablecloths, with magnificent heraldry adorning the high walls around us, somehow mocking those of us who were leaving historic England for fresh surroundings.

My last purchase was a slim book on Scott of the Antarctic, from the railway bookstall. Within minutes we were chugging eastwards to Tilbury docks, and as we reached the gangplank, I conducted my own little ceremony, slowly raising my heel from English 'soil' before proceeding on board.

RMS *Orion*, 24,000 tons, carried almost 700 passengers, some first-class, the rest tourist, with many emigrants among them. Those who were paying their own way (such as the Friths) seemed keen to assert the fact rather than be lumped in with those assisted migrants who had paid only £10 a head. They had mortgaged their freedom by having to stay in Australia for a minimum of two years. I only wish I had known at that time that *Orion* had carried the 1936-37 English cricketers to Australia. It would have enhanced the trip no end.

As the ship drifted away from the wharf, a bunch of sentimental souls on the quayside began to sing *Now is the Hour*, which caused most people in my vicinity, Mum included, to shed tears. I could have done without that.

White bread-rolls were a sight for post-war eyes, and helped assuage the feelings of homelessness and loneliness . . . to which was soon added sea-sickness. I'd woken that first morning, when we were almost clear of the English Channel, and pulled back the curtain fully expecting to have a good underwater view through the port-hole. Instead, there was cloud and choppy water. By mid-morning I was rugged up in a chair on deck, and suddenly bringing up all the puffed wheat I'd forced down at breakfast. The jolly old crewman who had just swabbed that section of deck made light of my mess. A day later it happened again, prompting my father to enter compassionately in his diary that 'David looked like a wet Nellie'.

I had enough pocket money to buy a Kodak Brownie box-camera, and immediately had to curse our navigator for getting us to Gibraltar too late for a well-lit picture, though I made up for this as the voyage progressed. My little brother had his sixth birthday, and kept his cake down despite the bucking and tossing in the still-choppy seas. Looking back, he was lucky to get this far, for not only had he survived a hazardous birth, but one afternoon, when still under a year, he had screamed so insistently and piercingly that Dad came seriously close to tossing him through the window. I was a witness. Now, he was bubbly, cheeky and a shipboard favourite . . . apart from when he roamed the decks yelling out 'Man overboard!' The ship's officers didn't like that.

One rough, grey morning I ventured into the ship's pool. There was no-one else around as I clung to the railing and eased my way round the four sides. Then I lost my grip and sank, bobbed up again, sank, took in half-a-lungful of Mediterranean sea-water, thrashed away in an effort to get within distance of the railing, sank again, got a watery view of a disappearing world, and then flailed away until the railing was just within reach. I manoeuvred my way back to the ladder, climbed out, brought up some sea-water, and went unsteadily down to my parents' cabin to announce that I'd taught myself to swim.

The first port of call came as a relief. Port Said was a mass of bazaars, which we explored after buying some cheap souvenirs at the Simon Arzt store. In one of the darkest and dingiest of them, there was muttering and furtive eye movement, and before I could know what was going on, Mum spoke out defiantly: 'Up the British!' One of the Arabs reached for his curved dagger, and Dad hurriedly led us from the shop. The way things were going, we would be lucky to reach Sydney.

There was further drama when a stowaway was discovered and put ashore at Port Said. And then one of the ship's officers died, and I happened to emerge on deck around dawn just as his body was being committed over the side into the depths.

Easing down the Suez Canal had been like a James Fitzpatrick travelogue: camels, Arabs, shadoofs; then the torrid heat of the Red Sea, before Aden, set among jagged rocks, where, unbelievably, rain had not fallen for eight years, or so we were told.

I put on my dressing-gown, applied some lurid make-up to my face, and strung my boxing-gloves around my neck, and came second in my age group in the fancy-dress competition. Mick won his in my old cowboy costume. Peggy Brooks, the singer, presented the prizes.

An early defeat

Then some of us boys went up to the captain's bridge and were interviewed on a tape-recorder, my own contribution – something about preferring chocolate ice-cream – a first-class example of tongue-tied self-consciousness.

Still the intense heat, reddened skins, deck games, entertainments like wooden-horse-racing in the evening (with a Tote), and bombast from an older boy named Bob who was returning to Australia and knew all about girls and dished out implausible stories about finding gold, wrestling with killer sharks and handling spiders and snakes. Then there was a Londoner named

Boyce whose genitalia used to hang from his misshapen bulbous swim-trunks as he posed on the railing before diving into the pool. By the third week it dawned on us that this was no accident; he was not unaware; it was called exhibitionism.

Colombo, Ceylon was a delight: launch to the quay, bus to town, thence to Mount Lavinia, to be escorted by a guide over his master's plantation. Afterwards we saw Kandy, and the Buddhist Temple of the Holy Tooth. Sinhalese lace, cheap fruit, lotus blossom and mimosa: Lynton Road was fast fading from memory.

We crossed the Equator, first time for all of us, and stopped, by tradition, off the Cocos Islands. Next stop Australia. On February 15, early, we espied a ribbon of land on the horizon to port, and slowly Fremantle came into view, an unprepossessing sight by the wharves, all cranes, stores and corrugated-iron roofs. But we had made it to Australia, and were soon sweeping through Kings Park in a taxi to Perth. The cleanliness here struck us, and the fruit (peaches five for 1/8d) and milk-shakes were symbols of Paradise.

Sydney Harbour, my little camera does the job: early morning, February 25, 1949

More rough seas in the infamous Great Bight spoiled our progress across to Adelaide, and even in that sedate city there was frustration, for it rained hard. Onward to Melbourne, shipboard activities now closed and the decks ghostlike. And here, at our third Australian city, was more rain. Sunny Australia. What a joke. Up to the Dandenong Ranges we went in a coach, having Devonshire tea and seeing a lyrebird on the way down. Due off at midnight, we found ourselves still tied up next morning, for the ship had got stuck in mud and a tug's rope had snapped and fouled one of our screws. Down went a diver, and more free entertainment was had. The new land was full of the unexpected, quite apart from the shop windows, brimming with great food.

On February 25, 1949, *Orion* swung to port into the opening to Port Jackson around five in the morning, with lights still twinkling from Mosman round to Rose Bay and beyond. As we ploughed up the Harbour and the light gradually lifted, the mighty Bridge came into view, and eventually we slid underneath it, the masts seemingly certain to crash into the world-famous expanse. Some people on deck actually ducked their heads.

We berthed at Pyrmont, and two of Dad's friends, Max Yager and Percy Thomas (the Fire Brigade Column Officer referred to in his diary), came aboard. For a while it was exhilarating, especially when the taxi-truck raced us over Pyrmont Bridge and into the city of Sydney, a sprawling colonial town of solid sandstone office buildings and shops that were somehow naive in their simplicity of display. Before long we were outside the People's Palace in lower Pitt Street, our new and, thank God, temporary home.

Percy Thomas had tried to line us up a house for rental and eventual purchase, but the arrangement had collapsed just as we were due to sail. At Aunt Flo's suggestion, Dad booked us into the People's Palace, run by the Salvation Army. For him, it must have seemed like 1926 all over again.

Mum was horrified. That evening she found a flea or two in their bed, and what with the peeling wallpaper and dull net curtains, the gloomy corridors, and the corpse of an old woman being wheeled on a trolley through the foyer, we must all have longed for the comforts and familiarity back at 80 Lynton Road. Auntie Edie would have cheered us up with the clink of glasses and her over-ready laughter. But she was now 12,000 miles away, and probably feeling just as empty.

There was much to be done next day: back to the wharf to clear the rest of the luggage, job enquiries by Dad (he knocked back an immediate offer of £7 a week as a fireman), arrangements at the bank and post office, time for a little diversionary fun at Luna Park funfair, under the Bridge's northern approach.

We also took the long train-ride down to Woolooware for a social visit to Percy and Gladys, whose hospitality was probably stepped up out of embarrassment at having failed to organise our accommodation. I must have looked fitter than when Mr Thomas last saw me in Lynton Road, for he said to Dad, 'Ted, your David's going to be a six-footer.' He overestimated by three inches.

Off we went to the breathtaking sweep of Cronulla beach, and while the adults talked in the evening, I read one of Percy's books on infamous crimes, which gave me a severe attack of the creeps on the dark walk back to the railway station, even though I had my parents and small brother with me. Buck Ruxton, and mother-killer Sidney Fox (my God, he did it in Margate), and Neville Heath the mutilator, and sinister Charlie Peace – they were all waiting for me behind the next clump of bushes.

Percy had given me an Ion Idriess book, about the central desert of Australia, which was hardly more uplifting than the murder book, and did nothing to raise my spirits in the confines of the People's Palace. Dad was the lucky one. He had plenty to do. Ever thoughtful, he was soon sending food parcels back to friends in England, and visiting people whose addresses he'd been given before leaving London. At one of them, in the exclusive Eastern Suburbs, Mum and we two boys were permitted to have baths, something unavailable at our 'hotel', where, disgusted by cafe prices, Dad had set up a small methylated-spirit stove, and we cooked for ourselves.

Then another blow fell. Max Yager, who was supposed to be setting up some kind of business proposition for Dad, told him he was going back to England. To our astonishment Dad quickly signed up for a job with the Water Board many miles away at the Warragamba Dam project. Before he left us, we went to Coogee beach and the zoo.

Then he was gone, and we were desolate. He must have been truly desperate to have left us like this. Mum's lips were tight, her anxiety painful to witness. She took us to the pictures. When we came out, the most familiar voice in the world greeted us. It was Dad. One day had been enough for him among the brawling, drunken Europeans. 'I wasn't going to dig gutters,' he scribbled in his diary, 'with a load of DPs [Displaced Persons] from the Bulkan countries. I was supposed to be a carpenter's mate.'

On my 12th birthday, Dad took me to my new school, Sydney High School, a stone's throw from the Sydney Cricket Ground. It was shut. The janitor told us it was sports day. So back we went by train and tram next day, and I started my month-long enrolment, feeling somewhat overawed, but made to feel welcome by one boy in particular, who, it turned out, was only interested in me for my English comics.

If one good thing came out of it, it was that Dad had learned from the janitor that the Department of Education had vacancies. Dad was no schoolmaster, but they signed him up as a paver and labourer at £7.18.0 a week, equal to £6.6.0 sterling. A week later we left the city, Dad having decided that we would be best placed in a caravan until a more conventional home could be arranged. There was no sadness at leaving Pitt Street, especially, in my own case, because it meant I would never again have to set eyes on the dirty old man who sold newspapers outside the People's Palace. At our first encounter he had placed his hand on my arm and asked if I had 'ever done anything naughty?' I wasn't sure what he meant. And then I wasn't sure that I wasn't sure what he meant. I washed my forearm until it was red-raw.

So the searching for flats and houses ended: for the time being, no more travel in trains with razor-slits in the leather seats and no more phantom journeys to accommodation that had never existed in the first place. That stranger had sent us miles, maliciously intent on causing a Pommie family maximum inconvenience.

We took possession of the Hunter caravan at Summer Hill, and while Dad sat up with the driver of the towing vehicle, Mum, Mick and I held on for dear life in the 'van itself as it bumped and sashayed along Canterbury Road and eventually Princes Highway, coming to a blissful stop in a corner of a caravan enclosure known as Prince Edward Park, in a suburb named Carlton, next to Kogarah.

Family life in the confines of a caravan is a severe test of patience and forbearance, even when a lean-to tent is added, something Dad swiftly felt the need to do. The fold-up table at one end made way for a small double bed, which my parents occupied without – to their eternal credit – ever attracting attention during the night. My young brother and I slept in single beds at the other end of the 'van, the recurring complication being that we were both still bed-wetters. This suggests that I suffered from anxiety. It only got worse with organic functional changes within my teenaged body.

Our first Australian home

It was a cramped existence, testingly inconvenient. A six-volt battery had to be lugged back and forth to be recharged at cheerful Snowy's garage on the Highway, and the water tank had to be refilled by the bucketful from the 'amenities' shed, where Mum had to cope with the washing in the communal sinks. Torrential rain nearly every day turned the park into a quagmire. I marvel at Dad's comment in his 1949 diary: 'It seems a lovely life from here.'

My snapshots were processed, and rekindled those feelings of anticipation throughout the sea voyage, an anticipation that now took on ironic undertones. Look at us! The warmth and comfort of Lynton Road, even with all those relations sharing, seemed Heavenly against this somewhat squalid accommodation. Dad had promised Mum that if she was unhappy after two years, we'd return to England. There were times when I felt a revolt would be in order, and that the three of us should demand that he took us back on the next ship.

Then came the rededication. We were getting used to the hefty American cars and canvas-hooded jalopies all around us, and the little boys in their absurd adult trilby hats. Some of the neighbours were kind and affectionate, Australian and non- Australian alike. And when our furniture arrived on the good ship Coptic, I was as glad to get my hands on my bike as I was indifferent to the smashed panel on the piano. In the darkness, the bakelite radio was our salvation: *Doctor Mac, Superman*, the daft, chuckling quiz shows of Bob Dyer from Tennessee and the much-loved and witty Jack Davey, *Quiz Kids* with John Dease, and nerve-shredding dramas like the tale of Jimmy Governor, the Aboriginal bushranger and murderer. Randy Stone, crime reporter, captured my imagination in *Night Beat.*

Left alone sometimes I was content, draping a blanket around my shoulders and studying the mass of seagulls out on the football field through binoculars. It was cosy, with rain pattering on the caravan roof, and my understanding of the gulls' behaviour patterns developing by the hour. How like humans they were, fighting over worms, taking offence when none was necessarily intended, and displaying unseemly vanity after the slightest of triumphs.

Auntie Edie sent 'comfort parcels' every few weeks, the problem being how to make the Rowntrees gums, Lyons Slams, Mars bars and KitKats last till the next intake. Cissie, too, the sweet cockney lass who was one of the waitresses in Dad's London restaurant, sent batches of newspapers which were balm to the pain of nostalgia, affection par avion. I had been stunned by the price of the imported *Knockout* comic in the newsagents at Carlton: double the English price.

My old school friend Colin also wrote, so the feeling of exile, banishment even, never quite overwhelmed.

There came that historic, seminal moment when my mother thought she detected a change in her elder boy's accent, the tender sidelong challenge generating nothing more explanatory than a slight blush. Same when Dad came across some of my sketches. I'd written off for a Brodie Mack drawing course, monthly lessons by post on pen-and-ink art, and had begun practising, once applying my imagination to the wilder extremes of female anatomy. Dad was unsparing: ice-blue eyes grilling me, cheekbones taut, the insistent questioning. How I wish he had laughed and joked about it, or better still, ignored his discovery. In those few embarrassing moments a wide gulf opened up between us. Yet my artistic efforts had not been in any way obscene. I should not have felt shamed.

I had already begun to doubt his love when he refused to get me a Hornby Dublo train set (five guineas) for my last English Christmas. Wait till

Australia, he'd said, probably taut with anxiety as our emigration approached – and I'd retorted that it would probably cost more over there. Now there it was, in a shop window in Castlereagh Street, at 10 guineas. No train set. Further shrinkage in the mutual admiration between father and son.

It was my age of discovery. George, a tough local, arranged for a few boys from the caravan park, for a charge of one glass marble each, to view one of the girls from the other side, who lay like a corpse on the trestle table in the football grandstand changing-room, minus knickers. That glance advanced my education, but I truly felt on the verge of adulthood when I reckoned to myself, one day in the toilet block, that now that I had a wrist-watch and pubic hair and was choking on a dog-end made up painstakingly from the sketchy remains of cast-off cigarettes, I was a child no more.

George even led one or two of us into the narrow gap between fence and corrugated-iron wall of the shower block, where he'd punched a few holes with a nail, creating viewing points for when the women took their showers. The over-riding emotion for me was terror: what if we were seen? There was no way we could have left in a hurry. We were wedged tight. Would Dad remove wood splinters this time if he'd known how I got them?

I grew up some more one night when there was a stir outside the gates to Prince Edward Park, and there, on the dusty verge of Princes Highway, a motor-cyclist lay prone by his overturned machine, blood pouring from his head. Next morning, at school assembly, my good-natured new pal Kevin remarked almost casually that his cousin had been killed the night before in a motor-bike accident. I struggled to come up with the right words.

I had soon been shifted from Sydney High to Canterbury Boys' High School, founded in 1925, motto (another good one) Truth and Honour. Instantly, I had run into trouble with a boy named Pinfold. Whether the friction stemmed from nationality or personality eludes me now, but our differences had to be settled behind the shed in the playground – unfortunately with about 50 kids encircling us and demanding action, just when perhaps we might have sorted our problem out with a few words. There was a lot of preliminary pushing and shoving and loud 'Yeahs!'. Then his small fist lacerated my lips as the flesh jagged against my buck teeth. So I whacked him back, rocking him, and we lost our inhibitions and waded into each other, to the shrieking of our expanding audience. It might have outstretched the Sullivan-Mitchell fight had not a master rounded the corner, raised his hands in disgust, and sent us to the headmaster. I felt Pinfold got his desserts when he was forced to repeat first year.

The school's cricket fame rested with Arthur Morris, currently charming hundreds for New South Wales and Australia. The solid, imposing establishment facing westwards across the suburban plain in time gave the world golfer Bruce Crampton, the only young man at school with a car (a little green Renault: the Rolls-Royces came later); a radio presenter, Russ

Walkington (with his Gerald the Grasshopper); Phillip Knightley, the investigative author; journalist Murray Sayle; Rugby League international George Peponis; and, in 1996, an Australian Prime Minister in John Howard, who was three years behind me.

All that concerned me was settling in and adjusting to the collection of youths around me and the fascinating array of teachers up there by the blackboard. One was known as 'Butch' because of his obsession with touching boys' backsides. Another, Mr Duhig, was related to the Catholic Archbishop of Brisbane, and, in an extremely serious manner, taught us geography. 'What,' he posed, 'is the climatic difference between Perth and London, Frith?'

It was one of those days when I hadn't managed to do much homework, but I did recall that when we left London, it wasn't all that cold, and the sky was fairly blue; and when we docked in Fremantle and went into Perth, conditions seemed not all that dissimilar. So I mumbled: 'They're very similar, sir.' That wild response cost me.

'Wimpy' Towner took us for French, and I felt some progress there, as well as in English, which was to be the prime subject as I sorted out what I wanted. For a time, having seen a stirring movie, I thought I'd be a barrister and save innocent men from hanging, and so I took special Latin lessons after hours for three months before letting it lapse. Mr Crausaz, with the thick S.Z.Sakall accent if not his gleeful warmth, was cane-happy, and Mr Gillogley's ferocious aspect turned me off science, just as Vocational Guidance had suggested that this could be my most propitious area. To complete an extraordinary set of names, we were taught mathematics by a Mr Wackwitz.

I missed Mr Hawkins back at Roxbourne, but the cricket influence now came from a strange, severe little man named Kentley. 'Slim Jim' had a long red nose, wore a black Homburg hat seemingly all the time, favoured a shiny black linen jacket, and used a pencil, held across his knuckles, like a conductor's baton. Not that there was anything musical about Jim Kentley. His high-pitched snarl pinned us to our desks in the library, which was his domain. 'See you three-twenty,' he would bark when a misdemeanour meant staying behind after school.

He had a fixation with the bullfighter Manolete, who had been killed in 1947, a classicist among matadors, so Slim Jim clearly admired style. In time, when he saw my attempt at Lindwall's bowling action at the nets, he uttered soft words of encouragement that cheered me greatly.

He had a large print of Laocoön on the library wall, the man wrestling with a serpent which was after his two small sons: Ted Frith in a loincloth, perhaps. Mr Kentley talked cricket too, and sneered at C.B.Fry's pre-war radio commentary. He said the illustrious Englishman had made silly remarks, like 'Well, Fleetwood-Smith needs only another 97 to reach his century.' If Slim Jim had lived long enough to hear some of the moderns he probably would have suffered a seizure.

With a couple of the lads, I played miniature cricket in the schoolyard: down on one knee, foot-long chunk of wood for a bat, dried peach-stone (seam up) for a ball. Proper house cricket followed, on concrete pitches with 'compo' balls. It was only quite late in my five years at Canterbury that I made a bid for the school team, and by the last year, 1953, I was doing my Len Hutton thing as 1st XI opener, also getting a few overs with my Ray Lindwall stuff.

Back in 1949, though, studies came first. Made to feel special at home, I tried hard to make a mark in class. And a certificate covering that first year indicated some progress: first place in English, French and Technical Drawing. Two years later, I managed eight passes in the Intermediate Certificate, and unhesitatingly lined up for two further years. There was a 'leak' before the results came out that someone had got 97% in Tech Drawing. Was it Bill Le Page, whose Dad had been killed by the Japanese? I hoped so. Or Graham Utley, the forceful future school captain, who had heard me speaking of England once and told me to 'f— off back to Pommieland'? Neither of these. The clever dickie who had managed a near-maximum in TD was me. So for a fortnight or so I felt I had to become an architect, an ambition that soon withered.

I had begun to feel more settled, for we eventually got away from the caravan park (where the mighty St George Leagues Club now stands), Dad having paid £250 for a piece of New South Wales, at the top end of Ecole Street, which spurred off the Princes Highway opposite Prince Edward Park. The corner plot was 50 feet by 120, and overgrown with canna lilies and weeds. My father and I were still on friendly terms, though I'd committed my first verbal offence when we were playing cricket on the expanse of football field and he became critical. 'We can't all be as good as you!' I blurted as I stomped away. His brothers, George and Alec, had by now arrived in Australia, and had crammed their families into caravans too. Uncle Alec was a genuine cricket-lover, and gave me one of my first books, Jack Hobbs's thick volume on the Bodyline series. Although Dad had won £1 by predicting Les Ames's century in the 1934 Lord's Test – or so he said – I felt it was Alec who really knew his cricket and had a feel for it. Sandy-haired and shortish of stature, he once watched a new batsman, clearly an exhibitionist, time-consumingly surveying the field setting before finally preparing to face. 'Bet he can't remember a thing he's seen,' murmured Uncle Alec drily, in his cultivated Home Counties accent. It amused me, and I've re-worked the remark often.

Uncle George and Auntie Harriet and their three children returned to England a few months after arriving, which cost me some companionship, for away from school Joey was a dynamic organiser of blackberry-picking expeditions and, more dangerous, birds-egg collecting. He would climb the tallest of trees while I, his accomplice, waited below to catch the falling eggs in my coat. I'd then blow them, while Joey did it the proper way: he sucked them. The raids ended when his forearm was fractured by an angry swan, out on the swamps where James Cook High School now sprawls.

One morning, on the way to the school train, I stopped by Jubilee Oval to get some branches of leaves for the Indian elephant, Gandhi, when Bullen Brothers' circus was in town. When I returned, Gandhi had torn my school bag apart and swallowed most of the contents: textbooks, exercise books, cheese-and-pickle sandwiches. I tried, but I could not hold back the tears of shock, shame and panic. Dad marched up and demanded compensation, but all we got was free tickets for the circus.

Other traumas included sunstroke, contracted while sitting fishing for hours at Carss Park with the sun playing on a bare neck, the price being two days of traumatic delirium (without the German U-boat) while Mum worried and prayed and worried; and then, wading with my neat little balsawood sailing boat in the pond at Scarborough Park, I trod on a broken bottle and left crimson crescents on the footpath all the way home, a route which took me close to the abode of a lad a year or so younger than myself called Clive James, later a clever wit on British television. We were never to meet.

The caravan having been towed the short distance up to the block of land in Ecole Street, Dad set about building a house. First, the land had to be cleared of foliage, and within minutes I had mistimed a swing with the sickle and sliced my left elbow. Trying not to faint, I watched my resourceful father at his best, staunching the flow of blood and applying a firm bandage. I hoped he didn't think I did it deliberately to avoid further labours.

As he dug the foundations, levelled the concrete and began the bricklaying, I admit that I could have done more to help. But there was homework to hide behind, and cricket in the roadway with Keith across the way. I had been listening to the Test matches of 1950-51 and had transferred my idolatry from Compton (who was to average 7.57 in the series) to Len Hutton (88). I was also getting interested in the beautiful smooth action of Ray Lindwall, having seen him on the newsreel. So Keith was Ian Johnson and I was Hutton, reserving the right to extend my repertoire of imitations as our long series of cricket contests progressed.

Caravan life was scarcely more tolerable on our own block of land, but at least I could escape to Keith's house to play table cricket, a compulsive pursuit: ball-bearing down a chute, small metal batsman with a finger-operated pivoting bat, metal fielders disposed to stop boundaries or even catch the ball in the trap between their feet. The ping-ping-ping of the ball-bearing after it had sped across the tablecloth and fallen onto the wooden floor was the music of the time – along with *Slippin' Around* and Burl Ives's *Lavender Blue*. Once I made Alec Bedser score 534 at that table-cricket game.

The cricket bat had taken over from the airgun, which had seen action by the storm-water channel at Prince Edward Park, picking off the rats, and down at the sandhills at Cronulla, where Raymond from Essex had actually wanted to kill seagulls, whereas I was content just to give them a fright. The 'Bee-bee' rifle had impressed Theo, my little friend from Poland. He could only have been about six, same age as my brother, but he fascinated me because he knew something I didn't, and that was how to speak Polish. So I'd let him fire a few pellets, then we'd have Polish lessons: aeroplane = samelot, etc. What a polymath I was becoming.

We still did some visiting – to Percy and Gladys at Woolooware, which was boring, and to their friends the Walters at Miranda, interesting only in that they had been shipwrecked on their way to Australia in the 1890s. The main family friendship developed with the Gooches, who had also been on our ship. Harry helped Dad with the building of the house while Et kept Mum company. Son John Gooch had had an early shock upon arriving in Sydney. They lived in Dowling Street, across Moore Park from the Sydney Cricket Ground, and one morning John was walking across the park when he found his eyes level with the feet of a man hanging dead from one of the giant Moreton Bay fig trees.

When we visited them, we played cricket in the street, just as if it were a London suburb, and listened to the Test match on the radio, and watched disapprovingly as our parents drank a little too much and got noisy. Mum in particular must have felt she had a puritan for a son, but I didn't like to see either of them 'loose' like that, and failed to see that the strain they had been under entitled them to do exactly as they wished.

All the same, I drew the line at Dad's loud proclamation when the Gooches, yet again, were teasing me for being so serious and quiet. 'David's embarrassed about his body hair.' Oh, great! Gold medal for clumsiness, father.

The house neared completion, though there were setbacks. One night a fierce gale caused a freshly-cemented brick wall to lurch drunkenly. The building inspector told Dad what he knew already: that misshapen wall had to come down. It was the closest I ever saw him to tears. He went out with the six-pound hammer and smashed it to pieces. Then he started all over again.

The unsewered lavatory was often more than I could stomach. The 'dunny man' came once a week. Although Mum splashed disinfectant liberally into the large receptacle, the blowflies came, and then there were maggots. My stomach churned, and I took to a secret spot in a far corner of the garden thereafter.

The second anniversary of our arrival saw the house almost completed, so no loyal and true wife was going to say to her husband 'Let's go back to England', pledge or no pledge. We stayed, and although I looked forward to the parcels and newspapers from England, and sought out English movies at the Odeon, I was happy. The furniture and personal possessions came out of storage soon after the last brick was in place (with a special trowelful of mortar mixed with whisky), and we all felt immeasurably more decent and secure to be living in a house of our own once again.

At fourteen, I had my first pair of long trousers, launched with a proud stroll down Ecole Street, the wearer unaware that he had not removed the colourful label from the rear pocket.

By the third Australian Christmas, a meal on the beach in near-century heat seemed as natural as the old snow-fireside-and-turkey scene, and as the local accent became familiar, so English and Scottish accents now stood out with almost startling significance. At school, I blended now.

The skies were unquestionably bluer, and I often looked westwards as the sun set over the distant vast interior, with perhaps Vaughn Monroe nasalising *Ghost Riders in the Sky* or Frankie Laine oozing *Cool Clear Water* on the little radio, and I shuddered at the thought of all that harsh wilderness beyond. Though summer evening light never extended to anything like 10pm, outdoor activities beckoned, with homework postponed. Into Jubilee Oval some of us climbed, for cricket on a perfect surface and to maul each other in quest of a rugby ball. We played tennis on hardcourts under lights, with the Kogarah district apparently boasting more tennis-courts, many in backyards, than any similar-sized district in the world. Mighty little Ken Rosewall was the best local product.

I even got involved in the school's athletics carnival at Blick Oval, though my heart was not really in it. I borrowed running-shoes, tripped over the spikes, decided to run the 100 barefoot, and slipped over at the start. The shot-putt seemed contrived. I was the wrong build for the long jump. And by now, anyway, there was every sign that cricket had afflicted me very seriously indeed.

I was to make it into the school's 3rd XV at rugby, playing as a breakaway (known later as a wing forward) feeling death was imminent on those hottest of afternoons, when the heavy jersey was like chain-mail or even a straitjacket. I was a rather ineffective footballer, trying to protect my own scrum-half, then clawing at the opposing scrum-half. But throwing myself about on the rock-hard grounds seemed crazy. I managed only one try in all the matches we played, and executed one copybook tackle, hurling myself through the air like Superman, bringing to earth some poor bloke over whom I then rolled, snapping his collarbone. Give me soccer any day.

I'd been taken on by St George as their ball-boy at Prince Edward Park, and took part in the night-time training under lights. I bought *Charles Buchan's Football Monthly* and listened to the Cup final from Wembley each year, very late at night. And inspired by visions of the clean-cut Nat Lofthouse, I set out to play for St George. First, though, I had to do something at junior level, so I joined Sans Souci, whose coach was a friend of Dad's at the Oddfellows Lodge. As a scheming left-half and sometimes right-wing, I made a bit of a mark and got into the representative side and won a sweet little silver cup, which I hugged lovingly all the way across the golf course on the way home that night. Soon I was playing in the glorious red-and-white of St George, in the reserves.

Essentially, football was merely something that helped to tide me over between cricket seasons. I found a boys' team to play in on Saturday mornings, on matting stretched over concrete, and after a year or two, found a men's team too, so I could play two matches in one day. Every run excited me and was replayed over and over again that night; every wicket swelled my heart; every failure plunged me into gloom.

Ignition really took place on January 8, 1951. The evening before, an invitation of the most profound significance had come my way. Keith asked if I'd like to go to the Test match with him and his grandfather and Mr Cooper. In the dust, he drew a plan of the Sydney Cricket Ground, and marked where we'd be sitting. So off we went, Keith and I in the back of the old Ford, with its long bonnet and canvas hood, as it bounced over the tramlines around Newtown all the way to Moore Park. Into the SCG we walked, the match already under way, past the rear of the Sheridan Stand, with the Victor Trumper memorial plaque high up almost out of sight; around the base of the Hill, with the cackle of barracking floating from it; along the humble Bob Stand, where we found space on the wooden stepped seating.

I looked up and saw a square-shouldered Englishman throwing in left-handed. This was substitute fieldsman David Sheppard, one day to be Anglican Bishop of Liverpool. And out in the middle, a hard-put England bowling line-up of Alec Bedser, Freddie Brown and John Warr were to toil away all day (with a few left-arm spinners from Compton), Bailey and Wright having been injured, while Keith Miller made most of his 145 not out and Ian Johnson scored a turgid 77.

I looked around me in wonderment, at the enchanting green 19th-century pavilion with its ornate roof and clock-tower, at the roomy and elegant Ladies' Stand, and the long, cosy Brewongle Stand. Far left was the Sheridan Stand, a confident structure which, at its extremity, faced down the pitch, so on future visits it became my preferred position. The Hill was packed. Beer-cans were a future invention still. Hundreds of men sat on that great grassy expanse, almost all wearing wide-brimmed hats, some of them yelling encouragement to the Australians, not that they were in need of it, some directing ribaldry and gentle derision at the Englishmen. It was a momentous baptism, a revelation, destiny-making.

I went home with my tour souvenir booklet and mental pictures: Godfrey Evans, the bouncy little English wicketkeeper; Alec Bedser, the heroic kingpin bowler, a tireless giant; Keith Miller, with his toss of the hair and slap of the back-cut; Lindsay Hassett, small and neat; Neil Harvey, so trim; and the sound, still in the ears, of Sam Loxton's pull-shot smacking into Bedser's huge hands. Then came the mesmeric study of those portraits in the tour booklet, and the perusal of the statistics: MacLaren the same number of Test runs as McCabe, Stoddart four runs short of 1000, Hutton, this Hutton, unbelievably the scorer of 364. Aladdin's cave was brassy by comparison.

Sydney Cricket Ground in the 1950s – a place of magic

Perhaps other interests were due to fade. We'd been to speedway at Sydney Sportsground. But only a few nights before my Test cricket debut, Ken Le Breton, the Australian known as the White Ghost because of his white leathers, was killed before our very eyes, and what made it worse was that the English rider with whom he had collided, Eddie Rigg, was being held responsible by some. Denis Compton, my old dream batting partner, was there that night, and I managed to get his autograph for the first of many times. I also noted how nonchalantly he walked, and tried it for a bit.

Now I found I needed to be near those Test cricketers, so I caught the train up to Sydney and headed for the Hotel Australia, in Castlereagh Street, where I'd heard the English team were staying. I stood by the marble columns at the entrance, unable to get past the commissionaire, and began to despair of seeing any of the great players. Another boy encouraged me, and even offered to sell me Freddie Brown's signature for two bob. That was a lot of money. I was tempted, but hung on. Then Alec Bedser came out, and I pounced. We even had a little chat. He spotted my Wembley Speedway badge, and responded. Within days I was writing at school about my encounter with one of cricket's giants and stating that my mind was made up: I wanted to be a cricket- writer. Nothing else.

Emboldened, I went back next day and got the lot more into the autograph-book, and actually saw the plane take off from Mascot as the train passed Tempe on the way home. There was a resounding, painful sense of loss.

There had been, however, one crucial meeting during my trips to town. That other lad had taken me along to Hunter Street, where there was a sports-shop run by a dapper little man named Bert Oldfield, who had been Australia's wicketkeeper in the 1920s and 1930s. He was hardly taller than me, oozed charm and spoke rather theatrically. He gave me a signed photo and was well into cricket chat about Wally Hammond and Tibby Cotter, whose life-size pictures adorned the shop window, when in walked the England cricketers Reg Simpson and Trevor Bailey, Bailey with his right hand in plaster after Lindwall had broken his thumb, on the opening day of the Test match. His signature in my book was indecipherable, and it was only after enjoying his friendship many years later, and getting him to sign all sorts of other books and items, that I realised that Trevor normally scrawled his name like that.

Bert Oldfield (right) tries on his Australian blazer in 1930, and Archie Jackson checks it for quality. Both players played a part in the author's life. And Oldfield gave him the blazer

I became a regular visitor to Oldfield's Sports Store, buying my first bat there, meeting briefly his old Test colleague, the shy and immortal Charlie Macartney, who had an office upstairs, and soaking up Mr Oldfield's flow of reminiscence. Unlike some of my school acquaintances, he respected England, having spent so much time there, and he talked nostalgically about the cricket grounds and the shops and the castles and dukes and theatres. I discovered that he had been buried by a shell at Polygon Wood during the Great War, and there was talk of a metal plate in his skull; but I never dared ask. That plate may even have saved his life when he was hit by a Larwood bouncer during the Bodyline series.

Such became our friendship that in due course he gave me a lift to the Sydney Cricket Ground, telling me among other things that he had scored centuries in every country in which he'd played, including Egypt. Then we had to part, he through the pearly gates of the members' entrance and myself through the public turnstiles, flashing the free pass issued by the NSWCA to all members of high-school cricket teams.

I even saw Bert Oldfield keep wicket. He was in his late fifties, but in a charity match at Glebe, his old stamping-ground, he played for the Pakistan High Commissioner's XI, and moved and handled with all the elegance I'd been reading about in books by Neville Cardus and Ray Robinson.

My investigations sent me further, to Stan McCabe's shop in George Street, next to Cricket House, home of the NSWCA, and to Alan Kippax's establishment in Martin Place. But these shops were impersonal by comparison, especially when Mr Oldfield took me aside on one visit and presented me with his 1930 Australian tour blazer and a ball from the 1930 Trent Bridge Test. That really started something. Sixty-odd years later I found myself with a cricket collection that needed almost a house of its own for storage and display.

Cricket had now well and truly taken over. Old Mr Doust across the road was telling me tales of Trumper and Bardsley and Collins; I was playing at school and at weekends and with Keith across the road whenever the rain let up, and crouched over one of the table-cricket games when it was too dark or wet outside. When nobody else was available, I'd put a cricket ball into one of Mum's cast-off stockings and tie it to the clothes-line and bop-bop-bop-bop-bop until I felt the off-drive was as good as Hutton's. Conveniently, there was the deserted school playground across the road, where a tennis ball could be hurled towards a chalked wicket (how was I to know I was about to start a 40-odd-year career perched at slip?). Then, throwing the ball from 15 yards, one could bat against the rebound. Who needed anybody else? The imaginary teams were brilliant, Trumper followed by Bradman, with Hobbs and Hammond opposing them. Soon I had whipped up a cricket jamboree such as few kids before me could ever have known.

When I was exhausted I'd climb one of the gumtrees by the school perimeter, with cicadas screeching. I'd look down across the empty playground and the silent street, wondering if I would ever be good enough to play in a Test match, and wondering whether to face up to the certain truth that of course I never would. Even if my technique continued to improve, perhaps one day touching the perfection of a Hutton or a Lindwall, I sensed that my temperament would always be an insurmountable handicap. I even got nervous playing against myself up against that school wall.

All kinds of variations presented themselves. I once tried a golf-ball against the wall, and it came back so swiftly that I came close to losing an eye. However, it assisted in the development of the hook shot – as did the join in the matting in the middle of our Saturday-morning pitch. An elephant of a fast bowler, left-arm over, dropped one on the join one day, and had I not got my first real hook-stroke to it, it would have killed me. And already I was hearing the odd fellow claim that cricket was a slow game.

There was, of course, another kind of cerebral cricket. I spent all spare cash on cricket books at Dymocks, the old, high-vaulted shop in George Street. The first was *Elusive Victory*, E.W.Swanton's book on the 1950-51 Ashes series, of which I could claim to have been a tiny part, having watched one day's play and listened to almost all the rest on radio, clinging to each word uttered by the friendly Johnny Moyes, Alan McGilvray, Arthur Gilligan and Vic Richardson. Then came the first *Wisden*, an incomparable delight to handle, with its chocolate binding and esoteric small type. And then came Neville Cardus.

I lashed out 12/9d for *Good Days* and 4/6d for *The Summer Game*, and tried to work out, as the train rumbled me to school or back, what was meant by Grimmett's name penetrating 'to the quiddity' and what sort of batsman must George Gunn have been if, as Cardus says, 'his bat was a swift rapier used not for warfare but just to tickle the ribs'. This Woolley must have been something if some of his innings 'stay with us until they become like poetry which can be told over again and again'. As for MacLaren, my old teacher Mr Hawkins' favourite too, what a vision of him glowed from the page: 'His bat swept down and, after his stroke, it remained on high, and MacLaren stood still, as though fixed by the magnificence of his own stroke.' To my credit, I hope, I never tried this. Such florid batsmanship is associated with the English amateur rather than the down-to-earth and usually victorious Australian batsman.

There was not a spare minute. Off to the SCG to see Sheffield Shield cricket; playing cricket wherever the chance arose; reading about it; listening to radio commentary; back into Sydney to see the English cricketers at the hotel before they went home, having won the fifth Test in the wake of all those painful defeats.

I paid some sort of lip service to my education, but there were other enthusiasms, such as flying: I joined the Air Training Corps, who issued me with a fine dark-blue uniform and gave me lessons in aerial navigation. There was a fortnight's camp down in Canberra late in 1950, where I had my first flight. The Auster two-seater was so smooth to handle that this 13-year-old was allowed to hold the joystick for a time. The sortie in the two-seater Wirraway A20-3 fighter-trainer, the first Australian-built warplane, was less serene. 'Have you got your safety-belt fastened?' called the pilot from in front of me. He had to repeat the question several times before realising I hadn't switched on my intercom. Having found the button, I said I was safely strapped in, but why? 'We're going to do a few tricks,' he said. I protested, but this time he had his intercom turned off.

Canberra suddenly swung from underneath to overhead. Then it twisted, fell away, disappeared. Clouds twirled. The aircraft contorted. My stomach swelled and churned, my head spun. There was Canberra again. Now it's gone. We fell rapidly to the left, stopped in mid-air, seemed to fall backwards. There was damned Canberra again, spinning this time. Such severe pressure on the head and neck. Gravity had gone berserk. Closing the eyes didn't help. Oh, God!

The tossing and gyrating stopped. We were gently, blissfully floating back to earth, and my benevolent pilot came through again: 'How'd you enjoy that, son?' I tried to speak but couldn't.

But I was proud, for I hadn't, after all, been sick. Then the undercarriage touched the runway, and as it did so, as if a switch inside me had been touched, I brought up my breakfast. Since the floor of the cockpit was all tubes and wires, it took me some time to clear up.

In contrast, I made a good job of my session in the Link trainer, the synthesizer in which you 'fly' by the cabin instruments according to the instructions on the earphones, a 'crab' tracking your progress in red ink on a glass-topped map.

Barrack-room crudities were all part of it, though one evening our small gathering was stopped short in our session of experimental expletives when a group captain put his head round the door and asked if we would use such language at home in front of Mum?

I valued this Canberra camp as much as anything for the trip we had to Manuka Oval, where MCC were playing NSW Southern Districts, and Sheppard and Close made centuries and Hutton 54. Our visit to the great white Parliament building was also absorbing. Arthur Fadden was in full cry on the floor of the House, but I was thrilled to meet, at a reception afterwards, Sir Thomas White, a diminutive, dapper, silver-haired gentleman who was an aviation pioneer and First World War hero. Married to a daughter of former Prime Minister Alfred Deakin, he had been captured by the Turks in Baghdad, and escaped after three years as a prisoner. Later he became Australia's High Commissioner in London. This lovely man talked to us cadets as though we were the most important people he had ever met.

The aviation craze often took me out to Kingsford Smith (Mascot) aerodrome by bike, where a few of us would clamber over the Qantas Constellations – security was so low-key as to be almost invisible – and then the old wartime Catalina flying-boat, which brought out the Errol Flynn in all of us. It didn't smell as foul as the Japanese bomber we'd been allowed to crawl through in the marvellous War Memorial and Museum in Canberra.

In spite of the Wirraway experience, the sky still seemed a wonderful place to be, apart from the cricket pitch, and I made a small aeroplane out of balsawood and tissue-paper, with a propeller driven by an elastic-band, and when it powered its way up into its brief flight, my spirit was up there with it. Later, I cycled to Mascot to see the first Boeing Stratocruiser land in Australia, and to Bankstown to greet the first Canberra bomber. Years later came the Britannia, the 'Whispering Giant', and the RAF Vulcan bomber, which looked so eerie as it flew over the city. It was to crash upon its return to England, all but two of its crew perishing.

I worked out a good way of compiling a scrapbook on the 1950-51 Test series. The local butcher used to ask for old newspapers, so I offered to stack and tidy them for him, while cutting out the cricket pictures. A lovely colour portrait of Denis Compton out of *Sporting Life* crowned the front cover beautifully.

A hand-cranked Minicine film projector filled another corner of my life, with additional film strips ordered from England. If I was not to become a cricket-writer, perhaps I could be a film producer. I certainly saw enough movies. We went to the Odeon in Carlton twice a week, the four of us, booking to avoid disappointment, for it was always full. Dad would pass me a half-melted chocolate bar as the curtains parted, and off we went to the technicolor world of singing, dancing, carefree, love-everybody Hollywood: Mario Lanza, Kathryn Grayson, Fred Astaire, Cyd Charisse, Frank Sinatra, Red Skelton the master laughtermaker, Howard Keel, Judy Garland, Van Johnson, and three ladies who competed for my hesitant juvenile passion: Jane Wyman, June Allyson and Jane Powell (doin' the *Oceana Roll*). Jane P. came closest to the divine girl I eventually was to marry.

Perhaps top of the magic pile was Gene Kelly for his broad, eternal grin (was he never unhappy?) and his incredible fitness (what a cover fieldsman he would have made). *Singin' in the Rain* sent a teenager out into the night in a state of bliss, while after *Brigadoon*, I went straight out next day and spent my pocket money on a green shirt and red undervest. The handsome clean-cut look was the fashion, and among the cowboy movies the square-jawed, steady-gazing Dale Robertson was the paragon. I was wishing I'd had an impressive nose like his.

Dean Martin and Jerry Lewis had us in fits, and we were only a few feet away from the Pacific war, in full colour, when *Men of the Fighting Lady* came on, with all the frantic drama of the aircraft-carrier. Australia's fighting tradition came stirringly through with *Forty Thousand Horsemen*, which had even more meaning when we found out that some of it was filmed down on the sand-dunes of Cronulla, just down the highway. In September 1951 (the films are all listed in my diary, mostly classified as 'VG' for very good) we saw *Destination Moon*, with John Archer. Walking home down the Jubilee Avenue hill, I looked up at the moon, and wondered . . . in my lifetime? Extremely unlikely.

Life went into reverse every time we saw English films – such as *The Blue Lamp*, with Dad's friend Jack Warner – for there were the very distinctive streets and clothes and speech patterns, the cosy smoking chimneys and peculiar native kindliness that we'd left behind. This and certain attitudes at school from the likes of Utley sometimes made settling down a difficult and complex business.

Randolph Turpin helped focus this. Early one morning in July 1951, hunched over the radio-set in the caravan, I listened to the 15-round world middleweight fight from England. To everyone's amazement the coloured Englishman, uncomplicated son of a Leamington woman and a black man from British Guiana who had been gassed in the First World War, beat the apparently unbeatable and highly glamorous American 'Sugar Ray' Robinson. Young Turpin, who went to the stadium by tube train, had caused the biggest sporting upset since the Ashes Test of 1882.

I floated on air all the way to school, where, to my mortification, nowhere could I find anybody to share my joy. Boys had either wanted Robinson to win, or felt frustration because the best middleweight in the world (in their opinion), Dave Sands, the Aboriginal from Kempsey, was being denied his opportunity. (Sands had given Turpin's brother Dick a fearful beating, but was killed in a truck accident near Dungog in 1952.)

I argued that Australians should have wanted Randy to win. Was this country about to become yet another State of the USA? 'You just want us to be like the Pommies!' said one. 'No,' said I, 'I'd like Australia to stand up for itself and not copy anybody.' A few years hence, though it was not a pretty sight, Australia embarked on just such an era of blustering jingoism and patriotism.

Anyway, I went home, mumbling to myself, and sent off a fan letter to Randolph Turpin, addressed, I think, to Earls Court, where he had earned his glory. To my amazement, some weeks later I received a signed photo of him, and for a time Hutton, Bedser, Lindwall and the rest were sidelined. I started a scrapbook of Turpin cuttings and found a brilliant portrait of him to place up on the wall. I searched everywhere, even in Bert Oldfield's shop, for a pair of satin boxing shorts like Randolph's, but in vain; and I tried to add that lightning ducking manoeuvre to my range in school boxing bouts. I got to the newsreel cinema early and watched him beat Sugar Ray four times in all in one day, blinking hard when finally ejected into the evening sunlight. (How strange now to reflect that the referee's name was Henderson, a surname that would make a sizable imprint on my life 44 years later.)

When Robinson beat Turpin to pulp in the return fight at the New York

Polo Grounds two months later, my schoolmates were at it again, figuratively waving Stars and Stripes. I could readily have belted into the lot of them. Randolph Turpin would have. This time I went to the newsreel house, but watched this fight through only the once. That beaten-up figure felt like a brother to me.

Randy Turpin: an inspiration

In 1966, now 37 and bankrupt and working in a transport cafe, Turpin shot himself. As soon as I could, I visited his grave in Leamington, recalling with gratitude the inspiration that he had unknowingly given to me.

Having, on the whole, good relations with my classmates, especially with Kevin – he and I, for no known reason, used to have a Lancashire-accent routine when we spoke to each other – I became, I suppose, inordinately sensitive to criticism of England and the English. This made England's soccer victory at the SCG all the more important to me. It was no ordinary victory, but a humiliation of world-record proportions: 17 goals to nil. Most rugby matches have lesser margins than that.

From my seat in the Sheridan Stand, it was clear that the ground was a sea of mud. England, on an FA 'goodwill' tour, had been winning by polite margins. But now, in the first few minutes, one or two Australian defenders got rough, and one rubbed a handful of mud into the face of Jackie Sewell of

Sheffield Wednesday, who was then the world's most expensive player, having been transferred for £45,000. Looks were exchanged, and the Englishmen decided now to pop in every goal they could get. Ike Clarke scored a three-minute hat-trick, Sewell himself put in seven goals, and goalie Sam Bartram hardly touched the ball. Seventeen-nil! Suddenly, none of the lads at Canterbury Boys' High School seemed to have had any interest at all in soccer.

Life went on. On the train to school, I tried playing chess. It might have worked had I not chosen, by sheer chance, to play against Emmerick on his lap-top set. Emmerick was about to emerge as school champion. So I read my way steadily through the Biggles books, all that were held by 'Slim Jim' Kentley in the school library. Somehow my hero's exploits read better on the days when I wore my blue Air Training Corps uniform to school. Other times, I lashed out on a newspaper, one edition of which carried the sad story of a young genius of a batsman named Archie Jackson who was, by all accounts, as brilliant as Bradman, but who died, like so many of my own forebears, of tuberculosis. I felt I'd like to investigate that story further one day. And I did.

We lost a youngster from our own midst quite suddenly. Returning from school holidays, we were told that a lad in our year, David Gurr, had died from leukaemia. It could have been any of us. And yet there he was now, looking out at us from the third-grade rugby team photo in the new school yearbook.

As the train passed Kogarah, the Victory Cinema could just be seen, where young Bradman received a presentation at a St George cricket evening after his triumphant 1930 tour. During the journey to school we often exchanged our homework efforts for mutual assessment. It was blush time again when John Bishop, my companion in hundreds of hours of cricket and golf and tennis around Carlton, chose to read out loud from one of my carefully-composed essays.

'Here, get this, fellas. Frithy's written a beauty here: "*superfluous belligerence*"! Huh! "Superfluous belligerence"! Where'd you get that from?'

There was no answer, and I didn't even try.

It came as something of a surprise several weeks later, therefore, when our English master, as was his custom, called upon one of the boys to read out his essay. His choice was Bishop, and within the first paragraph my mate had dropped in what he evidently thought, after all, wasn't a bad little expression: 'superfluous belligerence'. I was learning more about human foibles with each passing day. It was still a delight to meet up with John many years later: he had become one of Sydney's leading lawyers.

The matter of the hard 'a' and the soft 'a'was proving problematic too, a terrifying climax coming when I was asked to stand up in History lesson and read a chapter on the French Revolution. Of course, the word 'France' cropped up every few lines, and with each attempt at the word, hating the local hard 'a' and irrationally ashamed of my natural soft 'a', I became confused and tongue-tied. The embarrassment choked me, and, face aflush, I left the classroom. I felt I would never be able to stand up in class ever again, let alone address a mass of people from a podium. Life's difficulties were piling up.

Shyness brought me down again at Ted Amos's party. It was all right while everybody sat and talked, with plenty of corners to settle into, but when the command was given – and it was just that – for all the boys and girls to sing and dance in formation (*Everyone knows she's a rambling rose*, a brainless piece of music) I seized up. A pity because I quite liked Edna. All I could do in the circumstances to make myself feel better was to take tennis racquet and ball into the empty school playground next day and whack, whack, whack the ball up against the wall, murmuring her name with each contact. This was preferable to running amok with a cricket bat.

Dad let me work at the shop he managed in Rockdale, just Saturday mornings, cooking pigs' trotters and sliced heads and baking meat-pies, then clearing everything up afterwards, all for five shillings. I was very vulnerable at fourteen, for I decided I loved Miss Manners, who served out front in the shop. But she had a boyfriend who was away fighting in the Korean war, and all I ever got from her was a weary smile. What else could I have been entitled to, for she must have been at least three years older.

I'd actually decided, while moving bricks for Dad on the house site, that it was time to become much tougher. I'd had enough of the nonsense at school: the disloyalty to Randolph Turpin, the cheating over essays, the humiliation over pronunciations, the failure on the athletics track, the indignity at Amos's party. You can't really be brave unless you're scared. Well, I seemed scared – from mildly to seriously – a little too often. So now I was going to be braver than ever.

This meant asking a girl to dance on Saturday evening at the Paradance Ballroom in Rockdale, where the band played *Harlem Nocturne* and *One o'Clock Jump* and *Learnin' the Blues* and some of Glenn Miller's stuff, and the saxophonist was the envy of my eye. A shuffle barely related to the foxtrot got us all around the floor, and the energy was restored with sixpenny soft drinks. Afterwards, it seemed, everybody went home alone.

Lonely times were spent waiting for trains, walking to the far end of the platform humming, or even trying to sing Nat King Cole's *Somewhere Along the Way*. Dad couldn't stand his voice. In a flash, I was no longer in unthinking agreement. I liked that voice.

My confidence must have been growing. When caught, after school hours, hanging out of a first-floor classroom window, reaching for some eggs in a pigeon's nest in the high guttering, I coolly met the teacher's challenge, '*What* are you doing, Frith?' with a defiant, nonsensical 'Nothing!'

My golf was improving too, from a first-ever round of 145 (at Beverley Park) to 114 three months later, when still short of my 15th birthday, although sore at the financial setback of balls sliced into Kogarah Bay from the elevated fourth tee. As for tennis, I probably gained more enjoyment from listening on radio to the Davis Cup efforts of Sedgman and McGregor, and Hoad and Rosewall as trying to get my own serve in.

With every day that passed it became more obvious that cricket and I were made for each other. There was something supernatural about its grip on me. Every single day my diary entries carried the evidence even if there was room for only 35 words to be pencilled in.

Almost ready for the fray
There was something almost supernatural about cricket's grip

In November 1951 the entries tell it all: 'Saw Bert Oldfield at his shop. Saw 1st day of NSW v West Indies. Spoke to Frank Worrell on the fine-leg fence' – 'Did not go to school. Went to see West Indies v NSW. Got autographs. West Indies are stubborn but got 4. Came home with Ray Lindwall in his car. A great experience' – 'Went to the Test match. Doubtful weather on and off all day. West Indies got a good start, 6-286. Got 4 autographs' – 'Went on to Test match. Very crowded. Hottish. Went to dressing-rooms after. Only got three autographs. Went into stand and saw the photo gallery' – 'Went to last day of 2nd Test. Took Mick. He was a devil. Aust won by 7 wkts. Stopped behind after. Only got 2 autographs and Worrell signed photo. Warm all day. Went to Bert Oldfield's in the morning. Got cap, bat oil and bat grip.'

I framed the Worrell picture and hung it up. He was so charming, and his entry into the arena, white gear gleaming, red cap bright in the sunlight, black skin fascinating, was to be an enduring image. Affection for the man was coupled with resentment at the negative attitude of so many young Australians towards Randolph Turpin, and left me with mixed feelings when Bill Johnston and Doug Ring stole victory in the Melbourne Test with an hilarious last-wicket stand of 38.

Interest in cricket history was fanned by public film shows at Sydney Town Hall, where on a giant screen the 1920s were recaptured as Jack Gregory thundered in again to bowl, with whimsical little Arthur Mailey twisting his legspinners down at the other end, and Hobbs and Sutcliffe, revered England batsmen, manoeuvred their grey bats to place the grey ball across the silver-grey outfield. All this plus film of the 1901 Federation ceremony and the Diggers marching to war: a great shillingsworth.

And at last I got my first real cover-drive away. Having made it somewhat timidly into the school 1st XI, I went out to open with the growling extrovert beanpole, Rod Barton, who was to make a name for himself as a baseballer. The setting was the tree-ringed Chatswood Oval, where Macartney used to hit the ball over the railway line. Sick with nerves, as usual, I did Rod's running for him, pottered about a bit, and then found the glistening red ball coming along at a tempting width and rather a generous length. What would Len Hutton have done? Put his left foot across, let the bat swing down easily, keeping the head steady, eyes fixed on the ball. Crack! Away it went, smacking into the white pickets, and the umpire expressionlessly signalled four. I too tried to show no emotion. But inside I was exploding with ecstasy.

'Shot!' came Rod Barton's throaty encouragement.

Next week we played miles out in the south-west, at rural Glenfield, and I turned my ankle in a rabbit-hole at mid-on.

Still, it was great to be in Canterbury's senior team, and to psyche up with our anthem: '*Hail Blue, Red, Gold and Southern Cross. . .*'

It dawns on me, a trifle shamefully, that life's milestones are nearly all set against cricket events. I know Mum had her operation in 1952 because I read a magazine in the hospital waiting-room that carried a feature on England's new fast-bowling discovery 'Fiery Freddie' Trueman. And there he was on the newsreel, with this thrilling, power-packed run-up and cartwheel delivery. What would the boys at school think of that, then? And what if I'd been able to tell them that Fred would one day be a close pal? It was the most intimidating thing I'd seen on screen since the 1951 feature on mystery spinner Jack Iverson. When his freak finger action had the ball bouncing the wrong way, straight at the camera set up in the nets, some people in the Odeon audience ducked.

Two other major events of 1952 were the death of King George VI and my first shave. The sadness of the king's departure was practically universal. The emotion surrounding my first shave was very private.

The fluff had built up on my upper lip and in front of the ears, and I wanted to be rid of it. It was as embarrassing itself as the prospect of shaving. My parents must have sensed this, for the Gillette safety-razor set appeared without fanfare on my 15th birthday (like a sentimental fool, I took it out of the drawer and used it again on my 60th birthday, and then carried on using it). Back in 1952, after a few days of cogitation I slunk into the outside laundry and managed to perform the lathering and razoring without slicing lips or nose. Into the house I crept, eyes averted, and when Mum asked if I'd like a cup of tea, I blurted out: 'I've sold my violin!' Being unfamiliar with this expression, she looked at me askance. Slowly her dark eyes moved to my clean, fresh cheeks and upper lip. 'You've had a shave!' she cried. 'Ted, David's had a shave!' The way things were going, I would soon be running out of the fluorescent fluid of which blushes are made.

In passing the Intermediate Certificate exams, I secured a bursary which accorded me the princely sum of 35 shillings from school funds. I spent this on a dictionary, and now set my sights on a good Leaving Certificate pass in two years' time so that I could join a newspaper and write about cricket. The ambition to become a film producer became even stronger after seeing *Treasure Island*, with Robert Newton's captivating performance as Long John Silver, and young Bobby Driscoll acting out the part we'd all have loved to have played. But this was pie in the sky. Australia made barely one film a year. So good was *Treasure Island* that I sat through it twice – which was probably too much for my young brother, who was spectacularly sick in the train going home.

My first essay in print appeared in the school magazine, *The Canterbury Tales*: some not entirely accurate details about an English grammar school; but the photos of the cricket and rugby teams were an inspiration, as were the notices on Old Cantabrians who were doing well in the fields of medicine and education. I just had to get a good Leaving pass – and to keep pressing, too, in my quest to become a 'professor of cricket'.

I spent even more time in the dining-room studying, while Mum kept the cups of tea coming, and the chocolate blancmange, as the radio poured out sweet music. I even won £2 for a selected popular request (Freddie Gardner's *Smoke Gets in Your Eyes*) from 2KY's gravel-voiced John Harper. And I contentedly absorbed my studies while Sheffield Shield commentaries rumbled in the background.

The SCG continued to be a prime attraction, my first view of South

African cricketers coming in 1952-53, a year after the West Indians. Then, amazingly, there was only one Test series in Australia over the following five summers – England's exciting 1954-55 tour – so it was Sheffield Shield or nothing. And a lad might easily have been driven from cricket by some of the deadly slow batsmen on view: Sid Barnes, Jim Burke, Jack Moroney. They forever preached the necessity for a batsman to place survival above risk-taking. This eventually prompted the introduction of the dramatically shortened formats which folk in the next century, with their short attention spans, relished.

The SCG members' entrance, where DF became a regular 'stage-door johnny'

Leaning on the pickets in front of the Sheridan Stand concourse, I felt part of the play, and sometimes talked to the outfielders. One fast leg-glance by Ray Flockton during his wonderful 85 for NSW against the West Indians almost rapped my fingers. In the fifth Test, I imagined I could see the ball swing as Gerry Gomez used the breeze and humidity to take 7 for 55. Nineteen wickets fell on that first day, which helped a boy in his growing belief that there was no cricket to match international cricket – even if the debutant openers, Colin McDonald and George Thoms, were deadly to watch.

The autograph collection grew, with many an anecdote to go with them. Loitering for hours by the members' gate, and sometimes slipping in so as to catch the players before they reached the car park at the rear of the pavilion, paid off. Once, the great K.S.Duleepsinhji walked past: 173 on Test debut for England at Lord's in 1930 and now India's High Commissioner in Australia. Arthur Mailey and Jack Gregory were spotted. Then, Heaven help us, Sir Donald Bradman. None of us boys had the courage to approach him. One young player struck us as a bit of a swank, and there was argument as to whether his name was 'Benno' or 'B'noh'. At least he signed willingly. Clyde Walcott took offence at my pal's entreaty of 'Will you sign, please Clyde?', telling him not to be 'so bloody presumptuous' and to use 'Mister'. We therefore both missed out, for the time being, in getting all the fabled Three Ws. Managed Ramadhin and Valentine though.

Keith Miller, easily bored it seemed, left his initials till last: eith iller, then smacked on the K and the M. Cyril Washbrook, on the '50-51 tour, he of the cigarette-card image at junior school, impressed me greatly by ignoring my biro and taking a fountain-pen from his double-breasted jacket and planting his name in my book. The biggest surprise must have been seeing Prime Minister R.G.Menzies treading across the lawn towards his limousine. We ran over, were lined up, and with a friendly word or two to each of us, the gist of which was to pledge us to vote Liberal when we were old enough, he signed his name in stately fashion across the page: *'Robert Menzies, Canberra, 1952'.* What puzzled us was that we were in Sydney, not Canberra. The prime minister must have dined well.

Bill Johnston, the tall, bouncy left-arm fast bowler, was always cheerful with the kids, which meant a lot to us. And Ken Archer made us laugh when he signed near Allan Rae's signature. Beside Rae I had printed 'West Indies opening batsman'. Archer had just been dismissed for 11, following twin failures in the Brisbane Test. 'You can write "ex-Australian opener" alongside my name!' he quipped. Although he made 47 in the second innings, his prediction was accurate. It was some consolation that his young brother, Ron, made his Australian debut next season.

Most amazing experience of all was, naturally, the lift home with Ray Lindwall, who lived just beyond Carlton. Too self-effacing to discuss his own performances, he preferred to talk about history and geography, while I quietly prayed that his car would break down so that I could have more private time with him. The boys at school believed I was making it all up. As for Mum, she desperately wanted Ray to come in for a cup of tea, but he politely declined. He was eager to get home and put his feet up.

In the 1952-53 season, as I was to do for most of my active life, I swung between my own little world of cricket, playing as hard as I could at as high a level as I could, and then entering the big-time as reader, spectator, and researcher. I don't think I have ever seen – all aspects considered – a more remarkable innings than Ian Craig's unbeaten 213 for NSW against the South Africans. Small of stature but high of forehead (under his big blue cap), he was only 17 years of age, and yet he out-batted Miller during his six hours-plus at the crease, facing a Test attack. When 16-year-old Bob Simpson made his New South Wales debut later that month, I wondered what was going on. I was almost 16 myself, but could never hope to match that sort of talent.

Another reality was sinking in.

Ray Lindwall: perhaps the greatest of fast bowlers and certainly one of the most amiable of men

And again, the reminder of cricket's inherent dangers: Benaud, fielding at gully during the Test match, took a fierce cut from John Waite smack in the mouth. The blood on the grass was visible from my seat up in the Sheridan Stand 100 yards away. Poor Richie. Graeme Hole, fielding by the fence, shrugged when my brother asked him what had happened, and said with a devilish grin: 'Asleep!'

Off I went to find Victor Trumper's grave at Waverley Cemetery, taking the long tram ride and searching for hours before stumbling upon the resting-place of Australia's premier romantic sporting heroes. He, like Craig, made his first-class debut at a tender 17 years of age, and by the time he died in 1915, aged 37, he was thought by most to have been the most brilliant batsman of all, Grace and Ranji notwithstanding. It was not just that. He had a charming nature as well. Looking beyond his grave to the shimmering blue Pacific, I recalled that there was a cricket oval not far away where he played regularly and which was named after him. That interested me.

By now I was a junior at the famous St George Club, home ground Hurstville Oval, where Bradman and O'Reilly once toyed with Saints' opponents, where Morris and Lindwall played, and where now the best boy cricketer in Sydney, Norman O'Neill, was our captain in the Green Shield team.

The roll-up at club nets was awesome: State players and future State players everywhere: Bob Cristofani, who had scored a century at Old Trafford in the 1945 'Victory Test'; Eric Lukeman, who had made a debut hundred for NSW; Billy Watson, soon to score 155 for NSW against Hutton's MCC side; Brian Booth, a future captain of Australia; Warren Saunders, a considerate young man who was to captain NSW; Wally Yeates, a left-hander good enough to have scored 93 for NSW; and the suave, dignified first-grade wicketkeeper Ernie Laidler, who had kept to O'Reilly and Lindwall.

I bowled my Lindwall stuff and tried to impress, but the only comment I earned was from Yeates: 'Don't ever let me see you stop the ball with your leg again. A blow like that could give you cancer.' And all I'd done was to misfield; the ball had smashed through to my limb.

Our Green Shield campaign ended in heartache. In the conclusive match I held out against Waverley (after Norm O'Neill's one failure of the competition), but the draw left us a decimal place away from the championship. One edged four would have done the trick, if only we'd known. At least I got a crushing handshake from Norm for my efforts. In the first match, we had put on 54 together, but I'm afraid only 10 of those runs were mine. He was simply phenomenal: built like Tarzan, aggressive, with a sledgehammer of a pull, and drives and cuts that frightened all in the vicinity. I saw nothing to compare, apart from Walcott, until Robin Smith came along. As for the power of his throw, it was a guided missile.

We all had to suppress smiles when O'Neill's carnage with his legspinners was unexpectedly halted by a little chap at Bankstown who banged him all around the oval. But we knew Normie would make it to the top, and six years later, having provocatively been dubbed 'the new Bradman', he made a fine Test debut at Brisbane against England.

So, quite early in the piece, I saw how clearly defined was the Australian cricket structure. All I had to do was bowl a bit more like Lindwall and bat a bit more like Hutton and I too could make it into first grade, thence New South Wales, then the Australian Test XI. Simple.

There were other matters to be attended to, however, such as finishing secondary school on a high note with a good matriculation, even if I saw no purpose in going on to university (and had no wish to burden my parents any further financially).

There was a careers night, when Canterbury Old Boys came to advise on the best course for advancement. I made straight for the desk marked Journalism, where sat a young man who was to make a name for himself as a writer: Phillip Knightley, who was to achieve acclaimed exposes on thalidomide and spy Kim Philby. Phil currently worked at the *Daily Mirror* in Sydney, though his future lay in Britain. He promised to try to line up a cadetship for me at the Mirror, subject to a good Leaving Certificate pass. With a sniff in the direction of the Accountancy desk and the Science desk,

I went home happy.

Norm O'Neill, our local champion, who was soon to become a Test batsman

I had no real right to expect a good pass at the end of 1953. There were distractions everywhere. It was not just that my most important cricket season so far took me into April. I struggled with the bat, once coming as close to a 'pair' – 0 and 0 not out – as it was possible without actually sustaining the ignominy; but I did scheme a batsman out first ball of the match by bowling just wide of off stump and tempting him to tickle an edge to the keeper; and for Rockdale Social against Rockdale Methodists I took 8 for 26, mainly pitching leg stump and clipping off. Nor was it that soccer then gripped me throughout the winter months, though I was a player, a ball-boy no longer. It was not, either, that Elizabeth II was crowned, and Hillary and Tenzing conquered Mount Everest, and the Korean conflict ended (Miss Manners would have been pleased). It was not that Stanley Matthews won his Wembley winner's medal at last, or that Hungary caused the earth to shake by beating England at Wembley, or that Gordon Richards won the Derby at the 28th attempt, or that mass murderer John Christie met his come-downance with the hangman's rope. It was even distracting to learn of Stalin's death, with the accompanying murmurs that, far from being one of our co-saviours, he was a dirty rotten mass murderer. Two other deaths, both in England, distracted: dear old Queen Mary, seemingly made of crystal though she was; and Derek Bentley, hanged without justification.

But none of this kept a teenager from his studies. What did was the 1953 Ashes Test series between Hutton's England and Hassett's Australia, beamed to us from 8pm till 3am on the oscillating air-waves.

I was glued to a commentary that would never be matched ever again, from the clipped tones and dramatic timing of Rex Alston and the measured baritone of Jim Swanton to that fascinating Hampshire rhythm of John Arlott (plus, briefly, some input from my friend Bert Oldfield). I sat hunched over my scorebook, glancing through the tour publications, sometimes actually trembling with anticipation. My parents would turn in, but not once throughout the 1953 series did I miss a ball. The electric fire had to be turned on at times, but I stuck with it, half through the night, my admiration for Bedser and Hutton growing ever larger.

The Watson/Bailey rearguard at Lord's was the most nail-biting span of play throughout the series, though I could not find anyone wanting to discuss it at any length in the playground next day. The protests at Trevor Bailey's negative bowling which saved England at Headingley were not easy to repel, though Australia's subsidence to 35 for eight wickets at the end of the Old Trafford Test caused some local blushes.

There can have been no more bleary-eyed 16-year-old in Australia than I after the famous final Test, when England won the Ashes by eight wickets, at The Oval, 19 years after having lost them.

Trueman came steaming in in his maiden Ashes Test, and Peter May looked the part at last, and Laker and Lock gave marvellous displays of spin bowling, while Hutton, the quiet, masterly captain, scored an important 82 and got himself run out in the second innings just as so many of us were willing him to make the winning runs himself. Compton swept Morris for four towards the gas-holders, and, in Jack Fingleton's neat phrase, the Ashes had crowned the year.

Len Hutton has won the Ashes. Wish I'd been there. The newsreel cinema was the next-best thing

I felt my own stocks had risen somehow, and to confirm the phenomenon I raced into Sydney a few days later and saw it all on the newsreel – two or three times. Incidents would stay burned onto memory's slate forever: Harvey pulling Trueman, only for Hutton to run away from the gas-holder background to cradle the catch; Laker trotting smoothly in; Lock bending backwards in ecstasy as another catch is taken; Bedser pounding in and building up a record tally of 39 Australian wickets (I soon realised that in cricket you should never say 'and that will never be bettered'); and those admirable skippers, Hutton and Hassett, on the balcony afterwards, looking down on a sea of smiling, upturned faces. Hassett, small and whimsical, showed how to lose. He was all smiles and congratulations, and pretended to toss his Australian blazer over the balcony. Years later, we learned that he smashed the dressing-room clock with an empty champagne bottle. But no scandal-sheet picked that up, and the very thought of any necessity for match referees to monitor and punish misbehaviour by cricketers would have been branded absurd.

No 16-year-old with literary aspirations could let the 1953 Ashes series pass without attempting an epic poem, so I laboured for hours over a work of some 308 lines which sometimes struggled to scan, with the rhyming often touch and go. A sample of eight lines will suffice:

The joyous Evans heartily scored
His runs as if he thought
It was a village-green affair,
And he a lone dreadnought.

Laker came and went like Christmas,
Poor Bailey on his own!
No-one to help our hero calm,
His face as still as stone.

Soon it was time to sit for the Leaving Certificate examinations, and, Test series or no Test series, there was no time for further revision. I had concentrated on five subjects, abandoning chemistry, resentful at having been forced to choose one of the sciences in the first place. Pathetically nervous before batting, I was just as bad as the exams approached. The train-rides were purgatory. The long uphill walk was little better. But all was well once the cream-coloured papers were turned over at the starter's orders, revealing questions that, on the whole, seemed answerable.

When it was all over, there lay ahead weeks of waiting before the results were published in the newspapers. Out onto the cricket field and golfcourse I went, developing the arts of distraction and diversion without which life can be even more painful.

It was the fast bowling rather than the batting that was getting me into the local representative sides. After the 8 for 26, I'd taken 6 for 11, including the wicket of Norm Shannon, who was the grandson of Bill Howell, who spun offbreaks for Australia in the early 1900s. That had significance for me, even if nobody else cared. Norm and I got into the St George Juniors rep team, and so did John Cope, who scored a century and took a hat-trick against us in a club match, rendering us literally hopeless, and so did a cocky little youngster named Reg Gasnier, who amazed us all by growing into an Australian Rugby League player to rank with the immortals.

Since we lads now played occasionally on turf – a demanding transition from matting-on-concrete – we had to have spiked boots. I bought mine from Alan Kippax's shop in Martin Place, and at the first outing I found them unusually heavy underfoot. At tea I saw why: the spikes had not been properly tempered and had curled into something resembling fish-hooks. Without comment, that most charming of pre-war batsmen took them from me and gave me a fresh pair in a box. Next Saturday, my team-mates seemed concerned that I examined the soles of my boots after every delivery. There was no further cause to worry.

Norm O'Neill, almost certainly briefed by his elders at the club, had been the first to teach me about time-wasting. We seemed on course for defeat, and as I walked back to my bowling mark he called across: 'Do your bootlace up, Dave!' I looked down, and my laces were all right. So I told him so. Through gritted teeth, he repeated his command with a weight of urgency I could not ignore. So I bent down and played with my bootlace for half-a-minute. We could be blamed, perhaps, in infinitesimal part, for the later introduction of the 15/20 overs-in-the-last-hour regulation.

We had broken up at school for the last time, the traditional fancy-dress day climaxing the ceremonies. One chap dressed in Gestapo uniform and went round beating everyone with a rubber truncheon (33 years later, David Gower was roundly condemned for his 'insensitivity' when he chose similar Nazi costume for the England cricket team's Christmas fancy-dress party in Melbourne). The only other violence came when Bruce Crampton rammed one of the giant bottle-palms with his Renault, having got dizzy from driving in a dozen tight celebratory circles. I put on a false beard and stuffed a pillow under my shirt and went as 'W.G.Grease', recognised by probably 10 per cent of my fellow pupils, if that.

I was to regret being talked into drawing a colour caricature of the headmaster, F.C.Wootten, kicking a dog up the backside, the likeness then being pinned onto his study door. There were tales of his quick temper and black moods, and nobody had a good word to say about him, so the gesture (I was at my peak as an illustrator) was universally popular. But years later, I re-read his pages in the school magazines – something none of us could be bothered doing during schooldays – and not only were they particularly well-written and thought-provoking, but in the course of one of his essays he revealed that he had lost two brothers in the First World War, and had himself been in the harrowing action at Messines Ridge. Dark and brooding Mr Wootten may have been, but how I wish I hadn't lampooned him.

Now it was time for the exam results. I had plunged into an orgy of cricket, even catching the train to the SCG when it was raining, and passively writing in my diary that the gates were shut and so I had to go back home and play card cricket while listening to commentary on another Sheffield Shield match from another city.

January 5, 1954 was a remarkable day in that I saw Lindwall hit for six. Queensland's Mick Raymer was the bold batsman. And an extraordinary double was completed when Jim Burke, dourest of bats, also hit a six. It may have been that day that the wag on the Hill had called to Burke: 'Hey, Jimmy, I reckon you're a statue! Only wish I was a pigeon!'

January 13 was an even more remarkable day. I'd continued to pass the time by reading cricket books, and writing to Auntie Edie and Aunt Flo, and writing a murder mystery, complete with illustrations. In a match at Scarborough Park, I 'had a poor day, 0-21 and bowled for 4. Took slip catch & dropped two others. Bruised finger and chipped two others. Had a bash in mouth from return drive – cut inside.' Was it all a sinister omen? No: the entry for January 13 starts off: 'I have passed the Leaving!'

I had missed out on Economics, having tried so hard with a subject that did not come naturally (money has three purposes: as a store of value, as a means of exchange, and as a measure of value), but I was jubilant at getting four As: English, French (with oral), Modern History, and General Maths. The History exam had been touch and go, for we had been given the wrong syllabus. The study of the lives of Churchill, Roosevelt, Stalin, Lenin, Sun Yat-sen and Chiang Kai-shek, however, together with a general knowledge of things, got a few of us through. In English, Mr Cloran had been highly encouraging – almost flattering – though early in our acquaintance he had been forced to say that my style occasionally covered up my lack of understanding of the subject under review. Without question, the A pass in English meant most to me, and the dictionary had already become a loyal companion, sorting out the differences between 'acronym' and 'acrostic', 'elegy' and 'allegory'. . . and defining contentious words like 'superfluous' and 'belligerency'.

All I wanted now was a job interview. The diary records my listening to the Hassett testimonial match on radio, bowling alone against the school wall, noting the deaths of Warren Bardsley and Fred Root, and being concerned at England's performance in the first Test in the Caribbean. Current reading matter was *Close of Play*, Leslie Ames's story, but despite fights with my brother and a bit of golf and long walks, getting caught severely by the sun, I was obliged to write: 'Must think of something to do tomorrow or I'll die of boredom.'

Then came the interviews: at the *Sydney Morning Herald*, the *Telegraph* and the *Mirror*. I was doing all right with the man at the Tele, until he asked me who was my favourite batsman? I told him it was Len Hutton, and for some weird reason, as I recall, I dropped the 'H'. Whether it was that or the choice of a non-Australian player (much more likely) that prompted him to give me short shrift thereafter I can't say. But that's what happened.

Back to the cricket, further employment application letters having been sent off: saw Harry Lambert take 6 for 55 for Victoria v NSW and Keith Miller make 143 – separated by my own game in which I got 42 not out and bowled three eight-ball overs (complaint of under-usage registered) as we won by an innings. Unlike 16-year-olds in faraway England, we were not playing purely for fun. Winning seemed almost as important as breathing.

The wait for a favourable response from a newspaper seemed endless and perhaps hopeless. So, more cricket practice – often alone – with poor Bonzo, our mongrel dog, copping a nasty one in the eye from a hard ball; more cricket-watching at the friendly SCG (Neil Harvey now joining my select band of special heroes, but his brother Ray making a stylish century); and up at 4am to go into Sydney and camp in George Street, all of us, to await the arrival of the Queen and Prince Philip. They cruised past in a matter of seconds after we had sat kerbside for six hours, but no-one thought it wasn't worth it: 'Came home at 3.30. Mum felt sick. My forehead was blistered from the recent continual sun. A lovely day altogether.'

The need for employment grew daily: 'Heard NSW v WA match. Played a little Home Cricket. Killed a few ants. Read through papers. Did not go out as I've 3d in my box.'

On February 11, I rang the *Mirror* and was told I had a job as a copy-boy, to start the next Monday, the 15th, when I would be a working man at last, and probably only a couple of years away from reporting my first Test match.

Yet again, how merciful it can be that we know nothing of the future.

CHAPTER FIVE

You can go back to the Fifties, to your nostalgia, your Menzies, the Caseys and the whole lot. They were not aggressively Australian, they were not aggressively proud of our culture.

PAUL KEATING

IT was not the best of times to become a working man, for Mum and Dad had chosen now, February 1954, to take a fortnight's holiday up in the Blue Mountains, leaving me to 'batch' on my own. At least they took my bothersome young brother with them. But I had to live off tinned beans and cans of fruit, and do my own laundry. Even at seventeen I was naive enough to believe that a darkened shirt collar could be remedied with a dab of shoe-whitener.

My early duties at the *Daily Mirror* were to attend to the needs of Jim Mathers, the sportswriter, known as 'Poison Pen' for his vitriolic approach to cricket- reporting. He fitted the Hollywood image of the newspaper hack: hat on back of head, glasses perched on pudgy nose, stained cigarette hanging from lower lip, braces sometimes in a twist, thick forefingers attacking beaten-up old typewriter as if he were exterminating so many ants.

I related more to Phil Knightley, my guiding light from school, who gave me trial reports to write, which he later assessed. I studied Pitman's shorthand, consorted with the sub-editors (becoming particularly fond of the legendary Parkinson, who carried a hip-flask of gin), and stood transfixed by the teleprinter as scores came through from England's Test matches in the West Indies, where Hutton's team were fighting back after losing the first two Tests. The diary entry for April 2 reads: 'Len got 205 - that crowned my day.'

My assignments soon became monotonous. Each morning I witnessed the drawing of the State Lottery down in Angel Place and rang back the major winners, treating the task with great care, unlike Arthur Mailey, who had blighted his journalistic career at the start of the century by reporting a funeral and getting the name of the corpse wrong. I found listing the Stock Exchange prices even more boring, and began to grow impatient when no promised cadetship materialised. About the only high drama came whenever poor Mr Dreyfus, who compiled a full-page historical story each day from the thousands of books in his library, collapsed, often with alarming splashes of blood flecking his white shirt.

Spare time was taken up reading a succession of cricket books: John Arlott's enchanting little volume on Maurice Tate, A.G.Moyes's *Bradman*, Bill Bowes's *Express Deliveries* and Ray Lindwall's *Flying Stumps*, huge inspiration to an aspiring quickie; books by Freddie Brown, the John Bull figure of the times, and by Trevor Bailey, the Bedser twins' autobiography, Denzil Batchelor's imposing *The Book of Cricket.* More influential than these, though, was Moyes's *A Century of Cricketers*, a collection of short biographies that introduced the reader to cricket's illustrious, from W.G.Grace and W.L.Murdoch, through Spofforth, Ranji, Trumper and Jessop, and Macartney, Hobbs, Sutcliffe and Ponsford, and my friends Mailey and Oldfield, and Bradman and Jackson and Hammond, to the moderns, Compton, Hutton, Miller, Harvey.

I say 'my friends' Mailey and Oldfield because not only did I continue to call into the old wicketkeeper's shop, but soon I was to make the acquaintance of the fascinating Mailey. But that came after a change of career.

My pay at the *Mirror* was £3.18.6 a week after tax. Train-fares and 'keep' took up most of that, but the real problem was lack of progress. So I had an interview at the Commonwealth Bank and joined them, at a slightly higher salary, after only two months with the *Mirror.*

I was soon missing it: not just the train routine and that sweet aroma of beer between Central station and the newspaper office when Tooth's were brewing up, but the bustle and excitement all around me, even if none of it directly involved me. Now it was the staid interior of the bank, secure all right, and marginally better paid, but claustrophobic. After one day's service, I wrote: 'Was shown the ropes, & didn't relish the thought of spending lifetime there.'

From Arncliffe branch I was sent to King's Cross for training, and managed to instil some competitive life into proceedings by trying to win the adding races. These were times when it was all done in the head, with no calculators, let alone computers. Unfortunately, it was also a time when Saturday-morning work was mandatory, and racing from the bank to some football or cricket match miles away became an ugly problem.

It became worse when they shifted me to Cronulla, over 20 miles by rail south of Sydney. My clerical duties included calling out customers' names so as to give them their savings passbooks back, and I ran into another mental freeze every time a name like 'Mrs Schets' came up. For the lunch-break I would hurry to the beach and sit on the sands, gazing at ships on the horizon which were sliding to and from England, and watching the gulls. By the water's edge were young folk in their swimsuits, and here was I strangled by collar-and-tie and constantly checking my wristwatch.

The only break from routine came when a man collapsed near the counter. It shook me so badly that, as the manager and staff attended to him, I intoned: 'Well, this morning isn't without its little bit of drama', to which Wendy said, 'That's four times you've said that.'

The manager, a Mr Brown, was a tyrant. Reduced to jelly whenever his wife came in, to me, the junior, he was an uncompromising bully. When a cheque went missing, the week's salvage bags had to be tipped onto the floor and every piece of screwed-up paper examined. I did this from a chair, but Mr Brown forced me to get down on hands and knees, saying this was the only way to do the job properly. I have been forever grateful for the discipline taught me by bank routine - but not for this particular humiliating act of tyranny.

The greatest agony was to come. England's 1954-55 cricket team arrived, and I invested in the smallest portable (battery) radio then available. It was about the size and weight of a house brick, and it came on whenever the large flap opened. As Australia piled up 601 for 8 after Hutton had sent them in at Brisbane in the opening Test, I had the volume low as I attended to my counter duties, with an eye around the marble column to ensure that Mr Brown remained in his glassed-in office. If he emerged, I'd subtly kill the broadcast of the Test with a touch of my knee on the flap. Alas, and I suppose inevitably, he caught me on the hop, and my knee-jerk was a little too forceful. The radio clattered to the floor, the volume leapt to full-blast, and they must have heard out in Surf Road that Morris was 138 and Harvey 76 at lunch on the second day. Any chance of a bond developing between Mr Brown and me had also crashed.

There was no holding back, though, when the silver-haired Arthur Mailey came in. He had a butcher's shop in the area - though he preferred to lie back in his little boat on Gunnamatta Bay, hoping the fish wouldn't bite. On the shop window he painted, in white: 'I used to bowl tripe, then I wrote it, now I sell it'. In the 1920s he had spun out 99 wickets in Tests, audibly buzzing the ball, so whippy was the spin imparted from those strong little fingers and wrist. To this day no Australian has bettered his Test figures of 9 for 121. He remains the only Australian to have learned of his Test selection while sitting under a coolabah tree cleaning a water-meter. I warmed to this man.

He had presented us with caps at a St George Juniors evening in Bexley, but now was my opportunity to talk to him at length. What about his 10 for

66 at Cheltenham in 1921? Pure luck, he said. What else could he have said? Did I really expect him to talk me through each of those dismissals - as if he could have remembered them? And that 9 for 121 against England at Melbourne in 1920-21? His chief memory there was that the authorities had presented him with the ball, and a few days later he found his son bowling it against a brick wall, the engraved silver presentation ring having snapped off it. He seemed amused by the recall of Arthur junior's irreverence.

My two precious friends from the Test cricket world of the 1920s – Arthur Mailey (left) and Bertie Oldfield

Mailey made his way from the poorest of beginnings, his career as a cartoonist and writer superseding his spin-bowling fun-days, and always he seemed to grin through adversity. This small chap with the puckish countenance had turned up at matches still in a dinner jacket from the previous night's entertainment; he demonstrated his googly to Neville Cardus with an orange late at night on the pavement in Piccadilly. And, in due course, his ashes were scattered in Woronora cemetery, where my parents were eventually laid to rest. Bill O'Reilly is there too, which all helps make the losses a little less unbearable.

The frustration and boredom of life in the bank were already mounting. Escape came at times: soccer trials with St George one Saturday and my first cricket 'tour' on the Sunday, when the junior rep team took the train up to Gosford and we won by an innings. Two wickets, two catches and 12 not out gave me as much pleasure as Don Bradman's 452 not out must have given him. That biography I'd read both ways in the train was an inspiration.

A diary entry discloses that 'Everyone is getting worried about H-bombs'; but I further distracted myself through friendship with an Essex lad named Gus, a tricky little inside-left with round, pink face and shorts covering his knees, who went with me to the Tivoli to see Tommy Trinder. We waited by the stage-door afterwards and got the jolly cockney to sign our programmes, and we had a friendly chat, and felt English again. I was to spend a lot of free time with Gus, and we must have talked through millions of words. And then he found himself a girlfriend, Glenda, over whom he was extremely possessive: and that was that.

I used to speak to a nice-looking blonde girl called Pat in the morning train, but never managed to get up the courage to entice her out with me. She was responsive enough in conversation, but it was no surprise - even though it stung - when I discovered she was going out with one of the glamour- boys in the mighty St George Rugby League team. A 'romance', if it could be called that, with a twin who appeared in the Toni adverts, begun probably at that sanitised venue the Paradance, was also short-lived.

Thus, a typical Friday-night diary entry reads: 'Family went to pictures. But I stayed by the fire. Had an exciting game of card-cricket.'

News items such as George Hirst's death (May 1954) were duly noted, but plaintive entries such as 'Wish something would happen' dot the adolescent chronicle. The boredom and loneliness were offset by driving lessons, which Uncle Alec, over in Brighton-le-Sands, kindly gave me at weekends. He worked on the assembly line at General Motors, Pagewood, where the Holden cars were manufactured, and I kangaroo-hopped his neat little car along the service road beside General Holmes Drive. I disappointed him when he came to see me play cricket by getting out second ball. Now I was determined to show him I was a born driver.

Evenings still meant reading: *Wisden*, *The Cricketer*, *Everybody's* (with John Arlott's features on the county cricket clubs rousing a fever of homesickness). Then came the Empire Games, with England and Australia vying for supremacy (I won two bob on Roger Bannister's mile triumph). But back at the bank there was continuing unease. By way of rebellion I went in one morning wearing a high-neck sweater, and played right into Mr Brown's reproving grasp.

Making my first-team debut with St George soccer club at 17 gave me a lift, playing at Lane Cove alongside Billy Rolph, Cec Milne, Arthur Medbury and the legendary Johnny Wendt, with Scotsman George Swanson in goal. We won 3-2, and I walked on air for a while. Three days later, however, the diary entry is telltale: 'Spent train-ride just thinking.' It was not a worthless day, all the same, for I had another chat with Arthur Mailey in the afternoon and went into town to buy my first cricket 'box' at Bert Oldfield's. In fact it was a highly eventful day, for the death of Min, our canary, is also recorded.

Shamefully, I was soon writing 'Fed up with family good and proper'; but the cricket season was unfolding, and life brightened up as I had a net trial with St George again, facing Billy Watson (who was about to score 155 for NSW against the Englishmen), then went off that evening to Sydney Stadium to see Johnny Ray, whose hysterical tortured singing of *Cry* was thought by the elders to be outrageous and ridiculous but still gripped the hearts of the young.

The Stadium, built by Hugh D.McIntosh for the Jack Johnson v Tommy Burns fight of 1908, became as much a second home as the Sydney Cricket Ground. There I went to see boxing (Peter Keenan, Bobby Sinn, Andre Valignat) and some of the great names of showbiz: Billy Daniels, the Andrews Sisters, Nat King Cole, Frankie Laine, Lionel Hampton, and Guy Mitchell, whose joyous light voice had helped me through the early 1950s with *Truly Fair* and *My Heart Cries for You.* There was a mystic cross-identification in my mind between Guy Mitchell and Neil Harvey. Anyway, I went out, trancelike, and bought myself some socks in 'Mitchell blue'. It was a delight many years later to talk with Guy after his concert in Guildford (when he kept forgetting the words). I mentioned the Sydney event, and he said: 'Hey, can you get me a show back in Sydney? I loved that place.'

Later I learned that this poor chap who had made our hearts sing long ago was now an alcoholic.

One small gesture as the 1954-55 cricket season started restored my flagging ego. To preserve my right boot (the Lindwall drag would have holed it in two matches) I fitted a steel plate over the big-toe area. Then, when star local batsman Jim Marshall kept charging me, I asked my captain what I should do. 'Just drop it shorter and shorter,' he replied. So I did. And poor Jim ended up in hospital with a fractured cheekbone, leaving me with a cocktail of emotions: sorrow for him, a touch of guilt, and undeniably a shameful feeling of macho pride. I'd sent a bloke to hospital. When word got round, batsmen were bound to back away. Well, it didn't quite come to that.

October 28: 'Just thought cricket all afternoon' - a clue to the reality. A chocolate addict since wartime, I sometimes wondered when the girlfriend of my dreams would enter my life. And I was still often preoccupied with flying. Thus, the fantasy of the period was of circling high above the ground in a well-appointed private aircraft, with the prettiest of girls by my side, a carton of Cadbury's to hand, and the Test match commentary ticking away.

Dad was now attending to an unusual shortcoming in a man of 45. He took driving lessons, and bought a car. It was no ordinary vehicle. It was a pre-war Pontiac, a monster that could have housed half Al Capone's gang. Neighbours congregated when they heard Ted manoeuvring the Ponty out of the garage he had built as soon as the house was completed. Granted that Jack Brabham would have been hard pressed to get this automobile out and pointing up the street in a three-point turn in such a narrow passage. Dad needed at least a dozen manoeuvres, invariably taking some of the fence palings with him. Once inside, you sank into the luxurious leather seating, and then prayed as my father drove with characteristic awkwardness of limb-control. He had, after all, badly dented a fire engine at Shaftesbury Avenue in his first attempts at driving.

When the English cricketers reached Sydney, I trained and trammed out to Coogee to see them at the hotel. Brian Statham seemed very relaxed: he had his large feet up on the table. So, too, Denis Compton, who once raised his voice to call 'Four beers, waiter!' The top delight was chatting aimlessly with a throwback to the 1920s, England's scorer/baggageman George Duckworth. Next day, with Dad, brother and uncle - we all got badly sunburned - I went to the SCG and saw Billy Watson make his century, and wondered for the first time if the Hill really was such a repository of wisdom when I overheard a barracker tell his mate that this Peter Loader, fielding just in front of us, was a legspinner.

We hung around afterwards, but couldn't get near the players. And in any case, I was beginning to wonder if this autograph-collecting was right and proper, since I'd recently approached a player, Ian Craig, who was close to being the same age and height as myself. The reservation was soon overcome, and the pursuit (of signatures, known as autographs), in fluctuating degrees of devotion, was to continue for a lifetime.

Mum became ill that spring, and we all worried. It took a lot for her to take to her bed, where she now stayed for a fortnight, extending her reading of E.V.Timms's Australian historical saga. When she recovered, the spring returned to everyone's step.

It was my own turn to take sick as the Sydney Test match neared. I had mild pharyngitis, and managed to get a two-week medical chit from the doctor which enabled me to take in most of a match which remains the most vivid in what had become a very cluttered cupboard of cricket memories.

When Hutton and Bailey came out to bat, I was breathing with difficulty. The tension was like nothing I'd ever experienced, and if it didn't recede I feared I might not survive the day. The view was good from the Sheridan Stand, almost straight down the pitch, and the tightly-packed crowd was companionable and very civilised, men with their sons and grandsons, and an old chap in the row in front saying how 'fond' he was of tennis, which I found to be a strange remark in this electrifying cricket environment.

Caught by the newsreel camera, Sydney Test 1955: the author and young brother, near bottom of frame, with youngster passing in front

Ray Lindwall came swinging in, and I rode every pace with him, shoulders rolling, right arm paddling, and then that unique (well, almost, I might modestly observe) movement of the arms in the act of delivery. Then I was down the other end in a flash, raising Hutton's backlift with him and watching very carefully as the outswinger sizzled through to Langley.

This went on for a while, and I began to relax, while never losing the intensity of the moment and hardly daring to blink for fear of missing some slight incident in this drama-charged theatre. By the end of that opening day, under oppressive grey skies, I was aching from the tension. Bailey had been bowled for a duck by Lindwall after half-an-hour, and a back-cut to a rising Lindwall delivery by Hutton had thrilled. But a wondrous diving catch by Davidson at leg slip cut my hero down at 30, and May, Graveney, Cowdrey and Edrich did little more than display one glowing stroke apiece before Johnny Wardle came in to thrash 35 to help England to a miserable 154.

There was just time for Morris to glove Bailey to Hutton at leg slip, by which time I was viewing from in front of the Bob Stand, the icy suspense of the morning already a memory.

The rest of this extraordinary Test match was digested alternately through radio and return visits to the SCG, and on the Saturday evening I took brother Mick down to Cronulla to a barbecue at the golf club, where, according to the adverts, some of the England team would be guests. When none turned up, I recorded it as 'a horrifying fizz-out', although my allegiance to Hutton's men never seriously wavered. The third day saw England going in a second time, 74 in arrears, and Ron Archer and Bill Johnston had them 55 for 3 before lunch. Then came a stirring century stand between Peter May and Colin Cowdrey, the two young batsmen on whom their country's hopes were pinned for years to come. Through a sunlit afternoon, my view now coming from the Hill, they coped with Benaud's curling legbreaks and all that the pacemen could hurl at them, and it seemed to me that a shout of 'no-ball' from a spectator might have lured Cowdrey into a big drive off Benaud which Archer caught in the deep. This brought in the ugliest little batsman (in strokeplay terms) I had yet seen at high level - or was ever to see - W.J.Edrich, DFC. No further loss, and England, four down, were now 130 ahead. Pulsating, especially that pull by May off Archer.

I was in position early next day to see May get the two runs he needed for his first century against Australia, but Lindwall soon bowled him. In came Frank Tyson, and before long he was turning away from a Lindwall bouncer which flattened him, a lump coming up on the back of his head which even we could perceive, down by the Paddington Hill fence now. Tyson lay prone, raised his head once, then seemed to slip into unconsciousness, like a flattened boxer. I was not the only one who thought he was dead. An English sailor in front of me swore loudly as two ambulancemen ran to the middle. It was some time before the wobbly batsman was helped off, and a very shaky Godfrey Evans waddled out to take his place.

Mathematically, England's last-wicket stands in each innings were the decisive factor. Wardle and Statham belted and fiddled 43 in the first innings, and now Statham and Appleyard made a sensible 46 in the second. That left Australia to get 223, and before we went home they had made 72 of them, though Favell and Morris were out. Neil Harvey was in good shape, and creamed Wardle away for two fours at the end. But it was noticeable that, far from being retarded by the blow to the head, Tyson was bowling at the speed of sound. Side-on, he was completely invisible - or the ball was - to a 17-year-old's keen eyes; and by the way the batsmen hurried to get their bats down, they too were seeing - or scarcely seeing - something the like of which had never previously zoomed their way.

On the final day, Tyson completed the job. Despite Neil Harvey's classical 92 not out, and a heart-stopping last-wicket stand of 39 with Bill

Johnston, England scraped home by 38 runs to level the series. Tyson had taken 10 for 130, and I paid for my cowardice in staying home on the final day by needing to follow up the radio commentary with a trip to the newsreel cinema.

St George won the Club Championship in 1954-55. Seated on the left is DF. Top left is future Rugby League legend Reg Gasnier, and the gentleman in the light suit is Frank Cush, young Bradman's mentor in the 1920s. The picture of the fourth-grade team was taken at Hurstville Oval

There were two major upshots of this wondrous Test match: I think I was so inspired that I added half-a-yard to my fast bowling; and I decided not to try to get a job on a country newspaper. If anything was going to happen, it would need to happen here in Sydney. The drudgery of the bank, the daily war with my mischievous young brother, the widening gap between my father and me, with him now engrossed with his work at the shop and at the Lodge and Rotary and Lions International: all this would end some time and I'd be fulfilled. The wonderment of childhood had evaporated.

Adults were no longer seen as infallible and dependable. Security and the comforts and support provided by grown-ups were illusions, and always had been. I wanted a life in cricket. Desperately.

CHAPTER SIX

That age is best, which is the first,
When youth and blood are warmer.

ROBERT HERRICK

PLAYING, watching, reading, collecting in a minor way, idolising, compiling statistics – all these cricket activities were absorbing, but there was one further commodity which needed to be addressed, and that was the social side of the game. The Australian game has always been essentially businesslike and almost unnecessarily serious, with no after-match drinks in club/grade cricket. In that glorious summer of '54-55, however, I attended my first important cricket function, the St George club's annual dinner at the Cricketers Club in George Street, Sydney, where a pleasing Arthur Mailey oil painting graced the corridor. I must have been the only junior present. Boys don't usually go for this sort of thing. But to be seated near Brian Booth and Bob Cristofani and to discuss, seemingly on level terms, what made the ball swing and what constituted and caused a 'half-cock' stroke made me tingle inside. This was my natural habitat. 'Grand time,' records the faithful little red diary. 'Talked in saloon bar, then had good dinner. Introduced to crowd like everyone else. Chatted with all.' I did not realise until years later that the chairman, E.W. (Ted) Adams, who was Town Clerk of Sydney and St George DCC treasurer, had played for the club with Don Bradman and had represented New South Wales once. A genial old gentleman, Mr Adams, who had played for NSW Colts against the 1920-21 England touring team (toiling away to take 3 for 183), sat close to his bottle of VAT69 whisky all evening, his tonic propped securely down by his chair-leg, according to this keen-eyed youngster.

Life has teemed with opportunities taken and also missed. There that night was Albert Scanes, a gnarled figure, who had played alongside Bradman in his NSW debut match, at Adelaide in 1927, and had batted with Kippax and Jackson and Macartney. What little tales might he have had to tell? Same applied, on a more dizzying scale, for Harry Donnan, who played in five Tests against England in the 1890s, and once scored 353 locally for Bexley Oriental. Now, aged 90, he was living just a mile or two away from me in Carlton. That could have been a sensational maiden interview. Not until he died in 1956 did I discover that he had lived so near.

The 1954-55 Ashes series crackled on. England won at Melbourne, with Tyson crashing through again with 7 for 27 on the final day, and at Adelaide, England retained the Ashes with a five-wicket victory that swelled my pride and put one or two cocky tellers at the bank in their place after the gloating that followed Australia's innings win in the opening Test at the Gabba. Godfrey Evans hit the winner, but only after Miller had scared England by plucking out Hutton, Edrich and Cowdrey and diving to catch May. As the shocks hit the England dressing-room, the gloomy Hutton is said to have given up hope. Keith Miller had always caused him more anxiety than even Lindwall, and Len now believed the cavalier Australian was to prove literally irresistible. 'The boogers've doon us,' he is supposed to have exclaimed. Whereupon Denis Compton, ready to take his turn at the crease, said, 'Hang on, Len. I haven't had a go yet!' Cricket is largely about attitude.

The fifth Test was in Sydney, and I was up there like a shot. And back home again, for the heavy rain caused an abandonment. Next day was the same. Then Sunday, with no play scheduled, was brilliant. Monday, though, was wet again, and it was not until the *fourth* day that play began, before only a smattering of spectators. We were rewarded with a lovely century from Tom Graveney. First, though, came Len Hutton's last innings against Australia. Play began at 2pm, and within minutes he was gone: a two and a four off Lindwall, then a glance against the inducker straight into the hands of debutant Peter Burge, who told me years later that it was prearranged: and he was almost peeing himself in nervous anticipation. As Hutton left the field, part of my young heart went with him.

Graveney's display was worth every penny and all those hours spent waiting for this odd little Test to begin. On the slow pitch he drove masterfully. An old boy near me on the Paddington Hill kept saying how he reminded him of Charlie Barnett, but probably no-one knew who he meant, unless they had been here in 1936-37. The Graveney-May partnership of 182 was the most uplifting thing I'd yet seen on a cricket field. But then Graveney was caught-and-bowled by Ian Johnson, who also had Cowdrey (out of a sick-bed) held by Maddocks first ball. Compton came in and fiddled around scorelessly for 20 minutes, and May was caught at slip off Benaud for 79 in the last over. The highlight, though, had to be the manner in which Graveney reached his century. He was on 85 at drinks, his face florid, grin wide, hair flopping when he removed his cap. Miller then bowled, and those eight balls provided Graveney with the means to make his only hundred against Australia: two majestic drives, a sweep and a hook, all for four, got him there, and I joined the old boy from Cheltenham in cheering.

The penultimate day of the series was a scorcher, though Compton and Bailey played soberly, as if it were the opening day of a five-day Test. At one stage Compton offered his bat to a jeering section of the crowd, a gesture he could never have been forced to make at Lord's. Perhaps it was the cap. When, after lunch, Denis tossed it to the umpire and hit four fours in a Benaud over, we wondered if an impostor had been out there until now. Compton's 84 was his best against Australia for some years, and as the tea interval approached, with a declaration expected, Lindwall came up for his last over. He had looked very tired, and even Bailey took pity on him, which was another unthinkable concept. Not entirely without ostentation, the England batsman, after his patient 72, let Lindwall bowl him to complete 100 Test wickets against England. A little pompously, this 17-year-old wrote in his notes: 'I didn't like it. If a fast bowler can no longer bowl fast he should not be allowed to continue just for the sake of a record. It has been said, truthfully, that records are worth having only when they come naturally, and not by design.' Old Raymond had the laugh on all of us, for this wasn't his final Test. Four years later he inflicted a pair of ducks on Trevor Bailey in what really was his final Test.

Billy Watson, with whom, incredibly, I'd been netting at Hurstville Oval not so long before, now came in for his first Test innings. He and Colin McDonald put on 52 before Johnny Wardle diddled out the St George man for 18, which brought in former St George player Les Favell, who was quickly – in every sense – bowled by the broad-shouldered and balding Tyson. Still, at 82 for 2 that evening, there was no likelihood of a result. But only a catastrophe would have kept me away from the final day of the series.

Tyson was soon catching Harvey off his own bowling, and Miller was scratchy before being run out. He was capable of such grandeur at the crease, but when bothered, particularly by spin such as Wardle's back-of-the-hand variety, he could look cumbersome on the forward defensive.

Appleyard, like my ancestors a victim of TB, but unlike them a glowing recoveree, dismissed McDonald, and Benaud was bamboozled by Wardle, so that Australia were 147 for 6 at lunch, some way from safety.

The Englishmen had looked radiant with happiness when they took the field that morning, a condition not often apparent in the years ahead. They had every reason to be. It had been a stirring series win, and in May and Cowdrey and Tyson and Statham they had secured four richly-talented young men just as the post-war generation was going out to pasture. Down by the Hill boundary pickets, young Cowdrey was practising with his throwing arm (the older men occupied the slips positions for now), and it was noticeable that his flannels had not seen an iron since they had been laundered. Few of us appreciated the problems of living out of hotel rooms. And if one were to predict that one day this fellow would be in the House of Lords he'd have been told not to be stupid.

The Australians couldn't handle Wardle's left-arm wrist-spin, and as he teased his way to five wickets, and three more in the follow-on, some sailors from Yorkshire kept up a boozy chant of 'Coom on ye broad acres!'

The sound that really mattered to me was suddenly introduced via my portable radio. The ABC had passed the microphone to visiting commentator John Arlott. This was Heaven. How could I have known that a cherished friendship between us would one day materialise?

Farcically, poor Lindwall, coming in at No.11, sent his captain, Ian Johnson, back as Compton fielded the ball with one run needed to avoid the follow-on. So Australia had to go in again, with only two hours remaining. After an hour they were 29 for 3, with Harvey among the casualties. Were England going to take the series 4-1?

To expedite things, Tyson bowled off a shortened run-up – and still generated enough force to knock Miller's bat from his hands. But the pride of Sydney stayed in, supported by the trusty McDonald, until the Victorian nicked one from part- time legspinner Graveney. Miller had a slog at Wardle and was bowled, and as the clock approached the dreaded zero hour, Hutton himself walked the length of the ground and solemnly placed the field to have the final over himself. Benaud went along with the end-of-term spirit of it all and had a mighty swing at his sixth ball, aiming at the clock-tower, and was bowled. Poor chap had now scored 163 runs in 14 innings against England, to go with his 12 wickets at 46. No future, we said.

He may not have been alone in that respect. Having wormed my way into the sacred members' pavilion, I peeped into the England dressing-room and saw Tyson's powerful physique. Draped only in a towel, he looked like a cruiserweight boxer, and it dawned on me that with my unexceptional teenage body I had better give up hope of ever being an express bowler. The final fantasy came afterwards, when I stood on the pathway at the back of the pavilion as Tyson emerged. When he was precisely 22 yards from me I undertook a flash of imaginary combat. Had he been bowling at me the way he'd been bowling at the Australians, I'd have had about a third of a second to get the bat to him or duck. Wow! Another of life's sweet surprises was our friendship years later, when one evening I had a net with him. He became irritable that I was being defensive against his now-geriatric bowling; but he didn't understand that I had a good memory and vivid imagination. I was visualising the Tyson who blew Australia away half-a-century previously. But it is hard to duck a medium-pace half-volley.

Back to 1955 and the SCG, I sought comfort. I made my way over to the England captain, who had just emerged, wearing a pale-blue suit. Not for the first time, I got his signature – and searched in vain across Sydney in the days to come for a suit like Len's. No matter what it cost, this £400-a-year bank clerk would buy it. But of such a garment there was no sign. I'd probably have had to go to Bradford.

In a way, this was the best time of all. Patience was being rewarded as Test cricketers came thick and fast out of the pavilion doors after the end-of-series reception. I'd seen John Arlott with Ian Peebles, the broadcaster from Hampshire uncomfortable in the heat, as ever, his nylon shirt open at the neck, his voice impatient as he explained to one of the boys, 'I'm not a player, sonny.'

Some of us daringly scrawled cordial messages on the stickers on the MCC players' piled baggage, and I stole a handshake with young Cowdrey, whom I'd gone to see doing an ABC Radio interview, during which he joked and giggled, making cricket seem the most uncomplicated and pleasurable of pastimes, something he was to do for decades to come, even when in the hot-seat of international administration.

And suddenly all the England players were gone in their courtesy cars, and the Australians too, and I was left to wend my empty way home. The first element of bi-nationality had just presented itself when, seeing Arthur Morris come out, I felt an instant rapport because he was one of my school's Old Boys, a duality of allegiance that was to intensify in years to come, making me sometimes twice the man – and sometimes half. Caught by Australia, bowled by England.

The immediate problem – apart from the bleak outlook of having no more international cricket in Australia for four long years – was to get out of the bank and do something with my life.

It would have lifted the soul to have known that just about all the cricketers who had taken part in this glittering 1954-55 Ashes Test series – both sides – would one day become friends and acquaintances. But, as ever, the future was an impenetrable and tantalising secret.

So it was back to preparing for the new football season and finding a fresh job.

I was taken on by Overseas Shipping Representatives Association, an organisation responsible for Australian shipping tonnage records and administration, with offices in Bent Street, near Circular Quay. It was clerical work – from which I departed occasionally by editing a staff magazine which the boss thought good for office morale – and I was surrounded by an interesting collection of people. There was old Captain Graham, who had seen action at the Battle of Jutland, and Captain Adamson, who had been in tanks in the Second World War and was now in wharf security. Mr 'Wobinson', as he called himself, was the accountant, and eventually took me in as his assistant. He already had one, Barney, who extended the hand of friendship by saying that when he served in the Royal Australian Navy they called Englishmen 'kippers' because they had two faces and no guts. So much for Anglo-Australian bonds. A couple of old girls ran the general office, and I was tucked away, with my own desk, alongside three or four other lads, under the managership of Reg Friend, who had been a prisoner of the Japanese in Changi, and was bitterly marked by the experience. Jim, not quite as old, had fought the Japs in New Guinea, and delighted in telling of the trenches his patrol captured and of how they stank.

If there was an ulterior motive for joining OSRA it was that one day I might be fortunate enough to get a cut-price or even free passage to England, to see Auntie Edie and Aunt Flo and Colin again. No hurry, but it was something to look forward to. The view from the 10th-floor office windows was teasing. On one side was the magnificent Victorian sandstone clocktower of the Lands Department. But northwards lay the Harbour, with Fort Denison ('Pinchgut') clearly visible, with almost always a ship either bringing in more migrants or leaving with eager Australians – and disenchanted migrants – bound for Britain and Europe.

At 18, although I wished it otherwise, I may just have been a slightly better footballer than cricketer. Playing regularly for St George 2nds (and also juggling exaggeration and modesty in my match reports for the *St George Call*), I turned out midweek in lunchtime games on Sydney's grassy Domain (where H.H.Stephenson's 1861-62 ground-breaking English cricket team had played). I'd dash over from the office to line up with the Local Government team, returning to my desk flushed and sweaty, to fumble with a late lunch of peanut-butter-and-lettuce roll.

Back in Carlton, appreciably fitter by 1956, I played a further five seasons mainly in the firsts, after which St George merged with Sutherland when the old-fashioned NSW Association was overthrown by the new Federation, which was administered by European men.

Most matches were like full-scale internationals. Pan-Hellenic were all-Greek, Concordia were Germans, Hollandia all Dutch and playing in orange shirts, Hakoah were all-Jewish, Polonia not surprisingly all-Polish, Juventus Italian, and a bunch of Englishmen called their club Corinthians. In time, I switched to a lunchtime team by the same name.

Police and public wondered what was going on whenever Croatia's matches against Dalmatinac sparked riots. Eventually they realised that these people had been killing each other for centuries, so for them soccer was never going to be a peaceful pastime.

Our own matches sometimes plunged into violence. We were the guilty ones in one Hollandia match, when the Dutchmen pleaded with the referee to call the match off at half-time. We were only shoulder-charging, within the rules. But when a madman drove his car all over the field during another match, and the wife of a Hakoah player strode onto the field and whacked the ref with her umbrella, when another referee had his jaw smashed by a player's right hook, and when, as we gathered around Pan-Hellenic's goal for a corner, a spectator in a flat cap yelled out at our skipper, Dave McComish (formerly of Glentoran and an Australian rep centre-half) and pointed to a pistol in his shoulder holster, the point of it all was brought into question.

St George 1st grade soccer: a Dutchie, five Brits, four Aussies, and me (back row right)

Among the golden moments was a goal against Juventus which came after a run – which may have been a fluke – zigzagging past six sliding Italians, warmingly at Blick Oval, my old school ground. Another was taking the ball off Bobby Bignall, who was then captain of Australia, when we played Corrimal. But there was an hour- and-a-half of agony and frustration in the Leichhardt match when the task of getting past the knees and elbows of Joe Marston proved too much. There may have been a touch of awe too, for Marston had recently played for Preston North End in a Cup final at Wembley.

Soon after that magical goal against Juventus, I was brought down by one of the Italian defenders – he must have been 5ft 3ins and 13 stone – and as we disentangled our legs he made me a sweet promise: 'You weel feenish up een Caanterbury 'Os-a-pitale!' Thus the wandering-winger strategy was conceived.

The aroma of horse liniment and the splintery floor of the gloomy dressing-room of Prince Edward Park became an important part of life. The red-and-white of St George was worn with immense pride, even if the shirt was heavy-duty and you felt like ripping it off on stinking hot days. The report in the *St George Call* on the following Thursday somehow gave life extra purpose, and when celebrated European names began to play in the competition – Len Quested and Alex Jeffery from England, Leo Baumgartner, Walter Tamandl and the great Gerhard Hanappi from Austria,

Les Scheinflug from Germany – the tempo rose. Tamandl came to Carlton to coach us on training nights, and the stakes were raised during matches, even if these illustrious Europeans were elusive and hardly ever gave us a sight of the ball. The sophistication process of Australian soccer was under way.

As for support, none was more warm-hearted than 'Jock's'. He must have been close to 80, and was a fixture at Prince Edward Park, clad in an old hat, waistcoat and watch-chain and baggy trousers, always puffing at a pipe. 'Hulloa, Davey,' he'd greet me at the grandstand gate, before rocking into a coughing fit. Then he would wheeze more bonhomie, occasionally talk briefly of Scotland, and wish us luck. When the Saints scored, Jock would begin to cheer before inevitably collapsing into another coughing spasm. It sort of spoilt it all when somebody found out that his real name was Matt.

In 1958, Blackpool, with Stanley Matthews and Jimmy Hagan, played at Sydney Sportsground, and St George played Pyrmont in a curtain-raiser. One of the tragedies of my young life was that I was omitted, and I failed to come to terms with the old pals' act that saw a certain left back included in our side, a Yorkshireman who did a lot of committee work but was so shortsighted that hardly a match passed without the shuddering spectacle of him stunning himself in collision with a goalpost or almost disembowelling himself on the corner flag. I sat on the Hill and watched sullenly as Saints played, in my opinion, like donkeys, and was later transported by Stanley Matthews' wizardry in the big match, the only thing to irritate being Blackpool's goalkeeper, George Farm, who lay in the goalmouth, possibly half-asleep, for most of the match. This was cockiness on the grand scale, and I was delighted to see him have to get up hurriedly when the Australian centre forward broke away and came rushing towards Blackpool's goal. Needless to say, the kick sent the ball sailing way over the bar. 'Two points!' as we so often murmured scornfully.

Dad used to sit up in the stand during home matches at Prince Edward, and seldom had much to say other than a sentence or two of criticism, perhaps sometimes warranted. Later, after St George and Sutherland amalgamated, he came less often to the home games at Miranda, and I was sorry when he missed my one 'international', when we played against the full Fiji national team. Among other things, he would have seen his son almost decapitated in executing a defensive header against a cannonball shot. It wasn't easy to pretend you intended to head the heavy ball and that you were not at all dizzy, when all around you were twinkling stars and triple visions of team-mates and opponents.

Although we were paid £3 for a win and £2 for a draw, I retired at the end of the 1961 season, when only 24. I now had responsibilities, and the risks – with our Croatia match ending in a riot and the accent increasingly on the physical – were simply too great. I would try to compensate for this all-too-short soccer career (246 matches played, 108 won, 103 lost) by extending my cricket career into my forties if at all possible. If only I'd known.

CHAPTER SEVEN

Who serves his country well has no need of ancestors.

VOLTAIRE

IT was excusable for an 18-year-old to wonder impatiently whether life would always be this ordinary, strung together only with cricket and football matches, movies and books (and now records, since Dad had bought a quality radiogram: Cara Mia by David Whitfield was the first of numerous 78s I brought home). Hopes of writing about sport seemed doomed. The openings simply weren't there. I was soon to have a cartoon accepted by David McNicoll at the *Telegraph*, and then another, and the thrill of seeing someone perusing the page it 'graced' as I walked along the railway platform was indescribable.

Destiny preoccupied me. That youngster's question in the street – 'What are we made for?' – still hovered, legitimate, insistent and unanswered. Waiting for a train underground at St James one evening, I focused on a brick down by the rails: not so much the brick as the thick layer of grime that coated it. That, I thought, represents complete and utter obscurity. Who wanted to be like that brick? It will be trapped down there forever. Why, if I hadn't bothered to look at it, its insignificance would have been absolute.

The Royal Australian Air Force put paid to all this self-pitying desperation. Late in 1955, I was called up for National Service, and my ATC experience at school stood my Air Force preference in good stead. Cleverly, all the New South Wales lads were sent north to Queensland, and the Queenslanders were posted down to Rathmines, west of Sydney, making the comforts of home inaccessible for weekend leave. In Britain, young men were put in uniform for two years at this crucial stage of their lives, even if they were in careers or studying. Australia wanted its trainees for a mere five months, time enough to turn them into reasonably capable fighting men after concentrated training.

Seven years in Sydney, I had been no further north than Mum's favourite picnic spot, Bobbin Head, no further west than Katoomba, in the Blue Mountains, and no further south than National Park. And I had been no further east than about 20 feet into the Pacific. Now, seen off at Central Station by a large party of relations and friends, I embarked on the longest and most telling train journey of my life. On and on we strained, the carriages crammed with 18-year-olds, sleep elusive until the smaller men climbed up onto the luggage-racks.

At early light, a peep under the blinds revealed a fairyland scene of drifting mist across the bushland. We must be near Queensland by now. We weren't even halfway. On and on we chugged. This seemed a criminal waste of a young man's day. Why couldn't we have been flown up? Talk, read, gaze out of the window at bushland that became brain-numbingly monotonous. Attend to the inner man, try to sleep again. Then the State border, and a change of train because of the different rail- gauge. The winding track through the banana plantations had induced a headache, but all grim things come to an end, and we finally pulled into South Brisbane station – only to transfer to another train for a one-hour journey out to Ipswich. From there a bus carried us through the darkness to RAAF Amberley, the largest bomber base in Australia. Within a few hours, dozens of young men had been kitted out and were civilians no more. After 29 hours of wearying travel it was disorientating and slightly depressing.

Amberley had become operational in 1940, a staging centre for the US Army Air Corps and an important base for assembly, maintenance and salvage of combat aircraft for the Pacific theatre of war. I later discovered that Eleanor Roosevelt, Charles Lindbergh and General Douglas MacArthur had all visited the base in the early 1940s. All was quiet now. All fresh intakes were probably similarly subdued. And at 6 o'clock on a cool morning, reveille did nothing to raise spirits.

Aircraftman Frith, A214727, would like to have trained to be a pilot, but Aircrew was reserved for the elite: university blokes who had held rank in the ATC. Comfort soon came in the knowledge that the chosen ones worked extremely hard and were expected to join up full-time as career airmen. We – the RAAF Regiment – had greater freedom, though it was not immediately apparent. And by staying at Amberley I was on course for a supremely significant meeting that would point the way for the rest of my life. It wouldn't have happened if I'd been transferred up to Brisbane.

We swore allegiance to Her Majesty and to the Royal Australian Air Force and to our country, and then the conversion of self-indulgent young civilians into self-reliant and disciplined men began in earnest.

In dark-blue overalls throughout the long waking hours, we marched and marched across the parade-ground – the 'bull-ring' – and when that torrid exercise ended we ran miles along hard roads in full battledress, the weaker ones collapsing, the bigheads striving for victory while risking heart attacks, the smart ones doing just enough. Night manoeuvres brought other risks. Leopard-crawling through wild rain-forest under the moon's eerie light demonstrated the hopelessness of it all: come the real thing, what hope would a man have in the face of ambushes, trip-wires and mines? The current fear was not so much the discomfort of aggressive ants as the risk of disturbing a tiger-snake. It was all well and good to rub charcoal over the face. One still felt as conspicuous as a batsman walking to the crease at a capacity SCG.

We were a mixed bunch. The timid and scholarly got by by keeping themselves to themselves. Others, like McDowell, who had a supply of illicit booze and always returned from weekend leave late and with his trousers bearing vile stains, took their punishment. Mac even ventured over to the four Lincoln bombers which had been used in the 1952 Atomic bomb trials at Monte Bello Island and which were still radioactive. It was strictly out of bounds, which is exactly what made those contaminated monsters irresistible to McDowell. The worst accident at Amberley was also a Lincoln, which crashed in 1948. The bomber was loaded with explosives, and all 48 aboard were killed.

Boredom often cloaked our activities. Out in the bush, any goanna seen halfway up a gum-tree copped a bayonet. Peeling potatoes and digging trenches prompted thoughts that perhaps Aircrew might have been preferable. Letters from home were desperately awaited, as were weekend leaves, when we hitchhiked into Brisbane and relaxed at the Catholic United Services Club and at Cloudland ballroom (later burned down), which was like something out of *The Great Gatsby*, a glittering venue which even had a roped-off area for jitterbugging, a relic of the war, when Yanks flooded into Brisbane. There, Teddy Lloyd, a miner from Cessnock who was one of our hut 'gang', sang his Frankie Laine stuff and his Tennessee Ernie Ford. And I found myself bim-bimming the drums.

Down to the Gold Coast on weekend leave, as ever with a foot in each camp. Teddy Lloyd (left), Tony Cupit (right)

The RAAF trainees from Amberley and the Army lads from Wacol might normally have picked on each other, but the motor-bike gangs around Brisbane were such a concern that the two services readily united.

The pick of our instructors was Corporal Lilley, an Englishman who told us of his wartime exploits with the Marines: surviving the sinking of HMS Penelope, and the terrifying landings at Anzio and Normandy (some achievement). Nothing diverted him, not even mocking echoes of his strangulated voice, and when he felt it appropriate he began to reveal his sense of humour, winning us completely over, until – as intended – we would have died for him. He would have made a fair cricket coach.

There were lectures on seemingly everything, then theory was put into practice: bayonet charges, teeth bared, screams freezing the enemy's blood; and the stripping-down of a Bren-gun; and the throwing (or, rather, bowling) of a hand-grenade; weapons training: the firing of a Very-pistol to light up the night; and firing .303 Lee-Enfield rifles just like Uncle Bill's (and writing proudly to Auntie Edie over in England to say I'd officially become a marksman). The Tommy-guns were less scientific. Their kickback was like a horse's, and a short burst was enough. Anything more would have spun weak handlers round 180 degrees, killing Flight Sergeant Meacham, which would have been a popular move.

The upshot of all this was that my left ear ceased to function at all well, and in these days of litigation I often wonder what compensation I might have won from the RAAF. In later years I sometimes sat to the right of John Woodcock in Press- boxes and at functions, and with his deafness in the right ear we've had wonderful conversations where neither quite heard what the other was saying.

The inter-squadron cricket match was interrupted by Vampire fighters blowing up storms of dust on the adjacent runway, though I could not blame them for my dismissal for 12, bowled by Peter Allan, the local lad who went on to take all 10 wickets in an innings for Queensland in a Sheffield Shield match and played a Test against England in 1965-66. When the RAAF played the Army on the same oval, I found an excuse to be there, and saw Maurice Fenner, on loan from the RAF, a Kent player and future county club secretary, helping M.A.Noble's grandson (he made a century) to force a draw.

Juvenile pranks had to be endured. Beds were strung up to the rafters. Frogs, grasshoppers and beetles were hidden in bedclothes. Mosquito-nets were raided with heavy boots, meaning that the manly thing to do was just lie there and take the full brunt of the black mass of mossies when they descended from the ceiling as soon as the lights went out.

These skin punctures were nothing compared to the numerous vaccinations. Lads fainted, and with good reason when those long needles crunched into bones as the trainee Colombo Plan medics experimented on us. I had further good cause to sue when I was one of only five or six in the entire squadron who did not 'take' after a second smallpox shot. We later discovered that it should have been left at that, but we were then subjected to a *third* slug, a mega-dose, and this time we were flattened, sweating and delirious for two days. Once recovered, we had to be careful not to burst the shilling-size thick yellow scabs on our left shoulders.

Some of the best hours were spent gardening at the local hospital for disabled children, after which we visited the wards. Those kids who were able to stand and speak always grabbed our hats, for they knew that the young airmen usually had pictures of their girlfriends under the plastic lining. Mine was empty. But not for much longer.

We were flown home for Easter, and the family seemed to approve of the khaki uniform and blue peaked cap. I'd seemed to have grown, they said, and Dad thought I was probably fitter and would score more goals now for St George. When I flew back to Queensland, there was only a two-month stretch left – although so turbulent was the Ansett Convair flight back that some of us gave up hope of ever touching down safely again.

The remainder of the five-month course was infinitely more enjoyable. The instructors, apart from the born bullies, eased off a little and were noticeably friendlier, and the training became more constructive. There were still hazards, like the phosgene phial that snapped during the lecture on war gasses and had me gasping desperately for air, eyes streaming for an hour afterwards. Perhaps a case could have been made for trauma, distress and all that sort of thing? Somehow we were ready to accept that all this was being done for our country. The world wasn't as litigation-crazy as nowadays.

Brisbane's limitations having been exposed, we spent our leave down the Gold Coast, always readily picked up as hitchhikers in our uniforms. We got dumped in the surf at Coolangatta, marvelled at the only high-rise building along the coast, the half-built Lennons Hotel at Broadbeach, and played mini-golf, drank orange- juice and tried out the dance-hall. The alcoholics walked over the border to Tweed Heads where, under New South Wales licensing laws, they could drink at 18. You could have bought a block of land hereabouts for a fiver or tenner. This dreamy place was unrecognisable from the buzz and coarse city it became half-a-century later.

On April 21, 1956 we threw a dance of our own at Amberley, in the recreation room, with coloured lights on the lawn, a makeshift band, myself scarcely animate on the drums, and soft drinks and sandwiches on hand. All eyes turned to the incoming bus, full of local girls, and soon I was talking to one of them, who happened to be there only because her sister, Rosie, had urged her to go, if only to keep her company. Her name was as pretty as her face: Oriel Christina. She was only midway through her teens.

The nine-mile run in full battledress and intense heat the previous day, which I'd managed in 99 minutes, had left me with blisters and an excuse not to dance, even when dreamier records took over from the crude live band.

So we talked and talked, and compared our contrasting backgrounds and homes. A couple of my mates told me next day that I was very possessive, but they could never know how long I'd waited for this chance meeting. This girl was the perfect vision, so sweet-natured too. Within the hour I had made myself useful by responding to her doubts about her name. She reckoned Debbie Reynolds was the best thing on the movie-screen, so, without ceremony, 'Debbie' she became and Debbie she remained. Except in Queensland.

I asked her to the Anzac Day ball a few days later, where all around us were senior airmen, and I kidded her that those lights out there on the runway were all hand-held by junior airmen, who weren't allowed back in till morning. When I took her back to her isolated home out in the Ipswich suburb of Raceview, she had the last laugh by lending me the family bicycle, which was no racing model and squeaked. The creepy nine-mile ride back to RAAF Amberley passed through the cemetery and down endless moonlit country roads. The rather terrifying experience left me frozen and sore and exhausted. I had just enough strength left to shove the bike under my bed.

Waking from the deepest of sleep, I found the sergeant standing over me, with a grinning audience forming a crescent. What the hell was this woman's bike doing in the hut? Although never one to think fast before lunchtime, if at all, I miraculously found an answer. Yes, I'd bought it off one of the WAAFs. Alibi accepted.

For the rest of my days at Amberley – and beyond – Debbie was my obsession. Resting on a wooded hillside miles from civilisation, draped in a ground-sheet, rain dripping from the brim of the bush-hat, the alluring smell of the gum-trees all around, I watched a spider battling against the elements to make its web, and was besieged with hope and curiosity about my own lot. Several mountain-tops away and down into the town of Ipswich my girl was serving in a clothing shop. I wanted her here with me, and a haunting agony began to well up inside, allayed only by Corporal Lilley's shrill order to 'Pwepare to march!'

I took to stealing out through the fence at night to get to see Debbie, shunning the dreadful bike and employing all manner of means to cover the nine miles each way: lifts with those in the know, hitchhiking, costly taxis. We sat on the verandah of her old wooden homestead and talked and talked, and at weekends we talked more by the persimmon tree while her father exercised the horse. When Mr Pennell had his fill in Ipswich in two or three of the swing-door pubs on a Saturday night, Prince the horse would automatically bring him the three miles home. All 'Sonny' had to do was hold tight in the saddle. For our part, we prayed he would be too tired to make a scene. But sometimes he instilled terror into us all, and once he even wiggled his old army bayonet. And there was I, the boy from the big smoke, completely unarmed.

Debbie and I went to the pictures and talked, and played records and talked, and walked and talked. Parting was not going to be easy, especially when records like Johnny Ray's *Ain't Misbehavin'* and Don Cherry's *Band of Gold*, as well as the Platters' *Great Pretender*, became our theme songs, our anthems. Life had never been more worth living – and yet weighed down by complications.

I looked across at those Lincoln bombers which were marked with black crosses and were checked by experts with Geiger-counters, and hoped I had not been touched by the radiation – though if I had to forsake this girl because of the distance that would soon be between us, I might as well wander over to those dusty old aircraft and get contaminated.

I played a few soccer matches for Amberley as the weather grew colder, but always wished I was out at the old homestead with my beloved rather than blitzing around the damp turf under floodlights. Then some of us were chosen to serve in a guard of honour for General Jimmy Doolittle, who 14 years earlier had led the daring bombing raid on Tokyo off the American aircraft-carrier Hornet. We drilled for days, and spent hours on preparing uniform and weapons, knowing it would all be over in minutes. But it was a great privilege. Only with an effort of will did I refrain from taking my autograph-book along with me.

After the guard of honour to General Doolittle

Decked out in ceremonial white webbing, we were driven to Eagle Farm, and after a lengthy wait on the tarmac, we saw the Dakota land, and soon the little Pacific hero stepped out. 'These are orl National SURRvicemen, are they?' I heard him say. He was told by our Oxford-accented CO, Group Captain Deryck Kingwell (a Second World War hero himself: wounded at Port Moresby; decorated for piloting his badly damaged aircraft to safety) that indeed they were. He looked at each of us as he passed along the ranks, and I prayed for him to stop for a chat. I could tell him all about the Blitz, and Dad's heroic war. But he was already past and into the rear rank. Ah well, it was good to have seen this legendary figure at such close range. And he was nice enough to write to the CO afterwards complimenting him on the guard of honour.

The last major event was the week-long bivouac up in the mountains around Lake Manchester, where we camped four to a tent and found out now why we had been issued with five blankets apiece. They were barely enough. We had to shower under a perforated oil-drum in a freezing, fast-flowing stream, and shave without hot water. Starvation rations were to suffice, until an air-drop exercise, a dramatic and wonderful thing, with the Lincoln bomber emerging through low mist and dropping its canisters near the clearing.

I was 'killed' on one night exercise, my clumsiness yet again substantiating my pessimism. How could anybody stand a chance in enemy territory? It was much more fun when we were the ones in possession, concealed at the top of a gorge and waiting for the opposition to walk into the trap. I'd had quite enough of it on one compass march, and took time out to carve two sets of initials framed by a heart, into the trunk of a sapling. Maybe it's still there.

There was always the cosy copper full of steaming cocoa at the camp when we got back in the early hours of the morning, wiping off the cattle-dung from our overalls and searching for leeches about our persons. We were already asleep halfway down to the blankets.

Back at Amberley, our service was to end with the grand Passing-Out Parade: more intense practice and polishing of gear. Debbie came out on the bus, and brought her sweet and inoffensive mother, Esther, a lady of the bush who tended to all the needs of the family of four daughters, and well beyond, and made succulent rosella jam and scones.

The prizes were given out, and we did well. Group Captain Kingwell said that we would all miss the companionship and fun, something we already knew to be true. During inspection he spotted some traces of lipstick on the shirt of one of the boys in the other flight. What now? Expulsion? Bit late for that. The CO leaned across and said, in a stage-whisper: 'You want to tell your girl to be more careful!'

Some Vampires whooshed through in a low salute and, giving eyes right at the flagpole, we marched off the bullring for ever as the band blazed away. As we had tea on the lawn with our guests and the officers and airmen of the RAAF and USAAF, it struck me: would the switch from uniform to civvies affect Debbie's view of me? How insecure can you get?

I was very sad to leave Amberley, just as when it had been time to quit secondary school. No more friendly nights at Hungry Harry's, no more camp-fires on bivouac, no more entertainment from Corporal Lilley, no more hitchhiking.

Passing out parade, RAAF Amberley. Group Captain Kingwell is looking at the author (third from this end), whose uniform was free of any lipstick.

But worse by far, no more visits to Raceview and Debbie at the old homestead, with its shimmering, peaceful surrounds and the wood stove and the portraits of the pioneer family on the pinewood walls. This was the crisis of my life.

Handshakes all round at the base before the buses took off, with special regret at saying goodbye to some of the Queenslanders, a 'grand bunch' as recorded in my contemporary memoir. Most of us left with self-esteem enhanced and perhaps tempted to join up permanently, though the long initial period – six years – was a deterrent.

Last day in Queensland, RAAF service at an end. Shall we ever see each other again?

In any case, we were all in the General Reserve for five years, and the Suez crisis might well soon have us all back in action before we could resume our office chairs. If so, or if certain threats from north of Australia turned to outright aggression, I felt we'd be ready.

But nothing else mattered as I passed my last couple of hours with Debbie. She was too young to leave home; I could not expect to get work in Ipswich; all we could do was promise to write to each other. And as the bus conveyed me away from her I hoped that the driver, through his mirror, would think my watery eyes were brought on by hay-fever.

CHAPTER EIGHT

God gave us memory that we might have roses in December.

J.M. BARRIE

JIM LAKER's extra-extraordinary 19 for 90 in the Old Trafford Test of 1956 spawned many thousands of words then and probably millions since. However, the performance cannot have dominated the opening paragraph of many love-letters. It did in the one I wrote to my beloved Debbie on August 1.

Since that gut-wrenching parting I had written to her daily, and she to me – and there were occasional pulsating and expensive brief telephone calls via the long-distance manual exchange – over an entire three months, before her parents agreed to let their under-age daughter have a fortnight's holiday down in Sydney, over 600 miles away. The love-letters remain testimony to the anguish we both felt at being apart, though they are lightened by all manner of references to the music we loved – Kay Starr's *Rock'n'Roll Waltz* and all of Slim Whitman's records – and also my remarks such as this from the lovesick 19-year-old bull-calf: 'Boy, this cricket Test series sure is exciting. I'd like to explain it all to you, but if you know me for long you'll learn all about cricket.'

Against the monotony of work in the shipping office in Sydney, there were the nocturnal vigils by the radio as the 1956 Ashes Tests were broadcast from England, and the letter-writing, and the emotional slavery to country (hillbilly) music that would forever spell Queensland. The main variation came from a sensational new boy who crashed onto the airwaves and the hit parades with *Heartbreak Hotel.* Young Presley and the rest readily brought tears to the eyes of the lovesick. As for the cinema, the great new attraction, *Rebel Without a Cause*, turned out to be probably the most depressing film I've ever seen; and as we fell under the strange spell of James Dean, it seemed cruel as well as illogical that he was already dead, his neck snapped when his speeding Porsche Spyder topless racer crashed into another car on a California highway and wrapped itself round a telegraph-pole. That was in 1955, and many years later Dean's face still haunted as it was used to sell T-shirts in boutiques in London, Sydney and all over.

First car: Elvis.
Could it make it all the way to Queensland and back?

As Peter May's England pulled ahead of Ian Johnson's Australia, John Arlott's Beaujolais familiar voice describing so much of it, I bought my first car and surprised the family by naming it not after any cricketer but calling it Elvis. The bull-nosed Morris 8/40, fawn, with handsome white wheels and a canvas hood, brought independence – in between life-threatening brake failures – and became a royal chariot when my Queensland sweetheart finally came down in the Pioneer coach in September 1956. We became engaged. But a fortnight later she had no choice but to return to Queensland, leaving me desolate and inconsolable. Letters flew back and forth, the most telling going from my father to hers, persuading Mr Pennell to accept Dad as Debbie's guardian if she returned to Sydney.

Within a month she was back by my side, and we married the following May. I was 20 and she was even younger. There had been no formal proposal. It was a natural understanding.

That 20th birthday was the only one when I've shed a tear. The teen years had gone, and I was about to take on, with eager willingness, a huge measure of responsibility. I had very little money, and neither did either set of parents; but we had each other, and the future stretched out invitingly and mysteriously before us. I showed my girl Sydney in all its beauty, not least Cronulla beach and the sand-dunes, where we stretched out all on our own in the sun, my love having bought herself her first swim-suit.

It was no ordinary wedding arrangement. My folks couldn't get away, so Debbie and I madly undertook a 1300-mile round trip to Queensland in Elvis on rough and winding roads, up the New England Highway, back down the Pacific, crippled on the return trip after a gasket blew, average speed 30 mph, painstakingly logged. Total petrol cost £8.

Debbie and DF in 1957

We had no money for motels, so the 15-hour drive up as far as Glen Innes left us exhausted. There, late at night, we parked in a sidestreet, had a hamburger each, and tried to sleep. But frostbite threatened, so we moved on before dawn, with a milky fog draping the windscreen. Reaching the Queensland border gates was uplifting, and the views were breathtaking, but Elvis was over-firing long before we rumbled into Ipswich after a further seven hours on the road, sprinkled with dust but triumphant. I fired off a momentous telegram to the family in Sydney, which brought relief to their anxieties, and soon, out at the sleepy old homestead, we were washing away the dirt of the miles and tucking into bread and rosella jam and one of the greatest cups of tea of all time.

We were married at St Paul's, a charming and well-appointed old church built in 1859, the year Queensland was founded, an ancestor of Debbie's probably among the workforce. Then came a fright when old Reverend Cornish dashed round to the house to say that the paperwork was incomplete. My parents should have signed a permission. My parents were over 600 miles away, and the wedding was tomorrow. There were no faxes or emails in those days.

Somehow the problem was overcome, and after some relaxing cricket on the lawn with the local kids, and a quick beer in town with my best man and father-in-law, I got into the dinner-jacket I'd borrowed from Dad and reached the church in good time, to gaze nervously down the aisle until my beloved appeared, on the arm of her father, who was obviously even more nervous than I. Debbie, in her borrowed dress, was radiant, and we managed to raise our young voices sufficiently to complete the vows. The reception was a characteristic bush affair, the 'speeches' anything but elaborate or sophisticated, the telegram boys still racing in with fresh cables, and the bottled Bulimba beer gradually bringing ease to all the relations, whose names I was trying hard to remember.

Debbie – Laker's 20th victim.
A gift in 2018 from Maha (artist) and Arun Sengupta (concept)

Cousin Colleen played the violin; the MC sang *I'll Take You Home Again Kathleen*; Uncle Tom warbled *The Rose of Tralee*; my bride and her sister Rosie had the place swinging with *Caribbean*.

Then back to the homestead we went in a Customline limousine, to pack, change into our red sweaters, and dance the traditional bridal waltz before Debbie had a touching waltz with her father, who by now seemed to have accepted me and the impending departure of his sweet daughter. As the squeezebox whined, we loaded the car with heaps of gifts, mainly crockery, and set off for the mountains – after removing the tin-cans and Just Married sign Rosie had tied to Elvis's rear bumper. We hit a wallaby in the darkness on our way to Beaudesert, but Elvis proved slightly more robust than the marsupial, and near midnight we walked through the swing-doors of the hotel, the young cow cockies lined up at the bar all turning to stare at the young couple with suitcases who were obviously on honeymoon. Our blushes subsided as we checked in, and a marriage scripted in Heaven was on its way.

Debbie's parents, three sisters and two nephews were but a small section of a well-attended wedding

Trying to find O'Reilly's Green Mountains guesthouse next day was a nightmare. Lost in Lamington National Park, we worried for the mighty little Elvis as we bounced along gravel tracks and up steep inclines, harassed by cattle, hopelessly out of bounds. We eventually found a homestead, and who should have greeted us but Bernard O'Reilly himself, a national hero after his valiant search for the crashed Stinson aircraft in 1937: his bushcraft and stamina saved lives after days of fighting his way through the rainforest, up and down perilously steep gorges. He gave us tea and sandwiches and explained that the guesthouse was two miles away – by packhorse. So we had to navigate all the way back to Beaudesert and then head for Canungra: 25 miles all told.

Elvis roared and strained his way to our destination, which we reached late in the day, the motor apparently burned out. We were finally towed up the single track by a Landrover. At O'Reillys we had five blissful days, walking the tracks, riding horses around narrow mountain pathways with sheer drops to the side, sitting cross-legged by the campfire at night, listening to pioneering tales from O'Reilly elders – and worrying whether Elvis would cough back to life when the time came.

He did, but top speed on the marathon haul back to Sydney was even lower than coming up. Our honeymoon idyll over, we slid back down the

mountain tracks, loaded up with sixpenny pineapples, vowing we'd be back some day. We were to return a little matter of 31 years later, and saw our juvenile signatures preserved in the visitors' book. By then little had altered about O'Reilly's, much about ourselves.

Now began a series of Sydney suburban tenancies in rooms with landladies who were prone to bouts of hysteria. Our longing for independence went on for a few years, for it seemed impossible to save money. Of all people, it was to be Auntie Edie who came to the rescue.

Our first digs had been OK. In fact it was a thrill to be just a few doors from where young Don Bradman had lived, in Frederick Street, Rockdale, soon after he came up from Bowral in the 1920s to play for St George. His landlord, the club's current president, Frank Cush, was still living there, and had been helpful to the comparatively untalented colt Frith.

The going had remained tough with St George. So many bright young batsmen were on the scene that I was restricted to the lower order and regarded just as a promising fast bowler. The indications are that I was prone to occasional frustrated outbursts, for I remember that a cocky youngster named Joyner so annoyed me that in the process of tossing the ball back to him from slip to gully I decided to shut him up by hurling it flat-out at his chest. The throw was slightly high and almost smashed into his teeth. The skipper glared, but at least Joyner went quiet for a while. To this day I've abhorred mindless chatter on the field, now referred to euphemistically as 'sledging'.

Against Glebe, we were behind the clock in a late-afternoon run-chase, in days long before the 20/15-overs-last-hour regulation came in, and I was so disgusted at Glebe's time-wasting in the field that I appealed against the light, and off we all trooped. If they wanted a draw that badly they could bloody well have it. Again, skipper was not amused.

At least we won the Poidevin-Gray Shield for under-21s in 1957-58, under John Cope's mature leadership (he was later 12th man for NSW), with support from Reg Gasnier, who, like Joyner, was a bit of a smartarse. But I'll give it to Reg: he grew out of his teenage foibles to become a masterful Australian Test Rugby League player and captain, and an impressively mature fellow.

The heat was so great in the match at Bankstown Oval that, after three (eight- ball) overs with the new ball, I felt myself swaying at slip and slumped to the ground. It was only heat-exhaustion, but it alarmed Debbie, who was watching from the stand, with our budgerigar Bing in his cage.

My moment came in the Randwick match at Coogee Oval on New Year's Day 1958. On a dampish pitch we bowled them out for 52. Touching a never-to-be-repeated emulation of Ray Lindwall, I took 6 for 20, both these statistics being replicas of his demolition of England at The Oval in the 1948 Test match. What spoiled it all was being robbed later by a leg-before decision before I'd scored, and one of the newspapers spelling my name as 'Firth', a goof that was to be made often throughout life, until it was accepted with a shrug.

All that mattered was having my girl by my side. I kept a diary, which records that I listened to the Tests from South Africa in '57-58, when our 'hero' Benaud started to look really good at last; and that America launched the first satellite into space, five days before 'Plane crashed in Germany with the Manchester United team aboard. Byrne, Taylor, Colman & Frank Swift killed. I was stunned when I heard it on this morning's news. Don't know why, but I felt almost sick to think of it.'

A month later I was unhappy, without quite being griefstricken, when Len Hutton's cherished world Test record 364 went by the board: 'Sobers broke world record (365*) – darn him!'

I played football on my 21st birthday and launched the Voigtlander camera (valued gift from parents) with the first of thousands of colour slides. But the office job was seriously getting me down. Writing cheques, drawing salaries, recording fruit and wool rebates and levies, chatting aimlessly half the day was not my idea of a meaningful existence. *And I somehow rather fancy that I'd like to change with Clancy, / Like to take a turn at droving where the seasons come and go, / While he faced the round eternal of the cashbook and the journal – / But I doubt he'd suit the office, Clancy, of The Overflow.* Banjo Patterson had said it for me. And Debbie could recite all of it effortlessly.

We went to the recording of the Jack Davey show; but I was concerned about Debbie's stomach pains. A few weeks later we had the explanation. She was expecting. And we were thrilled.

The turmoil concerning the future persisted. Join the RAAF? Join the police force? Rejected: 'Too short & too light. It doesn't matter what's between the ears as long as you're a big fat gawk!' That entry eased the frustration. They'd offered a spine-stretching course, but I didn't like the sound of that at all.

The frustration of the office was getting serious: 'Undecided whether to go in today. Did a silly thing – went in.' Evenings were spent reading, listening to the radio, making model aircraft, all the while fulfilled at having my sweet Debbie with me. Winter was cold though, and the kerosene fumes in our small room couldn't be doing the embryo any good.

June 20: 'Douglas Jardine died.' How could I have known that one distant day I'd write the definitive book on Bodyline?

England's Bodyline Test captain merited an entry, whereas a year earlier Uncle Bill's death had had little effect on me, I'm ashamed to recall. Now, though, Auntie Edie had decided to end her loneliness by coming to Australia to be with her sister and family. It was a disaster from start to finish. At 51, she was a Londoner through and through, with a dependence on the special mutual conviviality that went with that environment. She continued to drink heavily, and when the initial excitement of reunion with Mum and the rest of us had subsided, she had nothing but scorn for the Australian way of life. There were outbursts and tears, and hopes that she would at least stay for the birth fizzled as spring approached. She boarded a Qantas Constellation four months after arrival, and we were never to see her again. We bought her walnut dining-room suite.

Although winter and soccer were always just impatient intervals between cricket seasons, the Australia v Great Britain Rugby League Tests were always compelling; indeed the tensions were even more concentrated than in the cricket Tests, with bigger, noisier crowds and explosive passions cascading over all of us. By now, when my loyalties might easily have been with Australia, I went with the underdogs, those who were on tour and thus were short of vocal support. When Great Britain won the Ashes in front of almost 70,000 at the SCG, I was overjoyed.

And four years later, when they did it again, I picked up a pearl of a quote from the British vice-captain Derek Turner. He said, 'Tha's t'give it and take it, and not t'groomble.' Terrific.

The Telegraph also published a letter of mine complaining that the SCG crowd had been blind to Britain's skill and were appallingly one-eyed. Of course, somebody wrote next day to say that the match I had been watching couldn't have been the same one he'd watched.

I was playing occasionally alongside my brother in St George seconds at soccer, which was a source of pride and pleasure, if only because he was forced to desist from vexing me for 90 minutes.

Life went on: I'd buy *The Cricketer* in Swains, and let nothing interfere with listening to *The Goon Show*, and pursued my oil painting, without ever working from nature. An exhibition of Winston Churchill's paintings at the Art Gallery in the Domain was rewarding. And what a lucky young wife I had, to judge from another diary entry: 'Read my psychology book to Debbie after she had fixed my cricket trousers.'

'Read all about poor Wardle being dropped.' The cantankerous Yorkie had written indiscreetly for the *Daily Mail* and had cost himself a second tour of Australia. Still, I felt an excitement rising as the English side was announced and set sail late in '58. So many great names did it contain that the retention of the Ashes seemed a formality. But some failed to play up to expectation, there was dissension in the ranks, and Australia generated a resurgence under new leader Richie Benaud. The only thing that spoiled it was the prevalence of bowlers in the Australian ranks with suspect actions, and the dragging which saw some of them bowling well forward of the front crease.

With the baby expected in December, we endured not only the cramped hardships of living in one small room but were unlucky enough to fall into the hands of one mad, screeching landlady after another and were compelled to move on. The tension was increased by my commuting into Sydney: public transport was costly and slow, so I bought a motor-scooter, a questionable investment. Bare-headed and clad in duffle-coat, I fell off every time the front wheel touched a slippery tramline in wet weather; and it often broke down for no apparent reason. Cricket gear piled on the rear luggage-bar did nothing to improve the vehicle's stability either.

Realising that St George 2nd XI was likely to be the limit, I switched to Paddington for the '58-59 season, using an address provided by my dentist in order to comply with the strict NSWCA residential qualifications then applying in grade cricket. I was now able to play home matches either at the elegant Rushcutters Bay Oval or, alternatively and thrillingly, at Trumper Park, where the old pavilion, with its splintery floor, was where the glorious and much-loved Victor himself had so often played. The classic Beldam photograph of him hung on the wall in the home dressing-room by way of inspiration, and, for me, a certain magic was embedded in the splintery floor, where Trumper's feet had once trodden. Surely there was some of his DNA still there?

Reading Arthur Mailey's confessions of knee-knocking hero-worship in his entertaining book *10 for 66 and All That* was a comfort, for it showed I was not the only bloke prone to idolatry and insecurity when it came to rubbing shoulders with top cricketers. 'Wonder what Trumper's doing this very minute . . . bet he's not ironing his flannels. Perhaps he's at breakfast . . . Wonder if he knows I'm playing against him? Don't suppose he's ever heard of me . . . Think I'll dig the garden. No I won't – I want to keep fresh. Think I'll lie down for a bit . . . better not, I might fall off to sleep and be late.'

When the little-known Mailey had Trumper stumped, he ended this passage, which has since deservedly been anthologised many times, by recalling: 'There was no triumph in me as I watched the receding figure. I felt like a boy who had killed a dove.'

When, at the Paddington nets at Trumper Park, Arthur Morris was breaking in a new bat, and punched three consecutive balls from me into mid-off's hands, I quietly enjoyed a hat-trick fantasy of my own. I knew Arthur was not serious, but to me he was no dove. Same when Ron Archer, coping with a serious knee injury, bowled me some 'dazzling offbreaks' (diary entry), one of which was short and got pulled to the far side of Trumper Park. The one-time Australian Test giant limped after it, leaving me, well, a little bit shamefaced.

One evening I sat down in the confines of our room and wrote to Jack Hobbs, who was then 75, a gentleman, I was led to believe, as well as the choice of many Englishmen as the finest batsman the game had known. To my astonishment, seven weeks later I received a long and friendly reply, together with a signed photo. It was uplifting, and it was also the first brick in the foundations of a cricket letter collection that was to grow to many thousands.

Other evenings I rode the scooter from work down to my parents' home, to be followed back to our room late at night by Dad in his formidable Pontiac with Debbie on board. In rainy weather this was the greatest ordeal of all: would my father's reactions be sharp enough to avoid running over his son when he slid off his precarious machine? Hair-raising stuff.

It was not just in the office that frustration hurt. Playing at Manly Oval, I was caught first ball (and later avoided a pair only through an umpire's inefficiency – or leniency), bowled four fruitless overs with the new ball, then discovered that our dressing-room had been robbed. Stripped of its contents (about £8), my wallet, with all the others, was floating in the toilet-pan. Of course, the scooter played up on the journey home, and I was in need of the comfort of my beloved more than ever.

There was always that other world. Off I went again to the Hotel Australia when the English cricketers came to town, confident enough now to walk into the foyer, past all the luggage with MCC colours, and sit in one of the leather armchairs. As recorded at the time, I saw Willie Watson trying not to show his limp; pale Fred Trueman leaning on the reception desk, glowering; Peter Richardson 'staring hard at me'; Tony Lock, bald and surly; friendly, eye-crinkled Colin Cowdrey; and a couple of Pressmen, Frank Rostron and Crawford White. What a wonderful life they had, I reflected.

I singled out reserve wicketkeeper Roy Swetman, because he was about my age and height. He looked me up and down with those cat's eyes of his and we had a very affable chat. Then I moved on to Tony Lock, whose remaining red hair was plastered down on the back of his head. He had a moan about the hotel service, said he was sure England would win the Ashes, but confessed that his knee was a bit stiff. I wondered what was going on when I saw Jim Laker ('icy' I thought) and Alec Bedser (writing on the tour) strolling along with Norm O'Neill. Was the young Australian being compromised? Surely not?

My financial worries were temporarily pushed aside by cricket, whether playing or watching or hanging about at the nets. Two new challenges emerged at the Paddington practice nets when I faced the bowling of the whippy Jim O'Regan, a young man with only one eye, who had played for New South Wales last season; and I bowled to Jeff Hallebone, who had scored 202 for Victoria on his first-class debut in '51-52 (and who had endured a most fearful going-over from Lindwall and Miller one dark evening at the SCG in a Shield match).

FST: 'It won't coom out, son.' But it did.

As for big cricket, there were the Englishmen's preliminary matches to be watched. I asked Fred Trueman, standing by the pickets at long leg, if he'd face my camera, please: 'It won't coom out, son,' he growled. But it did, and the nice colour image was published years later. At the nets, I found Peter May charming, and told him our baby, expected any time now, would be named after him. I'd always promised myself that my first son would be named after the world's best batsman of the time. I suppose 'Garfield' came close, or even 'Hanif' (though the two fs would collide). The suggestion that if it were a daughter she would be named 'May' was tongue-in-cheek.

The England captain stepped out of the hotel one afternoon with his pretty fiancée Virginia, and I was astonished to learn later that the English Press were creating merry hell over her presence.

One Saturday, I went with heavily-pregnant Debbie and Uncle Alec to the SCG to watch Laker, Lock and Trueman bowl against an Australian XI, having cast my first-ever vote in a Federal Election that morning, honouring my pledge to R.G.Menzies, who seemed to be doing a fair enough job in maintaining stability in the Australian economy. And the next day we went all the way to Brookvale Oval for a charity match which featured some great names: Keith Miller, Sid Barnes, Freddie Brown, and the lyrical New Zealand left-hander Martin Donnelly.

It would have been saturation cricket had not my boss put an office ban on the radio. I was back to sneak listening, and searching for shop-window television sets to watch play after tea.

For accurately predicting Australia's team selection for the first Test, I won a fry-pan that came in extremely handy, though the stroke of good luck was cancelled by getting a month's notice from our landlady, who did not like babies.

ENGLAND'S BLOODY NOSE read one of the street placards during the first Test, lost by England after Trevor Bailey's record slow fifty and O'Neill's last-day strokeplay which made ex-St George players proud. Australia won the second Test of 1958-59 as well, and the rumblings about certain bowlers' actions grew louder. It was confusing. How could a team containing May, Cowdrey, Graveney, Watson, Bailey, Evans, Trueman, Statham, Laker and Lock lose two Tests running, each by eight wickets? I went to Sydney for the third Test to find out.

By now we were parents. While we were at the cinema, watching *Dunkirk*, the first alarm came, and we raced home and then over to St George Hospital. But it was not until almost two days later that Peter arrived, my poor girl having been in labour much longer than the tedious Trevor Bailey had been at the crease in the Brisbane Test. Our son shared a birthday with Robert Menzies and Bill O'Reilly: a brilliant Aussie trifecta, and I was so euphoric that morning that I croaked *Soliloquy* from *Carousel*, Gordon MacRae-style, as I steered my scooter along the road that follows the railway track to Kogarah: *My boy Bill!* . . . Debbie looked exhausted but as beautiful as ever.

I rode down to Cronulla and took my first wicket as a father; dashed back to the hospital during the tea-break, and returned to the game to drop a catch. Still, we won; and the opposition was none other than St George.

Back at the Test, Cowdrey made the then-slowest Ashes century, and May scored 92, before 'Chucker' Burke bowled him. A rather strange-looking chap named Dexter came in, smashed a drive into the pickets right in front of me, and was then caught by Grout off Benaud. But the draw was ensured. I'd had my first sight of Ian Meckiff and Keith Slater, and their bowling actions worried me.

Paddington cricket was enjoyable. It was good to see Neville Cardus's name among the vice-presidents listed on the club's fixture card (he lived in Elizabeth Bay during the war years) and Cyril Docker's too, a member of the AIF cricket team after the First World War. An evening in his company was a delight. On the field, some wickets were followed by an 83 at Trumper, which was worth more than twice that on any anonymous ground, as we came good with 330 for 8 against Glebe.

But with Australia forcing a crushing 4-0 Ashes victory, and my accountant boss an even more depressing influence in the office, I was facing frustration on all fronts. We found another room to house ourselves and baby, and I failed an audition (reading racing results) for a job with ABC Radio in Hobart. Next door lived a friendly old couple from England who let us watch their television set whenever we felt like it, and life was lightened by *Gunsmoke*, Phil Silvers (fat, innocent, lovable little Doberman, always smiling, was the favourite), and Bootsie and Snudge in *The Army Game*, with a dash of mellowness from the Perry Como show. On radio, from nowhere came an episode of *ITMA*.

May 1959 brought another midnight date with the FA Cup final by radio from England, a further touch of homesickness from out of the blue. Writing soccer reports again for the local paper, I tangled with the universal problem of avoiding repetition and with the frustration of seeing my byline left off the report every couple of weeks. In one match, I let fly a speculative kick from the touchline near halfway and saw the ball bounce high over the goalie from the hard ground and into the net: 50 yards. But still life was flat enough for a diary entry three days later to read: 'Am reading *Diary of Anne Frank*. It's more interesting than this diary.'

'Dreamt about those Prague forwards all night' establishes that the football was being taken as seriously as the cricket, and when my 100th match for St George came along I was alert enough to recognise it. I played in the last match ever at Prince Edward Park, which we won 10-0. Back in the city, the magic of Royalty was sufficient to have me hurrying up to Macquarie Street during my lunch-hour to see Princess Alexandra pass by, just as I'd once been up to give the Queen Mother a wave.

In our little room Debbie and I watched our baby grow ounce by ounce, and worried about making a home. The £5 won on the Lottery wasn't going to ease our plight. Then I had a brainwave.

On Dad's 50th birthday, July 14, 1959, my parents vacated 27 Ecole Street, the House that Ted Built, and took a delicatessen down at Jannali. That tied up such capital as they had. But childless, widowed Auntie Edie over in London might just have had some cash lying idle. So I wrote to her, and she agreed to help us, without the slightest hesitation. Her signature for a loan arrived the same day the brilliant West Indies batsman Collie Smith died following a road accident.

Such was the uplift given by Auntie Edie's response that I had an idea for a play for television. I started writing it on my 1912 Remington typewriter, lost the inspiration just as quickly, and read 100 pages of *Room at the Top* instead. Mooching around Circular Quay during lunchtime produced no answers. Should I try to get a job in a country town? A 64 on a difficult pitch against University took my mind off things for a few days.

Then we moved to Connell's Point, tucked away down off the street, by the waters of George's River, where pelicans cruised and crabs made the sand move, and possums and kookaburras lived in the trees. It too was cramped and primitive, and our toddler had to be watched extra carefully, but it was an idyllic environment, somewhere good to be while we awaited Auntie Edie's loan and tried to find a house.

Cricket continued to rule thought. Australia's Tests in Pakistan, much to our surprise, could be picked up on radio, while a particularly silly diary entry reads: 'Mentally am playing cover-drives & hook shots all the time now.' Elsewhere: 'Oh, come on success!'

Then, suddenly, the 1950s were over.

They had been good years in so many ways. School had been fulfilling, and finding the serene and beautiful Queensland country girl had been the greatest piece of good fortune I could ever have dared to wish for. We now had a bonny, fair-haired boy, who had already been photographed while still in nappies with a miniature cricket bat in his tiny hands. And the housing problem was about to be overcome. What more could a 22-year-old want?

Merely to be a cricket-writer. It was the hopelessness of it all that ate into my soul.

CHAPTER NINE

Nerves play as important a part in batsmanship as skill.

GILBERT JESSOP

'NO pot-bellied, baggy-eyed bully will boss him around,' sang Gordon MacRae. And that went for my son too. He was going to grow 'like a tree', with his 'head held high'. But if, like Billy Bigelow, this father 'never knew how to get money', he certainly would not be going as far as the tragic figure in *Carousel*, who planned to 'go out and make it, or steal it, or take it; or die!'

There were two types of bliss: being with wife and baby son, and playing or watching cricket. January 2, 1960: 'Rode to SCG for NSW v Queensland game. Madden 99 & Flockton 97. Got very very burnt.' But back at the office: 'Bored stiff with the solitary confinement. Won't talk about the afternoon. May as well not have lived it.' Came the following Saturday: 'Went in 3 minutes from the end & am 2 not out. Pleased with myself. Stupid, isn't it?'

Improvement of the mind came from reading Somerset Maugham, and *Borstal Boy*, and the harrowing *Grapes of Wrath*. This led to a Steinbeck 'season', followed by John Dos Passos and the pretentious Hemingway. Cardus and Ray Robinson were not forgotten. They all helped allay the anxieties of real life. March 14, 1960: 'And still the bank balance dwindles.'

Sad to turn 23, I received a generous batch of cards, and at lunchtime 'had quiet little beer with myself at the Australia'.

There had been pronounced hopes around now that a book I'd written on my National Service experiences at Amberley would be accepted for publication, but a rejection by Angus & Robertson, followed by two further refusals, were dampeners. Then came luck and relief with a job in advertising, with Alan Davis, contractors for bus and tram ads: £22 a week. After five years at OSRA, it was like being let out of low-security prison.

My new boss was an ambitious but fairly humane chap from Manchester who reckoned he'd played football with Denis Viollet. I countered that by telling him I'd played cricket with Norm O'Neill. There was a detectable bond here that may have had something to do with origins.

The football season was another tough one. I actually played in both matches – 1st and 2nd team – one afternoon against Concordia (whose German shouting was understood by our own right-half, Popp, who kept intercepting passes, much to their bafflement). The police were called to our match against the Italians, so riotous were not only the crowd but the players too.

My weekday duties included supervising the erection of advertisements onto buses, sometimes designing the ads, liaising with clients, one of whom taught me a lesson that initially hurt but which has lasted through life. My response to one of his instructions was 'I'll see what I can do.' He swung round, eyes blazing: 'Don't "see what you can do", David. DO IT!' That's the Australian way of business – or it used to be: no bull, no procrastination, no excuses. I preached it in slovenly old England for years, losing popularity points every time.

With a little more money coming in, we got a TV, and the scooter gave way to a car, a green Morris Minor, with a canvas hood. It behaved all the way up to Queensland for a brief holiday, and back.

Evenings were agreeably filled with *Hancock's Half Hour*, *The Benny Hill Show*, *Perry Mason*, and *The Twilight Zone*. Quality of life had improved. But the big event was the buying of a new house. With Auntie Edie's loan, we bought an oblong block at Revesby, near Bankstown, and saw the neat little fibro house go up in a matter of weeks. We moved in just before Christmas 1960, a month before our second son, Johnny, was born (to be given Denis [Compton] as a middle name: it worked: he turned out to be the most debonair of all of us).

I was now captain of Paddington's third-grade side, and had to attend selection meetings at the Cricketers Club in George Street (October 17: 'Saw Benaud.'). The first crisis came when Jack Clark, who had bowled fast for both NSW and Queensland, was dropped from the 1st XI and demanded to captain the seconds. Seemed he would be lost to the club otherwise. I found myself giving the casting vote. Jack was made captain.

This was the amazing season of Australia v West Indies Tests, starting with the tied Test at the Gabba. On that last afternoon it looked like being a fairly tight finish, so I stayed behind in the office and listened. As Wes Hall bowled that lengthy final over, in which the last three wickets fell, thanks to supernatural throws from Conrad Hunte and Joe Solomon, I was grateful that the office was empty, for some strange noises were coming from my nostrils. The commentators were under stress too, and I recall Michael Charlton's faintly hysterical laughter as he announced that the strong sunlight stopped him from seeing much of the action out in the middle. At the climax, it sounded as if commentators Clive Harburg and Johnny Moyes were strangling each other.

All the way home in the train I was still trying to control a mild trembling which even the long walk from the station failed to fix. We had listened to top-drawer cricket history. There would never again be a Test match that ended in a tie. Not till 1986, in Madras, anyway.

A week after the Brisbane sensation, we were in our new home in Revesby, just down the road from where, 4 ½ years later, Steve and Mark Waugh were to be born, and where already a 10-year-old named Jeff Thomson was terrifying batsmen as he spearheaded the Padstow Pirates' attack.

The thrilling 1960-61 Australia-West Indies Test series paralysed the nation and restored international cricket's fallen stocks. Everybody was inspired by it, even when the occasional discord sounded, such as Solomon's cap falling onto his wicket at Melbourne. The Laws said he was out all right, but such was the popularity of the West Indians and so equivocal was Melbourne's attitude towards Benaud that the Australian captain was given the raspberry. After the Sydney Test – where West Indies levelled at 1-1 the day our son was born, and I saw Garry Sobers for the first time, as well as my 'old friend' Worrell – there was a finish at Adelaide even more taxing on the nerves than the Brisbane tie. Ken Mackay and the 'hopeless' Lindsay Kline held out for over an hour and a half to force a draw with just that one Australian wicket in hand. As Mackay took the final ball from Hall in the ribs, the continent of Australia seemed to deflate as the tension snapped. How much more of this could we take?

True cricket-lovers cast patriotism aside. The ideal outcome would have been a shared series. Unhappily it was resolved midst controversy when Wally Grout seemed to be out hit-wicket near the end but was allowed to bat on because neither umpire had spotted the cause of the dislodged ball. Perhaps even this early I had a perception that one day justice could be done if the television screen could be utilised to replay and demystify incidents such as this.

So Australia won this stupendous series, a success which was in keeping with the new mood of nationalism. Ampol's 'Be Australian, Buy Australian' was among the first strident bugle-calls as the movement to cast off the rather appealing Australian modesty and inferiority complex got under way. It was inevitable and it has sometimes been ugly and undignified; but this is the usual way in which a youngster transforms himself into a full-grown man.

When, two years later, Ted Dexter's England team toured Australia, there were new kinds of shouts booming from the Hill at the SCG to remind the gathering of Churchill's misguided Dardanelles campaign in the First World War and his intransigence towards Australia's military needs at home in the

Second. Updating the history lesson came a cry from the SCG Hill of 'Yeah, Dexter, and what about the Common Market?' It was the first time I'd heard the expression.

What did all this matter to a suburban bloke who hurried home each evening to his lovely wife and two boys in their new home which still smelt strongly of paint? There was a coarse lawn to be mowed and a TV to be watched. On it, we first saw and heard a group of Pommie kids who called themselves the Bee Gees, and on a late-night show there was a zany, up-and-coming hilarious Irish comedian named Dave Allen. Our 'estate' was shown proudly to visiting parents. All that was missing was a string of centuries to get me into first grade and then the New South Wales team.

Not that I didn't brush with greatness. Those Cricketers Club selection sessions had their high moments: January 3, 1961: 'Ron Archer bought me beer.' January 16: 'Got out of lift & Bradman got in.'

The Tests were sometimes watched in shop windows, and listened to on the portable radio on the long, uphill walk from the station, which became a creepy journey during dark winter evenings. Such was the tight financial position that I sold the car one Saturday morning – and used the £125 in notes as a thigh-pad when I batted that afternoon. I gave up buying cricket books and borrowed from the library instead. And to help with the food bills, I planted a large packet of lettuce seeds, which brought a good harvest.

In the quest for improved fitness I went down Beaconsfield Street to the gym run by Welsh boxer Ron James, who had once fought for an Empire title. And the wonderful friendship with Bert Oldfield, the gentleman wicketkeeper, was sustained by attendance at one of his lectures, for which I designed the announcement sign.

Suddenly I had a year up at Davis's, and began to feel I knew a bit about the essence of advertising, although that feeling of going nowhere was never far away. The diary also discloses that an outbreak of dandruff disturbed me.

It may have had something to do with nerves. They seemed on edge at the best of times, but when Australia opened their Test campaign in England in 1961, and I sat up for night after night of radio-monitoring, followed by viewing of the daily newsreels in grainy black-and-white, the tension was such that I recorded: '1st Test is starting now. My tummy's trembling!' Matters eased when the action began and John Arlott's reassuring voice flowed comfortingly over me as I sat alone in the lounge, by the kerosene heater, with a bottle of port and some bread-and-jam for company. 'Thought a lot about Dexter's 180,' I wrote after the Edgbaston Test.

The only consolation for not having become a Test cricketer at the age of 24 was that it spared me from dying from nerves. But there was another test just around the corner: without thinking carefully about the consequences, I had applied to take part in Channel 9's *World of Sport* quiz, compered by Ron Casey. My television debut came on June 25, 1961, after days of feverish study, and a morning of hideous stage-fright, when my mental contortions just stopped short of throwing up my breakfast or pulling out of the show. Yet it went all right, and I won enough points to be invited to return the following week, which, to Ron Casey's annoyance, I declined to do, for St George had an important soccer match against Blacktown. I took a beating in that match, as it happened, the doctor having to put a long needle in my knee and telling me that damage to the right thigh could finish my career.

And I still haven't received my £5 appearance money from Channel 9.

Reflecting on the TV ordeal, I submitted further a few weeks later, and got onto Reg Grundy's *Wheel of Fortune*, taking home a very welcome large basket of household provisions. Necessity is the mother of daring.

Diary entries seldom come more frank than that for July 20: 'My huge aim is to develop a supreme knowledge of my subject.' Had that aim concerned medicine and surgery, I might have saved a few lives by now. Instead, the concentrated study was applied to what I now feel might border on the frivolous or, at very best, is an allegorical substitute for real life. The commitment, already embedded for years, now intensified, and led towards an inviting world of recreation, companionship, travel and history.

Such could not be said for football. Our match against Croatia was cut short by a crowd riot.

A certain portion of Englishness was still intact, to judge from my written reaction to the Old Trafford Test of '61, when Davidson and McKenzie put on 98 for the last wicket to give Australia something to bowl at, and when all still seemed lost, Benaud went around the wicket and set up an odds-against victory with 6 for 70. It became a bit more acceptable later when I heard that the tactic had been suggested by Ray Lindwall, who was on tour as a journalist.

While the people in the office 'drive me insane', and August 28 was a 'day of deep thought; what of the future?', I did what I could to keep cricket's little flame a'flicker: borrowed a 16mm film of Don Bradman and somehow found a projector on which to run it; wrote a piece on this 1961 series and submitted it to Jack Pollard, who was then editing *The Referee*. He commended it, rejected it, and said I'd probably find more scope over in England. The thought was to grow.

I had fun whenever I could with my two little blond-haired boys, and found distraction when the firm sent me down to Wollongong and I met an elderly contractor who had been in San Francisco during the earthquake of 1906 which destroyed the city and cost over 1000 lives. I told him I'd survived the Blitz, and felt sure in myself that no natural disaster would touch me during my lifetime. Superstitious as my mother, I made sure to touch wood.

Out of all this came a flash of inspiration. Why don't we venture to England? Financially we could just about make it, and there was always

Auntie Edie there to lend a caring hand. Debbie and I studied the London map, and though her family in Queensland were understandably cool at the idea, and the Russian Atom-bomb tests were terrifying everybody, we advertised the house and waited for something to happen.

The advertising job was even more of a trial now that the office was shifted over to North Sydney, and when Dad drove off in his Holden van in the early-morning darkness to sell his meat-pies to local outlets, I knew I had to get out of this depressing situation. Family talk of a 'co-operative' shop or restaurant, with Auntie Edie involved, soon subsided. Only the Greeks and Italians seemed to have the knack of doing that sort of family thing successfully. We were loners. Worse, Dad seemed rather naive in business affairs, even a touch over-deferential when he was with the owner or the bank manager. I hated that and vowed never to kowtow to anybody, no matter how overawed I might feel.

In support of this, I did a week's Scientology course which was aimed at lifting confidence and spirits, cleverly lured to it after a free IQ test which flattered me with a 141 reading. I resisted any movement towards outside mind control, but voluntarily self-assessed and realised that I prized loyalty to an extraordinary degree and found betrayal unforgivable. Such principles, I sensed, would not make for a smooth ride through life.

For Debbie's 21st birthday we parked the kids, went to King's Cross for a lobster meal, then on to see the ultimate movie *Gone with the Wind*. It helped me forget the 'catastrophe' of our TV tube fizzling out a couple of nights before.

One Saturday, before I'd made a run, I hooked too soon and took a blow to the side of the head that hurt and rang bells. It also relaxed me sufficiently to score 95 before a cross-eyed umpire gave me lbw. Up into Paddington 2nds I went, and then into the 1sts for my debut. It was at Rushcutters Bay, and on a damp pitch we got Mosman out for 49, of which little Peter Kelly made 42. Kelly later scored twin centuries for Western Australia against M.J.K.Smith's MCC [England] side. I'd helped by falling forward at slip to catch David Lord, but missed out on a bat when we declared as soon as we had first-innings points. That 42 out of 49 (85.71 per cent) by Kelly seems still to be a world record in any 'significant' match.

I did get in second time around, and was bowled round my legs third ball by Cal Matha for a duck. The only consolation was that I wouldn't have to face the most terrifying bowler I'd ever seen – and that included Tyson – in Gordon Rorke, the king-sized blond who'd petrified the '58-59 Englishmen off about 18 yards.

So I was a first-grader – of sorts – though I expected not to be around next season, for we should be in England. Not much of a record: one innings, no runs, one catch. Never mind. One must never use the word 'tragedy' in cricket, any more than one should compare tough cricket matches with the slaughter at the Somme, as some have done.

There was real tragedy in 1962. Auntie Edie was ill as well as lonely. Bill had died five years before, and now she lived alone in a room in Gloucester Place. Incurably generous, she sent clothing for the little boys, and obtained a 1927 *Wisden* for me as soon as I expressed the need. But, having helped finance our house for us, she earned just enough for her needs without touching her post-office savings. She was thrilled at the news that we intended going to England but deeply regretted that she would not be able to assist with accommodation. And she warned of the very high rents.

My loving aunt fed the birds in Regents Park in the afternoons, but didn't 'bother with people, all I worry about is you all over there'. After her first major operation she endured severe pain in her legs – arthritis, she was led to believe – and got by on a steady intake of painkillers. Her sorrows poured into her airletters: she sometimes felt regret at having returned to England so hastily three years before. 'I wish I was 24 and know what I do now . . . It's the same old thing, work and sleep . . . I nearly went mad with the pain.'

How I wished we could get over there to give her company and comfort. Instead, when the truth of her illness became apparent, Mum flew to her sister, the cost of the air ticket loaned by a kindly, wealthy, Baghdad-born man in my office. In Auntie Edie's last letter she said how much she wished we could all be together again, and finished with: 'Well, Debbie, I am pleased to hear the good news, do hope you have a nice little girl'.

We did, on September 15, 1962, and we called her Julianne Edie. But by then Auntie Edie was gone.

I had switched jobs again, joining Abrahams Packaging in industrial Alexandria as a rep, with a swish, powerful, two-tone Holden car supplied. The phone-call about Auntie Edie was not unexpected, and when I got it one afternoon I went to the gents and the teardrops fell – until I could hear her voice saying, 'Come on, ducks, don't cry. I'm out of my misery now.'

Suddenly it mattered less that we could not get a buyer for the house. We prayed for Mum's safe return from her nightmare journey to England (naturally she brought back toys for the kids, from Hamleys, and a shirt for me from Austin Reed in Regent Street, 'where Mr Menzies gets his when he's in London'), and then we consolidated for a while with our expanded family, while Frank Ifield plaintively sang over and over *I Remember You.*

Our daughter was born – what a blessing – as a new cricket season began, and her father was mildly surprised to be graded in the firsts and to find himself opposing one of his heroes, Neil Harvey, in the opening match, at Chatswood Oval. After Sid Carroll, the NSW opener, had just failed to reach a career landmark of 10,000 runs, Harvey strolled in, head inclined, as always, and turned a ball to long leg. I chased, caught up with it, and stared at it: Neil Harvey had just hit this ball, the same Harvey who'd scored 118 at Headingley in 1948 on his Ashes Test debut. Wow! 'Come on, Frithy, chuck the bloody thing in!' came the cry. When Harvey was bowled for 10, I was severely disappointed.

On the second Saturday, ABC Radio's Bob Richardson came along to give live commentary. Our captain, Ted Cotton, who played six times for NSW, decided that my 'correct technique' now made me a No.3. But it didn't make me an attractive commentary subject, for my 29 took 100 minutes, and I've always believed that I helped the ABC make up its mind whether or not to continue to broadcast grade cricket. Dismissal came from a swerving offspinner from Harvey, a glittering consolation.

Toughing it out for Paddington against Northern Districts at Rushcutters Bay. Lyn Marks is at silly mid-on, John Phillips at gully

Against Glebe I had the chance to put my opinion of Frank Misson to the test. I really couldn't see how this lumbering blond fast bowler had been perceived as a Test player. His second ball, delivered with a distracting grunt, was surely going to be a bouncer? No. Off stump uprooted, with the batsman's feet glued to the crease. That evening, one of the umpires, Herb Elphinston, who had stood in that first Test match I ever saw, passed a helpful remark about my hesitant footwork, and never again could I stand accused of being reluctant to get in line to a quickie. The lessons were hard, and they were coming thick and fast.

Wisden, to whose editor I had just written with a list of errors spotted in the 1962 edition, continued to come to life. Against Waverley, I faced Gamini Goonesena (Ceylon and New South Wales) and Vic Jackson (Cahn's XI and Leicestershire); against Balmain, Dave Renneberg (soon to play for

Australia) and Ken Hough, who had claimed the wickets of Graveney, Watson and Cowdrey in his two Tests for New Zealand. Sixty-odd against them sent a young man home ecstatic. Against Petersham, we had to get Noel Hughes out. He'd played over in England, for Worcestershire. Against Cumberland, John Benaud (big Richie was absent) got me with a dubious lbw an hour after I'd caught a screaming flat hit from him at mid-off.

Paddington 1sts, 1962: DF, John Sweeney, Mort Cohen (former NSW opener and now club president), Rod Nicholson, Jack Cummins, David de Carvalho, Clarrie Pier (scorer), Graham Bastock; front: Eric Stockdale, Stan Gilchrist, Ted Cotton, Peter Davidson, Mick Burt (both cousins of Alan Davidson)

Then came Western Suburbs. Jim de Courcy played, he who had toured England with the 1953 Australians, and Ken Muller, one of Harold Larwood's sons-in- law (which somehow lent a thin veneer of awe). Most importantly, Bob Simpson and Alan Davidson were playing: a claw-sharpening exercise before the next Test against England. Simpson made a steady 134 not out and 'Davo' took 5 for 21. I should have been quaking with apprehension as I stepped out onto Pratten Park, our old school ground, but the recent runs had settled my fragile nerves. Davidson came cruising in, left-arm-over: the mind-blowing grunt; but the Misson grunt had cured me; the ball swung in late; I put a limp bat to it, and felt 20 feet tall. Having survived an over of fast swingers, I leant on my bat with what I hoped looked like nonchalance.

Later, when Simpson bowled a googly a trifle short, I pulled it for four. We were dismissed for 97, of which I made 31 – having held out against some leg-spin from Johnny Watkins, who was also to play (and freeze with nerves) for Australia.

When Simpson and Davidson went on to power Australia to victory over England at Sydney a few days later (Simpson 91 and 34 not out and 5 for 57 in the first innings; Davidson 4 for 54 and 5 for 25), Paddington's performance seemed a little less humiliating, and I fantasised about being perhaps not quite so far from Test standard after all. The delusion was not even destroyed when one of Jim Burke's bent-elbow offbreaks hit me on the thigh, and the umpire, who was now Burkey's best friend after all the preceding cheery chitchat between them, enthusiastically threw his index finger skywards.

Against Manly, cheap dismissal to a two-bouncer from Barry Rothwell was deflating. Stunned, I wandered back into the opposition's dressing-room. The giant Gordon Rorke, leading Manly in for the tea interval, gently steered me into the appropriate room.

Almost as exasperating was being barracked by some of Ted Dexter's England team from their motel balcony at Rushcutters Bay when we had a Sunday match. Mum and Debbie had come up for this one, and as they walked past the Travelodge, Freddie Trueman emerged. 'Oo, there's Freddie! Good old Fred! Come on, England!' cried my merry mother. Fred hurried away.

Given a bowl against Bankstown, I had both openers missed from stumpings as they piled on 264. One was Grahame Thomas, soon to make his Test debut. Swarthy grandson of Cherokee Indian who had fled the USA and made for the Australian goldfields, by all accounts his inclusion in Australia's 1966-67 tour of South Africa caused panic among local authorities. Now, against our humble attack, Thomas smashed 151: 302 for 5 was a challenge, but next Saturday it rained all day. When would life's next fillip occur?

Next week, actually, for Paddington played at the Sydney Cricket Ground, and this romantic dreamer heard his spikes crunching over the gravel in the members' area as the gateway through which all the greats had passed beckoned. Out onto the billiard-table outfield he went, to take guard and look around at this most captivating of cricket arenas, picturing Bradman as he composed his 452, and Hammond his rich scores, and MacLaren on his favourite ground. And what about McCabe . . .?

'Are you ready, batsman?' yelled the umpire, as bowler and fieldsmen glared, waiting impatiently for this newcomer who must surely have been in a trance. Never did a first-baller seem more likely.

I managed to avoid disgrace by scoring 17 in an hour's stay with Ted

Cotton, and never once threatened the paintwork on the picket-fence. We lost, and the last two Saturdays were washed out at Mosman. Then, in a social match, I had a finger badly fractured at short leg. But I'd played at the SCG, a phenomenon reserved just for dreams until now. Just as well that I had no future vision of the Sydney Cricket Ground of 2021, when television captured the action midst a heap of electronic adverts splashed across the field. How desperate cricket's money men have become. Today there are even flashing adverts around the boundary that instinctively draw the eye away from the game. This is unethical, and should be banned. It's all part of the global hysteria, and I can't see that any true cricket-lover would approve of it.

As for the 1962-63 Test series which ran in parallel with all this personal drama with Paddington, cricket-lovers of the future will scratch their heads when they ponder that the leaders in this dull and gruelling Ashes contest were renowned cavaliers: Benaud and Dexter. Then the names Lawry and Barrington will be seen, and much will be understood.

Before the first Test, New South Wales had beaten the Englishmen, with a remarkable spell from Benaud on the third day: a career-best 7 for 18 off 18.1 eight-ball overs. Short of blind attack, there seemed no clear way to get on top of him, so accurate were his legbreaks. Peter Parfitt top-scored with 22, and so often did the Middlesex left-hander thrust out his right pad that a desperate soul on the Hill shrieked out, 'Tie ya bat to ya leg, Parfitt! Then ya might make a run!' We had to laugh.

As Sheppard and Cowdrey batted England to victory at Melbourne, I ticked off the runs in my dingy little office at Abrahams. The only meaningful communication there was with Ken Cohen, nephew of Victor Cohen, who had managed the Australian team on their 1893 tour of England, and who said he had himself scored a double-century long ago for Paddington, apparently with Macartney in opposition. Most of the staff were Eastern Europeans.

I'd watched England at the nets at the SCG, and decided that David Allen's offspinners would trouble no-one, that Ray Illingworth's gentle outcurve was scoreable if you could drive, and that the huge David Larter was no great problem either, though he did bowl Dexter off the under-edge, causing the skipper to call out, 'Well bole'd!'

Barry Knight looked pretty straight too, while Ken Barrington's leggies were much too erratic. Then I caught sight of Statham. Oh Gawd, that's something else! Off five paces only, the Whippet almost took Tom Graveney's head off. And Titmus was making the ball speak, curving it out before it spat back. Even deputy wicketkeeper Alan Smith was wobbling the ball about. Meanwhile, Cowdrey, the old softie, was teasing and encouraging the net bowlers, defying them to make life difficult for him.

Yes, there was a gulf between us, of course there was, and I'd known all along that I wasn't equipped to bridge it.

Nonetheless, watching O'Neill, Harvey, Simpson, Booth and Davidson keep Australia in control during the Sydney Test was no longer like watching strangers. They were erstwhile team-mates and opponents, and it drew me nearer the core of the game. The complication now arising, of course, was that I'd enjoyed my chats with Parfitt and Cowdrey, and was starting to feel a confusion of allegiance. Doubts were held at bay in the final Test, also at Sydney and also drawn, when acute tension returned as Barrington approached his second century of the match. Where in the name of Grace was there a gap in the field? When would Hawke or Davidson give him a glimmer of a chance to score? Poor Kenny was virtually choked out. The outcome? c Grout b McKenzie 94. I could have wept.

But the real tears were for Auntie Edie still. And before long there came more shock and sadness as a close friend of my parents, a slave to drink and gambling, parked in the bush past Engadine and shot himself. His widow then tried to kill herself, survived, but was found in a railway waiting-room a few months later, staring into the distance, all life gone.

I Remember You. Too much sadness and frustration. Let's sell the house and get out of here.

CHAPTER TEN

We should not let our fears hold us back from pursuing our hopes.

JOHN F. KENNEDY

I THINK I was a good husband and father: food in the fridge, occasional outings, plenty of football and cricket in the backyard with the boys, pleasant pop music nearly always drifting out of the radiogram. I even invested in man's greatest invention, a movie camera, though the 8mm film was costly, and the priceless moments still preserved in moving colour sixty years later should have been part of a much larger collection. Undeterred by the lack of a telescopic lens, I shot away at the SCG, even capturing John Murray's leg-side catch off Lawry which severely damaged the wicketkeeper's shoulder. Video came at least 30 years too late.

And still the house wouldn't sell.

My sales job took me all over the North Shore of Sydney, tantalisingly close to some beckoning beaches, which had to be viewed from a distance. This was the weakest area for business, and that is why the young newcomer was put there. The most thrilling moment came at Dee Why when, as I idled at a crossroads, two cars smashed into each other. The large surf-board tied to the roof of one snapped from its moorings and came spinning through the air straight at my windscreen. It must have weighed a hundredweight or more and would have sliced my head off. I threw myself to the floor of the car – something I could not have done had seatbelts been in vogue – and shuddered as the board crashed onto the bonnet and bounced over the roof.

Having survived that, I wondered if we were all now about to be vaporised in a nuclear holocaust when the Cuban missile crisis was at boiling-point: President Kennedy getting tough with Khrushchev. With Roy Orbison, Gene Pitney and the Beach Boys still ringing in my ears, I pulled the car over to listen to a news flash. It must have been like this when Pearl

Harbor was attacked in 1941. Down there stretched Manly beach, with joyful, oblivious young people splashing about. And yet tomorrow we could all be cinders. Young parents in the early 1960s seemed to have become part of a Worry Generation.

The West Indies cricketers were taking entertainment with them wherever they went, and in 1963 they were in England, and we were lucky enough to get TV highlights in Sydney. The Lord's Test finish ranked among the most nail-biting, but the doings of Hunte, Kanhai, Sobers, Worrell and Gibbs, and Dexter, Trueman, Close and Barrington were soon forgotten as fresh tragedy struck.

Debbie's father sustained grievous head injuries in a road accident near Harrisville, close to Ipswich. She took the first available flight to Queensland and joined her sisters and mother in a hospital bedside vigil for two days. Then she rang to say that the hopeless wait had ended. Reuben 'Sonny' Pennell, 53, psychiatric nurse and Army Medical Corps veteran in North Queensland during the war, had been drinking with brother Gordon that afternoon. After a long session, Gordon had been at the wheel of the car when it failed to negotiate a culvert bridge on a bush road.

Leaving the boys with my parents at Kirrawee (Debbie had taken baby Julie with her), I flew to Ipswich, and acted as a pallbearer at the funeral, which was heavily attended. The forced acceptance that losses such as this are all part of life's chapters makes the coping no easier.

Only a few weeks later much of the civilised world was in grief when America's President was shot. News reached Sydney in the early morning. All who were alive at the time are said to have remembered vividly forever exactly where they were and what they were doing. I was about to venture down the pathway to the outside 'dunny' when first news of the shooting came over. As I re-entered the house, Debbie told me that John F.Kennedy was dead. We were stunned, like millions of others.

Would the big cricket at the SCG be cancelled that sad day? I still went, and before the NSW v South Africans match got under way, we experienced the old ground as it could never have been before: housing thousands of people, all standing for two minutes' silence, with the only sound coming from the pigeons that fussed around in the rafters of the old Sheridan Stand. Then Peter van der Merwe made a turgid century as the world cranked up once more on its axis.

I'd had the good fortune to be watching when a real star had burst on the scene a year earlier at the SCG No.2. They'd flown this 17-year-old lad up from Dungog when one of the batsmen broke down just before play in the NSW v Queensland Colts match. A waif-like figure under a large blue mushroom of a cap, he slammed 140 not out, striking one ball over the far wall and into Kippax Lake. Doug Walters was on his way.

As for the 1963-64 season, I played a further 13 first-grade matches for

Paddington, getting out to Test players with regularity – stumped by Brian Taber off Dick Guy (a renowned form of dismissal), out twice in one afternoon to the bewildering leg-spin variations of Peter Philpott, caught at leg slip off Alan Davidson, caught laughingly one-handed at slip by Jimmy Burke – but at least I made a top-score 20 against Davo's Wests, and a first-grade best of 70 not out at Glebe that took three hours and sent me home intoxicatingly satisfied. It was the highest score that day in first-grade matches. Another 70 came when I went back to Canterbury High School to play for the Old Boys, so at 26 it seemed that I was starting to get things right. It so happened that this was to be my last-ever season in Australia.

Sydney suburban family – with thoughts on England

The desperate search for a buyer for the house went on, until an enlightened estate agent claimed that no fibro house painted yellow would ever sell. So I lashed out on two huge cans of white paint, turned the transistor radio on, and slapped the first brushful on the wall as bubbly little Johnny Martin took up the attack for NSW against South Australia with his crazy left-arm twiddlers. By the time he had taken his sixth wicket (including Les Favell, Ian Chappell, Ian McLachlan and Garry Sobers) in 26 eight-ball overs, the house was transformed. Soon a buyer walked down the short front pathway, and we were able to book our passages to England.

That last summer, 1963-64, had produced an adequate ration of good Test and Shield cricket, some viewed live, some via shop-window television, the rest on the faithful radio on the front seat, between strategically-timed calls on clients and prospects. Once seen, Graeme Pollock was never to be forgotten. Nor was the tense conclusion to the last Test, eventually drawn after Tom Veivers and Neil Hawke had held on for an hour-and-a-half for the 10th wicket, rendering South Africa's task impossible. David de

Carvalho, my Paddington skipper, had wangled me into the SCG members' enclosure, and, believing cricket at this level to be an intense and unsmiling game – except when Wardle and Trueman were around, and perhaps Cowdrey – I was really taken back by Trevor Goddard's charming smile as he walked past us and through the gate to see if South Africa could make those 171 runs in 85 minutes to take the series in that final session. With him was that picture of pugnacity, Eddie Barlow, sleeves rolled up almost to the armpits.

The shock of the series had shaken Australia two months earlier, in the opening Test, at Brisbane, when Ian Meckiff was no-balled by umpire Col Egar for throwing. My team-mates were sitting on the grassy embankment when I came in from batting, and they seemed unduly quiet, even distracted. 'Hey,' I bleated, 'I didn't think I was *that* bad!'

'Shut up!' one of them said. 'Listen to this . . . Meckiff's been done for chucking!' In the aftermath I came to realise that being a good bloke in Australia – which Meckiff unquestionably was and is – had the effect of blinding people to certain stark realities. It was five years since the English Press had shown concern over the purity or otherwise of the Victorian's bowling action, and now the 'conspiracy' theories began to circulate. There was concern, too, about the bowling action of Charlie Griffith, the West Indian; yet when Benaud, O'Neill and Barrington all spoke out on the issue they were pilloried. The game of cricket was starting to look less than eternally radiant and chummy.

Years afterwards, I was taken back by Godfrey Evans' remark: England's manager Freddie Brown had wanted to lodge a formal complaint to the Australian Board over all these suspect actions, but was over-ruled by skipper Peter May. Bulldog Brown over-ruled? May, whose name had just been given to my baby son, wasn't the shy, mild and inoffensive young man that he seemed.

Now, our curiosity to see the sights of England and neighbouring countries was coupled with my desire to get into cricket journalism. So it was goodbye to Revesby's flatness, with its forest of clothes-hoists and flotilla of prams and cars roaring threateningly along Beaconsfield Street. From the house proceeds we paid Flotta Lauro £485 and we were Europe-bound on MV *Sydney*, the two of us plus three halves.

It was only later in life that the unwitting cruelty – but cruelty nonetheless – of my decision came home to me. We were taking from my parents, and from Debbie's folks up in Queensland, three of the loveliest children ever conceived. Perhaps it did not seem so bad when our headlong dash was halted with the question 'How long do you think you'll be over there?' We hadn't given that any thought. 'Ah, well, most people seem to make it about two years. Not much point going for less.'

Consequently, when two years had expired, the airletters contained pointed enquiries, particularly from my father. But we had no great desire to leave. England in the mid-1960s was simply a marvellous place to be.

The typically paranoid question had been 'Why d'you want to leave Australia?' The answer was simple enough: We didn't 'want to leave Australia'; but we did want to have a look at England. Was that such a crime? If we didn't do it now, even with only £700 to our name and three small mouths to feed, then the plan would have had to have been shelved for 20 years.

Even our taxi-driver was at it. He was from Lebanon, and as we drove away from the house, he piped: 'Why you wanna leave 'Strahlia, huh? Ees the grydest country in the world!' His commitment was commendable, doubtless the result of repeated questions like 'How d'ya like it in our country?' and encouragement such as 'You're an 'Stralian now!'

It seemed half of Europe was there on the wharf that night, jostling and barging, shouting, laughing, weeping. The Friths tried to keep their upper lips steady, but all along the tightly-packed passageways were mini-tornadoes of emotion. The farewells were heart-rending. It was too late to change our minds now. Wasn't it?

We were on the bottom deck, sixteen to a cabin, and I claimed a bunk in the men's quarters which backed on to where Debbie tried to get settled with 18-month-old Julie. That way I could tap on the bulkhead reassuringly through to her. Mum and Dad gave us touching little going-away gifts just before the dreaded All Visitors Ashore announcement boomed through the loudspeakers, and I could not bear to watch as my mother said goodbye to her moppet grand-daughter and golden- haired grandsons. This was distress I had been too dumb ever to have foreseen. Then my father withdrew, and my mother, so motherly, came to us one more time for a final goodbye. Then they were gone, and we were alone with the other occupants of this stuffy cabin, old women and young, many with children, with much crying and whispering.

We composed ourselves and climbed upstairs to join the smoky babble along the ship's railings. Far below were the folks, small figures in the crowd, waving helplessly as we stood helplessly and waved back, unable to touch each other any longer. When the ship's siren suddenly resounded piercingly above us, little Johnny burst into tears. Lucky fellow.

We prayed for the ropes to be cast off to ease our misery, and at long last we were drifting away, paper streamers stretching and snapping while the emotional Italian songs echoed across the water. Our faces must have merged with the night long before we finally lost sight of my parents and brother, waving faithfully still into the gloom.

Rough seas up the east coast made that first night horrendous. In Debbie's cabin a young Lebanese woman moaned and cried all night with sickness, as did her five children. When I went in at 5am the stench was dreadful. Debbie had tried to comfort the children, all of them, but the situation was hopeless. Our own kids complained of the odd feeling in their little stomachs. The thin coastline mocked. How lovely to have been on the highway in a good car, with a tasty motel breakfast on schedule, and Queensland mountain ranges up ahead.

In the male cabin, where men of several nations co-existed, some were groggy, but merely stayed on their bunks and prayed or made light of their discomfort, while up on deck footholds were treacherous and lines of washing flapped in the wind. The sour smell down below was even drifting up to the deck.

I went to see the purser, Sacha, a tall and smooth fellow who had much on his mind. I demanded some sort of relief from our predicament. He promised he would sort something out in Brisbane; the rotund commissario nodded in support; and a nurse gave the Lebanese woman a sedative needle. As a big Dutch woman emitted a monstrous retching which failed to produce results, I saw Peter, our five-year-old, staring at her with frightened eyes, and I talked to him about something stupid to divert him. It seared my conscience to think that I had subjected my family to such horrors.

We berthed in Brisbane, and had a picnic with Debbie's mother and sisters and other relatives at the Botanical Gardens. Then it was another trying time as we bade them farewell. And off into another cyclone we sailed.

At least now we were installed together in a cabin of our own. We clung to each other as the vessel pitched and tossed, crockery smashing, passengers down the corridor crying out. Our suitcases slid madly around the mosaic floor, and we groaned helplessly, praying for tomorrow.

Next day we paid close attention to lifeboat drill, for we had already twice faced the probability of being flung into the sea. As we sailed into calmer waters, and confidence and enjoyment levels rose, so three-year-old Johnny regularly disappeared, down in a cabin with one of the dozen or so girls who seemed to fancy him. Whenever he went missing we searched feverishly all over the ship and across the acres of waves, hoping to spot his blond hair before it was too late. Usually there were hundreds of thousands of white flecks on the surface of the sea, and only the reappearance of his swaggering little figure along the deck eased away our anguish.

Was it all worth it? England had better be good.

The lashing wind whisked clothes from the washing-lines on deck, and the food was always a bit too Italian, but we grew used to the routines and hardships, and forced ourselves to relax, and enjoyed the ports of call no end: Singapore, which we did thoroughly by taxi, spending as little time as possible in the bazaars, where money was a necessity, but walking miles, the little ones displaying a hardiness which made me proud; Bombay (Mumbai), where we took a gharri ride before footing it for miles, trailing a crowd of dumbstruck, curious admirers behind us, and angering some street people in their straw huts by trying to film them; then onward, past the haunting cragginess around Aden, into the sweltering Red Sea, and through the Suez Canal, fifteen years on since the schoolboy had last passed through it.

Young Peter had lapped it all up – even listening to the padre, who greatly resembled Burl Ives, telling long stories in Italian. We had stretched out on deck in the best of the weather, reckoning we owed ourselves a bit of this. I read Nabokov's *Laughter in the Dark* fairly quickly, and soon tired of my dark beard. We should have won the fancy-dress contest as Cleopatra and Mark Antony, except we were not part of the Italian 'in crowd' who manipulated the voting.

From Port Said we entered a choppy Mediterranean which was soon trying to upend the *Sydney*, not the most stable of ships. Once more the world was a ghastly place. Once more we were about to die, and wondering why we'd ever left our little Revesby home.

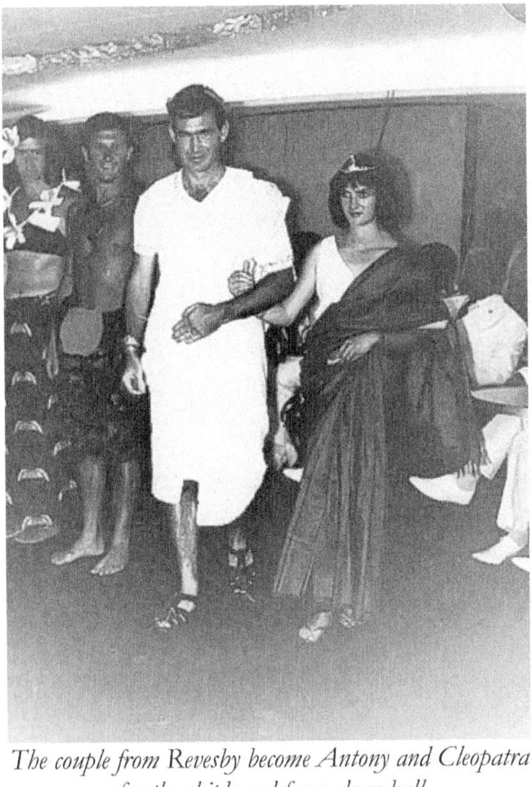

The couple from Revesby become Antony and Cleopatra for the shipboard fancy-dress ball

So turbulent was our progress and so close to death did we feel that when Peter manfully slithered over to the cabin door and announced that he was going to get us something to eat (he'd heard a steward urging us to force something down), we were too enfeebled to restrain him. The door slammed shut behind him as the ship made another violent lurch, and I feared we'd never see our elder son again.

We tried to raise ourselves, but fell reeling backwards. It was hopeless. As we were tossed and pressed down and slewed sideways, control of the mind ceased. What a way to die.

Then the door burst open and in stumbled our little boy, his arms loaded with bread-rolls. Though the violent motion continued, our hearts lifted. If only they minted gallantry medals for five-year-olds. After further heaving into buckets, the Friths fell into various half-sleeps.

A breezy, sunny morning brought recovery, and soon we were tied up in Valetta Harbour, Malta, watching the locals embrace in reunion and fascinated by the gondolas. Up the eastern coastline of Sicily we chugged, marvelling at the glow from Mount Etna in the evening darkness, and berthing late in Messina to a reception of blaring car-horns and flashing headlights. Soon the only sound was the unearthly wailing of a black-veiled widow on the quayside as a coffin was landed. Her husband's body had travelled with us all the way from Brisbane.

I went ashore with some of the other men and we walked miles through the parks and piazzas. I took in the wartime scarring from shells and bullets on the buildings and counted myself lucky to get back to the ship without having been kidnapped by the Mafia, who clearly were unaware that I had almost £20 on my person.

We slipped out of Messina, past the Garibaldi statue floodlit in green, and next morning our excitement grew as the sparkling Isle of Capri presented itself. The little camera whirred.

We nosed across the vast Bay of Naples, Vesuvius towering in the mist, the thousands of waving, sobbing, cheering Italians somehow making us feel lonely. Embarking on our customary pedestrian marathon, we could hardly believe the traffic chaos, Fiats and motor-scooters screeching and careering around so crazily that Sydney's rough-and-tumble driving seemed a treat by comparison. Then we met our con man.

He said he would drive us free of charge to the top of town and he was a prisoner-of-war in Lancashire and his brother lived in Sydney. Up the winding road we went, until we had a panoramic view of Napoli. We pulled up in Via Tito Angellini, and he led us into a cameo factory, despite our protests.

It took some time to convince him and his friends that we had no cash for cameos. Then he began his demands for money. Nervously, we got back into the car as he gestured menacingly, and throughout the five or six miles back to the city our escort was chattering and gesticulating. I managed to slide the few notes in my wallet down into my sock, and when he made his final demand, eyes now flashing menacingly, I showed him my small change

– four shillings – and Debbie, upon demand, handed him her purse, which had seven shillings in it. He hungrily grabbed the lot.

Shaken, we bought some buns and sat by the fountain near the fortress, and talked to an elderly couple from New York. Then it was time to rejoin our ship, the wharf now empty and silent.

As we throbbed further north it was like a ghost ship. Social life had ended and everybody was busy packing. Tomorrow the voyage ended at Genoa. Five quid for the taxi to the railway station (a five- minute journey) and our travelling allowance was nearly exhausted. Cold batter fingers made us feel sick, and as I sprinted back and forth relaying our luggage along the platform, Debbie was ill, while Julie's gastric condition became even worse. It was a relief to slump into the seats and feel the carriage moving us towards England.

Three uncomfortable hours later we reached Milan, and as we sat waiting for continuation of journey, two of the young Australians from the ship passed beneath our window. 'Where ya goin' to, Amsterdam?' one called out. Of course we weren't. 'Youse'd better change quick then!'

So we hurled our cases down to Doug and Merv, and after a hectic search for a currency exchange that would take Australian pounds, we made our connection with seconds to spare. I would rather have faced Muhammad Ali than subject my young family to all this.

Sleep came, shortly after we had rumbled through the Simplon Tunnel, with heavenly visions beyond of snow-capped Swiss mountains and the moon reflecting on the lakes. Stomachs were more settled, and next morning our spirits rocketed at the sight of French fields and villages and chateaux as we swayed and clattered north-westwards.

Using my Leaving Certificate French and enjoying the curiosity it brought to Parisian faces, I ordered us a pavement meal, and then a taxi, which, in the short transit time available, was requested to take us to every known attraction. But such was the traffic snarl, we did little more than circumnavigate the block before I was forced to tell our driver to 'retournez à la gare, s'il vous plâit!' Bit of a let-down, although at least we had seen Place de la Bastille and Notre Dame Cathedral.

Through the low country we purred, into Calais, now feeling as weak as mice, mother and daughter almost prostrate from the stomach ailments. When all the luggage had been heaved on board the ferry (which had taken part in the Dunkirk rescue in 1940), we got what we so desperately needed: the reassuring sound of English voices as the crew asked if we'd like some tea and strawberry-jam sandwiches. A little kindness at last.

It was 15 years and 106 days since the good ship *Orion*, bearing the Frith family, had steamed down this Channel, Australia-bound. Understandably, I was moist of eye and tight at the throat. And how did this new Frith family feel? The children looked eagerly ahead, and Debbie felt genuinely excited, an unexpected sense of 'coming home'. Years later we discovered that the first of her ancestors to journey to Australia (as a free settler) came from Lewisham, which in the 1850s was still regarded as being in Kent.

Another ancestral fact as yet unrevealed was that in 1915, here in Dover Harbour, my great-uncle Jim Frith, in Army uniform and with rifle over his shoulder, had drowned. He had enlisted in the East Surrey Regiment, and having returned one night, on leave from the fighting in France, he had slipped while disembarking from a torpedo-boat in Granville Dock and his heavy pack dragged him to the sea-bed.

I wish I'd been aware of this tragedy at the time, but I wasn't. What I did know was that we were seriously fatigued, perilously low on money, but close to 'home', which was to be temporary accommodation in Surrey with the family of one of Mum's cousins.

Down there on the wharf, was that policeman in the phallic blue helmet real? Surely not? He must have been put there as a symbol just for us. And were these fields sprayed with some sort of rich green intensifier, or had our sight been affected by the weeks of travel? We just sat there and let the train speed us Londonwards. Debbie freshened up in the powder-room, and poor Julie, in her cute green knitted dress, had come back to life. Just as brave were her brothers, heroes of five and three. The little film I made is a precious reminder.

Now it was all rooftops and flowering cherry-trees as we neared London; and finally, Victoria station. Off stepped the five daring travellers and out came the eight suitcases (containing, among much else, my cricket library of 60 books) and four overnight bags. We knew that nobody would be there to meet us: thoughts of Auntie Edie were whispering tantalisingly. But a West Indian porter came up, flashing a grin, and began to stack our luggage on his trolley.

We had a Chertsey address to find, and as we were very, very tired I thought we'd take a taxi all the way, so would he kindly wheel our stuff to the taxi-rank?

'That's fine, sir,' said the porter. And he looked at our three children, sleepy but still unprotesting. 'No need for you to tip me, sir. I mean it.'

'Thank you very much,' I replied wearily but oh so gratefully.

CHAPTER ELEVEN

To be happy at home is the ultimate end of all ambition.

SAMUEL JOHNSON

LORD'S was slightly disappointing. The Sydney Cricket Ground had been 'home' for so long, and now, after 11 days in England, I sat on a low-slung seat under a gloomy overhang, at the Nursery end, watching Price, Bennett, Hooker and Titmus bowling to Sussex in the 1964 spring bank holiday County Championship fixture, the temperature a touch chilly, the applause mechanical and lightweight, 'atmosphere' non-existent. At least there was the great Victorian pavilion, and the old Tavern, with its friendly congregation on the concourse, pints in hand. My birthplace was about a mile away. Perhaps, in due course, I'd be lucky enough to sample Lord's at Test match time. Maybe I'll even be in the Press-box one day.

From our stopover in Chertsey, we needed to move on, a problem resolved only when, in desperation, I rang Mrs Eve Heath, a jovial, caring Tory councillor and mother of Nigel, a pal of mine in Sydney, whose brother Malcolm bowled from a great height for the 1961 county champions Hampshire. 'You must come over, my dears,' came her jolly invitation down the phone-line.

So at leafy Walton-on-Thames, in Surrey's stockbroker belt, where blackbirds trilled in the trees and bushes that abounded, our recuperation from our travels continued, and our destiny as Surrey citizens accidentally was sealed.

From there, we secured a house lease in Worcester Park (future prime minister John Major was then living a street or two away) and I found work. Almost equally importantly, I found a cricket club, Cheam, where I was made welcome, regarded with a certain amount of curiosity, and took 7 for 36 with offspin on my first outing to show that they were being far too cautious in placing me in the 3rd XI. For the first of countless occasions in the decades of English club cricket to follow I was lbw to a short ball that shot through low as I instinctively aimed a pull shot. At 27, my batting technique was already 'in the blood', beyond modification.

I had written to Middlesex requesting a trial. A Sydney first-grader surely stood some chance of making the county 2nd XI at least? The kindly Jack Robertson, county coach and former Test batsman, put me in a net for 10 minutes on the Lord's Nursery ground and I patted about nervously at the five fast-medium bowlers (three of them West Indians) until Mr Robertson said softly that they'd let me know in due course. It was nice of him not to have issued a warranted 'Hope you have many happy years of club cricket' – which is what I did.

After a season with Cheam I switched to East Molesey, where half-a-dozen Inland Revenue employees held sway. There was then no league, and the cricketers seemed to fire themselves up only on the bitchiness that came from recalling how the opposition had batted on too long three years ago. This, and the nonsense talked over the evening gin-and-tonics and dishwater beer, and the lousy pitches that turned mediocre trundlers into 80-wickets-a-season 'stars', annoyed me.

Otherwise, though, we were extremely happy. Declining a packaging sales job with British Cellophane that would have taken us to Somerset, I took a punt on Servowarm, selling central-heating systems around Surrey and Middlesex and south-west London, working mainly in the evenings, when Mr and Mrs were both at home to listen to my spiel, and entering, in all, about 3000 homes before this 'career' ended. The worst of it was going out in the little red Hillman Imp on nights of blizzards and ice, when only a swig of cherry brandy gave me lift-off. Nor was it much fun when hours of presentation set up seemingly certain sales only for the prospective customers to say they wished to 'think it over'. I was never ruthless enough to brush this aside and demand signature and deposit.

Still, there was enough commission to keep us fed and housed, and the advantages of free weekdays were Heaven-sent. Having bought a 1911-built semi-detached in Tolworth/Surbiton (*The Good Life* territory), with only a tiny patch of garden to care for, we were surrounded by friendly middle-aged and elderly neighbours who all seemed to think the children darlings and Australians in general among the world's most acceptable people.

I reported to head office in Acton once a week, and there the reps gathered in the pub to tell of their triumphs, with one or two, in the characteristic English custom, getting very steamed-up and anxious about events around the world, chiefly in Vietnam. Their soapboxing, which would get them nowhere, got me down. It made me isolationist.

How long before I became a cricket-writer? I arranged to meet Arthur

Langford down in Cobham. He ran *The Cricketer*, and I tried to get him to publish my thoughts on English club cricket as compared to Australian grade cricket. He talked about Plum Warner and this and that, but never invited me in, and never accepted my article.

Writers, like batsmen, need patience.

I played for Cheam against an MCC team and fell to another quality dismissal: c Eric Bedser b Stuart Surridge. And when we all sat around at the bar later, Surridge, leader of Surrey to five consecutive Championships in the recent 1950s, gave me a crushing handshake and asked if I'd like a ticket to the Oval Test. I certainly would. So I gave him my address, and two days later the ticket arrived in the post . . . accompanied by an invoice.

I identified fairly strongly with Bob Simpson's 1964 Australians, without necessarily wanting them to retain the Ashes. Timing my Servowarm calls as best I could either side of Test broadcasts and television, I rode John Edrich to his Ashes-debut century in the Lord's Test (having seen him and Micky Stewart make a big first-wicket stand in the Surrey match at the grimy old Oval, when an old fellow next to me muttered that 'Wally 'Ammond's not playing today': it took a while to work out that the old boy in the cloth cap was fixed firmly in a time-warp and that he'd meant to say Ken Barrington, who was absent injured); I'd felt a thrill at Queenslander Burge's crashing 160 at Headingley, and was probably the only person in the land to feel equal delight at Bob Simpson's 311 and Barrington's 256 and Dexter's 174 at Old Trafford; and then it was time to present my expensive ticket at the Oval turnstiles. The Ashes were already safe for Australia, but England could still level the series. What did I get for my money? England all out 182 on a dull day, Neil Hawke 6 for 47, with Dexter's bat hilariously split in half from splice to toe. At least the car was still intact that evening, parked in Fentiman Road. Couldn't do that today – like so much else. Fred Trueman's famous 300th Test wicket was taken on the Saturday, but I was elsewhere, doing my bit for Cheam.

As the job settled down and friendships were made – like the one at Cheam with the fatherly former Surrey player Eddie Watts, from whom I'd bought a bat for £2 – the feelings of insecurity receded a little. Letters back and forth to family in Australia were never a substitute for the lost close proximity, but the enticement of colourful London and the historical attractions and the fresh beauty of the countryside repeatedly suggested that we'd done the right thing – though reminders of Auntie Edie, conjured by the sight of Swan & Edgar's building in Piccadilly and Selfridges in Oxford Street and Hamley's toy shop, taunted the soul with what might have been.

The libertarian yet cosy 1960s were Beatles, Stones and Kinks, the Aberfan disaster, Donald Campbell, The Seekers (who had arrived from Australia on the ship behind ours), Harold Wilson and pipe, *Z Cars*, Francis Chichester, England's World Cup triumph (when we dashed up to

Knightsbridge and saw the footballers and that manipulative Prime Minister on the hotel balcony). These years were Tom Jones (an obvious star from that first *Top of the Pops* experience) and George Best, the Hollies, Peter & Gordon, crackpot (but evil) Jimmy Savile, and Jimmy Tarbuck, and military uniforms illegally worn by long-haired lads. It was, for us, a decade of hope and impatience, curiosity and excitement; of recurring insecurity too, which is better coped with when you are young. And memory's long reel of unfading images takes in not only Ted Dexter's broken bat but the Moody Blues (*Go Now* another instant pointer), the Zombies and Lou Christie, and our welcome on-screen Scottish guests Bill Simpson (met him once at a cricket function), Andrew Cruickshank and Barbara Mullen, the *Doctor Finlay* cast, at the solid, reassuring Arden House; and the wonderful Pete and Dud; and the moving monochrome portrayals in *The Forsyte Saga*, which kept millions away from church on Sunday evenings; and the disturbing Alf Garnett, and the revolting Steptoes. We coasted along to the beat of the Spencer Davis Group and the Crystals, Herman's unimaginative Hermits, and the Bee Gees from good old Oz, the Righteous Brothers, who shivered the soul, and the Mamas & Papas, who challenged one's sense of responsibility. Buffalo Springfield's beautiful tone and delicacy caused a catching of the breath, and Bobby Vee restored high-school bounce just as Bobby Goldsborough elicited a gentle tear. The Association, too, rekindled that college concert-stage sound, an ongoing reminder that it had not always been an adult world of ominous pressures to survive. And the serious stuff, the television news, was brought to us by the smooth-haired, smooth-voiced Corbet Woodall and Michael Aspel – and the cheeky, rebellious Reggie Bosanquet, whose father popularised the googly early this century, and whom I had caught (Reggie) in a charity match.

Not quite the set of images that had drawn thoughts to England in the 1950s. Then, it was *Doctor in the House* and *Genevieve*, David Tomlinson and Margaret Rutherford and Cecil Parker, healthy, toothy Tommy Steele, *Dixon of Dock Green*, Dickie Valentine's clear, throaty voice, Lita Rosa and Ruby Murray, sweet innocence scoffed at by future neurotic generations. England was also the dashing Mike Hawthorn and Geoff Duke, whose escape into speed was the envy of many. There was the serious reminder of bravery and suffering in *The Cruel Sea*, and the unadulterated joy of *The Titfield Thunderbolt*. As Norman Collins wrote of London in his book with the tantalising title – *London Belongs to Me* – people are regularly 'savouring the simple but tremendous pleasure of merely being there'. Couple that with something Sir Don Bradman wrote in his autobiography and you have it: 'Nothing in this world has ever appealed to me more than England as nature made her.'

We pottered along, my customers in seven years of central-heating activity including a film producer, a Czech partisan, a county cricketer, a journalist, a mortician (I was ill-prepared for what I saw in the tiled room out the back), an actor, a chap named Mr V.Trumper, a lord, a count, the widow of Lord Brabazon, and a gentleman named Sir Gordon Covell who recalled colourfully one or two performances in the 1890s by the epileptic Lancashire spinner Johnny Briggs, whom he described as a 'funny little object'.

Cricket talk, of course, sometimes stretched my calls well beyond the two-hour average, though I was never exactly over-run by appointments. Those who hung around the office and drank with the management got fistfuls of leads – and probably many that should have come my way.

The first winter was a shock. Long before the lowest temperature was reached we wondered if it could possibly get any colder. It was simply terrifying. But Debbie and I couldn't let the kids sense our apprehension. The old sash windows let in knifing jets of freezing air. It was ironic that the paper I used to stuff down the gaps was the *Sydney Morning Herald.*

Peter came home from school highly agitated that first autumn, hollering that all the leaves were falling off the trees. Wouldn't the country be in a terrible mess. I comforted him, telling him it always had been in a mess. Then, after one of those long, boring spells of unbroken grey skies, three-year-old Julie pointed urgently through the car windscreen and screeched 'What's that!' She thought invaders from Space were about to land. But the 'gold ball' was only the long-lost sun.

The death of Winston Churchill in January 1965 was not so much a shock (he was 90), but it was the removal from our living ranks of a major symbolic foundation-stone. My tribute was to break a lifetime rule by rising voluntarily in the early hours. I drove through a chill, dark morning to take up position near St Paul's Cathedral and await the funeral cortege, 8mm movie camera at the ready, loaded with sombre black-and-white film. In the post-war years, Churchill and Montgomery had been superseded, I suppose, by Hutton, Bedser and others as heroic figures, but I knew that the impact and influence of the defiant wartime Prime Minister would always remain the greatest.

The snow was a delight for Peter, John and Julie, but a worry to their parents. How do you prevent the little car from spinning on the icy road? How do you stay upright on the icy footpath? I may have experienced enough of this stuff years ago, but fear of breaking a limb didn't seem to come into it then. Now, the safest thing was to be huddled over the fireplace. I was a stranger to England, a foreigner.

A leak in the roof caused the ceiling to crash down in the boys' bedroom and myself to think about selling up and getting back to the climatic safety of Sydney. But all this was offset by new places and people – as well as old ones, like dear Cissie and her family in cockney Bermondsey (she used to work in Dad's shop and had faithfully sent newspapers and gifts to us in Sydney for years), and like Aunt Flo, now in her seventies, youngest of Grandma's sisters, still serving the Salvation Army but just a few years away from senility. She was a marvel for no other reason than that she told us of her view of Queen Victoria passing in her open carriage. She also spoke about the traumatic experience when she was only three years old, soon after the death of her mother, of discovering her Fulham fishmonger father hanging from the rafters. Having recently lost his wife, he couldn't cope with the shop and looking after the seven children.

The adult DF back in England, with his Australian family: Hampton Court Palace

This was but one tragic episode among several in the ancestral archives. The horrific collision and sinking of the pleasure steamer *Princess Alice* on the Thames near Woolwich one night in September 1878 cost over 600 lives: two of them were female members of the Frith family, Emma and daughter Rose. I was gratified to read recently that the 1878 Australian touring cricketers made a sizable donation to the relief fund. They had done well out of that speculative pioneering tour, but their generosity is touching.

And there was another troubled ancestor: Tom Orrock came from a highly respected family, makers of exquisite and prized Orrock glassware, and was himself a cabinet-maker, and a chapel regular. But this young man was led astray: he aimed to rob a chapel in Dalston one foggy night in 1882, and shot a policeman dead. It was almost two years before he was re-arrested while in prison on another count; and he was represented in court by a Mr Willis. Found guilty of murder. The black flag was hoisted, and Orrock was soon dealt with by the renowned hangman James Berry at Newgate Prison. What had sealed his fate was smart police work: Orrock was one of a group of young men who had practised shooting on Tottenham marshes; the bullets were retrieved from the tree and matched against his pistol and with the shot which killed PC George Cole. Orrock was arrested while serving a prison sentence for jewel theft. Conan Doyle later used elements of this pioneering detective work in his book *A Study in Scarlet.* I declare my descent from the esteemed Orrock *family*, but not directly from the murderous Tom.

So up the M1 we went in 1965, to Scotland, five of us crammed into the little Imp, cries of 'Take him over, Dad! Take him over!' coming from the back seat, suggesting I had bred offspring a little more competitive than myself – more on a par with Stirling Moss. Four days we spent on the island of Mull, in the Inner Hebrides, without understanding more than just an occasional word from the locals: and vice versa. On the long drive home Whitby Harbour, on the Yorkshire coast, stirred thoughts of Captain Cook.

And as the years passed. more history was absorbed at Hampton Court Palace, and the favourite among castles, Bodiam, with its moat.

Down to Cornwall we went, stopping at Itchen Abbas, above Winchester, in an unsuccessful attempt to trace the grave of Squire Powlett, a founder of Hambledon cricket. But we located the grave of Felix (Nicholas Wanostrocht) in Wimborne Minster, and mighty Gilbert Jessop's in Dorchester. In the years ahead the search for cricketers' graves was to result in the discovery of hundreds more, a rewarding hobby, though certain people have unaccountably regarded it as 'morbid'.

In Lyme Regis, Dorset we had tea with G.D.Martineau, the learned and aged author of some cricket books. And in due course we touched the ancient columns of Stonehenge and stayed in Lorna Doone country. A weekend in South Wales made *How Green Was My Valley* come true. There really was much to write home about.

No experience was more mind-splitting than seeing the Beach Boys perform at the Finsbury Astoria. There they were, my special group, in their striped short- sleeve shirts, harmonising visions of surf-beaches and sun, while outside the theatre rain pelted down on the cold London pavements and the wind pushed people's heads down into their scarves and raincoats. Yet again, the soul was torn.

Life expanded. Debbie did some art modelling, and I played midweek cricket with Romany and Public School Wanderers, besides working on my golf at the driving range. Nostalgic trips to Rayners Lane were slightly disappointing, but were somehow compelling. There were no familiar faces of family or neighbours any more: people from other lands lived there now; and the once-vacant kerbs where we skinned our young fingers at five-stones were now given over to motor cars. Never mind: man's greatest invention, the camera, had done its job years ago.

Occasionally we drove up to London to see a West End show, and some winter nights I'd keep clear in order to go to Wembley, not for the speedway but to see England play soccer. They usually won. Other times the simplest pleasures were the best: sitting on the landing outside the kids' bedroom and listening to their enchanting conversation. I recorded one little epic:

John: *Pete, a boy in your clath told me thomething.*

Peter (surly, in big-brother tradition): What?

John: *He thaid he had a bag of gold.*

Peter: He's a liar.

John: *Yeth, I know, Pete.*

It might almost have been where Messrs Cook and Moore got their material from. Trying desperately not to giggle out loud, I recorded some more:

I'm not afraid of anything in the world. Are you, Pete?

No.

Julie ith, ithn't she?

Yeah.

Who'th afraid to eat Englith thnakes?

I'm not.

Who'th afraid to eat a crocodile?

(Hesitation) – I'm not.

Nor am I, Pete. Are you afraid of eating elephanth?

Yeah, a bit.

Why are you, Pete?

Because they blow water at you, and you might get pneumonia.

Several yawns, then: *I'm going to get rest.*

Me too, Pete.

At other times, when minor offences were committed, the parental inquisition was met with 'Not me!' followed by 'Not me!' followed by the little poppet's 'Me *neether*!', Julie's eyes wide as saucers, beaming innocence. How glad I am that we made the very best of them. An Englishness overtook them, of course, but they never forgot their Australian origins.

And my cricket? The whole family now went most weekends. The boys had been taken to the Hill at the SCG when still barely able to speak, spending the afternoon picking up bottle-tops (beer-cans were just about to be introduced) while their father was trying to interest them in Meckiff bowling to Simpson and so on. Now they both played promisingly themselves. Peter was a John Edrich-type left-hander and fast bowler and John worshipped Ken Barrington, cutting like him – straight into the garbage container, hence the 'dustbin shot'.

As for their father, I should have done better, should have shown more respect to the bowling, which was mainly ordinary. Showing contempt for it, I got myself out too often. Roger Harman, a slow left-armer, had taken 127 wickets for Surrey in 1964, and when I popped him over the sightscreen it seemed to symbolise how slim was the difference between club and county cricket. An illusion, of course. And instead of playing safe with off-spin, I should have stayed with the Lindwall stuff a few more years, exploiting responsive English club pitches, or else had the courage to bowl legspin/googlies, which were so successful in the nets, where I was relaxed. Concentration was sometimes a problem; yet it shouldn't have been, for I had undergone a dramatic lesson in shutting out distraction one Saturday at Rushcutters Bay in a Sydney grade match. As I walked the long walk to the middle, there were distractions all around me: RAAF Gannets doing an aerial display above; a regatta gracefully getting under way on the bay; exotic Continental women strolling along Waratah Street; tennis players whacking their soft ball around the adjoining courts; ballerinas and elephants preparing themselves outside the circus marquee in the neighbouring field; and the sound of *Be Bop a Lula* floating across the road from a Gene Vincent and the Blue Jeans rehearsal at Sydney Stadium.

Next thing I knew I was walking dazedly back to the pavilion, bowled first ball by Merv Black.

In 1965 I was bowled by Dave Gibson for nought in a benefit match for Micky Stewart at East Molesey, but was soon in good company as Ken Barrington also got a duck, bowled by a shooter. Dear old Kenny stomped off to his car and went home. Cricket the ruthless leveller again. John Edrich hit a century, mostly off me, in 44 minutes. I managed to see some of the England v New Zealand and v South Africa Tests in person, and much on TV, with radio commentary filling the gaps. At Edgbaston, where it was so chilly that hot drinks had to be served, Barrington made a century so slowly that he was dropped, leaving our little John puzzled. He was not alone. At Headingley, John Edrich made a stunning 310 not out to show what he thought about being dropped by England a year previously – and Barrington came back with another century, a bit faster this time. I was present when Edrich, in the next Test, took a sickening blow on his unprotected temple from a Peter Pollock bouncer. Helped off, he passed out later, and came to in a hospital near Lord's only to see nuns in white. It took a few seconds for him to establish that he wasn't now in the Promised Land.

By now I'd picked up some work from Reg Hayter, whose Fleet Street sports agency was flourishing. I did a few soccer and rugby reports for provincial papers, the fee barely exceeding travelling expenses, and at Lord's and The Oval I rang copy through for Learie Constantine (with whom I had a very meaningful chat about belonging to two communities) and one or two others, also running J.M.Kilburn's meticulous handwritten essays over Waterloo Bridge and down the road to the *Yorkshire Post* offices. Some of the best conversations and friendships began here: with Ian Peebles and Bill Bowes, England Test stars of the 1930s, and with Crawford White and E.M.Wellings and Alan Ross. The friendship which had by far the most telling consequences, however, was with John Arlott.

At the Old Sun, Alresford,
with friend and mentor John Arlott

His 21-year-old son Jimmy had been killed in a road accident early on New Year's Day 1965. A year later I'd got John to sign a book or two, and I joked about seeing him suffering in the heat at Sydney a few years earlier. There was a rapport here which may have surprised us both, and he became my warrant for entry to the Press-box until such time as I had my own credentials. Soon I became a regular at his home in Alresford, a privilege and delight that had a unique effect on me. There I met interesting people. There I drank all manner of wines, and first ate lampries. There I stood with my rear to the fireplace and talked of Australia and cricket and football, and listened to John Arlott on his favourites, Hobbs and Tate, Tennyson and Mead, Dylan Thomas and John Betjeman, and sometimes Nyren and Beldham and Walker. Valerie cooked and broadened the conversation. John sat at the head of that great oak table and delivered his opinions and impressions and reminiscences in a Hampshire light baritone that was the most famous voice in England. Seldom did a minute pass before another roar of laughter rang out, or at very least a chuckle, and seldom did an hour pass without a caller of some sort ringing the doorbell, and easily joining the gathering, even if he be merely the window-cleaner or the chap who'd come to fix the kitchen tap. It was, in its way, a royal household, and I rejoiced to be part of it.

I think we saw each other as vaguely father and son: I was some sort of vague substitute for the tragically-taken Jimmy, and I saw John as the Dad I'd left behind in Sydney and whose attitude towards me had changed, perhaps because he sensed that I could no longer maintain that adulation the small boy had once felt for his uniformed hero of a father.

This new friendship survived argument – that must have been the key – only once leaving me wondering if it was all over: we had a tense row in which I took a high – probably pious – moral stance on the matter of journalistic expenses, some time in the early 1980s. The breach was healed midst multiple slurps of Beaujolais.

Over the years, I spent countless days and nights at his spacious home, the best times being when we were alone, the noisiest times being the Alresford golf days, which coincided with the annual fair; and the Christmases, when around 20 of us (I dubbed us 'Men of Arlott') would dine exceptionally well at the George in Winchester and each of us would tell a funny story in an effort to win a strange piece of pottery, to be retained for a year. I won it once with an apocryphal and recently- borrowed (how many aren't?) tale concerning Keith Miller: in his twenties, so it went, the virile Australian had been capable of bending an iron bar over an erection, but now he's getting on in years and can't do it any more: his *wrists* have gone. At least it had the merit of being brief: some stories lasted five minutes. It took a lot to deprive the Arlotts of the prize, for John and his two sons usually insisted on being the adjudicators.

As I set about building up my cricket library, there were two other major influences. At intervals, and with as large a budget as I could muster, I called in at Epworth Books in City Road, London, where Leslie Gutteridge held court. Up and down the lines of secondhand cricket books I'd go, buying as many as I dared and, after a scholarly chat with the proprietor, taking the armful to the car, through the crumbling Bunhill Fields burial ground. Many of the classics came my way, and, of course, I would have been content to have invested in two or three times as many, had I the purse. The other main source was Joe Goldman, a famous collector who now lived in Egham and had books, booklets, pictures and letters stored in all sorts of unlikely places throughout the house. Here there were no marked prices, so this small, thick-set, venerable Jewish solicitor (who had been wounded at Passchendaele) would wheeze and ponder for a while before announcing his asking price. In time I came to realise that it helped to break his boredom if I summoned the nerve to bargain with him. At first I thought I'd angered him, but he was actually in a minor paroxysm of delight if I should ever counter his £5 demand with 'How about £4?' Today the Goldman bookplate signifies many a treasure in the collection.

Around 1970, our dealings for the day done, he excused himself and went off for a nap, leaving his wife to cook me egg and chips before I drove home. As I downed the meal, Mrs Goldman expressed her anxiety about the remaining collection, which was still substantial. 'When Joe dies,' she confided, 'I'm going to give it all away. And do you know who I'm going to give it to? I'm going to give a third of it to Tony Baer, another third to Irving Rosenwater, and a third to you!'

A few months later *she* died. Joe sold the rest of his stuff, some at auction, and invested afresh in foreign stamps, taking the albums with him into a nursing- home, where he died in 1978, at the age of 85.

Visits to Joe Goldman were sometimes family days

Continuing to make enough central-heating sales commission to keep us fed and housed, I played about 25 cricket matches each summer, and had a few seasons of soccer with Walton Terriers, enjoying a more cerebral kind of game played on more comfortably soft grounds, though with no crowd to speak of. One year I won a little plaque.

The differences between English and Australian cricket jumped out at me with every match: I guested for Hampton Wick against a Middlesex team in 1965, and after they had piled up 250 for the loss of only a couple of wickets – one of them Mike Brearley for 140 – we lost our openers quickly, and against an insistent attack (Herman, Stewart, Bick – whom I hit for a six) a chap from Melbourne and I batted defensively for over an hour. Having held the fort, we were then mocked not only by the opposition but by some of our own players, who all seemed to think that we should have taken risks and gone for the remote, probably invisible, victory even if it meant losing. So much for the contrasting attitudes in cricket.

With my final kick of a football began a gradual fading of interest in that game, perhaps because the playing of it was paramount – as with cricket. That was always the most enjoyable and important facet. But soccer had become spiteful, arrogant and petulant at top level. Some players were thuggish and exhibitionist, and the horrible behaviour of some of the supporters turned it into a living nightmare. Like the equally disillusioned John Arlott, I had no desire for an obituary that read along the lines that 'he was beaten to death outside Luton Town Football Club'.

So, back to the green and sometimes soggy fields of southern England, lapping up the scenery, enjoying the companionship, tolerating the tedious and predictable remarks about Australia.

But what about cricket writing? These little agency reports weren't satisfying, any more than the flimsy cheques that followed. Always it was the humanity of the game that captivated me. I could take on anybody in a quiz based on cricket facts and figures, but it was the personality of a cricketer that fascinated me more, his background and attitude, his family, his hobbies, his weaknesses, speech, dress-code, financial situation, attitude towards animals and children. Then, and only then, were his statistical achievements of any interest.

For some time I had wondered about the 'unsung', those who had made indelible marks on the game but who had since fallen by the wayside, their reputations lost in time. In a 30-year boom in publishing many cricketers from earlier ages had received belated recognition in biography form. One of the first – my own contribution towards doing justice to the legions of the forgotten – was A.E.Stoddart.

In the 1880s and 1890s he was, as a cricketer, every bit as popular as Gower and Botham in a later generation, and even more revered than Rory Underwood as a rugby winger. Stoddart captained England in both games, and drew people through the turnstiles, usually outshining the supreme W.G.Grace when in partnership with the Great One for England or the Gentlemen. However, details of his career and his life were difficult to find, and, starting in January 1967, I couldn't resist embarking on a detective mission. It lasted, on and off, for three years.

Two questions have been put repeatedly. The easier one is 'Why was "Stoddy" forgotten?' He was relegated to a mere name in the lists not only because he left cricket abruptly in the late 1890s, and did not hang around as a journalist or committeeman, but because he took his own life. The less easy question was 'Why select *him* as a subject for biography?'

It was not enough just to have felt sorry for him, for his wretched torment in later years, for the fact that he hadn't received his due. More likely it was amazement that the name of a man of such achievement meant little or nothing to cricket-lovers of today. Drewy Stoddart had forced law changes in rugby, so revolutionary had been his play. As a batsman, he once held the world record for any level of cricket with an innings of 485, for Hampstead in 1886; for 80 years his 173 at Melbourne was the highest score by an England captain in a Test match in Australia; at Lord's in 1893 he became the first captain in Test history to declare an innings closed; he was the first ever to score a century before lunch on the opening day of a County Championship match; and he scored 221 in his final match for Middlesex, in 1900 ('a consolation for my old age' – an old age that never transpired).

'Stoddy' – no longer forgotten

Today, instead of having poems written about him, Stoddart would have seen his name on many of the banners now in vogue on the outers of the Test grounds in England and Australia. It was from some verse in Melbourne Punch during Stoddart's sensational Ashes tour of 1894-95 that I took the book's title (from the final lines):

Then wrote the Queen of England,
Whose hand is blessed by God,
'I must do something handsome
For my dear victorious Stod . . .'

There were quite a few areas where subject and author had a lot in common (and admittedly many where they didn't): both married Australian girls; all-year-round sportsmen; both schooled a long way from their birthplaces; one born 37 years before 1900, the other 37 years after (and both in March); a north London/Lord's proximity, with Stoddart even having lived next door to the house occupied by the great Victorian artist W.P.Frith until his death in 1909. As the coincidences piled up, I was persuaded to see a psychometrist. With a photo of my hero concealed in a buff envelope, I let her 'feel' the subject and give her readings, which were far too vague and generalised for my sceptical mind. Then she suddenly said she 'saw' a coalmine. Now why should she have said that? I'd told her next to nothing about 'Stoddy'. But his father had owned Bedlington Colliery. I went home wondering. Debbie was probably right. His spirit was guiding me. I looked again at the 'For book' that he'd pencilled here and there in his 1890s scrapbooks. It seemed I was composing the book he never managed to write. It was never quite (as one reviewer much later so rawly put it) a case of 'Frith's apparent love affair with the eventually tragic Stod'.

Stoddart's tempestuous wife, Ethel
(a photograph which had not previously been published: courtesy of Debbie Beavis)

To peer into another's lifetime, to investigate and reconstruct in great detail somebody else's being, be it of a film actor, an ancestor, or a cricketer from long ago, can be almost transcendental as rewarding experiences go, a displacement, temporary or otherwise, of one's own personality. Months of intensive research in the newspaper library at Colindale and at Lord's produced the book's bulk, but I also travelled to see a niece and others who had known him, one the yachting writer Francis Cooke, who had gone to school with Drewy Stoddart as long ago as the 1870s, and was now about to reach his century of years. Mr Cooke was rather deaf, but fortunately lucid of speech and clear of memory. The last link, caught just in time.

The intensive search for Stoddart's burial site eventually took me to Radford, Coventry, where his ashes had been placed in his mother's grave. The pink granite monument, damaged by a Luftwaffe bomb blast, has since vanished. Vandalism in the churchyard has been so vicious that most of the monuments have been removed.

The last of the research expeditions took me all the way up to South Shields to find his birthplace. Westoe, its quiet streets covered by snow sparkling under the lamps, must hardly have changed since Stoddart's childhood in the 1860s. It was not only a thrill to be there, but something of a miracle, for my car had spun round in a sudden snowdrift on the A1 around Scotch Corner, and for what seemed an age I was speeding along backwards at 70mph, holding the road by fixing my eyes on the rear-vision mirror. Not daring to touch the brakes, I soon realised that this couldn't go on forever, particularly as I had no idea what lay over the brow of the hill up ahead (or behind me, so to speak). I had not been as scared since Elvis's brakes went, though on that occasion the ordeal lasted only a second or two.

The north and south carriageways were separated by a 20-foot wide expanse of snow under which presumably was grass. So I touched the steering wheel, zoomed off the road, spun round and jerked to a halt, windscreen-wipers banging furiously away, indicators flashing, and, for a shocked moment, horn blaring as I slumped forward.

A Morris Minor pulled up, and out leapt a vicar, who enquired after my health. The nervous after- spasms were made worse by the sight of heavy trucks and trailers roaring down the other carriageway. If the grass verge hadn't stopped me, these heavies would have chewed me up and spat me out.

Understandably, I was now wondering if the book would ever be completed, a view which intensified when one major publisher and another lesser one sat on the typescript and pictures for months before rejecting it. Stoddart, they said, was not well enough known. And yet this was exactly the flaming motive for writing the book. I later learned that the publisher's reader had been displeased with the mis-spelling of one word, which struck me as a flimsy pretext for knocking back an entire book. In the years that followed, whenever I was asked to 'taste' a manuscript for a publisher I was alert not only to the loving care and effort put into the would-be book by its author but to the financial risk about to be taken by the publishers. Assessment was therefore never easy. But you learn as you go, and I have found myself warning many an inexperienced author not to agree to derisory financial terms or any mean clauses. Years later, when I was planning another book, I rang a publisher whose hoity-toity lady asked 'Are you in print?' I told her I was indeed 'in print': I was responsible for something like thirty books. 'Who is your agent?' came the follow-up. I explained that I didn't have an agent. 'We can't possibly deal direct with an author,' she snorted. I was left wondering how many publishers had knocked back *Gone With the Wind* before Margaret Mitchell scored.

Sweat and toil bring their reward: the Cricket Society prize is presented by Sir Oliver Leese
Picture by Morley Pecker

Now, back in 1970, this particular inexperienced author seemed to have wasted the best part of three years with this haunting obsession, guiding spirit or otherwise. There was only one thing for it: publish it myself. The anxiety was eased by the loan of a few hundred pounds from Tony Baer, the Melbourne-based bachelor cricket-collecting stock investor, and I found a friendly printer in Northampton and committed myself. I advertised the 400 copies of *'My Dear Victorious Stod'* at £2.50 each, signed and numbered, had generous reviews by John Arlott and Ian Wooldridge, and sold them all inside a year. Copies have been sighted at huge prices on the Internet over the years since, and the book has developed into further enlarged editions, the last (*'Stoddy': England's Finest Sportsman*) as recently as 2015.

One autumn evening back in 1970 the phone rang. It was Jim Coldham of The Cricket Society, a gentle, cautious man who had served in the 'Forgotten Army' in Burma, now nervous not only from the weight of the news he was about to impart but from the hardly-serious breach of confidentiality involved: he made it clear that he ought not to be telling me this at this stage, but he was so excited and so keen to transmit the news that, blow it, he felt he had to ring (or 'wing' as dear old Jim put it). He then announced that my biography of A.E.Stoddart had won the first-ever Cricket Society Jubilee Literary Award.

I thanked Jim, rehooked the phone, floated into the lounge to hug Debbie, and then the phone rang again. It was another member of the judging panel, Irving Rosenwater, equally abashed at having broken protocol, equally excited on my behalf. I thanked him too, and felt that it now sounded like anything but a practical joke.

At the Cricket Society spring dinner in May 1971, I received the award parchment, plus a cheque for £25, from the president, Lieutenantt-General Sir Oliver Leese (which gave me special delight since he was Uncle Bill's commander in the Eighth Army) and then I had to overcome the challenge of making a brief thank-you speech, during which, at the expense of the current MCC president Lord Caccia, who had been one of Her Majesty's diplomats, I quoted the old chestnut about a diplomat being somebody who could convince his wife that a fur coat would only make her look fat. There was a gentle ripple of applause.

At last things were moving. We were now in a large, semi-detached Edwardian house in a quiet tree-lined street in New Malden; I had a loving wife who was prettier than Debbie Reynolds; we had three bonzer children; I was captain of Shepperton Cricket Club, Walton Terriers Football Club, and leader of the best team in the most successful branch of Servowarm; and my growing cricket library was now neatly housed in the box-room.

I remember walking down Chestnut Grove and admitting to myself that I was happy: so happy that I didn't think I could be happier.

Then, four hours after midnight about a week after I'd received the award for the Stoddart book, the phone rang. It was my brother in Sydney. Mum had been operated on, and had only hours to live. A couple of days later, truly terrible days, the telegram arrived. Mum was dead. The hollowness was unimaginable, made worse by remorse.

CHAPTER TWELVE

Everyone can master a grief but he that has it.

WILLIAM SHAKESPEARE

EVEN for my last days with Mum I had to thank cricket. Early in 1968 my application to go on *Double Your Money*, the television quiz show, was accepted, and nobody who had taken any sort of interest in cricket could have failed to get to the £64 stage: who is the heavyweight opening batsman who has dieted his way into the England team? ('Good old Colin Milburn'); nationalities of the following famous cricket players, Sonny Ramadhin, Neil Adcock, Richie Benaud?; what is a cow shot? ('want me to demonstrate?' – polite laughter); who scored 16 centuries in the season of 1925? And so on to the Treasure Trail.

Into the claustrophobic glass booth I went, and Hughie Green, the affable and popular quizmaster, solemnly spelt out the requirement: 'I will tell you the years in which players scored 1000 runs in May, and ask you to name each player: May 1895, May 1927, May 1928.'

W.G.Grace was no problem. In fact I blurted his name out as soon as Hughie had uttered '1895', causing him to caution me in the fashion of an avuncular barrister. The other two names were clearly in mind, but which came first? I agonised for a few seconds, which I suppose pleased the director, for the clock- hand ticked menacingly down, before reasoning that since Charlie Hallows was older than Wally Hammond, he probably achieved the feat before him, i.e. in 1927 to Hammond's 1928.

'I'm sorry. That is the wrong answer,' cooed Hughie, to a background of groans from the audience and mournful organ music.

I could scarcely believe it, and checked the *Wisden* in my glovebox as soon as I reached the car in the Wembley Studios car park. But there it was: 1927 – Hammond, 1928 – Hallows. Dammit, or words to that effect.

Winning by losing: Double Your Money with Hughie Green

I tried that question out on a number of friends in the days that followed, and none got it right. They all seemed to think it was a tough one for £64. So when the producer rang to ask me back a week later – without divulging a reason – I assumed they were wanting a reshoot. To that end I donned the same Stoddart-style high-lapel suit and the same tie. But there was no reshoot. Instead, after I'd sat alone sweating in the wings through an entire show, I was called on stage by Hughie Green, who announced: 'Last week saw a young man – his name was David Frith – and he lost on our programme, on Cricket, and he told us that he wanted to go back to Australia, or better still bring his Mum and Dad over from Australia. We have a little surprise for him tonight . . . Since last week a ticket has been sent to us by the Sitmar Line to bring your mother and father to this country. [*In recent times Donald Trump has reminded me so much of Hughie.*] I've got a picture right here of this very, very beautiful ship, which is the *Fairstar*, and your Mum and Dad, as soon as they can, can jump on the *Fairstar* and come on over here and have a wonderful time on this very beautiful ship.'

As I made my inadequate effort to thank everybody I caught sight of a nurse rushing down the aisle. Debbie had fainted.

Back at the house, beyond midnight, I put a call through to Sydney (charged at £3 for three minutes, at which point the call was forcibly ended) and told my father the great news. To my astonishment he said they'd think the matter over and ring me back tomorrow. Of course, he had arrangements to make with the shop.

They arrived in July, with the temperature in the nineties, though Dad's stubborn nature was never better displayed than by his refusal to take off his coat, even though he was melting from the heat (the 'it gets much hotter than this in Australia' syndrome), and we all had ten wonderful – if sometimes tense – weeks together. It was cramped in our Tolworth house, of course, but the togetherness, especially where my warm and jolly Mum was concerned, reminded us of what we'd been missing, and probably caused the youngsters to wonder why we had ever left Sydney and family.

Dad went off to explore his childhood haunts around Bethnal Green – and was shocked at the changes – and Bisley, where he was in the orphanage. And we all did Kew Gardens and Bodiam Castle, Kingston and Claremont, dear old London town time and again, and even Lord's, where Johnny ventured into the Tavern to get the autograph of an extremely tall, blond, young allrounder named Tony Greig who had just made a mark on the MCC President's XI v Australians match.

We all dreaded the end of their stay, and when it came we lunched sadly in Winchester before delivering them to the wharf at Southampton. I said we would not go aboard, for I had too vivid a memory of our painful Sydney departure four years before. So, with cranes and warehouses around us, we politely hugged and kissed goodbye, and I was actually sitting back in the car when Mum came over and grasped my hand again and held it for some time, a time which, logically, somebody had to terminate, and she showed no inclination to do so. I therefore withdrew my hand from hers. It seemed for some time afterwards that nothing I had ever done in my life was as callous as this. Through our lives I wish I'd shown her more affection. But we weren't that sort of family. The emotional Italians are sometimes to be envied. Patricia Frith was so loving and caring, so ingenuous and guileless.

The long drive back to Tolworth was utterly miserable. It was also thought- provoking. What were we doing here in England? In the days that followed we dredged up enough reasons – sightseeing, career, children settled at school, even better television perhaps – to justify staying on. We resumed the airletters back and forth. Love and best wishes . . .

My brother had made a trip to England in 1966 (Garry Sobers' great summer), but he was already in love, and reduced his stay. He had been startled by the weather. When we collected him from Southampton it was a wondrously sunny day, the fields all technicolour, the houses bright and clean. Next morning Mike was awoken by two nephews and a niece jumping on his chest and everything outside white and slushy following an April blizzard.

My club cricket continued to absorb, with all kinds of failures and triumphs blending with new experiences – and a resistance to the repeated assertions that Australians played too hard. League cricket was being introduced gradually to the south of England, to the horror of those who played solely for the pleasures inherent in the very rhythms of the activity. In the years ahead, their fears were substantially borne out as the worst manifestations of football's 'competitiveness' infiltrated cricket. Club cricket eventually became a hideously noisy pursuit, young men crying out for more effort before every ball and moronically clapping their hands. Superfluous belligerency, perhaps?

Summer '68 – Mum and Dad prepare to leave England for the last time

I would defend against generalisations about Australian 'sledging' and non-walking with a memory of Ian Craig, Australia's young former Test captain, which I often told my team-mates. In a Paddington v Mosman match Craig thin-edged to the keeper so finely that there was no real evidence for the umpire to consider as we launched into a middle-strength speculative appeal. Yet even as we stared at the pained face of the umpire while he deliberated, Craig was gone. Bat under his arm, he hurried away, peeling off his gloves. 'Worthy of an Englishman,' taunted one of my listeners. So I gave this pompous ass another reminiscence, just to confuse him: Terry Lee, a New South Wales allrounder who played for Manly and also over in the Lancashire League, played at the last ball of an over and it went through to our keeper Lindsay Getts. As we changed ends, a couple of us queried whether the bat had been anywhere near that ball. Gettsy, normally not slow in these matters, began to wonder too. So just as the new bowler was about to reach his mark, we appealed very belatedly, the umpire now having walked out to square leg. He was a man of courage, too, for up went his finger, a full minute since the ball had lodged in Gettsy's gloves, and Lee was out. I have seen some thunderstruck batsmen in my time, but none to compare with poor Lee.

So the bipartisan outlook prevailed. There was no real option. Some of my convictions would continue to stem from Australian experience and some from English proclivities. When, in a match at Shepperton, I had Russell Endean stumped, I was filled with memories of listening on the transistor to his unbeaten 162 for South Africa in the 1952 Melbourne Test, which had me reeling with admiration, and now feeling that nobody on this field could have treasured this wicket more. At the same time, anyone watching closely, whether English or Australian, might have had grounds for suspecting that the wicket was generously donated.

With the 1968 Australian tour of England well under way, a hilarious Test had been staged at Lord's (the 200th between England and Australia: why not, I suggested to MCC, issue replicas of the Ashes for public purchase? No thank you. Another idea ahead of its time). Milburn smacked the ball around on a damp wicket and got hit from throat to rump; then the tourists collapsed for 78.

By now, well into the Stoddart research and writing, I was asked by Reg Hayter if I'd like to ghost John Edrich's book. The fee was a princely £200 and the deadline reasonable. John lived not far away, so I signed up and bought some recording tapes, and away we went. We sound at times not unlike Pete and Dud, but we got the job done on time, and *Runs in the Family* was published on July 21, 1969, the day the first human landed on the Moon. Surely a good omen?

I spent the historic 1968 Oval Test sitting with Jack Fingleton in the old low-level Press annexe at third man, where the rain now trickled down the walls as a lunchtime cloudburst seemed to have washed out the final day with Australia five down and still 266 runs from victory. Since the tourists had won the only Test to be finished (Old Trafford: the kid in the blue cap, Doug Walters, having given a rare display of his gifts to English fans with a pair of eighties) Australia seemed to have won the series. At least one Australian journalist – not unreasonably – had cabled home to that effect. 'Throw her down, Hughie!' was the shout raised by the Australian camp when the rainfall was at its most intense.

Fingleton, whose experience as pre-war Test player, historian and parliamentary writer in Canberra, (particularly when coupled with his tetchiness), made him stimulating company, had indulged my constant questioning and perhaps occasionally inane observations (like tipping Edrich to pass Hutton's 364: he was out 200 short, but at least I'd stirred Fingo by making him remember Australia's worst-ever Test: The Oval, 1938, lost by an innings and 579 runs: Bradman, he rasped, had been carried off like an emperor when he damaged his ankle, whereas Fingleton himself, when he was injured, had to crawl up the steps on hands and knees).

He had had a good old moan earlier in this Oval Test when he spotted umpire Arthur Fagg chatting with the England fielders after an Australian wicket had fallen. It was disgraceful, he said. An umpire should keep himself apart from the players. And he was far from impressed when spectators answered the head groundsman's call by spiking and brooming away the water flooding the outfield. The lake gradually drained, and resumption actually seemed possible.

From the telephone-room I'd watched hundreds of spectators weaving their damp and forlorn way out through the Hobbs Gates. So much for the hopes of the opening day, a day which had been made memorable for me by bumping into Herbert Sutcliffe in Kennington Park Road. This smooth and dignified gentleman graciously stated that he knew the face but was dashed if he could remember the name. Of course, we'd never met before. With the utmost charm, he became one of the 1200-odd signatories in my sturdy copy of the 1165-page *World of Cricket*. Sutcliffe's century alongside Hobbs's on a damp pitch here at The Oval in 1926 had set up a famous Ashes victory, which made the chance meeting all the more pleasurable.

The Press-box tearoom made for a distinguished parade of former players: Bill Bowes, Keith Miller, Denis Compton, Bob Simpson, Sir Learie Constantine, Richie Benaud, Alf Gover. Of the other journalists, Jim Kilburn and Lyn Wellings let me sit with them at lunch and proceeded to paint brilliant pictures of pre-war cricket and cricketers, before spoiling it all by expressing condolences that I had been born when I had and thus had to endure all the substandard performances posing as Test and county matches in these post-war years. It took months to get over this. Then I converted their theme into a warning: that to depress the young by comparing their heroes unfavourably with your own was irresponsible. I was to discover, many years later, that this pledge was desperately difficult to observe.

And so the ground was cleared of water, and as we awaited a resumption I went into the England dressing-room with John Edrich to get some more signatures in the big book. Tom Graveney's deep brown eyes were fixed on a crossword; Ray Illingworth was affable enough despite his troubles with Yorkshire; Basil D'Oliveira, soon to be the political pawn in front-page stories across the world, was smiling and courteous; 'Ollie' Milburn, the universal favourite who was only months away from the road accident that would cost him an eye and a career, was nursing a shoulder bruised in the field that morning; captain Cowdrey was serene and accommodating; John Snow sat alone, looking boyish and glum; Alan Knott, stretched out on the seating, said five wickets would be too many to get in the time remaining; Edrich agreed, saying it would be a lifeless pudding out there; Derek Underwood, who wanted to sign the book under the Beckenham CC section, was persuaded to inscribe his name under Kent. A couple of hours later he had qualified for the Heroes section.

Amazingly, play resumed at 4.45pm, with 75 minutes to go. But after 40 minutes no further wicket had fallen. The sanguine words of the England players, of course, had been so sage. Then D'Oliveira bowled Jarman. Underwood replaced him at the pavilion end and immediately got Mallett, caught by Brown in the crowded close catching ring, and also McKenzie. The clock ticked on. There was no overs-minimum requirement in those days but the England fielders moved very, very smartly between overs, and the tension began to hurt. Gleeson padded away and swished and swung, until eventually Underwood, switching to around the wicket, knocked his off stump over. Nine down,10 minutes remaining.

I made it three minutes left, not six as was claimed next day, as John Inverarity, who had opened the innings, padded at Underwood and was hit on the back leg. The whole nation appealed, and umpire Charlie Elliott gave him out. The pandemonium must have been no greater when Australia beat England by seven runs on this ground in 1882, an upset that inspired the creation of the Ashes.

Afterwards, I slipped into the first of hundreds of Press conferences through the years, but in contrast to burning questions that had to be asked at various times in the 1970s, 1980s and 1990s, I could think of nothing pertinent to put to Cowdrey and Lawry, though I would have liked to have asked Messrs Kilburn and Wellings (both of whom I got to know well in later years) how many finishes like this they had in pre-war Ashes Test matches. These media gatherings are often, in themselves, fascinating events. There is always the unimaginative 'You must have...?' approach: reporter to interviewee: 'You must have felt pleased when you reached that century?' We've waited in vain all these years for a batsman to reply, 'No. It was a ghastly experience.' Graham Gooch came close, after his 333 against India in the 1990 Lord's Test. How did he feel? After a longish pause he drawled, with the faintest suggestion of a smile, 'All right.'

Graeme Wood, after batting all day for a Melbourne Test century in the 1978-79 series, responded to the most-asked question, how did he feel, with one word: 'F—d!' In a way it was refreshing when contrasted to some of the more loquacious cricketers who get carried away with their own verbosity. New Zealand's Jeremy Coney could go on a bit, and when miffed so could Mike Brearley. In 1981 he rounded on all 26 of us, saying he would give no more interviews if this nonsense continued to be written. Only one newspaper (*The Sun*) was at fault, so Brearley should have been more specific. Alternatively the offending writer should have done the decent thing and spoken up. Brearley also launched into something special at Sydney when I queried whether Rick Darling, who had just been floored by a Botham pull, would have been standing so close if fielding helmets weren't allowed. (Some of us felt that helmets for fielders were unethical.) That, he fumed, was just another crass example of muddled thinking. In 1981, as England captain, he told me I was not welcome in the dressing-room, even though David Gower had asked me in to pick up his latest literary effort. His irritation may have owed something to the fact that throughout that memorable series I had spent quite some time in the Australian dressing-room. Maybe he saw me as some kind of Kim Philby in the pay of Kim Hughes? Whatever the case, I have a lot of time for the man, often having protested at claims that Brearley couldn't bat while challenging other claims that he was a world-class slip fielder (I reckon he held only four, maybe five, of every seven catches offered).

By far the most entertaining guest at Press conferences, however, has been Pakistan's manager Haseeb Ahsan, who merrily sounded off against English umpires and the perfidious British media and anything else that entered his mind. In my experience, he holds the time record. At Old Trafford in 1987 we thought his response to a question would never end. Men were looking at their watches, even shaking them, while some shook with suppressed laughter as the dear chap went on and on. One or two excused themselves as they had to file. Others did so pretending they had to file. Haseeb's audience was halved by the time he stopped, probably with a sore throat.

My story has broken from its reins. Back in 1968, the bits-and-pieces sports journalism was proving frustrating, though I had the Edrich book to complete, and the Stoddart research continued pleasurably between central-heating sales. *The Observer* needed someone, so Reg Hayter got me to do a trial piece at the MCC v Australians match. But it came to nothing. Nor did two or three speculative chunks on Somerset's tough and ancient Australian, Bill Alley, make print – until, that is, I got a copy of his autobiography (ghosted by Alan Hill) the following year and found in it some oddly familiar phrases. Yes, they were mine. So what had been going on, Reg? In that charming, chuckling manner of his he 'explained' the oversight and sent me a cheque, which yet again did not overwhelm me by its weight.

Without fully realising it, the futility of much of what I was doing, together with an occasional longing for Australia, had turned me into a rather perturbed and restless young man. Naturally enough, Debbie was the first to sense it, and in her concern she decided to communicate with the Revd David Sheppard, who now ran the Mayflower Family Centre in London's East End (land of my paternal ancestors). He was not only the first player I had seen touch a ball in a Test match, back in Sydney in January 1951, but Debbie and I had got chatting to him and his wife Grace when we saw the 1962-63 MCC team fly out of Sydney. My wife, bless her, now got secretly in touch with this other David, my fellow Piscean, and I could hardly speak for astonishment when he rang. The conversation was perhaps a little cagey on both our parts, but an appointment was made, and off I drove through London's congested streets that could surely never get worse but certainly did.

It was mainly cricket talk, but it was somehow coded in parts, and like all good counsellors, David persuaded me to look into my own heart: no lectures, no pressure. No conclusions either, in all truth. But after a thoughtful drive home I was probably ready for a fresh start, and maybe even slightly ashamed that my lack of contentment had shown.

A house-move worked the trick. We managed a five-bedroom, three-storey Edwardian semi in New Malden, put some quality furniture into it, and proper heating (so vital), and looked forward to a good crop of fruit from the trees out the back. It was Christmas week, and we recovered from the removal effort by watching *Carousel* on TV, the tears trickling down my cheeks in my dark corner.

That same week I took Peter to Twickenham for his 11th birthday, and we saw England beat South Africa after political demonstrators had run along the Springbok line-out, addressing the players with a pertinent message. In went the ball and, with a minute or so left, England tumbled over for the winning try. The last time I'd been to Twickenham, Hancock had run the length of the field in injury time to snatch a famous victory against the Scots. Yet with all this and my Hayters rugby and soccer work, winter was still far, far too long.

I managed a century or two for Shepperton, and when Alf Gover brought a team down to our lovely ground, I bowled a teenage Geoff Howarth with an 18-inch offbreak which might have hit a divot. Still some long-hops failed to get up, catching me with my pants down, but if you play enough the compensations come along: the one-handed slip catch off a left-hander which brushed the keeper's pads, the fluke at gully when a slash at a full-toss finished in a set of fingers extended by reflex: all guaranteed to warm a fellow in old age. A peculiar feeling marked the day in 1989 when I passed Drewy Stoddart's lifespan.

It began to seem that the summer of 1971, after my mother died in May, would be our last in England. I returned to playing after a week or two, muttering cornily to myself 'That's for you, Mum' when I got my first boundary hit away. There were other delights ahead, like a match in the grounds of Windsor Castle, with the leaves turning golden on the massive horse-chestnut trees, and chestnuts cooking as the autumn evening closed in on us; and a match at The Oval, where I got a forty against John McMahon, the genial Aussie left-arm wrist-spinner who played for Surrey and Somerset. There was also a match at Westcott where we were conned out of victory. 'Don't think you're going to get these,' murmured their captain between overs. 'We've got 40 minutes yet,' I said. 'No you haven't,' he insisted. 'We finish here at 7 o'clock.' 'But we agreed 7.30,' I protested. 'No; 7 o'clock, in'tit ump?' The umpire – their umpire – agreed. Our left-arm slowie, a Yorkshireman if you please, persuaded me not to leave right after stumps were drawn, taking my team with me in disgust. 'Let's just have one drink wi'em. Then we'll go.'

Thereafter I always wrote everything down at the toss. So much for the Corinthian values of good old English club and village cricket.

Dad was now writing letters which caused us concern. He had gone to pieces after Mum's death. Then he went off on a cruise, which was probably a good idea, even if a mindless attempt at shipboard romance struck us as barmy. The poor man was so consumed by grief and so horribly disorientated after 36 years of marriage to an angelically loyal and caring woman that he seemed to have lost his will to live. It was years since I had first come to realise that grown-ups were not infallible and trustworthy and heroic. Nor are they unchanging. That secure vision of the world and the protective properties inherent in family elders is usually shattered in the years of puberty, if not before.

Ted Frith, orphaned at 11, widowed at 61, worked at his beloved handicraft until the steadiness of his hand began to fail him

We had gone ahead with a week's holiday in the Austrian mountains, booked just before the tragic news, and the break probably helped us cope. But the reality awaited us back in England, with Dad's sad airletters spelling out the grimmest of details of his grief, and slowly but certainly pointing us in one direction. We had to go back.

'If I thought you would like to come home (excuse the term),' he wrote plaintively, 'I would hang on to the house. That way there would always be accommodation waiting for you. Can't you both get it into your sad hearts that there are two families yearning to have your company, as well as

Queensland. We are all reaching out to give love and company to each other. Days are running out pretty fast for all of us. Give a thought to the cables and phone calls that will have to be made in future years. Please keep writing frequently.'

At 62, my poor father found himself in a plight similar to that of 1921, when, as a 12-year-old orphan, he looked around desperately for love and security. Gone now was his wartime fortitude. We had to go to him.

With the house on the market and every effort being made to raise as much central-heating commission as possible, I tried to see a range of county cricket while there was still time. Seven years in England, and still there were many grounds I had yet to see. I drove to Leeds and saw England win a thriller against Pakistan by 25 runs to take the three-Test series, and in August I was thrilled to be present at India's historic first-ever Test victory in England, when Wadekar's men scraped home at The Oval by four wickets, spin wizard Chandrasekhar, one of my heroes, fizzing through England's second innings with 6 for 38.

An extraordinary thing happened at Leyton. With Essex batting, Somerset wicketkeeper Derek Taylor took a bloody blow to the mouth. Off he raced for repairs, skipper Brian Close taking his place (no pads or box, needless to say; it was surprising that Closey even bothered with gloves) while Roy Virgin went off to pad up as replacement. An over later, Virgin came back on, duly decked out; but so did Taylor, his mouth stuffed with cotton- wool. By now, Close was so enjoying keeping that he was reluctant to hand back the gloves. So for a most memorable few moments we had three wicketkeepers staring at each other by the side of the pitch, none prepared to relinquish the gloves. It must have been a unique incident in cricket's vast history.

These little tours were pleasant, but I would never have wanted to be away from home for two-thirds of the summer, which is what fulltime county cricket coverage would have entailed. Back in 1967, I had been particularly lucky, seeing Yorkshire make runs at Kidderminster after Warwickshire, the day before, had taken first-innings points off Sussex at Edgbaston in most dramatic fashion. Jim Allan, the little Scottish left-armer, had teased out Sussex for 104, and in the evening it needed for the injured John Jameson to return to the crease with his side 97 for 9. Joining No.11 Jack Bannister, Jameson faced up left-handed so as to protect his broken left hand; and the runs were made. A Brummie by the gate, as I left the ground, memorably said to his mate: 'That's the best blimmin gyme I seen in eye-gees!' Indeed.

Goodbye to all that. We'd enjoyed England to the hilt. Now family needs were paramount. Who knew? Australia might now afford the opportunity for which I'd waited so long.

CHAPTER THIRTEEN

There is no security on this earth; there is only opportunity.

DOUGLAS MACARTHUR

THERE had been no blinding flash of light or bass baritone announcement from the clouds above. I had merely left the cricket at the beautiful Worcester ground and found my way into the Cathedral, hoping that the peacefulness and coolness inside would somehow create an atmosphere for clear thought. Having paid brief respects at the tomb of King John, I sat quietly on a pew and wondered why Mum, one of those very rare people who never harmed anyone in her entire life, had been taken from us at only 62. And the muddle in my mind was swept away with the powerful simplicity of the knowledge that our place was now in Sydney. Dad needed us.

We had grown to love that old house in New Malden, and had put some good furniture into it, Debbie's Edwardian chiffonier best of all. Now, little more than 18 months after moving in, we were selling our stuff at knockdown prices, having estimated how much we could afford to take with us. When the taxi honked its horn at 5am on the day of departure, we were all still fast asleep, victims of exhaustion. In the rush Peter forgot to grab his fishing-rod.

At Luton airport, the large, framed Philip Hermogenes Calderon's Pears print *Captain of the Eleven* fell over, shattering the glass, some of which left my fingers bleeding. Another omen? Not exactly light of heart, we took to the skies, only to come down not long afterwards at Stansted. Here we took on large stocks of fuel. Seemed that had we filled up at Luton we would never have got up off the short runway in time. Nobody had bothered to explain.

Kuala Lumpur, where we had an overnight, was blazing hot and sweaty, with plenty in the streets to excite and intimidate the three youngsters. Poor little John got sleeping sickness and could barely stand up. We now desperately wanted to be in Sydney. The plane simply could not fly fast enough for us.

Everyone, as we were greeted upon landing, fought to keep the storm of emotions under control, but the lunacy of jet-lag, when it touched the ongoing grief and sadness, pushed the vulnerable mind to the very limit. The reality of Mum's death struck home forcibly as we advanced from the cemetery roadway towards her grave. It was next to that of a young soldier who'd been killed in Vietnam, and the surroundings were too plain and too isolated for my liking.

In the weeks that followed, Dad, whose eyes filled with tears when we gave him a sprig of heather from Bisley heath, near where he spent his early orphan years, bared his soul with an almost unending torrent of words: describing in minute detail my mother's last days and reminiscing to lengths which came close to ad nauseam. Debbie listened compassionately for hour upon hour. We had little outings and numerous gatherings over cups of tea and stronger drinks, and the stories wore thinner and thinner for the retelling. So much had Mum meant to all of us that I began to fear that there could be no recovery from her tragic loss for any of us. Against this background I had to get out and find work and somewhere to live.

We hoped the youngsters would settle in readily at school, but Peter soon came home clearly disturbed after a bunch of Sutherland classmates had spotted his suede shoes and chanted 'Pommie poof' – this to a 13-year-old born just up the highway at St George Hospital, Kogarah.

We'd soon be putting all this behind us when I got that job in cricket. But such doors as opened were soon closing with no more than the frail promise to 'get in touch' if something should turn up. Once more we found solace in Queensland. Having bought, through my brother, a Holden which, on the whole, behaved itself, we undertook that great journey yet again, driving ever northwards, patiently ticking off the hours and relishing the sweeping views, an idea gathering strength all the while: why not become a truck driver? Then this carefree existence could be mine for all the days of my life: the bushland, the ranges, the blue, blue sea to the east, all my favourite music on the tape-player. But that would mean separation from Debbie. Or should we go one better and find an island in the South Pacific, where we could be self-sufficient, no bills, the sea at our disposal, the sun on our backs whenever we wanted?

At the end of our long northward haul waited a sweet lady who made good rosella jam and tea, who said comparatively little, but had a Mona Lisa smile and, like my own late mother, was the warm, undemonstrative heart of, in her own case, a wide-flung family. There she stood on the verandah of the old house, waiting for her daughter and her family to complete their journey from a place called England which might as well have been Venus. For the first time in months we were serene, as if laced with morphine.

Across the shimmering expanse of the land stood the hazy violet-tinged mountains, and outside the tumbledown shed the horse still stood munching. In ones and twos the friends and relations drifted in, expressing in their inadequate way their pleasure at seeing us all, with condolences at the cause of our journey.

Already, though, the signs were there that our mission was not turning our successfully. Whenever anybody asked about my job prospects I couldn't conceal my anxiety. If the subject of England were raised, we recalled all the enjoyment we had derived from our travels and friendships. They must have known we might well be gravitating back to England unless something turned up fast.

From this latest Micawber stance, I did at least snatch at opportunities to find old cricket names, and to walk with history and shake hands with some of its cast. While in Queensland, I thought I'd establish once and for all precisely when and where it was that the legendary Aborigine fast bowler of the 1930s, Eddie Gilbert, had died.

Questions dropped all around the Brisbane suburb where he was last seen pointed me back towards Ipswich, to Goodna, where Eddie had been in care. When I asked the superintendent about the cricketer's date of death, he staggered me by talking of Eddie Gilbert in the present tense. He was still alive! And right here! Please, I must see him! What a scoop!

Calm down, fella. That was the message in the superintendent's eyes. He couldn't let me see him. Against the rules. Instead, he asked Debbie how her mother was, and remembered her father (a fellow psychiatric nurse) with pleasure. I let them talk on for a while, before asking "*Now* can I see Eddie?" He picked up the telephone and told someone to 'find Eddie'. Soon, by the door stood a small white-haired Aborigine, long arms hanging limply, black shorts, T-shirt, eyes, when they finally lifted, bloodshot and nervous. This was the man who had put a thunderbolt or two through Bradman, who was said to have made the ball generate smoke when he bowled on the concrete pitches back home in Barambah, and who had left 'nufactured in Austra' (in reverse, of course) imprinted on the head of a batsman – one of many – who had failed to negotiate a Gilbert bouncer.

'Shake hands, Eddie,' the superintendent quietly requested, and he complied. But, as we had been forewarned, there was no conversation. Eddie was under sedation, having been violent in years past. He had been placed in care in 1949, and was 'bottled right up'. He wouldn't talk despite all manner of encouragement. When a cricket ball was placed in his hand he stared at it then let it drop to the ground.

'If he went out again he'd be back among the plonkies down at the *Adelaide* [pub] in no time.'

Nor, after agonising for a full minute over the first initial, would he, or could he, give me an autograph. The 'E' was all he could manage. I treasure it still.

So this was the popular little chap who had been denied a Test cap either because of racial prejudice or his bowling action off half-a-dozen steps (he was no-balled for throwing by umpire Andy Barlow in the ninth of his 23 first-class matches). Outside, when the superintendent was looking away, I took a photograph and tried to convey with a smile all the warmth felt by cricket- lovers who knew – or half-knew – the tragi-romantic story of Eddie Gilbert. I could only finish the article I put together that evening as follows: Eddie walked off, still breathing his wheezy monotone; he wandered through the meal hall, and the last I saw of him was as he drifted, an emaciated and desolate individual, across the parched grass.

Eddie Gilbert: in his heyday ...

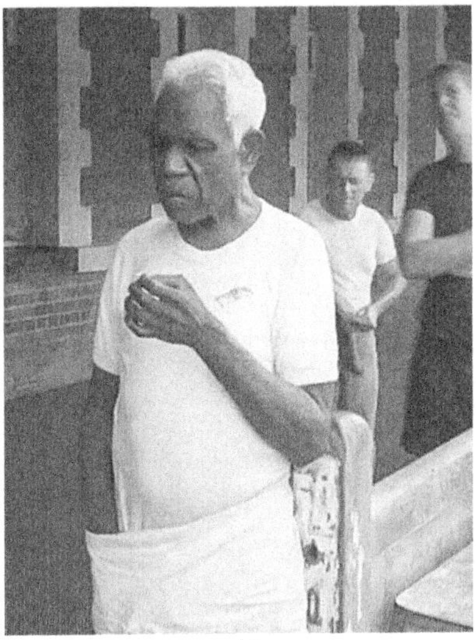

...and in care

Back in Sydney, I persevered with the research for a book I hoped to write on Archie Jackson, the contemporary of young Bradman who had come out from Scotland as a small child, grown up in poverty in Balmain, scored two centuries for New South Wales in one match when only 18, and made a glorious 164 at Adelaide on his Test debut for Australia when only 19. He was a member of the 1930 Australian side which toured England, and had an important stand of 243 with Bradman against Larwood, Tate, Hammond and Peebles on a lively Oval surface in the final Test match. But he was already fatally infected with tuberculosis, which took him in 1933, when he was only 23. His style and his genius and the magnitude of his achievements in that short life elevated him to comparison with Trumper. Like Stoddart, he deserved a book.

I tracked down Hunter 'Stork' Hendry, a genial and often blunt Australian player of the 1920s, who gave me some graphic recollections about Archie and a number of other contemporaries. (Hammond, for instance, who scored nigh on 1000 runs that summer of 1928-29 in close proximity to fieldsman and bowler Hendry, had about him an aroma that Stork had never encountered before in anyone: 'Might have had something to do with that illness he picked up in the West Indies,' he mused.)

Archie Jackson: doomed genius

Bill Hunt, who grew up with Archie Jackson ('We was so poor we had to spread coal-dust on our bread in those days'), was immensely helpful. A left-armer who reaped wickets – and hat-tricks – galore for Balmain, New South Wales and in the Lancashire league, Bill won that status-elevating first Test cap for Australia in 1931-32, at Adelaide, when Don Bradman made 299 not out. Bill, alas, took no wickets in his 16 overs and was dismissed without scoring, and forever more insisted he was dropped because the 'puritanical' skipper Bill Woodfull disapproved of his coarse language. Another fantasy was that one day he himself would burst into print with a biography of his youthful pal Archie Jackson. I can't see how Bill would ever have got round to it. He probably saw in me the next-best option. By giving full support, he ensured that Archie was 'resurrected'. Unhappily, when the finished book was in his hands, with fulsome acknowledgement for his invaluable assistance, he became what I can only describe as 'odd'.

Piecing together the Jackson story was absorbing, not least because I was steered by Bill Hunt to Phyllis, Archie's fiancée of all those years ago, a diminutive, vibrant grandmother now, and also his two sisters, the elder of whom, Peggie, not only added to the fund of family tales but gave me a few cherished books – *Lawrence of Arabia* signed by the young cricketer – which were once held and read by her beloved brother. I spoke with Bert Oldfield and Alan Kippax about him, and Bill O'Reilly and Frank Buckle, and began to enjoy the feeling that all biographers crave: that although my subject died before I was born, I was getting to know him.

Messrs Oldfield and Buckle took me to lunch at the Imperial Services Club in Sydney, and, Glebe players both of them, they told me that the great fast bowler 'Tibby' Cotter had been killed by a Turk's bullet near Beersheba in 1917 not while in the charge but when, doubting what he'd seen in his periscope, he raised his head from the trench to see for himself, and took a shot through his fair forehead. This conflicts with the 'official' record, but I had no cause to doubt these two friends of his, respectable gentlemen both.

As we threaded our way across the road afterwards, Mr Oldfield linked his arm through mine in a fine old 1920s gesture, and in return I tugged him from the path of a hurrying car, only too pleased and proud to have preserved the life of a treasured old Australian cricketer.

While visiting Archie Jackson's other sister, at Normanhurst, I learned that Ernie Toshack, the left-arm bowler who had been just as unplayable on sticky wickets as Bert Ironmonger pre-war, lived just up the road. Though weakened and thin from recent illness, Ernie was grand company. Out came the scrapbooks and one memory triggered another: 3 for 17 and 6 for 82 against England at the Gabba in 1946-47, and 5 for 2 and 6 for 29 on the same gluey surface a year later against India. He had good memories of Lord's too: 5 for 40 as Australia chalked up another massive victory in 1948. Like all who played under Don Bradman and toured England, Ernie recalled those experiences with fond gratitude. And he'd recently survived a charge of stealing copper wire from the railway company. He wore his Australian blazer in court, and Keith Miller testified to Ernie's good character.

Nearby lived Arthur Chipperfield, renowned for having been dismissed for 99 in his maiden Test innings, at Trent Bridge in 1934. Like so many of his generation, 'Chippy' was warmly welcoming and keen to talk of the halcyon days. He brought out a newspaper placard which marked his only century for Australia, at Durban in 1935, and then recalled his shipboard duties on the way to England in '34, when he 'signed' autograph sheets with near-perfect impressions of all the players' signatures. I got him to demonstrate, and the old touch was still there: recognisable O'Reillys and Grimmetts and Browns. From that day on, I've felt sceptical about team autograph sheets.

Living off dwindling capital, such as it was, was none too nice an experience, but relief came when, upon Jack Fingleton's recommendation, I was taken on as a journalist, Grade B, with the Australian News & Information Bureau. I was sent out on riveting stories concerning European and Asian migrants who had set up successful businesses in Sydney, and forthcoming 'cultural' events. Didn't they want some cricket coverage? And when would I get my first posting? The answer to that one was uncertain, and as to where it might be, I could forget London or New York. Those places went to seniors. My first two-year posting would probably be to somewhere like Djakarta.

I threw myself into further discovery of cricket people: Clara Macartney, sister of the brilliant Charlie and now the last of the family (she was almost as glad as I that someone had turned up to take possession of the 1909 tour photograph album presented to her brother by its compiler, Frank Laver, and of some postcards Charlie had sent home from tour). 'Do you know,' Miss Macartney confided, 'Charlie never drank. And when he went on tour one year, and Mother wasn't very well, he left behind £100 for any emergency.'

Victor Trumper's son, who had bowled fastish for New South Wales, was a generous host, and showed me all that remained of his father's memorabilia, another of the Laver albums and a large, framed photo of the 1909 Australians. There was also a dark-brown bat, with half-perished rubber grip. To hold that was akin to touching the Turin Shroud. I told him that I had, as a boy, gone out to Waverley to see his father's grave, and also to Crown Street School to see if I could find his initials, said to have been carved into one of the desks.

Not far away lived the widow of A.G.'Johnny' Moyes, who told me of her husband's everlasting pain from wounds sustained in the First World War, and of his gratitude for a life in cricket, with its treasured friendships. Without warning, she took down a copy of Moyes's *A Century of Cricketers*, inscribed by him: 'To my wife, once again the inspiration, 12th April 1950'. And to my astonishment she handed it to me, saying it was mine to keep. Before I left, she bade me join her in a prayer. Somehow I managed to cover my confusion and embarrassment at all this generosity and devotion. The main problem was how best to show my gratitude. I think a few flowers did the trick.

Harold Larwood, the Bodyline villain, was the biggest prize. Already resident for over 20 years in Sydney, he was apparently rather reclusive, but was known to have seen occasional visitors. I tried my luck, and was made welcome. The name of Archie Jackson helped. It was from a rare Larwood half-volley that the youngster had creamed the boundary that brought up that Test-debut hundred at Adelaide in 1929. Would Harold write a foreword to the biography? Agreed on the spot.

'Never be a fast bowler, son,' he advised my young son John – not all that sincerely, for it was obvious with every remark that the old pride of Notts and England would gladly have done it all again if the years could have been rolled back: smashing stumps out of their holes, instilling fear (and negative footwork) into batsmen, and even unleashing a glorious cover-drive of his own. Wife Lois tended us with tea as the souvenirs and cuttings came out for examination. 'Leg theory' Harold called it pointedly. He would have none of this term 'Bodyline'. And he tried not to be impolite as he classified the bravery or otherwise of the 1932-33 Australian batsmen. And, of course, there was the presentation ashtray from Douglas Jardine, 'The Skipper', for whom Larwood, the odd friction aside, would have walked through a blazing field. There was, too, that cherished congratulatory telegram from Archie Jackson, from his deathbed in 1933. All this came in so useful years later when I undertook to write a definitive book on that most renowned of all Test series: *Bodyline Autopsy*.

'Never be a fast bowler, son,'
Harold Larwood jokingly told Johnny Frith

Larwood had been generous in his assessment of the latest Australian fast-bowling sensation, Dennis Lillee. There was a Rest of the World tour in progress, and Lillee had ripped the visitors apart in his hometown, Perth, taking 8 for 29. I had seen some of the Brisbane match, when Ian Chappell scored a century in each innings, and umpire Tom Brooks kindly gave me a bail as a souvenir.

During that match, Bill Jacobs, who was managing the World team, strode into the Press-box one morning, all 5 ½ feet of him, and proceeded to rebuke us all – even those of us who were innocent – about the way skipper Garry Sobers was being 'persecuted' for playing too much golf. Jacobs, a Melbourne man who had managed Australia in South Africa and who had been guilty of a little bit of physical aggression in his wicketkeeping days way back in Melbourne sub-district cricket, threatened some kind of retribution unless the Press laid off Garry.

In the third match, at the MCG, Sobers hit a heavenly 254 which made his point emphatically enough. That glorious performance had to be watched on black-and-white television, and later again via the treasured film recording. He gave Lillee a belting all right, and was harsh on Bob Massie too, the swinger who was to take 7 for 76 in the Sydney match and many more on his Test debut at Lord's a few months later (Massie's emergence for the Press conference at the SCG set new sartorial standards: he wore a bizarre pair of red-and-black briefs). But the other bowlers massacred by Sobers that day were the high-tossing Terry Jenner and scarcely-turning Kerry O'Keeffe, plus medium-pacer Graeme Watson, which leaves doubts in my mind as to whether it really could have been the greatest innings played in Australia, as asserted by one eminent source.

Pat Mullins: warm host

While in Brisbane, I made contact with Australia's premier cricket collector, Pat Mullins, and secured a friendship to be treasured. Generous and unquenchable of spirit, even in later years when his sight began to fail and his collection had been sold to faraway Melbourne Cricket Club and he was forced to submit to extensive heart surgery, Pat had been an inspiration to all fellow collectors. Now, in November 1971, he invited me to his cricket supper, and while the lights of east Brisbane twinkled, and his eight children displayed impressive manners before scattering, Pat and Betty hosted at a large table on the verandah: Tony Greig, who talked entertainingly, sharing the bulk of the chat with Bill Jacobs; Farokh Engineer, who had to rush off early; Richard Hutton, son of my early hero, who had refused to fasten the seat-belt when I drove him from the Gabba to Coorparoo; umpire Lou Rowan, the detective who had a clash of wills with England captain Ray Illingworth in the Sydney Test only a year previously and now made some extremely emphatic points about matters that hardly mattered (a few years later he was forced to retire hurt after shooting himself in the foot); and Kerry O'Keeffe, who spent most of the evening browsing through Pat's impressive library.

Though no permanent job beckoned, it was a delight being on the fringe of the cricket fraternity, and I further developed the activity by writing two pieces for *Australian Cricket*, the magazine set up a few years earlier by schoolboys Eric Beecher and Dean Banks: I called to see Alan Kippax in his Martin Place shop and made a few notes before he set me aback by inviting me round to his Bellevue Hill home for a further chat in more relaxed surroundings. And I had tracked down Syd Smith junior, who had served the NSWCA and the Australian Board during his 60 years of administration, and had managed the 1921 and 1926 Australian tours of England.

Kippax, then 74, softly-spoken and silver-haired, had watched Trumper as a schoolboy and recorded his runs in an exercise-book. He also bowled to the great man before formal net practice began, wore his sleeves half-rolled, like Victor, and in time inherited the mantle as the most elegant and artistic contemporary batsman, a lineage which he passed to his own protégé, Archie Jackson, in due course. At 29, Kippax should have toured England, but was not selected for the 1926 tour. 'I felt like throwing myself off the Gap,' he told me. 'I opened this sports store instead.'

Among 'Kippy's' greatest achievements were an unbeaten 315 against Queensland, 260 not out against Victoria, when he and Hal Hooker put on a record 307 for the 10th wicket, twin hundreds against Sussex at Hove on one of his tours, and 250 at the same pleasant venue on another, and the first Test century ever for Australia v West Indies (Adelaide, 1930-31). He led NSW when Victoria piled up the world record 1107 against them, and again in the return match when the same opposition (minus some of their stars) were swept away for 35. In his soft voice and with an enduring smile, Alan Kippax recalled all this, besides the 1932 fun tour of America, where there were some bizarre Hollywood parties thrown by the likes of Boris Karloff, Leslie Howard, Norma Shearer and Tom Mix. There was an insistent feeling that this quiet sophisticate and his special pal Vic Richardson would have extracted every drop of enjoyment from those parties.

Then he showed me the scar on his temple. Queensland's 'Pud' Thurlow inflicted it. Eddie Gilbert had run amok – 'one bouncer hit the sightscreen on the full' – but Kippax over-assessed Thurlow's pace at the other end, and hooked too early. It was said that this injury and the horrors of Bodyline a year later (he and Eric Barbour wrote *Anti Body-line*, a now-rare book) reduced his effectiveness as a batsman. If so, he concealed the loss well in 1933-34 when he and Bradman put on 363 in 135 minutes against Queensland at the SCG. In 1930 this NSW pair, Kippax the senior by 11 years, had stands of 192 in the Lord's Test and 229 at Headingley, when Bradman made his 334. A recent book had suggested that Kippax felt no great personal admiration for The Don, resenting the records he was appropriating. 'Kippy' declared the innings perhaps a shade unnecessarily when he was 452 not out, and then brusquely instructed him to take the field with the rest of the team upon resumption of play. If this be so, Kippax did not utter one derogatory word about Bradman in all the time I was privileged to be in his company.

Alan Kippax: huge stands with Bradman

Visiting Syd Smith in Chatswood was to venture even further back in time. He spoke even more familiarly about Trumper, and then Armstrong, that demanding bully of a skipper on Australia's 1921 England tour. Of course, what I wanted most to hear was the eye-witness account of the scandalous brawl between Test selectors Clem Hill and Peter McAlister in 1912.

Remembered by post-war cricket aficionados as a reactionary man, short of stature, with a Mr Magoo face, Smith, though it cannot have been obvious, was young once. I was taken aback to learn that the first Test he had seen was the one in 1894 which Stoddart's England side won after following on, and he could still picture Peel's catch to end Syd Gregory's innings of 201 – off 'Stoddy's' bowling.

He told me of a third-grade match he had played for Gordon against St George in 1923 when he and Frank Fordham added 116 in 25 minutes, their side totalling 416 for 8 in 140 minutes. Thereafter, he was figuratively wearing a suit, collar and tie in all his anecdotes. He even knew Bill Howell, who took 10 for 28 against Surrey days after getting off the ship in 1899, and Jack Marsh, the fascinating Aboriginal fast bowler of the same era, who wore his NSW blue cap proudly under his straw boater and held a newspaper up (sometimes upside-down) in the tram even though he couldn't read. Accused of throwing, Marsh tied a splint to his arm, under his shirtsleeves, and still bowled at breakneck speed.

Syd Smith: witness to the 1912 punch-up and much else besides

Now Mr Smith was visualising Bert Oldfield's sensational leg-side catch off Jack Hobbs's bat in 1925, and Macartney's century before lunch in the

1926 Headingley Test ('Is it possible for him to keep this up?' an alarmed Yorkshire committeeman had asked Smith). Then he recalled how Macartney, during his 345 in a day against Notts, had called for a heavier bat when in the 200s.

But the Hill/McAlister punch-up: what about that? Would he decline to talk about it? Far from it.

We were back in 1912, in Bull's Chambers, and what happened next renders every subsequent squabble between selectors insignificant. The mighty Clem Hill, captain of Australia as well as a selector, had been insulted and provoked by Peter McAlister, a Victorian batsman of much lesser ability and repute. Sydney Smith recalled: 'I had arranged for the Australian selection committee (Hill, Iredale and McAlister) to meet there at 7.30 to select the nucleus of the team for England. I intended to acquaint the selectors with the names of the players available, and then to leave them to their deliberations. I planned to carry on with some work elsewhere until the names were ready for Press release.

'Before I could begin, however, Clem Hill and Peter McAlister began arguing over the use of several bowlers in the recent Test matches. McAlister, when asked by Hill what experience he had ever had as captain, replied that he was as good a captain as Trumper, Armstrong, or Hill himself. Hill retorted that McAlister knew nothing at all about captaincy, and McAlister stated that Hill was the worst captain he had ever seen.

'At this, Hill stood up and leaned across the table. He told McAlister that he had been "looking for a bloody punch in the jaw all night" and that he was going to give him one. With that, he dealt him a terrific blow in the face. They came to grips, with Hill, the younger man, having the better of the struggle. He eventually pushed McAlister almost through the open window – three storeys up!

'Frank Iredale, who had been jammed in a corner with the table pressed against him, grabbed McAlister's arm and I pulled at Hill's coat-tails. We finally separated the duellists. McAlister was in a bad way, bleeding copiously. It took some time for Iredale and myself to get him presentable.

'This was my first experience of Test selection,' Smith reflected, seemingly still in mild shock 60 years afterwards, 'and I was somewhat shocked, especially as the two concerned were most likable men.'

During my visits to Mr Smith I bought from him copies of pre-war Wisdens and a few rare books such as C.T.B.Turner's *The Quest for Bowlers* (signed) and Iredale's *33 Years of Cricket*, together with some early Australian cricket annuals, and some cobwebby framed team photographs, glass mostly cracked. And since we now felt certain we would be heading towards England again, the job, house and family-relations situations all seeming fairly hopeless, I bought from Syd Smith the huge cabin-trunk that he'd taken on his two tours of England in the 1920s. It still had 'Ashes' labels stuck on it.

It was thrilling to be in the presence of these men who were part of cricket history, Eddie Gilbert, 'Stork' Hendry, Archie Jackson (per medium of his relatives and fiancée and Bill Hunt), Bert Oldfield, Arthur Chipperfield, Macartney's sister, Trumper's son, Johnny Moyes's widow, Harold Larwood, Alan Kippax, and Syd Smith junior – and since they would all be dead within such a short time, the encounters were beyond price. It helped me, in due course, to come to terms with the massive financial loss incurred by our 1971-72 Australian expedition, which in so many ways spelt anti-climax and desolation.

And there was one more interview to be set up, one which would have fateful consequences. It was not an 'interview' in the true sense of the word, for Jack Gregory, the Keith Miller of the 1920s, had flatly refused to give an interview to anybody for over 40 years, ever since a Sydney journalist had betrayed him in 1926. Why, he had asked Gregory, did he think Charlie Kelleway had been left out of the Australian touring team? 'Blowed if I know,' said Jack, not wanting to get involved. So the paper ran a story along the lines that Jack Gregory simply could not understand how the Australian Board could possibly have overlooked Kelleway. That was it. Thereafter, if he saw a reporter he'd turn his back or disappear.

All this had been established in exchanges of letters. He lived in Narooma, over 200 miles down the south coast. Now a widower (he'd married a Miss Australia), he lived alone, fishing and playing bowls, watching cricket occasionally on television. Without any prior arrangements, on impulse one morning I got into the car – the petrol-tank was full – and headed south.

Had I stopped for petrol I would have missed him. As it was, I found his elevated shack only with difficulty and called through the fly-screen door just as he was about to leave the house. He was completely unimpressed by my reminder that we had corresponded, and I announced that I had just driven 170 miles in the hope that he would sign these books for me. I had President Nixon to thank. Jack had been watching the American president's historic arrival in China on the little television set in the kitchen, and had forgotten to switch it off. 'You'd better come in,' he murmured.

As he signed the books, now, how could I lure him into conversation, delay him, interest him, get him reminiscing? Had he been to America? That was an unlikely bait, but it did the trick. Well, yes, he had, in 1921. Prohibition was in force, but 'somebody organised some King George IV [whisky] for us through a bootlegger'. And away we went.

His last Test was Bradman's first. His knee gave way, and even as I verified the tearful 'I'm finished, boys' I could smell the liniment. Vivid imagination? No: there was the tube, on the table. Jack Gregory saw me looking at it, and said, 'My knee's like a barometer. I had to put some of that stuff on. It's going to rain soon.'

In the early 1920s, having shown his dynamic allround skills when playing for the Australian military teams, he smashed centuries – left-handed and without batting-gloves – and bombarded batsmen with a furious mix of bouncers and yorkers, delivered off a bounding run-up which culminated in a kangaroo leap. When not doing this, he was pocketing all manner of catches at slip, standing extraordinarily close for the spinners (his 15 catches in 1920-21 still a Test record).

He hit the fastest century in Test history (in terms of minutes at the crease), at the old Wanderers ground, Johannesburg, in 1921. This cricketer was very special.

'I didn't know it was a record till my son told me some time later. Seventy-five minutes.'

'Seventy,' I told him. 'Jessop's was 75.'

'Yes, well, I just enjoyed batting. Never bothered about records.'

He really was so like Keith Miller; just as tall too.

Jack Gregory never bothered with batting gloves.
Here he books Larwood during the Oval Test of 1926

There were no cricket books visible, or trophies or bats or balls. Here was a cricketing Garbo. And if I'd dared to show a pencil and notepad he would surely have shoved me out through the door and down the steps. We talked on: his pride in belonging to such a large clan of cricketers: Australia's first Test captain, Dave Gregory, was his uncle, and little Syd, who played in a record 52 Ashes Tests, was his cousin; his keen approval of this modern 50-overs cricket ("I tried to amuse the public; they like to see bright cricket"). And when I lamented the fact that his old club (and mine), Paddington, had gone out of existence, his reply was as unsentimental as anything that had gone before: 'Oh, I played for lots of clubs – North Sydney, Manly, Paddington, Waverley, Randwick, Sydney.'

I knew when it was time to go. He declined the opportunity to be photographed – but was too late. I got a half-smile, but sensed that any plea for a few more seconds to take another, just in case, would have been pressing my luck. I thanked him, descended the steps with no great certainty of tread, got into the car with key slightly atremble, and drove to the nearest beach. There, while Jack Gregory's words were still freshly imprinted in my brain, I scribbled it all down: an interview that had been forbidden and yet which I felt would do nobody any harm, and cricket-lovers – so long as I could reach them – perhaps some appreciable good.

Jack Gregory: the forbidden photograph after a momentous meeting

A 1000-word feature typed, I sent it to Tony Pawson in England, and he did a double with it for me in *The Observer* and *The Cricketer*, from where it was picked up by BBC Radio. Mr Gregory, I Presume? was to be my very own Livingstone/Stanley.

All this lay weeks in the future. With heavy hearts and no little bewilderment, we packed our stuff into 37 suitcases and boxes and extricated ourselves from Sydney and what was left of the family. We sailed on Fairstar on March 19, 1972, the 40th anniversary of the opening of the Sydney Harbour Bridge, whose chief designer, Dr John Bradfield, was one of

Debbie's ancestors. Parting, as always, was a choking experience, made all the flatter this time against the background of hope which had been our sustenance a few months previously, but which was now spent. In reality we had nothing tangible to draw us back to England other than the gentler kind of friendship we had known in the 1960s, and the less ebullient society. At 35, it was still permissible for a man to nurture hope. But only just.

CHAPTER FOURTEEN

The only thing to do when life gets difficult is to take it on the chin.

TONY HANCOCK
(who later committed suicide)

IN my hour of desperate need, it was John Arlott's warm voice that came down the telephone line again. What was that, John? 'Would you be interested in becoming Tony Pawson's successor at *The Cricketer*?'

Of course, but that could never happen. For a start, I didn't drink gin-and-tonic; I hadn't been to public school; and I didn't have a hyphenated name.

'I've spoken to Jim Swanton, and he'll talk to you,' John went on, disregarding my cynicism. 'Will you do it?'

I would. I most certainly would.

It was now August, and we had been in England over three months. The voyage from Sydney had begun almost disastrously, for the ship sailed into a cyclone of great ferocity, the pallor of our faces being matched by the anxiety etched in the faces of those who lined the wharf as we tied up, many hours late, in Auckland.

Thereafter, it was divine. The Pacific, I'd long felt, was the best part of the globe, with its warmth, its smooth (usually) blue waters, and its alluring islands. Besides that, it had been the stage for some of the most dramatic episodes of the Second World War, the evil doings contrasting potently with the natural beauty in a way that can seldom have been so in the European theatre. As *Fairstar* cruised sedately north-east, with a predominantly young complement of passengers, I would gaze north across the endless surface of glass and picture the American and Japanese carrier-borne aircraft spitting red cannon-fire, and the landing-craft surging beachwards, the countless helmets masking men atremble and at prayer. Tarawa, Midway, Guadalcanal, Saipan: slaughter in Paradise.

Or the daydreams might turn to Captain Cook and other explorers of this hemisphere, and there would be a yearning for just such excitement and purpose, preferably without the discomforts.

Visiting our luggage in the hold, I would procure a book such as Luckin's South African cricket history and curl up in the convivial stuffiness of the library. Half-an-hour of sparring with the speed-ball in the gymnasium fed the conviction that I had never been fitter. And we were all glad to go ashore in Tahiti, where, in my advanced state of desperation, I stopped short of checking out real-estate prices.

In Panama we accepted an elderly American's offer to drive us around (he said he did this every time a ship came in: it eased the pain of separation from his own family), expecting a repeat of our unfortunate experience in Naples eight years before. But Charlie was genuine; and we were grateful.

Once through the Panama Canal, and after a day in Curaçao, we were into choppier waters, and I was already pining for the Pacific. We made it to Lisbon, shuddering at the temperature of early spring in Europe and taking a magical ride up to Cintra. Then came Rotterdam, with its vastness of cranes and canals and heavy topcoats; and finally the slow chug into Southampton. There was no elation in our hearts, but we knew how all the young Australians on board would be feeling now that the first stride of their European tour was about to be taken.

What could we possibly do about accommodation? I'd wired John Arlott to ask if he could fix up some emergency shelter for us, and he booked us into the Northlands Hotel. I went up to London to borrow a 15-cwt van from Servowarm (getting my old job back from dear old Reg Hirst, who always claimed he was related to George of Yorkshire and England) and I drove all the way back to the wharf to load up our 37 items of luggage, which miraculously had survived intact despite having been poorly taped up (a very rare signed photo of the 1912 Australian team was water-damaged). All this went into the Arlott barn in Alresford, and while Debbie helped John's wife Valerie about the house, I set about finding some accommodation.

We couldn't inflict ourselves on Mrs Heath again, but another Samaritan materialised now in the shape of Murray Hedgcock, an Anglophile Australian career journalist who had lived in London since the 1950s. We had met through cricket, found ourselves to have much in common in terms of attitude to the game and to matters Anglo-Australian, and although I had only rung him to say we were back and had he any suggestions as to what we might do for a roof over our heads, we were soon under instructions to deposit ourselves at Chez Hedgcock in south-west London, where we were welcome to remain as long as necessary. Since Murray and Petra had a house almost full of children themselves, this struck me as the finest gesture to come our way since Auntie Edie had loaned us that money for our first house.

We were all happy together for just over a week, and then I secured a three-month rental on a detached house, with large garden, in West Byfleet. There, I'm afraid, numbness set in. It was the reaction to what had happened to us over the past 12 months: Mum's death, the loss of the house we adored and so many of our possessions, the traumas of Sydney, where so little had gone right, and now the demoralising experience of being back where we started, now without a house of our own. Worse, I had lost seniority at Servowarm, so sales were hard to find. And even worse than that, house prices while we had been away had leapt by 40 per cent in a winter of property madness. We could not have afforded to buy the house we had recently sold even if it had been available.

Among the few cheering episodes was my return to my club, Shepperton, marked by a knock of 92 down in Brighton, though I regret I gave a mouthful to the buffoon who ran me out. And I wanted to attend the Cricket Writers Club dinner for the 1972 Australians. Brian Johnston said that all seats were taken, but he would ring if there was a cancellation. Good as his word, he telephoned to say that one of the Australians, a lesser-known called Massie, was indisposed and I could have his seat.

The Skinners' Hall might have had a strange hue about it that night because of reflections from Ian Chappell's suit, which was purple. But the captain made a good, defiant speech, and when the minstrels in the upper gallery played a faintly familiar refrain in medieval style, Rod Marsh, sitting opposite me, began to twitch about the nostrils. The pain of unsolved mystery clouded his features. 'What the f—'s that tune?' he lip-messaged. It took me a time to register it, but the embarrassment was Rodney's when I pointed out that, of course, it was obvious. Why the hell hadn't we spotted it straight away? It was our revered *Waltzing Matilda*.

But there weren't many light moments. Income was low. Property was frighteningly expensive. We were all bewildered by our recent experiences. It seemed, from the estate agents' house details, that we should have to consider going 'bush', to somewhere such as Guildford, a long 30 miles from London. I had made calls there, but we knew no-one in the area. Still, there was little choice. We settled on a small semi in Onslow Village. It was quiet and neat, in sight of Guildford Cathedral, and with a sizable mortgage, we could manage it for £12,000. Without any distinct enthusiasm we waited for the legal procedure to take its course during the summer of '72, while I played some cricket, watched some cricket, and cherished the items I'd managed to secure in Sydney.

Then came that fateful phone call from John Arlott.

The formidable E.W.Swanton would see me on the opening day of the Oval Test match, where shrewd Ray Illingworth and his England side would try to resist any attempt by young Chappell's desperadoes to level the series.

I thumbed a lift from West Byfleet and cursed my luck when my saviour's Morris Minor proved to have a top speed of around 30. It was like our constricted progress on that honeymoon drive back from Queensland in 1957.

On the roof of the broadcasting area on the old structure to the left of the pavilion at The Oval, Jim Swanton and I had a long conversation which was in reality no conversation at all. It was a gentle inquisition. I knew it was incumbent upon me to reinforce John's recommendation by displaying my knowledge of and love for cricket in support of my claim for the editorship. Thus, EWS might have commented on Lillee's field-setting, and my response would have been not just a nod of agreement but observations on how far Evans stood back for Tyson, and how wonderful it was that Bodyline field-settings had long since been banned, and how Lillee had mistakenly believed he shared Sobers's birthday but actually shared with WG.

Despite pessimistic forecasts from friends,
I always hit it off with Jim Swanton

Halfway through this probing discourse I blushed at the thought that we might be overheard. We must have sounded like a pair of 12-year-olds trying to impress and outdo each other. But this was EWS, not Ralph Lidyard.

Two things sealed the matter. I mentioned the cricket identities I'd tracked down recently in Australia, and Swanton suddenly swung round and said, 'Oh, you're the fellow who did that piece on Jack Gregory!' He then told me that the Australian had been one of his favourites. There soon followed another of his casual questions: 'Do you know who Jimmy Cannon was?'

'Yes,' said I, with renewed confidence, 'he wrote on cricket and football under the nom de plume of Tityrus.'

'No! No!' gurgled Jim. 'That was Jimmy Catton. Jimmy Cannon was chief clerk at Lord's – served MCC for over 60 years!'

With that small amusement I felt that the job was sealed.

But there was one further crucial formality. I needed to meet the owner of *The Cricketer*. His name was Benjamin G. Brocklehurst, and he was one of those amateurs that Somerset, among others, used to take on as captains. They weren't first-class cricketers in the true sense of the word (this one averaged 15.62 with the bat), and if he was a born leader it didn't show in the county's results while he was captain: in 1953 and 1954 they won four and lost 37 of their 56 Championship matches.

I had to go to Tunbridge Wells to meet Brocklehurst, and he seemed uncertain despite the presumably firm recommendations of Messrs Swanton and Arlott. After a general discussion, I waited patiently, but no invitation to take up the appointment was forthcoming, despite the seemingly urgent nature of Tony Pawson's position. Perhaps I should have asked for a gin-and-tonic? Perhaps I should have evoked Mum's maiden name and become a handsomely hyphenated David Frith-Thomas?

The days passed. This couldn't go on indefinitely, so I rang him from the corner phone-box (we had just moved into Onslow Village), asked him to decide now on whether I was his man, and suggested a start in September. Back at the house, I gave Debbie a big hug. It had been a long, long wait, an apprenticeship of absurd length, but at last I was in cricket full-time. I had inestimable quantities of stored-up energy and loyalty to impart. My 'scholarship' would not be wasted after all.

It was to last almost six years, and it was quite feudal. I was a long time getting the promised company (second-hand) car; had no secretary, no editorial assistant, and much negative influence from the general manager; the advertisement manager rang only when he wanted to air grievances; derogatory comment from within about the design and layout took no account of the fact that my training and acclimatisation amounted to 20 minutes with Tony Pawson when I took the hire-van to collect a filing cabinet and baskets of papers from him over in Sevenoaks. Tony showed me how to size up a picture, handed me some copy and some galley-proofs for next issue, and wished me luck.

It was soon apparent why Pawson had wanted to leave. The workload was too much for one man plus a (recently-departed) assistant . . . unless, like me, he was willing to devote nothing less than all the time and effort necessary to get the monthly job done. Then would come the next edition, pressing hard and urgently on the last one.

Matters became worse with a change of printer. The new foreman was a thin-lipped, hook-nosed and beady-eyed type, a Northerner who claimed to have played Rugby League for St Helens (the records didn't support his claim) and who, it soon emerged, was conspiring against my best interests. What had I got myself into?

A few friends had forecast difficulties between Jim Swanton and myself, but they were wrong. We got on all right: I respected him and made it clear, while he extended his own kind of respect towards me, based, I think, on the freemasonry of cricket and the background connection. Jim had shared brutal wartime captivity under the Japanese with many Australians.

Our house was small, but I now had to convert the dining-room into an office and clutter the narrow garage with the cabinets. The hours needed to get the job done totalled anything between 45 and 60 per week, and as time went on and the salary proved inadequate (salaries rose 100 per cent over this six-year period; my *Cricketer* pay was increased by 35 per cent in that time), I was compelled to add to my workload by writing a book here and there, as well as doing liaison work at Benson & Hedges Cup matches.

It was at one of those matches, at Taunton in 1974, that I became the first person ever to interview a lad named Ian Botham. This 18-year-old had dismissed Barry Richards for 13 and then gone in at No.9 with Somerset 113 for 7, still needing 70. Another wicket fell immediately, and only 15 overs remained. It seemed all over when an Andy Roberts bouncer struck the new boy in the mouth, causing him to spit out tooth fragments and blood. There was surprise when he refused to leave the pitch in this seemingly hopeless situation. Yet not only were Botham's innate aggression and bravura scarcely known beyond family and local neighbourhood, but few even knew how to pronounce his name. From Charles Barnett, the Gold Award adjudicator (with whom I'd had long and absorbing discussions about Hammond and the Ashes series of the late 1930s and much else during a couple of these B&H matches), to the journalists and random spectators, opinion was divided: Bott-ham? Boath'm? Borth'm? And did it matter? No person at the charmingly dilapidated Taunton ground that evening – not even the youngster himself – could possibly have foreseen the ultimate scope and magnitude of his career let alone the off-field sensations that were to go with it. As for this young bloke ending up in the House of Lords . . .

He now made his first headline by belting 45 not out to see Somerset into the semi-finals with an over to spare, and as he sat with a cigarlet, hand trembling from his efforts, I found him in the dim, cool dungeon of the dressing- room, congratulated him, asked him when and where he was born and, yes, before I forgot, how was his name pronounced? He was polite and accommodating – just as he was in signing one of his biographies for me about 15 years later: 'To David, From one convict to another!! Best wishes' followed by that indecipherable signature.

To see him strut onto the Test stage in 1977 and steam his way to all sorts of allrounder records in the years that followed was a delight, with the 1981 Ashes Tests marking Botham as the Lion personified, the towering cricket identity of his era, the name on all lips. His colourful lifestyle bulked up the legend, rendering the Jessops of long ago almost boring by comparison (for some).

He was good to have around in a hotel bar in New Zealand when a pair of large and flabby German drunks were getting over-attentive. And it was nice to catch a couple of his skyscraping hits aimed at a cluster of us cricket-writers at the nets in Christchurch (where England were soon to be bowled out for 82 and 93). There was a moment of pathos, too, when he was recalled to the England side towards the end of his playing days, the heartfelt 'It feels like old times' met by his 'I hope you're right, mate. I hope you're right!'

His flightpath subsequently has not always been impressive. Granted that his name will always be heavyweight, television producers might almost be excused for signing him up as quizleader and commentator. Almost. Not that his voice and spontaneity and natural wit are by any means the most wanting among cricketers who have stepped, with little or no training, into media activity. And that his very-best-selling autobiography was unduly self-justifying matters little to the masses who relive the great days by flicking through its 400 pages. I thought the most significant thing he wrote was that life might have been better if Brian Close, Ken Barrington and Mike Brearley had been around longer. Is there one among us who would not be more secure for having a dependable 'father figure' regularly on hand?

Back in late '72, I inherited a *Cricketer* magazine which was very plain in design and mediocre in content, so unimaginative, in fact, that it was often shamed by its only rival, *Playfair Cricket Monthly* – put together, boasted its editor Gordon Ross, from only one morning's work a week by him (and it showed). I was tied to a shoestring budget, and, as Alan Gibson once observed, only the very rich or the very poor wrote for *The Cricketer*.

I kicked it off with a couple of unusual personal items: the discovery of the ashes of Charlie ('Terror') Turner in a small, blue, cardboard box in a Sydney funeral director's office (Carters, set up by the old-time wicketkeeper Sammy Carter), and a confession by Clarrie Grimmett that he was a year older than the records had always shown. In an effort to brighten the illustrative quality, I laboured away at the occasional sketch, the best probably being an imagined musical evening featuring Bradman at the piano, Nyren with violin, in the presence of W.G.Grace, with Cardus looking down from a framed portrait. Later, to animate a letter about umpires' dress-code, I caricatured David Constant in boater, striped blazer and brogues, which delighted him, to judge by his effusive greeting when next we met. But they're no less odd than wicketkeepers or legspinners, these umpires, for after (in 1986 at Headingley) I'd revealed in print that England had claimed a wicket (Shastri lbw b Lever) while illegally having three fielders behind square leg (quickly substantiated by TV producer Nick Hunter), when next I encountered Mr Constant, who had been implicated as one of the umpires in that Test, he sniffed and walked away.

This was one of many times when I unwarrantedly began to doubt my own judgment. When I called out in the Press-box that there had been three behind square, nobody was able to second me. John Woodcock suggested that I must have imagined it. A few more overs passed, then I dashed down to the BBC Television van in search of producer Nick Hunter, a friendly, co-operative chap. The process of wiping everything bar the highlights tapes was already under way. Nick shouted for the wiping to be stopped, and we then began the laborious business of tracking through that dismissal from several angles. It was inconclusive . . . until a long shot from behind the bowler revealed a fieldsman on the long-leg boundary, in addition to the leg slip and the square-leg fielder who had drifted absentmindedly behind the umpire. Vindicated!

What further embarrassed the umpires in this match was that for one whole over India had 12 players in the field, Lamba, the 12th man, having failed to notice the return of Srikkanth. What fun.

I had contributed to *The Cricketer* in the 1960s: features on cricketers' graves and an article on the cricketers whose replicas have been displayed at Madame Tussaud's waxworks. In October 1972, I began compiling the monthly news round-up. But the December issue was my first full edition, and I hurried to Guildford station to take delivery of the advance copies with the same kind of excitement felt on those stomach-churning childhood Christmas mornings.

In the following spring I was appointed editor of this magazine that I used to buy 20 years ago in Sydney, a logical move in that Jim Swanton had for some time resided in the 'upper house', while I was in the engine-room, giving it day-and-night effort, a 'hands-on' editor if ever there was one.

It was a busy, stimulating time. In March '73 I had spotted that *The Cricketer* was about to outstrip *The American Cricketer* as the longest-running cricket magazine of all time, and signalled the fact. And when Brocklehurst picked up *Playfair Cricket Monthly* on the rebound when Dickens Press sold all their titles, there was the prospect of expansion.

It was not an easy transition. Gordon Ross, suddenly unseated, spent a lot of time at Tunbridge Wells bent on convincing the owner that he was indispensable. Out of that several things sprang: the absurd title of 'executive editor' and a place on the board for him, and a new quarterly statistical publication under his editorship, and a continuation of the *Playfair* readers' dinners at the RAF Club under a new banner.

Renowned more for the red carnation at his lapel than for his prose, Ross, a flashy, silver-haired egocentric who, to his undeniable credit, had served in

Bomber Command, behaved like an editor who had taken over a minor title rather than the other way round. He had no conception of what went into the magazine until he received a finished copy, but as his demands mounted it was clear that he expected all his dreary *Playfair* columns to be incorporated into *The Cricketer* (including his own, of course, which was usually very ordinary: he probably still holds the record for most first-person-singulars on one page: exactly 100 – and he has had some formidable challengers in this respect).

So I rang Swanton: 'Jim, this chap seems to think we're killing off *Gallery* and *In the Press* and much else to make way for *Playfair Cricket Monthly* stuff.'

'We must stand shoulder to shoulder, David,' came the reassuring reply. So relieved was I that I felt it was time for a quip, bearing in mind our relative stature: 'Perhaps you mean shoulder to *hip*?' The old boy gave that chuckle which, while reasonably long-lasting, never bore the warmth of an Arlott chuckle. I think I knew where I stood already.

Of course, as editorial director Swanton was empowered to issue the odd order. And one was just that: odd. 'Now look heah,' he said in that sealskin voice, 'I don't like to see the sweep shot on the front cover – or anywhere else for that matter. It's an abomination.' There spoke the author of a tender 1948 booklet on Denis Compton, the master sweeper.

Poor Gordon Ross, the Ernie Wise of cricket-writing, died in 1985, aged only 67, in the car park at Lord's, a demise many a cricket-lover might envy, though I wouldn't count myself among them.

After the amalgamation, it was still not a magazine I could feel proud of, for its seniority should have ensured its supremacy over all others globally (there was no longer any rival in Britain) in terms of production quality and cast of writers, to say nothing of bulk. The owner was surrounded by nodding, soothing toadies; it was I who took the brunt of criticism from readers. When I slipped in a few colour pictures, trying to make the magazine look like a modern publication, the owner became very angry. He baulked at the extra cost.

One gets used to pompous letters from readers. Several came in when I included photographs of Colin Milburn, Derek Underwood and Glenn Turner with their fiancées. But the most serious problem in 1973 was the temperamental Jack Fingleton's objection to my use of the word 'mischievous' in respect of his role in persuading Harold Larwood to emigrate to Australia. 'Fingo' was at his worst. First he accused me of inventing the story, then he objected to my preference for Larwood's version of what happened to his own. And then he refused to communicate with me at all, which left Jim Swanton as the ham in the sandwich.

There were a few more 'Look heahs' and letters back and forth, and eventually peace was restored, at the second attempt. In the first, I gave my evidence, through Larwood's own testimony, that he believed that Fingleton prompted him to start thinking about emigration by writing of a visit, with George Duckworth, to Larwood's Blackpool sweet-shop. The old Bodyline express bowler was forever grateful that Fingleton had planted the possibility in his mind. Fingleton now insinuated that it was Duckworth (who had died in 1966) who publicly raised the possibility of Larwood's moving to the land of his former enemies.

Where I played into Fingleton's hands was in trying to explain that to me the word 'mischievous' was harmless because my grandmother had often used it, the sense then being no more sinister than 'naughty little boy'. It was commonly heard in a particular environment at a particular time: mine. 'Fingo', in contrast, chose to view the word as potentially 'damaging to my newspaper reputation and integrity'. What a distortion. He scoffed at the grandmother reference, writing a letter twice as long as the first, and I replied with a reiteration of my apology.

'Fingo': friend and adversary

That was the end of a good friendship. Or so I thought. Four years later, during the 1977 Ashes tour, I played for the Australian Press against the English, and Jack Fingleton umpired. We had in our midst Kerry Packer, the man of the hour, and Ian Chappell. Five hundred locals had turned up at the Harrogate ground to heckle Packer, the heavyweight who was in the process of hijacking big cricket. Red-faced from a half-century alongside Chappell, I found myself still in when Packer strode to the crease.

He prodded the first ball to short cover and looked up enquiringly. There was never a single in it, but I tried to extend the lightheartedness of the occasion by giving the old Compton panic call of 'Yes! No! Wait!' (but without the customary 'sorry!'). Kerry came slowly down the track, and I wondered for a second or two whether he was about to add to the 60-odd writs he now had out; but all he said, in that gentle baritone of his, was: 'Look, I'm in your hands.'

Packer! In my hands! Wow! Did everybody hear that? Overwhelmed, I got out next over.

Then we fielded, and Fingleton teased Chappell with a multiple call against one of his legbreaks: no-ball, wide, running down the pitch, a swing of the arm as the ball reached the boundary rope, and then a warning for bad language. I stood at mid-on, laughing but minding my own business, and my heart leapt when Fingleton turned to me and winked. Was this the start of a thaw?

K.Packer first slip, D.Frith second, I.Chappell third, Harrogate 1977.
I scored 58 and had a good stand with Chappell, but no WSC contract materialised

Next morning, back at the Headingley Test, all was quiet in the Press-box when 'Fingo' entered, looked across, caught my eye, and drawled nice and loud, with great generosity, 'Ah, Cover-Drive Frith!'

In 1980 he responded readily to my request for an article (no fee) for the Lord's Taverners' Centenary Test commemorative booklet, and for another magazine piece. Tram-driver's son to dining companion to the rich, influential and famous, Jack Fingleton was not only one of the most prickly men I have ever known: he was among the most interesting. I was glad to be able to find for him a replacement copy of his *Cricket Crisis*, which must still be ranked among the very best of cricket books; and I was sorry he ventured into a Trumper biography, published in 1978, for it was a poor effort, employed as a tool against the reputation of his bête noire Don Bradman. Further, his admonition to me in 1968 never to publish a certain story was rendered redundant when he told (in the Trumper book) his version of the leak of Woodfull's sharp words to P.F.Warner in the Adelaide dressing-room during the Bodyline series. He always insisted he was wrongly blamed for passing this to the newspapers, claiming that Bradman had divulged it. Fingleton also never forgave The Don for being an influence in Fingleton's omission from the 1934 tour of England. He seethed and seethed, and there were those who condemned him for doing so. But if you seethe uncontrollably, short of regularly taking tranquillisers or consulting the Maharishi, while the irritant continues to hover, you go on seething. As it turned out, years later I was given handed the true story of the 1932-33 Adelaide leak and used it in *Bodyline Autopsy*.

Without actually seething, I was none too pleased to be summoned as a matter of duty to the final of the village competition at Lord's and also to Burton Court, Chelsea for the Cricketer Cup final. Not only had I always had a heavy week's work behind me and ahead of me, but my meagre salary was not subject to overtime. I'd have preferred to have been playing rather than standing around with strangers at the yawn-making village bun-fight. In the Old Boys' match, at least there was dear old Lt-Colonel 'Buns' Cartwright to chat to, specks of breakfast debris on his Eton Ramblers tie, and memory reaching back to the Great War and the 1907 Eton-Harrow match. Now *that* was worthwhile. The Maharaja of Baroda was good company too. But, as so often through the decades of cricket-watching, the limbs began to twitch. It would have been so much better to have been out in the middle actually playing.

It was not all proofreading until the eyelids were red, or monitoring a late correction on the machine, the new characters shining among the fields of hot metal already set and locked in and smeared with ink. It was not all condemnation for declining to risk my life through the snowdrifts at Newlands Corner, which was almost impassable: the trip to the printers simply had to be held over for a day. My life was worth something to me and my family. Nor was it all gratuitous advice from other members of (non-editorial) staff who had never had their fingers touched by cow-gum or known what an 'em' was.

I decided to show the readership that they had an energetic and enquiring editor who knew what it felt like to be embroiled in a serious game of cricket. With coach Alan Oakman's agreement, I set out one morning at 5.30 to join Warwickshire, the reigning county champions, at net practice at Edgbaston. With only a chocolate-bar to sustain me through the three-hour journey (overnight accommodation expenses were never on offer), and fighting to come alive in what for me has always been the most difficult part of the day, I jumped straight into it, running with the tracksuited Warwickshire lads, somehow managing to get over Willis's great arched form in the leapfrog parade, and then spewing into the gutter, a distressing upshot captured on film by the eagle-eyed Ken Kelly. Vigorous exercises brought an ominous tightening of the diaphragm, but this was the sort of preparation that provided for enough quick singles to steal a Gillette Cup match.

After a pleasant lunch, during which Dennis Amiss described some of the umpiring decisions on the recent England tour of the subcontinent, we headed for the nets: 'Mic' [Steve] Rouse whistled a ball through John Whitehouse and clipped the leg stump. Norman McVicker slammed Peter Lewington for six. Willis measured out his full run and did his mesmeric knees-up . . . Some leg-spin variations to a courteously respectful Amiss and John Jameson preceded some time at the crease, with circumspect reactions to A.C.Smith's wrong-foot swingers and Bill Blenkiron's nagging medium-fast. Willis had by now withdrawn from the practice area, much to my relief.

So, readers had an active editor as well as one who cared deeply about providing them with as enjoyable a read as limitations permitted. Thus, inclusion of Irving Rosenwater's provocative piece on Montague Druitt as cricketer as well as a possible Jack the Ripper. The title of the article cheekily gave a nod to E.W.Swanton's recent book: JACK THE RIPPER – SORT OF A CRICKET PERSON?

In 1973 the Bermuda Tourist Bureau and Bacardi offered me a few days on that charming island for the rum company's international cricket tournament, and it was there that Australian fast bowler Graham McKenzie taught me to body-surf, a pursuit in what we were led to believe were safe waters. When a mammoth stingray rose out of the sea like some amphibious Concorde, no more than 50 feet from us, we swam fast to the shore. We then went to pay our respects at the grave of the recently assassinated Governor. All movement was by motor-scooter, and with no trams on the island, I managed to stay in the saddle – though the hospitality at the receptions, especially that at the Bacardi headquarters, rendered scooter travel hazardous. Still, with tales of nocturnal pot-shots circulating, it needed some sort of Dutch courage to travel around at all after dark.

After one such hospitality session in Hamilton, we were ferried back across the harbour. 'Mischievously' the pilot made the launch swing on its axis and rear. I franticly grabbed hold of England's premier batsman, D.L.Amiss, as he was about to be thrown over the stern and mangled by the boat's screws, thereby entitling me to stake a share of the credit for his eight Test centuries that followed over the next 3½ years, especially the monumental 262 not out in Jamaica. The three ducks with which he ended the 1974-75 tour of Australia were nothing to do with me.

The cavalcade of interesting people flourished. Here, the 'king' of Bermuda cricket was Alma Hunt, an affable gentleman who was still saddened about succeeding in a trial before the West Indies tour of England in 1933 and then being omitted when it was decided that Bermuda was not really part of the Caribbean. Of the modern brigade, Seymour Nurse, Keith Boyce, Younis Ahmed, Ron Headley and Maurice Foster were, along with Amiss and McKenzie, good tour companions.

I had my MCC membership by now, proposed by as influential a member as one might find, EWS himself. And on my first day in the Long Room as a member, who should I bump into but my proposer, who was with the MCC secretary, Jack Bailey. Congratulations were extended, and in my characteristic desire to say something felicitous in reply, I mumbled something about standing for President next year. They both seemed a little uneasy in their half-smile response.

Access to Long Room and dressing-rooms was useful, not least when Neville Cardus was around. He held court, leaning against the oak table, his back to the play, his thoughts mainly concerning his favourites from way, way back: MacLaren, Tyldesley, Spooner, Makepeace, and the odd non-Lancastrian. He agreed to write a foreword to a book I was hoping to write on Trumper, but it never came to pass. Even if I'd started then, Neville would have been dead before it was completed.

He was glad to write for the magazine. In all truth, he needed the money, such as it was. One suggestion was a discourse on a team chosen on entertainment value, and he naturally spun together an enchanting essay, with probably not a fresh word to be found. It was actually Cardus who not only first had me, in my teens, spellbound with his creative and unusual writing but also, years later, awakened in me an awareness that there must surely come, in every writer's life, a time when he has little alternative other than to recycle himself: in the worst cases, it became self-parody, however unwittingly. This spectre can haunt. Turned outside oneself, it leads to a fascinating study in others, the bright sparks who write cleverly, slickly, inventively, energetically. How long before . . .? It is a problem the dull writer never faces. He has no mountain down which to slide.

I took all my Cardus books to his basement flat in Bickenhall Mansions, close to where Auntie Edie used to work, by Baker Street tube station. The patron saint of cricket writing implanted that frilly, spidery signature for me in each slim volume, hesitating only when he came across a second copy of *The Summer Game*. He signed after I'd explained here were two separate editions, but I think he suspected I might have been getting a duplicate signed in order to sell. In *The Noblest Game*, a handsome pictorial book he prepared with John Arlott, Neville penned a lyrical little inscription combining two of his classic titles: 'With my best wishes for many *good days in the sun*'.

Cardus: never hurtful

I saw him for the last time when a cricket-lover from the Australian outback sent me a bat which he particularly wanted Sir Neville Cardus to sign. Neville said he'd be in his customary seat in a certain steakhouse in Baker Street. I found the frail octogenarian ensconced with an Australian musician, female. I didn't stay long, though yet again he was all charm and cordiality.

A certain amount of Cardus-debunking has gone on of late, and I have contributed my share, though I hope in kindly fashion. His exaggerations and inventions were never damaging or hurtful, and his whimsical defence for fabricating a quote by a player would have won over many a jury: 'Ah, but that's exactly what he *would* have said!'

Perhaps the most amusing contrast between what probably happened and what Cardus's romantic bent made happen sprang from the 1896 Test at Old Trafford (when John Frederick Neville, son of a lady of the night in Rusholme, Manchester, was only eight – not seven, as he claimed). Having bowled 544 balls against Australia in this match, taking 13 for 244, the titanic Surrey fast bowler Tom Richardson, according to Cardus, 'still shook from the violent motion. He stood there like some fine animal baffled at the uselessness of great strength and effort in this world. A companion led him to the pavilion and there he fell wearily to a seat.'

One who unquestionably was there reported a different scene: shattered though he must have been by Australia's three-wicket victory after his stupendous effort, Richardson apparently was first off the ground and had sunk two pints of ale before any of the others had taken their boots off.

There will always be those who prefer the first version.

A blurry mixture of fact and fantasy ran through Cardus's life, even to a latterday claim that he was a closet Nazi. Perhaps, with his *Guardian* connection and fondness for the National Liberal Club, he had all the qualifications for the most unlikely of spies. Happily, the matter seems to have been resolved with the recognition that many an Australian musician was stung by a scathing Cardus review, and that one of them was seeking revenge. These things happen.

In 1974, the belief that the day was imminent when one cricket magazine could girdle the earth grew stronger, and I suggested to the owner a modification of title. The May issue thus saw the extended name-tag of *The Cricketer International*, which, on reflection, sounds rather pompous – and therefore rather apposite.

Lord's continued to produce shocks. The 1973 West Indies Test was interrupted on the Saturday by a bomb scare which had spectators flocking onto the grass (keeping umpire Dickie Bird company as he sat minding the pitch-covers) or flooding out through the gates. My two sons were somewhere in the crowd, and showed heroic indifference to evacuation. My vivid imagination saw me out of the Press-box in a flash, but I was a long time agonising by the Warner Stand before they sauntered into view, the elder son, now 14, tossing away his beer-can just as I caught sight of him.

Out in St John's Wood Road, it was the oddest of sights as Lance Gibbs and a few other West Indians strode down towards their hotel through the milling throngs of numbed spectators. Had this not all happened, I would have remembered the match chiefly for having been in the West Indian dressing-room when Garry Sobers came back in with a stomach problem. He was already 132 (one of three centurions in West Indies' eventual 652 for 8) and it was to be the last of his 26 Test centuries. He gets my vote as the greatest allround cricketer of them all, and the vote is tendered with extra conviction because he has always been such an even-tempered, friendly and modest chap. Hurt by the vilification across the Caribbean after his generous declaration which let England in for victory at Port-of-Spain in 1968, he once confided that vengeful umpires in several of the territories gave him out to stiff decisions in the wake of his captaincy error. He was also mystified to a certain extent and wounded by the hostility which greeted his decision to appear in a match in Rhodesia (later Zimbabwe) in 1970 when that country was in political isolation. What puzzled him most was that coaching black youngsters was part of the agreement, and surely no-one could object to that?

The Lord's bomb scare in August was followed by something rather more real and terrible in October, when the IRA campaign took in Guildford, which had long been a Saturday-night haunt for off-duty military personnel from nearby Aldershot barracks. On the night of October 5, the *Horse & Groom* pub in North Street was blown up. Two female and two male soldiers and a civilian were killed and over 60 people injured. Forty minutes later another planted bomb exploded in the *Seven Stars* in Swan Lane, injuring several people. We had been alerted by a phone-call from elder son Peter. He had been in the youth club a stone's throw away. At first I thought he was joking: a bomb in Guildford, people dead, police cordons? Come off it, Pete! But an ITN newsflash was now on the screen, and nausea assailed all of us.

Viewed up North Street, beyond the police tape cordon, it looked like something out of the Blitz. Arc-lights revealed rubble and dust, stretchers and walking wounded, a scene of horror as the emergency services went about their grim duties. The old town, pre-eminent in the history of cricket for its many 'firsts', had been classified as a 'hotbed of rest'. Now it was going to be a long time before the reputation for peacefulness and tranquillity would be restored.

As Lillee and Thomson inflicted shellshock on most of Mike Denness's 1974- 75 England team in Australia, I received two interesting invitations to cricket countries, one 'above board', the other not. I was condemned subsequently for accepting one, though not the other, even though my aim was the same for each: to find out about each country and its cricket set-up. The acceptable freebie was Pakistan. The disapproved one was South Africa.

I was flown to Lahore by courtesy of PIA's London representative, Haseeb Ahsan, no less, the joker who was to make such an impact as Pakistan's manager on the 1987 tour of England. The first problem presented itself while I was still at Heathrow airport. The televised highlights of the Ashes Test in Australia were about to be shown, and there was just time before take-off to watch them – if only I could find a TV screen. PIA had a lounge, but no TV set. Now, would Qantas or British Airways, my own 'national' airlines, help? BA were nearer.

'I am sorry, sir,' said the lady in red, white and blue, 'but if you are not flying with British Airways we can't possibly allow you use of our passenger lounge.'

Fair enough. I'll try Qantas, I thought. But as I wandered around the terminal, with the clock approaching zero hour, I spotted PanAm, and asked at the desk if I could watch the cricket on their TV, being a cricket-writer, and appreciating that I wasn't flying with them, and probably anyway everybody was watching baseball up there, etcetera.

He looked a lot like Edward G.Robinson, and without a word he reached for the telephone and said, 'Frank. Now listen. There's a guy coming up to watch the cricket on TV. Pour him a Scotch.' A wink at me, then he moved away.

The Test in Melbourne was like no other in the series, for Thomson and Lillee were both injured, and England, their maulings now a thing of the past, won by an innings. Leather armchair, whisky-and-ginger, peanuts: how, I wondered, could I ever repay PanAm? They were to go out of business before I had a chance. I could have wept.

Two hotels in Lahore proved intolerable before I sought shelter in the expensive Intercontinental. There it was, at the end of a long street. One paving-stone was missing, and it was precisely when I was a step away from it, weighed down by suitcase and overnight bag, that one of the three-wheeler taxis frantically tooted his horn, wanting my patronage. I turned to see what the racket was . . . and plunged into a hole in the pavement. My foot was submerged in a layer of unidentifiable muck and my shin was ripped half its length by the concrete. The taxi man took pity on me – or was perhaps concerned at my verbal outburst over what had happened – and he took me, free of charge, to the steps of the hotel.

'David! How nice to see you! How are you?' exclaimed my cherished friend Hanif Mohammad as I staggered, a messy, bloodstained vision, across the lobby.

How did I look? I asked.

Hanif was seriously concerned, and sent for the hotel doctor. The hour was late, and the ancient medico's hand shook as he ministered to me. He smelt of brandy. After a nervous half-minute, I took the cut-throat razor from him and undertook to shave my hairy leg myself. For all I knew, he might have thought he was working on an amputation. He splashed a bottle of spirit over the wound, bound it up, and said I'd be OK in the morning.

It was a restless, disorientated night, but next day I mixed with the West Indians at breakfast, and Clive Lloyd, their skipper, readily agreed to my taking part in the net practice down at the Gymkhana ground. I picked up a couple of wickets, but only against batsmen who were nursing injuries, such as Gordon Greenidge, whose back was playing up. They generously gave me an innings, ended when two local lads joined in and aimed everything at my forehead, but not before I had sampled the left-arm mystery spin of Elquemedo Willett, and the even more bemusing bowling purveyed by Viv Richards, who, like Greenidge, was a recent Test debutant. Richards slid his fingers over the top in an offspin action, but the ball consistently carried on to slip. He was very amused at my confusion.

That Lahore Test match saw Intikhab Alam, bareheaded, felled like an ox by an Andy Roberts bouncer. It saw Roy Fredericks cop two lbw decisions, one at least of which was very unconvincing, and I sympathised with him completely when he vented his anger in the dressing-room, where I had been made welcome. A century by Mushtaq Mohammad propped up Pakistan's second innings, and then Leonard Baichan, one of four Guyanese left-handers in the side, made a century for West Indies in his first Test to ensure a draw.

I was impressed by the manner in which Lance Gibbs, a senior player, acted as chaperon to Baichan at the Press conference after the match. Elated at his performance, the batsman chattered excitedly in response to questions which became more and more probing. Gibbs made sure the newcomer fell into no traps.

Few matches fail to offer up oddities. Here, at the unfortunately-named Gaddafi Stadium, the world's most recent quadruple-centurymaker, Aftab Baloch (428 for Sind, and now housed in Room 428 at the hotel), scored an important 60 not out in Pakistan's second innings, after being showered with bouncers. We also saw play held up when kites fell onto the outfield, the celebration of Basant finding the majority of citizens attached to the strings of high-flying kites of all descriptions. And, most curiously of all, 10 of the 31 wickets which fell were to lbw decisions. On the third evening, when about eight leg-befores had already been given, I shared a car back to the hotel with the two umpires, both of whom were standing in their first Test, and one of whom leaned across to me and said: 'Excuse me, but what is world Test record for lbws?' He was a man who had a date with destiny – and Mike Gatting – at Faisalabad 13 years hence. His name was Shakoor Rana.

In the pavilion it was a pleasure to talk with the Little Master (Hanif), and Jehangir Khan (a mighty cricketer now remembered principally for having bowled the ball that killed the sparrow at Lord's in 1936), and those pioneers of Pakistan Test cricket, Fazal Mahmood, Imtiaz Ahmed, Mahmood Hussain and merry Maqsood Ahmed.

Then there was A.H.Kardar, the Big Influence in Pakistan cricket for so many years. I was granted a formal audience with him, and learned that the Pakistan Cricket Board wanted to encourage cricket all over Asia and also were intent on ending the international dominance, on and off the field, of England and Australia. Kardar wanted 'neutral' umpires in Test matches, and reiterated the hard line on South Africa: recognition would not be forthcoming so long as apartheid existed.

Why, I then asked him, was Younis Ahmed banned for life for playing with Derrick Robins' XI in South Africa whereas Mushtaq Mohammad, who also toured, was out in the middle now scoring a match-saving Test hundred?

The answer came: Mushie had had his medicine: a carpeting, an apology by him, and exclusion from ever being captain or vice-captain of Pakistan.

Nineteen months later, Mushtaq Mohammad, bless him, became captain.

My injured leg turned all the colours of the rainbow as infection spread, but West Indies' English physio, Len Pink, fixed me up, and I was able to join Clive Lloyd, Lance Gibbs and Intikhab for a memorable Chinese meal on the final evening that was heart-warming in its fellowship.

There was an even more international flavour about the visit to South Africa a month later, but before leaving Pakistan I had one further assignment, and that was to see Air Marshal Nur Khan down in Karachi. The former Air Force commander-in-chief and Governor of West Pakistan had structured a support system for cricket, hockey and squash which amounted to State sponsorship and which was already producing results. The English system, vast and loose, seemed so amateurish by comparison. Nur Khan explained the national scheme with great patience, and after Omar Kureishi had escorted me back to Lahore, I found myself telling a young man in the bar all about my excursion.

'And what did you think of the Air Marshal?' he asked.

'Wonderful man,' I replied, without hesitation. 'So welcoming and helpful.'

'Good,' said the young man. 'He is my father.'

Sometimes, at least, one managed to say the right spontaneous thing.

The Derrick Robins team in Johannesburg consisted of Englishmen, Australians, a Pakistani, a Sri Lankan and a West Indian, captained by Brian Close and managed by Ken Barrington. My opportunity came through KLM, who were launching a new route to South Africa.

Again, there was the pleasure of joining in at nets, and seeing close-up Eddie Hemmings' face as Max Walker whacked him over the distant hedge. 'You bludy pillock!' growled the bowler, while big Max just stood there grinning, bat aloft.

Eric Rowan, the cantankerous old Test double-centurymaker, was helping with arrangements, and took every opportunity to vent his impatience with world attitudes: 'We've fallen over backwards to please the outside world,' he stormed, 'and the outside world just tells us to get stuffed. Some of the people who grew fat from Africa are now its sternest critics.'

Over the years, anyone who went to South Africa prior to the rebirth of the country following Nelson Mandela's release was branded 'sympathiser' by hard-line anti-apartheid commentators. Many of these had had to rely on what they had read or been told. My mistake, it seems, was in not stating very loudly and clearly that I disapproved strongly of the oppression inflicted on the non-white communities and all the deprivation that went with that oppression. My reason for never asserting this in unmistakeable terms is that I was suspicious of many who ostentatiously made this clarion call to all who would listen. I've always felt that to shout the obvious sounds phoney. I was quietly sincere in my conviction that I was no racist (I could name many who are, though you'd never guess), and that was what mattered. Nor, I dare say, was Brian Johnston a racist, though he managed the previous Robins tour of South Africa. From that early hero-worship of Randolph Turpin to the pleasure of being now among cricketers and associated people from all cricket's territories, I judged a man solely on the percentage of goodness apparent in him.

I failed to comprehend the criticism directed at people like Don Wilson, who was coaching black youngsters in Transvaal. The same went for Phil Carrick, another Yorkshireman, coaching in Soweto. There was so much that was good and inspiring on the cricket front in that deeply disturbed land. Cricket was showing the way. That is why those of us who had been there and looked and listened appeared to understand a little more than those who focused solely on the apparently unshiftable Afrikaner rulers, whose resistance to the world's demands that apartheid be swept away pointed to a siege that must surely last well into the 21st Century. That it didn't is one of the more astonishing turn-ups of our time. Aside from all the cant and hypocrisy, the pressures from the outside world were effective. But through it all, cricketers in South Africa who defied their government and bravely broke through the colour barriers brought credit to themselves and the game which has not been adequately recognised.

Back in England, there was still despair over the bouncer bombardment undergone by the 1974-75 England side in Australia. The team had set out high in optimism after three crushing defeats of India and three draws against Pakistan in the summer of 1974. High among the days of unreality in Lord's Tests was when India were bundled out for 42, rendering even my pal Bishan Bedi practically speechless. On top of all the euphoria of this loss-free season, England seemed unwilling to believe that Dennis Lillee's back had mended – or at least that he could ever again bowl as ferociously as in 1972 – or that this new chap Jeff Thomson could possibly be as fast as was being reported. It was surely typical Australian propaganda. The Englishmen came home five months later like Napoleon's battered legions out of Russia.

The eminent Lord Philip Noel-Baker, a Quaker, Labour MP, and 1959 Nobel Peace Prize-winner, wrote in anguish to *The Times* urging cricket umpires to seek more power to control fast bowlers' belligerence. I fired off a letter in reply, pointing out that cricket's Laws already afforded the umpires considerable authority in this area; the problem was simply that the men in white coats seemed to lack the will and courage to enforce restraint among over-aggressive fast bowlers.

And that was how *The Fast Men* was born. A Sydney publisher, Richard Smart, saw the letter in the paper and wrote asking if I had a special interest in fast bowling (who hadn't?) and whether I'd like to write a book on the subject. It seemed a good idea . . . until he told me it had to be written in three months flat.

Although I had to continue to keep *The Cricketer* going single-handed editorially and was having an extension built onto the garage to take the filing cabinets, and although Debbie was in hospital briefly for a minor operation during that time, with the three youngsters mainly taking care of themselves,

I took the task on. Burning up the nights, propped up by a thousand cups of black coffee, surrounded by reference books, I met the deadline, producing the first-ever full-length study of the fast bowler's 'art', his methods, mentality and, in some cases, madness. A by-product of any project such as this is that the author himself – apart from ending up punch-drunk – learns so much along the path of his researches.

The book was launched during the Oval Test, with Lillee and Thomson among our guests, the pair of them having had a preview of the book down in the dressing-room.

'Ay, look at this bloke. He's bowling with his cap on!' said Thommo. 'He must've been real quick, *he* must've!' He was looking at a picture of the nippy West Indian legend Learie Constantine.

Meanwhile, Lillee had gone straight to the index and naturally enough checked out all the references to himself. I grew tense. Were there any inaccuracies? 'Yeah, not bad, Frithy,' said the demon bowler. 'Except that beamer at Willis was not deliberate! The ball slipped!' I readily concurred.

Launching of The Fast Men at The Oval, summer '75: Richard Smart (publisher), Barry Norman, author and wife Debbie, Jeff Thomson, John Arlott, Dennis Lillee

A friend relayed a strange story about The Fast Men when it was on sale in a store in Adelaide where English screen heartthrob Stewart Granger was promoting his autobiography. He sat for an hour or more and not one copy of his story was purchased. As the world-famous actor stormed out and jumped into the waiting limousine, a thoughtful shop assistant handed him a copy of *The Fast Men.* As the car took off, the actor (whose face comes to mind whenever I see Mitchell Starc) shouted 'F*** Australia! F*** Adelaide!

And f*** this book!" Then he tossed it out of the car.

A few years later I wrote the natural companion volume, *The Slow Men*, and found them an even more interesting lot. But just as the book on fast bowlers was written fast, so the volume on the spinners took a long time. My overall workload was taking its toll, fatigue was reaching ever more deeply into my constitution, and the research was somehow more consuming than with the fast men's stories. For the one and only time, I failed to meet a deadline, and had to plead for an extra six months.

Back in 1975, the compressed energy from all the years of frustration and aspiration was still gushing forth. I even had time to make regular visits to the Australian dressing-room for after-play beers. So friendly was Ian Chappell that I sometimes went in while play was in progress. 'What's all this crap [or something similar] you've been writing about us now?' was a common Chappell question. But although I was duty-bound to condemn over-aggression and other elements of the 'Ugly Australians', he knew I had feelings for the corporate thing which was the Australian XI and what it represented, which was unadulterated team spirit and a pride in one's country.

After England's drubbing in the first Test at Edgbaston, of course, there had been a stirring revival, with the grey-haired and bespectacled David Steele, an unlikely newcomer, batting awkwardly, bravely and successfully at Lord's, as did John Edrich (175). England's entry into the field, at something of an infantry charge, behind new captain Tony Greig, was a stirring sight. The lads on the old Tavern concourse burst into *Rule Britannia,* and at last we had two real teams contesting the Ashes. The problem for me was that I wanted them both to win.

As far as I am aware there had been no reservations about Basil D'Oliveira's playing for England from 1966 (apart from the taunts from one or two Pakistan players who asked forcibly why he was making runs and saving the match for a country to which he did not belong: they didn't realise he slept with his England cap under his pillow, so proud was he). But in 1972 there was a certain amount of disquiet among the Australian journalists that this extremely tall South African, Tony Greig (whose father was Scottish), was making sizable contributions to England's cause.

I made a point of enquiring again during the 1975 series, and the reaction was a fairly consistent 'What are you on about?' So long and so well had Greig now been playing for England that he was considered a natural member of the Test XI, though I cannot be so sure that the English cricket public universally felt that way. Certainly, after he defected to Kerry Packer's breakaway unit, the sense of betrayal manifested itself in all manner of derogatory reaction, summarised in more gentle terms by John Woodcock's monumental observation that Greig was not 'English through and through'. Greig was the first modern cricketer to be identified as a 'mercenary'. D'Oliveira, of course, was not. His story was one of romance, dignity and a stout heart.

The first World Cup was staged in that 1975 summer in England, and everywhere I went there was drama. At Lord's, Sunil Gavaskar batted through 60 overs to make 36 not out after England had piled up 334 for 4, a demonstration of Indian iron will with few comparisons. At The Oval, Thomson's terror tactics against Sri Lanka, which kept the local hospital casualty department fairly busy, earned him the sobriquet of Our Ambassador to Sri Lanka. Same venue, three days later, and Alvin Kallicharran smote Lillee for 35 off 10 balls. And in the final, the longest day's cricket ever, surely, and one of the most taxing, West Indies beat Australia in the twilight, with Lillee and Thomson rattling off 41of the 59 needed in their last-wicket stand. Clive Lloyd's hundred, Viv Richards' three run-outs (there were five altogether in Australia's desperate reply), and the persistent tension left nobody in any doubt: the World Cup was here to stay, even if it was only limited-overs cricket.

On one of those London evenings I stayed in town, having been offered a room where the Pakistan players were staying. I valued the gesture, especially when I found the room to be spacious and neat. When I came to in the morning, however, I was not alone. Half-a-dozen Pakistan cricketers were asleep all around me, and there were lots of cheerful good-morning exchanges. I lathered up for a shave, and found a young man beside me who had only wisps of facial down to dispose of. He spoke with a husky voice, though not with any great command of English, and he said he was seventeen. His name was Javed Miandad, and he was to remain a favourite throughout his long career. His was the kind of resourceful batsmanship I envied, and he only just missed out as one of my choices in a favourite theoretical exercise I used to put to friends in the late 1970s: Which two batsmen and two bowlers would you choose if you were compelled to sit and watch them into eternity?

My contemporary choices were Ian Chappell and Gordon Greenidge against Jeff Thomson and Chandrasekhar. You could tell a lot about a person by his or her selections. And it was even more fun if your players could come from any era.

As for the daily grind, the punishing solo deskwork was lightened by contact with some of the best people in cricket, men like Bill Bowes, the studious and amusing Yorkshire and England fast bowler turned journalist, and Ben Barnett, former Australian wicketkeeper (and prisoner of the Japanese [Bowes had been a "guest" of the Italians]), now resident in England. There were, too, magazine contributors from the old playing ranks, like Harold Gimblett, the 'tormented genius', and Jack Young, the Middlesex and England left-arm spinner, now struggling painfully on sticks but defiantly perky. There was also Alan Ross, most elegant of writers, who never made the mistake of immersing himself solely in cricket; and Ray Robinson, kindliest of men, dextrous cricket-writer; and Gerald Brodribb, painstaking researcher of the old school, the perfect companion when 19th Century cricket was on the agenda.

Then there were the nice, gentle people who became staunch friends – free of the competitive pressures and ego-flashing that I soon came to realise were part and parcel of the cricket media world – men like Sam Canynge Caple and Dennis Castle and G.Neville Weston (the WG expert), Ted Brown the book-dealer, Arthur Gibson in England and Denys Heesom in South Africa, who both kept a stream of encouraging correspondence coming to alleviate any self-doubt and exhaustion on my part, and collectors and aficionados like Pat Mullins and Murray Hedgcock and Gordon Phillips and Richard Williams and Bob Jones and Mike Smith (despite the fact that he dwelt in Tunbridge Wells) and Yorkshire's David Wells. David Rayvern Allen, who shared my affection for John Arlott and for the quieter byways of cricket research, had become, like all of these, a valued friend in the late 1960s. The pursuit of cricket in the ultimate terms which I had chosen would never have completely satisfied without such friendships, and innumerable others besides. I never bought a friendship. These have been friendships that money couldn't buy.

Meeting Ian Peebles was a special pleasure, especially when he talked of bowling to Archie Jackson in the 1930 Oval Test. When, in 1974, I asked the urbane Peebles to write an obituary of New Zealand batsman Stewart Dempster, I was impressed by his integrity as he politely declined on the grounds that he had never had much time for the chap.

The grind was further broken up by occasional speaking engagements at dinners and cricket-society gatherings. It was an ordeal at first, for not only had I had no training, but unhappy memories lingered still from those bad moments in the classroom. Still, the challenge was there, and so determined was I to banish nerves and make a success of my first address that I went on and on for well over an hour. The subject was easily presented: it was the life and times of A.E.Stoddart.

Confidence grew as the engagements came and went, and the groups were welcoming and generous. There were minor exceptions, such as when I chose to advocate competitive club cricket in Somerset, before the baleful glare of the old county skipper 'Bunty' Longrigg, who turned out to be very old-school; and also when I suggested to the members of Sussex Cricket Society in 1977 that the Packer revolution might benefit the game in the long run. Most cricket-lovers in that neck of the woods considered Tony Greig to be in disgrace for defecting to Packer. Only the smooth summing- up by the charming president, George Cox, got me out of that frozen hall in one piece.

The further north I went the more I liked it: Wombwell, Leeds, Manchester (200 attentive members at Old Trafford), Boston in Lincolnshire (audience of nine, including four schoolboys), Uppingham (teenaged Jonathan Agnew and James Whitaker wide-eyed in the front row).

Dinners were a different matter. Cricket was incidental. Jokes were what counted, no matter how familiar. It was an opportunity to display the lifetime predilection for accents, and to tease a gathering by not always making it clear whether remarks were serious. I was not always sure myself.

Outdoor pleasures could hardly have been bettered than by strolling round the Hove ground with John Arlott and Keith Miller, or Portsmouth with John again (how those spectators did look upon him as their Messiah) and with the elegant and doomed Clive Taylor, and the genial giant Bill Shepheard, whose public-address announcements at Hampshire matches fooled many into thinking JA was at the microphone. Bill's most outstanding performance was when he drilled through all the teatime scores before signing off casually with: 'And President Nixon has resigned.'

My own cricket continued to produce extremes: Shepperton all out for 26 on a glassy pitch at Uxbridge in the National Club Knockout; a call from Surrey coach Arthur McIntyre (who happened recently to have branded my elder son a chucker at the schools trial nets) for me to captain Surrey 2nd XI at Motspur Park, where we framed a four-man pace attack (David Smith, Andy Mack, Otto Verrinder and Bob Lowe) two years before Clive Lloyd thought of it.

Even in freezing February I managed to get a cricket match going, an annual charity match in the depths of Surrey, featuring Test players like John Snow, Geoff Arnold, John Inverarity, and Pat Pocock, and showbiz people like Tom Courtenay and Pete Murray, Ed Stewart and Colin Welland. Here Tim Rice made one of his earliest public appearances. And when Jim Laker was lured down to umpire, he was persuaded to bowl the ceremonial opening over, just for old times' sake. Snowy kept wicket. Basil D'Oliveira played, and so did Ted Dexter (it was a privilege to act as his runner). We prayed for snow, but it was usually mild, though one year the rain was heavy, and poor Patrick Moore looked like a drowning whale out there in his capacious sweater. Urged to take shelter, he refused, probably lifted by the one banner, which read PATRICK MOORE FOR ENGLAND. Before taking the field for the February Fools, the astronomer extraordinaire had entrusted Debbie with his wrist-watch, delivering the memorable line: 'Do take care of it. It was given to me by Neil Armstrong, and it has been to the Moon.'

Occasionally I wrote match reports for newspapers: Guildford matches for *The Guardian*, some, including a Gillette quarter-final at Southampton, for *The Times*. It was from the sun-fried trestle table at the Hampshire match that I saw what looked like a stumping miss by Bob Stephenson. The evening sun was half-blinding, but it seemed beyond doubt to have been a critical error, and I wrote to that effect. A few hours later, back home, I watched the TV highlights and was mortified to see that the ball had shot out of the rough, and no keeper in the world could have done much with it. So I rang the paper. But it was too late. So I wrote a letter to Stephenson, apologising for my misreading of the situation. By return, I received one of the nicest of letters from Bob. Often, he said, he had been wrongly accused of missing chances, but never before had a journalist bothered to tender an apology. For days afterwards I suffered a sharp headache from the tightness of my halo.

It was gratifying, too, to get a letter from the secretary of MCC (Jack Bailey) after writing a *Gallery* feature on Dennis Lillee. Bailey welcomed the strictures that ran alongside the columns of praise, balancing Lillee's great talent against his verbal aggression. Had we all but known it, a horde of very vocal and belligerent fast bowlers was about to emerge to dominate the game and change its face forever, and not simply in forcing the need for batsmen's helmets and visors.

That *Gallery* series was obvious material for a book, since all the major players of the time had been honoured, the essays usually written by eminent writers. So Lutterworth agreed to publish, and I chose 50 Gallery items and added footnotes. It was one of these that produced perhaps the biggest howler I ever made. 'With Greig's appointment,' I wrote, 'Brearley's name finally ceased to be spoken of as a possible England captain.' In 1976, who could have foretold the Packer phenomenon of '77, much less the second coming of Brearley in '81, Botham's year? Anyway, although it took me several years, I managed to get all 50 *Gallery* cricketers to sign my copy of the book, and as I write, 44 years later, they are all still alive apart from nine of them.

I co-wrote another little book around this time, *Great Moments in Cricket*, though there were problems: Gordon Ross heard about it and said it clashed with something he was putting together. He went running to Brocklehurst, and if ever I needed further evidence that we were no team, this was it. The publishers had already spent money on its production, and I needed the fee, modest though it was. So a weird compromise was reached: I used a *nom de plume*, 'Andrew Thomas'.

Every effort I could make was directed to the creation of as bright a *Cricketer* magazine as possible in those non-colour days, and with so much dead wood having to be accommodated in the permitted number of pages. But to feed us and pay the mortgage I had to take on other work, such as editing *Arlott and Trueman on Cricket*, a book based on the BBC TV series, and working on *Cricket: More Than a Game*, an attractive publication edited by John Sheppard. And some happy hours were spent in the Arlott household at Alresford working with John on the Oxford Companion to Sports and Games.

But one project had a vice-like grip on my imagination. For 10 years, probably more, I had dreamt of putting together a large pictorial history of England-Australia Test matches, and to that end I had built up a copious index of illustrations. With the centenary of these matches fast approaching and ambitious plans having been put in place for the celebrations in Melbourne in March 1977, I had to get weaving.

I gave Brocklehurst first refusal. It was too big for him. Then I tried two or three mainstream publishers, to no avail. Then Richard Smart, confidence boosted by the success of *The Fast Men*, secured a deal with Lutterworth. There was last- minute resistance to such a mass of illustrations – why not be satisfied with 500? – but my mind was set on creating the first cricket book ever to contain 1000 pictures, banking on its success being assured by riding with the Centenary Test excitement and by its very bulk, which, with luck, would render price unimportant, even though £12.50 was rather a lot to pay in 1977.

So every night for weeks in 1976 I found pictures to bring back to life the 224 Anglo-Australian Tests played since 1877, laid down the pages, wrote the text and captions, and counted myself blessed when the two great knights of Ashes cricket, Don Bradman and Len Hutton, agreed to write forewords.

Production was carried out cleanly and efficiently by Jolly & Barber in Rugby, and on publication day Frank Bough brandished a copy of the finished book on BBC's *Grandstand programme*, which was no bad way to alert the nation to a new cricket title.

My big problem was getting to Melbourne for the big event. No-one from *The Cricketer* would be there, and the magazine was not going to finance me. So I cobbled together a deal with Qantas whereby the airline took (all too many) copies of the book, and I funded my own accommodation. It was money well spent, for, to this day, there has never been a cricket party to compare.

I need only look at my file copy of the England v Australia pictorial history if any reminder be needed as to who was there, for I obtained the autographs of 234 old and not-so-old players from Ashes Tests. Percy Fender was England's oldest, Jack Ryder Australia's (he died a few days afterwards). The number, 234, was all but a maximum for those still living at that time, bulked up as it was during the not-quite-so-magnificent 1980 Centenary Test celebrations in England. From Gubby Allen to Bob Wyatt, Ted a'Beckett to Tim Wall, there were both amusing and dramatic stories aplenty.

No more cheery cricketer ever played than 1930s Victorian fast bowler Ernie McCormick, and he quickly captured the spirit of the jamboree by telling everybody how a chap had come up to him and said, 'Hey! Didn't you used to be Ernie McCormick?' Eddie Paynter, the little Lancastrian, who had needed financial assistance to get to Melbourne, was heard to ask the barmaid whether she had any warm beer. Hard-nosed characters like Brian Close roamed around getting autographs as if they were schoolboys again, and Sir Don even had his picture taken with Harold Larwood. It was a cricketer's Heaven.

If it was the 1930s you wanted, there was 'Bull' Alexander, and Jack Badcock, Bill Brown, Len Darling and Hans Ebeling, and so on through the alphabet. Clarrie Grimmett, frail as meringue, spoke softly of his distant days in the sun, while his big mate Bill O'Reilly provided brass and percussion. 'Nip' Pellew and Bill Ponsford ('Autograph? It'll cost ya!' he joked) took us back to the 1920s, and it was even possible to talk – though not to any great depth on such a sensitive subject – to the umpires in the Bodyline series of 1932-33, George Hele and George Borwick.

Among the English contingent who had undertaken the marathon flight (during which John Arlott won widespread approval by giving Bill Edrich a black eye) to meet their old opponents, Les Ames was in fine form, and sat with us in a friend's room at the Hilton to watch the commemorative programme on television. As Larwood footage loomed, I alerted Les, and when that now-notorious clip of Larwood filmed from long-off was shown, the elbow seemingly bending and straightening in delivery, wicketkeeper Ames, who was in that old film himself, taking the bumper down the leg side, gasped. 'Well, I never!' was all he dared say. Harold Larwood was not only never called for throwing throughout his career but there had never been a serious murmur about the purity of his action. It was just that this camera angle seemed to have revealed an irregularity. But no-one dared to seek the old Notts and England man out to ask for his opinion.

During one of the lunch intervals in the great commemorative Test it was arranged that Larwood and Voce should walk out to the middle of the MCG, and as they did so, symbolically removing their coats, the huge crowd gave them a mighty (and forgiving) ovation. Yet in this superbly well-organised week, one oversight occurred. And I happened to be standing next to him in the crowded players' enclosure. Big Bill Bowes was also a member of that England team of '32-33, and although he played in only one of those heated Tests, it was here at the MCG: and he took a wicket: Don Bradman for a famous first-ball duck, dragging on an attempted pull. Bill would have loved to have strolled out to the centre on this day in 1977 when all hearts were singing.

Before leaving for Melbourne, I had put a special March edition onto the presses, with a period front cover (free, as usual) from my collection, and among the extra-special contents the result of the All-Time England and Australia XIs, chosen by John Arlott, Jim Swanton and myself was announced. This had been fun, with much horse-trading: EWS wanted Godfrey Evans, but JA pointed to all those straightforward catches Godders allegedly missed, so Ames got in, his batting a major factor; I had to fight to justify Trumble, and only got Bob Simpson in ahead of Ponsford on account of his slips fielding and legspin bowling. Oldfield beat Tallon to the keeper's position mainly on sentimentality. Grace and Hobbs meant no place for Hutton. But on the whole the teams came close to selecting themselves. It would be interesting to see what amendments a further 40-odd years might demand. Botham for Tate? Border for Harvey? Warne for Trumble?

Naturally, thoughts turned to those who had just failed to make it to the Melbourne Centenary party, like Herbert Sutcliffe, whose health was against him, and dear old Bert Oldfield and Arthur Gilligan, symbols of the warm sportsmanship that they helped make a feature of Ashes Test cricket in the 1920s, both now dead. But the handshakes, the reminiscing, the laughter, the clinking of glasses went on and on . . . while one of the greatest of Test matches proceeded out there on the historic MCG turf.

It was all nerves at first: Australia 138; England 95. Then it settled down, with Rod Marsh (Blackham's photo in his pocket) making a century and Derek Randall surviving a Lillee rocket to the skull and going on to 174 in his maiden Ashes Test. It was not quite enough. Lillee finished England off, taking 11 wickets in all, the eventual margin being 45 runs, the same as that in the first of all Tests here a century earlier, when the MCG was little more than a paddock. I tried very hard to summon the ghosts of Dave Gregory and Jim Lillywhite, but must have been a few pints of grog short.

Randall had wandered off grinning after his dismissal and seemed to be heading for the Royal enclosure. 'She's gonna knight him on the spot!' gasped one of the VIPs. But the Nottingham lad changed course just in time. That evening, in the hot and bustling lobby of the Hilton, Randall burst in, still in his flannels and MCC touring blazer, and shouted to the first familiar face he saw, which happened to belong to David Lloyd of Lancashire and England: 'Hey! Fancy me gettin' 'oondred'n'seventy!' Whatever had we here? Something approaching genius, that was what. And it was sad that England's selectors over the next few years treated him so inconsistently.

Visiting the vast, empty ground on the eve of the great match, I had marvelled at the souvenir stalls and been moved by the canvas name-placards from the old scoreboard: dotted about the place with studied randomness were to be seen TRUMPER, MacLAREN, HOBBS, HILL, BRADMAN, COMPTON, WOOLLEY, GREGORY. It must have been intimidating for the 1977 players, for even the dimmest of them must have known something about a few of those oldtimers.

The one nearest in essence to God was Sir Donald Bradman. We had corresponded for several years already, and when he went to London in 1974 as guest of honour at a Lord's Taverners dinner at the Hilton, he had brought over a pair of his batting-gloves for my collection. Since one of his blazers fetched £750 at the auction that night, the measure of his generosity can easily be understood. I also took about 30 books for his signature, a task he attended to without complaint. Now, in Melbourne, he invited me to sit and chat in the members' area, in the warmth of the sun, at this ground where he had piled up multiple-hundreds and been serenaded by pre-war crowds. We talked as much about the economy as cricket. But there would be plenty of other occasions in the future, hours of relaxation, hours of privilege.

And when my friend Don heard it was my birthday – and the weighty 40th at that – on the fourth morning of the match, he insisted I join him and Jessie for breakfast at the Windsor Hotel, the five-star old-world establishment where they customarily stayed. It was to be a working breakfast in that DGB had prepared a number of suggestions for discussion (and possible publication): leg-side fielding restrictions, reducing long run-ups, timekeepers controlling the length of overs, and so forth. Did the man never relax?

I relaxed that evening. I found myself having a few beers with Neil Hawke and some of his mates. Then there was a 40th-birthday meal somewhere, and a few more beers, and imagined sightings of Dave Gregory and Jim Lillywhite, and probably Charlie Bannerman and old WG and Stoddart too. And suddenly it was morning again, and I barely had time to get from the motel to the MCG for the start of play.

Never was the end of an event so sadly contemplated. Though Virtual Reality was an expression in the future, that was it. Every hour brought faces to life from cricket's history books. A video-camera was the greatest need, though there were quotes that would only have been embarrassments: such as mine own when I bumped into Rick McCosker in the lift at the Hilton; his jaw had been broken by a Willis bouncer on the first day, and he was now wired up and bandaged, unable to speak and not all that mobile from the neck upwards at all. And what did I blurt out automatically when I came face to face? 'G'day, Rick. How are you?' Yet another good bloke, he managed to make a positive mumbling sound through the bandages by way of acknowledgement.

Finally, I flew up to Brisbane and Sydney to see relatives, having just failed to interview the ailing Jack Ryder, whose voice had gone on him. Then came the dreaded long night across the world, in a Jumbo half-filled with old Test cricketers. I was longing to see Debbie again, and tell her all about this event of a lifetime.

At least the England-Australia pictorial book seemed to be selling well. In fact, in time, it ran to a dozen editions, and became the first cricket book to gross £1-million.

Meanwhile, back at *The Cricketer*, I steamed into my workload, ever with an eye to averting its traditional blandness. I had Richard Hutton writing on the progress being made in South Africa, and David Rayvern Allen compiling an April Fool's Day spoof on cricket in Tibet, a completely convincing piece which, when revealed later for what it was, brought in a few sniffy letters: 'not the sort of thing we expect to see in *The Cricketer* . . .' and so on.

Then there was the matter of the John Ward prints. This charming Royal Academician had painted Cowdrey, Illingworth, Greig, Bedi, Knott and Clive Lloyd and the magazine was about to offer prints at £10 each. With most of the *Cricketer* people sitting around the table, opinions were sought. There was much cooing and congratulation. But, true to myself, I expressed disappointment at the Bedi, Lloyd and Knott impressions, which seemed to me to be too stiff, inanimate. This did little for my popularity within the organisation, though it was a relief to hear Colin Cowdrey condemn his own image. With over 2000 prints to be sold at what was then a fairly steep price, it seemed to me unwise to get carried away on waves of mutually comforting optimism. As with most editions in recent years, there were plenty of unsolds after the initial interest had waned.

With the July 1977 issue I began the demanding daily summary of the complexities of the war between established cricket and Packer's World Series, all of which gave Gordon Ross something convenient to feed off when he did something similar for *Wisden*, then edited by his friend Norman Preston, a Pickwickian character with a guttural delivery and a splenetic temper. (To hear Preston arguing with Irving Rosenwater about the status of the 1970 England v Rest of the World matches was worth more than a seat at the Opera House.)

The August issue had the normally genial Brian Johnston after me. He had spotted my review of John Parker's book *The Village Cricket Match*, which was an attempt at a sequel to Hugh de Selincourt's 1924 classic. I found it cliché-ridden, and referred to the 'trite, trite, trite speech'. 'We don't write that sort of thing in *The Cricketer*,' Johnners expostulated. Don't we? Well, what right had he to act like a 'senior pro' towards somebody who was working to the limit, unaided and devoid of encouragement, to produce this publication month after month, and to review books honestly? Every right, of course, for he was a close social pal of the proprietor.

It all seems so long ago, that era of flared trousers and sideburns. How did I manage to keep my head up while there was so little team spirit, with *The Cricketer's* interest in Corfu seemingly outweighing the Ashes Test series? For years I was the only member of the staff not to be invited to the island, and when I was finally asked (the lure seemingly being to drink with Bill Edrich), I put my son's school exams first and declined, a decision which was evidently another black spot.

I funded myself to the 1977 Test matches and co-wrote *The Ashes '77* with Australia's captain, Greg Chappell, not the easiest of tour books to compose, since the touring team was split into two camps, those who had signed up for Packer's breakaway cricket and those who hadn't. Weakened by the absence of Lillee, Ian Chappell and a couple of others who would greatly have strengthened the side, the Australians were crushed 0-3 in the Tests, with Boycott, back from exile, averaging 147, Willis blasting out 27 wickets at under 20, and newcomer Ian Botham showing promise. Jeff Thomson (23 wickets) led the Australian bowling, backed up mainly by his wild mate Lenny Pascoe and the popular Max Walker. But the off-stage rumblings were neverending.

With my restricted budget, I spent the first night of the Manchester Test curled up uncomfortably in the car, entering the ground early for a shave at the wash-basins beneath the pavilion. The situation eased when Sydney journalist Brian Mossop let me sleep on the floor of his room, and became positively luxurious when the skipper arranged for use of the odd spare bed, one in David Hookes's room, another in Gary Cosier's. And so the book got written.

The authorship partners take a breather: DF and Greg Chappell, Trent Bridge 1977 Patrick Eagar

It was written to a tight schedule too, and so up to date with the action was I at Trent Bridge that John Arlott leaned forward from the bench behind me and asked, 'And what have you written about the next half-hour's play?'

Some evenings there was more activity in the hotel bars than there had been on the Test field, with Thommo, David Lord, the agent, Len Maddocks, the manager, and sundry others being paged for telephone calls. With feigned casualness, reporters would sidle over towards the telephone booth, hoping to overhear something that would have telling effect on the saturation war between organising factions which clouded this summer and the one to come. David Lord got Thomson and Kallicharran to pull out of Packer cricket, but the after-effects were unnerving. It was a turbulent time, reflected in Greg Chappell's moods when we went out after dark for a meal and a drink. Out of this near-desperation was created one of the finest Ashes centuries of our time: Greg's 112 at Old Trafford.

Boycott's 100th hundred, registered in the Headingley Test, was effective as a prime piece of history. But there was little else. There was too much worry in the air, too much bitter division, too many threats of ultimate domination by one faction or the other. Some of those divisions were understandably to last through protagonists' lifetimes.

Some of the best times were passed late at night, in the hotel lounges, discussing lighter matters, such as Rod Marsh's breaking of wind during the mayor's speech at the golf that afternoon, or how good was Bradman? Once, manager Maddocks came back from some function in the early hours, spotted some of his players still up, and stood disapprovingly by the doorway, hands on hips, for a full half-minute. It seemed that poor Len, Australia's wicketkeeper in the mid-1950s, was there now just to attend to the bills and the laundry.

And one evening, after waiting over an hour for the night porter to bring me a hot cocoa, its arrival was greeted with curiosity by Doug Walters (the boy from Dungog, in the big blue cap, vintage 1963, now grown up, though not by much), who reached across as if to prevent the cup from toppling – and downed my drink before I could stop him. All pals together.

This Australian year was rounded off with a glimpse of the Under-19 team currently on tour in England. There in the gloom of the pavilion at Weybridge were long-haired teenagers named David Boon, Geoff Marsh, Wayne Phillips and Greg Dyer, all destined to wear the full Test cap in years to come. Their manager was none other than Warren Saunders, my old St George contemporary, who might have had a Test cap or two of his own in another era.

To end this turbulent year, I 'interviewed' Victor Trumper for the November issue of the magazine to mark the centenary of his birth. There was no seance, simply an exercise in imagination, incorporating all the pointers to character and personality gleaned over the years, since I had stood by his graveside as a 14-year-old and played on that turf named in his honour in Paddington. I told my phantom interviewee about some of the problems facing the modern game: restricted-overs cricket is widespread, legspin is almost dead [as it was in 1977], we usually get well under 100 overs in a day's Test play. . . 'Stop, please!' my phantom Trumper cried. 'Goodness, does anyone get any enjoyment out of cricket?' And I asked him about the boy whose eyes settled on his bat after he'd scored a Test century with it: 'You gave it to him cut-price because it had been used!' 'What else could I have done?' was the reply I felt certain he would have uttered.

By the spring of 1978, Kerry Packer and a group of his players having triumphed in the High Court in London in a restraint-of-trade action against the TCCB and ICC, things were desperate. Cricket-lovers deplored the dilution in quality of Test cricket, with many star players contracted to World Series, while traditionalists could not stomach many of the innovations of the Packer version of the game. How long could the damaging division go on? In the March edition I found myself, for once in my life, pleading for compromise. As ever, the game of cricket and its well-being were the sole consideration. But the agony had to be endured for some time yet.

It would be a very different world for me by the time cricket's greatest rift was to be healed, for in the early summer of 1978 I was summoned to Tunbridge Wells, where the proprietor said, within seconds of my arrival, 'We've reached the end of the road.' He had already made arrangements for the Reg Hayter agency to take over, and I was to keep the old car and get a year's salary. I drove home in a rather terrifying daze.

During that brief meeting, Brocklehurst gave no explicit reason for my dismissal, but confessed that for some time now he had been hoping I would move on, perhaps succeeding the late Clive Taylor at *The Sun* or joining *The Guardian*. It was as if a bright light had been switched on: of course, they had been going out of their way to make life difficult for me. The modern expression is 'constructive dismissal'. As for his remark that the directors were 'unanimous' in this decision, when I saw Colin Cowdrey at Lord's soon afterwards he said he had no knowledge of it. But then again, Colin was revealed in due course as a man with a mystic smile.

So, with the new lad, David Gower, on the front cover, I'd created my 68th and final edition of the magazine, and soon a van came to take away the filing cabinets.

What angered me more than anything else was the effect this shabby dismissal had upon my wife. Debbie's health was severely affected by the sudden insecurity, and even if a newspaper job had been on offer, I would have been reluctant to take it, for I had no wish to be away from home for days and nights and weeks on end. And I certainly had no desire to write about soccer during the winter.

For the time being I did some editorial work for publishers, and the occasional piece for obscure publications. The only slight lift we got during the weeks that immediately followed was sight of the next edition of *The Cricketer*, which was an atrocity. There were errors and inconsistencies galore, starting with a bastardised word on the front cover: HELMET HERESAY. The Edgbaston Test scorecard did not add up; words such as 'sean', 'archtype' and 'Gloucestshire' appeared; and Gordon Ross apparently wrote that 'C.C.Case is a name impregnated on my mind'.

Proofreading is a punishing pursuit which, like motoring, entertains no relaxation. To do it thoroughly is a gesture of respect towards the reader, and although standards have dropped grievously, it has remained important to me that the best job possible should always be carried out. It was not easy, late at night (thanks to the broken schedule, courtesy of the uncooperative printer), when all was quiet at last but the eyelids sagged and the brain throbbed, to comb through columns of text, flushing out blatant clichés, checking facts, applying a necessary house style (e.g. right-hand batsman, County Championship), searching for mis-spellings, dangling participles, and lost commas, questioning absolutely everything – and then, in due course, checking it again to see that corrections have been properly applied. The hazards were much greater in the days of hot-metal printing.

Over the years, though, I have wondered if the world really cares, just as I have wondered if it is inevitable that a chasm must exist between people in the creative sphere and those in non-creative business.

Reflecting on my *Cricketer* years, I can claim to have been the first to publish cricket writings by, among many, Scyld Berry and David Lemmon in the early 1970s (respectively articles on lob bowling and Stuart Turner), and I got a few cricketers writing by setting up features such as *The Captain's Column*. There, the irrepressible David Lloyd gave traces of the humour which, allied to his knowhow, took him to the position of England coach 22 years later, and then a very popular character on television commentary. 'I have thoroughly enjoyed my first venture into column-writing,' he wrote, 'even if it did take three days, and 50 sheets of paper.' I'd asked him only for 700 words.

Outweighing all else were probably the interviews with old players, which embraced a wealth of cricket insight and incident across much of the century. All seemed grateful to have been remembered and were usually free with their recollections and opinions, even if it was wise to check out details which the decades might have blurred.

George Geary in 1973 and (left) many years earlier, around the time (1929) he held the world record with 10 for 18

George Geary, 80, then one of only two survivors from pre-First World War Leicestershire cricketers, once held the world first-class bowling record with an analysis of 10 for 18 (against Glamorgan at Pontypridd) and had bowled Bradman in 1934 with a perfect leg-cutter. George made me very welcome in his cosy abode in 1973, when nine of his 15 brothers and sisters were still alive and he himself was struggling to get used to a replacement hip. The most famous of his Test matches had been the one at The Oval in 1926, when the Ashes were regained. He spoke of matters which the history books never disclosed, like the bruises on the *backs* of his hands from slip catches taken off Larwood's bowling, and the robbery on the final morning at the team hotel: 'Someone got into the bedroom and pinched all my money.'

In a match in Perth at the start of the 1928-29 tour he was smashed in the face and had to be carried off on a wooden table, no stretcher being available. Two pieces of bone were removed from his shattered nose, and his sense of smell improved vastly. Later, he hit the winning boundary, and let somebody have the bat for £10. Jack Hobbs later told him he could have got £250 for it in London: 'the bat that won the Ashes'. Another record came with a marathon 81overs by Geary in the fifth Test, at Melbourne: 'Oh, I didn't feel too bad.' Young men of today may scoff.

More stories followed of Ashes Tests of the between-wars period, and of his benefit match in 1936, from which he took a mere £10, and of coaching at Charterhouse, Peter May the towering young figure ('I used to make him pick his bat up as high as he possibly could').

There, on the corner of a picture of George Geary meeting King George V, hung a limp and worn England cap. 'How tempus fugits,' was his memorable remark, with that ever-present grin. When I next tried to visit him I was told he had gone into a home, and there I found him, still smiling but beyond communication, for he had Alzheimer's. I'd found him just in time.

'Stork' Hendry, the 1920s Australian Test allrounder, remained in correspondence after our meetings in Sydney in 1972, and was now very easily persuaded to write for the magazine. He was clear of memory and punchy in his opinions ('The most extravagant assertion was that Garry Sobers was the greatest cricketer ever. Did W.G.Grace, Alf Noble, Warwick Armstrong, Wally Hammond, Frank Woolley never play?'), biassed fairly understandably towards the claims of his own contemporaries but willing to give the nod to the Lillees and the Chappells, though scathing towards the money-grabbing attitude of many modern players.

Scorer of 325 in a first-class match against the New Zealanders and of a 'mere' 100 in Victoria's record 1107 at the MCG in 1926-27, Hendry had a vivid recollection concerning Jardine, not on the Bodyline tour but of the one four years earlier, when he became neurotically anti-Australian. 'Stork' had tried to cheer him up when the Englishman (Bombay-born Scot, to be precise) was being coarsely barracked at Melbourne. For his trouble, he was addressed by Jardine thus: 'All Orstralians are an uneducated and unruly mob.' 'If that's what you think,' said Hendry, 'then you can go to buggery!' They don't sledge like that anymore.

He then reckoned that in the next Test, Jardine tried to spike his water with whisky. The Australian was 96 at the time, and Patsy Hendren, the cheery Londoner with the Irish grin, warned him. Hendry drank it all the same, and was soon pushing a ball from Hammond away and galloping to his one and only Test hundred.

'Stork' Hendry bats in the 1921 Lord's Test, using his height to get to the pitch of the ball. Below: Hendry with wife Vida on a visit to England over half-a-century later

With my incurable penchant for fantasy, I greatly enjoyed a few hits on the lawn with a tennis-ball against this survivor from Armstrong's illustrious 1921 Australian side before we took him and wife Vida to see Guildford Cathedral. In the nave, Hunter Hendry looked up at the high-vaulted ceiling and was so impressed that he intoned loudly: 'Gee, Dyverd, what a bloody lovely church!' The passing verger stopped in his tracks, smiled, and probably gave his blessing to Anglo-Australian relations.

From the same era came Arthur Gilligan, whose brother Harold also captained England (and whom I'd visited in Surrey for a pleasant chat at the behest of his son-in-law, one P.B.H.May). Arthur lived in Sussex, and had first impressed me with his warmth of character during Test broadcasts in the old Ecole Street days. How could I have known in the early 1950s that one day I would be driving Gilligan halfway across England to Lansdown CC's 150th anniversary dinner, talking all the way about Herby Collins, Jack Gregory, Bert Oldfield, Maurice Tate, Herbert Sutcliffe, Jack Hobbs? And when I called at his home, he rolled his sleeves up and recreated the scene at selection before the final Test of 1926, when he urged the inclusion of Wilfred Rhodes, who was then 48, a heroically successful choice.

Arthur Gilligan had many a jolly memory to impart in the 1970s about cricket 50 years ago and more. In the happy 1924-25 series in Australia, he tosses (below) with H.L.Collins before the third Test, at Adelaide, where England lost by 11 runs on the seventh day

A.E.R.Gilligan understandably enjoyed reliving the 1924 Edgbaston Test too, when he and Tate bowled South Africa out for 30. He held the seam upright and the ball darted this way then that. He not only looked like

Douglas Fairbanks, the laughing screen swashbuckler, but he could be a fighter too. When the malevolent Armstrong bumped into him and chipped his shin with his bat while running a two, the gargantuan Australian rasped: 'Didya think I did that on purpose?' After a well-timed pause, Arthur said, 'I had the great pleasure of knocking his cap off next ball.'

But the most intense unreality was sitting with a man who had watched, when very young, Jessop's 75-minute century at The Oval in 1902, almost three-quarters of a century previously.

Not that this was a record, for a few years prior to the Gilligan interview I had made several trips down to the south coast to talk with Wilfred Rhodes, who played in Jessop's match. Now blind and in his nineties, this grand and gentle old Yorkshireman, taker of a world record 4187 wickets with his slow left-arm craftiness, now rocking gently in his armchair, spoke in his pumping, gravelly voice about bowling to W.G.Grace 75 years earlier, in 1898. Thank God I took the tape-recorder. He talked for an hour-and-a-half, putting the lie to that silly story about 'getting 'em in singles' when he and Hirst stole 15 runs for the 10th wicket to win one of the most celebrated matches, the Oval Test of 1902.

Yet it might have been an even greater source of pride to him that when he batted at No.11 in the Sydney Test of 1903, he kept pace with R.E. 'Tip' Foster (287) as they added a swift 130 for the last wicket. Wilfred rose to opening the batting for England, and featured in the Ashes record opening stand of 323 with Hobbs, at Melbourne in 1911-12, a benchmark finally passed by Mark Taylor and Geoff Marsh at Trent Bridge in 1989. I was sitting close to Jim Swanton then, and his anguish was palpable. I too spared a thought for old Wilfred, though he was by now but a ghostly figure in cricket's Valhalla.

As I left Wilfred Rhodes at his daughter's house, he shuffled to the door to say farewell. Although blind, he knew his way across the drawing-room, but I supported his arm, the one which had teased so many batsmen to their doom. And I was surprised at its softness. The sinew had gone with the years. His husky chuckle followed me to the car, reassuring me about directions to the Ringwood roundabout.

I was furious to read soon afterwards that the house had been broken into and his cricket memorabilia, mostly silverware, had been stolen. I supplied Dorset Police with a photograph, but none of it was ever recovered. That Edgbaston 1902 ball (7 for 17), those used at Melbourne when he took 15 wickets in a Test, and the one with which he took his 100th Australian Test wicket: all these I had been thrilled to touch. And now they were gone.

I last saw Wilfred in the nursing-home in Parkstone, and still he talked cricket non-stop. There had been very little room for anything else in his long life, and who was to say that he wasn't happier for that?

It was my privilege to have taken him to the last cricket match he ever attended, a B&H match at Dean Park, Bournemouth. Safely seated near the pavilion, he was still passing fairly reliable judgment on batting strokes from the sound made by ball on bat. I alerted Peter West to Rhodes's presence, and upon cue the PA announced his presence and the camera picked him out as he slowly got to his feet and lifted his trilby-hat in response to the best applause of the day.

Talking to a 19th Century cricketer:
Wilfred Rhodes was clear of memory and keen to talk.
Although he was blind, his head was swimming with historical images

His funeral was a private affair, family only, apart from Sir Len Hutton, representing Yorkshire, and Desmond Eagar, Hampshire and MCC, and myself. It was a bright summer's day, which might have caused the young Wilfred Rhodes indecision as to whether he would prefer to be batting or bowling. As the casket slid out of sight beyond the curtains, I felt I was witnessing the end of the Golden Age.

Always I shall regret not taking the tape-recorder on trips to see two other legendary characters, S.F.Barnes and Herbert Strudwick. A number of times I drove to Shoreham-by-Sea to sit with little 'Struddy' by the fireplace, having toast and tea while he remembered keeping wicket to Tom Richardson when he first joined Surrey at the end of the 19th Century. Up would go the most gnarled hands I have ever set eyes on as he demonstrated how far Richardson jagged and bounced the ball down the leg side from an off-stump line.

Strudwick was badly missing his great friend Jack Hobbs, whom he had seen almost daily before The Master's death in 1963. His 'memoirs' had been published long ago in book form, but always you feel that there are interesting stories that haven't made print. Struddy gave me a few, one concerning the voyage to Australia for the 1903-04 tour. He was challenged by some of the other professionals to tap on the porthole window of skipper P.F.Warner's cabin, for inside it was thought that Warner was enjoying the company of his fiancée. It was an amusing lark . . . until the curtain swished open just as the little Surrey cricketer was tapping. 'Plum' Warner gave him a dressing-down. How aerial commuting has reduced the scope for such leisurely fun.

Herbert Strudwick, who gave a lifetime to Surrey as player, coach and scorer (and who did not put raw steak in his wicketkeeping gloves), was truly one of Nature's gentlemen, one of a breed now reduced to rarity in the England of the 21st century. Still, he could get fired up – by his restrained standards – when a certain matter came to mind: on the successful England tour of Australia in 1911-12, he kept wicket in the first Test, but gave way to E.J. 'Tiger' Smith of Warwickshire for the remaining four. This was because, he said, Frank Foster, the sharp left-arm bowler, wanted his own county wicketkeeper behind the stumps. Warwickshire, after all, were county champions in 1921.

Foster, an unusual individual in so many ways, ignored Strudwick's signal to fling one down the leg side (in the hope of a stumping). The ball was taken by Woolley at slip. Struddy lost his place. Bosanquet's googlies in 1903-04 were all over the place too, but he couldn't help it.

E.J. 'Tiger' Smith also lived to a great age, and sat on match days in the dining- room at Edgbaston, peering through the thick lenses of his glasses, leaning on his stick, fist usually wrapped round a glass of good ale, grinding out ribald stories of tours and adversaries from long ago. Like most English pros, there was a native cunning about him. In the old Ashes battles, as with Rugby League clashes, it was often the shrewdness of the Poms against the raw skill of athletic Aussies.

It cannot be said that I wasted opportunities. While they were still available, I tracked down so many great names from the annals of cricket. P.G.H.Fender was another. I called on him at his Mayfair office (he dealt in wine) and later, when age was telling on him, at his daughter's home in Sussex, where he sat, hunched, in his First World War flying-jacket, hardly able to see now, an affliction today's cricketers may be fortunate enough to avert now that sunglasses of high quality are widely used.

Percy Fender had firm opinions about most things, as demonstrated in Richard Streeton's outstanding biography of him. From all our conversations, two things stood out. There was his recapitulation of his world record 35-minute century for Surrey at Northampton in 1920, made in genuine circumstances, when he claimed actually to have slowed down to let 'Podgy' Peach reach his double- century, for he feared a declaration the moment he reached his own hundred. And there was his sore memory of leaning on the ship's railing as the vessel steamed down the English Channel on its way to Australia a few weeks later. J.W.H.T.Douglas, England's bull-headed leader, made it patently clear to Fender that he had little regard for him as either batsman or bowler: 'I wondered what I was doing on board that ship!'

Another blind veteran cricketer sits and reminisces: Percy Fender in Sussex garden

S.F.Barnes was the most disturbing interviewee. He was renowned for his cussedness, this greatest of all bowlers (in all probability), even when in his nineties. I had written to him to line up the call, and duly drove 170 miles up to Cannock, in Staffordshire, arriving punctually. 'What do you want?' growled the tall, gaunt figure. I explained our arrangement, and without the trace of a smile he said, 'You'd better come in then.'

He beckoned me to sit down, but I had a feeling that this was going to be short and not so sweet. So I began firing questions: what had he said to England captain Johnny Douglas when he took the new ball at Sydney in preference to Barnes himself; why hadn't he played more county cricket; why, with 49 wickets in the first four Tests in South Africa, did he refuse to play in the fifth? His answers were brief, uncompromising and charged with feeling, even all these years later.

If Barnes was famous for anything, it must be for his spell of 5 for 6 in 11 overs against Australia on the opening day of the New Year Test at Melbourne in 1911-12. What was the background to that?

'I was sick the day before and thought I might not play.' He frowned as he threw his mind back. 'Syd Gregory [the tiny Australian veteran, who was not playing in this match] helped me. He got me some whisky and I went to bed to sweat it off, with plenty of blankets.' And next day over went Bardsley, Kelleway, Hill, Armstrong and Minnett – Australia 38 for 6 – and England were well on the way to levelling the series. Barnes (34 wickets) and Frank Foster (32) led England to a decisive 4-1 Ashes victory.

Sydney Barnes: he teased me in 1967 ...

Questioned about his control of the ball, he dismissed the new jargon of the 1960s. Seaming it? Cutting it? None of these. 'I SPUN the ball!' he roared, twisting that long, bony hand of his by way of demonstration, the fingers seemingly still capable of making a cricket ball hum. He spun it at medium-fast pace. And he had the look of the devil about his brow. No wonder he swept all before him, even when into his sixties.

Now came the really difficult bit. I had carted my big book up there to add his signature, but he refused point-blank to use the ballpoint pen I proffered. 'Can't use *that*!' he croaked in what may have been mock-contempt, or it may have been the real thing.

And if I supposed he was going over to the Staffordshire Council offices to get his own pen (he still worked there), with which he wrote a beautiful copperplate, I had another thing coming.

This was disappointing, and unique in my experience. It was also embarrassing. And as I put the book back into my bag, a wicked smile crossed his lower face, though the eyes seemed incapable of joining in. His tease had worked. He had taken yet another 'wicket'. And now he relented.

An exquisite 'S.F.Barnes' joined the hundreds of other signatures in the creaking volume.

He agreed to a photograph of us both and seemed almost warm as he crunched my hand and bade me farewell for the long journey home. In later years I came to realise how similar he was in personality to Bill O'Reilly, Australia's leading candidate for Greatest Bowler of All Time. Good to be with, both of them, though one could never truly relax.

... just as he'd teased thousands of terrified batsmen.
Here he is at his fieriest best in 1912

Of all the interviews in the 1970s with men currently in the game, two stood out. Talking with S.C. 'Billy' Griffith on the eve of his retirement as MCC secretary was a pleasure not only because he was warm and receptive but he was also a hero of the 1944 Arnhem landing. He was in no doubt about the most stressful item in his 22 years in administration: the South African question. 'One got no rest from it – sometimes seven days a week, 24 hours a day. I was often seen as the decision- maker when, after all, one was merely the spokesman. It was very distressing that many people assumed that I had some sympathy for the policies of the South African government however often I stated otherwise. Just like everyone involved in cricket at the time, I wanted the same end – namely that cricket was played wherever in the world on a multi-racial basis, knowing no barriers of race, colour or creed. The argument was just how those ends could best be achieved.' I can sympathise with this now, many years later, more than ever.

In his other capacity at Lord's, as secretary to the International Cricket Conference (later Council), he led me to a filing cabinet and withdrew papers among which was an ICC statement from 1972 which made it clear, once and for all (though certain woolly-minded people never grasped it), that the 1970 matches between England and the Rest of the World were 'not official Test matches'. I would only quibble with the word 'official'. A cricket match – like a pregnancy – either is or isn't.

In that same issue of *The Cricketer*, a full-page picture of Intikhab was reversed, making him a left-arm bowler. I had passed a correct proof, but negligence at the printers at the final stage of production made me look foolish. I wondered if it was deliberate.

Beyond question, the most poignant interview during that time was with Colin Milburn, the rotund and jolly Geordie who had belted the new ball all over the place in Northamptonshire, Western Australia and England colours. The loss of his left eye in a car crash in 1969 was conceivably the greatest individual tragedy to befall English cricket since the war. A wave of grief swept through the game, and for four years speculation about a return to playing was persistent. After all, the young Nawab of Pataudi did it.

Colin Milburn, one of the most beloved of cricketers, and victim of the cruellest of accidents

Then, early in 1973, injuries caused Northants to give Milburn a trial after promising performances in friendly matches in which, amazingly, he had hung on against the likes of John Snow, Graham McKenzie and Alan Ward. He was never going to belt centuries in Tests again, surely, or even come close to emulating his blitz in a Shield match at the Gabba in 1968, when his

243 included 181 runs in the second session (against four Test bowlers). But the one-eyed, ever-laughing Billy Bunter figure managed some thirties and forties, between heart-rending failures, before I caught up with him at Guildford.

Cricket is studded with ironies, and the one this day was that Northants had been due to play Surrey the following day when that terrible accident occurred in 1969. We all could easily have wept when Geoff Arnold now bowled Milburn for a duck in Northants' first innings.

Later that day, the visitors followed on, and even the Surrey boys must have dreaded inflicting a second nought on 'Ollie'. The Guildford pitch was still doing a bit, and there were none better to exploit it than Arnold and Jackman. But soon the Milburn forearms that so resembled legs of lamb were thumping the ball square on either side, and we all clapped like hell when he swatted Jackman for six into the groundman's garden. Milburn's fifty brought applause the like of which I had seldom experienced. So much of the clapping heard at county matches is mechanical and bloodless. This was the opposite. How did the man do it? Was a hundred in the offing? I was so glad to be here. The power of prayer was effective after all.

Then Intikhab bowled, Milburn swept, and the stumps collapsed. The ball had turned a lot. It needed to.

The comeback attempt, of course, was shortlived. He went off to Perth again that winter to play and coach for Mount Lawley, to sell cars, and to open the batting against the shiny red ball in brighter light. His Northants testimonial proceeds had been placed in trust (it would have been 'chaotic', he admitted, had they given him the lump sum), and he did a bit of this and that, including radio commentary, where I thought he was as good to listen to as any of them. Alas, he was engaged only spasmodically before being dumped.

Years later he came on a Wisden tour with us to Barbados, distressed alarmingly when his suitcase went on to Trinidad – 'Ah'm gooin' hoam! Ah couldn't get clawthes to fit me here, maan!' But luckily he recovered, and drank the *Jolly Roger* dry, singing his way to oblivion every night. Through the 1980s he was a welcome fringe figure, sleeping on the settee in many an old pal's hotel room, the centre of ribald gatherings at the bar, a merry companion in the car.

He never sought sympathy, so there was plenty of the alternative: teasing. I pretended to confuse his accent, and called him 'Scottie'. In return he was lukewarm when I played a Jethro Tull tape in the car just when I thought the frenetic guitar in *Aqualung* would stir him. There was not so much as a flicker of badness in him, and he was deeply mourned when a heart attack took him in 1990. 'Ollie' was only 48.

Blessed are those, I suppose, who make it to 91, as did Frank Woolley and Andy Sandham. I caught them both just before it was too late, the legendary Woolley for a three-part interview late in 1976 and Sandham (Jack Hobbs's 'shadow') two years later.

Woolley and his Canadian-born wife Martha were in England on a holiday from their home in Nova Scotia, and the idol of Kent (1906 to 1938) and England (1909-34, 64 Tests), though now frail and ailing, was happy to submit to taped interviews at Lord's and in the rooms where they were staying. Sharpened by repetition, his memory darted from year to year, player to player, and, it has to be said, from moan to complaint, often justified. Who would not have been annoyed to be given out lbw at 99 after C.B.Fry had shouted an appeal from extra cover? (*Wisden* and *Cricket* show that Woolley was actually bowled by Leach the only time he made 99 against a side which included Fry, but this would not be the first old player's reminiscence to have been fogged by time.) And was it fair that he got less talent money than he deserved because the Kent committee felt he was hogging the fund with all his runs, wickets and catches? He told Lord Harris he was tempted by an American baseball offer, to which His Lordship said he would guarantee him a testimonial, from which he would probably get more than WG's £10,000. 'I got £900,' he rasped, with all the scorn he must have felt at that time.

Frank Woolley, 89, back at Lord's,
with wife Martha, in 1976

He spoke feelingly of the menace of the Australian fast pair Gregory and McDonald, and the fizzing spinner Arthur Mailey, all of whom had been bowling, less than 100 yards from where we sat, in the 1921 Lord's Test in which Frank Woolley made two nineties; and he paid glowing testimony to Jack Mason among his Kent captains. He even thought back to his first-class debut, 70 years previously, in 1906, when Johnny Tyldesley gave him words of encouragement as he left the field.

Woolley, like so many others, including Arthur Gilligan, had no great affection for Warwick Armstrong: 'Armstrong took a ball at slip after I'd cut it towards him. It hit the ground first, but he threw it up. I said, "Now then, Warwick, you didn't catch that." He started swearing. But the umpire gave me out.' This was almost certainly in the fifth Test of 1911-12, at Sydney, Woolley having made an unbeaten 133 in the first innings, surprisingly one of only two hundreds in his quarter-of-a-century of Ashes Test matches.

As for keeping wicket for England in emergency (Oval Test, 1934, when he was 47: Australia made 327 to follow their first-innings 701, and there were 37 byes): the tall Kent veteran had stood at slip most of his life (the only fieldsman to have held 1000 catches), but had never kept wicket. 'Nobby Clark, the fast left- hander, let me down. He started bowling round the wicket and wide down the leg side.'

It was not all unhappy memories. Harold Larwood was the best and fastest of them all; 1911-12 saw the best England team, with Barnes and Foster the best pair of opening bowlers; the 235 with Arthur Fielder for the 10th wicket, at Stourbridge in 1909, was still a wonderfully fresh vision; he cherished his left-arm spin partnership with 'Charlie' Blythe, who was to become one of the ghosts of Passchendaele, and he admired Trumper, whom he was proud to have dismissed; he was contemptuous of excessive protection for batsmen (in 1976, helmets had yet to appear); and much relieved to have missed, purely by chance, the Battle of Jutland. He lost much memorabilia when his home in Kent was bombed in the Second World War.

It was a thrill and an honour to have spent time in the man's presence, assisted by his cheery and charming wife, a lady of some literary accomplishment, whose manuscript based on Frank's boyhood recollections I was glad to edit into the limited-edition booklet *Early Memoirs of Frank Woolley*. Frank died in Chester, Nova Scotia in October 1978. Martha, the first female graduate of the London School of Economics, lived on till 1992, when she died at the same place, aged 92.

It was all very different when I went to see Andrew Sandham, born, bred and always resident in London, the little Surrey (1911-37) and England (1921-30, 14 Tests) opening batsman. In the corner of the small room was propped the bat with which he had scored Test cricket's first triple-century, in Jamaica early in 1930, when he was in his 40th year. He was out in the middle for 10 hours, and the bat had been loaned to him by the England captain, the Honourable Freddie Calthorpe. It had too long a handle for his liking, 'and I didn't like the balance of it.' He borrowed Patsy Hendren's boots, one of which kept slipping off, and he was annoyed every time a fresh batsman came in and wanted to sprint quick singles, for poor Andy's feet were killing him. England amassed 849, did not enforce the follow-on even when 563 ahead, and Sandham went in at No.7 in the second innings and made 50.

'I believe even now that is the record for most runs in a Test match,' he modestly whispered, with tangible pride. And I had to decide whether to break the news to him that Greg Chappell had recently overtaken the mark with 380 runs. I told him, and instantly regretted it, though he took it in his stride.

Andy Sandham, the first Test triple-centurion

Chivalry and good manners have waned in cricket, as in real life, but there remains no room for immodesty. And I have never met a more self-effacing cricketer than Andrew Sandham. His sight was failing, but we made it down to the local pub for a beer. He fitted in perfectly, just a little old Londoner in a smoky public bar, shoulders slightly stooped, dark grey overcoat, flat, slow voice spinning out memories from the depths, and peering through thick lenses that may, for all I knew, have been somehow focussed still on faces from long ago.

He detested the boredom inflicted by 1970s bowlers with long run-ups, and the surfeit of bouncers, and he spoke with authority, for he made over 100 centuries, most against the new ball and with Jack Hobbs at the other end. Whether Hobbs succeeded or failed, his was the name in the headlines: 'I quite understood,' smiled Andy, 'but it used to annoy my wife!'

He spoke of team-mates and opponents, injuries, highlights and disappointments, and even his Army experiences in the First World War, when he served with the Royal Fusiliers (he might even have passed my Granddad and great-uncle in the mud) until an appendix operation had him repatriated.

'I'm 87 years of age, you know,' he mused, 'and it's a bit of a job trying to remember some of these things!' Again, for me, it had been a magic-carpet ride.

Yet even as I sat with Andy Sandham, the plot to replace me as editor of *The Cricketer* was in full swing. While I'd tried with all my might with such limited resources to create an appealing magazine each month, I'd been undermined. There was simply no feeling of support. I would be better out of it, though this was emphatically not my feeling when the axe fell. The next ('Heresay') edition included the bluntest of announcements that I had moved on, and my name scarcely ever appeared in the magazine thereafter, not even when its 75th anniversary occurred in 1996. *Virtus Non Stemma.*

CHAPTER FIFTEEN

A particular generation of cricketers thinks in a certain way and only a change in society, not legislation, will change the prevailing style.

C.L.R. JAMES

WHAT a time to be out of work. We had just moved into a new house, on the edge of Merrow Downs. Teenage son and daughter were still with us, but elder son Peter had returned to Australia, land of his birth, to 'find himself' (he's still looking). The words from the *Soliloquy* in *Carousel* still haunted me.

The despair which followed my dismissal from *The Cricketer* cut deeply into Debbie as well as myself, more so in fact, which ruled out any possibility of forgiveness on my part for that callous behaviour. The severance payment was a short-term buffer, but what was to come next? Back to selling central heating? Back to Australia?

There was one small assignment to be carried out straightaway, and it turned out to be an exercise in absurd futility. I was asked to act as one of the Man of the Match judges in the England v New Zealand one-day international at Scarborough. Car expenses were met, plus accommodation for two nights, and a modest fee. I watched the game diligently, decided that Bev Congdon (11 overs for 25 and an unbeaten 52 which took the Kiwis close to victory) deserved the award, and I searched all over the crowded pavilion at the end to convey my thoughts to my chairman, Alec Bedser. When I finally bumped into him on the staircase he said, 'We're giving it to Cairns.' Lance Cairns had taken 5 for 28 and belted 23 towards the end, but it was worth at least a minute's discussion. The third judge was still trying to find us, so it struck me that my old England bowling hero was acting somewhat unilaterally. But that's the way it was, and I drove the long road home next day wondering at the economic stupidity of it all. Over the years I've learned to accept that in cricket as in government, quite as much money is wasted as is usefully spent.

My state of mind was reflected, not surprisingly, in my results for Guildford in that summer of 1978. After a rewarding 1977, I could now hardly get a run. Even in the beautiful surroundings of the Whitbread ground in Bedfordshire, I managed to miss a Jim Parks googly when 4. When the Press XI defended our 246, a young Australian came in and belted 90-odd to see the All-Stars home. We chatted with him afterwards, and with great curiosity tried on a batting helmet for the first time. He said he was playing as much cricket as he could get all over England, seeking experience, having played a game or two for New South Wales already. The chunky left-hander had quite a future, as it turned out. We remembered his name: Allan Border.

It became obvious that the only way I could make a living during the forthcoming winter was to write on the Ashes series in Australia. I managed a commission or two from papers, but the foundation would be a tour book. I did deals with Qantas and the internal airline TAA, prepared for a 13-week absence from home and family, with the aim to eat little and find cheap accommodation, and to make the best of seeing son, father and brother again and Debbie's folks in Queensland. All the same, I felt sick with sorrow as Heathrow airport came into view that cold early morning, and came perilously close to asking my neighbour to turn back to Guildford. For all life's exciting hellos, the recurrent goodbyes were close to being unbearable.

I had been trying to map out plans to start up a cricket magazine of my own. I felt that I knew what the British public wanted, and it was something appreciably better than *The Cricketer.* I had approached William Gray of John Wisden & Co, and he was enthusiastic, though they would not finance it. The use of the Wisden name seemed to me to be a guarantee of a magazine's integrity and purpose, but it would mean paying a royalty on every copy sold.

The sums in the forecast and budget seemed to add up, and I made presentations to several interested parties, publishers Collins and EMAP and office-cleaning tycoon and cricket 'nut' David Evans (later an MP) among them. They all liked the concept, but could not see big profits coming quickly. I would have settled for modest profits coming gradually, but then dull old me has never been a swish and rapacious figure in the City, with mobile phone, expensive haircut and *Financial Times* tucked ostentatiously under the sleeve of mock-Savile Row suit.

When all hope seemed dead, an acquaintance put me in touch with a local-newspaper publisher who had money to invest, and although he did not have quite enough to meet the launch costs plus first three months' running, another party made up the difference, and by the time I set off on the 1978-79 Ashes tour, provisional plans had been laid for a new cricket magazine in the spring, subject to certain other matters being settled.

I had already started recruiting. John Arlott, bless him, promised without hesitation to support me. Jim Laker, dear old phlegmatic Jim, actually said it all sounded 'excitin''. Ted Dexter confirmed that he could never resist a challenge, and he too would be delighted to be part of the Editorial Board. The new laid-back blond-haired sensation David Gower, 21, was eager, perhaps sensing that one distant day he might like to put away his bat and become a media-man. And Bob Willis, now in his 30th year and sometimes finding cricket a rather painful pursuit, signified he would be glad to be part of the new magazine. Patrick Eagar, whom I promised much greater exposure and earnings for his photographs, was torn between the new concept and a long-term loyalty to E.W.Swanton, who had given him encouragement at *The Cricketer* when he was young. He finally came round.

There was only one refusal. During the tour of Australia I invited England skipper Mike Brearley to join, but over breakfast one morning he explained that he was already stretched, and any further commitment would need to be extremely well paid. This I could not offer.

Thus, there seemed a future after all, though with so many proposals already having collapsed, there seemed no reason why I shouldn't get an airletter one day in Adelaide or Hobart to say that my prospective backers had changed their minds. Then, well, I could examine once more all the other options: zookeeper, film archivist, military historian, psychologist, long-distance truckdriver. It would be like being fourteen again, though without that absence of responsibility.

England won the 1978-79 Ashes series 5-1, but there were plenty of days to remember, though few based on Australian performance, although the likable and amusing Rodney Hogg earned 41 wickets in the six Tests, the most by any bowler in his maiden series. Another record was Australia's dismissal for under 200 on nine occasions, while their average of 19.18 per wicket lost was the lowest by either side since 1912.

The victory in the first Test was England's first at Brisbane for 42 years: that's to say, in my lifetime (if only by a few weeks). But the most gripping was the fourth, at Sydney, where England retained the Ashes, for it was there that Derek Randall, a principal favourite of mine, showed extraordinary concentration, shored up at times by Brearley, in batting for just on 10 hours to make 150 after England had allowed Australia a first-innings lead of 142. Though the scoring rate was low, it was a duel to cherish as Jim Higgs spun down 60 eight-ball overs. Poor Graham Yallop, Australia's captain, moaned at the defensive play but was apparently unable to see that England were looking at it as the longest arm-wrestling contest in memory. John Emburey and Geoff Miller eventually spun Australia out for their devil's number of 111 to bring England victory by 93 runs. And part of that disciplined rearguard had seen an amazing 90-minute period at the crease by Ian Botham in which he had confined himself to six singles.

That summer, of course, witnessed competing big cricket matches from start to finish. It was the second season of Packer cricket, which I needed to see and assess whenever the opportunity arose. So I found my way out to VFL Park in outer Melbourne for a WSC 'Supertest' ('Superficial Test', Bill O'Reilly contemptuously dubbed it), played on the hothouse-grown pitch which had all the spring in it of the dancefloor at the old Paradance in Rockdale. With most of the world's best playing on it, the cricket was unquestionably 'fair dinkum', and the run rate was barely above two per over, dispelling the accusations of 'circus' cricket.

The one-day matches were much more intense. The one at the SCG was overwhelming in terms of noise and bright colours and unaccustomed behaviour, which persuaded me to write: 'For the first time in my life I did not feel at home at a cricket match, did not feel part of the occasion, even though almost every single player was a personal friend or friendly acquaintance.' I sat with my son and brother by the players' gate as Gordon Greenidge came back in, having failed to score. He looked to me like a cricketer who had been run down by an express train: a gory sight in his red cap, pink shirt, white sweater, pink trousers, patchily-painted pink pads and white boots. Out there on the dazzlingly-lit field, the fielders resembled so many petrol-station attendants.

I could not pretend. This was not my type of cricket. I could not be more honest than to write: 'If I'm prejudiced at all, perhaps it is in favour of playing cricket in God's sunshine.' That prejudice may have subsided slightly in the years since, but not by much.

I kept scribbling away at *The Ashes '79* and at short pieces for newspapers and magazines, stayed lucky with the cost of accommodation, and encountered all kinds of unpredictable experiences. There I was, bowling for 40 minutes one evening to Geoff Boycott at the SCG nets, my Lindwall imitation long since pensioned off in favour of leg-breaks and wrong'uns, which 'Boycs' played according to desserts, smashing the crap balls and applying a measured response to the others, with a polite nod for anything that was decent. I was on $10 for every time I got him out, and not surprisingly came away penniless.

Poor Boycs went boundaryless on this tour for what must have been a world-record length of time by batting on and on, tight as a drum, through 857 minutes: that's over 14 hours, without even an edged four. With this tug-of-war going on between the establishment and the rebels, this was the last thing the conventional administration wanted.

Chatting to Kerry Packer (my subservient batting partner in the 1977 Harrogate 'Press Test'), I spotted on the giant TV monitor in his guests' area at VFL Park that Gary Gilmour's name was mis spelt. I knew that many in his position would have said something like, 'Haven't you got anything better to worry about?' But instead, he got a short, sharp message sent through to the control-room, and the correction was effected instantly. Not that Australia's richest man, with his meaty grip unrelentingly on cricket's throat, felt any obligation to be polite to people like me. Later, back at the SCG, he looked down at my Australian Cricket Board/Benson & Hedges overnight bag and scoffed: 'Bet it doesn't last to the end of the season!'

The England manager, Doug Insole, thoughtfully sought me out to hand me extremely welcome letters from home, which Debbie was addressing care of the England touring team, and to break up the loneliness and homesickness there were highlights such as a call into the Bundaberg shop of Don Tallon, considered by Bradman to have been the best of all wicketkeepers (I bought an ice-cream but couldn't get Tallon to say much; his deafness was an impediment); and a visit to Old Melbourne Gaol during a fierce thunderstorm, only to hear that evening that Ned Kelly's skull had been stolen that very day (Not guilty, m'lud); and then to be part of a magical evening with the Primary Club of Australia at a gathering in honour of the 1948 Australian touring team, and to listen to Lindwall, Johnston, Harvey and company compare notes on their physical shapes 30 years on.

An opportunity arose to fly up to Papua New Guinea between Tests, to see how the enthusiasts there – some nationals, some temporary residents – were getting on in their preparations for the 1979 World Cup for non-Test countries. This necessitated having a net against some of them, and the local paper filled some of its sports page gleefully with a picture of my discomfort. The cricket community in PNG had serious worries about financing the World Cup trip, glancing enviously eastwards towards Fiji, where some very wealthy person had underwritten their costs. But they made it in the end.

With all due respect to PNG cricket, I came away with dramatic mental images of a non-cricketing kind, for my hosts had kindly driven me up to the Kokoda region, where I walked through the flights of heavyweight mosquitoes and along the rows of white gravestones of the gallant Australian dead, poignant testimony to one of the most courageous and dramatic combat episodes of the Second World War. There in the ranges the Japanese advance had been halted in 1942 at the last hurdle, the terrain and the ever-present tropical diseases proving almost as lethal as the enemy. It would still not have been possible without the support of the brave 'Fuzzy-wuzzy Angels', and whenever I saw a local with white hair I found myself gazing and imagining.

Back in Port Moresby, in one sweeping view from a hilltop could be seen the harbour the Japs so coveted, and even now evidence of an Australian hospital ship they had sunk, and the remains of an American Lightning fighter. For a time, it was anything but easy to get back into the spirit of the 1978-79 Ashes Test series.

There were two other outstanding occasions, one when a couple of hundred people from the cricket fraternity descended on Wyndie Hill Smith's

Yalumba vineyards in the Barossa Valley on the rest day of the Adelaide Test, to drink his wide range of products, plunge into the pool, whack a tennis ball around, and talk languidly down the afternoon with players, umpires, administrators and journalists, the 'King' himself, Sir Don, holding court in the shade with Lady Jessie. My dear old pal Alan Shiell, writer and former player (who had scored a double-century against the 1965-66 English team), had been driven home early by his wife after 'Sheffie' had got ahead of schedule with the imbibing. Since my clothes had been placed on the rear seat of their car while I dived to catch flying lemons in the pool with David Bairstow, I was left to find my way back to town (late) in only my swim-trunks and thongs – not even sunglasses to shield my embarrassment.

And the other day to match any in the Ashes Tests came when the return 'Ashes Press Test' was played in Kensington, Sydney. Here, I did a 'Midwinter', playing for England, having already played for the Australian Press in 1977. I went in to what even Trevor Bailey might have classified as a crisis, for the ABC's Peter Meares and Jim Tucker, a fiery redhead and colt reporter, had disposed of Messrs Whiting, Martin-Jenkins and Blofeld for ducks. As I took guard, I saw the reassuring figure of Ken Barrington at the other end, and after I'd survived a Tucker bouncer which touched my nose, Ken and I restored order. The Surrey and England batsman already had one heart attack on his cv, so even the longest hit, if it stopped short, was worth a mere single, walked not run. We put on 60 or 70 and Kenny went on to 80. Bob Simpson made quite a few in reply, and Australia won, but I wasn't too distraught. After all, I belonged to both countries. Full commitment to both, too.

As for the serious business of the '78-79 Tests, the most significant moment in the sense of destiny came when a chunky little left-hander, the same one who had helped himself to those runs at the Whitbread ground a few months earlier, jabbed his first Test run through point on the opening day of the third Test, at the MCG. What odds could one then have got that Allan Border would add an awesome, unthinkable 11,173 more runs before retirement?

A couple of hours after Mike Brearley had hit the winning runs in the final Test at the SCG, I wrote the last words of *The Ashes '79*, bar the afterthought chapter, which was tapped out as I sat in the old stand at the No.2 ground then handed to publisher Richard Smart. We aimed at least to be the first out among the tour books. Bill O'Reilly had already handed over his inordinately generous foreword, so now I could board that Qantas flight to freezing Europe and back to my family.

The journey was facilitated with the ready supply of Tooheys – for long my first choice among beers – withstanding the irritations of Randall wandering up and down the aisle warning everybody that the aircraft was infested with woodworm, and Botham working out his Test figures.

Bairstow made history by cutting himself while using an *electric* shaver. And, somewhere over the Alps, conscientious manager Barrington saw to it that all his players were smartly attired for the landing.

Gerry Rafferty's *Baker Street* was playing through the headphones as we broke through the clouds and had our first sight for over three months of England, now dark, drab, and leafless. A few hours later, with the warmth of a suntan still radiating, I was stepping through the snow on Merrow Downs, relieved to be reunited with my dear Debbie, Julie and John, and wondering if I could now produce the best cricket magazine ever conceived by man.

CHAPTER SIXTEEN

Originality and the feeling of one's own dignity are achieved only through work and struggle.

DOSTOEVSKY

TO indulge in a gross oversimplification, I went out and found a printer, a distributor, an advertisement sales manager, and some contributors, and soon the first edition of *Wisden Cricket Monthly* was on sale. And it sold very well. Within days a reprint was called for, and altogether over 50,000 copies were sold. Still many did not become aware of its existence until the second issue went out, and today copies of that Vol.1 No.1 can fetch as much as £25.

It was an auspicious time. World cricket authorities were forging a peace settlement with Packer's World Series, and Margaret Thatcher became Britain's first female Prime Minister on May 4, 1979, three weeks before *WCM* was born. What a treble.

My associates and I launched the new baby with a party at Lord's during a one-day match between Middlesex and Yorkshire. John Arlott was there to oversee the wine situation, and all kinds of people popped in during the day, including the Yorkshire lads, with Ray Illingworth leading them that evening to the Victoria Sporting Club, where we had another party. Phil Edmonds had come, out of curiosity, but none of the other Middlesex players came up, perhaps because Brearley, having declined a place on the Editorial Board, did not wish to appear hypocritical.

Boycott and Hogg graced that first front cover, and for 50 pence the reader got 52 pages, of which only eight bore advertisements. There would always be over 40 pages of editorial, later 50 or so. And there were colour pages, which will have sent tremors through the opposition.

We soon discovered that mischievous rumours were circulating, making life hard for the ad manager: *WCM* was purportedly using *Wisden's* name without permission; *WCM* was backed by Packer; *WCM* was backed by Arabs. But the 'product' was vibrant enough to survive, and it was with huge relief that, after the first year or so, it seemed that we had not only made it but we were now first in the field and well into profit.

So much had depended on policy, and I had tossed and turned for weeks as the character of the upcoming magazine formulated itself in my mind. I banked upon its being devoted to first-class cricket and its storehouse of history, excellent pictorial reproduction, and an editorial viewpoint that sided with no faction or administration but simply projected a protective concern for the game I treasured.

A day I'll never forget. Spring 1979, and Wisden Cricket Monthly is launched – with the help of my Yorkie pals Ray Illingworth and David Bairstow

Book reviews were to be incisive, obituaries detailed, news columns far-reaching, and readers' letters were to be considered sufficiently important as to take prime position up front. As far as proofreading went, the aim was simple: perfection. And to ensure we were on the right track, every once in a while there would be a survey – a 'parliament' – for readers to express their views on the magazine's style and content. Of course, month by month I was picking up reaction through reader-contact by letter, phone and wherever cricket-lovers gathered, at matches and cricket society meetings. It was a great relief to sense, by the end of the first year, that the formula was just about right.

The benefits for magazine-readers were greater than at first met the eye, for the opposition now had to try to kick back with an improved product to stay in business.

The first illustration inside the first edition was aptly a portrait of John Wisden, the diminutive fast bowler turned publisher, whose Almanack was launched, doubtless just as speculatively, in 1864, and I pledged that the magazine would augment *Wisden Cricketers' Almanack*, adapting the words from that first, slim book of 1864: that 'we have taken great pains to collect a certain amount of information which we trust will prove interesting to all those that take pleasure in this glorious pastime'.

The content would seldom be quite as stuffily worded as that, but the ideal was the same.

Writing Editorials has never been the lightest of tasks. The irritating and unpleasant things that buffet cricket can cause people to be serious and ill-tempered, the game seen as a business, humourless, headache-making. Nonetheless, the incoming tide would bring debating points, problems and crises that sometimes came close to flood level, and the responsibility had to be faced, though always my instinctive preference was to write about people and emotions and the human drama that goes to make up the contest out there in the middle. What happens in the corridors of power is often boring, sometimes disgusting. It had to be contended with, and it was, for just on 17 wearying years. No wonder most Saturdays it was a relief to get out on the cricket field, to be reunited with the physical side of the game which had had a grip on me since I was in short pants.

All the big guns fired in that first edition of *WCM*: Arlott, Dexter, Gower, Laker and Willis, big John levelling some provocative comment at *Wisden* in his review of the 1979 *Almanack* ('a sorry lack of historical perspective') that may unwittingly have ignited an ambivalent, at least, and possibly hostile view of the magazine from the *Almanack's* editor of the time, Norman Preston, and at least two of his successors. But it was the truth: and the truth, like a torpedo, sometimes cuts through even steel plate.

When, in the fourth issue, I published a longish list of corrections to the 1979 Almanack, which was intended to be a service to the more scholarly readers of *Wisden*, Preston exploded, even though I had observed the basic courtesy of advising him beforehand.

For years, the task of constructing an attractive magazine each month, summer and winter, working at high speed but with a high degree of accuracy, was punishing, but most fulfilling. The demands of the business side of the operation added to the weight of editorial responsibility for years left little scope for relaxation or proper holidays, and the only long-term incentive came from the knowledge that as finances improved, so the budget for taking on some assistance would surely materialise. It was just as well I was unaware that it would be several years before that assistance materialised, and even longer before the right man entered stage left. Looking back, I wonder how I found the strength to sustain the effort imposed by the first nine or ten years. Debbie's loving support was a major factor.

It was absurd that a man should wake at 2am wondering if it was too soon to put Botham on the front cover yet again, or whether the *WCM* hoarding should remain at such high cost on the Tavern Stand at Lord's now that the BBC cameras seemed too coy to dwell on it. But the general excitement kept fatigue in check, for my efforts to reach all corners of the game were rewarded with regularity, with such gems as Paul Gibb's gripping diary from the 1946-47 tour of Australia, followed by A.E.Relf's 1903-04 diary, and guest columns from the likes of Patrick Moore, Brian Clough, Simon Gray, Frank Swinnerton, Sir Don Bradman, Roy Hattersley, Bill O'Reilly, Barry Norman, Ben Travers, Laurie Lee, Richard Ingrams, Arthur Askey and others, until the well ran dry, with promises to write piling up in the pending file. It was time too to wade through the vast collection of pictures I had built up over the years, aiming for special exposure in an illustrative feature called Picture Gallery.

That first summer of publication embraced the second World Cup, won again by West Indies after Boycott and Brearley had dawdled in setting up a platform in the run-chase. And we had our first *WCM* Editorial Board dinner, when all attended, even David Gower, our 'baby' at 22, who that very day had scored a double-century against India in the Edgbaston Test. 'You're excused,' I told him. 'I know you'll be wanting to go out and celebrate.' But he came, a gesture much appreciated, though he became harder to persuade as the years passed and the demands on his social time increased.

Interviewing England's favourite cricketers at Wembley, 1979: Derek Randall (left) and Ian Botham

The idea of setting up winter tours for readers seemed to have some merit, so the toe went into the water that first off-season, and we took a number to Australia that in due course would swell significantly, particularly when Caribbean series were being played. It kept the flag flying and enabled the editor of a low-budget magazine to go along as escort, broadening his experience to the point where he saw Test cricket in nearly every territory, met many old Test players, and made countless friends. The 1979-80 tour of

Australia, when England played (and lost, under Brearley) three Tests, and when the WCM forecast of 'Lillee c Willey b Dilley' was fulfilled at Perth, began with a huffy Editorial, for I was ashamed that the TCCB tried to put the Ashes aside for this series on the basis that the tour had been hastily arranged. So what? The Ashes were not theirs to withhold. The urn was the property of MCC, and in spirit belonged to the cricket communities of both England and Australia. The spineless attempt to lock away the Ashes did England's image great harm in Australia.

The first WCM Editorial Board dinner: Patrick Eagar, Ted Dexter, Jim Laker, DF, John Arlott, Bob Willis, David Gower (fresh from his 200 not out against India)

A year later we were in West Indies, and for those of us who believe there is more to cricket than tomorrow's headlines, the gathering of dozens of former West Indies and England players during the Barbados Test was a joyous event. Here was the chance to converse with Wes Hall and Rohan Kanhai and Gerry Gomez and Jeff Stollmeyer from my own time, and Andy Ganteaume (112 in his sole Test innings), Derek Sealy (still West Indies' youngest debutant, at 17, on this very ground in 1930) and E.L.G.'Teddy' Hoad, another from 1930, when he captained the side.

The greatest catch was George Headley. Weekes, Worrell, Sobers, Lara notwithstanding, there are still those who contend that Headley was the greatest of all West Indies batsmen. Certainly he had inferior batting support in his day, and his reputation among contemporaries (always a primary consideration) was simply towering.

He welcomed my company, but not the tape-recorder. So I put it under the seat. 'I don't want to do that,' he whispered, patting his chest. 'I had a little heart trouble a while back.' So we simply talked: all through the morning session and well into the afternoon, never missing a ball out there in the cauldron as England, still reeling from the death of their manager Ken Barrington, slid to defeat. 'Oh no!' exclaimed the impartial Headley as Peter Willey got a clearly dubious lbw decision when facing Croft. 'That spoils my day.'

Though he was not a hard-liner on racial matters, he grew serious, close to heated, at the recollection of the West Indies team filing through the immigration counter in Australia in 1930, when he wrote 'African' automatically and with pride on the entry form, but then spotted a team-mate writing 'European' on his, when he was anything but.

With the great George Headley, Barbados '81: cooling off after the pepper sauce

As if in apology for getting serious, he laughed at the recall of his early attempt to play Clarrie Grimmett, the grizzled little legspinner. Down the pitch he sailed, only to be stumped. He gripped my forearm and shook with laughter, his eyes hidden by creases of merriment.

George Headley, one of the many to lose good years to the war, averaged 60.83 in Test cricket. And in 1948 he became the first black man to captain West Indies. 'It wasn't altogether a popular appointment,' he reflected. Would he have worn a helmet had they been in vogue in his day? He thought for a while before drawling, 'I might; I might.'

I was privileged to sit with him at lunch, and he warned me about the pepper sauce, which I consequently reduced. But still half-a-teaspoonful was like dynamite, and as I writhed and howled, he chuckled deeply. Never two minutes went by without somebody asking him to sign a postcard or even a napkin. If only he'd let me switch on that tape-recorder.

During the previous summer in England, West Indies' slow over rate – 74 in six hours one day at The Oval – generated remonstrations, and it was widespread, to be echoed again and again over the next dozen years, the protests broadening to take in the grave matter of intimidation. Umpires and, less excusably, administrators dithered, and the game suffered, while those of us who condemned it in print were accused by the 'defendants' of being poor losers (it had nothing to do with the match result) and worse. Many a time I wished I had been born into an earlier era, but I was not now going to shirk a clear and insistent editorial responsibility. There were others who ducked it, and others who were mealy-mouthed about the problem, while some of the high-circulation tabloid newspapers profited by it. But all the while, true cricket-lovers wept at the outrages: batsmen in fear of their physical – and mental, come to that – well-being, no place for slow bowling, with the consequent monotony, and few strokes forward of the wicket.

Someone who cared for cricket but not a jot about what people thought of him was E.M.Wellings, recently retired from the *Evening News*, and glad of the invitation to contribute to *WCM*. Readers were never in two minds about how welcome or otherwise were Lyn Wellings' views on current topics. 'More right-wing than Franco' was one chap's slick verdict. But Wellings had 60 years' experience as player and writer, and cared almost rabidly for it. It was, after all, about the only friend the poor fellow had, having upset almost everyone who had ever entered his orbit. And when he died, he left instructions that his ashes were to be cast into the English Channel; then, but not before, was I to inform the world of his passing.

Not many genuine scoops come the way of a monthly journal. Much that is privy has been seized by others in the tedious days of countdown before we published. But there were two special items in 1980: we were sent a photograph of the umpires being jostled in the Lord's Long Room during the Centenary Test match, taken illicitly by an MCC member. And I had secured a copy of the confidential 1979 report of the ICC fact-finding mission to South Africa, which was still the forbidden land. It revealed that, against all supposition, the subcommittee had recommended that 'some recognition and encouragement' be given to those who were working for integrated cricket, and that a representative ICC team ought to be sent to South Africa to signal that recognition. These findings were swept under the carpet.

Already it was noticeable that many more cricket books were coming onto the market. I had contributed a couple more myself. *The Golden Age of Cricket 1890-1914* came out in 1978, and contained over 300 pictures from that enchanting era, with a text that aimed to show that there was more than one man – Dr Grace – playing the game around that time. I was fortunate enough to obtain a foreword from J.B.Priestley, who was then the greatest living English literary figure, and, crucially, a survivor of the blood-splashed conflict which closed that chapter of life, leaving the world in 1918 in such a state that it 'could never again be trusted' in Priestley's words. He went on to acknowledge the benefits of television as far as cricket-watching was concerned, and then, privately, asked me to organise his fee in the form of the best Havana cigars, to be left on his doorstep.

Then, in 1980, *Thommo* was published, a book written with the 'world's fastest bowler'. It was no easy assignment, since Jeff Thomson is more a man of action than words, but the project was enjoyable all the same as I chased him with the tape-recorder out to the family home in Bankstown (the Sydney suburb where my daughter had been born) and to the SCG No.2 ground, where he was shattering a plastic screen meant to resist a cricket ball (how the helmet visor manufacturer was red- faced!), and even into the dungeon of the dressing-room at VFL Park, where Thommo was putting in a World Series 'personal appearance' despite still being on the Australian Cricket Board's books.

J.R.Thomson, man of action

The best and only honest way to get this thing written, I swiftly concluded, was for me to write my bit and Jeff to tape his. Somehow the combination gelled, and the world now knew that he wasn't the slightest bit evil, just capable of being carried away at times. And his love of nature – the surf, sunsets, fishing, wrestling with wild pigs – was genuine. He really had needed to be dragged onto a cricket field as a youngster. Many a bruised Test batsman wished he hadn't been.

His memory for cricket incident was poor. What about his Ashes debut, when he took nine wickets at the Gabba in 1974? 'Ah, you'd better check with Dennis about that one'; or, 'Greg'd probably be able to help on that.' He did become very animated, though, when it came to uproarious descriptions of a bank hold-up (he was a victim, not the perpetrator) when he was a teenager, or nearly being killed in a rough surf when fishing from the rocks. It struck me that a tape of the 'interviews' would probably be a preferable option to the book.

Cricket film night at the NFT, with some of the 1950-51 England team as guests: Alec Bedser, Reg Simpson and Godfrey Evans. Clyde Jeavons is in the doorway

Alongside the demands of the magazine and the occasional book, a developing interest in cricket on film became near-obsessive. The fascination had long been present, but now, under the flag of Wisden Film Search, I stirred as much interest as possible in the ranks of the public, launching the crusade with the first of many Wisden Film Evenings at the National Film Theatre in London, with the backing of the National Film Archive curator Clyde Jeavons. With those long-ago public film recitals at the Sydney Town Hall firmly in mind, I was so pleased to be able to retrieve silent film and pre-war newsreels, and also features from the early post-war years from the vaults, and films made by cricketers on tour, and run them on the big screen before twice-nightly audiences of almost 500, the majority of whom might never have imagined that they would ever see WG and Ranji and Hobbs and Bradman batting, let alone Grimmett, O'Reilly, Tate and Larwood bowling. After 30 years or so of these recitals, the National Film Theatre curtly terminated them. I could only gasp to the shiny-bum who imparted the news: 'How the English hate success.' A pal of mine hazarded a guess that the administration would prefer to stage a film show for the delectation of two dozen Patagonian hermaphrodites.

By natural progression, I had set about compiling a film history of batting – *Golden Greats* – supported by Benson & Hedges, a video programme which incorporated film sourced from private and institutional collections, with John Arlott presenting it. I asked David Puttnam, a known cricket enthusiast, fresh from his *Chariots of Fire* triumph, to act as executive producer. We had some encouraging early meetings, but he was called away by another blockbuster, and the only communication for weeks was a terse postcard from him stating that he'd read my script, and why hadn't I mentioned in it that Victor Trumper was killed in the First World War. Since Australia's sainted batsman had been too ill to join up, and died in 1915 from Bright's Disease, my response was brief and uncomplicated.

I hired Broadhalfpenny Down, Hambledon for the Arlott sequences, and the blustery, chill conditions had John shivering, although he was usually more sensitive to heat: that's to say, anything above 55 degrees Fahrenheit. So I lent him my jumper. He then devised some extra script and referred to the dreadful non-cricket weather; and he was brilliant. Inside the historic Bat & Ball Inn he was again at his best, surrounded by warm, copper lamps. He memorised all of Hammond's scores in the 1928-29 Ashes series, reeled off a long passage to camera without the need of autocue, and closed with reference to the England captain of the time, 'Gubby Allen'. Unfortunately it should have been Percy Chapman, and as the crew and stray customers at the bar clapped spontaneously and heartily, I had to make myself unpopular by suggesting that it all had to be reshot so that the correct captain was named.

This was just about the last major professional performance by John Arlott before his health went into serious decline. The memorable tracking shot of him walking through the Oval Long Room, talking about his beloved Jack Hobbs, worked only after the sound engineer had managed to delete all the gasps emitted by poor John's tortured lungs. Still, we had some grand lunches and dinners.

The logging of film went on, with shot-lists entering a swelling catalogue of discoveries. A video on bowlers was a natural follow-up, and appeared six years later, a technically superior production, and presented in part by another very capable old pro in Peter West. It surprised many that film of S.F.Barnes existed, even though he was 80 when it was shot in 1953, his arm still almost brushing his ear. The pace of the programme built up naturally, with the slow bowlers dealt with first and the crash-bang-wallop of the modern West Indian fast men bringing the cavalcade to a bruising close.

Meanwhile, back at the editorial desk, I continued to work single-handed, with huge, loyal support from Debbie, doing all that had to be done even if it meant many hours of weekend work, while a free evening was practically unheard of. Two convictions fuelled this workload: that to all of us are given 10 to 15 years at the peak of working life when the Big Effort is there to be made; and perhaps only once does there come along an opportunity to show clearly what we are worth. Burn-out would be inevitable, and the cleverest among us probably knew when to ease off and avoid heart attacks that spell the saddest of epitaphs: he worked himself to death. My case was unusual in that I had my chance comparatively late in life. Had it have come earlier, burn-out would have come that much sooner. Further, who would dare to complain about overwork in cricket, when thousands would – or so they have claimed – have done it all for nothing?

Life early in the magazine's existence would have been smoother had not the printer gone broke and closed down. This necessitated an emergency dash to Portsmouth to retrieve film and original material, and finding somebody else to set and print *Wisden Cricket Monthly* without interruption to the flow of publication. Again, it was nothing a few nocturnal extra shifts wouldn't secure.

The reviewing of books became a prime item on my agenda. Some authors dare not do this, the old glasshouses and stone-throwing principle applying. But I stuck my neck out, wrote the reviews frankly and as informatively as I could – and made a few further enemies. Not that some authors were not appreciative. After a review of Gordon Greenidge's 1980 autobiography *The Man in the Middle*, I received a letter from his collaborator, Pat Symes, which read, in part: 'We've had some strange reactions to the book but yours was one of the best. The people who have enjoyed it most are those who have been able to identify with him in some way. I believe you have an Anglo-Australian background, and your review is one of the few to show any sympathy towards his traumatic early years.' I was to think back on this during my own traumatic year of 1995.

If ever I won a few dollars on the poker machines at the St George Leagues Club or at the trots, I quit. In fact I hardly ever gamble with real money. But how I wish I had done in a sizable way when I think back to 1981. The 'Botham Ashes series' was the series of our lifetime in so many ways, and helped ease the shock and pain of the loss of Ken Barrington only a few weeks earlier. The Headingley Test, when Ian Botham, freed from the captaincy, carved 149 not out off 148 balls, and Willis stormed to 8 for 43, England won after having followed on, an achievement only ever seen once before in Test history, when a certain A.E.Stoddart led England to victory by an even narrower margin, 10 runs, at Sydney in 1894 after having followed on.

I was writing reports during the 1981 Tests for the *Indian Express*, and as Botham plodded belligerently to the crease in England's second innings, the score was 105 for 5, still 122 short of avoiding an innings defeat. Teatime was deadline for me, so I dropped in the throwaway comment that as Botham entered, it would need 150 from him to make this a match. I was one run out with this flukey conjecture. More importantly, had I had the wit of a Lillee or a Marsh, I would have put 50 pence on England at 500:1.

The other speculation which would have served me handsomely with a wager attached was back in the second issue of *WCM*, when Somerset skipper Brian Rose declared in a B&H Cup match in order to preserve his side's wicket-taking rate, which was good enough to get them into the quarter-finals. They were expelled, and their president apologised. No rule had been broken, but the spirit of the game had been traduced. Indeed, a period was unfolding in which the spirit of cricket was to be bruised time and again, forcing caring writers and broadcasters to sound quite pompous at times. But they – we – meant well. It was a beautiful and honourable game, and still is, on the whole, but there is a fragility about its natural code of conduct that has forced legislation to be brought in here and there as a sort of splint.

At the time of the Rose incident, I wrote, without serious expectation of its ever happening: 'I have been waiting, with trepidation, for the moment when, with six runs needed off the final ball and a lot of money at stake, the bowler informs the umpire of a change of action and rolls the ball along the ground.' That is precisely what Trevor Chappell did in a one-day international at Melbourne less than two years later. I have never thought to check with his skipper, brother Greg, where he picked up the idea. He lived to regret his dire action, saying he was in some kind of mental crisis at the time. There were, however, pragmatists who excused him. The loophole was there and he drove through it, just like 'Shock' White, with his grotesquely wide bat just over 200 years earlier.

To have been present at all of Botham's buccaneering performances in that summer of 1981 was some experience, though the jubilant scenes at the three cricket grounds (Headingley, Edgbaston and Old Trafford) contrasted somewhat with the subdued atmosphere in the Australians' hotels, where I stayed. The tourists were in siege, with their own Press not sparing the rod, while the British papers were not the best of breakfast reading.

One of the few lighter moments came when John Snow came into the bar in Manchester, and I had the chance to introduce Test cricket's latest fast-bowling recruit, Mike Whitney, to one of the immortals. As he shook hands with the still-slim Sussex man who had taken 202 Test wickets for England, the best that the awe-struck 'Whit' could offer was: 'Hey, you're the bloke they threw the beer-cans at the SCG! I was there!'

After that Test, I had the dubious pleasure of informing Allan Border that he had just recorded the slowest century in Tests by an Australian. Then I caught sight of Dennis Lillee's sweat-soaked headband hanging on his suitcase. He had promised to let me have it for my private cricket museum, but throughout the series he kept saying, 'Later, mate, later.' So now I simply grabbed it. Having bowled 46 overs in England's second innings and now batted for an hour-and-a-half, the world's greatest fast bowler was too spent to resist. 'Go on, Frithy, you can have the bloody thing. And don't forget, it's got my original sweat on it!'

Still every opportunity was grasped to trace old-time players who would make for good interviews. One such was Fred Bakewell, the pre-war Northants player whose career was destroyed by a road accident in 1936. He really took some finding, having lived a shadowy existence for many years, but he turned out to be friendly and down-to-earth, and astonishingly free of bitterness. He was 27 when the car crashed, killing the driver, team-mate Reggie Northway. Bakewell had just scored 241 not out against Derbyshire at Chesterfield. He described his injuries, finishing with: 'and my hands, there wasn't any flesh on them at all. I was a helluva mess.' A few days later, Dallas Page, the young captain of Gloucestershire, was also killed in a car accident. Dangerous times.

Bakewell: bright colours with a dark thread

Fred Bakewell scored a century for England in the 1933 Oval Test against West Indies. Reaching three figures, he said, was just like reaching a century in a county match, or even a village match. He was, as Robertson-Glasgow wrote, good enough at times to have batted with Bradman on not uneven terms. 'Crusoe' also wrote that 'among the bright colours there lurked a dull thread of negligence, even apathy'. I sensed this myself. For days after our meeting I couldn't get Bakewell's moving mixture of melancholy face and brave words out of my mind.

I managed to get to Sri Lanka to witness their first-ever Test match, when they gave England a fright over the first three days at the P.Saravanamuttu Stadium in February, 1982. Incurably romantic, I thrilled at the first ball ever bowled in this newest of Test countries: Willis to Warnapura. Among the photos I took was one in colour of the 18-year-old left-hander Arjuna Ranatunga, who, alone, was the only member of this inaugural team still playing for Sri Lanka 14 years later when they won the World Cup at Lahore. He had a paunch and little white sideburns by then, but was still soft of voice, modest too, if slightly less shy.

Keith Fletcher led England to victory in Colombo, after Emburey and Underwood had spun through the Sri Lankan second innings like borers through a log, and Tavaré and Gower saw England to a seven-wicket win just before the close of the fourth day, leaving everyone free to swim at Mount Lavinia (which I'd last seen in 1949, as a boy on the voyage to Australia) or Negombo, where the Wisden tourists were staying.

If anything, the ultimate highlight was the official banquet, presided over by the Honourable Gamini Dissanayake, then Minister of Lands. He was to be assassinated in a bomb outrage 12 years later as that gorgeous island reeled from civil violence.

None of the unrest was apparent to us as we listened to the speeches that night, Mike Gatting's wife suffering a fit of the giggles which spread slowly round the table, inspired chiefly by MCC president Hubert Doggart's repeated references to *'Sri Lonka'* in his thunderous voice. I came home with a bagful of souvenirs, thoughts yet again overtaken before reflection was complete because another sensation was upon us: an English 'rebel' team immediately set off for South Africa. There was predictable uproar: one faction saw the players' huge fees as 'blood money' while others saw them as champions of freedom of movement, taking encouragement to the beleaguered ranks of South African cricketers. Other rebel tours followed, until there was one too many, in 1989-90, led by the disillusioned Gatting. By then the political scenery was being moved fast and furiously, and the new South Africa was just about to emerge.

The event which dominated my thoughts in early 1982 was a house move. For once the cricket world had to take second billing for a few days. At last we had trees all around us, and room for my burgeoning cricket library. When the pressure of work became almost intolerable, I could now lift up my eyes and see the restful ruins of a 14th Century chapel in the middle distance, while at the top of the lane, in the old cemetery, was Lewis Carroll's grave, a source of reassurance when the world of today really did seem to be rather too lunatic and distorted. As Debbie and I were settling in to the new home, the Falkland crisis turned into open warfare, and the mind reverted weirdly back 40 years to a childhood in which apprehension featured very anxiously. The casualties were grievous, and for a time the risk of global escalation seemed serious.

Above and beyond the buzz of all this, Debbie was devoting all her free time to helping women with PMS (Premenstrual Syndrome) and related problems, counselling with all the unique sensitivity of one who herself had suffered severely. She co-founded an organisation called the National Association for Premenstrual Syndrome, which expanded to the point where hundreds of women were being comforted and helped each week. Debbie's exhausting input lasted for four years, and her efforts drained her. It made my own cricket media activities seem frivolous by comparison. I felt immense pride and admiration for what she was doing.

Some of those recruited into NAPS allowed their ambitions to get the better of them, conspiring to control the running of the charity and to resist any movement towards broadening its policy, into which much thought had been invested. Debbie, Queensland's gift to Britain, was incapable of acting bossily and after several years she walked away, exhausted and in tears, unable to comprehend the deviousness. It was at least two years before she felt she had come to terms with the experience. At least she had a thick pile of grateful letters as testimony to the good she had done. I didn't think that this sort of iniquitous behaviour was to be found in cricket, I naively told her.

The shape of the magazine was now well settled, as was the house style, which is more difficult to establish than might be supposed. Among the regular features was coverage of the cricket memorabilia auctions, which proliferated, with prices rising beyond belief. I went to them all, primarily as reporter but sometimes as would-be purchaser, missing out on countless occasions when ludicrous bids were made, but getting the occasional choice item, such as Victor Trumper's fob-watch and three original photographs from the first English tour of Australia (1861-62). Interest grew to such an extent that some enthusiasts from Manchester, Tony Sheldon and Keith Hayhurst, set up the Cricket Memorabilia Society, and I was gratified to accept their invitation to become a vice-president. The more we learned about institutionalised collections the more we felt that cricket owes much to the army of private collectors, who pay big money because they cherish what they acquire, and they take good care of their treasures, major and minor, before selling them on – or having them resold after death.

An article with explosive consequences appeared in the September 1982 issue of *WCM*. It was written by a Scottish schoolmaster named E.J.Brack, and it challenged what some considered to be a privileged phenomenon, the BBC Radio cricket coverage, *Test Match Special*. No-one would seriously have suggested that John Arlott, who had gone off to self-imposed exile/retirement on his island, could ever adequately be replaced as a commentator. Unlike the crowd of ex-Test players now signed by radio and television – few of them with tolerable voices, command of the language, or knowledge of cricket's folklore – Arlott was a trained and gifted broadcaster. And he became a major legend.

The self-indulgence and self-satisfaction permeating *TMS* was disappointing some and exasperating others. It was an institution and therefore prone to smugness, unthreatened as it was by competition. In fact, so sacredly was it regarded that none dared to criticise. Until Mr Brack offered his thesis.

He had digs at Brian Johnston and Fred Trueman and Henry Blofeld, and believed the programme was being held together by Trevor Bailey and Bill Frindall. The response was phenomenal: bags of letters, six in favour of the kick up the backside for every one defending the conduct of the programme. The waffle about cakes and pigeons was mocked, and one correspondent even pointed out that Percy Fender, now blind, preferred to listen to the television commentary.

Two of the regular broadcasters, Don Mosey and Tony Lewis, came up to me during the next Test match and confided that they believed the criticism had some justification. But I was soon picking up two dismal rumours: that I was actually E.J.Brack, and the attack on *TMS* had been launched in *WCM* because I was frustrated in my ambition to become a commentator myself.

One: E.J.Brack exists, and had written for *WCM* before; two: I have never had any ambition to be a radio commentator, and can think of few worse ways of passing a day at the cricket than having to chortle on publicly about it for 20 minutes at a time. Some who do, in my experience, suffer from verbal diarrhoea even in the evening, after a long day behind the microphone, and are quite often incurably opinionated.

My mistake was in falling for John Arlott's suggestion to approach *TMS* producer Peter Baxter around 1980 after John and Don Mosey had met to discuss possible new candidates for cricket broadcasting. Mine was one of the names put forward. 'See Peter [Baxter] about an audition,' was John's near-command. So I did, out of curiosity, only to be told that everybody, it seemed, was seeking an audition. The enthusiasm wasn't there, so I walked away and let the matter drop. Occasional TV and radio appearances have always been fun enough.

The second batch of published letters focused on the preponderance of clichés and also blamed *TMS* listeners who wrote in 'egging them on to yet further ridiculousness'. But while the obsession with chocolate cake continued to be condemned, there was an insistent glimmer that Brian Johnston's good-natured banter was much appreciated. As we were to see, that appreciation mushroomed into something almost too enormous to be comprehended. And the complacency diminished as the programme's slot in the schedules became less secure. The format tightened up, and the only modest conclusion had to be that it probably would have done so without *WCM's* 'unfriendly act'.

Around this time, I was able to engage my first assistant, a self-assured

Yorkshire lad named Simon Wilde. While I trained him, my workload actually increased, though he eventually worked with a minimum of supervision. The repetition and isolation got to him in the end, and he joined *The Times* and wrote a book or two, his *WCM* apprenticeship serving him as well as those undergone by David Gower and Bob Willis.

There was a slight and amusing printing error in the Christmas Quiz that I compiled in 1982. Wicketkeeper Dick Lilley's name was *just* visible on the colour postcard reproduced, so that eagle-eyed readers, faced with identifying him, must have wondered whether it was a trap.

By now I was off to Australia again, following the Melbourne Test in my mother-in-law's lounge in Queensland and bellowing in frustration when Channel 9 were busy displaying a lucrative commercial while failing to show the ball which dismissed Thomson and gave England a thrilling three-run victory.

Australia were overall stronger than England, and won the 1982- 83 series. Apart from a memorable meal Debbie and I had with the Bradmans at Stoneyfell, however, when we were the last to leave, so pleasantly engrossing had been the conversation, the defining moment of the entire season was when John Dyson was run out before having faced a ball in the Sydney Test – but was given not-out. Television showed him clearly out, as did the front page of the newspaper next day. But he batted on for five hours to score 79, and it substantially helped Australias to win the series. I choked on the injustice of it and the lack of logic. With millions clearly having seen Dyson fail to make it to safety, how could his continuing innings ever be justified? This cardinal moral/technical principle was to take an unduly long time for some supposedly intelligent administrators to grasp.

I was distracted for the rest of that Test match, and launched a crusade to have the replay facility employed officially in the most useful manner: simply to determine whether a batsman was out or not.

It was painfully repetitive, but at every opportunity, in several parts of the world, I urged umpires and administrators to consider at least giving it a trial. At first nobody seemed to like the idea. Fred Goodall, the New Zealand umpire, listened patiently before snapping back angrily that I seemed to want to take the umpire's authority away. No, became the stock response, I would like to see umpires never again look stupid as they got it wrong while the truth was hitting TV-viewers between the eyes. There'd be too many hold-ups? A risk, yes, but it would be worth it if the game's injustices were eliminated. And think how it would remove grumpy batsmen's grounds for dissent. They would know they were out. The smouldering would be drastically reduced.

More than one international umpire feared that their role would be reduced to that of mere coat-hangers. Perhaps, they said, you'd like the game umpired from a room up in the stand? Years later it occurred to me that if that were possible it mightn't be such a bad thing. The paramount need was for justice to be done.

With a tinge of embarrassment (because it's against the grain to be repetitious) I returned to the theme at every opportunity as bad decisions had to be recorded in *WCM*, all avoidable, many of them 'perverting the course of justice'. And as the years slipped past, and the anger persisted as batsmen were either erroneously given out or wrongly reprieved, I felt that a gradual awakening to the beneficial possibilities was beginning to stir in the umpiring fraternity and among cricket- lovers generally, if not among batsmen themselves, who probably already realised they would no longer benefit from close run-out and stumping calls – without seeing that would also often benefit. South Africa finally had the courage to try it out, and it proved an instant success. They had led the way in other innovations, such as the fielding ring and players' shirt identification in the limited-overs game. Now the world could contemplate the wastage that had occurred with every decision wrongly given while the truth had been available and ignored on that little screen upstairs.

The most moving hours of that 1982-83 series were spent at the Sydney Cricket Ground. It was now already over 30 years since my first visit, and as the ground developments piled up, I found myself picturing George Gunn walking bow-legged to make his Test debut hundred here in 1907, and MacLaren and Trumper. I gazed hypnotically at the old 'showboat' pavilion, relic of the 1880s, supposedly protected by a heritage order, and slightly intimidated by the concrete edifices all round the oval. In a Disney film the characters would all sway and chorus a deep-chested dirge about the inevitability of Time's conquests.

The only conflict for the moment, though, was with Bill O'Reilly, whose company was always stimulating, even if tales of pre-war Test battles, always enthralling, had to be interspersed with argument over Northern Ireland and, now, the Falklands war, with 'Tiger' speaking for the greater mass of Australians, it seemed, in condemning British 'colonialism' – up to their old tricks again. I held Bill at arm's length by asking him how he thought Australia would react if the Indonesians occupied Lord Howe Island?

More to the point, I asked Norman Cowans, England's Jamaica-born fast bowler, to write a piece for the magazine, since he seemed keen to do so. But he said, a day or two after deadline, that he hadn't been able to write a word. 'Writer's block!' he claimed, with a huge grin. So it wasn't just us day-to-day men who suffer?

One writer who did get more than he bargained for was Richard Cashman, who was interviewing an England supporter on the SCG Hill. The Pom had been waving his flag, and a bunch of locals threatened to hurl beer-cans at him, some not empty either. 'Coom on, chook it at me!' he teased. And they did. And they missed him. Instead, Cashman copped one between the eyes, and staggered back to the Press-box with what could only be termed the researcher's ultimate bleeding badge of honour.

Nothing like a robust discussion with Bill O'Reilly first thing to wake a man up

A wonderful meeting in Melbourne was with Leo O'Brien, who, among many sporting accomplishments, had batted for Australia during the Bodyline series of '32-33. Here was a true, old-fashioned Aussie sportsman. He was modest and spoke ill of nobody, chuckling at every opportunity, beating me to the bottom of the glass every time we attacked a 'pot' in the Sportsman's Bar at the Windsor, Leo yarning non-stop with fascinating tales of cricket and Aussie Rules football and baseball and boxing and horses and India. Later, I took my notebook when we had another session at the Australia, and I was close to trembling as he prepared to tell me about the Adelaide Incident.

This was the most explosive moment of all the Bodyline Tests, with Bill Woodfull sending the England management packing with fleas in their ears. Argument has raged ever since as to who leaked the story of that historic verbal exchange. Leo O'Brien now eliminated both Fingleton and Bradman. He himself was there, and he recalled that the stone-deaf physio was in the room when Woodfull spoke, as were Alan Kippax and Jack Ryder, as well as the old Australian fast bowler Ernie Jones. Further than that Leo would not go. And it was too late now to go back and question Kippax or Ryder or Jones (long dead). A few years later, while working on my Bodyline book, I was bequeathed the solution to this mystery.

Having explained that the only protection he wore against Larwood, apart from box and gloves, was an old singlet stuffed inside his trouser-leg, he then produced a gnarled old batting-glove, the rubber-pimple kind, and gave it to me, saying he had worn it during that infamous series. Just before we parted he said he had recently finished his 61st playing season, some achievement for a 75-year- old. I wondered if I might one day match that.

On another tack, though, there was still just time to telephone an octogenarian named Jack O'Hagan, composer of *The Road to Gundagai.* I needed to use his merry jingle *Our Don Bradman* on the soundtrack of the Great Batsmen video now nearing completion. The cheerful voice of this legendary man assured me that he would consider himself honoured if the tune were to be used. No reference to money was made. (The music publishers took care of that in due course anyhow.) I had just been in direct touch with the 1930s. Emerging from the Flinders Street phone-box, I found it hard to cope with the reality of the rush-hour crowd.

Around this time I fell foul of R.S.Whitington, and again it was over a book review. Dick, an affable companion, six times married, with much of the devil-may-care of his pal and sometime co-author Keith Miller, had produced a slipshod illustrated history of Australian cricket in 1972, and it was now reissued with an even bigger array of misidentifications and misprints. There was no escape for a reviewer. The truth had to be told. It was. And I had a stream of abusive letters from the author. We were friends no more. Ah, well.

I despaired at times, for the producers of the Bodyline drama-documentary, Kennedy-Miller, had written to me in search of film and the addresses of surviving players and even blazer and badge manufacturers in an apparent quest for authenticity. There was no fee, but I devoted as much time as it needed and sent them a fairly sizable file. The completed programme, high in dramatic impact, was littered with inaccuracies that discredited it in the eyes of anyone with even a passing acquaintance with the era and the personalities. Even the crease markings were wrong. The sweaters were ridiculous, characterisations often laughable, historical reliability shaky, and as for Bradman reaching the crease and raising his bat in a prolonged gladiatorial salute to the crowd, in reality he used to walk slowly enough to attune his eyes to the light, take guard without fuss, and score, usually, at least a single off that first ball. Didn't anybody care about historical fidelity? Again, a man began to wonder it if was all really worth it.

In the summer of 1983, another cricketer with journalistic aspirations got his chance in *WCM*, Mark Nicholas showing a neat turn of phrase which, when added to his creamy voice and range of vocab, made him one of the more acceptable new faces midst the stampede of glottal-voiced ex-cricketers into plum media openings. One of them even disconcertingly reminded me of Heinrich Himmler more with each passing summer.

That 1983 season will be remembered, of course, for India's victory over West Indies in the third World Cup, the final at Lord's being a pulsating event. It seemed so predictable, with India seemingly broken at 111 for 6, and then little less hopelessly finishing with 183 all out. West Indies were 50 for the loss of only Greenidge in reply, with quite a lot of batting to come.

And then the clatter of wickets began. None was as unexpected and decisive as that of Viv Richards, who in popular parlance was an 'emperor' on most of the cricket grounds he strutted, but none more than Lord's. Now, on 33, which was incredibly to be top score of the innings, he cracked Madan Lal towards midwicket on the Grandstand side, and Kapil Dev ran as if his shirt was on fire and clung to the high catch.

That evening, the hotel across the road throbbed to the drums and clapping of hundreds of Indian supporters as Kapil elegantly danced a bhangra. When I'd got all the players' autographs in the match programme, I went home happy. It was very late.

Unpalatable meal: I devour my own words after India's delectable World Cup triumph in 1983

In the following month's *WCM* I was shown chewing on my ill-advised words, written pre-tournament, focussing on India's dismal approach to previous World Cups. Though it didn't show on my face, I was truly thrilled for them, and for the millions of fans back home. I felt I was entitled to claim that I had inspired India to their memorable victory.

On the same spread, my Editorial dealt with the issue of qualification rules for overseas-born players in Test cricket, sifting out genuine immigrants such as Roland Butcher and Norman Cowans from others who were in England playing professionally and qualifying for Test cricket for England while their native country, South Africa, was excluded. It was to be one of those topics that, far from resolving itself, was to become a hot potato. The debate had begun.

On the field, the other sensation of the summer was New Zealand's first Test victory on English soil, their seamers, Hadlee, Chatfield, Cairns and Coney, beating Willis's England line-up at their own game. The Kiwis were a very likable bunch, particularly in the evening, when John Wright plinked his guitar and Geoff Howarth showed how a skipper could sip with the best of them in a democratic battalion. Ian Smith was joke-cracker-in-chief, and Lance Cairns kept laughing even though his deafness sometimes meant missing the punchlines. At the end of the series, Bruce Edgar, the brave and easy-going (even by New Zealand standards) opening bat, tried to compare for me the fast attacks of the various countries. He did it with WHOOSH sounds of several degrees of pitch and duration, and the final noise, illustrating Holding, Roberts & Co., blew us both off our feet into the Trent Bridge dressing-room seats.

The season closed with a match between some illustrious oldtimers at The Oval, and I drove John Arlott up the A3, headlights blazing, roaring up the hard shoulder when miles of cars had jammed in front of us. Once at the ground, John took a while to get his breath back, and was then overwhelmed with nostalgia as Ray Lindwall and Bertie Clarke bowled. It was 1948 again as the revered Aussie came in from the Vauxhall end – except he was 35 years older, grey and more heavily built, and he wasn't going to take 6 for 20 today. My own feelings might be imagined too, for here was my hero, as friendly a cricketer as I'd ever known, the one who gave me lifts from the SCG when I was fourteen. And now he was old, and could only manage a six-yard run-up. No.

And there was Neil Harvey, picking up cleanly in the covers and firing in a flat return to the bails. He was only 55. It was exquisite to see these two again, but also bordering on the tearful. What eased the situation for me was that JA, on the public-address microphone, was alternating between being weepy over Lindwall and envious of Clarke, the pre-war West Indian spinner, who had just become a father again at 65.

That autumn we took a Wisden All-Stars pro-am cricket party off to Barbados. Supported by some talented club cricketers, we had the genial services of Graham Barlow, Richard Illingworth, Barry Dudleston, Basher Hassan, Ricardo Ellcock, John Childs and Alan Ormrod, and we won two and lost three matches in an enjoyable mini-tour. The best day came with victory over the renowned Wanderers club, who seldom lose. 'Charlie' Childs took 5 for 8, little realising, perhaps, that in four years' time he would be playing against stronger West Indian players when, in his 37th year, he first wore the special raiment of an England player.

We also had Monte Lynch, of Surrey (and Guildford), along with us, and by the poolside in the evenings we took it in turns to discuss his dilemma with him: he was in possession of a contract to join the rebel West Indian tour of South Africa, but could not for the life of him decide whether to sign it. He had just been to Guyana to see his grandmother for what he felt would be the last time, for if he went to the forbidden land, he would be banned indefinitely from his native land. It was a teaser. I think I was not alone in suggesting that, with all due respect, he was unlikely to play Test cricket for England, or for West Indies for that matter; so if he wanted the tempting fee on offer for joining Lawrence Rowe's band of outlaws, he might as well take it.

We were sometimes given a tough time in the shops, where people wanted to know why 'your Mrs Thatcher' wasn't helping out by sending troops to Grenada to deal with the uprising. One had to think quickly: well, the Yanks are there, it's only a small island, and if they need help, which is unlikely, well, the Brits will follow up – the Aussies too, if necessary. Why do politics always have to intrude into cricket? I went off to Kensington Oval and bashed a half-volley into the top deck of the Sobers Stand, almost into Debbie's lap, finishing up on my backside and earning a new nickname, 'Rohan'. If the ball had been three feet to the right it could have killed my darling Debbie. She was unperturned, but I had nightmares for some time afterwards.

Later that winter I made it to New Zealand in time for the sensational Christchurch Test, where England were wiped out by an innings in 12 hours of play. Hadlee scored 99, more than Willis's men made in either innings, and the newspapers sagged with all kinds of allegations concerning the England players' off-field activities.

I followed the tourists to Auckland, and got a ticking-off from Captain Willis for handing over yesterday's sheaf of letters from home just an hour before play began. How was I to know whether players would be inspired by this mail or distracted by it? Anyway, this utterly miserable team got its utterly miserable desserts when the Kiwis won the toss and batted well into the third day, John Wright, Jeff Crowe and Ian Smith all making centuries.

It took me over 40 hours to get home, and I was relieved to have written a tribute to John Wisden on the centenary of his death (April 1884) before departure. I had also persuaded John Wisden & Co. to fund a handsome new headstone for Wisden's grave at Brompton Cemetery, where the Archdeacon of Middlesex gave a brief address after Bill Gray had unveiled the memorial. We then adjourned to Queen's Club for a commemorative lunch, where 'the Little Wonder's' toast was drunk – with me secretly coupling his name with that of someone who was secretary at this very club many years earlier, none other than A.E.Stoddart.

Next problem? This time it was an outbreak of short tempers and indignation in the trade when David Gower appeared on our front cover using a bat with both Gray-Nicolls and Newbery markings. He was having such a successful time of it at the crease in Pakistan that he'd run out of bats: hence the bastardised version. But this was one I decided to renounce. It was somebody else's problem, and nothing that an explanatory paragraph next month wouldn't fix, all involved being adults.

Bill Gray unveils a new memorial over John Wisden's grave at Brompton Cemetery

In all probability, having come this far down the publishing track and having had to take on so many people whose intentions were either hostile or negative, I had somehow become stronger: because I had to. I'd needed to insulate myself against criticism, some unwarranted, and the undermining efforts of the unfriendly. There was never any shortage of encouragement from family, friends and readers. It was just that every day seemed to bring something that needed tough reaction, whether internal (and the management did not always operate sensibly or smoothly) or external, be it a recalcitrant advertiser or reader, or insistent would-be contributor, or disappointing distributor, or moaning player (the heyday of the lawyer was looming). It was so often a relief to review a book in the silent time approaching midnight, or to work on another set of cricket questions for BBC TV's *Mastermind*, which I prepared for a number of years. (The programme today is boringly formulaic, many questions unduly long, numerical answers dubiously included: not a good idea.)

Morning brought a heavy post, over an hour combing the newspapers, digesting every match report, extracting News Register and Microcosm scores material, answering all kinds of telephone calls through the day, before turning after lunch to whatever writing needed to be done and reading galley proofs before laying down page paste-ups. Picture searching always took much longer than expected, often because I went on stubbornly seeking something just a little bit better. All this activity and perfectionism, every day of the week and over much of the weekend, plus Press conferences, meetings and dinners, was only possible when built around 20-minute meals (usually and indigestibly coupled with watching the television News).

I typed all my own letters, well over a thousand a year, fielding all manner of queries: can you give me details of my great-uncle's career with Somerset? (it often transpired that he'd never played any first-class cricket). What is this signed bat worth? Who are the cricketers in this photograph? Will you publish this article of mine on freckled left-handers who wore spectacles. When were pitches first covered? Who invented the box?

Then there were the innovations I unwrapped in *WCM*: identifying on scorecards fieldsmen responsible for run-outs; interspersing touring players' figures in the national averages; ranging batsmen in batting order rather than numerical ascendancy in the abbreviated scores; crediting photographers alongside their work; standardising spelling and terminology; all done in defiance of the sloppiness welling up all around us.

I tried not to complain. Why should I? It was my magazine and I was proud of it. I knew instinctively, without bragging, that it was the best. It was a platform for original thought. I probably wanted it to last forever; and with reasonable advertisement revenue, healthy sales figures, and strict control of wastage there seemed no reason why it should not have an indefinite life. The prospect of still being on this treadmill 20 years hence, when in my late sixties, neither thrilled me nor horrified me. It was the high summer of *Wisden Cricket Monthly* and of my life.

CHAPTER SEVENTEEN

To hoard anything is to have a feeling of comfort and well-being.
Like a squirrel with its nuts, like Kerry with his billions, you are consoled.

PHILLIP ADAMS

JOHN ARLOTT directed his hooded eyes towards each corner of my cluttered study, curled that expressive bottom lip, and murmured, 'Uncritical.' He had taken in the piles of newspaper cuttings and booklets and relics and crowded shelves holding several thousand books. He had peered into the display cabinet and seen the Lillee headband, the balls of hard Bulli soil from the SCG, Jim Laker's 1956 cigarette-lighter, old belt-buckles, a 1948 Oxford v Australians poster. There was an ivory miniature bat, an MCC tie once owned by Fred Bakewell, Leo O'Brien's shrivelled batting-glove, an 1880 Surrey membership card. There were lapel badges and medallions, a brick from the old Oval wall and a chunk of concrete from the old Tavern at Lord's, a pâté jar decorated with Nicholson's Alfred Mynn, Goss cricket bags, a miniature of the 1963 Wisden Trophy, and two Kinsella figures. Alongside Joel Garner's West Indies tie was propped George Robey's 1920 Middlesex membership card, behind which was Neville Cardus's passport. Here was Ross Gregory's wartime diary, and the penny used by Ivo Bligh in the first Ashes series in 1882-83. Pillboxes, goblets, cufflinks, ashtrays, tankards, plates, beercans, decanters, tobacco-jars, keyrings and Edwardian buttons, all bearing cricket motifs, festooned the cabinet, which also held Boycott's MCC card and a daguerreotype, and a selection of miniature signed bats. And somewhere in there was the wrapper from John Arlott's last cigar before he abandoned the habit.

Uncritical indeed, for while I had always sought the most interesting cricketana available, I never said no to even the most fatuous bauble, partly because my affection for cricket knew no bounds and partly because you never know . . .

John did not intend to be unappreciative. In fact, when we turned to the old bats and I singled out the one used (and signed) by Archie Jackson in 1930, he gave a deep 'Aaah' and handled the relic reverently. Only when he raised it in a crude backward defensive was the spell broken, for he banged the cabinet accidentally, and was profuse in his apologies.

Bert Oldfield can take the blame for starting me off with that 1930 Australian blazer back in the early 1950s. With a ball from the 1930 Trent Bridge Test and his New South Wales cap (the one he was wearing in the famous Hammond cover-drive photo) thrown in, I was on my way. I rescued an extremely rare 1907-08 tour booklet from my young brother soon afterwards, and spent all I could afford on new books, never, of course, having the slightest inkling that one day my cricketana and book collection would amount to half-a-houseful, the excesses of enthusiasm running me into the complex territory of investment, protection and high insurance premiums, and also that recurring and difficult and slightly depressing question: What's going to become of all this?

There came a time when the archive needed to be justified. Unlike most of the other committed collectors, I was constantly drawing from the material in the course of research, and, in the case of pictorial matter, for fresh publication. That in itself was probably sufficient justification for building a collection of such magnitude. But the sheer joy of being surrounded by these pieces of history was justification enough for any cricket nut, as shown in the picture in *The Wisden Book of Cricket Memorabilia*, by Marcus Williams and Gordon Phillips, into which I was glad to have some input. There I sit, unselfconsciously at last at the seventh attempt, wearing Duleepsinhji's England cap, the Oldfield blazer, Bradman's gloves, Max Walker's large boots, and holding the Archie Jackson bat.

From auctions to dealers' lists and private sources, I spent many years building the collection, and for too long it was housed in chaotic fashion, mushrooming to the alarming stage when I first realised I no longer knew exactly where everything was.

We are all merely custodians, and the major decision is whether to dispose of it all before you go or to leave the unwelcome task to someone else. Anyone clever and brave enough to dispose within his lifetime then has to cope with the resultant emptiness. I recall how John Arlott instantly started to refill the gaps. Once a collector . . .

Hardly ever did I go to a cricket match without a few books in my bag that I hoped to get signed. It greatly enhances a book to have an inscription on the title- page, be it as brief as 'T. Dexter' or as conscientiously and lovingly penned as 'To David with all my very best wishes Ken Barrington'. Sometimes the opportunity comes along to buy a signed book, such as

Charlie Macartney's autobiography, which means having to sell the unsigned. But since the preponderance of content in most cricket libraries is modern, the hard work befalls the purchaser. To single out just five books of recent vintage: Geoff Boycott, with whom I had always been on friendly terms, refused to sign the critical biography of him by Don Mosey, which in itself made for an interesting inscription, for I pencilled in the fact and dated the refusal: June 24, 1991 – years later he refused to sign Leo McKinstry's GB biography, saying, 'I haven't read it. It's rubbish!' Omar Henry, the South African Coloured Test player, inscribed a thoughtful 'Life and cricket should improve on history'; soon after his knighthood, the greatest of all allrounders unwittingly gave protocol a flick by signing himself '*Sir* Garry Sobers'; then R.E.S. 'Bob' Wyatt, most serious and ancient of England captains, signed his biography (by the charming Gerald Pawle) and added 'With best wishes to a student of the game whose views coincide with that of the subject. Lord's June 29 1985'; and Shane Warne greeted an unauthorised biography with the incisive inscription 'Nothing to do with me!'

At the marathon Lord's sale, with Charlie Watts

As important as anything in this library – including G.B.Buckley's annotated books – must be the first edition of *Scores & Biographies* in which Fred Lillywhite, the somewhat ruthless publisher, has penned, on July 18, 1862: 'Presented to Arthur Haygarth Esq as a small token, in acknowledgment of the services rendered the publisher, in publishing this 'Large Work'.' Underneath is the plaintive retort of the man who slaved away at this monumental work for years, with scant recognition: 'Arthur Haygarth compiled himself the whole of the work Vols 1 to 14 inclusive.' He spoke for all who have been exploited in the literary field.

The little treasures were picked up as the years passed: Arthur Mailey's *10 for 66 and All That*, complete with all the original drawings tipped into the book; and 19th Century classics and rarities, which will always afford an escape from the torrid modern world; rare Liebig menus, and an inscribed Cricket by W.G.Grace (1891), and early Australian annuals, and the almost unobtainable *The Secret History of the Coningham Case by 'Zero'*, a detailed account of the bizarre goings-on when Australian cricketer Arthur Coningham, at the turn of the century, got involved in a sectarian conspiracy in Sydney, complete with court case, when he conducted his own brief, revolver at hip. For a time I seemed to have the only surviving copy. Then my delightful Brisbane mate, Pat Mullins, rang to say he'd picked one up – and it was, unlike mine, in pristine condition. The friendly rivalry was often as pronounced as in the onfield game itself. I know of no other collector, though, who has an inscribed copy of C.T.B.Turner's extremely rare book.

The prime section represents books on Ashes series alone, surmounted by a replica of the legendary little urn, given me by Rolling Stones drummer Charlie Watts after I'd acted as his 'consultant' through the 11-hour MCC sale at Lord's in 1987, where not every item was a duplicate, though this was the club's excuse for selling. Beyond the biggest section of all (the biographies) reside the fiction volumes (how little of cricket fiction is convincing) and the coaching and the club histories and the humorous (again, such a small proportion here achieve the aim). There are limited editions, some properly scarce, others mere publishers' pretensions. There is the largest book of all, *Men in White*, the glorious New Zealand production by Don Neely and Richard King, almost, it seems, as big as the North Island itself, and safe only for a very fit person to lift. And there is the outstanding exercise in exposing hypocrisy, Bruce Francis's *'Guilty': Bob Hawke or Kim Hughes?* Shamefully many bookshops decided that this book was too hot to handle.

And, of course, the *Wisdens*, 1864 to the present day: with a preference for facsimiles of the early issues, for one cannot work out of originals without fear of costly damage to page or spine; besides which, it helps keep the valuations and insurance premium down. Not that there aren't some special editions here: I bought three of G.L.Jessop's early *Wisdens* from his son, and elsewhere was given one (signed) which was formerly in the ownership of A.E. Stoddart. Percy Jeeves, brilliant Warwickshire cricketer, killed in the First World War, and whose name was adopted by P.G. Wodehouse for Bertie Wooster's valet, left two *Wisdens*, signed and annotated, which his brother eventually passed on to me, a big custodial responsibility.

The collection fills drawers and shelves, and grows up from the carpet: piles of scrapbooks (none more special than Stoddart's) and photo albums (from which *WCM* greatly benefited), table games, videotapes, scorecards from the past 150-odd years, autograph books (which nowadays mostly seem to be sliced into separate pages for profit), and wine bottles bearing cricket labels, tour booklets, greetings cards, postcards, cigarette-cards (I once knocked back a mint set of 1896 Wills for £21: then unaffordable) and over 6000 letters, the earliest by the Earl of Winchilsea, a founder of MCC in 1787, many from Victorian cricketers, and, of course, the majority from 20th Century players. Letters are preferable to signatures (commonly referred to as autographs) because they are extremely unlikely to have been forged, and they say so much about the writer. There are 6000 letters in this collection (scarcely any by modern cricketers, who use handheld devices for their communications), each one revealing a great deal about the cricketer who wrote it.

Prints and posters galore have accumulated, the task of displaying them quite hopeless. The biggest outlay went on Victor Trumper's fob-watch, won after a hard-fought saleroom battle. It holds special significance because it was given him by his Paddington team-mates of 1897-98. Two mounted cricket balls were purchased long ago from the son of Tom Richardson, one with which he took all 10 for 45 for Surrey v Essex in 1894, and another which accounted for eight Australians for 94 at Sydney in 1897-98. You don't have to be unduly romantic to be able to feel something special when touching these and closing the eyes. Same goes for that penny which Ivo Bligh tossed in 1882-83. For an MCC podcast, I flicked the coin into the air and it reverberated on the oak committee-room table for several seconds: a beautiful historical sound effect.

Enough 'props' have been acquired to equip a theatrical hire agency: Australian caps worn by Ted McDonald, Clarrie Grimmett, Jeff Thomson and Allan Border (who also gave me the shirt off his back after the 1989 Oval Test); Majid Khan's Pakistan cap, Derek Randall's and John Edrich's England touring caps, and not only Bishan Bedi's Indian cap but one of his patkas too. And Mike Atherton's parents, Alan and Wendy, kindly presented me with their son's Lancashire Schools cap, which he tried on in 1995, and it still fitted him. One distant day it will be an antique.

The McDonald cap came in an odd way. Debbie and I were in Kendal, Cumberland in the late 1960s, and took a deep expectant breath at the entrance to an enormous antiques arcade. But the proprietor, probably Italian, spoiled it all, as sometimes happens, by asking what we were seeking. 'Sport,' I responded noncommittally. What kind of sport, he persisted? So I came clean and said 'Cricket'. He had nothing, he said.

But as we sloped off down the pavement, we heard footsteps. He scurried after us with a moth-eaten green object in his hand. Was this cricket, he asked? I spun it round, and there was the Australian coat of arms, sewn in wire thread. At this sort of moment, the hands usually begin to tremble and the voice quavers. 'How much?' I blurted out as I spotted the 'McDonald' written inside the old cap. 'Five shilling,' he boomed. '*Five bob*?' I cried, mock indignantly. 'Oh, all right then.' Out came the coins and we walked abnormally fast back to the car. It was a terrific find, unexpected even when it was remembered that the Tasmanian fast bowler, who with Jack Gregory had destroyed England in 1921, had spent his last years in the north-west of England, playing for Lancashire, 'his aspect,' as Cardus described it, 'sinister but princely'.

Years later, I had the chance to acquire another great fast bowler's gear when he had no further use for it. On the eve of Sir Richard Hadlee's final day in Test cricket, in Birmingham in 1990, I took him to dinner, and we had a wide-ranging discussion. I almost forgot, but threw my question in over coffee: would he care to swap something for a copy of my deluxe *Pageant of Cricket*? He played it carefully. Might he see the book at breakfast? He seemed to like it. 'Come and see me at the end of play,' he said.

When it was all over, he was sitting reflectively in a corner of the Edgbaston dressing- room. And when he saw me, he pointed towards a small bundle. There, for me, were his New Zealand sweater, shirt, trousers, gloves and boots. While I thanked him, he picked up a bag and said, 'You've forgotten this.' In the bag was his helmet. I'd scored just about everything.

It was in that same room four years earlier that I'd asked Sunil Gavaskar if he had anything ready for dumping that I might add to my private museum. I had in mind perhaps an old sock or jockstrap, but my Indian friend, then the only batsman at that time to have made 30 or more centuries in Test cricket, beamed that slightly mystic smile as he slowly removed his blazer and handed it to me. I really did think he was joking, but he was not. And although I was in my 50th year by then, I felt just as weak at the knees as I had when Bertie Oldfield made his gesture of destiny in that Hunter Street shop all those years before.

Steve Waugh, with whom I'd struck up a rapport, for he had an untypical (for a Test player) interest in cricket history, gave me a sweater and his gloves at the end of the 1989 tour, together with a short-sleeve shirt, which briefly I played in, hoping that some of the magic would saturate me. (It didn't.) And elsewhere in that heavenly pile of garments is Willie Watson's 1953 England sweater (purchased the hard way at a Cricket Memorabilia Society auction, an exquisite item of history for one who sat and trembled through the night back in 1953 when the Watson/Bailey stand saved the Ashes Test at Lord's). Alongside are T-shirts, some garish, some dreary, some special, such as the Lillee-Thomson propaganda issue, and the one marking Robin Jackman's expulsion from Guyana in 1981.

There has to be a careful vigil to detect any woodworm, for the row of bats includes that one with which J.T.Brown slammed 140 in the decisive Ashes Test at Melbourne in 1895. Inscribed with a thick pen by the solid little Yorkshireman, it is dark brown with age, and still stands as the weapon with which the fastest fifty in Test history was made. In 1997 this bat had an airing on BBC TV's *Antiques Roadshow* and earned a dizzy estimate.

Equally valuable is a bat used by R.E.Foster during his record Test debut score of 287 at Sydney in 1903-04. Lord's has one from this innings too, donated by 'Tip' Foster's widow, and there is another at Malvern College. Mine, with Sotheby's provenance, was handed down by his brother, H.K.Foster.

Long innings in tropical conditions often meant more than one bat being used, with cracks appearing. Having bought a bat used by Patsy Hendren in his knock of 169 at Brisbane in 1928-29, I compared it with a photograph or two from that innings, and began to feel decidedly chilly when the patterns didn't match. Then another picture did show him using a bat with identical taping around the blade, good as a fingerprint. Relief.

Once, a woman rang me to say her late husband had left a bat signed by an Australian cricketer called 'Mr Singleton'. The signatures were from the 1938 team, and the owner had been, of course, Jack Fingleton. I gave her a fair price. Other bats in the line-up include one signed by C.B.Fry and, representing the moderns, one given by Craig McDermott, in whom we've always been especially interested since he was born just around the corner from Debbie's family home in the Ipswich suburb of Raceview, in Queensland. Shane Watson also was born in that town.

Perhaps the last bat to be incorporated into the Frith Collection was the one used throughout the 1953 tour of England by jolly Bill Johnston. He famously batted 17 times, usually at No.11, and was not-out 16 times, amassing 102 runs at an average of 102, thus joining Bradman. It is one of the biggest laughs in cricket. As he handed me this legendary willow, Bill drew attention to the repair along the inside edge of the bat. 'That shows class, getting cracks on the inside edge rather that the outside. Don Bradman told me that!' And he roared with laughter, as was his custom.

Few things acquired have been more transfixing than Ross Gregory's wartime diary. The young Victorian, who had been a glorious contributor to Australia's 3-2 Ashes victory in 1936-37, served in the RAAF (Wellington bombers) and was the only Australian Test cricketer to be killed in the war. I managed to secure that animated diary at auction, and turned it into a book. With the diary came several of his trophies and his Victoria and Test sweaters, very rare items. He was, incidentally, part of the saddest scoreline in Test history: R.G.Gregory c Verity b Farnes. He and the two Englishmen all were to lose their lives in thc looming war.

I've built up this treasure-store as a kind of tangible object of worship, with so much of it proving highly useful for research. So many authors have to carry out their research at Lord's or Melbourne, or in public libraries. To have it all this source material under one's own roof has been a very useful facility.

Still there seems a need to justify collecting. Only those who build collections truly know how much part of oneself a library and assortment of historical items can become. Collecting in the purest sense is steeped in affection.

This separates those who collected for love of cricket and those who moved in as speculators. When money seemed too frail a commodity to be holding long-term, from the late 1970s onwards, certain people with little understanding of cricket's true values moved in and paid silly prices, believing they would profit. Cricket made fools of them. Even one or two genuine cricket collectors got swept along by this fever. As values rose steadily, even the proudest of collectors began to wonder if the bubble might burst, and whether they ought perhaps to be selling. This thought pattern coupled with that dreaded question 'What's going to happen to all this?' inflicts unwanted pressures on the keenest of collectors.

But of late perhaps the best motive of all has presented itself. That outstanding social commentator Paul Johnson once wrote of the 'new disease sweeping Britain': he called it 'shufflitis', the 'compulsive urge to introduce change for its own sake, to take an institution or a belief or a product which has stood the test of time and transform it simply because it is old.' He condemned, on behalf of the silent majority, the 'fanatics of the religion of change', who love 'the jargon of market analysis and management powerplay'. And it has only grown worse.

The antidote, for cricket-lovers at least, is a chapter or two each night of Cardus or Robertson-Glasgow, a glance at a few of the better cricket engravings and photographs, and a gentle swing of a bat once held by a champion, preferably out of range of the glass-fronted cabinets. If those who know nothing of and care little for cricket history feel threatened by the game's culture, that's their problem.

As for that dreaded question, 'What's going to happen to all this?', a friend once offered a solution. 'Have you got a bit of lawn?' I told him there was enough to keep an athletic cat (Javed) exercised. 'Well,' he suggested, 'why not build a pyramid and load it with all your books and stuff? Then, like the Pharaohs, you can take it with you!' I may be seeking an architect shortly.

CHAPTER EIGHTEEN

Toughness is a form of honesty, let's face it.

DAME NINETTE DE VALOIS

EACH season brought its quota of drama, but 1984 was one of the most torrid in that the West Indies four-man bouncer blitz was in full swing and their over rate was a disgrace. Many of us who had the responsibility of protesting on cricket's behalf were branded as whingers, and worse. The Caribbean community said that all who condemned their mighty fast-bowling brigade were poor losers. But when there was nothing on view all day but short-pitched fast bowling, and no batsman was able to play off the front foot, and only 75 or so overs were bowled by the conclusion, it was impoverished viewing, resented by those who were accustomed to variety in bowling and a decent allocation of overs. The tension grew, and continued to grow right through the 1980s, until relations with the previously admired West Indian cricket team had fallen away.

England were beaten in all five Tests in that nasty summer of 1984, their troubles beginning on the first morning, when Andy Lloyd was felled by Malcolm Marshall. When umpire Dickie Bird decided to have a word with Clive Lloyd about the intimidatory level of bouncers, the West Indies captain stood stubbornly at slip, obliging Bird to walk some distance to speak to him. This was no more impressive than Lloyd's tossing the ball away after the first warning against the short stuff.

There were claims, of course, that this West Indies XI might have been the strongest side in the history of the game, unless their 1976 combination was even stronger – and it was unquestionably a source of immense pride to all West Indians, at home and overseas. So invincible did this group seem that even when Marshall sustained a broken hand he went in to bat and saw Larry Gomes to his century at Headingley. Then Marshall amazed everyone by taking the field, grabbing the new ball and running through England with 7 for 53, his broken bone in plaster on his non-bowling wrist.

In the fourth Test, viewed from the old chicken-coop of a Press-box over long leg at Old Trafford, a fiasco was brewing as Allan Lamb approached his century, escorted by Paul Terry, whose arm had been broken by a bouncer and who now returned at the fall of the ninth wicket, with England still 222 behind West Indies' 500 (Greenidge 223, Dujon 101). Would Lamb get his third century of the series? Would Terry avoid further injury? Would England save the follow-on? Equally interesting, where was the captain, and what were his instructions? David Gower had been under fire for allegedly not paying attention at Lord's when a declaration seemed imminent, and now the sharpening of knives could be heard again in the Press-box. With both batsmen looking up to the balcony, with seemingly nobody there, it was an absurd situation. Surely they knew their objective when Terry had gone to the crease? If not, why was Gower not signalling? There was about to be another messy back page in tomorrow's tabloids.

So I raced across to the pavilion and up the stairs into the dressing-room to alert D.I.Gower of England and *WCM* to the fact that the wolves would be after him again unless he immediately did something positive. But Lambie had already scampered a two to reach his hundred, exposing the injured Terry needlessly to face the music. In fact it was clear from his gestures that Lamb thought the innings would be closed as soon as he was into three figures (even though the follow-on had not been avoided). What a mess. And the papers understandably said so. Gower later said that Lamb's hundred had been the only reasonable aim when Terry, arm in sling, had gone back in: 'the avoidance of the follow-on would have been a bonus'. So would the abandonment of the series, I felt.

West Indies recovered from a first innings of only 190 in the final Test, at The Oval (when Botham took his 300th Test wicket) and won again, sealing their 5-0 'black-wash'. I found myself sitting between Fred Trueman and Clive Lloyd, looking back over the series of '84 for Channel 4 News. With the events of almost 40 years ago rising from the depths of memory, I could only say that I now knew how the Germans must have felt in 1945.

Quotes dangled everywhere. There was Pat Pocock telling everybody that before going in to bat at No.10 (he bagged a pair) he had reassured team physio Bernard Thomas that he had cleaned his teeth and gargled, just in case he should need the kiss of life. David Gower diplomatically described the tourists as 'a very well-organised and talented side'. But independent onlookers whose love for cricket was beyond challenge pulled no punches: 'I would have thought that Clive Lloyd, with his wealth of experience, might have had a quiet word with his Bouncing Billies' (Sir Len Hutton); 'the current West Indian method . . . is deeply offensive to the essence of cricket' (Robin Marlar); 'It was not, I believe, cricket as it was intended to be played, and for that the umpires, specially Constant, who stood at Marshall's end, must take some of the blame' (John Woodcock).

As for myself, I concluded that the fundamental sadness was in the fact that West Indies must have won the series even without the relentless diet of bouncers. That would have earned praise from all sincere cricket-lovers. It was the brutal way in which their crushing victory was achieved, not the victory itself, that upset so many onlookers – something they and their supporters declined to grasp as the years passed and their tactics remained unchecked until the authorities, fearing for the game's future, tried to clamp down on intimidation by rationing bouncers to two per over (still potentially 180 per day). Then it was the turn of fast bowlers everywhere, not just in the Caribbean, to squeal that their virility was being fettered. Cricket's salvation, fortunately, owed more to the rise of brilliant spinners such as Shane Warne than to the restrictions placed on the fast men. Balance was restored as the 1980s gave way to the 1990s, though too late for many traditionalists, who had angrily turned their backs on the coarse type of spectacle served up since cricket lost its innocence after the 1977 Centenary Test match.

Even thirty years later, Michael Holding was still complaining at the criticism directed at that fast-bowling overkill, and was still not calmed when I handed him a list of the 40-odd batsmen he and his colleagues had sent to hospital in those fifteen brutal years.

My own view of life had been altered following a disturbing chat with Viv Richards early that summer of 1984. Since we had had that fun session in the nets in Lahore in 1975, there had been little opportunity for conversation between us, but at a Texaco Trophy party in 1984 I asked him if I could discuss a few things with him, such as his Rastafarian wristband, and his attitude towards South Africa. I'd have understood had he declined, but he seemed quite keen to give me his views.

There was already an air of unreality about the night, for I had spotted film star Robert Wagner in our midst; he was a friend of Texaco boss John Ambler. Now, only four days after his spectacular 189 at Old Trafford, I listener keenly to Viv Richards as he spoke with great passion about the Lion of Judah and the Rastafarian movement, grew agitated when I asked if his feelings for Africa meant that he wanted to die there one day ('Don't talk about dyin', man!'). Then he worried me by giving the impression that he felt I should feel guilty for being white. I told him that while I had sympathy for the oppression inflicted on his ancestors (by blacks as well as by whites), I could not hold myself personally responsible since I was sure that there had been no slave-traffickers among my ancestors. He did not seem satisfied, and his manner persuaded me that it was time to part. Bob Willis steered me away.

I went to Viv Richards' book launch 10 days later, and as our eyes met by the entrance, he smiled and said, 'Let's let sleeping dogs lie, Dave.' That suited me.

There was a somnolent conclusion to that furious summer as Sri Lanka declared twice in their first Test on English soil and Sidath Wettimuny batted for 642 minutes for his 190, which I calculated (after hours of research) to have been the longest innings ever played at Lord's. Then, another English winter, the prospect of which still tensed up the Frith muscles even after all these years.

I escaped for a while, joining the *WCM* tourists for the Madras (Chennai) Test, where Graeme Fowler and Mike Gatting both made double-centuries and Neil Foster, soaked in perspiration through 51 valiant overs, took 11 wickets as England went ahead in a series which had seemed close to abandonment at the start when Mrs Indira Gandhi was murdered, and then, on the eve of the first Test, Percy Norris, Britain's Deputy High Commissioner to Western India, was gunned down in Bombay. These events, and not England's defeat at the hands of Shivaramakrishnan (12 for 163), were tragedies.

On the rest day of the Madras Test, I played in the 'Press Test match', decked out in Gower's sunhat, Phil Edmonds' shirt, Norman Cowans' box, Mike Gatting's trousers (which, I was delighted to find, were then so much too capacious for my waistline that they slid down at the first step), and Paul Downton's shoes and bat. My only innings in India amounted to 7 before I optimistically tried to late-cut Bishan Bedi's faster inswinging yorker. Still, it was a delight to share the field with India veterans such as Chandu Borde, Ambar Roy and Kripal Singh.

I sat at the extremity of the Press-box during the Test at the Chepauk Stadium, so that when Gatting began to employ the reverse sweep during the 190s, a few of the wide-eyed young onlookers leaned across and enquired what sort of shot that was. I told them, repeating the phrase to be sure, and soon this information – 'Reverse sweep! Reverse sweep!' – was sweeping right round the upper stand and, it seemed, back towards us from the left, full circuit. It was a stroke that chairman of selectors, Peter May, was soon banning from use.

Back at the hotel, 'Foxy' Fowler celebrated his 9-hour 201 with a frantic spell on the drums, and later, at the bar, I spotted one of the last faces expected in these parts at this time: crooner Engelbert Humperdinck. He asked if he could talk with the England cricketers, and I got him permission from manager Tony Brown to enter the team-room on the top floor, but as far as I could make out he just gazed at them in awe and they just gazed at him and there was no memorable conversation.

Six hours of waiting from midnight in Bombay airport lounge, then back to snowbound England and a massive backlog of mail, messages and newspapers. More multivitamin pills, please, Debbie.

A few weeks later I was again strapping my seat-belt on in a Boeing 747 and heading for Australia for the closing stages of the so-called World Championship, marking Victoria's 150th anniversary. The chance was taken, of course, to meet up with family again, but the anticipated Australia v England encounter in the final vanished with the failure of both sides to emerge from the preliminary group. Not many Australians took kindly to an India v Pakistan final, but it underlined the current paucity of Australian talent, so soon after Border had been rushed into the captaincy following Kim Hughes's tearful resignation. And there was further erosion with the unauthorised tour of South Africa, which meant the loss of Hughes, Yallop, Alderman, Dyson, Hohns, Rackemann, Maguire and the highly promising Michael Haysman. The upcoming 1985 Ashes series looked to be England's already, two years after the 1982-83 thrashing.

If England had a worry it concerned Ian Botham, and the anxiety about his fluctuating form and courtroom appearances was expressed in *WCM* by none other than E.J.Brack, he who had dared to attack *Test Match Special.* Now, he wondered if Botham would go the way of George Best. 'Too often these days,' he scarily wrote, 'Botham tries to buy wickets with a series of ill-directed long-hops.' And he feared that all the off-field traumas must have 'conspired to have a debilitating effect on the player's cricketing form.' The nation joined in waiting to see where England's Most Exciting Cricketer Ever went from here.

It also held its breath over what happened next to the national cricket team, and by the end of the summer the welcome news for all long-depressed Englishmen was that, in the wake of the splendid victory in India, the Ashes had been regained, and David Gower was a winner again. As Ashes series went, the 1985 encounter was actually the biggest runmaking bonanza by England that either side had ever achieved in the 108 years of competition. Gower, Gatting, Gooch, Robinson and the rest had chalked up their runs at the unprecedented rate of 60.67 per 100 balls. Tim Robinson, in the opening Test at Headingley, displaced Derek Randall with the second-highest score (175 to R.E.Foster's 287) by an England batsman on debut against Australia. In consecutive Tests, England had triple-century stands (Gower/Robinson 331 at Edgbaston; Gower/Gooch 351 at The Oval). And Botham was still there: averaging 31 with the bat (and whacking a record 80 sixes in all first-class cricket this season) and taking 31 wickets in the Tests, more than anyone else.

Battling Border averaged 66 for Australia, with a memorable 196 in the Lord's Test, and McDermott from Raceview, still only 20, took 8 for 141 at Old Trafford. He (30 wickets) and Geoff Lawson (22) carried the Australian attack, and it was sad to see Bob Holland, the legspinner, operating as a stock bowler, often around the wicket. Even sadder was the fact that the series was effectively swung England's way with a disputed catch in the fifth Test at Edgbaston. Wayne Phillips cut Edmonds hard and downwards, the ball bouncing up from Lamb's boot for a dolly 'catch' into Gower's hands. The umpires consulted, and a bewildered, inconsolable 'Flipper' had to go. That evening, after Australia had collapsed to defeat, Allan Border was still trying to come to terms with this decision as the media grilled him.

There had to be doubt about the decision, and even though Jim Laker leaned across and whispered 'Wait till you see the slow-mo on BBC TV tonight', the pictures were blurred. It was an uneasy way to decide a Test series, even though England were beyond doubt the better side.

Still, Thommo had managed to take his 100th England wicket (and 200th in all Tests), despite his bleached hairdo, and there had been a superb Lord's Taverners dinner before the Lord's Test in honour of Ray Lindwall and Keith Miller, for which I organised some old newsreel film. That gala event also enabled me to pay Ray back for all those lifts home in the early 1950s by driving him back to his hotel in the early hours.

There had been a very friendly spirit between the two sides in the 1985 Ashes series, which pleased all Anglo-Australians, be they hybrids, 'misfits' or, in the latest attempt to coin the perfect description, 'kelpies' (half British border collie, half Australian dingo). Perhaps the presence of Miller and Lindwall had somehow set the tone.

Whatever the case, Allan Border took some stick for being so friendly – with Botham in particular – and was never again to be so amiable among adversaries. I understood utterly his position. As Dirk Wellham wrote in the summary I asked from him for *WCM* at the end: 'I have found it refreshing to see such competitiveness and achievement being linked in such a good-natured way.' Might this have been the last of the truly friendly Test rubbers?

As winter came on, foreboding descended, for England were once again Caribbean-bound. All members of the cricket fraternity were exposed nakedly as either optimists or, more numerously, pessimists. Nobody seemed undecided.

Meanwhile, as the never-ending quest to make *Wisden Cricket Monthly* fascinating every month, we revealed, courtesy of Andrew Lamb, that Neville Cardus was actually christened John Frederick Cardus (father unknown), and was born not on April 2, 1889 but on April 3,1888. Man of mystery. Furtherance of our knowledge. And proof that NC had fibbed (or was the inaccuracy the result of ignorance?) in knocking a year off his age in his passport.

Strengthening of the magazine was always paramount in my thoughts, and as 1986 unfurled, I took on Steven Lynch as deputy editor. Employed in the MCC office at Lord's for 10 years since he had left school, he had impressed me with the neatness, accuracy and speed of his entries to *WCM*'s annual quizzes, so he bade farewell to the gruesome commuting to London every day and seized his opportunity. This time I was in luck. He proved to be responsive to training, unafraid of work, an alert proofreader nine days (or nights) out of 10, and possessed that rare and golden asset, loyalty. Nursed for a couple of years, he developed good wings of his own.

The flow of cricket books was unabated, and reviewing continued to take up much of my time. I sometimes considered taking a speed-reading course, so careful, almost plodding, was my approach to the job. Still, if anyone should challenge criticism levelled against them in a review, I was able to go back to my review notes and demonstrate that I'd actually let them off lightly. 'Always hold something in reserve,' had been one of Keith Miller's wisest gems of advice.

I'd invited Matthew Engel to write quite a few pieces for the magazine, and eventually to join the Editorial Board as a member of the newer brigade who brought whimsy and quite a bit of thought to the 'industry' of cricket-writing. In reviewing his book on the 1985 Ashes Tests, I found myself writing that he 'is certainly not one of the Press-box's clever dickies'. But then I didn't as yet know him all that well.

I was an extra special clever dickie myself at a reception at the House of Commons to mark Les Ames's 80th birthday, hosted by Earl Attlee (son of Clement), when one of the many Members of Parliament buzzing among the cricketers present stood squarely in front of me and said: 'I've been waiting for years to put this question to you. You know so much about cricket, but I bet you don't know who scored the fastest fifty in the history of Test cricket?'

This was a dream come true. I drew a deep breath and replied: 'J.T. (Jack) Brown of Yorkshire; Melbourne, 1895; 28 minutes, though he claimed it was only 27. *And I've got the bat at home*!' I suppose there have been plenty of similar retorts in the House over the years.

It may have been that summer – he was certainly past 80 – when I asked Les Ames, lumbago or not, whether he could still get down on his haunches in the wicketkeeping crouch, and in a flash he was down and back up again, supple as a teenager. We were passing along behind the Mound Stand, and I thrilled at the connection, for it was here at Lord's that he had scored a famous century against Australia in 1934, winning my Dad a little bit of welcome money in the process.

A footnote to that Parliamentary reception: Ames's wife, Bunty, a charming and lively lady, was absorbing all the kisses on the cheek as guests crowded in, until she'd really had enough of it: 'Les,' she called across, 'these people must stop all kissing me. You never know with all this Aids about!' The world was still trying to comprehend this latest threat to mankind.

WCM went on uninhibitedly and caringly exploring the game from all angles, but still one of the favourite avenues was the tracking down of oldtimers, and none was more surprising than Wilfrid Timms, who lived near me, having retired from schoolmastering at Charterhouse. This mild and gentle old man had scored 154 in six hours for Northants against Essex back in 1921, when he was only 18. At that tender age he had also captained the county while still at school, being the only amateur available. He made runs off the terrifying Larwood by stepping back and cutting, and did not allow his colleague Vallance Jupp's uncharitable remark (he inferred he was a coward for stepping away) to upset him. Charming man. He died a few months after the interview. He was 84.

No sooner had the ugly West Indies v England series of early 1986 drawn to a merciful close than two illustrious names entered the obituary columns: Jim Laker and Bill Edrich. They died within a day of each other that April.

Edrich's game is inextricably linked with Compton's in the annals of the game, but he had a most distinctive obituary, for his last day on earth would have been the envy of many: 'Mr Edrich, 70, was a guest at a St George's Day lunch in London and was driven home 7 ½ hours later.' *Seven-and-a-half-hours!* And the coroner found that he had drunk enough to register more than four times the legal driving limit. 'Apart from the hip replacements,' he said, 'he was a very fit man.'

Bill Edrich was an RAF wartime hero, with a DFC, and that was enough for me. I already knew how tough he was when I watched him at Sydney during the '54-55 tour, and found him pleasant enough in later years, playing alongside him in a charity match at Goodwood when he carted 61 runs, one for each year of his life to date. But he turned snarly later, and told me I was a lousy editor (was it a coincidence that he had a Norfolk connection with Brocklehurst?) and asked aggressively what I'd done during the war. I explained that I had tried to comfort Mum, had a Fire Service hero as a father, but had fired no shots in anger myself because I was only eight when the conflict ended. He did not seem satisfied.

With Jim Laker it was very different. He could be sulky and mildly cynical, but he was essentially gentle, and it was always good to see him saunter up to the doorway of the Press-box when his commentary stint was over. He'd stand there with his hands plunged deep into his pockets, catch sight of me, wink, smile and move sedately over for a sit-down and a chat. Time and again somebody would slip into a nearby vacant seat and raise the 19 for 90 – or, if they wanted to be mildly original, the 8 for 2 in the 1950 Test trial. Jim 'arm-balled' us all by explaining that he bowled better in Bombay during a Commonwealth tour, taking 5 for 88 in 65 overs on a perfect batting pitch.

He had almost died a couple of years before his eventual much-mourned demise, and that was when an emergency aorta operation saved him. I called on him in his mock-Tudor Putney home afterwards. He sat, weak and wan and under-weight, in his dressing-gown, that distinctive voice that seldom bothered with the final 'g' now but a whisper, and spoke sadly of the theft of some of his trophies. Pointing to a silver salver on the wall, he said, 'But the daft buggers missed that. Thought it was a mirror when they shone their torches on it, I s'pose.' He asked if I'd like to see his scar, and I demurred;

but it was too late: he showed me all the same, the incision running almost the length of his body. I had to sit down.

Those grainy pictures of Laker running through the Australians on that sawdust-flecked Old Trafford pitch in '56 will be reshown till Eternity, but I picture him in colour, trotting up to bowl with pinpoint precision at the SCG, with Ken 'Slasher' Mackay stretching forward, trying to erase the humiliating memory of his 'pair' against the Greatest Offspinner two years before.

While I continued to hope for closer links with John Wisden & Company, there was a change of editorship for the *Almanack*, John Woodcock stepping down after six years of worthy stewardship ('not wanting to die in service'), his assistant, Graeme Wright, taking over after years of solid backroom work. It was gratifying to be told by both big John (Arlott) and little John (Woodcock) at the time that I would have been the natural choice; but I wasn't asked, and had I been, I could not have accepted, for the magazine was, and would seemingly always be, a fulltime job.

Wright, originally a New Zealander, had had a spell as my deputy, but it was not to his liking, and he did not last long, which may explain why, during his six years as editor of the *Almanack*, he never once asked me to write for it. Indeed, his attitude had been sometimes aloof, for his association with the parent company seemed to have persuaded him that the magazine was permitted to go about its business only by some sort of royal decree; and sometimes his attitude was, well, twitchy. I had that uncomfortable feeling that he was not inclined to speak his mind. It was sad that he and his successor after six more years (Matthew Engel) both seemed to feel that the magazine was some sort of threat to *Wisden Cricketers' Almanack* when all along it was meant to be – and, I believe, was – a strong complementary publication. To be told that Engel, in 1994, told a prospective contributor that he edited the 'famous' one (as opposed to the less famous monthly) caused me further despondency. This was an example of self-importance unmatched in the Press-box, which is fertile territory.

In that spring of 1986, I enlisted Jack Bannister and Tony Lewis onto the Editorial Board, Jack for his broad connections in the game and his analytical talents, and Tony because he too seemed a likely asset, though he stressed he did not want to be overworked. Months later he resigned, saying I hadn't asked him to write enough, but reading between the lines it was quite clear that his old Cambridge buddy Richard Hutton, who had married the daughter of *The Cricketer's* owner, had expressed disapproval of his association with *WCM*. I was learning more about English (and Welsh) attitudinal manoeuvring with every passing year.

England lost to India and then New Zealand in the Tests that summer, but magazine sales were not affected. It was to be several years before Britons began to follow the Australian pattern by discriminating in this respect. As reversals piled up, only the truly masochistic wanted to read full analysis of them. That was why it was essential to keep finding an attractive mixed bag of contents every month.

David Gower lost the England captaincy after the defeat at Lord's in the opening Test match, when Dilip Vengsarkar scored his third Test century at the old ground. Afterwards, we sat in the writing-room awaiting the new England captain. In he walked, a muscular slab of self-consciousness, Michael William Gatting, a stormy time ahead of him, if only he'd known it, but now so abashed that throughout the Press conference he did not for once lift his gaze from the oak table-top. He was to be a strong and often successful captain, and when he was removed in 1988, English cricket was to enter an era of writhing confusion and depression that made following it and chronicling it a depressing experience.

Concern felt earlier by E.J. Brack for Ian Botham now turned to something stronger as England's most charismatic cricketer began a suspension for writing a confession about pot-smoking. Former golden boy Frank Hayes penned something for *WCM* entitled The *Tragedy of Ian Botham.* Where had all cricket's traditional happiness gone?

David Gower expressed deep disappointment at being stripped of the Test captaincy, filling his editor with dread by announcing that he would now go back to the subject of gastronomy, 'leaving the cricket to the experts'. I will admit that I could never have foreseen at this stage what a media 'star' Gower would one day become. I didn't think he had quite the voice for it or the writing skills. He has been branded 'prolix' ('tediously wordy'), and Don Mosey, for one, was irritated by the suave left-hander's airs and graces in society. But just as it would have been counter-productive to have tried to perfect his batsmanship by urging the elimination of risky strokes (many still tried), I saw no point in editing him heavyhandedly. Writers sometimes had to be cut to fit, but never would I reach to rewriting anything submitted. Corrections, yes; interference never.

Around this time I began to use the offerings of a young journalist named Rob Steen, who tried hard to be different and entertaining, even if some of his jargon was so deliberately 'new-age' that I feared a good 90 percent of our readership would be playing down the wrong line. Steen hopped from paper to paper and crisis to crisis, but I stuck by him, feeling he was worth encouraging. In time, though, he was to cause me to apply iodine to teethmarks on my hand, the hand that had fed him. No matter how cautious one may be in human dealings, there is no way of eliminating the risks.

Unwittingly, all kinds of precursors found their way into *WCM's* pages. Towards the end of the 1986 season, George Eykyn interviewed a promising black player with Gloucestershire, Tottenham-born Mark Alleyne. The headline was CRICKET IN THE BLOOD. The lad himself was quoted as saying that all he ever wanted was to play cricket for a living: 'It's in my blood.' Such phraseology, in a slightly different context nine years later, was to prove inflammatory, perhaps because times had changed, perhaps because there were axes to grind.

Botham, having served his time, came back and usurped Lillee's Test record of 355 wickets; Boycott's career ended, low-key fashion, with a *WCM* prediction that he would now remove his creaking armour and spend the rest of his days watching old videos in his ivory tower, unless he joined us in the Press-box, 'to tear strips off the faulty techniques of the batsmen of today'. It was a pleasure to see him become one of the last of the critics who were prepared to give unbridled opinions.

We continued to keep an eye on the South African situation, with Jack Bannister bringing back quotes from Dr Ali Bacher to the effect that apartheid was now seen to be doomed, and it was only a matter of time; but why did ICC continue to ignore South Africa?: 'Our cricket is now completely non-racial, and I think that ICC should at least acknowledge that.' World cricket, Bacher urged, 'should know who we are, how we feel and think, and what we are trying to do.'

Not least fascinating, Dr Bacher referred to a signed letter of intent in which Ian Botham, David Gower and Graham Dilley agreed in principle to the proposed tour of South Africa planned early in 1981. All withdrew their interest, 'the difference being, in the subsequent withdrawal of all three,' wrote Bannister, 'that two of them did not mount a self-righteous pulpit'. Botham, he wrote, was offered £50,000 and then half as much again, but this was 'still not enough to convince the player's legal and business advisors that it was commercially viable because of the fear of losing other sponsorship contracts, including one with SAAB. His final back-out was because of financial, not moral, misgivings'.

As for Viv Richards, the South African Cricket Union managing director said they had met in Taunton in August 1983. Money was never discussed. 'He said that for moral reasons he could not come, and he came across to me as a genuine and righteous person.'

Botham announced his long-distance plans hereabouts, saying he wanted to spend half of each year in Australia. And he was about to leave Somerset for Worcestershire. For the moment there was an England tour of Australia to excite us all, with Rob Steen contributing a rather woolly piece about Graeme Hick's hopes of qualifying for England, during which the author wrote: 'The counties depend on Test match receipts and, therefore, a strong England team with an identifiable devotion to the flag.' Quite.

Britain was cheered up immeasurably by that 1986-87 Australian expedition. Gatting's side won the Perth Challenge of one-day matches and the World Series Cup, but, most important of all, they retained the Ashes, with three centuries from Chris Broad. I joined the *WCM* tour later on, and sat again with Bill O'Reilly in the SCG Press-box, teasing him with questions like, 'Did you bowl even harder at Protestants such as Sutcliffe?' I gathered that he might have. He could dish it out, but he was vulnerable as any of us to the tease. 'Going up to Brisbane for the one-dayers, Tiger?' someone asked, and had to duck away from a cuff around the ear. How O'Reilly hated one-day cricket, and all the modern razzmatazz.

I brought Australia luck for that Sydney Test. Their victory ended a record sequence of 14 Tests without success. Dean Jones made 184 not out and legspinner Peter Sleep took 5 for 72 to snatch a win with only one over remaining, Gatting's fall for 96, caught-and-bowled by Steve Waugh, proving the turning-point. Earlier, Peter Taylor had taken 6 for 78 in his maiden Test. It was good to see the two spinners together in the hot, sweaty, arc-lit interview-room afterwards.

More top-quality time was spent with brilliant cricketers of the past: Bill Brown in Brisbane. Don Bradman in Adelaide. Brown, as modest and cool a man as you could ever find, even in cricket, said that his grandchildren were not inclined to believe he had been a cricketer, and he wanted to get hold of some *Wisdens* to prove that he had been. A touring batsman in England in 1934, 1938 and 1948, Bill was another who disliked limited-overs: 'vaudeville' he called it. He made elegant Test hundreds at Lord's (one of them a double-century) and elsewhere, but sought to give others the credit for Australia's triumphs. After the war 'a lot of the rosy glow had gone'. Still he made eight centuries on the 1948 tour and averaged 58, yet still was only fourth in the table. And how was life today, at 74? 'Let it be known,' he said softly, 'that I devote my full time to keeping my wife happy.'

Good laughs were certainly possible with Sir Donald Bradman, but the conversation is always meaningful

The position was similar in a suburb of Adelaide, where The Don lived contentedly still with the lady he married way back in 1932. Not that he seemed to regard relaxation as permissible. He greeted me with some queries out of *The Slow Men*, including a quizzical comment about the alleged full-toss with which he bowled Walter Hammond. It was a robust discussion, with sources quoted almost as if in a court of law. It was only after Don had died that I unearthed confirmation that it had indeed been a full-toss. Here was Opinion in cast-iron terms, spread out slowly and carefully, to produce a case that would be as formidable as his bat once was. Names, places, incidents: it was a kaleidoscope of cricket's last 60 years, sometimes even earlier. Those eyes glinted defiantly as he awaited my remarks on a certain subject, and if I moved in what he considered an ill-advised direction, I'd figuratively be struck for four. But it was all very enjoyable – for both of us, I'd like to think.

As I wrote in the introduction to the 1988 Pavilion edition of *Farewell to Cricket*, 'it is a spine-tingling experience to look upon the countenance of the elderly Bradman and see in it the virile young man from the flickering greyness of the newsreels, the leathery dynamo who conquered legions of bowlers and floundering fieldsmen, and left millions of cricket-lovers slavishly spellbound'.

DGB was not too pleased at my reluctance to support his campaign to have the old back-foot no-ball law restored. The ultimate put-down was to be asked if I felt I knew better than the likes of Benaud, Lillee, the Chappells and himself. I had to insist that under no circumstances should bowlers be allowed to go back to the grotesque transgressions of old, where a Curtly Ambrose might be bowling off 18 or 19 yards. Tennis servers had to be behind the white line; so did athletes, whether runners or jumpers or javelin-throwers. It remained little me against all the big boys, but I was not going to change direction just to be popular.

In an attempt to cool the argument, Jessie asked: 'Have you written Don's obituary yet, David?' I had never been that well organised, I said. It was all I could do to keep up with immediate requirements, without writing for possible future needs. 'Anyway, he's going to make another century, isn't he?' I asked. And hurriedly we moved onto the next topic.

I reciprocated with dinner at my hotel, and although we had a table quietly tucked away, the young waitress knew who this septuagenarian welterweight was. When it came to dessert, she challenged him with the question, 'Would you like some apple pie?' The Bradman eyes twinkled above the rosy cheeks. He put on a mock sternness. 'Now do I look like a man who likes apple pie?' Boldly, she came straight back: 'Yes!'

'Right! I'll have some apple pie then!' And he rocked with laughter, which proved to be very contagious.

On another visit, he kindly drove me back to the hotel, and as the car emerged from Holden Street, just after midnight, we were all but in collision with a vehicle that was speeding from our right. It would have been easily the most glorious way for any cricket-lover to die.

I suppose the strangest thing about Don Bradman is that, greatest of Australians though he may well be, and weighed down with honours and accolades, it is by no means certain that he has been the happiest and most contented of men. His marriage to Jessie has been a superlative in itself, but there has been family grief, and the non-stop nightmare of having scarcely any privacy or freedom from public demands. There is, too, the matter of the incessant pressure placed upon anyone possessed of an enquiring, perfectionist mind such as his. He must have the answers, the truth, the ascendancy in any debate. What might he have done, as his nation's true leader, in Canberra? Or even in Westminster, had Great Britain been so lucky, had his forebears never left Suffolk?

During that 1986-87 Australian visit, there was a meeting of supreme significance in Sydney too. It was with my father, and it was to be the final meeting.

The wartime fireman and the little boy on his knee: neither of us was the least recognisable as that now. We had continued to grow apart, briefly drawn closer by Mum's death in 1971, but there was still a problem. We were happy for him when he remarried. But it was a disaster, and he divorced. Now he lived alone, visited by my brother and his family and sometimes by Percy Thomas, his old firefighting mate, who was even older than Dad.

So after the Test, Debbie and I broke away from the Wisden group and had a memorable afternoon with my father down at Sutherland. He put some of his tapes of pre-war music on, and joked about the long line of pills, each captioned, which had to be downed each day to keep him going. With those large, trembling hands, he made some characteristically strong tea and cut some cake as we listened to familiar stories and had a few laughs. He was at long last able to poke fun at himself, mocking his failing eyesight and shaky fingers, and cursing that long column of pills of all colours and sizes that enabled him to live on. Thirty-odd years later, I know precisely how he felt.

Sensing, I think, that this could be the last time we would ever be together, he handed me his wartime diaries and other priceless family documents, and when it was time to go, we stood by the roadside and he gave me a handshake that was almost as strong as it used to be. The only way I could get through this departure was to calculate when I was likely next to be back in Sydney, and to convince myself that he would still be here. Countless times since that afternoon I have dwelt on questions I should have asked Ted Frith about his childhood and so much else. My belief that future regret is what one should strive to prevent in all life's actions was always going to prove vulnerable.

Perhaps it was the medication, perhaps it was a sudden capitulation to mounting bitterness at his physical plight, possibly fanned by outside influences, but he began to drop unpleasant lines into his airletters to us, the resentment at our living in England now welling up bitterly (and, I acknowledge, quite understandably). Deeming his two sons to be well enough placed financially, he had put his six grandchildren as beneficiaries in his will. Now, though, he struck out the names of our three. He accused them of not writing to him (despite the fact that they had written, but received nothing in return). He sent back to me the inscribed books I had proudly mailed over the years, and eventually wrote a letter which he said was final. He wanted no further correspondence. I went on sending him birthday cards, the last one reaching him on his deathbed in July 1989. This war hero was 80, and had passed exactly half his life in England and half in Australia.

The final hour with my father

CHAPTER NINETEEN

What is human life but a game of cricket.

DUKE OF DORSET

PLAYING cricket has long been a kind of lifeblood, and among the things for which I feel the deepest gratitude to Our Maker (be He above the clouds or in that crystal powder-pot) have been my marriage, my offspring, and the continuing liberty to walk onto a cricket field to bat, bowl and catch even when twice the age when some men find excuses to hang up their boots. It was a privilege, at 60, to have sufficiently clear vision and muscular ability to make a duck, get hit for six and muff a catch, for this was the one surviving link with the colt you once were.

The pain of failure recurs, of course, offsetting the ecstasy of success. And it was after messing up yet another innings somewhere down in scenic Sussex one Saturday afternoon in the 1980s that I turned to verse as a source of comfort. Shielded again by the *non de plume* of 'Andrew Thomas', I foisted this upon my readers:

Along green lanes;
Signposts to the afternoon
Of sport; and tight breathing
In the visions of what triumphs are to come.

And hours afield, from a lifetime, irredeemable,
Run down to the dusk,
When deep shades of unfulfillment
Dim the mind, and the soul
Is pressed low in dreams of what might have been.

It takes me back to a discussion long ago with John Arlott, when he modestly shrugged aside any suggestion that he wrote 'poetry'. Well, then, what was it he had written? Doggerel? 'Oh, I shouldn't think it was as bad as that,' he smiled. We finally settled on 'verse'.

The 1977 season had been challenging. Cricket would surely not be easy once the 40th birthday had come and gone. If only I had had the wit to imagine that at least 20 further seasons lay ahead, with some undreamt-of experiences to garnish them by way of reward for braving it against ever-younger, ever-faster bowlers and an ever-growing undermining of confidence (much of it, foolishly, self-inflicted).

The Press games – nowadays all but extinct because of the abandonment of rest days in Test matches – brought opportunities to play with and against some of the most illustrious names. Imtiaz Ahmed, once a double-centurion for Pakistan, hammered a quick fifty on a damp Harrogate greentop when aged 50, Bill Frindall's fiery, snorting bowling off a 20-yard run-up notwithstanding. On the umpiring roster that afternoon were the 1954 bowling heroes Fazal Mahmood and Mahmood Hussain, with a comical interlude with Brian Johnston.

Imagine the delight of batting with Rohan Kanhai at Lord's (even if it was on the Nursery ground, and our partnership failed to advance the score). Better still was a match, again at Harrogate, against the Old England XI, when I managed 34 in a stand with Reg Simpson, hero of that magical, long-ago 1950-51 Ashes series with 156 not out in the fifth Test, at Melbourne. The calm and elegant Reg was now 62 and well above his old weight, so we didn't run many singles. Fred Trueman had taken himself off, which was a relief. Every minute in the middle was sublime. Before holing out to Eric Russell off Fred Titmus, I'd found David Allen hard to get away; played doggo to Basil D'Oliveira's accuracy; banged one back past bowler Ted Dexter, just missing his nose; swept a four off Titmus; and had no trouble from the chuckling Peter Parfitt. Mushtaq Mohammad should really have batted ahead of me, but had gone missing. When he eventually took my place, it was all he could do to find the pitch. A medicinal brandy intake had fogged his navigation. Earlier, though, he had spun his legbreaks beautifully when Dexter and Graveney were together (a stand that caused another writer to say he really could not believe he was on the same field as these two gods of his boyhood). We all felt that.

That winter, in one of Bertie Joel's charity matches, on Kew Green, I was very disappointed when Mike Gatting threw his wicket away because the rain had started to intensify. I'd had visions of a stand well in excess of that one with Kanhai.

Then there were the annual Gray-Nicolls XI matches on the lovely Saffrons ground at Eastbourne, organised by Jock Livingston, the once-prolific NSW and Northants left-hander, who became such a staunch friend.

We always had a contingent of young Australians in our side: Trevor Chappell, who got hit to all corners, and Mark O'Neill, son of my teenage St George team-mate Norm. I became sentimental when taking my turn to umpire. If Mark got hit on the pads in front, it would have broken my heart to have had to give him out. I did at least have a chance to offer some advice to Richard Williams, the nuggety 15-year-old who played for Northants: every time he cracked a ball straight to a fielder he unleashed a string of expletives. While envying his range of strokes, I had to urge him to be more philosophical.

It was a privilege to be hit for four by Sunil Gavaskar, then the leading runmaker in Tests, and a delight to hit him to the rope in return. He loved bowling, and rated himself. Jim Laker came along, just to watch, and I pinked with pride when he murmured just one word after I'd had a spell off the longer run: 'Raymond?'

Jim umpired one of our matches at Tim Hudson's idyllic Cheshire ground, and at tea I said to him, through my unreceding exasperation, '*One* of those lbw shouts must have been out?' In slushy conditions that made batting almost impossible, I'd half-rolled, half-slid down the slope with some more 'Lindwalls', and screamed at least six times for leg-befores against Steve Wundke. 'Come on Jim, admit it! One at least!' Half-closed eyes, barely-moving lips, and a hint of a wicked smile: 'Oh, they were all out,' he said.

In the second half of my playing time I lost a front tooth (it was only a top-edge off a slowie), broke a few bones in feet and fingers, and copped one in the eye which left a white background cloud every time I moved the eye from side to side. 'You will be all right,' said the doctor when he first examined it. When I went back to him a month later, the cloud not having dispersed, he calmly told me: 'You will get used to it.' And I have, until the relief brought by wondrous cataract operations in 2020.

The Cricket Writers played against a Texaco side in 1984, and in our XI we had Sarfraz Nawaz, the heavyweight Pakistani, and Chandrasekhar, the Indian wizard. I waited keenly, desperately for a slip catch from my hero Chandra's bowling. No luck. Meanwhile, though, Sarfraz was pounding the office-workers' ribs to pulp. One coughed up blood. We prevailed upon Sarf to slow down, bowl offbreaks or something, but he looked stonily at us and said, 'I cannot', adding a wheezy chuckle.

This was the same big fellow who, one evening over a drink, put me in charge of the design and erection of floodlights at Lahore's Gaddafi Stadium, even though I protested that I had no experience in this field. Sarf was a government agent of some sort, and it was as if he somehow knew about my 97 percent in Technical Drawing in the 1951 Intermediate school certificate. Needless to say, the fine set of lights now illuminating the ground where Sri Lanka captured the 1996 World Cup is nothing to do with me.

At the advanced age of 47, I offset much of the heartache of failure by following up a century with seven wickets in a match for Guildford, a club record. It would have been nice to have had a video recording of the afternoon's work to soften old age. I sometimes wonder if the players of today realise how lucky they are to have so many television highlights of their antics freely available. Still, it happened: the cutting from the local newspaper affords proof.

Well past 40 now, I need never had had those doubts, for enough morsels of encouragement continued to come my way to convince me that I was not yet making a complete fool of myself. So well did things go in a Media XI match in Yorkshire that I was banished from the team for a time. Having opened on a wet, grassy pitch against two mean local seamers who made the ball dart, I then took up with my old pal Qamar Ahmed in a longish stand as things eased. For once, I didn't chuck it away after having done the hard work, and when we declared I was into three figures. What I hadn't realised was that on the faraway boundary had been waiting eager batsmen of the calibre of Mark Saggers, Jeremy Thompson, Graham Otway, Colin Bateman and Graham Morris. I duly paid my debt to society.

The very next match I played was a good'un. It was part of The Times' bicentenary celebrations. At Broadhalfpenny Down, Hambledon I captained a Collins Publishers' XI against *The Times'* XI, who were led by Mike Brearley, with John Woodcock umpiring and John Arlott presiding over lunch in the historic Bat & Ball, where he proceeded to recite passages from Nyren that bewitched the gathering. Rain spoilt the day, though not before I'd had the pleasure of batting with that great record-holder (most not-outs in Test history) Bob Willis. Later, when Brearley came in, I set a Bodyline field for Willis. I think he felt we were serious, for he never so much as blinked or smiled.

How could one leave all these treats behind simply because of the aggregate of the years? I remained perplexed whenever I bumped into an old friend who said that he no longer played because he had a lawn to mow or a fancy car to wash at weekends. To each his own.

Had I given up in 1985, I would have denied myself the experience of bowling Nicholas Parsons with a wrong'un, a deed which I dedicated to the nation. I would also have missed the close-up taste of dear old Brian Close's tendency to be somewhat overbearing. A long-time admirer of the mighty Yorkshireman, I was not going to be intimidated by him as he strode across Hudson's picturesque ground, Birtles Bowl, resplendent in his multi-coloured blazer, and announced that his side would bat. Pig's bum, I told him. We're going to toss properly. And we did. And I batted first. And when it began to drizzle, and we passed 200, Closey, bless him, was spitting chips. Like Derrick Robins once at Eastbourne, he even attempted to close our innings while captaining the fielding side. With Dilip Doshi spinning nicely, we won that one.

Our mystery guest player (standing, left) at Tim Hudson's ground.
Front row: Dilip Doshi, David Norrie, DF, Stephen Thorpe, Qamar Ahmed

But there was no more remarkable Hudson match than when we were a man short, and I phoned on ahead, begging for a local man to be lent to us. When we arrived, there he was, dark and brooding in the corner of the little pavilion, which was festooned with posters and photos and ties hung from the rafters. Our guest player didn't say much, except that he was tired, having taken nine wickets in yesterday's league match, which sounded promising. So we gave him the new ball, and he earned his early respite by whipping out both openers. So off he went to long-leg (never was there a more apt fielding position). England rugby player Steve Smith then held us up, and a couple of hours later we needed to finish things off, so I asked our guest if he would be so kind as to knock over the last three wickets for us. He loped in, and was repelled. Match drawn. Never mind. What was that bowler's name again, one of our crowd enquired. I told him: Curtly Ambrose. A year later he made his West Indies Test debut.

In another match at Tim Hudson's meadow, Phil Simmons, also still unknown, caused a buzz with a century in less than an hour, mostly driven off photographer Graham Morris's disingenuous bowling. It was disappointing later to find Simmons claiming a catch at forward short leg after I'd pulled the ball downwards and was convinced it was gathered on the half-volley. Farokh Engineer, who was keeping wicket, urged me not to go, but the umpire felt that the fieldsman's insistent claim was good enough, and up went the finger.

In Surrey Club Championship cricket, and later the Fullers Surrey League, it was gradually becoming apparent that the noise level was rising (clapping and shouting before and after every ball, irrespective of its merit or the state of the game) and morality was curdling. Players acting in emergency as umpires often cheated blatantly. This, and this alone, caused me to hesitate as one springtime followed another. But the shirt still fitted, even if the trousers had to be let out a fraction. If you are truly transfixed at the age of 12 or 13 there is little chance of wriggling loose.

At 50 it seemed even more dangerous. The quickies in the league matches were almost young enough to be grandsons. But had I quit at 50, I should never have taken the field with 1954-55 giant Frank Tyson, who was to become a long-time friend. There we were, with Brian Close again, playing for English Press against Pakistan Press at Kirkstall, Leeds, on a sweltering day in 1987. With eight overs limit per bowler, I asked the Typhoon whether he wanted four-and-four, to which the 57-year-old replied that he'd settle for two-two-two-and-two.

It was an exceptional thrill for all on that field to have Probably the Fastest Bowler of All Time in our midst, and off a restricted run-up Frank pinged down some sharp medium-pacers, puffing and heaving by the end of the over, for oxygen was scarce in that airless dustbowl. For his second over, our intrepid little wicketkeeper, David 'Toff' Lloyd, whose association was with a village near Basingstoke, came up to the stumps. Frank Tyson did a double take. This was conceivably the first time he had ever peered down a cricket pitch and not seen his keeper in the far distance. In he strode, and with a grunt such as we'd heard at the SCG over 30 years before, he banged down a shortish ball. In that split-second we feared for the batsman and we feared for the keeper. I even feared for Frank, for he must have taken quite a lot out of himself. To his credit, the batsman swayed away, and to his even greater credit, 'Toff' took the ball above his head. We won, but for once it hardly mattered. It was the company we had kept. The only problem had been Brian Close. He had declined to field at short leg, so I had threatened to report him to Lord's. It was about time that something like that happened to him again.

For all these years it has been an odd existence, hopping back and forth between the world of watching the big-time and writing about it, then hopping around in the fresh air, playing at my own modest level, whether for Shepperton, Guildford or finally Godalming, or in Press and charity matches. It brought strange looks so often in the Press-box during Tests when I got the 'jumps' and wanted to be out playing rather than watching mediocre international cricket.

Then, when trying to bat on the crude pitches prepared for club matches, I would envy the pampered batsmen at top level for their placid pitches. It was underlined when we played at The Oval occasionally. How I wished I was still young enough to bowl my Lindwall-understudy stuff, especially when I might have taken advantage of club cricket's 'cabbage-patches'.

The seasons with Guildford, where Surrey played each summer, saw quality pitches, if on the slow side, with the exciting emergence of young locals who went on to play county and Test cricket. I recall chauffeuring a 15-year-old Darren Bicknell to a match in which I made nought and he scored his first century. What a thrill it was, a dozen years later, to read of his 235 not out at Trent Bridge, which was the longest innings ever played (638 minutes) in a county match. I stood at slip, where I spent so much of my life, but appreciably deeper, as another 15-year-old, Martin Bicknell, steamed in for Guildford, this younger Bicknell brother one day going on to play for England. With better luck with fitness, he would have done so many more times. We also had Adam Hollioake for a short time. His father, John, from Melbourne, was for a season or two my conversation partner in the slips. And perhaps the biggest surprise of all was a 14-year-old with large feet who bowled fast left-arm with considerable skill. At 50, reasoning that nothing much was coming to slip these days, I adapted to wicketkeeper on occasions, which relieved the boredom, despite a crack on the eye which had the specialist telling me I'd get used to the white floaters. Along came this lad, Ashley Giles, an impressive left-arm quickie, who once shed a tear when a batsman smashed one back and bruised his hand. In time he switched to spin. I suggested he might save that for his old age. But, he explained, he had a bad back. He had certainly given the ball a tweak, and bowled a good length. Lo and behold, a couple of years later he had grown several inches taller and was in Warwickshire's colours, and then in the England A touring team, and then the Test team (being a vital cog in the famous 2005 Ashes series). Then, believe it or not, 'Gilo' ended up as England cricket's highly-paid supremo. West Surrey was proving fertile territory.

I was honoured with the appointment of president of Guildford CC in 1988, the year that half-a-century of county cricket was celebrated at Woodbridge Road. I compiled a heavily-illustrated A4 book to mark the event. Equally memorable was the visit of the Australian Aboriginal team, 120 years on from that quaint first visit by Dick-a-Dick, King Cole, Twopenny, Red Cap, Bullocky and the rest. The 1988 team was led by Mark Ella, Ian King and John Maguire, and given a civic reception in Guildford, where one of the lads climbed up and sat on the mayor's 'throne'. Everyone chuckled, even the mayor herself, refusing to regard it as an irreverent act. The lads played good cricket, and expressed fervid hopes that some of their number might rise to the very top in due course. Of one thing I was sure: never before could the corroboree have been performed in this ancient town by aborigines in red loincloths.

Young Maninder Singh guested for us at Guildford one Sunday, not long before his Test debut for India. He bowled three immaculate overs on the spot, each ball spinning fast towards slip; but I began to wonder if he had any variety. 'What about an arm ball, Manny. Haven't you got the arm ball?' First ball next over, he speared out the leg stump, almost killing the wicketkeeper. Down the pitch strolled the young Sikh, grinning from ear to ear: 'That was my arm ball.' Pity we couldn't have signed him fulltime. In due course he played for India, and was last man out in that famous tied Test against Australia at Madras in 1986.

The annual match at Tim Hudson's was steeped in tension in 1990 when Sunil Gavaskar and Bishan Bedi both accepted invitations to play before I discovered that they were not speaking. Both had issued statements to the media criticising each other for what they saw as misdemeanours. However, they both honoured their promises to play, and although urged by mischiefmakers to place them side by side in the slips, out of respect to both my friends I kept them well apart. Sunny didn't make many runs, but he so enjoyed bowling that it had been almost impossible to get the ball off him. The only potential flashpoint came when he was inside-edged and Bish, at leg slip (vice mid-off: no need to move all afternoon), could only stick out a desperate hand to touch the ball as it sped past him. No exchange ensued. That's Indian cricket for you. I remained very fond of them both.

That was the last of the 'Lord' Tim Hudson matches in his dream world. The former manager of the future Lord Botham had to relinquish his cricket ground, and summers became duller for it.

But a year later, in between the serious business of league cricket against fit, strong, voluble youngsters, there were some enjoyable games, reward for my slavish perseverance past the half-century of life. At Collingham I played in a Bruce French benefit match, startled by the range of deliveries sent down at speed by Franklyn Stephenson before being allowed to take over Frenchie's gloves and grabbing a legside catch off Tim Robinson's bowling. Still aglow, I then missed a stumping off one that leapt, and witnessed at close range the famous Robbo scowl. The highlight, though, had to be keeping to an alltime favourite, Mr Derek Randall: 'Stand back, Dave! Here cooms me boomper!' It bounced three times. It all helped cloud the memory of my earlier fourth-ball duck, bowled by a Merv Hughes lookalike. Qamar Ahmed, patrolling the boundary, said: 'You reminded me of Graeme Hick.' This rather pleased me – until he elaborated: 'No footwork.'

But the greatest experience of all – perhaps of a cricketing lifetime – was to play in the first cricket match ever staged at Wembley Stadium. Ralph Dellor gave me the call. I was certain he was kidding. Not until we walked down the tunnel that day did it fully register that I was about to play on that same arena where Dad had brought me every summer Thursday evening 40-odd years ago to be thrilled by the speedway. Our 'All-Stars' were pitted against David English's Bunburys, and in spite of the persistent rain we gave the crowd of 2000 something to jeer before the main event (which was to be cancelled anyway). I flighted a few to Chris Broad, was presented with John Morris's wicket at the third attempt as he spooned catches to heavyweight boxer Gary Mason, and was hit almost out of the stadium by Roland Butcher. I caught a skyer from Dennis Waterman, and became the first man to spill blood while playing cricket at this world-famous venue when Rory Bremner's big hit settled into my hands as I stood slightly uncertainly by the midwicket boundary with half the West Indies Test team standing behind me. The catch looked and sounded good, but when I looked at my fingers, a thin slice was missing from the top of the right index.

I won't pretend I wasn't affected by the sight of my name in lights on the Wembley scoreboard when it was time to bat, or that I was unaffected by the possibility of Joel Garner bowling to me. Instead, I faced Mark Nicholas, a seasoned flatterer who said, 'Oh, jolly well played: shot of the day!' as I hit him straight. He had his sweater pulled over his head at the time, so intense was the rain. I puffed a few quick singles with Colin McMillan, who was shortly to take a world featherweight boxing title. But what meant most to me that wonderful day – more even than being given guard by Dickie Bird at one end and David Shepherd at the other (and having Bird, another masterful flatterer, exclaim 'You can plaaay!') – was climbing up to the presentation-box with the rest of the players, soaked through, and shaking the hand of Group Captain Leonard Cheshire, VC, Lord Cheshire, an exceptional hero of both wartime and peacetime. This right hand of mine has shaken with many of the world's eminent cricketers, but nothing has meant more than the clasp of Leonard Cheshire's hand and that of Douglas Bader, the legless air ace. For a time, heroes such as these make you forget cricket.

But not for long. Monthly deadlines, controversial issues (such as excessive commercialisation of the game: will they next place an advertising logo on that sacred space in the centre of the pitch?), all these pressures kept the mind concentrated. England, as I'd always believed, was the place to be for round-the- clock cricket. Trouble was, there seemed too much of it at times. The appetite can dull.

And then it can be resoundingly restored, as it was in the summer of 1993 when David Richards, a friend of many years and now chief executive of the ICC, asked me to join him in an Australian Lord's Taverners team to play an English Taverners side at Paul Getty's ground in Bucks. My club team-mates seemed reluctant to believe me when I told them the following Saturday that I'd been keeping wicket to Dennis Lillee and Greg Chappell, with Bob Simpson at slip and Bob Cowper at gully. Another touch of Heaven.

Lillee came close to disfiguring Rory Bremner that afternoon. The impressionist had kept up an amusing running commentary in Boycottspeak ever since he arrived at the crease. It annoyed the great fast bowler, who without warning dug one in. Bremner got his glove in front of his face with about a thousandth of a second to spare, and the ball ballooned to the third-man rope. His bizarre commentary seized up, and we tried to cheer him up by telling him he could brag to his grandchildren that he had once hit the great Lillee for four. As for Dennis himself, that ball demonstrated that he was still as headstrong at 44 as when he had burst on the scene 20-odd years earlier.

So was I: when we needed a lot in very few overs at the end, I had a swish at Brian Close's slower ball and was through with the shot about half-a-minute before hearing the fatal click. I don't recall ever having been dismissed before by a 62-year-old.

And so, with increasing trepidation, each season is unveiled: No.44, No.45 (one more than WG!), No.46. Would the 50th be achieved? You hear about that man in Gloucestershire still tossing down his offbreaks at 80. Now that was some target. I discovered that batsmen attract more bouncers in their 45th and 46th seasons. Launched in the early 1950s, I've survived long enough to have batted occasionally in a helmet and dabbed the odd touch of zinc cream on the 'titty' nose. But I flatly refused to add to the insidious modern noise pollution of loud and prolonged clapping after every ball.

The seasons were now like rounds of golf, where so much is disappointment, but the few good strokes are treasured. Thus, a fifty at Roehampton, eerily so close to where my grandparents used to be in service, included 12 fours: another new experience, justification for continuing. And fun cricket with the Bunburys, batting with Aussie rugby maestro Michael Lynagh, and football hero Ian Wright, and Spandau Ballet's drummer, and Dirty Den from *Eastenders*. And then participation in a televised match at The Oval to mark the 50th anniversary of VE Day brought the opportunity to bowl a few leggies with cricket's most prolific wicketkeeper, gentleman Bob Taylor, behind the stumps, and to stand at slip as England's heroes of the 1968 Oval Test, Derek Underwood and John Snow, bowled again, scarcely touched by the years either of them. Past merged with present and future as Liam Botham, son of 'The Greatest', ran through his paces in an attack that included David 'Syd' Lawrence, his shattered kneecap rebuilt, and Euro-sceptic Bill Cash, and Rolling Stone Bill Wyman, whose crab-like legspin action, not unlike Grimmett's, earned him a hat-trick (the legendary Gary Lineker, the legendary Trevor McDonald, and Charles Colvile). It was probably achieved by the first bowler ever at The Oval to operate with a cigarette dangling from his lower lip. Watching it all from the committee balcony were Denis Compton and Keith Miller, who must have yearned still to have been out in the middle. Alec Bedser handed out our commemorative tankards, moaning to me that he'd seen my dismissal, and I'd played across the line. 'I know,' I told him, 'I know. But have you ever looked up and seen 14 fieldsmen on the off side?'

That's how life sometimes is: opposition stacked across your pathway. You have to find a way around it, through it or over it, or else retire from the fray. But only when the enjoyment has died.

CHAPTER TWENTY

I wasn't there that morning/ When my father passed away;
Didn't get to tell him/ All the things I had to say.

MIKE AND THE MECHANICS

THE greatest ambition of all had been to compile a book which told cricket's story on a giant scale, in pictures and words. For perhaps 20 years I'd been working towards this, indexing every significant image I came across, in my own and other private collections and in institutional and agency archives. Thus was conceived *Pageant of Cricket*, a volume containing 2000 illustrations surrounded by 120,000 words, and weighing over 6 lbs. For the final run-in I commandeered the dining-room and worked 55 nights straight until 2.30am, laying down picture dimensions on the grid-sheets and handwriting the captions and chapter intros. From half-a-million images viewed, 50,000 had been short-listed and indexed, from which the final 2000 were selected, the idea being that no cricketer or incident of reasonable significance should be excluded. It was a draining experience, but the determination to see it through was consuming. The first indication that it was a worthwhile undertaking came at the end of Sir Donald Bradman's generous foreword for the 640-page book: "Thank goodness the cricket world," he wrote, "has always thrown up men like David Frith, who seems to regard a contribution to cricket history as a duty to mankind." I confess he was right. And I might add that I refused a sizable bonus on offer if a sponsor were to include its name in the title.

Former prime minister Harold Macmillan, head of the publishing house, died on publication day. Someone observed that perhaps he'd caught sight of the massive production bill. Richard Smart had orchestrated the publication through Macmillan in both the UK and Australia, and a superb printing operation was carried out in Hong Kong. There were two celebratory dinners, the first at Blenheim Palace, when I was seated beside Macmillan's son. Never had I relished an eve-of-publication dinner as much as this. There was then a more intimate dinner in London with principals of the Macmillan office. And never had such an occasion heralded such a chain of disaster.

As Debbie and I drove home from London on that night in October 1987, the winds were so violent that trees of some girth were bending. The house was being machine-gunned with seasonal beechnuts that normally fell lightly to the ground, and battered by a gale such as we'd never known. Sleep would not come. We were waiting for the storm to pass. Instead, it grew more ferocious. It became a hurricane, and the 100mph blasts from the south made the brick-built house shudder. Vegetation debris thumped against walls and windows. Was this old WG's way of acknowledging *Pageant of Cricket* from his pavilion up above?

At three in the morning came an almighty crash. The building trembled, windows shattered, and the howling wind and gushes of cold rain roared into the house. It seemed a limb had come off one of the trees, but through the darkness I could now see a gaping space in the dark sky which proclaimed the absence of one of the biggest beeches in the area. The massive 'grandfather' tree had come down!

The morning after: was it a hurricane or was it WG launching the big book?

Other trees had been ripped from the soft earth too, their branches heavy with leaf, their roots shallow. With wife and daughter holding onto crazily swinging bedroom doors and trying to block out the elements through shattered windows, the chief danger area was my study, where stacks of papers had been blown across the room and rain was splattering my cricket books. For about an hour I held the billowing curtains together against the gaping south-facing hole in the windowpane, glass splinters drawing globules of blood from fingers and knees. Finally I managed to secure the curtains with heavy old books, an 1898 Ranjitsinhji metal cigar-cutter and clothes-pegs. By now the rescue services were clawing their way through the jungle of fallen trees, and the firemen seemed to have spotted my silhouetted thumbs-up signal. Miraculously we had escaped death or injury, though Pongo the cat went missing for four days. The rescue team scrambled on, fighting their way further along the road.

With gas-pipes torn up and more trees threatening to collapse, we were evacuated to a safe house at the end of the road, with not even enough time to face that melodramatic question concerning which item above all one should take for safekeeping in a situation such as this. I grabbed my wallet and shepherded my wife and daughter down through the darkened mass of concrete-hard tree-limbs and wet, aromatic foliage. In the half-light of dawn, our street was a disaster area. The Blitz, 40-odd years on.

Repairs to roof, balcony, windows and contents cost over £10,000, but the traumatic effect on our nerves was incalculable. For years afterwards, whenever a strong wind came up we had if not panic attacks then headaches and flushes. It was some time before we accepted that there was a major benefit in the removal of half the beech forest around us: much more sunlight now shone through. The owls had fled, but we stayed.

This natural disaster could hardly have come at a more inconvenient time, for I was due three days later in Australia to promote *Pageant* before jetting across to the World Cup in India. Instead, I didn't leave the property for eight days as the initial repairs and clearing-up were carried out, with the lawn turned into a logging camp. We'd acquired overnight enough firewood to keep us going for 20 years, but this was small comfort. Among the things lost was a beautiful magnolia by the lounge window, crushed to pulp and still dead, it seemed, a year later. I was too busy to dig out the roots. And just as well, for two years later it began to grow again, and then blossom. It became our principal symbol of defiant renascence.

So Bombay/Mumbai it was, to the amazing semi-final of the World Cup in which Graham Gooch swept almost everything (too many arm balls from Maninder?) in a matchwinning century against India, and then to Eden Gardens, Calcutta, an immaculate ground with a five-star Press-box worthy of better dress-sense than that displayed by many of the English Press contingent. As in the 1882 Test match at The Oval, out of which the Ashes were created, Australia beat England in the final by seven runs, to launch an era of revival and eventual world dominance. Poor Gatting took most of the blame, messing up a reverse-sweep against Border's spin. Two years on from his Madras double-century there were no queries this time as to the name of the stroke, only condemnation.

An hour with the celebrating Australians was treasured, courtesy of manager Alan Crompton, a few teardrops emerging as Simon O'Donnell led the singing of *I Still Call Australia Home*. This young man, like all his team-mates, was in a state of ecstasy, and when I suggested they would be singing in the streets of his birthplace, Deniliquin, he said, 'Gee, that must be the first time Deniliquin ever got a mention in India!' Shortly after his return home, it was revealed that 'Sod' had a cancerous growth on a rib. Surgery and further treatment worked, and the cricket fraternity was relieved.

I wasn't too well myself by the time I reached Australia for the book promotion. Still shaken by the hurricane experience, I'd picked up a chest infection in India, which rendered 30 or more radio and TV interviews something of an ordeal, the worst being on the early-morning television programme *Good Morning, Australia*. Never at my best before lunch, I had to help my Vietnamese taxi-driver find the studio, then pump enough strength into the lungs to keep up with the hyper-enthusiastic, teeth-flashing host and hostess, and all before breakfast.

No such problems back in unimaginative England. I was called upon to do a mere three interviews, though the printed reviews were reasonable. Much more interest might have been shown in *Pageant* by the British media had I been a member of the 'inner circle'. My consolation came from a conviction that in all probability no member of that inner circle had the patience and wherewithal to have produced such a book.

If my wife, too, remembered 1987 for all this, there was something of much greater and sadder significance. Her mother suffered a stroke in July, and all else was sidelined as we sought to get Debbie on the first available flight to Queensland for a nightmare journey, never knowing until she landed whether she might ever see her Mum alive again. The dear lady did survive, though she was never afterwards able to converse lucidly. She lived in care for a further eight years, and since now we made a point of spending a few weeks annually in Queensland, there were many hours spent in glad proximity by her bedside and sometimes under the poinciana and jacaranda trees on the lawns.

On the cricket front, the major upheaval of that 1987 summer had been the crowd violence during the England-Pakistan one-dayer at Edgbaston, where several serious injuries were sustained. Officialdom was so disturbed that it buried its collective head in the sand; and when I placed BLOODSHED AT BIRMINGHAM on *WCM's* front cover, with an anxious editorial inside, the over-zealous authorities at The Oval and Edgbaston banned this issue of the magazine from being sold at those grounds. What mattered was that security and stewarding were subsequently reinforced as the spectre of the hooliganism and either-way racism which had cruelled football now threatened to ruin cricket.

Anglo-Pakistani relations were at their best at a dinner reception in Shepherds Bush at the end of the tour, with many of the touring team present, mobbed by their London-based supporters. I was asked to say a few words, and rejoiced in a rare chance to be the diplomat. Some sort of quip was called for though. So I explained that my wife and daughter were thrilled to be here in the presence of cricket's greatest-ever sex symbol. Eyes turned to Imran Khan, who controlled a spontaneous flicker at the mouth, then resumed his warrior countenance. I then put a name to this sex symbol: Haseeb Ahsan. The outrageous Pakistan manager screamed with delight, as did his cronies. We were friends for life; but I thought Imran rather cool when next we met.

On the social scene with the mighty Imran.
He did not think Haseeb's sex-symbol image was funny

As for Debbie, she had not been 'thrilled' at all, any more than she had been impressed when the heir to the throne had accidentally stepped on her foot while we were all attempting to dance at a Lord's Taverners ball at the Grosvenor House. She simply continued to support me staunchly, sharing my aims and pleasures.

Out in Pakistan, Gatting's England side faced another set of problems stemming from atrocious local umpiring. Reporters, captain and manager estimated that nine England wickets had fallen to poor decisions by the men in white coats during the Lahore Test. The unseemly and unsightly confrontation between Gatting and umpire Shakoor Rana in the next Test, at Faisalabad, seems to have become preordained. The eventual introduction of 'neutral' or 'third-country' umpires probably drained a lot of the sting out of the accusations of bias, though in reality it has merely internationalised incompetency.

Perhaps stung by something Hugh McIlvanney wrote, the TCCB gave each England player £1000 'hardship' money, a gesture roundly condemned. McIlvanney had merely written: 'By demanding that Gatting and his players accept being screwed on a daily basis as a patriotic obligation, the TCCB are not honouring any real sporting tradition.' How true.

The Bicentennial Test in Sydney, in January 1988, was less than memorable, apart from Chris Broad's hot-headed smashing down of his stumps (£500 fine) when he played on for 139, and David Boon's unbeaten 184 which sealed the draw when Australia followed on. For me the highlight was being perched next to Bill O'Reilly in the Press-box in this his final match. At 82, detesting much of what he had to watch, he was retiring. He undertook far more interviews than Gatting or Border, and Mike Coward presented him, on behalf of all the Press corps, with a copy of *Pageant of Cricket*, which Bill promised to 'read with pleasure for the next 30 years'. He was to be spared for only another four.

Australia's fastest bowler in the 1930s,
Ernie McCormick – a laugh a minute

From there we crossed the Tasman Sea for England's series in New Zealand, but not before a quick trip to Queensland, where I did a very happy interview with Ernie McCormick, Australia's pre-war fast bowler, who chuckled through numerous stories, the best-known concerning his first over in England on the 1938 tour, when he kept over-dragging. The umpire called him 19 times for no-balls in his first three overs in that Worcester match, and 35 times in all. Were they all really no-balls? 'I don't reckon so,' said Ern, serious just for a few moments. 'When we got off the ship, Don Bradman told the English Press that I was the fastest bowler in the world. The English umpires must have said to themselves, we'll soon fix him!' He claimed the no-ball shouts dried up eventually because the umpire went hoarse.

One amazing revelation was that he had been fit enough for the 1938 Oval Test (England 903 for 7 declared), and told vice-captain McCabe so. But he wasn't chosen. Earlier in that series he had shaken Len Hutton up a bit. Hutton now batted for almost 2½ days for his 364.

The 1987-88 series in New Zealand was tedious, though tedium can actually be welcome once in a while. It began with the expectation that Richard Hadlee, locked in top position with Botham in the Test wicket-taking table, would pull away supreme, but a calf injury on the opening day saw the end of him for the three-match series before he had taken a wicket. From Christchurch to Auckland, where the umpiring was abysmal, and Mark Greatbatch scored a century on debut, while poor Martyn Moxon was out for 99 after having had a sweep shot for three given as leg-byes. Then more yawns at the Basin Reserve, Wellington, and home we went, to interpret the latest news on Botham: Queensland had sacked him after an alleged series of indiscretions. I wrote in fear for his future.

The magazine continued to be served by mellow pieces from John Arlott, from his island of Alderney (we spoke often by phone but our inability to meet, either at home or in Press-box, left a sizable hole in my life). There were also strong offerings from E.M.Wellings, who was even more isolated in Basingstoke by his very lack of personal friends. I continued to give space to previously unpublished writers when the topic and treatment warranted, and faced up to the crises that seemed to be bearing down on cricket with increasing weight and frequency, feeling that by tossing ideas about (including the third umpire/video concept) we might one day have a perfect cricket world.

The South African question was never far away, and nor was the matter of intimidation by fast bowlers. But at Trent Bridge, during the first Test of the 1988 summer, I was taken aback at something the West Indies manager said to a group of friends as they stood by the members' enclosure. England were collapsing (again), and as Phil DeFreitas went out to bat at No.9, one of the group said to manager Jackie Hendriks: 'Who's this man, Jackie?' Back came the reply: 'He's another one of our boys – DeFreitas – he's from Dominica.' Was this the sort of teasing remark made to the England allrounder out in the middle? And if so, how undermining might it have been?

It wasn't all heavy going, thank God. Off I trotted to the annual Cricket Society dinner to receive the Jubilee Literary Award for *Pageant of Cricket* from president Hubert Doggart, 17 years after that honour for the Stoddart biography. Inevitably, I made reference to the tale concerning Phil Mead, whose tours of Australia (1911-12 and 1928-29) were 17 years part: no, it wasn't my father who'd received the award for the Stoddart book all those years ago.

A few months later, I was proud to take delivery of a Highly Commended certificate for *WCM's* page design, an award decided by the Sports Council and the Sportswriters Association. Returning to the luncheon table and still tingling, I was summoned back to the platform minutes later and presented with the British Magazine Sportswriter of 1988 award. It was a shock all right, but suddenly the labours of the years and the pressure on family and social life seemed almost justified.

After that torrid summer of 1988, when the mighty four-prong West Indian fast attack had again crushed England, and the background of political rumblings over South Africa grew more discordant, I was in need of a rest, and with a good deputy comfortably ensconced, I could begin to utilise the 40-odd weeks of holiday that had piled up over the past nine years. Back to peaceful Queensland we went, to the enchanting rainforest and beaches and sanctuaries and pestilent cane-toads. And, of course, space and peacefulness.

Never one to miss an interview opportunity, this time I persuaded Bill Johnston to submit. He and wife Judy had moved from the south to the Gold Coast some years earlier, and this wonderful left-arm fast bowler, the often forgotten key member of the all-conquering 1948 Australian team, was great to be with, for he laughed with almost every sentence. I remembered his jollity from my boyhood days, when I'd first got his autograph.

Bill Johnston smiles bravely after discovering the worst

We talked for hours – and were to be firm friends for years to come – but the real drama came when I persuaded him to open up the cabin-trunks in the garage so we could examine all his caps and blazers and other memorabilia. To my horror, but Bill's great amusement, the contents were riddled with moths and silverfish. In time, much of this treasure-trove was salvaged. The lesson was clear: keep a regular eye on things.

As 1989 began, those who knew Wilf Slack were distraught at the news that he had collapsed and died while playing in Gambia. He was 34, and had played three times for England. West Indies-born, he had moved to England when 11, and I had a close look at him when High Wycombe came down to play Guildford in 1976. I got a finger to a sizzling return early on, but two hours later he was 150-odd not out, cool and calm, pleasant and modest company at the bar that evening. In the return fixture he was out cheaply, but was a problem with the ball on a dim evening, with no sightscreen. But I shall remember Wilf most of all for helping out at a reception for *WCM* tourists in Sydney during the '86-87 tour. A tall, blond member of the England side, not entirely unconnected with the magazine, could not be bothered joining us for cocktails, even though it was not intended to last long. Wilf Slack and Graham Dilley, however, agreed instantly, and stayed till the end, giving untold pleasure to the tourists.

Now, early in 1989, it was time to have a fresh look at South Africa, 14 years on from that first visit. There were howls from a certain section of the media, of course, but it seemed to me irresponsible not to take the chance of being there and seeing first-hand if an impending transition from doomed nation to one reborn, as was being bruited, was an exaggeration.

We were shown the townships – Soweto, Alexandra, Atteridgeville – and joined in the cricket training with hundreds of black kids who had laughter in their eyes and hope in their hearts. We met up with so many old South African cricketers who had gathered for their Test Centenary celebrations, and listened to stirring speeches at the banquets. And we encountered lingering scepticism, though nothing compared to that which awaited us on our return to England, much of it from people with closed minds. F.W.de Klerk was on the verge of the big breakthrough, spurred by the release of Nelson Mandela from imprisonment and recognition of the African National Congress party. It was an exciting time, and I, for one, was proud of cricket's part in it. That is why I gave it as much as eight pages in *WCM*.

Ali Bacher had secured a wide range of Test veterans among the invitees, including a batch from Bradman's 1948 immortals: Lindsay Hassett, Ian Johnson, Ray Lindwall, Bill Johnston, Neil Harvey and Keith Miller. My old skipper Norm O'Neill turned up, as did Bob Wyatt, Fred Trueman, George Mann, M.J.K.Smith, Alec Bedser and Peter May among the English contingent. Walter Hadlee, Bert Sutcliffe, Merv Wallace and John Reid represented New Zealand's yesterdays. Dr Bacher had struggled to get guests from West Indies, India and Pakistan, but this was understandable. There was much yet to be proved. But Sri Lanka's first Test captain, Bandula

Warnapura, was there. And so were many old local heroes.

The quietest and most venerable was Bruce Mitchell, now 80, and still top of South Africa's runs list, his first Test having been played in 1929, 60 years previously. His voice was so soft as to be barely audible above the chatter rising from the gigantic barbecue. 'Tuppy' Owen-Smith was another celebrated name to materialise in the flesh during the Currie Cup final at Port Elizabeth, scorer of a famous hundred against England when he was only 20, in that 1929 series.

The gladness of the days blended with serious nights, when South Africans gathered with their visitors and talked and talked. 'We need help,' said Mike Procter, the world's finest cricketer 15 years earlier. 'The outside world owes it to us now. People should come here, see what we've done, what we're doing. Why doesn't Ian Botham come here to see? Why not Viv Richards? And Clive Lloyd?' It was going to take time.

Less seriously, MCC's Jack Bailey cracked the remark of the tour: at a nocturnal tribal dance attended by most of the main event's invitees, he spotted Alec Bedser (a lifelong bachelor) in the gathering, and said in a stage whisper: 'When did you last see a female breast Alec?'

Much was crammed into those days, including a dawn expedition into the Pilanesberg game reserve, where I could almost stroke a rhinoceros, my favourite animal, from the vehicle. At the crocodile farm I kept a safe distance. The neverending search for cricketers' faces continued to produce jackpots, among them Hugh Tayfield, perhaps Laker's equal as an offspinner. This five-times-divorced Natalian materialised at Parys, where black cricket coaches were being trained, and was soon displaying his renowned stubbornness, recalling the advice given him long ago in England by S.F.Barnes: 'Never take any notice of anything anybody ever tells you!' I took this on board.

Then there was the amazing Bob Crisp, the only bowler twice to have taken wickets with four balls in succession. Not that this was his greatest achievement by a long chalk, for he had conquered Kilimanjaro twice in a fortnight, swum Loch Lomond naked, taken 107 wickets with his fast stuff on the 1935 tour of England, survived a lethal, frantic tank war in North Africa, and won the DSO and Military Cross. Among other things he had conquered were countless women and, in middle age, cancer, which he said he'd repelled with wine and by canoeing his way around the Greek islands. This was the sort of bloke I wanted to write for *WCM*, and he duly agreed, having been a journalist and editor himself for many years. Some of his paragraphs inflamed a few of our readers, and I suppose that had been predictable.

Once again I had a birthday while on tour, the unique feature this time being that the coachload of old cricketers, including six former Test captains, sang *Happy Birthday* for me, many of them having spotted the bottle of vintage port I'd brought on board. We drank it from paper cups. Not the least pleasure was to hand Ossie Dawson (nine Tests late 1940s) a copy of *WCM* containing the feature on his gallant wartime exploits.

If one event had to be singled out from all this to demonstrate what the jamboree was all about, it must have been the historic first cricket match between an Afrikaner (white) school (Randburg) and a school for black children (Alexandra). It was like the coming-together of two different planets, a heartwarming pointer to the future.

In search of a successor to Allan Donald: Soweto 1989

Matthew Engel, of course, wouldn't have a bar of it, and wrote a liverish letter which I published. Next month came an offering from Scyld Berry which at least had the good grace to acknowledge that 'good work, for whatever motive, is being done in the townships towards multiracial harmony', though he puzzlingly went on to state his belief that this work would lead to the prolongation, not the termination, of apartheid. And old E.M.Wellings came in with the view that Engel 'surely had no need to write last month defending himself. He has visited South Africa, seen for himself and formed his own opinion about their cricket. That it differs from that expressed in the May issue could most certainly not number him among those then termed hypocrites.'

It was a relief to turn to the 1989 Ashes series now unfolding, straight after we had celebrated 10 years in business, with *WCM* now flourishing. That was more than could be said of English cricket, for the '89 series went down the pan from the opening day. Mark Taylor (136) made an instant stamp on Ashes cricket, batting all day at Headingley and doing the same in the fifth Test, at Trent Bridge, where he and Geoff Marsh put on 329 for the first wicket, breaking the record in England-Australia Tests, 323 by Jack

Hobbs and Wilfred Rhodes, Melbourne, 1911-12. ('Oh, poor Jack; poor Wilfred' lamented a sentimental Jim Swanton.

It was Steve Waugh's series as much as anybody's. He recorded a record unbroken haul of 393 runs before Gus Fraser got him out in the third contest, by which time he had been batting in the series for just over 13 hours. I kept him posted statistically as the series progressed. My reward was his gloves and sleeveless sweater.

Terry Alderman (41wickets), Geoff Lawson (29) and the colourful pantomime creature Merv Hughes were too much for England most days, and the sound of Roy Orbison's *Mystery Girl*, *Windsurfer* and *Not Alone Any More*, which blasted around the Australian dressing-room throughout the summer, will forever bring back the feel of that time. For it was an emotional time. Not only was I feeling pride and admiration for Border's boys and genuine sympathy for Gower's lost souls (29 players represented England in those six Tests) but I had some real grief of my own.

Around 6 o'clock one morning the phone rang. I stumbled across the bedroom, eyes refusing to focus. It was the voice of an Australian woman, a telephone operator. She had been asked by my brother to relay some sad news. My Dad was dead. She was very apologetic, and I found myself feeling sorry for her. I lay down, numb, and as Debbie stirred and asked who it was, I told her. Thank God I had sent that birthday card three weeks ago to the 80-year-old father who had rejected me.

I bottled up my feelings and drove to Manchester for the fourth Test, a match overshadowed by the revelation that England would be losing players to a disapproved tour of South Africa in the winter, all drawing long Test bans down upon themselves. For the Australians, none of this mattered. Another crushing victory won them the Ashes, for the first time reclaimed in England since 1934. When I took my perfect replica of the Ashes to the dressing-room (awash, thanks to Merv, with beer and mushy bread), it was all I could do to get the urn back from Allan Border. In his euphoria he offered me £500 for it. Even as I turned him down, Merv was approaching, his great fist outstretched. He just wanted a touch. He didn't get it. Orbison's unreal voice rose above it all, and I got a good front-cover picture.

There had been just one moment during that Test match when the events of recent days and months came into poignant focus, and I almost succumbed to tears. I took a stroll during the afternoon's play, always thinking of Cardus whenever I smelt Old Trafford's frying onions over by the Wilson Stand, and I suddenly caught sight of the elderly folk in the wheelchairs enclosure. They were escorted by young chaps, perhaps nurses, perhaps volunteers. But in an instant I saw both my aged father and my long-lost son, who was nursing now in Adelaide. Alderman bowled to Botham and had him lbw. I headed back to the Press-box, where I belonged.

In truth, this had not been the sort of Ashes series anyone of dual allegiance could really have enjoyed. It was far too one-sided, from that first Test at Headingley, when David Gower 'skated away on the ice of a new day', putting Australia in and seeing them make precisely as many (601) as they did when Hutton put them in at Brisbane in 1954, through to the drawn final Test at The Oval, where Border allowed his side to bat rather too long. I forgave him, for he gave me the shirt off his back for my collection when it was all over. It felt like receiving Henry V's vest after Agincourt.

Captain Gower of England, in contrast, continued to give me a hard time. He was under severe pressure that summer, which showed at Lord's, when he stomped unseeingly out of the Saturday-evening Press conference, nearly crowning me with a palmed-off spotlamp in his haste. I'd sensed his tension on the eve of the first Test as a few of us sat in a quiet corner of the *Fox & Hounds*. But when he faced a potentially hostile media conference halfway through that Headingley Test, I tried to divert that hostility by bringing up the matter of his arm injury. Through his shirt could be seen the patch covering the injection-marks. It was hardly something he himself could draw attention to, so I raised it more or less on his behalf. He misinterpreted the gesture and became quite ratty. I backed off, and saw him slightly differently thereafter.

Poor chap was ditched as skipper for the second time at the end of that '89 season, and we entered the Gooch regime, with the uncompromising Micky Stewart calling the shots too. Ted Dexter, chairman of the England Committee, was another who'd had a bad summer, lampooned mercilessly by newspapermen and editors who deliberately misunderstood the nature of that fascinating man. Cricket, I still believe, was never intended to shoulder more than a modicum of misery. Of late, it had borne only a modicum of happiness for those closely involved and the game's helpless followers. If, as *Daily Mail* columnist Peter McKay has shrewdly speculated, the British dislike success, then their needs had been well met by the England Test XI for some years.

As the 1980s drew to a close, *Wisden Cricket Monthly* became part of John Wisden & Company, to my immense and innocent relief. It was supposed that the joining together would strengthen both the magazine and the *Almanack*. Whatever difficulties might later occur, this seemed to be a reality.

With 1989 having claimed, besides my father, Laurence Olivier, Tommy Trinder, Henry Hall, and Dr Charles Hill, the BBC's wartime Radio Doctor, the decade, in its final weeks, also saw the passing of Gubby Allen, for some years transformed by knighthood almost unrecognisably into Sir George Allen. A dominant figure in English cricket administration for decades, he was regarded by many of us as a captain and player who best symbolised Anglo-Australian relations. He had refused to bowl Bodyline (the Northerners said, plausibly, that he hadn't the accuracy to do it properly anyway) and he refurbished England's image on the next tour, in 1936-37, when the tourists went two-up only to lose the next three, Bradman scoring heavily in each. If I remember one thing from several absorbing sessions of conversation with 'Gubby' it is that he insisted that Bodyline didn't start until halfway through the 1932-33 season. I politely pointed out that not only did that seem to be in contradiction of all that every other participant and observer believed, but it was to deny Stan McCabe's glorious 187 not out at Sydney in the first Test some of its due. Furthermore, Bodyline had been unleashed in Perth and Melbourne before the Test series had started. The old England player then delivered a put-down of nuclear dimension. Placing his hand on my forearm, he purred: 'My dear chap, I was *there*!' Perhaps he was, but weren't his eyes open?

Those who were *there* (not I) at Sabina Park, Kingston, Jamaica early in 1990 blessed themselves for being so, for England beat West Indies (and comfortably) for the first time in a Test match since 1974. Graham Gooch was England's commander-in-chief and most of the runs came from Lamb (132) and Robin Smith (57), with Fraser taking 5 for 28 in the first innings and Small and Malcolm four each in the second. Malcolm's dismissal of Viv Richards twice was significant. A video-tape of the match was on the market a week later.

A major new facility now to be enjoyed was coverage of overseas Test series such as this, live by satellite on BSkyB television. The hours of play when a Caribbean series is beamed to the UK are not anti-social. Other activities can continue while watching. And the intrusion of commercials was sparing, shaming Australia's Channel 9 for its unbreakable principle of at least one ad between each over, and even commercial strap-lines at the base of the screen during play: greed beyond belief. One should not have been too complacent. Sky's subscriptions soon started to creep up remorselessly.

After a washout in Guyana, England were kept from going two-up at Port-of- Spain by Gooch's broken hand, rain, and some truly shameful time-wasting by West Indies after Malcolm had taken 10 wickets in the match. The home side levelled at Bridgetown, with 13 of their wickets falling to England's West Indian-born pace bowlers Malcolm, Small and DeFreitas, and Rob Bailey notoriously falling to a 'catch' off his thighpad, and they crushed England in Antigua in the final Test, where there was at last a warning for intimidation, but laughably dished out to the gentle David Capel for a couple of long-hops to Ambrose. England v West Indies cricket was undoubtably in a parlous state, and it was difficult to see how a restoration of the spirit of old could ever be effected.

The summer of 1990 brought soothing – even snoozing – scorelines from the county game in an extraordinary year for batsmen when a near-seamless ball simply came onto the bat, from early May onwards, when Ian Greig made 291 in Surrey's 707, to which Lancashire replied with 863 (Neil Fairbrother

366, Mike Atherton 191, Gehan Mendis 102). But the most noteworthy innings of the summer came at the end of July when Graham Gooch scored 333 and 123 in the Lord's Test against India, most runs by anybody in a Test match, highest score in a match at Lord's (passing Hobbs's 316 not out), but not, to widespread disappointment, a new Test innings record. Sobers remained No.1.

Atherton had scored his first Test century in the opening match of the season, against New Zealand at Trent Bridge, prompting the daring prediction in *WCM* that he 'will probably bestride the 1990s'. This freshfaced schoolboyish figure certainly seemed born to Test cricket.

John Arlott, now beset by recurring illness, came back to write a rather gloomy piece for us in which he sensed little hope for England's Test prospects in the longer term, though he was far from being alone in this. The surrounding pessimism sometimes got to me. Where had that innocent fun gone which had attracted so many like me to cricket in the first place? Everybody now seemed to want to debate the Problems of English Cricket. It was downbeat, depressing, self-consuming.

I got on with the task of balancing the books, squeezing expenditures to a minimum and maintaining a proper level of advertisement revenue by holding rates when all around us it seemed that space was being all but given away. *WCM* was a strong specialist showcase, and was entitled to appropriate payment for advertisers' exposure.

Another of the irritations that seemed to encircle the game was the ever-expanding public-address 'service' at big matches. The booming voice seemed to drown all other sound every minute that play was not in progress, even interrupting Press conferences half-an-hour after close of play (with many interviewed players prone to whisper their responses anyway). One media man was so angered by the noise as we strained to hear what Jack Russell was saying that he got up and ripped the loudspeaker from the wall: there was much laughter when tinny words continued to leak through the dangling wires. Alan Curtis, whose mellow voice provided this service, was so stung by criticism that he wrote to the magazine to explain and justify his vocal outpourings. We ran the letter, although it needed to be abbreviated.

We were just about to go to press early in September 1990 when Sir Len Hutton died. The tribute should not be delayed a month, but most of the edition was already made up. So I loaded on a late extra four pages, lit my pipe that evening, and wrote. Len, a symbol of my boyhood, had stood for all that was admirable and heroic about English cricket, for he had style and toughness and was also a shade mystical. And, of course, there was the glamour of his 364 against Australia in 1938, which brought him godlike status; and then all those beautifully-sculpted centuries since. In the classroom I used to press a thumb against my nose through the lessons in the hope of reshaping it into a Hutton profile, and at nets I worked hard at glancing the legside half-volley as he did, while not worrying too much about the cover-drive, so little chance was there of emulating the master's poise and mechanical perfection. It was the *weight of responsibility* that he carried through series after series that impressed me most, especially in view of his comparatively slight physique and apparent vulnerability.

I saw him twice in his final weeks. He looked so worn and tired. At his Kingston-upon-Thames home he signed some books for me. I stacked them on the boot of the car, and Len stood there in baggy shorts and wrote that familiar signature in each, enquiring after the authors: John Arlott: 'How's John these days?' 'And how's Lyn Wellings?' And the replies, I realised too late, were all less than uplifting, for everybody seemed at that time to be unwell.

With the two great knights of Ashes Tests: Sir Len Hutton and Sir Don Bradman, London 1974. Len's death in 1990 affected generations.

Sir Leonard left Godfrey Evans's gala 70th birthday dinner at Swiss Cottage before any of the other guests. I saw him, through the shadows, crossing the room, a small, unobtrusive figure. Uncertain as to whether he might return, I hurried after him and asked him to sign the menu. It seemed that for 40 years, on and off, I'd been obtaining Len Hutton's signature.

And now he was gone, and I was left in no doubt that when certain people leave us, a small part of us perishes too. At Len's funeral, I chatted with Keith Miller . . . and started to worry about his health now.

Genius, fortunately, continues to sprout from the good earth, and I had just come from a Test match at Old Trafford in which six centuries had been made, for the Indians one by the magical Azharuddin and another by the youthful Tendulkar, and it was amusing to hear him respond to the presentation of a huge bottle of champagne just before his Press conference. In a falsetto voice the 17-year-old piped, with a shy smile: 'I do not drink.'

A big hundred by David Gower helped save England in the last Test, at The Oval, before all eyes turned to another Ashes series in Australia. We had acquired new premises for *Wisden*, oddly enough in the same street in Merrow where we had lived in the late 1970s. With more space for offices and storage it looked like being a happy move, with an uplift in team spirit.

Over at the Gabba, though, England were fighting to retain their own team spirit as they went down in the opening Test in three days, Alderman rolling them over after they had secured a first-innings lead of 42. It was a disappointment to all who wanted a close-fought series, this first post-Thatcher encounter for England. *Wisden Cricket Monthly* had thus outlasted Britain's first female Prime Minister, and the faint sadness was balanced by interest in the fact that the new man at the crease, one J.Major, was said to be a cricket fanatic. As it turned out, so regularly did he turn up at Test matches in the following half-dozen years that a Test without him almost took on a special hue.

Australia won the second Test too, again after England had taken a first-innings lead. Gangling left-armer Bruce Reid took 13 wickets, and England's batsmen scored few compliments for the way they tried to deal with his late swing. Captain Gooch was back after injury, but it made little difference.

Having seen this Melbourne Test on TV, I flew down from Queensland to Sydney for the third Test, which was at my spiritual home, the SCG. There, Greg Matthews (128) took Australia to a daunting 518, only for England to get close before declaring. Gower made another handsome century and Alec Stewart was unlucky to be given out lbw for 91. But the most riveting performance came from Atherton, whose century took 424 minutes. He was still cool and fresh after dismissal, and was not the slightest bit rattled when I informed him that he'd just made the slowest century in Ashes history. It had made for viewing every bit as absorbing as Randall's marathon on this same ground 12 years previously.

England wrongfooted Australia now, but their second innings did not slide away as quickly as it might have done, for Gooch seemed unaware that Rackemann could not handle pace. The Queenslander prodded and padded against spin for a vital 107 minutes for nine runs, and although Gooch and Gower smashed 81 in the first 11 overs, the overall target of 255 in 28 overs proved hopeless. Australia retained the Ashes again.

Now, before the fourth Test, there was time for the England team to register their first victory – against Queensland – and to see one of their longer-lasting stars effectively put paid to his Test career.

The match was at the vast and shadeless Carrara Oval, and when David Gower got out disappointingly, and subsequently became bored, he went down the road and signed up for a joyride in a Tiger Moth. He took John Morris of Derbyshire with him, a young man flushed with pleasure after his first century in England colours. What upset team manager Lush was that, without telling him what it was for, Gower had touched him for a $75 loan against his wages so that he could reach for the sky.

The biplanes came in from the sea and dipped low over the arena. If Gower had had his way he would have dropped a water-bomb on Robin Smith, who was still batting. The aircraft gargled off into the distance, and that seemed that . . . until photographer Adrian Murrell dashed over and asked if I had my car there. He'd been told there were two cricketers on that flight, and he wanted to get to the airstrip before they landed. So off we dashed, just being beaten by the returning 'planes. Biggles and his pal readily agreed to hang around for photographs. They even went back to pose for more that evening as a favour to Graham Morris, who had missed the landing.

David Gower and John Morris, having been passengers in separate aircraft, pose for me in one of the Tiger Moths upon landing

Graham Gooch and Peter Lush were furious, and it was said that the manager wanted to send Gower home to England immediately. But the anger took some time to find its target. Unaware of the gravity of their prank, Gower and Morris lingered at the airstrip as Queensland's early dusk fell. I was not feeling all that patient myself, for Gower and his fiancée and Gladstone Small were our guests for dinner, up in the hills, and I was keen to show them the beauties of the place and its birdlife before darkness settled. Devon Malcolm was sitting by the dressing-rooms, and I asked if he'd like to come up for some steak and wine, but he wasn't interested.

At last our miscreants returned, and with the Gowers and 'Stoney' on board, I got us to the hill-top as night fell. We had a good time – until the phone rang. It was Chris Lander, speaking on behalf of the English Press corps. 'Crash' pleaded to speak with Gower, who interrupted his flow on South Australian wines and seemed to enjoy his chat on the phone. But minutes later it rang again, and this time it was John Morris, and the news was grim. The management wanted to see them both at 8 o'clock sharp next morning. Our dinner gathering lost its bounce.

The cricketers were each fined a walloping £1000. Poor Gower got further into his captain's bad books by getting out to a careless shot in the Adelaide Test, falling to McDermott's leg-side trap. This Test still turned out to be a thriller, with Gooch and Atherton making a swift 203 for the first wicket when England were set 472 in the fourth innings. Of course, wickets then fell, and the vision of obtaining this astronomical target fizzled out. In the final Test, which followed right away, England reverted to the third-rate and lost again, in little more than three days, after McDermott sealed his comeback with 8 for 97 in the first innings. All this was watched on TV back in shivering England, with renewed disappointment that Ashes cricket was still lop-sided.

Coinciding with that Perth Test was one in Wellington in which Martin Crowe (299) and Andrew Jones (186) set a new record for any wicket by any country in Test cricket: 467 for the third wicket against Sri Lanka, whose Aravinda de Silva, in spite of making 267 himself, was overshadowed. This 467 partnership at least fired the imagination of cricket-lovers the world over. If there's any schoolboy left in you, whatever your age, you cannot help but swoon at statistics like those.

Another statistic that might induce faintness is the one showing that apparently more cricketers commit suicide than participants in all other major sports added together. Over the years I had built up bulging files for every conceivable facet of cricket, and when the file housing details of players who had killed themselves reached a thickness of some four or five inches, it seemed to me that something had to be done with it. A thesis was beckoning to be compiled, with the added hope that an explanation might be found. Could cricket be entirely exonerated?

And so *By His Own Hand* came to be written. It was the least enjoyable of all my written projects, and the resultant book was probably viewed with a mixture of distaste and suspicion by many. However, those who have read it and discussed it seem to have replaced curiosity with compassion. If there was a message within it might have been that we ought to make allowances for those who have either failed at cricket as professionals or have otherwise left the game without really having been able to let go.

The research reading was extensive, and I endeavoured to write the case histories in an arm's-length fashion, nothing too maudlin, letting the stories tell themselves. I found that there are three classic forces behind most suicides: financial anxiety, marital/sexual problems, and health worries. And Jim Burke, the Australian batsman of the 1950s, was an example of a man who was afflicted with all three sources of depression at the same time. He coolly bought a gun, wrote a note and carried out his tragic deed, with friends left to rue the fact that Jim's problems would probably have dispersed in time. In his despair, he could never have been made to understand that. In any case, it was considered sadly typical of the Australian male that he would have been too embarrassed to talk his concerns over with his family or pals for fear of being branded weak.

The tally of cases known to me in 1990 – about 80 – was viewed as stunning. How much more so did it become after a lot of further cases were uncovered during the 20th Century? Some wonderful cricketers are on this darkest of lists: Stoddart, Faulkner, Iverson, Shrewsbury, Gimblett, Albert Trott, Sid Barnes, Leary, Zulch, Scotton, Relf, Joe Partridge, Creswell, Bill Bruce, Tom Wills, Noel Harford, and writers Berry Sarbadhikary and R.C.Robertson-Glasgow.

In 2001 I wrote a revised and updated edition, *Silence of the Heart.* The Cricketers Association had reacted to the alert and set about providing counselling for any players who were beset by depression, which was gratifying. It had not been easy to find humour to lift the recurring pall, but something from the priceless Dorothy Parker's pen brought a grim smile: *Razors pain you; rivers are damp; acids stain you and drugs cause cramp. Guns aren't lawful; nooses give; gas smells awful; you might as well live.*

CHAPTER TWENTY-ONE

The important thing is not to stop questioning.

ALBERT EINSTEIN

THE spring of 1991 was loaded with distraction. While Australia fought hard in the Caribbean, losing two Tests and winning one, a *WCM* Editorial caused a stir. I was awoken around six in the morning in my hotel room in Birmingham by BBC Radio and asked if I'd care to talk about my Editorial in an hour's time. But why? I asked. Ah, the man said, so it seemed I hadn't yet seen the *Daily Mirror*? As I said, I'd only just been woken up, and I never read that paper anyway. Would I mind if they rang me back after I'd seen the paper? Fine.

In essence, the *WCM* June Editorial had expressed a distinct lack of pleasant anticipation at the return of the West Indians for a series in England only three years after the last tour. Tired of the monotony and brutality of the day-long bouncer attack and slow over rate, I had exercised my right as a cricket-lover (and, I knew, on behalf of many, many others of the same viewpoint) to articulate a dislike of that kind of cricket. Five or six bouncers an over is violent cricket, and I said so. And vengeance is not such a rare commodity in international cricket, or even in the lowliest class of cricket for that matter. Clive Lloyd confirmed it, and so did Viv Richards, every time they explained how their experiences in Australia in 1975-76 hurt them and galvanised them. In a later television appearance, Lloyd, asked about my accusation of arrogance, replied that any team as good as the West Indies XI for that period of 15 years or so was 'entitled to be arrogant'. That was fair enough by me; but I was impatient with anybody who tried to tell me that it had been an unwarranted suggestion.

The Mirror's attack on the *WCM* editorial was wild and irresponsible. Reprinting 300 words from *WCM*, enough to warrant a sizable syndication fee (permission to quote from the magazine at such length had not been sought), the *Mirror* made another mistake in quoting with grievously sloppy inaccuracy. One of their reporters, Colin Price, wrote that the West Indians 'are accused of being vengeful, violent, arrogant and racist', a hugely clumsy and damaging misquote. Within days our lawyers were informing the editor of the *Daily Mirror* that I had been seriously libelled: it was totally untrue that I had accused West Indies cricketers of being 'racist'. An apology and retraction were demanded. Hereabouts things got slippery as the cowardly editor and sports editor both became 'unavailable', and before long, new names were being substituted.

Equally mischievous was the sidepiece in the *Mirror's* May 23 edition by Ted Corbett, who repeated the grotesque claim, in quotation marks that spuriously made it seem legitimate, together with a reaction from Clive Lloyd, who, along with numerous others, still had not read the original Editorial in *WCM* later that day when he was giving interviews. As someone I considered an old friend, I asked for a few minutes of his time. We had a gentle argument over the number of bouncers we felt was reasonable (yet again), and parted with a shrug apiece.

If the *Mirror* was so desperate to sell its newspapers in a fiercely competitive climate, why, I wondered, did they have to stoop to distortion? Corbett may have written his sidepiece with relish because I had relieved him of his *WCM* column a few weeks earlier after he had refused to let me see his copy. What might he have been trying to conceal in that article? I had to take the trouble, quite unnecessarily, to get my deputy to fax it from England to Sydney for perusal: absurd. Corbett was paid for the piece but it was never published. We had better use for our space than giving a page of tribute to one of his old journalist mates who, as far as I was concerned, was an unrivalled pain in the backside.

Down at the ground on the morning of the match at Edgbaston, I was asked to do several radio interviews. On Michael Parkinson's show he had a West Indian stating an unequivocal view: 'Mr Frith, you are a disgrace!' And then he went on to say that I would not be aware of Lindwall and Miller. What about them? Well, they bowled lots of bouncers at Everton Weekes in 1951-52. I pointed out that I was around at the time and remembered it clearly. It lasted perhaps 15 minutes. The West Indian bouncer fusillade which had made me and most other observers unhappy had been going on unchecked by hesitant umpires for over 15 *years*.

There was also a discussion on BBC Radio in which my old pal Tony Cozier spoke. Here, West Indies' senior commentator bemused me by going on and on about Patrick Patterson having once taken one wicket for over 100 runs in a Test match in Calcutta. So what?

The Cricketer hopped on the bandwagon – and fell painfully off it. Their conveniently unsigned 'Bouncer' column insinuated that *WCM* was part of

Robert Maxwell's 'ownership complex', which embraced the *Mirror*, and that the sensational splash had 'all the hallmarks of a set-up'. They had to apologise for that in print and pay substantial legal costs.

By now, lawyers were darting all over the place, and it seemed that Desmond Haynes was considering legal action against me for my criticism of him in an incident with Australian wicketkeeper Ian Healy in the recent Bridgetown Test. It was puzzling that, with over a dozen journalists and commentators having expressed serious concern at this players' confrontation, I was being singled out for possible litigation. Our counsel was shown a video-recording of the incident from my collection and instantly concluded that I was entitled to have expressed that opinion. The matter died, and it was reassuring to see a competitive but controversy-free England-West Indies Test series played out in 1991. Soon bouncers would at long, long last be rationed under the Laws of Cricket, and spin bowling made a comeback, to the indescribable relief of all who cherished the game. It only remained for West Indies to discover more Ramadhins and Valentines, and the world would be close to perfect.

As for 'Desi' Haynes, I saw him some time later and asked if he was prepared to sign a copy of his biography for me. 'Sure,' he said, 'you're my buddy.' I accepted that. It gladdened my heart.

In that spring of 1991, among the unsolicited articles that often found their way into *WCM* was one from a certain Robert Henderson, who looked at something termed 'national cricket identity'. England's sliding fortunes in international cricket were causing all kinds of excuses and theories to be tossed around. This one examined the composition of the England XI, allowing that birthplace in itself was unimportant but urging that a qualification for inclusion ought to be that a player had spent his childhood in England or had had a British upbringing abroad.

It was a mildly interesting viewpoint and analysis, and it generated little reaction: which is phenomenally strange when the explosive events of four years later come to be examined.

Only one major letter came in following the Henderson article of 1991. It was from Nasser Hussain's mother, who responded to the claim that her son had thought of himself as 'Indian' while for cricket purposes he considered himself 'English'. Mrs Hussain stated that her son had been 'grossly misquoted' in a *Daily Telegraph* interview by Rob Steen (August 1,1989). She stressed his pride in playing for England. She also pointed out that Nasser was one of the first cricketers to bring Norman Tebbit to book after his provocative Who Do They Cheer For At A Cricket Match article. Lest proof of her son's commitment be sought, she reminded everybody that he had given his all in the recent Antigua Test while nursing a broken wrist.

Otherwise, there was little reaction. We ran a letter from a Mr Rooum, who pointed out that Devon Malcolm and Gladstone Small received at least part of their education in England: 'They are English and no doubt proud to play for England, and any residual allegiance with their native countries is entirely compatible with this.' He then referred to players of South African origin, calling them 'mercenaries', and suggested that there should be a limitation at Test level along the lines of county cricket's restrictions on the overseas-born. The point he missed was that only England qualification regulations come into it, not birthplace.

Slight though the reaction was to this article by Henderson, it can be seen now as the seed of something unimaginable in due course.

Excessive bouncers, slow over rates, Test-match qualification: all heavy stuff that commentators on the game had to live with, in contrast to those lucky chaps who covered cricket years ago, when the worst worry was seasickness on the long and lovely cruises to farflung parts for the winter.

Hence the fervent desire to get away from it all whenever possible; and this summer I slipped in a few fun games of cricket between the league fixtures, the most unusual being at Burton Court, Chelsea, a match between a James McNeil Whistler XI and a John Ruskin XI to mark the centenary of the court case wherein the American artist sued critic Ruskin after he had written some harsh things about his work (though not in the *Daily Mirror*). Whistler was successful, but was awarded a mere farthing (quarter of a penny), so tempted had the judge been to accept the legitimacy of the criticism. We played in costume, and partook liberally of the drink laid on by the Chelsea Arts Club. After a sparkling glass or two, it was small wonder that I missed my first ball, twisted down by former Hampshire skipper Nick Pocock. I popped the next one into the bushes for six, just missing a Daimler, and then had to take off my false moustache, which kept slipping. I strode out to square leg and asked the umpire to hold the moustache, and for once that notorious gentleman, Jeffrey Bernard, was speechless. Ian Hutchinson belted a century, and Mike Hooper did likewise against us, mainly off me, for which he apologised, though I assured him that this was what I was there for. So many matches bring original experiences. Here, Ralph Cowan (Oxford Blue,1980-82) drove his first three balls for four, off the front foot, most unusual; and one of our bowlers released the ball while airborne, something I'd thought not only inadvisable but physically impossible.

Around this time I played for the Cricket Writers against a Melbourne touring team down at John Woodcock's village of Longparish, where another brand new experience awaited me: I'd never before been confronted by a herd of cows grazing in front of the sightscreen as I asked the umpire for guard. Vic Marks and I had a century stand that day, with very limited conversation between us. He was, of course, associated with *The Cricketer.*

Back on the battle-front. I was clearly still persona non grata with the West Indians. My old friend Gordon Greenidge glared and walked past me.

Lance Gibbs, the manager, gave me five minutes of discussion, but still seemed sore at the desultory over rate of England's spinners, Illingworth and Allen, way back in 1959-60. For the rest of the series I abandoned my custom of staying in the same hotels as the touring team.

England won the opening Test, with Graham Gooch carrying his bat for 154 through the second innings, a display that ranked with the finest batsmanship in Test history, for the opposition included Ambrose, Patterson, Marshall and Walsh, and there was something in the pitch for them. It had been 22 years since England had last beaten West Indies in England, so the feeling of having witnessed something exceptional was patent. In the same edition of *WCM* which covered this Test there was a letter from Robert Henderson in response to letters in the preceding issue. He referred to 'cultural belonging' and 'cricket patriotism'. Nobody seemed to take much notice.

The next crisis concerned the Cricket Writers Club. E.M.Wellings put together an article which picked up on a piece by Matthew Engel the preceding month concerning qualifications for CWC membership, with special concern about the 'he's in, he's not, he's in again' admission of Tim Rice. Wellings gave the historical background to the formation of the 'club' during the 1946-47 Ashes tour, and went on to condemn the election to membership of 'unqualified celebrities', the nepotism 'which I gather is still rife today', and officers who had used their positions for their own ends. He also expressed disgust that a second vote should have been allowed at a recent AGM, and advocated 'a new set of officers to sweep the stables clean'.

The secretary of the CWC wrote a challenging letter for publication in *WCM* by way of response, but before that could be published, the Wellings article was on the agenda for the CWC committee meeting during the Edgbaston Test match. We convened in a tiny room attached to the Press-box, and I looked up from my chair to find Chris Martin-Jenkins towering over me and Robin Marlar parked menacingly near the doorway. 'Why haven't you published the secretary's letter?' barked 'CM-J', like some deranged schoolmaster. From the doorway came Marlar's near- hysterical cry of 'Out, Frith! Out!'

What struck me as peculiarly ironic was that Martin-Jenkins himself had not been above flattering Wellings in trying to poach him for *The Cricketer*. 'I always think,' he had recently written to the 81-year-old writer, 'you lift *WCM* above the banal whenever you contribute.' He could never have expected that letter to be seen by another person, least of all me. Oh, dear, dear, dear.

Now 'CM-J', as far as I was concerned, had come by the chairmanship in a peculiar way. He had attended only one of the previous *seven* CWC committee meetings before taking over, and yet was named as the man to succeed Marlar in 1991. I was unable to identify the proposer or seconder. Thus the ever-expanding CWC hierarchy was extended, following three-year terms for Peter Smith, and then Brian Scovell, his fellow hack at the Daily Mail, and a four-year term for Robin Marlar. In reply to the question, I explained that the letter could hardly have been published before we had all had a thorough discussion on the matter, and that is why we were here now. When play began in the Test match, John Woodcock, CWC president, came over and asked gently whether I intended to resign. Of course not, I told him. What sense would that make?

The knock-on consequences were revealed a couple of years later when Scovell put up Jack Bannister, a relative newcomer to the ranks of the Cricket Writers Club, as prospective chairman, with me as the other candidate. Jack, a man of feverish ambition and force of character, won the ballot, so I was told, by one vote. That was the last time the committee was to vote on such a matter. Henceforth it was agreed that the membership should have a vote.

My hopes were renewed in 1996 when Bannister's time was up, though I was amused to contemplate one of the reasons put forth for his original selection: he would be taking the chair for the Cricket Writers Club's 50th anniversary dinner (which was staged almost a year early, in spite of my warning about this). As it happened, Jack Bannister did not turn up at that gala dinner in the Long Room at Lord's in the spring of '96 (when Jim Swanton and Sir Colin Cowdrey made admirable speeches).

I was not unduly surprised when, in 1996, another candidate to oppose me was found – Patrick Eagar, the photographer – and he would probably have succeeded Bannister had it been left to the committee, which, besides our two selves, consisted of Messrs Bannister, Hodgson, Lee, Martin-Jenkins, 'Toff' Lloyd, Bateman and Scovell, with treasurer Wendy Wimbush and president John Woodcock (who had put my name forward, bless him). I felt I might have enough support among the membership of 250 – as long as everyone voted.

They didn't. I was told that Eagar had twice as many of the votes cast. Far be it for me to believe that his support had been orchestrated. In his 'election statement', which referred to 11 books of his photographs, he said he once 'even filed a 1000-word match report from Lahore'.

So Patrick Eagar got the necessary majority, many votes doubtless from CWC members affiliated to *The Cricketer*, and the Oxbridge mafia, and from fellows who felt I was too Australian, or whose books maybe I'd reviewed, in their view, harshly. The CWC committee, I later reflected, could probably have blocked me out just by putting up Bill, the Irish steward who presided over the Lord's Press-box. Any anti- Frith candidate would serve. My name would never now go on that Cricket Writers Club office-bearers' board. Personality politics and power-play had won the day again. E.M.Wellings may just have been right about the old-boy network. I recalled, too, John Woodcock's response years before, when I had complained at the chaotic way in which the 'club' was being run: a shambles. 'But, David,' chortled

Wooders reprovingly, 'that's part of its charm!'

In the spring of 1997, I was flabbergasted and sort of touched to be elevated, along with Richie Benaud and Peter West, to honorary life membership of the Cricket Writers Club: kicked upstairs, as they say.

What am I doing here? The dinner was to honour an Old Boy of Canterbury High School. No, not me. Arthur Morris. Among the famous faces at Claridges that night were (back row) Ted Dexter, Michael Bentine, Brian Johnston, Peter May and Jim Swanton. Seated are Sir Roger Bannister, Trevor Bailey, Denis Compton, Sir Edward Heath, Sir Len Hutton, John Warr and Arthur Morris, and in front: Raphael Djanogly (our host), Sir Michael Marshall and David Lodge

In July 1991 there was a vote of immeasurably more significance at the International Cricket Council. South Africa were readmitted. Ali Bacher, for years the figurehead and so much more in his country's efforts to rejoin the world cricket community, understandably was moist-eyed before speaking on this notable occasion in the Long Room at Lord's. It had been 22 years and 122 days since Bacher's catch at Port Elizabeth had sealed off South Africa's membership among Test nations. Now, suddenly, there was an undignified scramble to arrange tours to and by South Africa.

There were other ICC motions of significance. The bouncer was to be restricted, beamers were to be called as no-balls, and international match referees and a code of conduct were to be introduced, a necessity but a sad commentary on the abject level of conduct in world cricket.

Robin Smith's grand 148 not out ensured a draw in the weather-hit Lord's Test, but West Indies drew level at Trent Bridge, where Richard Illingworth took a wicket with his first ball in Test cricket, extending that elite list to 11.

West Indies won again at Edgbaston, so England had to win the last Test, at The Oval, to square the series. And a memorable match it was, with another century from Smith and a second of the series for Richie Richardson. Botham fell over his stumps when destabilised by Ambrose, reducing Brian Johnston, Jonathan Agnew and most of the nation to tears of mirth; but it is Phil Tufnell's spell of teasing left-arm spin that stands out most. The bad lad of English cricket ruptured the visitors' first innings with a spell of 6 for 4. Viv Richards made 60 in the follow-on, his final Test innings, and on the fifth day Botham hit the winning runs, and an absorbing series was over, one which, to widespread satisfaction, had seen repairs made to the tattered image of Anglo-West Indian cricket.

Such is life. The exhilaration was soon overtaken by the uncertain feelings of English autumn: a reduction of pressure now that the bustle of the cricket season was over and the beauties of golden leaves were all around, but the prospect of long, dark, cold nights proved as distracting now as in those first English winters of the 1960s, when chunks of that Sydney newspaper were stuffed desperately into the gaps in the window-sashes.

This year had seen the passing of Freddie Brown, not everyone's favourite (John Arlott was certainly no great admirer) but a symbol of my first Ashes series of any seriousness, 1950-51, when he was no mere John Bull lookalike. He *was* John Bull.

And then, on December 14, what so many of us had dreaded for so long came to pass. His body and for that matter his mind unable to take any more, John Arlott slipped into eternity. I could only liken the loss to the falling of a great English oak, the landscape now bare. He had meant so much to me: voice of my boyhood years, presenter of the beloved game in the written word and, even more impressively, in spoken words which were warm, reassuring, shrewd, even existential. To have become a member of his inner circle for 20-odd years enhanced my life beyond measure.

After his 35 years on the circuit, John retired to Alderney in 1980, and thereafter we saw little of each other. The telephone was the link. And when his chest condition worsened, even phone-calls were not easy for him. Writing became a struggle, but nothing gave me more pleasure than to prepare his work, ridding it of any obvious confusions. Understandably he always seemed keen to write again about his favourites – Tate, Mead, Tennyson, Miller – and had little rapport with the modern game, a reaction which I now know to be a natural process: one gets less excited about today's 'sensational' deeds, for they will all soon be history, or perhaps even lost in time.

The afternoons and evenings spent with him in his 'Long Room' and in the snug in his cosy Alresford home, with the Hampshire fields spread all around us, had long been things of the past, as had the annual golf days and the Alresford Fair and the Christmas gatherings in Winchester, when Debbie joined the womenfolk. It was years since I had last driven him through English countryside, after a hot afternoon at the microphone and over the battered typewriter, or dined with him in a rural pub, always preferred to the noisy plastic palaces in the cities. Always people were coming up to speak, whether in those warm pubs or walking along the concourse of Waterloo Station, a quick glass of dry white on his mind even though his train would be pulling out in three minutes' time.

He had ceased to be active some years ago, and yet at least he was still there. And now he wasn't. I was the last to visit him from the mainland, three weeks before he died. No longer able to speak at any length, he had to sit, sometimes with the respirator on, and listen to others. When our eyes met, he'd give a crinkly smile and a wink that seemed to be saying 'I've done my share of talking; now you lot can all indulge yourselves.'

On that final visit, I took him for a drive around the craggy coastline of his beloved little island, settling near Fort Clonque, which was being lashed by a violent, grey, wintry sea. I poured us some brandy into polystyrene cups (there was no-one there to see and mock us).

'I shan't live much longer,' John said. It was like a needle in the heart to hear him say that. And yet it seemed certain not only that he knew what he was saying but that he had had enough of suffering and frustration. After our farewell handshake next morning at the little airfield, he looked straight ahead through the car windscreen, a diminutive figure now.

His son Tim rang me early on the morning of John's death, and I flew back to the island for the funeral, along with Ian Botham, Leo Harrison, Mike Brearley and John's anthologist and biographer David Rayvern Allen. Standing alongside the coffin in St Anne's Church, I thought of my own father, whose place John Arlott had taken for so many years, and I felt shame mixed with loneliness, and a faint despair at the challenge of repairing these holes that kept appearing in life's tapestry. Dad, following Mum long ago now, then Len Hutton, Freddie Brown, and all the men in uniform from their generation who helped save us and who are now featuring in newspaper obituaries almost daily. And now John.

Spirits lifted dramatically when we adjourned to the church hall to pass the three hours before departure and drink the copious quantities of red wine laid on by John's widow, Pat, and the boys. Then, and only then, could his presence be felt, the old smile restored to his face.

Finally, we were wedged into the quaint Trilander aircraft, Botham applying a playful stranglehold from the seat behind, the combined output of vinous breath probably stupefying the pilot. We rumbled down the runway, and as the small island vanished beneath us I reflected upon, of all things, a walk along Kogarah railway station in 1953, when I was humming Nat King Cole's *Somewhere Along the Way* while reading John Arlott's slim volume on Maurice Tate. It was then an innocent world, so full of promise – 'happy highways where I went and cannot come again' as A.E.Housman once put it. Years later, I had got John to inscribe that little book. 'Done in the evenings of one week from memory and affection,' he wrote. Memory and affection? Those things are probably the key to life.

CHAPTER TWENTY-TWO

Every new opinion, at its starting, is precisely in a minority of one.

THOMAS CARLYLE

OUR Queensland sojourn of 1991-92 was lengthy. Besides the restorative holiday weeks, I monitored the World Cup through television by day and evening, and by viewing highlights from other matches taped nocturnally, and by radio and newspapers. Some of it I witnessed 'live', with Pakistan seemingly out of it after defeat at the Gabba, when Jonty Rhodes did his famous horizontal Superman impression to run out Inzamam, and then the Sydney semi-final, when South Africa's luck ran out, rain at the climax producing an eventual requirement of 21 runs off the one ball remaining. Yet again, cricket's administrators went back to that sagging drawing-board.

Even though Australia were out of it, Melbourne was *en fête* for the final, many of the locals, it seemed to me, wanting Pakistan to beat England. A Royalist v Republican feud had been developed during the season, and Botham and Gooch had walked out on a 'comedy' skit at the eve-of-final function, objecting to Gerry Connelly's 'drag' impression of the Queen. 'Beefy' had even worked out a way of numbing the hordes of barrackers in some of England's earlier World Cup matches: he simply held his wrists aloft as if manacled. From one convict to another, as he once inscribed a book for me. If you'd have suggested that one day he'd become Lord Botham you'd have been laughed at.

It was Gooch's spilling of a catch from Imran, a difficult diving affair, together with Botham's dismissal, given caught off his forearm, that swung the World Cup final as much as the madly bending deliveries from Wasim Akram. From the awesome MCG arena we went afterwards to the interview room and listened to Imran Khan as he explained how he had won the World Cup, how he had told his men to feel like 'cornered tigers', and how he was now hopeful that there would be enough money forthcoming for the completion of his cancer hospital in Lahore.

As always, it was sublime to feel the aircraft losing height as the Gold Coast and wooded hills came into view. A few more days' relaxation with Debbie, then back to chilly England and the backlog and the demanding season ahead. I brought back with me some delectable stuff written by Gilbert Mant, who was almost 90 and the sole survivor from the press-box during the 1932-33 Bodyline series. I *almost* brought, too, some interesting material from Barbara, wife of Australia's elegant batting maestro W.A.Brown. She was giving me all the gossip – brilliant stuff it was – about the players of the 1930s, and some of the wives, when Bill returned, and said in his droll way: 'Now what are you telling this chap, Barbara?' Nervous laughter all round, and we concentrated on the match now being played.

I had invited dreamy Frank Keating onto the *WCM* Editorial Board, for he was a writer of felicitous touch and wide experience, and he also happened to be a friend of long standing who had been constantly and loyally supportive of the magazine. It was as strong an editorial team as ever, with Jack Bannister full of energy and ideas as his journalistic and broadcasting career developed apace.

But any hopes of a stable summer were soon dashed as ball-tampering accusations against the Pakistan fast bowlers soured the air around us. When, after a classic Lord's Test, there was a flare-up at Old Trafford when Aqib Javed was found guilty of intimidation towards England's No.11, Devon Malcolm, unhappiness spread, tempers were lost, and the lawyers were centrestage yet again.

The match referee at Old Trafford was Conrad Hunte, the humanitarian former West Indies opening batsman, and although he was governed by the ICC's code of confidentiality, he might have defused the situation had he demystified it, even just slightly. It had become known that he had issued a polite warning to the England players about their behaviour, but this misguided attempt at even-handedness simply inflamed the local players, who had said or done nothing controversial. The Pakistanis were upset and expressing themselves by word and gesture after umpire Roy Palmer's warning to Aqib, who claimed that Palmer did not hand him back his sweater in a proper manner at the end of the over. And still Hunte maintained his silence.

A Heaven-sent opportunity to develop this story presented itself a day or two later, for Conrad Hunte was due to play for a touring Georgia team at my club, Godalming (the founder of the American state, James Oglethorpe, came from this little Surrey town). Hunte, now 60, made that many runs, in the same methodical way that we saw in the 1960-61 series in Australia, and he was as sociable as ever in the clubhouse in the evening. I asked him what measures had been taken or would be taken after the unpleasantness at Old

Trafford, and why. True to the binding terms of his ICC appointment, he gave nothing weighty away, but he did explain why he had cautioned the Englishmen. He said he had detected signs that they were losing patience, and he felt the matter might have escalated had he not 'cooled' them.

The atmosphere for the series was now sprinkled with cordite, and there seemed little hope that it could all be pacified, for the newspapers had the bit between their teeth. Among the more respected writers, Simon Heffer so let himself go as to classify the Pakistanis as cricket's new 'pariahs', taking over that role from the South Africans. It was around now that I began to suspect that the Foreign and Commonwealth Office must have had a quiet word in the ears of the game's rulers at Lord's. After all, that sort of government intervention had happened when the provocation was scarcely worse than this back in the days of Bodyline.

A smooth Test at Headingley was called for. We didn't get it. Another highly impressive century by Gooch gave England a first-innings advantage, and England eventually faced a target of only 99 in the fourth innings. Atherton and Smith were out with 27 on the board, and Gooch was given not-out when well short of the crease. His departure would have rattled England seriously. He batted for a further 24 overs. Gower's cool 31 not out saw his side home by a misleading six-wicket margin.

Of course, the unfortunate Gooch decision had to dominate coverage of the final day of the Test in the papers and in *WCM*, where I wrote: 'The crusade for the adoption of television assistance for umpires' line decisions took a giant step forward . . .' Oddly enough, I had spent a lot of time during this match in the company of the umpires, who were staying at the same hotel, and as we sipped and chatted through the evening, I was enthralled to hear the trade talk and glad to make some occasional input of my own. It transpired that Don Oslear, the reserve umpire, was keen on my idea of TV assistance. Merv Kitchen was unconvinced. And Ken Palmer, who reprieved Gooch, was dead set against it. When he looked back on this incident, however, he started to see the virtues of having somebody watching a monitor 'upstairs' and relaying to him down on the field of play the golden truth that was now openly available to millions of viewers at home. It might just be that the unruly gathering of Pakistan supporters who awaited him when he returned to the hotel (in a car bearing his name on the side) helped Palmer to see the point.

It wasn't just that run-out miscarriage that upset the Pakistanis. They were by now suspicious of every lbw and bat-pad decision that went against them, and I began to wonder if there was any future for Anglo-Pakistan cricket, so hostile had mutual feelings become.

Suspicion also raged in certain sections of the England team and the English Press. Were Pakistan's bowlers gouging the ball? How come it suddenly began to swing so much when worn, having moved little while new, traditionally the premium time? Limitations imposed by the Laws forced many to hint, flash their eyes, and weave innuendoes, but some TV footage materialised, and those close to the action exuded some strong convictions. Then, in amazing circumstances, I had a close-hand sniff or two myself.

The Texaco Trophy matches that wound up the tour included one at Lord's which ran into a second day, August 23, 1992. Pakistan won thrillingly by three runs, and then many of us hurried to our vehicles for the long drive to Manchester for the next match, which started next day. The M1, even well out of London, was clogged-up and fuming, with jam upon jam, so I desperately broke off westwards into unknown country, Shropshire or anywhere. It was a relief to be lost in such pretty countryside. The Beach Boys and Roy Orbison had seen me through most of this awful journey, and it was only when on the outskirts of Manchester that I switched over to radio and heard of a 'sensation at Lord's'; and it was not the three-run margin they were talking about.

So when I walked into the Copthorne to check in, and saw Ian and Kathy Botham in the lounge-room by the bar, I said to him, 'What's all this about a sensation at Lord's?' 'Sit down,' commanded my old pal. He explained with a tale that has now become fairly familiar to readers of Allan Lamb's 'exposé', which cost him so much, not only in terms of cash: the ball rolling down the pitch, Lamb's spotting of what he believed to be gouge-marks, his referring the matter to one umpire, who was not all that interested, then to the other, who was; the replacement of the ball and the smokescreen that swiftly enveloped everything.

This left the ICC referee, Deryck Murray this time, in an awkward position. If he said the ball was changed because it had been tampered with, all Hell would have exploded. If, on the other hand, it had been changed because it was merely out of shape, why did he not say so, and defuse the situation? (We later learned that his official statement, when finally issued, had been edited.)

After the Old Trafford one-dayer, at the Texaco reception, I went across to Derryck Murray, whom I had known since the 1973 West Indies series. Why did he not tell the media that it was an innocent ball-change, because of its shape? Before he had even begun to smile that pleasant smile and light the twinkle in those eyes that had once seen 22 catches into his gloves in a Test series, I knew he could not answer this conundrum of a question without either lying or blowing cricket sky-high.

That evening, Channel 4 transmitted a programme recorded a few days earlier. It was an edition of *Devil's Advocate*, and when they invited me to share the 'hot seat' with Trevor Bailey, I agreed to do so, though had I known about the 'court-room' format I might well have declined. It was a trap, with some bear-baiting about it.

We sat beneath an array of red lights, and the studio audience consisted of a bank of seats to the left, peopled by white folk, and to the right, where Asian and West Indian folk included Clive Lloyd and Haseeb Ahsan. The interrogator was the burly Trinidadian Darcus Howe, known as the 'sage of Brixton', and also known to have a way with words (of Imran Khan he once said 'there's a kind of innocent stupidity about him'). The show started with some film clips of unhappy scenes on the cricket field, and then some condemnation of excerpts from *WCM* Editorials across the years.

Then came the first postulation: that England and Australia can't stand third-world countries beating them. Aqib's bouncer attack on Devon Malcolm at Old Trafford seven weeks earlier was featured – and defended. When I could get a word in I ventured that there were people in this studio this evening who used to be able to bowl fast, and it was more than their honour was worth to try to knock a man's head off at No.11. But, said Howe, Malcolm was not helpless. 'Come on,' I said, 'we both know that he can't bat!' I was fed up already.

'I don't think anybody wants to kill anyone,' said Clive Lloyd feebly, before challenging me on what I had thought when Willis went round the wicket and bounced one into the teeth of Pakistan nightwatchman Iqbal Qasim in 1978. I said it had sickened me; but I wanted to return to the main issue, to discuss the forty batsmen that West Indies' fast bowlers had sent to hospital in the past 17 years. I was drowned out.

Fred Trueman now emerged from the left side of the audience and thundered that there was no need to bowl short at tailenders. 'If you can deliver the yorker, which 90 per cent of fast bowlers today cannot, you don't have to bowl short. Knock their stumps over!'

Towards the end of the segment I had a chance to throw the challenge back at the 'prosecution'. Howe made an accusation: 'You represent the kind of bulldog mentality that would not respect the elevation of these people [third world].' While I would not wish to disown the bulldog reference – was quite grateful for the Churchillian allusion actually – I was not having it that I did not appreciate good cricket if it was the work of non-English or non-Australian players. That was racist talk, and beneath contempt.

'You couldn't have said a thing like that if you'd known me,' I told Darcus Howe, having to lift my voice to pierce the mocking jeers coming from the right flank. 'Some of my best mates over the 20 years that I've been involved have come from what you call the third-world countries, non-white countries. I think too many people from those countries have a hang-up that the moment someone from Australia or England criticises West Indies, India, Pakistan, Sri Lanka cricket it's got to have deeper motives. In other words, we can only criticise people from the "white" countries. Is that what we are supposed to do?'

Howe cried, 'No, no, no! . . .' but was drowned out by encouraging applause from the *left* side of the studio, which seemed to have woken up at last.

When it was Trevor Bailey's turn he chose to try to humour his inquisitor and audience, but he played and missed a few times. 'I never toured Pakistan. I think I was *probably* [pause] fortunate.' He then went on to express amazement at how the Pakistan bowlers made the old ball swing. Howe: 'Are you suspicious?' Bailey was cautious. Fred Trueman then re-entered the fray with a very reasonable: 'I would like to sit down with Wasim and Waqar and say, now come on, as old fast bowlers, tell me how you do it!' He was heckled from the opposing flank of the audience, so there was only one thing for it: tailenders or not, they had to have a bouncer: 'And if you lot want to start talking about umpiring with that load of rubbish you've got in Pakistan . . .'

Murray Hedgcock's crisp voice came near the end with the nearest thing we were going to get to a reasonable summing-up: 'What David and Trevor and all of us who love the game surely are saying is, it's not a matter of a country which is a country we dislike or which consistently misbehaves. It's a matter of an individual cricketer, an individual team, at a particular time misbehaving.'

I was 10 miles down the A3 that night before the uproar faded from my ears.

Then, of course, it was time for another heartfelt Editorial, this time on the ball-tampering allegations. All around us was fury and muddled thinking. As with the intimidation debate over the years, people seemed to have overlooked the crucial fact that umpires had the power to deal with the problem. The worry was that they were not necessarily backed by the game's authorities.

The principal topic of conversation now concerned what could be done, in secret, to a cricket ball. And I had my own private demonstration from a county bowler, who picked the quarter-seam on both sides, stressing the need to point the 'shark's fin' backwards, and to press the fins back with the butt of the hand after four balls.

Umpires now scrutinise the ball at regular intervals during play, and the hubbub has faded. It was a pleasure to see Anglo-Pak relations repaired during the 1996 series.

Later that year we had to run two major obituaries, one of them actually a 'scoop'. Bill O'Reilly died after several miserable years of being homebound, and was given a big send-off by most publications. I got what I could into three pages, noting that he believed that 'the English couldn't handle legspin so they decided to destroy it'.

The final quote came from Len Hutton (while we were filming *Golden Great Bowlers*: he rang me next day to ask if I really thought his fee reasonable; Ray Lindwall, meanwhile, had said he would have contributed for nothing). Sir Len said: 'Every time that ball left his hand it was O'Reilly's intention to get somebody out.'

'Tiger' probably was the Greatest (vying with S.F.Barnes). The quote I liked best of all came from the *Sydney Morning Herald's* Greg Growden: 'He stressed to me bush basics, like being your own man, always standing up to your convictions, and being honest in life and on the written page.'

A month earlier, in September 1992, E.M.Wellings had died, having sworn his wife to keep the news from all but myself until his ashes had been scattered in the English Channel. I went to the funeral at Aldershot, and was asked as we entered the chapel if I would say a few words. Now Lyn Wellings was probably the most provocative and unpopular cricket-writer in the history of the game, so the request imposed difficulties. I collected my jumbled thoughts as best I could, and addressed the congregation, which consisted of three people plus the vicar. Evelyn Maitland Wellings, I told them, was a man of uncompromising views, who loved cricket and respected it deeply and always fought to protect it. Of necessity, I kept it short.

Wellings: provocative

Two strong-minded figures gone in a month. The world was changing.

'Accurate umpiring at last!' That was the exuberant headline on the January 1993 edition of *WCM*, alongside a picture of Cyril Mitchley examining a TV replay in the Durban Test match in which Sachin Tendulkar became the first batsman to be adjudged run-out after the third umpire had scrutinised the replay. It was a happy time for someone who had been preaching the virtues of this system for a decade. No more miscarriages of justice, no more dissent – on run-outs and stumpings at least. In this respect the game was now immensely improved.

My first look at South Africa on the Test field for 27 years came with a visit to Cape Town, reached on New Year's Day 1993. It was the slowest Test match in history (1.83 runs per over, though Steven's proofreading, for once, let me down: '1.83 runs per *hour*'!; but we had an intelligent readership, and they must have known . . .). The slowness didn't matter to me. I had never expected to see South Africa return to Test cricket, not until well into the 21st Century at any rate. Straight off the aircraft, I had played for India in the 'Press Test' at scenic Uitsig, keeping wicket without pads, then, properly protected, facing Robin Jackman: a single to third man.

We had Sunil Gavaskar with us, but again he disappointed with the bat. I should have played in the previous media match. He scored 130.

One evening we had the experience of a lifetime in cable-carring to the top of Table Mountain; on another, Allan Lamb and Denys Hobson were our leaders down to the Waterfront, a huge bar by the water that reminded me of Sydney; and then Graham Barlow, late of Middlesex and England, took me out to his little spread at Franschhoek.

From there, via Harare, to Perth, for welcome hours with elder son, then Adelaide, to see The Don, and hand him the 1864-78 facsimile *Wisdens*, and enjoy some more stimulating conversation and a kind of living newsreel that had to end, dammit. He made it clear, again, that it annoyed him that I would not support his campaign to revert to the back-foot no-ball law, but the charming Jessie steered the discussion into less turbulent waters. DGB drove me sedately down to Adelaide Oval, a slow and somehow royal chariot ride, which even now I can scarcely believe happened. Legend of legends, this elderly but wiry man caused me to commit a slight excess: 'To hear that distinctive voice now is to hear an overlaid echo of the sensational young Australian talking to the newsreel camera in 1931, or the revered Test captain addressing a high-powered gathering at a London club in 1948. To see the venerable Don in his armchair, full-face or in distinctive profile, is to cross-pollinate with visions of the fresh-faced kookaburra who tore the flesh off English bowlers.'

I gave Matthew Engel plenty of magazine space as he jostled his way to the head of the group concerned at the ICC's attempt to delete retrospectively first-class centuries scored during the disapproved tours of South Africa in the 1980s. He then explained the changes he had made in the soon-to-be-published *Wisden Cricketers' Almanack*, changes which traditionalists were bound to regard as unnecessary and unwelcome.

But the biggest change of all was upon us. In the May 1993 edition of *Wisden Cricket Monthly*, which heralded the arrival of Border's Marauders, and in which I did a long interview with feisty 1948 tourist Sam Loxton (now a Gold Coast neighbour), there was a picture of the new owner of John Wisden & Company, J.Paul Getty jnr KBE. In the official announcement it was stated that his acquisition 'was prompted by his deep affection for the game coupled with a desire to ensure that the Wisden tradition is maintained.' Five pages further on was a news par to the effect that *WCM*'s editor had received a Highly-Commended award from the Sports Council. An intriguing juxtaposition. I was most gratified.

CHAPTER TWENTY-THREE

I believe that the able industrial leader who creates wealth and employment is more worthy of historical notice than politicians or soldiers.

J.PAUL GETTY I

'AND how long have you been with the magazine?' The question took me by surprise, for the man who benignly asked it was none other than J.Paul Getty jnr, who had recently purchased John Wisden & Company and had surely read through the bulky disclosure document, or at least had his accountant explain the vitals to him. (In turn, upon learning of the purchase, I had made it my business to read Robert Lenzner's disturbing book on the Getty clan; a Queensland hillside was as good a place as any to flip the pages.)

'As a matter of fact,' I replied, with what I hoped was a tone of mild amusement, 'I launched *Wisden Cricket Monthly* 14 years ago today.' It was the first day of April.

I was later to pick up a rumour that JPG thought he had bought just the *Almanack*, and the magazine came as a surprise extra. But then everything hereabouts had seemed wreathed in secrecy. I had no reason not to be looking forward with pleasure to the new regime, for the understanding seemed to be that JPG cared about cricket and its traditions, and saw Wisden as an institution that needed ongoing protection.

Paul Getty, then 60, was said to be worth £1.6-billion, which probably returned him growth of around half-a-million quid a day. Small wonder that he felt impelled and free to endow all kinds of causes. Who, in that situation, would not feel good after having disbursed large amounts of lolly?

It was a time of conflicting emotions for me and my small staff, for while the prospect of having such monstrous wealth behind the company was exciting, bemusing, reassuring, any hopes that salaries might be elevated a little after years of enforced monetary restraint were pinned to the dangerous backdrop that the world would *assume* this was to be the case anyway, perhaps even to the point of excess. Ill-feeling could also be generated among contributors (who might now expect appreciably higher payment) and among readers (who could want even more pages and a reduction in the magazine's cover price).

As it turned out, there never was any danger that I would be lavishly rewarded for my efforts: during the three years of Getty ownership, my pay was increased by 8 per cent overall. Every member of our small staff had all kinds of light-headed visions of new horizons. The reality was something very different.

The weeks preceding completion of the purchase had been fraught with anxiety. The *Wisden* offices in Guildford were crawling with accountants, and one of them was overheard by one of the staff as she made a phone-call to Ben Brocklehurst, of all people.

That had us speculating that *WCM* might be about to be merged with *The Cricketer*, a prospect that induced nausea. So I asked what was going on, again and again in the months ahead. But straight replies were not forthcoming, and that increased the anxiety, even though we had been assured, through my departing fellow directors, that the employment of all of us would be secure.

Having tried to put Paul Getty fully in the picture as far as the magazine's foundation and history were concerned, I gave him a few of my books. It was a simple courtesy gesture, to show him what, in modern parlance, I was all about. I recognise that this was wide open to misinterpretation, but he fondled the deluxe *Pageant of Cricket* like a true bibliophile, and chuckled at the sight of the *England v Australia pictorial history*: 'Brian Johnston told me I should have this one. Now I shan't need to go out and buy it!'

Having drained the expensive teacup brought by the butler, I sensed it was time to go. It was early springtime in Green Park, and I felt it might just be a fresh springtime for my beloved magazine.

But how come there were no board meetings, no communications between owners and the Wisden office – except, as I soon discovered, with Chris Lane, the office manager? Still in his twenties (and now styling himself 'Christopher'), he had been hired in 1988, and soon proved to be an unusually self-contained individual, scarcely brimming with charm or humour, irredeemably unshiftable in his opinions, and possibly harbouring journalistic aspirations. He took umbrage at my suggestion that he should remove sensitive material from general view when the Merrow office was about to shut for the night, and bridled at the remark that we did not need outside help to cope with a surge of orders following a back-issues promotion. I'd forgotten, of course, that not everyone was prepared to roll up the sleeves and stay at a tough job until it was done, never panicking, refusing to acknowledge tiredness.

Chris Lane was a talented cricketer, but when we played in a publishers' match at The Oval, and we had to get rid of just one more higher-order batsman to be through the opposition, he somewhat irrationally wanted to save his final two overs until the very end, when, he assured me, he'd get this chap out. 'But by then,' I pointed out, 'he'd probably have 150 to his name!' So he was coaxed into bowling his last two overs now, in a win-or-lose gamble (we had no other bowlers), and the batsman duly holed out at midwicket without further ado. They then collapsed, and we won with some ease. But all I got from Chris Lane was the cold eye. In fact I can't recall him ever smiling.

His preference was golf, anyway, and he was soon making it clear that he wouldn't be playing any more cricket. It was therefore surprising to hear that he had been lured to play at the Getty ground, on the owner's 3000 acres at Wormsley, together with Steven and our ad-man Colin. I was not invited. Same went for a dinner at Lord's. I recognised the cold shoulder, but couldn't comprehend its cause or significance.

Graeme Wright also went to that dinner. His role was interesting. He had worked for Wisden for just about as long as I had, edited the Almanack from 1987 to 1992, and was now a member of the new Wisden management committee, alongside J.P.Getty, Mark Getty, Richard Charkin (Reeds International), Matthew Engel, company secretary Malcolm Ridley, Chris Lane and myself. The gentle rustle of flexing egos was a familiar sound around that table. Wright later resigned, but was enticed back. My most vivid image of him now was the one seen through my binoculars from the Lord's Press-box as he attended to the needs of none other than B.G.Brocklehurst, owner of The Cricketer, in the Getty box during the 1994 Test match, to my unblinking amazement.

It was in that Mound Stand box that I sat watching a county match with Paul Getty, Matthew Engel and sundry others, including Mick Jagger, when some question concerning published material came up, and Wisden's new owner made a classic remark: 'I never interfere with my editors!' Well, that was reassuring.

All the same, it was disconcerting to learn that Graeme Wright was embarking on some sort of survey of the magazine, from which he prepared a paper. After reading the draft, which I found ominous, I composed a response, and since he seemed to think poorly of almost everything about *WCM*, its editorial balance, its range of contributors, its design, its typefaces, my response was firmly worded. Going down in the lift after the meeting, Richard Charkin said to me, 'I really felt for you in there.' So I was not yet totally isolated.

The magazine may not quite have been torn to shreds, but the analysis was uncomplimentary on almost every front. Acknowledging a couple of points that had some merit, I adopted them. But readers of a successful and thoughtfully-prepared magazine do not like mass change. It's unsettling. And the latest survey from readers, in July 1993, had produced another resounding vote of approval.

Still there were gnats around the flame. When Peter Hayter (son of Reg) took it upon himself to evaluate the various cricket magazines in a BBC Radio programme, he slipped over in the greasy pool of national identity by remarking absurdly that it was a pity that *WCM* couldn't have been edited by an Englishman.

It was impossible not to notice that Matthew Engel was often feverishly engaged in keeping the new owner amused. I thought he came dangerously near the knuckle during an early meeting when, in comparing the limp-cover and hardback versions of *Wisden Cricketers' Almanack*, he drew an analogy with hard and soft drugs. But whimsicality was the keynote. With wit and morsels of ostensible publishing wisdom he elicited indulgent beams from Getty father and son.

Mark Harris Getty, who for all I knew had been given the magazine by his father as some kind of plaything, seemed to have taken an instant dislike to me. Completely against the run of play in the first management meeting, he addressed me bluntly on the subject of employing somebody to conduct a marketing survey of the magazine. And when my very capable deputy sensed his role was being undervalued and that he was sliding down the ranks, he wrote politely to Mark Getty, and as weeks passed without a response, he grew quite concerned. Colin was also worried. So I spoke up feelingly for my loyal little staff, and knew I had lost more ground as a result. It seemed to be another case of principals who preferred to surround themselves with fawning yes-men rather than develop a team concept. That first Christmas all the staff got bonuses – except me.

Morale was plummeting. One employee had been made 'king', the same one the previous chairman and I had privately agreed was the most easily replaceable member of staff, the one with the least specialist knowledge and experience. Our cottage industry, it seemed, was being trampled underfoot by 'big business' thinking, against a background of that age-old conflict of the Creative versus Business. Each nonsensically felt threatened by the other. To worsen matters, it soon emerged that the company secretary, Malcolm Ridley, was a close acquaintance of Richard Hutton, who was now editor of his father-in-law's magazine, *The Cricketer.* The air was clouded by insecurity. The plot, as they say, was thickening.

Much of the time it was as if I didn't exist. Just about all the discussion at Wisden meetings revolved around the Almanack. There was much salivation as the reviews of the 1994 *Wisden* were passed around. Promotional ideas and expenditure were debated, while the magazine, which still had to fight its fierce monthly battle against rival titles, barely came under discussion. At the last gathering I attended there was absolutely no call for me to speak or make any contribution; so I decided late in 1995 that I would resign from the management committee. Events were to overrun that intention.

I gave Mark Getty the benefit of the doubt back in 1993 when he rang me on the eve of my departure for Australia and, without warning, said he'd had papers drawn up for the sale of my stake in Wisden Cricket Magazines Ltd and wished me to sign them before departure. I wondered if he was joking, but when I heard how unrealistic was the offer I was stung. Debbie and I flew to Queensland in a very distracted state of mind.

Correspondence ensued. M.H.Getty was at last prepared to write to me. I sought a sensible (though anything but excessive) figure for my shares, though I didn't really want to sell, and at one point even asked if I could buy them out. I could have raised an appropriate sum for purchase through a couple of cricket-loving friends. But over the years, *WCM* had fed a great deal of money into Wisden's coffers by way of royalties. The agreement would collapse if the parent company were to have demanded a doubling or trebling of the royalty percentage. It was probably a relief when Mark Getty said they were not interested in selling.

We eventually agreed a figure for the disposal of my shares in February 1995, and that was that. I was no longer a shareholder, which saddened me, though in all truth I had reservations about the long-term future of cricket magazines, for a range of reasons.

Still I could get no guarantee that the Gettys were going to retain and develop *WCM* or that my job as editor was safe. On June 14, 1994, I concluded a long letter to Mark (copy to his father) thus: 'Let me offer you the assurance that, health permitting, it is my hope and intention to continue to serve *WCM* in the same multiplicity of ways and with the same commitment of time and effort that have kept it successful for over 15 years.'

Three months later I received a letter from Paul Getty stating that our bookkeeper Chris Lane was now 'managing director' of *WCM*, and Steven Lynch was now a member of my Editorial Board. I had no prior knowledge of any of this. I was still a director, but evidently in name only.

The pressing need was for the show to go on. Chris Lane dwelt in his ivory tower, with its direct line to M.H.Getty; Steven was pleased to be on the Editorial Board but rueful of the reality that it wouldn't buy any extra bread; and Colin, the only family man among them, was still worried. All this time, the readership could never be permitted to pick up even the faintest whiff of the undermining of morale. Once again, only my longsuffering Debbie knew of the anguish radiating from her husband's being, a cauldron of anxiety and mystification, distracting almost beyond endurance. It felt like constructive dismissal in the offing, so I asked, in a letter, if this might be so. No answer. So much for all the initial joy and expectancy.

Just where was Mark Getty getting his information, and how was he forming his opinions from afar? Why was I being cast as a pariah? Why did Matthew Engel insinuate that the onus of blame was on me for the 'personality clash' with Mark Getty? What was being said behind closed doors? This was not my game.

In another sense, it wasn't Mike Atherton's either. When I asked him how he'd enjoyed a practice game at Wormsley, he simply said, 'Talk about grovel!' He had quickly picked up on the ambient flavours.

I began to wonder seriously where J.Paul Getty stood in all this obfuscation that was enveloping Wisden, and so I wrote a plea to him to resolve the situation. Why had his son adopted this line? I was invited up for 'tea and a chat'. Looking more than ever like the older Frankie Laine, he made a note or two. Whether the paper slipped down the side of the sofa I know not, but nothing came of it.

At that last management committee meeting, Paul entered the room, sat in the vacant chair next to me, and stroked my back as he greeted me. Wow, this was all right! I must simply have imagined all the freeze-out of the past two years? Perhaps they had only been teasing?

In reality, I couldn't reconcile how a man like this could save *The Literary Review*, plough £50-million into the National Gallery, £20-million into the British Film Institute, £3-million into the Mound Stand at Lord's, £1-million for Hereford Cathedral's Mappa Mundi, and Lord knows what else, but still could not come straight out and say: 'Look, my son's not comfortable with you around. You started up a good cricket magazine and gave it 16 years of your life, without taking a day off sick (you lucky creep). With my *Cricketer* friendships, you're an embarrassment to me. I have a very efficient little genius on hand who already edits the senior publication, the *Almanack*, so here, pay off your mortgage, invest the rest, and enjoy your retirement.'

There was something likeable about JPG – his apparent tranquillity perhaps – but overall I felt disappointment of soul-destroying magnitude. He couldn't be as ruthless as *his* old man, surely? Back in 1956, when I was a young airman wooing my Queensland sweetheart, J.Paul Getty II was an underfunded petrol pump attendant in a Tidewater uniform, working for his half-brother George in America. We could probably have talked and understood each other then. Now, almost 40 years later, we sat in the same room but were planets apart. At various times I had put proposals to him: that he might help the Bradman Museum and Trust, finance an ambitious film history of cricket, buy for himself an early artistic gem featuring White Conduit Fields; and I expressed an opinion that the diaries and watercolours of Felix (Nicholas Wanostrocht) would be eminently worth publishing. All these ideas were rejected or ignored. A rare cricket film which I copied for him on video was never acknowledged.

Perhaps an early *faux pas* was the problem: I'd innocently asked him if he'd like me to bring a Press XI to play at Wormsley, to help fill his fixture list. 'That's the last thing I'd want,' he gasped. Of course. Then again, might he have been miffed that his pal Mick Jagger had been ejected from the Lord's Press-box a few years ago while a guest of mine? Surely not?

I could have given Paul Getty fairly intelligent cricket talk all day and half the night. Who had poisoned the atmosphere? By late 1995 I was past caring.

CHAPTER TWENTY-FOUR

Sisyphus was basically a happy man

ALBERT CAMUS

SO the 'famous' *Wisden* went on its refashioned, well-promoted, profit-making, once-a-year way, while the magazine month by month fought for its place in the market, having a large band of loyal regular readers after all these years but still facing competition from other cricket magazines, expanded newspaper coverage, and even cricket 'magazines' on television and in video form. I still had a feeling that we were at the forefront of all this because of a quality I could best describe as 'soul'. The founder/editor had devoted his life to cricket, and appreciated the game in a multi-faceted way. The pages reflected this, not least in the matter of depth: history where it was entertaining or significant, enlightening the young and striking nostalgic chords with the older readers; and unfettered handling of the many – too many – problems facing the game, particularly the English game.

The visit of the Australians helped get me through 1993. I'd hoped for a tight Ashes series, but again Border's men were superior in so many ways. They touched dizzy heights at Lord's. Taylor, Slater and Boon made hundreds, and Mark Waugh, at No.4, missed out by one run when Tufnell bowled him. First four in the order making centuries would have been unique. Poor Atherton also made 99, slipping as he turned and suffering a long-drawn-out nightmare as the ball zoomed in from Merv Hughes to Healy's gloves. Not only was it Australia's heaviest defeat of England in that they lost only four wickets throughout the match, but they did it with 10 men, 'Billy' McDermott having been rushed to hospital with a mystery stomach ailment which soon had him on a flight home to Queensland. The players kept a cardboard cut-out of him on the team bus and in the dressing-room, and Merv picked up the extra load despite his bad knee, never complaining.

'Two sides in it now' was the optimistic headline I constructed as a kind of wish fulfilment after England had drawn well at Trent Bridge, though they should not have let Steve Waugh and Brendon Julian hold out on that final day. Graham Thorpe made a century here on Test debut, and Nasser Hussain also looked the real thing. It was Thorpe's achievement that brought out the worst kind of national dualism in me yet again, for while I felt much at home with the Australians – we had some memorable evenings at the bar, players and journalists – I recognised Thorpey as a kind of neighbour too, for he and his brothers came out of Farnham, just down the Hog's Back from Guildford, and I had played against most if not all of them. Such nice blokes too, and I remain prone to allowing that to colour the issue.

This propinquity factor got worse in the next Test, at Headingley, for my young Guildford team-mate of the mid-1980s, Martin Bicknell, won his first England cap. All the wishing in the world was pointless, for the tall, tall colt took 1 for 155. 'AB' made 200 not out and Steve Waugh 157 not out, and their fifth-wicket stand of 332 was second only to the 405 marked up by Bradman and Barnes at Sydney in 1946-47. It was odd, therefore, to hear Border, late that night, saying how distressed he was at Neil Harvey's constant criticism of him. The Australian skipper ought, at that moment, to have been the happiest man alive, for the Ashes had surely been retained again. But he wasn't. And Ian Chappell was trying very forcefully to get it across to him that he was as pathetic as Harvey if he was going to go on taking that garbage seriously.

Chappell, of course, was always unstoppable when he had a point to make. One evening in Leeds I went out for a bite with him and his brother Greg, David Gower and Allan Border, and I cued Greg for that great anecdote about the clumsy Ashley Mallett getting on a flight and knocking his drink over, which turned out to be a good move, since he'd just accidentally set light to his newspaper, and so on. Young brother Chappell embarked on the story, but every sentence brought a butt-in from Ian: 'Nah, it wasn't Air India. It was Qantas!' Then, 'He was readin' the *Herald*, not the *Age*!' Poor Greg managed to get it all out, but it wasn't as fluent as on the printed page. We all dissolved in laughter.

One of the saddest of Press conferences came at the end of the Headingley Test when Graham Gooch gave up the England captaincy: gave up in the fullest sense, for he now felt he could do nothing further for the team in a leadership capacity. I felt as choked as he did, watching those hangdog features and lugubrious blue eyes from my position on the floor in that crowded room. Soon Mike Atherton was appointed, and it was a delight to have his ready acceptance of a place on the *WCM* Editorial Board. He was to write with a directness that was refreshing, and typical of this remarkable young man. His place in the cricket media years hence seemed assured.

A Press conference that lifted (and we had at least one every day of every Test with the respective heroes or captains or coaches) came at Edgbaston after Shane Warne and Tim May had bowled Australia to another victory with five second-innings wickets each. As expected, all the questions went to the glamorous Warne, who gave some sparkling replies. 'Maysie' sat quietly through all this, with amusement dancing around his eyes. When finally someone was polite enough to draw him into the discussion, he started like a man roused from sleep, and within the minute had made history – by my reckoning, anyway – by becoming the first cricketer ever to use the word 'tautologous' at a Press conference; not even Mike Brearley.

Again, I seemed to be alone in feeling delight for one side and, in equal measure, pity for the other. Now, for the first time in the history of Anglo-Australian Test cricket, Australia were ahead in victories on English soil (38-37).

It had been a one-sided series since that opening Test, at Old Trafford, where, right in line from the Press-box, Warne strode in for his first ball in Ashes Tests and spun it from outside leg stump to clip Gatting's off bail: the 'ball from Hell'. It ranked with the supreme thrills in my 40-odd years of Test-watching, for it was the first time anyone had hit the timbers with a maiden delivery in England v Australia combat. I worked out that this embraced 447 previous bowlers in the 275 Tests. 'Yeah?' said 'Hollywood' when I broke the phenomenal news that evening in the Cornhill marquee. 'Fair dinkum? Gee!' A few years later a researcher found that, untrumpeted, Tom Horan had scored with his first delivery in Tests in January 1883, bowling Walter Read at Sydney. Never mind.

There are those who think that single crazy missile from Warne won the series by draping a shroud of apprehension over jittery England. The corn-haired Victorian was without doubt the answer to cricket's prayers, amazingly talented, equipped with a vibrant personality, a young man who fired the imagination of would-be legspinners all around the world. And when he started bowling batsmen like Gooch around their legs with balls that spun miles out of the footmarks from around the wicket, the game was into another and exciting revolution.

Gooch, of course, produced his own specially memorable touch to that opening Test of the 1993 series by punching the ball away and becoming the first to be given out handled the ball in an Ashes Test.

The funeral turned into a christening in the final Test, when England earned a comfortable victory. Devon Malcolm's pace brought him six wickets, the easy-going Welshman Steve Watkin got six, and Angus Fraser, the Old Gaytonian (Harrow County Grammar School), took the match award with eight wickets to mark a great comeback from serious hip injury. There were six England half-centuries, the most satisfying probably from Mark Ramprakash (another fellow Old Gaytonian).

I left my quest for souvenirs rather late this time. In the new Oval dressing-room, I checked with Merv Hughes, but the big fella said 'Too late!': he'd already packed and locked his bag. Then he said, 'Hang on a tick', and thrust a bat in my hands. Then came a pair of batting-gloves. 'Go easy, mate,' I said, hardly able to believe my luck. 'No, go on, have it!' he insisted, adding a batting helmet. I couldn't help but notice the crown and lions on the blue helmet (all the Australians wore green ones), and realised that he was playfully raiding Nasser Hussain's bag.

Just before that final Test we had shown more cricket films at London's National Film Theatre, and Steve Waugh, Michael Slater and Ian Healy had come along. They were fascinated by what they saw on the silver screen, and the audience loved having them in their midst. Merv said he would have come too if we'd been showing *Jurassic Park* or *Terminator*. He could afford to relax now after a hard tour, and was making it clear to all who would listen that he had a love-hate relationship with the English crowds: he loved them and they hated him.

Brian Johnston came to that film night, and saw himself on the big screen interviewing the triumphant England players after the 1953 Oval Test. The auditorium rocked with laughter as Johnners congratulated Len Hutton on 'Australia's' victory. Oops! Afterwards, reduced to limpness, as always, after a demanding four hours on stage, I was comforted by Johnners' kind remark: 'Jolly well done, Frithers.'

Within the half-year we were laying out his obituary in *WCM*, ironically allocating more space than his beloved *Cricketer* gave him.

It had been a year of sad farewells, with Ted Dexter, the England Committee chairman, following Gooch out of the side-door, the cruel mockery of the newspapers still fresh in his mind. Then Botham and Randall, who were so much part of all our lives, announced their retirements, and, after another episode of muddle headed selection, David Gower hung up his boots, stepping into all kinds of media roles and, like Willis before him, having to pump out the words with absolutely no scope now to simply switch off when the mood overtook him.

As for the underlying discomfort about not only England's poor Test record but the composition of the side, Jonathan Rice, in his *WCM* column, picked up on the public disquiet at the large number of overseas-born players in the team. He considered the special pressures facing these cricketers, while referring to the England XI as an 'international hotchpotch'. It was a theme that would only gather momentum – and end in a nasty crash.

Derek Randall even got serious for once, and was quoted as objecting to anyone other than 'proper Englishmen' playing for England. He was not keen on the idea of players 'swapping flags'. When a Ken Dodd character like 'Rags' Randall gets serious about something, it must be a topic of some significance, and it would be irresponsible of any editor to ignore it.

Before heading off to Queensland for the annual restorative, I sat with Keith Miller as he saw the final touches put to Michael Corkrey's painting of him (in the inappropriate garb of lounge suit and tie) for the Long Room at Lord's, and we talked, mainly about the war, for an article for *WCM*. It was not dissimilar to being with Miller's great predecessor in the Australian side, Jack Gregory, 22 years earlier, except that Keith knew full well that he was being interviewed, even if he didn't make the most comfortable of interviewees. There was little cricket talk, and we finished up having tea with two of his old wartime drivers, women now in their seventies too, in a cosy room, appropriately near the Imperial War Museum. There were times, as I listened to them, when it felt like 1943 again. 'Dusty' now moved with difficulty. It broke my heart to see him struggling with his sticks, but his courage and pride were still abundantly on show. And his affection for Lord's, where his cricket career had really taken off in wartime matches, was patent and extraordinary.

Two Keith Millers are better than one. We talked as the artist put the finishing touches to the painting, and then we visited two wartime pals

Another substantial gain for the magazine was a series of articles by another old hero, Frank Tyson, not only the fastest of bowlers in those brightly-lit 1950s, but an interesting and pleasant man, and now a near-neighbour on Queensland's Gold Coast.

While in Queensland for those few weeks in 1993-94, I saw Allan Border play in a Test match which was unimaginably his 150th (he made a century against New Zealand to mark it). And in Border's testimonial match at the Gabba, we were able to see Barry Richards bat again, and Richard Hadlee bowled an underarm to Greg Chappell, levelling off a particularly painful piece of history. All this and walking with Debbie through the rainforest eased some fresh air through the overheated brain.

England were now touring West Indies, and it was no surprise when tempers rose again. The main flashpoint came when Courtney Walsh set about Devon Malcolm in the Jamaica Test that opened the series. The bouncer assault on England's myopic No.11 was roundly condemned. We all fished for words to express our disapproval, and it seemed to me best classified as a case of cricket's moral rules of engagement having been broken. The overuse of the bouncer at Atherton also struck most observers as dismal and unwarranted, though England's young captain gamely went on record as saying he found it exhilarating. He didn't have to watch it! It was like the time Robin Smith withstood 15 short, fast deliveries in succession, and went on professing that he enjoyed it. If so, it didn't show in his ashen face and haunted, sunken eyes when the camera closed in on him.

It turned out to be a dramatic series, and not one-sided after all. It was so impressive to see the genuine smiles on the faces of Atherton and his crew when they arrived fresh from having been floored for 46 in the Trinidad Test. It really did seem that they had bounced back up off the floor and were ready to counterattack. When they beat Richie Richardson's men at 'Fortress Bridgetown', where West Indies had not experienced Test defeat for 59 years, the moaning now came from the side less accustomed to it. Alec Stewart's glorious twin centuries elevated him for life, and the back-up from Atherton, Hick and Thorpe, plus Fraser's 8 for 75 and Caddick's 5 for 63 ensured a historic victory perhaps remembered as much as anything, in terms of a single incident, as for Phil Tufnell's sharp running catch to dismiss Brian Lara.

Now there was a name which we all knew would be with us for some years to come, but within weeks, the svelte Trinidadian left-hander had feasted his way to 375 in the Antigua Test and 501 not out for Warwickshire against Durham (everybody's whipping-boys, though nobody else whipped them anything like that hard). It took weeks to sink in that the cricket world's two most significant records had been annexed by one young man. Among the emotions was a pinch of sympathy for those two most friendly and gentle of men, Sir Garry Sobers and Hanif Mohammad, who were now in second place on those tables. It teaches you never to regard any cricket record – other than a first or an ultimate – as immune.

What did 1994 season bring? First, a big win over the New Zealanders (a likable bunch of chaps, as ever) at Trent Bridge, a century by Martin Crowe, and 11 wickets and a fifty by Dion Nash at Lord's, and promising debuts for Craig White and Darren Gough, with Phil DeFreitas seeming to have reached a career peak at last. England's march to respectability seemed to be under way.

Then came the first Test against South Africa for 29 years, and demolition by 356 runs. England capsized for 99 on the fourth day. And yet Kepler Wessels' century and the relentless bowling of South Africa's four fast men were overshadowed by the 'Atherton Affair', a shameful crucifixion of a man who sprinkled some dry soil on the ball, having saved time by putting the dirt in his pocket to save keep going over to the footholds to dry the hand. No cricket law was broken, and though it all looked dodgy, his one real 'crime' was in not giving match referee Peter Burge an open explanation.

Atherton was fined £1000 for 'having soil' and £1000 for withholding information from Burge. It seemed to me that it was the natural human reaction to plead innocent when asked if one has any 'substance' in the pocket, for this conjures up visions of all sorts of nasty things. I suggested to Ray Illingworth that he ought to give Mike £1000 back, at least, since 'having soil' was not an offence. Illy said he was inclined to agree, 'but he's not getting it back!' It was later apparent that the measure saved Atherton's position, for Peter Burge, if it had been left to him, would surely have issued a suspension, which would have made it difficult for England to hand Atherton back the captaincy.

The self-righteousness that swept the country turned my stomach. It was understandable that most foreigners, on principle, would pillory Atherton, but to hear and read English opinion, nearly all of it led by pompous columns in the tabloids and broadsheets, turned it into a kind of death-wish. Hysterical calls for his resignation took Atherton to the brink of tossing it all in, but close friends and father Alan tapped his innate toughness by pointing out that if he quit now, that would be pretty well all he'd be remembered for. English cricket was very fortunate that he stayed on after this monstrous mountain-from-molehill episode.

Peter Burge, of course, got him at The Oval, when a poor lbw decision before Atherton had scored had him briefly shaking his head in disbelief, and looking instinctively at his bat, the way thousands of batsmen have done when they've nicked the ball. The fine this time was £1250 (with further penalty for slow over rate in the match), which left him suggesting that he might play as an amateur in future. Never mind: in the years ahead Mike Atherton was paid a mint by Sky TV and a newspaper.

We had a *WCM* Editorial Board dinner in St James's that evening, and I was quite surprised when Atherton turned up. But it was probably the best place to be. He was still slightly stunned, gently shaking his head, and confirmed that the fine came out of his pay-packet *after* tax. We all managed a few laughs around the table – Willis was already primed, having been doing 'hospitality' during the afternoon – and when a telephone enquiry came through as to the England captain's whereabouts, it seemed prudent to suggest that he was unlikely to have come here after such a traumatic incident. When he did leave, the right side of midnight, it was by the back door. The manager explained that they were accustomed to the patronage of members of the Royal family, after all.

Later, bleary-eyed, three of us, Frank Keating, Jack Bannister and me, had a furious argument over the rights and wrongs of the soil-on-ball business and Burge's punitive action at The Oval, and, not surprisingly, I was outnumbered. But I fought my corner as long as my voice lasted, and next day we all smiled upon each other.

The last supper: the WCM Editorial Board get-together has the fugitive England captain in its midst just after his unpleasant experience with the Test match referee at The Oval: from the left: Patrick Eagar, David Gower, Frank Keating, DF, Bob Willis, Mike Atherton, Jack Bannister

Those smiles spread to almost every face in the vicinity when Malcolm stormed to 9 for 57, the sixth-best figures in Test history, and England beat South Africa by eight wickets to level the rubber and find new heart for the Ashes series now looming.

The 1994 season, the 16th and what was to turn out to be the final 'normal' summer of my *WCM* years, had the usual stock of highlights and an unrelieved level of work pressure (made no easier by the dark tensions concerning the new management). Master commentator Don Mosey was expressing fresh concern over the direction taken by radio's Test Match Special, mourning the loss of Brian Johnston, and majoring with a remark that seemed spot-on: 'There is a poverty of vocabulary that drives one to despair.' But is it that surprising, in a world slowly sinking into the mire of junk expressions: the misused 'hopefully', and repetitive 'issue' and 'at this moment in time' and 'at the end of the day' and 'I mean'? It suggests that the standard of teaching in schools has slumped grievously.

As pleasant a memory as any was the Lord's Taverners' Eve of Test Match dinner. In our midst were not only the likes of Mike Procter from pre-isolation South Africa but distinguished figures from that land who did so much to change it: First Deputy President Thabo Mbeki, Archbishop Desmond Tutu, Dr Ali Bacher, Omar Henry, and players from several generations. I happened to be seated between the bubbly Omar Henry and another of South African origin, Sir Alastair Morton, chairman of the Channel Tunnel project, who must have wondered which was greater: the project's deficit or the new South Africa's national debt, with the rand so feeble.

With the 1994-95 Ashes series looming, I had constructed, 100 years after the event, a book on the 1894-95 series, when Stoddart's English team toured Australia and engaged in some sensational matches in what turned out to be the first 'great' Test series. Much additional material had emerged since the Stoddart biography a quarter-of-a-century earlier, thanks in part to my son Peter's research among Australian newspapers from the period, and so *Stoddy's Mission* was created, with a fervent wish that the centenary of that series would be just as competitive and exciting.

Well, it was, but only up to a point. It was never going to be two-all with one to play, as in 1894-95. Sharne Warne seemed unplayable at Brisbane, taking 8 for 71 (11 wickets in the match) with legspin and laughter. 'How many of them came from the new mystery ball?' 'Aw, a fair few, mate!' - eyes gleaming, spiky hair defiant, fingers twitching. The man was top of the world, and deservedly so. Then, in Melbourne, he took the first hat-trick in an Ashes Test for 91 years (if only tailenders), when Hugh Trumble did it in his final Test. English folk, including those in our Wisden tour party, were already wishing that young Warne could find some reason to retire. But he was only 25, and appeared well on course to become the first to take a stupendous 500 Test wickets, and more.

Injuries and uneven umpiring – as well as Warne's genius – were telling against England in a big way, and they were particularly unlucky not to pull off victory in the Sydney Test. Among the ill-fortune they had to absorb there, Mark Taylor was just short of the crease when Gooch broke the wicket from Malcolm's throw, but umpire Darrell Hair unwisely declined to refer it to TV scrutiny. Taylor batted a further 160 minutes, and it was 1982-83 all over again, when John Dyson was so wrongly reprieved. Debbie suggested that Mr Hair should have been fined $2000. Australia hung on with three wickets in hand, the light having failed, as did the umpires in calling play off after 15 overs had been bowled in the last hour, though the hour had not elapsed yet. Atherton had to point this out as the tractors were speeding to the middle with the covers. Another over was bowled, but Malcolm had spilled a catch from Warne, and it was asking too much now. Warne and May had stuck it out for 77 minutes, and once again we had seen a pulsating Sydney Ashes Test. As always, I managed to conjure some visions from that first of all Tests for me, back in '50-51. But it was getting harder now that the SCG had grown so tall and the cast of characters on the field and off had changed so drastically.

The Melbourne Test had been overshadowed – for those of a certain age – by news from England that Peter May had died, close to his 65th birthday. By coincidence, he had scored a century in difficult conditions against Australia down on this very MCG around the time of his 29th birthday, which was just 11 days after the birth of my first son. My Peter and PBH could scarcely have been more dissimilar, but the thought was there: the best. Stricken by a brain tumour and beset by financial worries, Peter May told a friend towards the end that he felt he was staring into a huge black pit. It was too awful. He had once been so fresh, strong and commanding, and shy with it. It was noticeable even a year before his death (we stood together talking, with an almost-empty Lord's stretching out below) that his outstandingly boyish appearance was still there. It was that quiff of hair and angled smile that fooled us into thinking that England's greatest post-war batsman would always be around. Does one ever get used to the inevitably on-going toll?

Before heading back to freezing Surrey, I was privileged to be invited to a reunion dinner for the 1945 Australian Services cricketers at Sydney's Cricketers Club. Half-a-century on, here were the men who had fought and played (and in some cases married British girls) and were now keen to reminisce and laugh and to display a generosity of spirit that would confuse many a mean modern.

Ross Stanford, who as a schoolboy had scored 416 not out in 1931, sang *Along Came a Bloody Blackbird*, a bouncy tune which, when sung by a group of Aussie airmen in wartime London, had high society rocking away, bobbing up and down in their expensive dresses and jingling their diamonds. Bert Cheetham was proud of his Lord's duck, while Colin Bremner wanted to talk about the English countryside. Catalina pilot Stan Sismey went into the intricacies of organising the tour matches in that first post-war English summer. Bill Brown and Ray Lindwall were there, though their duties in the Pacific war had prevented their travelling to England for the Victory 'Tests' of 1945, but Keith Miller was too poorly on the night. (It could have been that he did not trust himself to hold back the tears as fallen comrades were remembered.)

And who should I find myself chatting to in George Street just after midnight, when this memorable evening was fast fading, but Martin Donnelly, that most urbane of New Zealanders, one of the best left-handers, up there with Bert Sutcliffe and Neil Harvey in terms of natural talent. He had to his credit the glorious Lord's treble of 206 in a Test match, a century in the Varsity match, and another for Gentlemen v Players. Martin had a fund of stories, midst which he quietly pointed out that Keith Miller's famous 185 for the Dominions at Lord's served to overshadow completely a century that young Donnelly himself had managed to carve out.

The last two Tests of 1994-95 were monitored 'live' through the night on Sky television, and Ashes credibility was partially restored by England's victory at Adelaide (century to greybeard Gatting, eighties from Atherton, Thorpe and DeFreitas, and an impressive 71 by John Crawley, following his 72 at Sydney; and a handsome debut century for Australia by Greg Blewett). Then, at Perth in the closing Test, England reverted to their worst shape, downing nine or 10 catches and absorbing a 329-run thrashing. Slater made his fourth century against England, and Blewett scored another, Thorpe having stroked 123 for England, Ramprakash a heartening 72. In the fourth innings, England were haemorrhaging at 27 for 6, but managed 123 in the end, still a tails-between-legs performance. Nothing was more poignant than Steve Waugh's 99 not out. He was marooned when his twin brother, acting as runner for McDermott, reversed but failed to beat the throw. Reminded me of just how often I used to be out of tune with my own brother.

Australia went on to beat West Indies in the Caribbean in a tough series which saw Steve Waugh at his best, and the unofficial Test world champions title was theirs. Meanwhile, Queensland at last managed to win that elusive Sheffield Shield after 63 seasons of endeavour. I felt almost as much joy as those on the spot. All we wanted now was a decent Ashes series. But we would have to wait till 1997.

CHAPTER TWENTY-FIVE

The world is governed by opinion.

THOMAS HOBBES

There was an item right out of the ordinary in the July 1995 edition of *Wisden Cricket Monthly*. Earlier in the year, I'd published a pair of articles by a young and promising Gideon Haigh based on some typically forthright interviews that Bill O'Reilly had given John Ringwood for the Oral History Unit in Canberra. O'Reilly had always been prone to denigrate Sir Donald Bradman, and here he was again, at his harshest. Now DGB wrote me two letters, one private and one for publication in *WCM*. So rare were his public utterances, especially on matters as controversial as this, that I fed the non-private letter in advance to the Sunday Times, who duly ran part of it. I was relieved that the Bradman side of the story would reach a wider audience.

However (perhaps the weightiest 'however' of my life), it was not this *WCM* item at all that made headlines. Instead, it was an article by a 49-year-old retired tax inspector in North London named Robert Henderson that was taken up by *The Observer* and then just about every other publication and broadcasting outlet in the country. Before long, the matter had swept around the world on waves of hysteria.

Henderson had written along similar lines in *WCM* previously, most recently in the April issue, when he exercised his right to criticise by objecting to the selection of Gooch and Gatting, and, on separate grounds, to the inclusion of Craig White, the Australian-bred Yorkshireman, among Atherton's 'motley crew' (with its 'cultural foreigners') on the recent Ashes tour. There had been no noticeable feedback to this article.

I was subsequently told by many readers that this next article, in the July issue, was 'boring' or 'unattractive'; some of them gave up on it halfway. Henderson was now asking whether cricketers born or brought up overseas might sometimes find it difficult to muster total commitment when playing for England. He wondered whether 'a changing-room comprising say six Englishmen, two West Indians, two Southern Africans and a New Zealander is going to develop the same camaraderie as 11 unequivocal Englishmen'. He later acknowledged that 'perhaps even some of the unequivocally English players lack a sufficient sense of pride in playing for England', a point endorsed days later by Geoffrey Wheatcroft in the *Daily Telegraph* when, in one of the more enlightened features following the *WCM* 'earthquake', he wrote: 'DeFreitas and Malcolm have both been unreliable performers for England, it's true, but then so have numerous pure-born Saxons from the shires'.

Wheatcroft drew a comparison between Henderson's postulations and those aired in 1990 by former Conservative Party chairman Norman Tebbit: When Tebbit proposed his famous (or notorious) 'cricket test', he was thinking of supporters rather than players. Could an immigrant to this country, Lord Tebbit mused, be considered truly British if he still instinctively supported Pakistan, India and West Indies against England? No-one could identify more strongly with that poser than myself. So the matter of cricketing loyalty had been raised again, in a more specific way, and one which asks larger questions.

Enter Mr Mike Marqusee, self-described as a 'deracinated Marxist of American Jewish background' – to which might now be added 'a mischief-making *demagogue'.* He circularised copies of the Henderson article to newspapers up and down the country. It was a quiet time of year. So, with scant heed to the fundamental theme, which was an assessment of the England Test team and its *national identity*, off they went with their irrational outbursts about a 'race row' stoked up by Wisden.

It seemed preposterous. No one who had seen the article prior to publication had questioned it. My deputy editor, Steven Lynch, had included an article by Henderson in the February *WCM* while I was in Australia. Now, Steven rang me merely to discuss which illustrations should accompany the piece, since he was now making up the pages. Who got a mention in the article? Geoff Greenidge. Right. There's a picture of him here. Phillip DeFreitas: Steven had a good Eagar of him on his desk. OK. Let's use that. Room for any others? Seemingly not.

For some reason the general manager, Chris Lane, customarily looked at the page-proofs. But he made no attempt now to query anything. And, not least significantly, there was no objection or query from the printers, who had been quick to object to the contents of a letter from the writer Geoffrey Moorhouse which was due for inclusion in our November 1994 edition, headed 'Pompous Benaud'. The managing director of the printers felt it needed to be diluted, so revised wording was agreed – to the subsequent fury of the author of the letter. Later, a letter attacking Rupert Murdoch was vetoed by the printer.

For over 20 years I had been fully aware that among my many responsibilities was the need to guard against libelling anybody. Perhaps only those who have undertaken similar duties could fully understand the weight of this when balanced against the desire to protect freedom of expression in an apparently 'free' country. The outcome of this Henderson article was absolutely beyond prediction, and suggests quite forcibly that free speech in Britain was being driven underground.

The heading used by Henderson was 'Racism and National Identity'. He did not realise that it is conventional for editors or subs to create the headline and the details of the by-line. Many a professional writer puts his own suggested title above his offering: sometimes it serves and sometimes it needs improvement. In all innocence, I gave this feature the heading 'Is It in the Blood?' The thinking was: is bravery in the blood; is athletic competence in the blood; is cricket in the blood? Are we stuck with what we are born with, or can we acquire qualities that take us to the top, no matter what our origins? For instance, can a lad born to humble parents in London become a Test player for Australia? Or set up a magazine that earns popularity in the cricket world?

This 'blood' thing played right into the hands of those who wished to turn the Henderson argument/postulation/question into something exclusively about biology and racial prejudice.

'Race row blackens cricket' was the July 2 headline on a column entitled 'Inside Edge', in *The Observer*, written by its newly-promoted chief sports feature writer Kevin Mitchell (ex-Sydney, 20 years in London). He described Henderson's article as 'a Talmudic ramble that staggers past logic, trips over common sense and ends up arse up in the bushes of confusion'. Mitchell acknowledged that 'the article addresses an intriguing subject' but branded it 'quite the most unpleasant editorial beast allowed out of its cage in some time, largely because of its tone'.

Mitchell had spoken to Matthew Engel, as a member of *WCM's* Editorial Board, who told him: 'I can't go along with everything that Mr Henderson says, as I'd never heard of him before. [Come again?] But the question of nationality and sport is a legitimate one, as anyone observing Wimbledon or Test cricket can see. There is a problem of how you marry the wider question of race and nationality into the narrow issue of sporting patriotism. I'm not sure it helps if you scream 'racist' when someone makes a contribution to that debate.' [Well said.]

Then the phone-calls started. At first I couldn't quite comprehend the feverish agitation coming down the line from many of the reporters. Paul Foot, the *Guardian* columnist, conducted a high-pitched third-degree, quoting back things I had written years ago about West Indian short-pitched bowling and related matters. This was starting to smell like a collaborative manoeuvre.

Other journalists who spoke softly went on to write vituperative stuff. I tried to explain the background – the years of recurrent public disquiet about not just the failures but the very composition of England's Test team (as long ago as 1981 I had speculated that by 1993 England could have three West Indian-born fast bowlers and three South African-born batsmen in their ranks) – but these critics filled their allocations of space with hysterical and often sloppily inaccurate material.

Same with the radio stations. 'Race row' this and 'race row' that, blind to the white Southern African and Australasian cricketers who have played for England and were also under consideration in the article. Had these reporters actually read it? (I had deleted Henderson's reference to Nasser Hussain, since a letter from the batsman's mother had challenged the statement he was alleged to have made to Rob Steen, then of the *Telegraph*, about his 'feeling Indian', which had been reproduced in *WCM* some years earlier. Henderson was miffed at this deletion, claiming that it reduced the 'Asian content' of the article and thus shifted the balance. Steen was now acting as Marqusee's fellow agitator.)

Robert Henderson, the author (who had previously had letters published in the *Sunday Telegraph* and, that very month, in *The Cricketer*), was all but invisible and inaudible through all the uproar. It would have been so different had a leading and accessible writer penned the article. Instead, I, as editor, was taking a double blast, and the perception eventually became so ludicrously blurred that I was considered by some of the more careless as having been the actual author. The *Telegraph Magazine* later gave me a 'Flying Duck Award' as Editor of the Year, asserting that I 'cast doubt on the patriotism of black and Asian England players' and that *Wisden* subsequently attracted a flurry of writs and had to pay out undisclosed damages to Devon Malcolm. I suggested they should publish a correction and apology for this particularly idiotic piece of journalism, and they did so, though it took them two months. I should have pressed for compensation.

I soon lost count of the people for whom I spelt out the disclaimer at the front of each issue of *WCM*: 'Views expressed in *Wisden Cricket Monthly* do not necessarily always correspond with those of the Editor or his Board'. It would have been a rather staid magazine had they always done so.

There was much confusion between 'commitment' and 'temperament'. I have seen occasional shortfalls in commitment at club level, and heard about it in county cricket. But it seems inconceivable at Test level. The highly-strung Harold Gimblett may well have suffered a psychosomatic carbuncle on his neck just before the 1950 Nottingham Test, causing him to miss the match; but reduced commitment, deliberate or otherwise, would take some finding in the annals of Test cricket.

My chief concern was over the unfair extra pressure placed on the likes of Roland Butcher when he entered the baying cauldron of Kensington Oval to bat for England against West Indies in his maiden Test. Born just a few miles up the coast of Barbados, Butcher was billed in the local paper as 'Our Boy, Their Bat', a taunt that might equally have inspired or oppressed him. Martin McCague, the heavyweight but gentle (off the field) Ulster-born Australian, was another who was intimidated by spectators when he represented England against Australia at Brisbane in 1994.

On July 9, 1995, the *Sunday Times* covered England's innings defeat by West Indies on an atrocious Edgbaston pitch upon which Jason Gallian, the Sydney-born 'Pom', became the newest overseas-born to make his England debut. This paper, like most of its competitors, also gave much space to the Henderson article, its repulsive headline reading 'How *Wisden Cricket Monthly* injected itself with poison'. Ian Hawkey observed that the *WCM* item had become 'second only to the Tory leadership election as food for broadcast and broadsheet discussion'. He had managed to track down Henderson, who told him: 'This is obviously the sort of subject that the liberal left will go screaming on about.'

Hawkey, who rang me several times, wrote that my Anglo-Australianism was a significant factor. 'The phone has not stopped ringing,' I had told him, 'and maybe I've given some of them too much time.' He gave the last words to Henderson, who said: 'In five years' time, when the sociological wind has blown to the right, people won't raise an eyebrow at this sort of thing.'

On July 4, I had issued a statement through Press Association to the effect that much of the coverage of the Henderson issue was distorted and that Wisden's lawyers were watching the situation. '*Wisden Cricket Monthly*,' the statement concluded, 'has always been an open forum for views on cricket and associated topics. Any critics who have felt that the magazine may have been used for extremist views are assured that the next edition will carry much that takes strong issue with Mr Henderson's point of view.'

The barrage of criticism grew ever more thunderous. Working as best I could – midst a torrent of calls and interviews – at preparing the next (August) edition of *WCM*, the only escape was to walk up to the Hog's Back as the day mercifully faded and to try, with my ever-comforting Debbie, to interpret what was happening. It was the hurricane of 1987 all over again. Gazing across at the cathedral, red-brick and solid on Stag Hill, we contemplated all manner of possible consequences.

The 'sensation' spluttered on as a media plaything day after day, though the tabloids were mysteriously restrained. Finally I left the phone off the hook.

What if DeFreitas and Malcolm did sue? The Cricketers Association, via general secretary David Graveney, had been critical of the Henderson article but said that not only was *WCM* a 'respected cricket magazine which has done a lot for the game' but that the CA's lawyers had advised that *there were no firm grounds for legal action*. But these two cricketers in particular, encouraged by a sizable lobby, including their county club, Derbyshire, and the Professional Footballers Association (who apparently have frequent recourse to the sorting-out of racial contretemps), were now taking the first steps towards seeking redress.

I had tried to telephone Phil DeFreitas when his displeasure became known, but could speak only to his solicitor. What did I want? Merely to ensure that the player was aware that the space was available to him if he wished to respond to Henderson's comments. No reaction.

I was even more surprised at Devon Malcolm's apparent intention to sue, for his name had appeared only once in the article, and that only passingly; and it was obvious even to the most casual cricket-follower that, principally when he took that 9 for 57 against South Africa at The Oval in 1994, he was without distraction, and committed to England's cause, even though he was Jamaica-born and even though he told *The Cricketer* in an April '95 interview that his heroes were Viv Richards, Michael Holding and Richard Hadlee, and that his favourite music was rhythm-and-blues, soul, funk and reggae. In *The Cricketers' Who's Who*, he added Malcolm Marshall and Allan Warner as favourite players. I admired his honesty. Some might have slipped in a token 'Atherton' or 'Botham' and stated that their favourite music was Vaughan Williams or *Greensleeves*.

It was infuriating to read in Malcolm's 1998 ghosted autobiography that 'David Frith kept making desperate calls to me, trying to reach some sort of compromise'. I made only one call. It was not to Malcolm. It was to DeFreitas, and it was not returned. Never once did I try to contact Malcolm. The only time in my life, to this day, that I have spoken to the man was when I invited him to come with David Gower and a couple of others (including Gladstone Small) up to my place for dinner at the end of the day's play at Carrara Oval (the day of the Tiger Moth fiasco). Malcolm had brusquely declined the invitation.

In the *Financial Times*, a fellow named Michael Skapinker had urged Malcolm and DeFreitas to sue. He chose to quote from *The Independent* after England had beaten West Indies in the recent Lord's Test: 'What made it additionally pleasing was that England's attack did not for once look like a United Nations strike force. Not since the Old Trafford Test of 1989 (Fraser, Foster, Emburey, Cook and Botham) have England fielded five bowlers . . . with undiluted allegiance to the country they were representing.' And he introduced a welcome note of levity by writing: 'Is there a nation anywhere on earth where national self-hatred is as commonplace as it is in England? [I think I can reliably say No to that question.] Gather 11 Englishmen together and they are more likely to whinge about what a ghastly country it is than they are to plot victory over Australia.'

This reminded me of a steamy evening in Madras in '84-85, when England were 611 for 5 and, as we all sat in the bus, the Pom press were searching for something to moan about. I suggested to them that if this were the Aussies in a similar situation we'd all have been singing Waltzing Matilda.

Skapinker was the latest to quote Matthew Engel in the 1995 *Wisden Cricketers' Almanack*: 'It cannot be irrelevant to England's long-term failures that so many of their recent Test players were either born overseas and/or spent their formative years as citizens of other countries . . . It is not a question of race.'

Engel was understandably irritated that much the same quote was used in the original Henderson article and was just as incomplete. Here, then, are the missing bits, where the dots appear above: 'In the heat of Test cricket, there is a difference between a cohesive team with a common goal, and a coalition of individuals whose major ambitions are for themselves. Successive England captains have all been aware of this.'

And following 'It is not a question of race' came: 'And of course there have been many fine and committed performances from players with all kinds of disparate backgrounds. But several of these players only came to England to play as professionals. There is a vast difference between wanting to play Test cricket and wanting to play for England. The overall effect has been to create a climate in which, as *The Independent* put it, "some of our lot play for their country because they get paid for it".'

There it was in a nutshell, in the 'famous' *Wisden*, an opinion which, I estimate, represented the majority view in the Press-boxes of England. This *Wisden* passage was just 30 pages prior to a tribute to Devon Malcolm, who was one of the Five Cricketers of the Year in this 1995 edition.

Matthew Engel was now ringing me almost daily, and to judge from his stuttering he seemed even more distressed than I. Struggling for coherence, the poor chap made me feel almost in control. He seemed to have convinced himself that *Wisden's* good name, built up over 131 years, was now irretrievably besmirched. And now he was apparently convincing others as well. Caught between old writings and present hysteria (as was I), he found himself in a complicated position in that he wrote for the 'left-wing, liberal' *Guardian* newspaper, some of whose other writers were now giving him a hard time.

Marqusee misrepresented him in that paper on July 4, 1995, and Engel put a letter in next day correcting him. Engel endeavoured to defuse matters by saying that his own ancestry entitled him to play for Belgium, and finished seriously with the remark that 'national teams perform best if they retain a keen sense of identity. How this might be achieved in Britain should be a subject for discussion at a calmer time, preferably between people who genuinely care about the problems. But there are no circumstances in which this could ever involve the exclusion of genuine migrants, still less home-born blacks, from English or British teams.'

I especially liked the 'people who genuinely care' bit.

The attack by Marqusee had been fired at Engel's article in *The Guardian* on July 3, 1995 which was headed 'Curious case of cricket's national affront', and which branded part of the article by the 'possibly obsessed' Henderson as 'drivel', and amusingly asked: 'At what point does one become a biological Englishman – after one generation, two, 10 or 20?' Engel then asserted that *Guardian* colleague Paul Foot was also talking drivel in that he seemed to have no conception of the difference between team games and individual sports.

'Nationalism may not be rational,' Engel went on, 'and it fits uneasily into Marxist theory, but it exists. International sport would be meaningless without it. And teams that flogged their guts out for their country habitually do better than collections of individuals whose sole aim is to further their own careers. This is one of the reasons England cricket teams lose more often than they win.'

He made profound point after point, including one concerning Michael Slater's much-remarked-upon kissing of his Aussie badge when he reached a Test hundred at Lord's. 'It is hard, not impossible,' mused Engel, 'to imagine either Graeme Hick or Phil DeFreitas doing the same – in the unlikely event of them [sic] summoning the resolution to produce a similar performance.'

Though I suspected this might have inflamed DeFreitas further – and Hick too for that matter – the article prompted one enthusiastic response. J.Paul Getty wrote to Matthew Engel complimenting him on the piece (with a copy to me) and saying that the magazine should be a forum for debate. I could not help thinking time and time again about this remark as the days passed and the plot deepened.

By now, I was absolutely fed up at the way Marqusee was big-timing it at my expense, so I wrote to him, pointing out *inter alia* that I was proud of the elders in my family who had fought against Nazism, and was not unaware that his lot had sat on the fence for a costly two years before entering the Second World War. I don't know whether he reported this to fellow American J.P.Getty. 'What English cricket has done to deserve him is anyone's guess,' wrote Marcus Berkmann of M.Marqusee in another context.

Meanwhile, another *Guardian* writer, Francis Wheen by name, a self-proclaimed 'Old Harrovian Trotskyist', decided to have his two-penn'orth. Noting that my own 'Englishness' is 'called into question by the fact that he speaks in a broad Australian accent' [really?], he strained his imagination further by suggesting I should be punished for publishing Henderson by being sacked by Getty, or, better still, facing a few overs from DeFreitas and Malcolm.

It so happened that I forgot to pack my helmet that Saturday, batted for two hours on a damp pitch in a league match against Southern Railways' attack of three West Indian fast bowlers, and got to 64 before my age (58) told against me. Not quite Malcolm and DeFreitas perhaps. But the days of crisis seemed to have sharpened the mind.

The 'media-inspired witch-hunt' (in the words of mild-mannered Cricket Writers Club secretary Derek Hodgson) continued avidly. I felt very alone. My distressed wife and family stood by helplessly as the tirade of vilification was sustained and the threat of legal complications swelled. And all the while, my Wisden 'colleagues' – apart from Steven and Colin – remained silent. There must have been much chatter going on among other members of the management committee, but there was not so much as a phone-call to ask how I was coping. Graeme Wright, when approached by one paper, piously told it that the Henderson article should never have been published. What I had feared was now a reality: this was no team. Never had been.

One complication followed another. Vic Marks, a member of the editorial panel of *The Cricketer*, gleefully wrote in *The Observer* that Mike Atherton had resigned from *WCM's* Editorial Board and that David Gower was likely to follow. No such thing happened. I rang both of them immediately, assured them that I was about to make it clear to the world that, for what it was worth, neither of them had prior knowledge of or responsibility for the Henderson article, and I was gratified to be told that they had no intention of leaving, the 'open forum' principle having been accepted by both. So much for sniggering Marks's claim that I was losing more England captains than Peter May.

As a matter of fact, Bob Willis had stood down prior to the appearance of the July edition. His attitude had changed over the years, so, given his shrinking enthusiasm for writing, I popped off the same sort of letter I'd had to write to Ted Dexter in 1986: no words, no point. So Willis stood down, at last revealing his grievance: as a member of the Surrey CCC committee, he said he had been embarrassed at some of the things written about the club's affairs by Rob Steen (that man again) during the Downing/Woodman regime. I was surprised and disappointed that Willis hadn't said anything to me. The space had always been available for him, and he'd been notably loyal and reliable throughout the first dozen years of *WCM*. So now off he went into the golden sunset of Sky TV, to drone on slavishly about the *Foster's* Oval.

Robert Henderson, whom I have never met, now wrote pleading to be allowed to respond to the media attacks on him. I was unable to give him the opportunity, which greatly upset him. But he continued to correspond with many leading cricket identities, and referred to past letters to them. He sent me copies of their replies and they made fascinating reading. I would have brought them to court given the chance.

'In general,' David Gower had written in 1991, 'it is always a mystery trying to analyse what creates "team spirit", especially when a side is struggling, and your [i.e. Henderson's] points must certainly be relevant.'

'You may be right about the lack of identity/loyalty in the England team,' wrote the inimitable John Thicknesse of the *Evening Standard*, 'but if so (which actually I doubt) it is an occupational hazard of our tradition of welcoming people of all races to our shores – which I consider one of the United Kingdom's most attractive characteristics.'

Both David Foot and Dick Streeton, much-respected veteran journalists, suggested in their replies to the 1991 Henderson 'circular' that *WCM* might be a ready outlet for his views on the England team's identity problem. The man was proving to be persistent if nothing else.

Then there was the little matter of quotations from past work by cricket-writers who now, in 1995, were apparently wanting/needing to distance themselves hurriedly from Henderson as if he breathed a deadly disease.

Christopher Martin-Jenkins, it seems, had consistently aired anxieties. Back in 1990 he had said, on BBC Radio 2 *Sportsdesk*: 'The selectors seem to be obsessed with West Indian-born pace bowlers.' And in the *Daily Telegraph* in 1994, he had written (June 27): 'Over the weekend both Robin Smith, born and schooled in South Africa, and Graeme Hick, born and schooled in Zimbabwe, have had their recent form closely analysed. You could easily have made a case for neither being retained for the third Test this week, when Graham Thorpe and John Crawley seem ready. Apart from a debate based purely on cricketing criteria, the latter two have been English since birth. Will not their dedication to the cause of England be that much deeper when they are tied to it by blood as well as by money?'

So I was not the only one who considered that this interesting discussion was worth further examination. There were other ripe quotes which the agitators seemed to have missed:

'CM-J' on May 23, 1994, same paper: '. . . we shall not have a consistently successful England team unless we get a proper balance between youth and experience [and] until we produce more Goughs; that is to say English born, English bred products of English schools.'

Fledgling journalist Simon Hughes had something to say on the matter (*Daily Telegraph*, March 30, 1994): '. . . there is still a doubt about his [Andy Caddick's] commitment – some of his English colleagues find it irritating that he still habitually turns to the New Zealand score first in the papers.'

There can be no doubt, then, that the composition of the England XI had been a burning topic for some time, in the Press-boxes, on the terraces, in the committee-rooms, at the breakfast tables. So despite the furore of July 1995 part of me still sensed it had been right to give the article some space in the magazine.

On the whole, though, the disturbance – the price of it all – was too much. Midst all the puffed-up outrage there seemed to have been some genuine upset, which caused me regret. After another panic phone-call from Matthew Engel, I decided to issue an apology for publishing the Henderson article, firstly through Press Association, then in the August *WCM*. I was reeling now, head flushed, stomach churning, after days of ceaseless interrogation, explanation, and some abuse (and there was more spite to come, in the London-based black Press and the grubby, unfunny cricket 'fanzines'). Matthew Engel's phrase 'error of judgment' found its way into my draft, and stayed there. When an apology is called for, I suppose it has to be the consequence of an error of some sort. Few had the good grace to accept my *WCM* apology, which demonstrated how nasty this thing had become.

In the August *WCM*, which contained my centenary tribute to Jack Gregory as well as reports on the dramatic Lord's and Edgbaston Tests against West Indies, and which was published after the longest month of my life, I laid out a selection of letters protesting at Henderson's views, together with a copy of my statement and Editorial, and articles on the hot topic by Mike Brearley and David Gower.

Opening the array of letters was one from left-wing MP Jeremy Corbyn, who suggested that a good way of restoring national pride would be to encourage children of all races to work together to create a new sense of what 'being English' was about. Just over a year later he became front-page news himself when he took 'togetherness' too far for the liking of the Labour Party's big boys, who condemned him for his persistent links with IRA sympathisers and former convicts. This time he wanted to meet Sinn Fein president Gerry Adams at the House of Commons. When persuaded to abandon this inflammatory idea, he told journalists that a 'right and freedom' had been denied him. So this man apparently believed in freedom of expression?

Brearley's article was neatly worded and wide-ranging of thought, conceding that some of Henderson's speculations might be worthy of examination, though on the whole he considered them over-speculative and offensive. 'There have been times,' England's cerebral captain wrote, 'when I have failed the Tebbit test (though, as far as I know, only as a spectator). Such failure may, as he suggests, arise from guilt. I may feel that I, or we, deserve defeat because of the injustices perpetrated in our names; or I may have problems with taking unmixed pleasure in success because I unconsciously equate doing well with contempt and gloating.'

He closed with an intriguing paragraph: 'The unconscious is a hybrid and above all elusive beast. Mr Henderson's attempt to expose it in others reveals more about his than theirs.'

As for my own statement of apology, the keynote read: 'My particular hope in respect of this article was that the plight of foreign-born cricketers in this country and those with immigrant parents – whether from West Indies, Australasia, southern Africa or Asia – might be better understood when their difficulties were considered. Publication of this particular article was, I now realise, not the best way to have gone about it. The national-identity element was drowned out. I had hoped that the article would be a springboard for beneficial debate, but have been deeply disappointed at distortions in certain sections of the media . . .'

Voltaire came into the most difficult Editorial I'd ever had to compose. 'Whoever serves his country well,' the Frenchman once wrote, 'has no need of ancestors.' To his credit also stood the better-known 'I may not agree with what you say, but I would defend to the death your right to say it.' It was this sacred maxim which was now under very serious threat from the Thought Police.

I referred to the outburst of a phone-in caller to a BBC Radio 5 programme onto which I had been invited to discuss the matter. 'I haven't read this rubbish, but . . .' the caller foamed. And he was permitted to go on for a couple of minutes.

Later in the Editorial I wrote, with relief, about the gradual emergence of reactions from calm and thoughtful writers who identified the compassionate side of the matter.

There was the letter in *The Guardian* from a black English-born lawyer who had no significant connections with any other country and yet did not feel he belonged in England. 'Public anger,' I wrote, 'should be focused on the fact that a devoted citizen of this country has always been made to feel like an alien. The letter's heading refers unerringly to "a nation ill at ease".'

That Editorial could easily have been many times the normal length, but that would not have solved anything. The most depressing aspect was that the most vociferous were the least likely to look at the problem from all angles.

But there were now some encouraging efforts that showed that, painful though the process had been, constructive debate was not only unfolding but was revelatory.

Mark Lawson, in *The Guardian*, explained how he wanted England to win but Gatting (because of his disapproved South African tour) to fail. Lawson disliked Allan Lamb because he seemed 'a juvenile yob whose accent was the full howling Springbok horror', but was right behind Robin Smith because 'his media image is that of a sensitive, even neurotic, oenophile with a soft voice'. Talk about prejudice.

'From the playground fight to the corporate power struggle,' wrote Lawson, 'to the family row to the country at war, the most terrible of questions has always been, "Whose side are you on?"' He closed with: 'The piece *Wisden Cricket Monthly* should have run is the one about how it is that supporters sometimes forget which side they are on.'

Peter Simple, in the *Daily Telegraph*, wrote that 'among the "anti-racists" it [Henderson's article] set off automatic yells and screams of hysterical fury. When the editor of the magazine said mildly that the writer of the article was entitled to give his views on an interesting subject, he was also abused . . . Behind this routine display of "anti-racist" bigotry loomed the larger subject of Commonwealth immigration and the virtual ban, reinforced by law, of open and honest discussion about its effects.'

I considered that Ian Jack produced probably the most constructive essay – 'In pursuit of Englishness' – in *The Independent* on Sunday (July 9). He sought to gather opinion on what England today means to people, and concluded that 'the nation clings fondly to a distant rural image because it cannot embrace the present.' A writer from Devon told him: 'The trenches in Flanders are in there somewhere. Soldier poets like Sassoon. That double nostalgia, where you are nostalgic about their nostalgia for an England that probably vanished in 1914. But now England tends to mean Little England, and I'm not very keen on that.' A London poet said, 'I don't know an English person who doesn't feel slightly marginalised by the word in some way, and anxious to find something that slightly separates them from it – ancestors from Cornwall or Ireland.' A young woman told Jack: 'I'd almost prefer to be from somewhere else.'

Jack (of Scottish descent) regarded much of Henderson's thinking about an instinctive desire to succeed and about 'unequivocal' Englishness as 'absurd', but conceded that 'at the height of empire, which is where so many ideas of Englishness still come from, it would have seemed normal enough.'

Hooray! We were getting some calm and sensible analysis at last.

Giles Coren, in *The Times*, quoted former England fast bowler Neil Foster as saying that 'when you play against Australia you are facing national pride. We don't have a truly national side.' Coren swiftly pounced on that one, noting that Foster had relinquished his England place to go on the 'rebel' tour of South Africa.

Had he consulted his newspaper's back issues from 99 years earlier, Coren would have discovered that times might well actually have improved, for on June 22, 1896 *The Times* said of Ranjitsinhji: 'Although the Indian prince has learnt all his cricket in England he could scarcely, if the title of the match were to be adhered to, have been included in the English eleven.' MCC having declined to select Ranji for the first Test, Lancashire CCC's committee had no such reservations, and after courteously seeking the acquiescence of the Australian captain they picked the little Cambridge and Sussex maestro. He scored 154 not out, though England lost the Test by three wickets.

In *The Spectator*, Leo McKinstry, a former Labour councillor who years later was to write an admirable biography of Jack Hobbs, was as anti-Henderson as almost anybody had been, and concentrated on foreign-born England sporting heroes from Ranjitsinhji through Plum Warner, Prince Obolensky, to the current headliner, Canadian-born Greg Rusedski. 'The row over British qualifications has been given a vicious twist,' McKinstry wrote, 'by an article in the current issue of *Wisden Cricket Monthly*, a magazine edited by an Australian, David Frith, and owned by an American, John Paul Getty II.' He was also loose with the facts in saying that England manager Ray Illingworth came across Devon Malcolm in the dressing-room listening to *Land of Hope and Glory* on his headphones. As Illingworth explained in his 1996 book *One-Man Committee,* he reminded Malcolm that 'he was playing for his country' and had been picked as 'a nasty, big fast bowler, and it was time he focused on that'. 'Illy' was not impressed at seeing him with the 'cans' on. 'I tapped him on the shoulder and when he lifted one can to listen to me, I heard the pop music coming out and said: "You should be listening to *Land of Hope and Glory*".' Before long, Malcolm was taking his unforgettable 9 for 57 to rout South Africa.

There is an interesting comparison to be made here with Greg Matthews, who was spotted on the Old Trafford balcony in 1985 before going in to bat, his head nodding away to the beat of whatever was pouring from his headphones. It transpired that this almost manically patriotic Australian was twitching to the rhythms not of *Advance, Australia Fair* but of *Midnight Oil.*

The young right-wing historian Andrew Roberts entered the growing debate about British pride later in July, following Government advisor Dr Nicholas Tate's much-publicised plea for national identity to be put on the school curriculum. In the *Daily Mail,* Roberts, lamenting various stupidities that have accelerated Britain's decline, ended with a particularly interesting claim: 'The liberal believes that a man, once stripped of his national and cultural identity, will become Everyman – Citizen of the World. The conservative knows that, in fact, he will become bewildered, schizophrenic, unhappy and alone.'

As I waded through all these feature articles, morning after morning, I wondered how many letters these writers and their editors were receiving. It was still taking me all morning to deal with my own postal intake, some of it hostile, some supportive.

The remarkable John Taylor, a black barrister, a moderate, soon to be elevated to the House of Lords, recalled his father's hardships as a Jamaican cricketer and coach in 1950s Britain (he eventually became one of the best-loved figures at Warwickshire CCC). Victim of humiliating racial prejudice, Derief Taylor 'didn't get angry and call everyone racist, he just quietly got on with things . . . The way to fight is with the pen, not the sword.' He might as well have added 'nor with the divisive writ'.

The whole nation, it seemed, was hopping up and down with red-hot opinions, many trite, some profound and provocative. 'The premise of Henderson's article,' wrote Robert Winder in *The Independent,* 'is that national pride is the supreme motivating force without which nothing is possible. Is that true? It would be lovely if it weren't. But almost all of international sport drinks deep from the poisoned well of political and racial animosity.'

Some months later, in a penetrative *Daily Telegraph* contribution, American-born Janet Daley suggested that although 'the elimination of unfair treatment of individuals on grounds of race or religion is an admirable aim', it seemed that 'anti-racism has gone far beyond this. It has become a form of religious dogma and, in that tradition, it has noted what is a genuinely universal human characteristic and ruled it inadmissible.'

As Geoffrey Wheatcroft observed, the Culture of Complaint (a phrase neatly coined by Robert Hughes) was 'founded on an obsession with victimhood and self-pity'. But 'victimhood is nonsensical because we are all the victims of our history'. I myself was now most certainly afflicted by that feeling.

Kevin Mitchell, who first fanned the coals of Henderson's piece into flames, came back on the subject in *The Observer* a week later, on July 9, 1995: '*WCM's* editor, David Frith, admits: "I've been up there like a dartboard on Henderson's behalf, and I've had enough of it." So much has he had of it, in fact, that he issued a statement on Friday night expressing his regret at giving space to such a loose cannon. Finally, I can agree with Frith. He had asserted that the debate was healthy, which it is; he has shown the courage now in conceding it should not have been left in the hands of an obsessive racial purist. All of this represents some volte face – not only by Frith, whose protestations that Henderson's argument did not wholly sit with his own view and whose determination not to have his editorial freedom compromised ought to be taken at face value.'

One interviewer, from ABC Radio, Sydney, began with an enquiry as to whether I was beginning to feel a bit like Salman Rushdie, the Anglo-Indian writer who had been under constant guard since the late Ayatollah had put a death sentence on him. I tried to muster the flippancy of a Gower in my response.

The fourth edition of an ambitious but short-lived cricket magazine called *Third Man* capitalised constructively on the burning topic with a six-page feature headed 'Patriot Games' in which Ian McQuillin put together a treatise combining history and philosophy, itemising Gordon Greenidge's dilemma in the early 1970s (he was abused in both his homeland of England and his native land of Barbados), the increase in intermarriage in Britain, and quotes from several professors, which introduced some overdue intellectual content.

Having spotlighted a self-contradiction in the Marqusee book, *Anyone But England*, which is muddled in more than one place, McQuillin asserted that a black Briton would fit into an England XI more readily in some ways than a Zimbabwean, a South African or a 'de facto Australian', and concluded by referring to remarks in Graeme Hick's autobiography. The Zimbabwe-born and -raised county cricket run-machine listed 'a number of hard-nosed business reasons behind his decision to qualify [for England]. Not once does Hick mention that he shared some kind of common cultural bond with England which spurred him on.' He is compared with Bob Woolmer (born in India), whose dearest ambition at school was to play for England. 'There may be many reasons why Bob Woolmer made the most of his ability,' concluded McQuillin, 'and Graeme Hick has so far failed to make the most of his. Nationalism may, just may, be one of them. Hick chose England. But England claimed Woolmer.'

He might have added a throwaway line that Woolmer, one of the world's very best coaches, was allowed to sell South Africa his exceptional services. English cricket caught napping.

Two other quotes from the bulging dossier are, finally, worthy of reference. The first is from a remarkably insightful summing-up, in the *Jamaica Gleaner*, by Clayton Goodwin, a Kent man with a West Indian wife, who had been writing for Caribbean newspapers for 35 years and contributed from time to time to *WCM*, some paragraphs from which were challenged by Henderson in his now-notorious offering. Goodwin felt it was wrong to have published Henderson's piece, but went on to say:

'There was nothing in that article to justify the extent of the ensuing brouhaha or the vilification of Mr Frith personally or of *Wisden Cricket Monthly*. The editor became the subject of much abuse, with detractors from the public seeking him out in the Press-box and a visitor there during the Test match against West Indies at The Oval described the magazine as a "right-wing racist rag". That is not a view shared by West Indian cricket-writers and their colleagues, or by those who have taken the trouble to read the offending article and not to feed off the invective of others.'

Goodwin continued: 'His pugnacious remarks that he did not care for "political correctness", delivered in an Australian accent which, unfairly, to most pukka English ears, gives a hint of belligerence, has made him appear to be more confrontational than is the case. Furthermore, his biting book reviews in *WCM* – yes, David, they do hurt (even when, especially when, they are true) – and frank expression of opinion have ruffled many feathers.

'Because he is used to the cut-and-thrust, give-and-take of debate, he adopted the same attitude with interviewers, without apparently first doing his homework in ascertaining who they were, what was their standpoint and how the remarks would sound to a listener who did not know the details of the argument. Some of the interviewers had an axe to grind, which wasn't exactly connected with a frank expression of the specific principles of cricket. The *WCM* editor appeared to make the error of an injudicious opening batsman [how did Goodwin know that?!] who goes for his shots before he has adjusted to the bowling, the light and the pace of the pitch. It was exciting while it lasted, but Cammie Smith, Colin Milburn and Keith Stackpole evoked a similar frisson of expectation when they cut loose in the first over of the day, but their stay at the top of international cricket was not prolonged.'

Clayton Goodwin then dropped in two images from the summer of 1995:

'An elderly West Indian claiming to be a bona fide journalist sought membership of the Cricket Writers Club. With one exception everybody gave him a wide berth, suspecting that he was a confidence trickster. That one exception was David Frith. He preferred to give the man the benefit of the doubt and sponsored his successful application to the club. Before the end of the summer he too admitted that the man was a charlatan, but it enhances rather than detracts from the fact that David was prepared initially to believe the best of a West Indian.

'My last image is of him [me] at the Test match at The Oval sitting among Tony Becca, Horace Helps, Bryan Davis, Qamar Ahmed, Khadim Baloch and William Whyte – it would hardly qualify him for membership of the Ku Klux Klan!

'David would be surprised to be compared to any black man, especially in the current context. All the same, I believe that the Anglo-Australian of Guildford has much in common with the Moor of Venice. If Othello 'loved not wisely but too well', Mr Frith expressed his opinions, perhaps not wisely but too well.'

And, lastly from the fat, groaning pile of cuttings, comes a summary by Murray Hedgcock in his weekly column in The Australian, this one published on August 16, 1995. He took it from the beginning: 'All hell erupted. Columnists, feature-writers and sports correspondents bought into the debate, some simply recording a good controversy, others making it highly political, slating the magazine and its editor as racist. Left-wing polemicists delighted in this proof – as they saw it – that England was a racially-prejudiced country, and its cricket dominated by middle-class fascists.

'Here I must declare an interest: *Wisden Cricket Monthly* editor David Frith is a friend of 25 years' standing. We share a mirror-image Anglo-Australian background, Frith being born in London, but growing up in Australia before returning to Britain, while still spending part of each year in Queensland. I was born and brought up in Australia, but have lived half my life in Britain. We each have mixed feelings about both nations, both backgrounds: we are not quite one nor the other, finding much to like/dislike in both the countries where we have shared our lives . . . Over the years I have argued that sporting identity should be based on close association with the community, the city, the country for which you play, or for which you barrack.

'However, in an increasingly internationalist world, where mobility is a key to personal choice and career opportunity, the roving sportsman clearly is part of today's life, as he offers any hungry team the prospect of winning trophies. It is in English cricket, the only country operating a full-blooded domestic industry in which hundreds of players can find fulltime employment, that the import for years has been accepted.

'That might be fair enough if he stayed in the county game – but he does not. The England Test team long ago decided to recruit from the best British-based foreigners, once they fulfilled increasingly flexible qualifications – and so recent XIs have included a string of South African- or West Indian-born players.

'This to my simple mind is quite wrong; as an outsider I'm not interested in the commitment to England of a Hick or a Malcolm (the argument put by Henderson), but in the correctness of their being in the team at all. No other Test team so blatantly uses imports: impoverished New Zealand has taken in one or two [their South African intake was to bulge in the 2010s] . . . and Australia once to its shame called Kepler Wessels an Aussie, but that's about it.

'But to return to Robert Henderson: his argument brought fury down upon editor Frith, who duly apologised because he had no intention of offending black cricketers, having published the article in the naive belief that it would start serious and justified debate. Fleet Street got very excited at hints that England captain Mike Atherton would quit the *WCM* Editorial Board in protest: in the finish he did no such thing, which to some extent helped to settle the dust.

'As usual, the lawyers will do best out of the whole unhappy affair,' concluded Hedgcock. 'Indignant Phillip DeFreitas and Devon Malcolm have their legal eagles still talking to the *WCM* solicitors – and the only thing certain is that Robert Henderson will never make it into mainstream print again.'

The rest of that turbulent summer was heavily punctuated with faxes and letters and consultations after solicitors acting for DeFreitas and Malcolm threw writs for libel at Wisden Cricket Magazines Ltd – though, interestingly, not in author Henderson's direction. Wisden's counsel, having studied the vast media coverage, noticed that there was no shortage of humbug around the fringes of the case, but concluded that with juries often being unpredictable and capricious, an out-of-court settlement might be advisable.

I had no idea what, in detail, the Gettys were thinking. There must have been many a huddle between them and Messrs Engel, Wright and Lane, but I might just as well have had the plague for all the contact between us. Eventually I picked up on the decision to agree acceptable damages, and Malcolm and DeFreitas duly accepted sums which the newspapers surmised to be £25,000 and £50,000 respectively, together with published apologies to each, and apologies read out in open court. There followed settlements with Chris Lewis, who, like the other two, directed a donation to charities of his choice (and had some very interesting days ahead of him), and with Gladstone Small.

It had been an exhausting and dispiriting experience, leaving me, as David O'Reilly put it in Australia's *Bulletin* magazine, 'upset that there seemed no room for free expression' and resentful at 'being vilified by people who had not read the original article but were merely reacting to the tabloid media coverage'. I had remarked to David that you no longer heard people say 'It's a free country'. The thought police had taken over, and there was no telling if freedom of speech would ever be restored. That was the most depressing part. The only welcome thing about all this was that I had lost a stone in weight.

Meanwhile, what no-one outside the family knew was that on July 21, three weeks into the commotion, we had a call from Debbie's sister Rosie, in Queensland, to say that their mother had had another stroke and was not going to make it this time. Dear Esther had survived for eight years in a nursing home since the first stroke, with severely reduced mobility. The phone was still ringing as eager journalists sought more details of *WCM*'s cause célèbre. Then it jingled once too often: Debbie's loving and uncomplaining mother had been taken from us.

We went this time not to that seat up on the grassy slopes of the Hog's Back but for a random drive to Windsor and Runnymede, where we had taken Esther Pennell on her 1976 trip to England. I could not recall ever having had such a wild mixture of emotions awash in my head and my heart as now: grief for 'Mum', concern for Debbie after what she had endured as a helpless onlooker through these nasty weeks of uproar; also bitterness at the sickening manipulation surrounding the Henderson affair, and anxiety over where all this left us.

The outstanding England v West Indies series of 1995 drew to a close at The Oval, the sides locked together two-all in the end, and we were left with memories of Dominic Cork's sensational first few Tests (and his gormless gesturing); of the terrifying injuries to Nick Knight in the field at Trent Bridge and Robin Smith while batting at Old Trafford in the tensest of all the Tests; of the disgraceful Edgbaston pitch; of Graeme Hick's masterful and long-awaited first Test hundred off West Indies bowling; and of Brian Lara's three enchanting centuries in the second half of the series. West Indies' reliance remained on pace, Ambrose, Walsh, Bishop and Kenny Benjamin taking 97 wickets between them in the series (in which England were up to their old tricks again, utilising 21 players); but less often were the critics stirred to condemn excessive short-pitched bowling. It was fascinating to learn that at one point Michael Holding, from the commentary-box, sent a plea down to coach Andy Roberts (who, of course, was once one of Holding's co-assassins) to get his fast bowlers to bowl a fuller (and more profitable) length. But it really had been a stirring series, and if I were to choose one supreme moment it would not be Cork's hat-trick ball, even though it's been shown a thousand times since. Instead it would be Alec Stewart's diving, turf-level, left-handed catch to dismiss Lara in the second innings at Lord's. Given its acrobatic nature, the state of the match, and the eminence of the batsman, it was the best wicketkeeping catch I'd ever seen in all my years.

Elsewhere, I'd helped Charlie Watts acquire Don Bradman's 1934 Australian blazer at Christie's for £3670, and was tickled to get an excited call from the sleepy-eyed drummer that evening to say that he'd tried it on, and 'it fits!'

As the evenings grew darker, there were obituaries to write for two legendary England cricketers, Harold Larwood and Miss Molly Hide. England prepared themselves for the tour of South Africa, the first for 31 years, and then for the World Cup on the Subcontinent. And the January 1996 edition of *Wisden Cricket Monthly* was to be the 200th, which sparked a proud inner glow.

The season closed with the annual Cricket Writers Club dinner, and as usual I had arranged for the speedy preparation of a trophy for the Young Cricketer of the Year. The 1995 winner was none other than Andrew Symonds, the Birmingham-born, Queensland-raised youngster who in August, while batting for Gloucestershire against Glamorgan at Abergavenny, had broken the world first-class record for sixes: 16 in his first-innings 254 not out and four more in the second innings. 'Roy's' name had first appeared in *WCM* back in December 1992 following his partnership of 446 with Matthew Mott in a competitive youth limited-overs match (at least it was intended to be competitive) in Brisbane. Suddenly he was hot property.

The young giant asked nervously if he was expected to make a speech. No, just say thank you. Then I realised David Graveney, now an England selector, was standing with us in that crowded room. So I said, 'Yes, you'll have to make a short speech, but it'll be good practice for when you're Australian captain one day!' Graveney looked down and said, 'Hey, steady on!'

Symonds was chosen for the England A tour that winter, but withdrew. He was a mass of confusion, speaking to his adoptive father, Ken, almost daily by phone to Queensland, and wondering whether he should keep his Australian Test hopes alive. After all, he had told the English Press after his century for Queensland against the 1994-95 English side at Toowoomba: 'I'm no Pom, mate. I'm a fair dinkum Aussie. I couldn't be persuaded to become English. When you're a baby, you don't know where you're born, do you?'

In order to return to Gloucestershire as a 'home' player, Symonds had to sign a declaration that he would accept England selection, by his birthright, should it be offered. He thus returned to Bristol for 1996, having failed to tempt the Australian selectors, even for their one-day side.

I began to wonder if, after all, I'd got the splash wrong on our October '95 front cover: 'The Pom who wasn't'. Then Andrew Symonds was interviewed for television in the spring of 1996. 'Do you regard yourself as English or Australian?' he was asked. The poor fellow, not wishing either to invalidate his contract or to be untrue to his inner self, just stared blankly at the camera. And as the tape rolled and rolled, he continued to say nothing.

I was one of very few people who knew exactly how he felt at that moment.

CHAPTER TWENTY-SIX

Our liberty depends on freedom of the press, and that cannot be limited without being lost.

THOMAS JEFFERSON

'I WON'T beat about the bush,' said Wisden's company secretary, having beaten about the bush for several minutes, lamenting England's performance in South Africa. We were seated in a cold and barren conference room in Coopers & Lybrand's huge block by Charing Cross station. Malcolm Ridley had asked me, soon after my return from Australia just before Christmas 1995, to meet him for a discussion 'about the future of Wisden'. Now I recognised that he was no decisionmaker, more the messenger, but for all my hopes and all my apprehension before this meeting, I was not quite prepared for what came next.

'The board have decided to replace you as editor.'

Every drop of blood seemed to turn to ice. I'd heard him clearly enough, but resisted the chilling reality of his words. A maelstrom seemed to be tearing my head from my body as I tried to grasp the likely consequences. They were snatching my magazine away from me, removing my livelihood, threatening my security, terminating my working life. Or were they freeing me from a 17-year devotion which had been slowly soured by controversy and personality friction, and a sense of drudgery?

The company secretary went on talking, but for a time I heard none of it. How could they be so callous? Whose final decision was this? Why hadn't they had a man-to-man chat with me about it?

Ridley pushed some typed papers across the table and explained that I was expected to sign them. 'Not right now,' I said. 'And when is all this supposed to take place?'

'It's with immediate effect. Or at least, at the end of this month. That's to say, two days from now, January 31.'

I imagined the indecent haste was because my successor was waiting to take his place in my chair, but in fact they had not yet even begun to find one. The immediacy of it all was because 'they' felt I would not have the heart to carry on writing and editing.

'But I'm halfway through an edition,' I pointed out, adding that they had underestimated my professionalism.

'Well, then, perhaps we can make it the end of next month, February,' he responded, and said he'd refer back to the board.

He expressed some slight sympathy for how I must be feeling and explained that this was not the first time he'd had such duties.

I had to get out of there. The bare walls were pressing down on me. It seemed my intestines were oozing down into my legs. I felt disgust. I felt anger, horror. And mystification.

'Why have they done this?'

Ridley mumbled something about my not having contributed to the last management committee meeting; to which I wasted more breath: 'But I was isolated, shut out. There was nothing for me to say. It was all *Almanack*. They didn't really want me there. I was thinking of resigning from the committee anyway.'

There had to be more to it than that? 'And,' Ridley went on, 'there was that business last year.'

So why hadn't something been said then, six months ago? What, for God's sake, has been going on? Were they just *using* the Henderson fiasco?

He had nothing further to say. We got in the lift, and in the cavernous marble lobby I regained my calm sufficiently to extend my hand. His own was cold and clammy.

Outside, in the narrow, jostling street, the chill January air stung my face and cleared my head, though not for long. My legs, which might normally have been regarded as the sturdiest part of me, now became unreliable. I decided to walk all the way back to Waterloo station.

The midwinter afternoon was darkening as I walked, in a half-trance, through the bare gardens and along the Thames Embankment. Incongruously there was a flicker of excitement deep inside me as I registered the fact that I had been, in a manner of speaking, liberated. But it was soon blown aside by fury and tumultuous insecurity.

What huddles my 'colleagues' must have had while I was in Queensland. And I had no reservations about the likely unanimity in the decision to get rid of me: Paul Getty, through his screen of advisors, could overrule anything and anybody, so it seemed. And he hadn't done so. Mark, his son, whether *Wisden Cricket Monthly* had been a birthday present or not, was certainly no admirer of mine, particularly after I had spoken up in my staff's interests and held out for an acceptable deal on my *WCM* shares. His sidekick Ridley, like Graeme Wright, was also highly unlikely to speak on my behalf. Chris Lane, in his new, privileged 'eminence', was almost certainly content with the decision. And as for Matthew Engel, some of his casual remarks from past months now took on significance: 'Are you really?' he'd queried after I told him my age. 'Fifty-eight? *Really*?' Suddenly, perhaps, I was conveniently perceived as an oldie, ripe for redundancy. And when he enquired after my well-being some weeks later, he seemed surprised that we were not in the process of selling up and heading off to retirement in Queensland. There had been too much guesswork all along. And here was I now, reduced to contortions of guesswork of my own.

I reached Cleopatra's Needle, first seen when I was waist-high to Dad long ago in the war years. And I wished crazily that he were here now, to place an arm on my shoulder, to tell me not to worry about those rich buggers and to think instead about starting up another cricket magazine and to write more books. But I just wanted to wake up now, and find that this was just another silly dream, a variation on the familiar nightmare which had visited me most of my life, perhaps six or eight times each year: a wicket has fallen, I'm next man in, but I am still in civvies, and the crease was far away. Rush, panic, quickly, tie up those laces: and they're all waiting, and gesturing, and I'm not going to make it. I gather this is the cricketer's version of the 'running hopelessly for the departing train' dream. And the analysts would have us believe that it represents a fear of death.

Across Waterloo Bridge I walked, getting a flash vision of us all 30 years ago, when Debbie and the three little ones first set eyes on London, seeing to the left the City of London which my courageous father had helped save over half-a-century ago, and ahead of me the National Film Theatre, where I had presented cricket film shows for 15 years. That's when I began to count the things I seemingly would never do again: the film nights, the Editorials aimed at spotlighting the game's hypocrisy and woolly-headedness, seeing Test matches through in the flesh from start to finish, interviewing the stars of today and the heroes of yesteryear, reviewing books conscientiously, scooping up every morsel of news throughout the month, corresponding with readers and evaluating their requirements, covering the auctions, selecting people to write for us.

I stared sightlessly through the window throughout the train journey to Guildford, and hoped that by the time I'd walked home, along the noisy Portsmouth Road and then up the silent hill, my mind would have eased. But it was not to do so for months, if then. Randolph Turpin must have felt a bit like this after Sugar Ray Robinson had half-killed him in taking back the world title in 1951.

A Press release had been prepared. It euphemistically referred to my 'early retirement', which I decided not to challenge for the time being, though to an even greater extent it made me feel about 85. It disguised the fact that I was the scapegoat for the hysterical reaction to the Henderson article and its legal consequences.

Somehow I kept the facade in place during the remaining month, while I completed the March edition of *WCM* and worked for half-a-month on the April. The March number recorded the retirements of David Boon and Martin Crowe from Test cricket, and Dickie Bird, Bruce Reid and A.C.Smith from their centrestage cricket activities. It seemed best to keep my own farewell remarks to a minimum: 14 lines. Appropriately, the England and Australian teams at the World Cup were featured on my final front cover. I saw to it, too, that a small item was included about a V1 doodlebug that had interrupted a game of cricket in 1944.

It took a while to ascertain that I could remain on the Editorial Board of *WCM* and would be trusted to write occasionally, though restricted to obituaries and perhaps the odd book review, deemed safe territory. And a stronger Engel presence in the magazine was soon apparent. He took a regular back-page column, one of which was devoted entirely to 'Cricket the Israeli way'. (He had recently delivered grace in Hebrew at the Wisden dinner.)

I was permitted to pursue my intention of covering the sixth World Cup, out to Pakistan and back in five days, the first, my birthday, spent mostly airborne. This afforded a few last morsels of the career involvement which had been ripped away on January 29, though it felt strange as never before to be in that hectic Press-box, the babble at record levels as Australia let it slip, out there under the lights, while Sri Lanka won hearts by taking the crown. As Arjuna Ranatunga coped with a crushing crowd of reporters afterwards, my mind flew back to the happy days of 1982 when, as an 18-year-old, he took part in his country's first-ever Test match. He was chubbier now, slightly less shy, and with silver tinges to his sideburns.

Equally memorable was the haggard countenance of Shane Warne as the Australians' team bus rushed them back to their hotel late that frenzied night. Still sweaty and unchanged, he sat at the front of the bus as we overtook it on the inside. I could see his usually laughing eyes glazed as if in shock. Every few seconds that famous face was hidden by another outflow of cigarette smoke. But this glorious spin bowler, to whom cricket owed so much, would bounce back another day. It was more than I could feel about myself. I had been tossed into a void.

It had been 21 years since I was last in Lahore: that absurd leg injury, Hanif's caring consideration, nets with Viv and all that, and dinner with Clive and Inti. This time, I felt remote from the cricket. I felt battered. I also felt absolutely no shame. That was for others.

The report of the World Cup final needed to be written next morning, and it took ages to get started. Finally, I broke down very rare writer's block by promising myself a trip to Lahore Zoo. The best part of three hours later I had earned my prize: midst exotic people and diverting exhibits in the enclosures, I felt a tranquillity I had not known for many weeks.

A night flight took me out of Pakistan, back to reminders of the recent traumatic events, but at least I had accomplished my mission. After travelling all that way, I had nearly missed the final for want of 'media accreditation'. Letters and faxes galore had gone off, but of a pass there was no sign. So dear Colonel Shuja Ud-din, who was so helpful during my visit (he was the slow left-armer who got May, Compton and Graveney out in the 1954 Old Trafford Test), drove me to the Gaddafi Stadium on the eve of the event in search of that vital piece of plastic.

The entire Lahore police force seemed to be encircling the cricket stadium, reinforced by half the Army, with tons of weaponry between them. How were we to penetrate this defence and reach the stadium to get my pass if we didn't already have a pass? In desperation I waved the clipboard through the car window. We were waved through. The relief was intense. It was calculated that only six or seven people in the entire world had witnessed every cricket World Cup since the first, back in 1975. Who knew? One day a man could be the only one left standing. And that very thought brought it home to me that I was not ready yet to turn my back on cricket entirely.

The next challenge was to decide whether to accept the invitation to the annual Wisden dinner, early in April, at the East India Club in London. It was always an enjoyable and meaningful affair, and I had been to the last 20 or so, none having been more memorable than in 1979, when Robert Maxwell, who then held the printing contract, boomed from the top table, like some South American dictator, though with the physique of a Sumo wrestler, that never again would diners get free *Wisdens*. It was a statement he was soon forced to retract, with a cackle, after an aide had pointed out that we were all potential reviewers, and they had saved much on postage. (Twelve years later Maxwell mysteriously drowned from his yacht off the Canary Islands.)

As the Wisden dinner approached, I was wrestling with a sense of having been betrayed by the management crowd, and this weighed heavily. My impulse was to stay away. But two close friends urged me to go. I left it until the last afternoon before deciding.

To my astonishment, Mark Getty greeted me like a long-lost friend, beaming and extending an eager hand. Was he scared that I was going to launch into a shouting match, or land one on him? Unlikely. I was greatly taken aback, and struck by his 'as if nothing had happened' behaviour, but managed to conjure up a verbal morsel in response. I congratulated him on the Gettys' recent acquisition of the Hulton Deutsch picture library (for around five times what they paid for Wisden).

Mark Getty, as dinner chairman, made perfunctory reference to my recent departure 17 years after founding the magazine (a gold watch was neither expected nor proffered). He then introduced my successor, *Independent* 'rock music' and cricket journalist Tim de Lisle, an Old Etonian aged 33, who was at that time in the throes of making *WCM* just about as different as it could be from the 'product' I had overseen. Even the front cover was unrecognisable, somebody suggesting that it now looked like *Gardeners' World*. Not least among the lost features was the *Wisden* logo, removed from *WCM* after 17 years, perhaps as a giveaway that Matthew Engel, editor of the 'famous' Wisden (the *Almanack*), regarded it as his personal fiefdom.

I was not sorry when this particular Wisden dinner was over, though I greatly appreciated the hands extended by true friends afterwards, plus that from Rugby legend Cliff Morgan, whom I scarcely knew, but who took the trouble to cross the room on his way out. Perhaps he somehow knew something I didn't yet know, and that was that I had a Welsh great-grandfather.

There followed a very strange summer. There was the compilation of the first edition of this autobiography, then *Test Match Year*, a new annual launched in the pleasant company of Warren Bagust, a long-ago St George cricketer in Sydney, and fellow Old Cantabrian, long time resident in London. This publication seemed to have a future until killed off, seemingly because the publishing house, we were to discover, also had an interest in the distribution of *Wisden*. Our annual posed a threat. A few other bits and pieces kept me fairly busy, but almost daily I had to fight acute disorientation, a pressing feeling that the past 20-odd years had been wasted, that I was on the scrapheap, my successor's scornful reference to 'getting rid of some of the junk' from *WCM* doing nothing to alleviate that impression. My senses of direction and professional purpose had been assaulted. Then came news of Ray Lindwall's death, which I could not escape feeling as badly as a family loss. Soon, Alan McGilvray went too, another piece of the golden years chipped away. And then the beloved Denis Compton was gone.

The world, a close friend stated, would look a much more pleasant place after a couple of months had passed. But he was at least a couple of years out. I forgave him for underestimating the depth to which the monthly routine and the creativity had gripped me over the seventeen years since 1979.

How was I to weather this and survive – and not just financially? Three things made it possible: the comfort and support extended by my faithful Debbie, as always, and by our family; generous letters from true friends (nine months later the admirable Gilbert Mant, last survivor of the Press corps in the 1932-33 Bodyline series, reflected on the Henderson affair: 'I would have thought that the author would be in the firing line, not the editor'); and, unsurprisingly, the game of cricket itself helped: not that which is watched so much as being out there on the field. In my 60th year, I was glad just to be out in the middle, trying to cope with a new ball propelled by a man less than half my age; or floating down a ball which could just as readily finish up in the bushes as flick the stumps behind a scything bat; or pocketing a catch that suggested that my recent numbness had actually enhanced the state of relaxation so crucial to slip-fielding.

From the hurricane of '87 to my dismissal from my magazine in '96: this was without question the toughest period of my life to date, embracing as it did two major family deaths, controversy by the bucketload, several other unrelated traumas, and now, following the insulting treatment of the past two years, the somewhat unfathomable mystery of the break-up of *Wisden Cricket Monthly*. What *now*?

CHAPTER TWENTY-SEVEN

Time goes, you say? Ah, no! Alas, Time stays, we go.

AUSTIN DOBSON

THE future came too fast. It always had seemed to have an unpleasant habit of coming at me with indecent haste. Suddenly the anticipated years of work on the magazine were blown away. I was left emasculated, stunned by a sense of obsolescence. I was destabilised, isolated, exposed, struggling to hold onto shreds of self-esteem. It was the scrapheap syndrome which I'd heard so much about in this youth-obsessed age. It has to be experienced for its demoralising impact to be understood. Next stop death?

I was on the outside again and dispossessed, coping with bouts of emotional disturbance. After such intensive involvement in the game which I had studied devotedly for almost half-a-century, I was cut off from the hundreds of friends and acquaintances and from the avenues in every country where cricket is played. I don't know how I managed to negotiate those terrible months following my ejection. I deeply regretted that my soulmate was forced to share the suffering as the closest witness.

The full truth, of course, had initially been disguised. I went along with all that 'early retirement' nonsense in the *WCM* press release. Stunned as I was, I refrained from lashing out publicly in anger. As the spring of 1996 turned to summer, with cricket activity resuming at a high pitch all around me, I tried to reshape my life and 'redefine' myself: the first opportunity for many years. Clouded daily and especially nightly by financial concern, I sought to reclaim the old self, the untrammelled person of long ago, when I had simply wished to acquire scholarship in cricket, before being drawn into a strange world where a thousand happy memories and treasured friendships were to be bruised by sporadic enmities, and where the suspicion, jealousy and tension deadened the eye and tightened the jaw.

There had been far too much hostility. I concede that there were times when I became so fraught, so combative and defensive that I might have given offence to one or two in the Press-box and elsewhere. But this was rare, although the burden of provocation and unfriendly actions towards me had amassed, perhaps induced by jealousy of my independence or by resentment at my perceived 'foreign' origin. One pony-tailed Fleet Street smart-arse smugly wrote that Frith had made history by being sacked by both cricket magazines. In these strangulated times cricket is as prone to *schadenfreude* as any other pursuit. An absurd perception of me as an Australian intruder seemed to have sparked ill-feeling not unconnected with Australia's painful dominance in Ashes cricket over the years.

How I wish I could have been like Don Bradman as defined in 1948 by John Arlott, who wrote that he 'ignored the spite of those who grudged him that [which] he had earned'. I've taken my responsibilities seriously, ever since marrying my wonderful Debbie when we were so very young, and experiencing the joys of fatherhood. As life advances, you have fewer elders to rely on for guidance, until you are exposed, completely responsible for your own fortification and that of your dependants. I've long subscribed to that old Rugby League warrior's assertion that you take it and give it without grumbling. (And I gladly registered my gratitude and surprise at never having had a night in hospital to that date.) When you're ganged up on you have to react. Don't you?

Just as the 12-year-old consciously tried to make himself stronger in 1949, when he found himself in a new land, often lonely, and stalked by unfamiliar fears, so in my thirties I aimed to take on the characteristics of the rhinoceros, my favourite animal, whenever my dream world of writing about cricket and circulating among cricketers was gatecrashed by people of ill-intent, English cricket's version of the Mob. I willed my hide to thicken and was prepared where necessary to charge at them at the gallop.

It has sometimes, not always, been practicable to adopt Jack Charlton's policy: 'When I don't like somebody I just completely ignore them. *They cease to exist!*' That's the honest way. People have pretended to be friendly while engaged behind the scenes in manipulative actions. This deceit, disguised as 'good manners', is disgraceful, dishonest, a symptom of the moral decline.

An abiding problem has been my propensity to evaluate and judge my fellow humans. I can't help it. It's all part of the doomed quest for perfection: 'suffers from an over-development of the critical faculty' as the Head of Fighter Command once said of Douglas Bader. At least my friends are certain of our bond. I am probably the product (or victim) of the age in which I grew up, when a boy saw Good and Evil defined crystal-clear in the shapes of Churchill and Hitler, and knew instinctively that loyalty and chivalry were sublime commodities, and that to fight and condemn the bad was the honourable thing to do, and that you can only truly be brave when you're scared; to turn away is cowardly. All a bit outmoded now. That time-honoured remark 'It's a free country': people don't say that any more. Our forefathers would have been indescribably sad.

I was greatly taken by something written in 1983 by Jeff Stollmeyer, the elegant West Indies batsman (savagely murdered in 1989). He recalled how his father used to return from business in Port-of-Spain and say, 'People are too devious. I'm returning to my trees.' I, too, often patted the sturdy trunk of one of our mammoth old beeches after returning from a meeting in London or a Test match where the Press-box atmosphere might have been 'divisive'. Stollmeyer snr was surely right? Well, perhaps up until October 1987, when some of those arboreal giants were torn from the ground by the ferocious hurricane and smashed our home. Betrayed again.

I have to smile at Brian Scovell's gall in once describing me as 'divisive', while Peter Roebuck saw me as 'cantankerous' – perhaps not altogether inappropriately, as it happened, when my disapproval was aimed at him as he strutted around, ignorantly blocking the view of others in the Press-box; or writing a book which was largely the fruit of the research of others, without due acknowledgement. 'Shrug it off' was a friend's wise advice.

My dismissal in 1996 from the magazine I'd created and nurtured was carried out without the slightest remorse. It seems now to have been an irrational violation, change for the sake of it. 'All change is for the worst,' said the old Duke of Cambridge. While I wouldn't endorse that totally, there have been times when I've wondered. The 'new' *Wisden Cricket Monthly* now went all-colour, something I had wanted the Gettys to sanction – without success. But the magazine was now seen as slick and hollow, edited by a youngish man who brought a few design touches but whose knowledge of the game – like that of the owners – was rather thin. His refusal or inability to incorporate the previous broad span of cricket's culture in *WCM's* pages was regretted by many long-term readers. It now cost much more to produce, contributors' fees suddenly soared, and sales were falling. It disappeared for a time, then emerged as a revamped magazine, with a questionable black and yellow colour theme.

These were no longer my problems. I wondered if one day I might find it possible to forgive those responsible for manipulating an early end to my editorship, or even to see the deed as a favour, however unintentional. But if they knew how much anguish they caused, then may God forgive them.

Through all those years my workload had stretched into the evenings and weekends: pressure which demanded non-stop concentration, with clearest thought in front of the mirror while shaving with my precious antique 1950s razor. Never was determination allowed to falter as *WCM* kept going against sizable odds. The eventual owners ought to have appreciated that. How tedious it was to be told by one telephone caller after another that I sounded weary. How uncomfortable it felt to reflect on the extent to which family life was disrupted by the recurring avalanche of the 90-hour week. And for what? 'Early retirement' for a conscientious fool. I probably took as much out of myself for each edition as a player might in a Test match. On that basis, I had 'played' 202 *WCM* Tests, 46 more than Allan Border's record at that time, two more than the record held by Sachin Tendulkar to this day.

Now, no longer did I have to monitor every news and feature programme in search of cricket matter, or read every book, magazine and newspaper to comb out information, though the habit tended to die hard. And no longer should I be bothered by the insouciance, even indifference, of an editor of *Wisden Cricketers' Almanack* who went off on his overseas holiday during a Lord's Test match. Nor would I concern myself at the duplicity of people who sheltered behind cricket's clean image.

Those problems at last had been buried, and I was flying free. The relentless monthly throb and the weight of responsibility were left behind. The emptiness faded. And cricket had no need to apologise to me. I would always be in the game's debt – notwithstanding the unwelcome storms – for it has given me incalculable pleasure and many friends around the world, together with a sense of purpose.

Fruits of my labours.
Was it worth it, I wonder?

Had those two estimable Yorkshiremen, Len Hutton and Jim Kilburn, not already utilised them, I would have taken *Cricket Is My Life* or *Thanks to*

Cricket as the title for this book. But, though I shall forever be proud of *Wisden Cricket Monthly* (as long as it should last under new regimes), henceforth cricket would cease to flood every corner of my existence.

There was one larger and indestructible problem that long pre-dates those foisted upon me from 1994 to 1996, one which will haunt as long as I live. This is the curse of being torn between two worlds. It dates back to January 20, 1949, when RMS *Orion* steamed out of Tilbury.

Affection for England and Australia should be complementary but is often actually conflicting. Comparisons, almost daily, are inescapable and insistent. How does one get by? Perhaps by reading Australian history on days of heavy English skies and drizzle during long winters, just as I used to bring England into my life in those Sydney days by reading London newspapers and drifting into the cinema to watch those nostalgic English films of the 1950s, cosy, heroic, uncomplicated, whimsical. It has been a two-way trade in nostalgia, firstly for a 1950s England I didn't know first-hand, then for a carefree Sydney suburban age, when future crises blissfully were unimagined.

Which country do you prefer? That question is the stuff of nervous twitches, when even the hairs left in the bath all seem to have taken on the configuration of question-marks.

Dad – to whose spirit I shall forever be a hostage – had every justification in asking once in a letter whether England, for all its village prettiness and historic sights, was more important than family togetherness. We knew the answer would never be clear-cut. That's why, through the first dozen years in Surrey, Debbie and I bought only second-hand furniture. Were we staying? We could never be sure . . . until I started my cricket magazine.

Not that even this prevented the feeling – fanned by casual remarks – that I was a 'hybrid' or a 'misfit' even, absurdly and rather vituperatively, an 'interloper'. Standing on the steps of the team's hotel in Aldwych, London one evening, the Australian Test batsman Graeme Wood asked me, with touching incredulity: 'How can you live here *all the time*?' I had to admit that it sometimes lost its appeal. But then so had Sydney.

Since 1950, Test cricket between England and Australia has been an overwhelming catalyst for all the thought and passions of my bi-national existence, its symbolic continuity reflecting an inner conflict that can never be resolved. We tried growing Queensland poinciana saplings in Surrey, but they withered in the coldness. I can smile as readily at the digs about keeping your wallet under the soap for safekeeping when a Pom visits you as the one about Aussies preferring thongs so as to escape the intellectual challenge of tying laces. *Sing you a song/Won't take long/All Pommies are bastards. Second verse/Same as the first/All Pommies are bastards.* The privately amusing thing for me about that scurrilous ditty is that 'Aussies' can be substituted at will – or anybody else you may choose.

Loving two polarised countries must be more emotionally draining than loving two women. While it permits of a kind of objectivity whenever England scrap with Australia at cricket or anything else (watching Lindwall bowling to Hutton, or Trueman to Harvey, or Thommo to Randall, or Warne to Atherton have been excruciating experiences) it can also lead to guilt attacks. Just as you start to feel that perfection is a cricket net on a golden English evening midst handsome greenery, or becoming immersed in the study of local history and archaeology, and sensing contentment in the pages of 18th and 19th Century cricket, some sudden upheaval, springing from meanness or snobbishness or terseness, hurls thought into a whirlpool. Visions emerge of blue distant hills, and a long, clean seashore, with the sound of carefree Australian laughter. The mind blanks out to a Dwight Yoakam tape or Billy Ray Cyrus's *Trail of Tears*. And you wonder how these things could ever have slipped from your mind. Crowded, stuffy peak-hour trains out of Waterloo and fume-filled London traffic snarl-ups are ideal places to tease the mind with visions of a silent Queensland highway stretching down the valley and winding up into wooded hills; or a ferry creaming its way across Sydney Harbour. Between a Namatjira and a D'Arcy Doyle on the wall hangs an equally symbolic print of old London Bridge. Nothing is more evocative than the kookaburra's cackle. The favourite bird has a Bradman profile and a sound that channels the last few decades, the past few millennia, into this day. Then you sizzle as the temperature soars past the century mark, the eye picks up a mean-looking snake on the track, and the ear is assailed by raucous Australian shouts, or the rare channel-billed cuckoo with its terrifying screech, and the national aspiration droops. And for the several-hundredth time you are confused.

When it's my turn to vaporise into that crystal powder-bowl, and assuming my sins are not deemed too many, I look forward to puffing my pipe with 'Stoddy' and hearing more about his days and nights in Australia with his cricketers over a century ago, and chatting to Archie Jackson about his short, notable life. It will be a time to address all those questions to my mother and father that I never bothered to ask while there was still a real-life opportunity, and to check out with Grandma how she managed to care for all those siblings as an orphaned teenager. At last I can seek out that son of a Welshman, John Valentine Thomas, my grandfather, in that photograph with the horse. I know we'd get on well. And my other grandparents, poor Susan and George Frith: could he find the words to describe his time on the Western Front with the East Surreys? Warming to see Debbie's parents and sister again, and the pain of the loss of Ray Lindwall and Len Hutton will be soothed. And in that timeless state there will be no need to fret at the prospect of leaving John Arlott's convivial table to drive home through the hazardous fog; no further cause to worry about financial security, or the passing of the years; forever onwards; the bliss of choice of company and environment; the elevation of a beautiful marital partnership to a state of perpetuity: I'm ready for all this when it comes.

But, please Captain, maybe not just yet.

Now that the incessant jangling of the phone had receded, I could be moved by the sunset with an indulgent, leisurely view, not just a hurried glance; and read books that are not about cricket, just as I did long ago; weave my cautious way back onto the golf course; write a bit – just a bit – about cricket; take Debbie to a non-cricket lunch or dinner; browse through junkshops; watch the disc of *Treasure Island* or *The Titfield Thunderbolt* whenever I felt like it; linger over the tree-lopping and hedge-trimming; see as much of my precious offspring as distance and their movements allow; try to see enough of both my two countries; and play cricket as long as my eyes, heart and legs collectively permit. That's where it began, at the crease. All else in cricket was subsidiary. Most of it had been enjoyable. I did my best. I had to if I was to be true to the bewildered little boy who all those years ago wondered what we were made for.

CHAPTER TWENTY-EIGHT

And a small cloud passes overhead
And cries down on the flower bed
That Honey loved.

BOBBY GOLDSBORO

So much for my state of mind a quarter of a century ago. Debbie and I had adored England in the 1960s and '70s, but the changes seeping through society dampened our feelings. While Carnaby Street and the Beatles and Stones and all that went with it had fascinated us, England was turning into an angry country, destabilised, greedy, raucous. So-called recreational drugs addled the brains of millions and drained through to the generations that followed: the outcome is clearly visible in today's chaotic, ignorant and frighteningly unreliable society. The kindness and gentleness of the older generations has long evaporated. Freedom of speech has been crushed. Social media has given rise to incredible nastiness. Warm and innocent humour is rare. Television and newspapers ache with 'celebrities' of whom most of us have never heard. 'Wokeness' is often as objectionable as the Covid-19 menace.

Nor has Australia escaped, though there were still enough quiet retreats in that huge country where one can relax in tranquillity.

Should we return to Queensland? We couldn't very well leave our loving and caring son John. He had entered into a terrible marriage to a woman who had become a violent alcoholic. The abuse and suffering John experienced culminated in a heart attack which left him crippled and with memory loss. He was taken into the care of a Leonard Cheshire nursing-home many miles from us. Mercifully I could foresee none of this years before when I'd been privileged to shake Group Captain Cheshire's hand at that charity cricket match at Wembley Stadium. Johnny has always been a warm-hearted, bubbly and fundamentally good person, so like his mother, unfailingly kind and considerate. To see him bed-ridden with little prospect of full recovery was utterly heartbreaking, as well as infuriating.

Daughter Julianne had married a charming Australian-Irishman in Queensland. Her John was a music-lover, incapable of anger or anything other than good humour and love. We were all so happy at their wedding gathering, when Debbie and I escorted our radiant daughter in a horse-drawn carriage to the quaint little wooden church in Mudgeeraba. But poor John was doomed: Julie nursed him bravely and selflessly, but the brain tumour proved to be terminal.

Daughter Julianne on her wedding day, with her mother

Meanwhile, elder son Peter had chosen a reclusive life in Adelaide, content in his solitary existence, reading a stream of books and studying the daily weather and Covid-19 reports. What a lecturer he might have become.

In considerations about where to spend our retirement years, a serious complication had been my cricket library and museum, several tons of it. The thought of shipping it halfway around the world was forbidding. And the sad losses among the Queensland branch of the family lessened the attraction. The good old days were beyond recapture, and we knew it.

Debbie had moved on from her noble but exhausting work helping women who suffered from the soul-destroying problem of Pre-Menstrual Syndrome. She set up the National Association for PMS (NAPS). She now turned to interviewing former Servicemen for the Imperial War Museum's Sound Archive, fulfilling work which involved talking to some very fine men and women who had served in the Second World War, one of them a veteran of the Great Escape. I was so proud of her for the painstaking way she carried this out. With her silken voice, so sensitive was she in interviewing traumatised soldiers and airmen that several of them ended up recounting terrible experiences which had been locked away in their tormented minds for decades. Some broke down, but later thanked her for coaxing them into releasing those bad memories.

Historic moment: the author meets W.G.Grace's last surviving grandchild, Primrose Worthington, Lord's 1997

Then, from our belated interest in ancestry, an extraordinary fact emerged from the research: Debbie's mother's father's birth certificate listed his *mother* as 'Unknown'. This, we discovered, could mean only one thing: that he was taken from his mother soon after birth, and she must almost certainly have been Aboriginal or Polynesian. This was not uncommon in Queensland in those times. We all felt good about this revelation. And the supposition was strengthened when I invited a full-blood Aborigine in Sydney to take a look at a photo of my daughter Julie. After gazing at the portrait for a full half-minute, he stated simply 'She's Koori.'

While my own work has not been as significant as Debbie's humanitarian output, I continued to write books as well as features, reviews and obituaries for *The Cricketer*, an ironic turnaround in the wake of the earlier bitter magazine rivalry. When my old magazine *Wisden Cricket Monthly* arose from the dead in 2017, I couldn't bring myself to write for it, though the new editor did leave the door open. The bad smells and lingering visions of the back-stabbing would never disperse. Nor did I think much of the overwhelming colour theme of black and yellow.

The author recovers from a fifty at Longparish, 1997

I suppose that if my work output were to be evaluated, above and beyond the 23 years of cricket magazine editorships, it must be in respect of the books I have written, over 30 of them across half a century. Following the first edition of this autobiography in 1997 came the first-ever book describing in detail the inaugural English tour of Australia, in 1861-62, titled unsurprisingly *The Trailblazers*. The research, much of it carried out in Sydney's Mitchell Library, was extensive and fulfilling. It was surprising that nobody had previously written anything of length on that landmark venture. Surrey County Cricket Club had instigated that significant tour, so it was rather a downer to find that, incredibly, the bookstall at The Oval was unwilling to stock the book. Former Prime Minister John Major, a Surrey fan, told me he'd have a word with them. Nothing happened.

Silence of the Heart came next. Since my 1989 book on cricket's suicides,

By His Own Hand, there had been further instances, and quite a few other earlier cases had been uncovered. People now knew where to come, and the extra data had piled up in a shoe-box, leaving me feeling a responsibility to return to this dark subject. The cricket authorities had already been alerted by the book and had set up counselling facilities for players who felt the need. Hence the dutiful update. Since then, although the research notes in the shoe-box have continued to pile up, I confess to having grown weary of the subject. I've done my bit, so there the matter rests. It was never a comfortable assignment.

Bodyline Autopsy followed, a heavy volume, exhaustively researched, and designed to be the definitive book on cricket's most famous, or infamous, episode. I had spoken to quite a few survivors of that sensational 1932-33 Ashes series over the years, which enriched the research, but now the intensive reading of books, cuttings and magazines resulted in a huge mound of material before the first words could be written. I laid out hundreds of reference pieces across the lounge carpet and was staring at this jumble, slightly lost, close to panic, when Debbie came in. She was stunned too. How could this avalanche of notes ever be turned into a book? Just by assuring her that it could be done I found myself reassured. The job was completed, as was an ABC DVD to accompany the book. And that book came within a whisker of taking the William Hill sports book prize; was Wisden's book of the year; and Cricketweb's book of the decade, although the judges at the Cricket Society this time didn't consider it worthy of inclusion in its short list of a dozen books.

Soon, though, they were giving me the annual award for *The Ross Gregory Story*, which was based on the young Australian's wartime diary. A very fine batsman and legspinner (he got Bradman out twice in one Shield match), this lovable Melbourne lad was the only Australian Test cricketer to be killed in the Second World War, having made a valuable contribution to Australia's 3-2 victory in the amazing 1936-37 Ashes series. He is pictured on the front cover coming back to the pavilion with skipper Don Bradman at Adelaide. Oddly, this third Cricket Society book award came 17 years after the *Pageant of Cricket* award, which had come 17 years after that inaugural award for the first Stoddart publication.

Next, I embarked on a book on what developed into a sensational Ashes series. *The Battle for the Ashes 2005* turned out to be one of many books on the subject, others having jumped on the bandwagon as the excitement grew. A year later, as I asked Michael Vaughan to inscribe my personal copy of my book, I enquired how many of that shelf-full of 2005 books did he have on his shelf? Without raising his eyes from his plate of salad, he snapped a blunt 'None!' Charming chap.

In the summer of 2006, my pal Andy Collier persuaded me to come out of retirement to play in one last cricket match. A couple of precautionary net sessions caused no pain, so off I went for the formality of my farewell innings. I was itching to bowl, but the captain kept looking elsewhere. At my regular post at first slip I dropped no catches: none came my way. My final innings was equally uneventful. One on-drive to the rope, a few singles, then an attempted hook: thin edge down onto boot; the ball spun back and clicked against the stumps; a bail fell off. I comforted myself with the silly thought that it bore a similarity to Don Bradman's dismissal first ball against Bill Bowes at Melbourne in the Bodyline series. Son Johnny, bless him, had taken a blurred long-distance picture with his mobile of me at the crease on this pretty emotional occasion. It was historic for me, although I accepted that it meant nothing to anybody else, apart from my precious Debbie, who'd always been there to share the alternating pleasure and misery.

The conclusion, however, was memorable: this very last cricket match after so many in a lifetime ended in a pulsating and uncontrived *tie*. This exciting final match over, I hauled myself from the field very, very slowly, looking across at the lowering sun, seeing flashes from the decades of playing the beloved game, and preparing to walk through a tunnel of commemoratively raised bats. But my team-mates, alas, were already in the clubhouse downing their beers. Perhaps it was best that way. They couldn't see my moist eyes, and they would not have understood my thinking: gratitude for the decades in the sun and the rain, excruciating sadness at the reality that I'd never play cricket again.

That meant that I was now condemned to travelling to watch big cricket matches or gazing at the television screen – for an exorbitant, ever-inflating subscription. Like many others, I often turn the volume down. The Sky Sports commentators are employed on account of their past on-field achievements, certainly not for their literacy or voice quality, qualities that used to be fundamentally and logically an obvious standard necessity. Gone are the mellifluous voices and much of the intellect of old. Not least regrettable is the absence of historical perspective: for the myopic production people, cricket did not exist before Shane Warne came on the scene.

The coverage from Australia is even worse: relentless, frantic jabbering by ex-Test players, even as the ball is bowled and the batsman is dealing with it. The star-struck producers miss other basics too, such as stating the match venue at the top of the on-screen scorecard. The volume control button is a vital function, though the sub-titles are often unintentionally hilarious. Oh, where did you go, John Arlott, Rex Alston, Alan Gibson, Alan McGilvray?

Aside from gazing at a television screen choking with commercials, with 400 channels from which it's often a challenge to locate one worth watching, I continue to file the cricket pages from the morning paper, a ritual that goes back decades, a compelling custom I'm loath to end. One day these bundles may prove useful to somebody, or perhaps make a monumental bonfire.

My old friend Richard Smart drew up another contract for a book on the upcoming 2006-07 Ashes series in Australia. It was a shock to discover on the opening morning at The Gabba that Cricket Australia, as the Board now called itself, had set up an exclusive rights deal with the all-pervasive Gettys for photographic coverage of the series. The chap who had been commissioned to provide us with pictures for the book therefore had to return to England, much out of pocket. Greed was gnawing ever deeper into the game's soul.

I'd already begun researching for a detailed and authorised history of the Australian Cricket Board, to be co-written with Gideon Haigh. We put all we'd got into this substantial work, and were pleased with the result, and gratified further when the Australian Cricket Society gave its annual book prize to us for *Inside Story: Unlocking Australian Cricket's Archives*.

There followed the biggest project of all: the detailed chronicling of every single item in my own vast cricket library and memorabilia collection. Michael Down took this one on, and after an estimated six thousand hours of labour I handed him *The David Frith Archive*, a heavyweight volume of over 1000 pages which Boundary Books published in an understandably expensive edition of only 60 copies, with a deluxe version of only 15. Crucially, I've maintained a scrupulous record of everything I've acquired since this volume's completion in 2009; but still I cannot persuade myself to start selling off.

Across these years I often sat in my library, filming with Charles Colvile for Sky Sports, speaking on all manner of aspects of the game for their lunchtime features, from the controversial coloured clothing (with a reminder that cricketers wore striped and spotted shirts in the 19th century) to, inevitably I suppose, the subject of cricketers' mental health and suicide statistics.

Returning to books, next came *Frith on Cricket*, a sizable selection from my output of words, whimsically starting with the school essay from so very long ago and drawing from numerous publications. Then came Cricket's Collectors, a slim illustrated volume tracing the history of the sociable and inspiring Cricket Memorabilia Society, profiling the collections of many members and their predecessors.

Guildford's Cricket Story was written in 1998 to mark the 60th anniversary of County Championship cricket in the town in west Surrey where we'd lived for so long. Fifteen years later I updated the book. I established that to its great credit Guildford had many more significant cricket foundation landmarks than any other area in England (or the world, come to that). This justified a claim that it had a stronger right to be referred to as cricket's 'cradle' than Hambledon. This reality will take decades to sink in, so long has dear old Hambledon been regarded as being most steeped in cricket history, thanks to John Nyren's celebrated volume. Yet Guildford has the earliest surviving documentary record of the playing of the game (albeit by schoolboys: 'creckett' – mid-16th Century), alongside first evidence of leg protection and of shoe spikes, and the local man (Lumpy Stevens) who forced the introduction of the middle stump, in addition to the first formal women's cricket match, and the coining of the expression 'test' match (by a Guildfordian), and the earliest surviving laws (set of articles). No other area in England can lay claim to anything remotely approaching this bundle of pioneering firsts. When I spoke at a lunch in the Bat and Ball Inn, laid on by members of the Hambledon Club, I stated my case, and they absorbed the 'news' in gentlemanly fashion.

I was less 'poised' at another gathering, in 2011, when at the Cricket Society's dinner in London, I was presented with the Ian Jackson Award, a silver salver, for 'distinguished services to cricket'. So choked-up was I at the presentation that words simply would not come, and my eyes were anything but dry. Later, when I stood to deliver my talk on famous cricketers I'd known, I tried to make up for my earlier inadequacy, and went on for so long that many of the members had to dash off to catch the final train.

Three years later my friend Patrick Ferriday published *Frith's Encounters*, a large bundle of essays portraying the many renowned cricketers who had been part of my life, from S.F.Barnes and Wilfred Rhodes and Frank Woolley to The Don and Cardus, Compton, Bedser, Hutton, O'Neill, Eddie Gilbert and dozens more. It was a time to pinch myself in wonderment as I reflected on this catalogue of acquaintances. How might Ralph, my schoolpal from so long ago, have reacted? And I explained to Debbie that I hadn't included her pet player, Joe Root, because he was still playing.

As a follow-up, the publishing house of von Krumm then took my final expanded offering on my romantic, tragic all-time super-hero 'Stoddy', launched in the Hampstead pavilion to coincide with the unveiling of Neale Andrew's splendid bronze of A.E.Stoddart's smooth off-drive. Andrew Strauss spoke, as did club president Jim Carter, the *Downton Abbey* head butler. I would have spoken at a little more length but the president cut me off soon after I'd started. Mustn't upstage these professional actors. I'm sure that 'Stoddy' smiled, for he too was once a passive conversationalist.

Then there was *Touring with Bradman,* a book based on the diary that Alec Hurwood penned during the 1930 tour, Don Bradman's sensational first visit to England. Queenslander Hurwood was a fine offspinner, who had come within a whisker of bowling Bradman early in his recent world record innings of 452 not out. But skipper Woodfull had little regard for him. Grimmett and Hornibrook were entrusted to do the spin bowling in all five Test matches. It was a tender story, based on Hurwood's well-observed diary: an enjoyable editorial undertaking.

Next came the updated edition of the inspiring but heartbreaking Archie Jackson story, numerous snippets having accumulated since the original 1974 book.

But the later stages of the writing were overshadowed by tragic poignancy such as I'd never experienced. Debbie was rushed to hospital before dawn on April 4, 2019, precisely 55 years to the day since we had steamed out of Sydney Harbour with our three youngsters on that grand 1964 venture.

Our daughter Julie and I went to Debbie's hospital bedside two or three times every day over six weeks as she faded away. We all somehow managed to remain calm: Oriel/Debbie was as brave and uncomplaining as ever. My love and admiration for my wife and for my daughter was boundless.

Early one morning, my beloved was taken from us. What we had all endured cannot be put into words. We had lost someone who was gentle, caring, selfless and self-effacing, beautiful in appearance and voice, beautiful in her pure and gentle Queensland country-girl soul. My deep gratitude for our many years together served as a crutch.

It was a monumental and dreadful loss, so unexpected. Life is temporary. I'd understood that all my life, but this was the most starkly emphatic proof of it.

The pressing formalities that needed to be dealt with are now blurred. Brave Julie guided me through them: bundles of paperwork, many pressing decisions, including one that few people confront in advance: burial or cremation? The nearest available burial ground was eight miles distant. I couldn't bear the thought of my Queensland princess lying among strangers in the cold earth so far away. We therefore accepted cremation. The ceramic urn rests at home, where we can place a warm hand on it and try to smile, for Debbie's beautiful smile was her everlasting signature.

These are words I had never expected to write. I'd always blankly assumed that I would die before my angel: a coward's anticipation perhaps, for which I hang my head. I found some comfort in recalling something that my father figure John Arlott had murmured when we were musing about the hereafter: 'It can't be a bad place if my mother and father and aunts have gone there.' I pray that he was right.

The carriage was drawn by two fine black horses, and I was touched at the way oncoming motorists slowed down, some flashing their headlights: it was almost as if those strangers had been fortunate enough to have known my beautiful Debbie. Selecting music and readings for the funeral had not been difficult for us. Every item had strong resonance: *A World of Our Own* (The Seekers); *Songbird* (Eva Cassidy); *Angel* (Sarah McLachlan); *Clancy of the Overflow* (read by the Welsh minister); *Amazing Grace*; a verse by son Peter; *Song of the Old Water-Wheel* (Slim Whitman); *The Warmth of the Sun* (The Beach Boys); closing with *Nuns' Chorus* (Joan Sutherland). Doubting my own capacity to deliver my Eulogy, I had asked a friend to read it.

There had always been music in our home. But no longer. To revisit that gallery of sweet sounds would open floodgates of tears.

I've always striven to justify my place on this planet. Yet my output is as nothing compared to my pretty Debbie's: loving and selfless daughter, sister, wife and mother. She brought relief and comfort to countless women PMS sufferers, and securely recorded many war veterans' recollections. Everybody who knew her loved her. She had bravely endured long-term health problems, not least cruel fibromyalgia and allergies. Now, after 63 years together, how could I go on without her? I'm trying to learn. I must not fall apart like my poor father all those years ago. Daughter Julie, so strong, so loyal, so competent, so loving, continues to sustain me. Debbie/Oriel would have been so very proud of her.

'What are we made for?' that bewildered boy plaintively wailed so long ago. Without wishing to sound like the manic-depressive Tony Hancock, I'm still not certain, though I am haunted by a vision of Man's fundamental stupidity and aggressive instincts slowly dragging us all to the cliff-edge. The curse of the Covid-19 pandemic, with its threat to sanity through the inescapable hell of lockdown and anxiety, has brought with it echoes of the fear and doubts and deprivations of the Second World War. I'm wondering if it might have been inflicted on the world as some sort of punishment.

The negativity and spitefulness of wokeness/wokeism, with adults behaving like petulant children; the scarcity of relaxed humour: I know what Keith Miller and Spike Milligan and their contemporaries would have said about it. The world has ditched its sense of humour. People are forever seeking to take offence. Names are no longer abbreviated, and nicknames are shunned by the po-faced. Filthy language is rife on television. Racial sensitivity is flooding the world with tension. It's all too grim. Might the Covid plague have been sent to punish people who insist on taking offence at everything? It seems that there are gangs of grim-faced vigilantes, unwilling to enjoy the simple things in life, prowling around on the lookout for something more to seize upon and howl about. At long last the authorities are doing something to rein in this madness.

I give deepest thanks to Our Maker for that distant evening in 1956 when Rosie cajoled young sister Oriel/Debbie to the airmen's dance at RAAF Amberley, Queensland. 'The power of the bond of love ran between us the night I met Davey, the man in my dreams' wrote my beloved on a piece of paper which I keep close to me. As my grief swirls around me every dawn, every day, every night, I accept that it was ludicrously unrealistic to have prayed for that lovely partnership never to end. I gaze at the evening sky. If I believe that she is there, she is there. The nearest thing to any kind of faint consolation is that Debbie, with her fragile health, was spared the horrors of the Covid-19 pandemic.

I find myself queueing for an anti-Covid 'jab', with lots of other people of pensionable age, in Guildford's huge concert hall. Here, long ago, Debbie and I saw (and met after the show) Guy Mitchell and then Howard Keel; years later we saw the Hollies. Most recently there had been the Abba tribute concert: Debbie, fresh-faced with joy, arose with the packed audience to clap her hands and sway to the rhythm, prompting me to haul myself up from my seat too. Now, years on, the music has died, and here I am, at that same place, being given a life-saving inoculation.

It's strange to reflect that at one end of my life the Luftwaffe was trying to finish me off, and at the other it's been this lethal Covid-19 thing: isolation, tedious repetition, writing book reviews and obituaries, trimming bushes, gazing at screens, watching the *Talking Pictures TV* channel for its haunting old feature films as an escape from the false values, spite, greed and hysteria of the modern world, trying hard to enjoy soulless international cricket played in soul-destroying empty stadiums.

In that dark summer of 2019 (pre-Covid), in some desperation I'd continued to honour my pact with cricket by driving up to the Ashes Test match at Lord's, where I watched the proceedings in a zombie state: feeling perhaps not all that dissimilar to Steve Smith after he was cracked on the helmet that afternoon by England's Barbadian bouncer merchant Jofra Archer. I managed to stumble through an interview with Jim Maxwell for ABC Radio, and was then greatly relieved to come across Keith Stackpole in the MCC hospitality area, where we had a claret or two and chatted as if we were back in the 1970s. Later I went searching for Neil Harvey – that chap who'd made my heart sing in Tests of the 1950s and then bowled me in a grade match almost a lifetime previously, and now the last player still standing from the 'Invincible' 1948 team – but to no avail. I continued to weep inside for Debbie every few minutes.

The traffic jams were sinful driving home. Our wonderful daughter had a good meal ready. Instinctively, helplessly I glanced around the room in search of Debbie. The house is garlanded with her portraits, her beautiful natural smile lighting up every one of them. Already three months had passed since she had been taken from us.

Forever prone to reflection, I think frequently of my beautiful life partner, triggering a kaleidoscope of images. How long before this anguish will ease? Another year? A decade? Probably never.

I needed to search for acceptance – that same kind of acceptance I'd ventured to urge Don Bradman to try to find a long time ago in his darkest hour. I now completely understood what it was like for him when his lovely Jessie was taken from him after many decades. Words do seem rather pointless. What else can one do but look back? That's what I've done in these pages. And notwithstanding the painful reverses in life, which we are all called upon to bear some time or other, I find myself simply grateful for what life has delivered.

'What are we made for?' whispered that bewildered lad so long ago. The answer seems clear: I was born to serve and enjoy the noble game of cricket: but also, more meaningfully, to rejoice in the privilege of spending those many years with my divine Debbie/Oriel.

PUBLISHER'S NOTE

David Frith has perhaps forgotten more about the game and its history than most of us will ever come close to knowing.
He started writing his first book on cricket in 1968.
He did not stop for the next 53 years.
38 books encapsulating the history of cricket, and thereby snapshots of society and life.
And then there is his collection of cricketana, memorabilia and films.
The letters alone amount to more than 6000. There are more than 500 VHS tapes, over 350 Betamax cassettes, hundreds of DVDs films and sound tapes, and an uncountable number of photographs.

"Makes me feel like Methuselah," he once said.

In 2020, he also said, "If I have one more book left in me it might be my autobiography, which seemed to have been blanked by much of the cricket world in 1996, and now needs to be amended and updated."

Here is that amended and updated autobiography.

DF c DF b DF: a clever compilation by the author's son John (lacking only DF the wicketkeeper)

Front paper picture:

Lord's Test match 1899, Jessop hitting Jones to leg

Photograph on back cover:

DF and Debbie after an enervating flight in the Tiger Moth which cost David Gower so dearly. Photo: Mark Ray

Printed in Great Britain
by Amazon

61579278R00254